W9-BWR-417

WITHDRAWN

PN
4145   PARRISH   09927
.P35   Reading aloud
1966

Wayland Maxfield Parrish, Ph.D., Cornell University, is Professor of Speech, Emeritus, of the University of Illinois, where he taught for twenty years. Dr. Parrish has also taught at Dartmouth College, the University of Pittsburgh, and the University of Florida.

Reading

Aloud

Wayland Maxfield Parrish
UNIVERSITY OF ILLINOIS

FOURTH EDITION

THE RONALD PRESS COMPANY · **NEW YORK**

Library of Congress Catalog Card Number: 66–22848
PRINTED IN THE UNITED STATES OF AMERICA

PREFACE

During the years since *Reading Aloud* was first published, there has been no slackening of interest in oral interpretation, and the opportunities for practicing it seem to have increased. It is still one of the chief interests of teachers of speech and is apparently getting more attention from teachers of English literature. But, since there have been no developments or discoveries that call for radical alterations in methods and principles, this revision is in the literal sense merely a re-vision, a re-examination of the subject growing out of additional reflection and experience. Those familiar with the earlier editions will find that, while the main stem of development remains unchanged, its branches have been extensively pruned and it has put out new shoots of such number and vigor as to make what may seem a new approach.

Nearly all the chapters have been completely rewritten, and two have been consolidated with others. Within the chapters, there are, besides the addition of new materials, a good many shifts in arrangement. On the assumption that voice and pronunciation are now adequately covered in general speech courses, I have treated them less fully than in earlier editions; but, in view of the present muddle in diacritics, I have compared the markings of pronunciation in the four principal dictionaries intended for college use and supplied a table of variants.

The principal innovations are two: First, the leading theories of literary production developed in recent times are examined, along with the classical theory of Aristotle, and adapted to the problems that arise in the oral interpretation of poetry. Second, both analysis and expression are based largely on I. A. Richards' exposition of attitude as an essential element in meaning. This formula seems well suited to both analysis and expression and helps greatly to give unity and coherence to our somewhat amorphous discipline.

While drawing materials from all related disciplines, I have tried to keep the writing simple and readable, studiously avoiding the jargons of semantics, linguistics, criticism, psychology, anatomy, phonetics, the theater, etc., and not attempting to create a jargon for interpretation. While this restriction may not please the specialized scholar, it will better suit the understanding of the average student—for whom this book is intended.

Most of the selections for reading in the third edition have been retained, especially the poems, and there are about fifty new ones, drawn from such authors as Kingsley Amis, James Baldwin, John Betjeman, Morris Bishop, John Ciardi, Robert Frost, Robert Graves, Aldous Huxley, Jean-Paul Sartre, Dylan Thomas, and John Updike, and from others less well known. All the drill selections have been retained, simply because after twelve years of search I have found no others so satisfactory for my purpose. Teachers may find them shopworn, but students will not, and, of course, any teacher may use others and make his own analysis of them.

This revision was begun in collaboration with Jerome Landfield. Unfortunately, the press of his other duties made it necessary for him to withdraw, but, while we worked together on the earlier chapters, he helped greatly by supplying new materials and points of approach, checking redundancy, freshening the style, curbing dogmatism, and contributing in other ways to making this a better book than it would have been without his assistance. I am very grateful for his help.

I am very grateful also to the many teachers—and students—who have expressed their approval of the earlier editions (I wish they had been more critical) and encouraged me in the preparation of this one. It is gratifying to know that there has been sufficient approval of the book to keep it in use during thirty-four years of radical change in all aspects of our culture. I would like to hope that this is an indication that the principles and pedagogy set forth are sound and of continuing, if not timeless, value.

W. M. PARRISH

Gainesville, Florida,
April, 1966

CONTENTS

READING ALOUD

1

INTRODUCTION

To begin with, we should understand that reading aloud to others is not an activity of recent development. It has been going on as long as man has been literate. Indeed, if we include the early reciting of tales and poetry, composed as uttered, or repeated from memory, it began long before man invented letters to represent speech sounds and so could preserve his compositions and enable others to recite them too. One thinks of the well-developed poetry that circulated orally among some tribes of American Indians long before the white man arrived with his alphabet. Even today, we are told, the Somali tribes of northeast Africa have a rich poetic literature, which may be lost if an alphabet suitable for recording it is not found before the few old men in whose memories it lives die off.[1] When writing was new and few knew how to read, and fewer still possessed the tablets or rolls on which literature was recorded, these lucky few were expected to share their riches with their less fortunate companions. Herodotus first published his famous history by reading it aloud in his home community, and later, to a larger and more appreciative audience in Athens. In a good translation, it still makes lively reading. Through a good deal of later history, laws and regulations were promulgated by having them read aloud in the marketplaces. Our grandfathers, having fewer books and diversions than we, often read aloud to their families, generally from the Bible, and, no doubt, the beautiful cadences of the King James Version, heard with the ear, helped to form the taste of many generations of speakers, writers, and others.

[1] See Jeanne Contini, "The Illiterate Poets of Somali," *The Reporter*, March 14, 1963, pp. 36–38.

3

The Prevalence of Oral Reading

And today, in spite of the ready availability of printed matter, the occasions for reading aloud are legion. Preachers read their sermons; politicians, their speeches; and professors, their lectures (often very badly). Speakers, announcers, and commentators on radio and television commonly read from a script, prompt card, or Teleprompter. At meetings of the thousands of organizations that call for our attendance there is reading of minutes, reports, resolutions, recommendations, and the like, and who has not suffered on such occasions from the fumbling attempts of an unintelligible reader. And, in the unbelievable number of conventions held almost daily in city hotels and on college campuses, the programs consist largely of the reading of papers to the long-suffering delegates. Even at conventions of speech teachers, there is endless reading of papers and very little spontaneous speech.

Let us note also that, in spite of the dominance of television in our lives, there is still a great deal of oral reading in our homes. Children must still have their bedtime stories, and in some circles there are adults who take pleasure in reading to each other, some, be it noted, who even in college dormitories gather occasionally to share with others their favorite bits of poetry, drama, or story. And those who visit the dives frequented by "beatniks" find that even these scorners of modern conventions sometimes read poetry to each other, perhaps to an accompaniment of bongo drums and finger snapping.

The late Charles Laughton, a distinguished actor, lent his voice and his example to encouragement of oral reading.

I plead for more reading aloud [he said]. It is a friendly, quiet and thoroughly refreshing thing to do. It makes us participants rather than spectators. Instead of sitting by to let the professionals amuse or enlighten us, *we* can get into the act, make contact with new ideas, exercise our imagination. More than that, it is a shared experience which draws people closer together. Husbands and wives, families or groups of friends can enjoy the comfortable satisfaction that comes from laughing together, learning together—from doing the same thing at the same time, together.

Other actors besides Mr. Laughton, among them Emlyn Williams, Hal Holbrook, Henry Hull, and Cornelia Otis Skinner, have at times taken to the road to give recitals from the works of such writers as Shakespeare, Dickens, and Mark Twain.

The Problem of Good Taste

We should also note the public recitations of small children instigated by their doting mothers, the prevalence of recitations on all kinds of school programs, and the widespread speech contests in which oral reading is a regular feature. Although these performances are generally wholesome and valuable, there are times when they are marred by bad taste, both in the choice of selections read and in their rendition. Some of us may have been turned against any tolerance of public reading by schoolday experiences in which innocent children fell into the hands of incompetent coaches with results that were truly dreadful. In public performances of all kinds, the problem of good taste is always with us and very likely will never be solved. Apparently it has not been solved in England either. John Masefield, Poet Laureate and an ardent champion of the public recitation of poetry, deplored the harm done, especially to child reciters, by the elocutionists, who, he said, "have made a child in a pinafore on prize-day a thing that strong men fly from screaming."[2]

It is well to recall that one of the reasons why Plato would have excluded poets from his ideal republic was because of the vulgarity of their public readings. There is a type of character, he said,

who will narrate anything; . . . nothing will be too bad for him: and he will be ready to imitate anything, not as a joke, but in right good earnest, and before a large company. . . . He will attempt to represent the roll of thunder, the noise of wind and hail, or the creaking of wheels and pulleys, and the various sounds of flutes, pipes, trumpets, and all sorts of instruments: he will bark like a dog, bleat like a sheep, or crow like a cock; his entire art will consist of imitation of voice and gesture.[3]

So it is not only in modern times that some oral readers have shown bad taste.

Earlier Studies of Vocal Expression

The wide prevalence of oral reading, its long duration, and its frequent failure to achieve effectiveness have led many teachers and others to try to define its method, develop its techniques, and improve its quality, and many are the treatises that have been published on the subject in the course of its long history. Even the austere Plato was aware of its importance and devoted one of his dialogs to its examination. (See "Ion," page 484.) The famous Roman teacher Quintilian, in his influential treatise on education, gave special attention to teaching boys to read well. The nineteenth century released a flood of books on what had come to be called "elocution," some dealing with general improvement in speech but most of them concerned primarily with reading aloud. The McGuffey and other school readers gave elementary instruction in the art. And the present century has brought many more texts, mostly intended for college students.

[2] John Masefield, *With the Living Voice* (New York: The Macmillan Co., 1925), p. 19.
[3] *The Republic*, iii.

Examination of this extensive body of theory and instruction could well occupy us for a year or more, and an adequate summary of it would fill a volume, but such a summary will not be attempted here. We will use the best of what has been learned and taught through past centuries with little attention to who learned what first and who taught it. You will not be asked to range widely over a broad field of theory, but rather to focus sharply on a few brief specimens of good literature, assimilating their meaning and learning how to translate it into effective oral expression. You will not be urged to develop the habit of rapid reading, valuable as that habit is, but rather to follow the advice of a great teacher of literature, Lane Cooper—"Read aloud; read slowly; read suspiciously. Reread."[4]

Mastery of the Language

It is a tired but well-tried truism that he who reads to others must understand what he reads. It is assumed that the behavior of the reader's voice will be controlled by his mind, that the pattern of his expression will reveal the pattern of his thinking while he is reading. But it seems plain enough that we *can* speak without thinking, and frequently do, and, of course, we often think without speaking. Whether we can think without language is, however, a question that scholars are still disputing. The conclusion of the eminent philosopher Alfred North Whitehead was "Human civilization is an outgrowth of language, and language is the product of advancing civilization," and "the mentality of mankind and the language of mankind created each other."[5] An oral reader, then, should know the nature of his language, its structure, its conventions and idioms, its relations to thought and to speech, and how thought is communicated by it. This involves, of course, finding and understanding the meanings of words, both in isolation and when combined into phrases and sentences. It involves also another aspect of meaning, and one that is frequently neglected. As Ogden and Richards pointed out in their very influential work *The Meaning of Meaning*,[6] parts of the meaning of a linguistic statement by a writer or speaker are his attitude toward the reader or listener, his attitude toward what he is saying, and his intention in saying it, the effect he desires.

The foundation of our study is mastery of the language with which we communicate. This must come first. Only from this foundation can we attempt the oral interpretation of literature, which is our chief aim.

[4] Lane Cooper, *Two Views of Education* (New Haven: Yale University Press, 1922), p. 118.

[5] Alfred North Whitehead, *Modes of Thought* (New York: G. P. Putnam's Sons, Inc., 1958), pp. 49, 57.

[6] C. K. Ogden and I. A. Richards, *The Meaning of Meaning* (8th ed.; New York: Harcourt, Brace & World, Inc., 1946), pp. 226–27.

Complaints of Students' Language Ability

It is a common complaint of college professors, editors, journalists, and employers that young people do not have mastery of their mother tongue. A distinguished professor of English at Harvard reports that a question always raised in meetings of his department is "Why are the graduates of Harvard University incapable of composing simple declarative sentences?"[7] Most of our high school and college graduates, it is said, can neither read with understanding, write with clarity and precision, nor speak with fluency and ease, and they have no capacity at all for the reading, speaking, or appreciation of poetry, and it is in poetry that the best of our linguistic heritage is preserved. Another university professor laments that many college graduates have "fine intelligence [that] is not matched by strength of intellect," that they have "no knowledge that is precise and firm, no ability to do intellectual work with thoroughness and despatch," and that they "cannot read accurately or write clearly, . . . cannot utter their thoughts with fluency or force . . . range conversationally over a modest gamut of intellectual topics . . . [or] address their peers consecutively on one of the subjects they have studied."[8]

Remedy Through Reading Aloud

Without feeling bound to accept these complaints as valid, let us note two things about them: Modern students have been exposed to influences that might well cause the deficiencies complained of, and one of the best ways to remedy them may be by carefully disciplined exercises in oral reading. When a child's oral reading in school is stopped at the fourth grade, his further linguistic development is driven underground where it cannot be observed. Oral reading brings it out into the open. The heavy modern emphasis on rapidity in reading encourages superficiality and weakens comprehension. Oral reading will slow the reader down and make him understand what he reads. Difficulty in composing simple sentences may be due to de-emphasis on grammar. Oral reading requires careful attention to sentence structure. It also requires careful attention to word patterns or phrases, some of which will pass into the reader's permanent vocabulary of phrases and grammatical structures, just as many word patterns from the Bible and from Shakespeare and other poets have passed into the common stock of the language. Vocabularies may be meager because students have never been required to examine words closely and learn to define and pronounce them. "Fine elocution," that is,

[7] Archibald MacLeish, "What Is English?" *The Saturday Review*, December 9, 1961.

[8] Jacques Barzun, *The House of Intellect* (New York: Harper & Row, 1959), pp. 98–99.

vocal expression, said Ruskin, "means an exquisitely close attention to, and intelligence of, the meaning of words, and perfect sympathy with what feeling they describe."

Many have tried too early to read literature that was beyond their capacity at the time, and, baffled by a strange vocabulary and unusual word order, have struggled along only half understanding until they have become resigned and habituated to a merely partial grasp of what they read. As John Dewey once said, "We are easily trained to be content with a minimum of meaning, and fail to note how restricted is our perception of the relations which confer significance. We get so thoroughly used to a kind of pseudo-idea, a half perception, that we are not aware how half-dead our mental action is." No habit could be formed more deadly to intelligence and growth. Such laxness will be corrected by the "exquisitely close attention to . . . the meaning of words" required in the reading class.

Other Harmful Influences

There are other educational and environmental influences that may have contributed to the alleged failure of students to master their mother tongue. A misguided interpretation of democracy assumes that, since all are equal, it is not proper for teachers to point out either excellence or inferiority in their pupils. If the dullard is made aware of his condition, he is unhappy; if the merits of the superior are made known, he becomes unpopular. It is thought that encouraging an intellectual elite, or making students aware of their limitations, in undemocratic, and perhaps un-American! Related to his misinterpretation is the current emphasis on pedagogical philanthropy—a reluctance to hold students rigorously to the hard tasks of learning because taking pains is painful and school should always provide pleasure (the more popular word is "fun"). In the background is the horrid picture of cringing pupils driven to their tasks to the tune of a hickory stick. There is also the invasion of the schoolroom by the romantic-expressive theory of art, the notion that all self-expression is art, and therefore sacred, that a child's work, if he ever does any, is precious, the manifestation of his individual creativity, and not to be criticised adversely. In addition, we cannot escape being influenced by the general lack of firmness and precision in use of language by politicians, journalists, advertisers, fiction writers, dramatists, and educators, with the result that much of what we read and hear is a loose conglomeration of turbidity, pseudojargon, doubletalk, "Newspeak," and plain gobbledygook.[9]

Some of us may escape these influences, and the better minds may

[9] On these influences, see *ibid.*, especially Chapter 4.

rise above them—and will probably go into science. But it is well to be aware of them and reflect upon them. The course in reading aloud should help to counteract them.

Accuracy of Observation

The key that opens the door to effective reading is the habit of close observation, the simple but difficult art of paying attention. "The first rule of study," said a great teacher, "shall be—*observe*." (See page 43.) Ruskin said, "You must get into the habit of looking intensely at words, and assuring yourself of their meaning, syllable by syllable—nay, letter by letter." (See page 41.) But, said another great teacher, "The process of making monotonous black characters on the page vividly stir the latent sense-perceptions is relatively slow and irksome. Few people have ever learned to do it consistently; and hence, it is fair to say, few have ever truly learned to read." (See page 44.) Close observation requires time and effort. No substitute has ever been found for taking pains, and we must learn to endure such pains. Just as one cannot become acquainted with a country by flying over it, so a jet-propelled reading of the printed page will not satisfy the requirements of the reading class. The habit of close attention to the meanings of words is the foundation of our study, and of many other studies.

Whether the habit of close observation developed in a reading course can be transferred to other studies is a question. But, if it can, elocution must be a very valuable discipline, for close observation is fundamental to all artistic and scientific method. Bennedetto Croce said, "The painter *is* a painter because he sees what others only feel or catch a glimpse of, but do not see." (See page 93.) And let us note the emphasis placed on observation by the great naturalist Louis Agassiz. To an eager student who came to study in his laboratory in Cambridge he assigned a vile-smelling preserved fish with the brief injunction that he should study it (without damaging it); he paid no more attention to his pupil that day, nor the next, nor for a week. At the end of a week, he called for a report, and, when it was given, he sent the student back to his task with the curt comment "That is not right." At the end of another week of ten-hour days, the student had really learned something about the fish, enough to astonish himself and satisfy his teacher. Agassiz' method was severe, but his pupil learned how to observe.

One of the surest marks of mediocrity in students is a certain dulness of perception, an imperfect understanding of ideas, a vagueness of emotional impression, and a general mental flabbiness, which, in book studies, seem to have their roots in failure to read with understanding. On the other hand, the surest marks of excellence, in art or science, in business or the professions, and the certain marks of genius, are a vivid sharpness of perception and a corresponding definiteness of impression. The reading class affords an unrivaled opportunity for detecting mediocrity and stimulating clear-headedness.

Uniformity of Meaning

It is true, of course, and it is a much labored truth at present, that all of us do not get the same meaning from a given statement. Words are understood as each individual has experienced them, and a writer's attitude and intention may be variously interpreted. A host of semanticists are engaged with great assiduity in exposing these differences. But, in spite of their findings, it must not be supposed that each reader is entitled to take from a statement whatever meaning he pleases. All of us are bound, and very strictly, by the nature or genius of the language that is our medium of communication. This will become clearer as we proceed. For the present, we will have to be content with saying merely that what we *seek* in our reading, though we may not find it, is not *a* meaning but *the* meaning.

Uniformity in Vocal Expression

Once meaning is determined, there will be a high uniformity also in its utterance, for among educated speakers of English there is a norm of elocution, as there are of grammar and pronunciation, and, though flexible, it allows little room for individual caprice. Otherwise we should not understand each other. Our perception of meaning in listening to speech depends very largely on the speaker's pattern of vocal expression. Certain intonations, rhythms, and gradations of stress are built into all languages and are used naturally and uniformly by literate native speakers. We become more aware of this when we try to speak a language different from our own. We can readily learn the vocabulary of French or Spanish, but we have trouble with their tunes, rhythms, and accents. And the native speaker of French or Spanish has similar trouble with English. Take a very simple instance of stress pattern: "To be or not to be." Both the genius and the logic of our language dictate more stress on "be," "not," and "be" than on "to," "not," and "to." Despite the oft heard declaration that no two actors interpret alike, in *this* respect their interpretations will be identical. Each of us acquires his speech at his mother's knee, or, as some wag has said, some other low joint, and neither of these joints may be a favorable place to acquire standard vocal patterns. The reading class is the place to detect and get rid of substandard expressional habits.

We have been considering chiefly the bare bones of meaning, to be perceived alike and expressed alike by all. But what if these bare bones are fleshed by various moods, attitudes, intentions, and feelings that are not so readily perceived alike and expressed alike by all readers? If the writing is clear, and the reader is alert and intelligent, differences will be slight. Moods of contemplation, geniality, indignation, horror, etc., are readily identified, and each has, within limits, its standard method of expression. Sometimes a writer announces his feeling and there is no mistaking it; sometimes it is only implied or suggested and has to be gathered from the context. But, because it is occasionally unclear, as in Lady Macbeth's much debated "We fail," one must not assume that feeling and intention may generally be understood and interpreted as the reader pleases.

Because of differences of background, experience, voice, and personality, and sometimes by defensible differences of opinion, there are bound to be some variations in the oral interpretation of all forms of literature. These can be tolerated only so far as they do not violate or confuse essential meaning, just as regional variants in pronunciation are acceptable if the general listener is not puzzled or confused by them. For instance, if a Southerner directs you to go *way-east* when he intends to say *west,* regional custom has become a serious barrier to understanding, and something ought to be done about it.

The Plan of This Book

When we listen to speech, whether spontaneous or recited, we should be aware of three separable elements that determine both its effect and our judgement of whether it is good or bad. First, there is the quality of the speaker's voice—whether it is pleasing or irritating, harsh or pure, shrill or mellow, and the like. Second, there is his pronunciation—whether it conforms to conventional "correctness" and whether his articulation is precise or muddy, clean cut or blurred, etc. Third, there is elocution—the pattern of vocal expression, its modulations, rhythms, accents, tempos, and phrasings. We shall begin with this third element, because it is the much neglected foundation of all our study of reading. Some teachers do little more than urge that modulations be varied, neglecting the fact that variety may be artificial and capricious. Vocal expression must be determined at every point by the action of the speaker's mind while he is speaking. It must not be divorced from meaning. We will begin with the study of plain prose, for at the start we do not want our mental and vocal responses to be complicated by emotion, verse, or dramatic action. This will occupy us for two chapters. In preparation for reading poetry, we will give some time to voice, pronunciation, and verse rhythm, since these are very important in bringing out the meaning and the beauty of poetry. Later, we will take up impersonation and the reading of plays. We should learn to speak as ourselves before we attempt to speak as other persons.

The Selections

In the next chapter, and in each succeeding chapter, I will present a body of principles, theories, and techniques, and then a brief paragraph or other selection, fully analyzed, with which it is expected that all the class will practice the application of these principles, after which each will read the selection before the class and submit to criticism from class-mates and teacher.   Then, a number of similar selections are provided (some of them loaded with booby traps), from which it is expected that each student will choose one to his liking, or have one assigned by the teacher, which he will analyze independently, read before the class, and again submit to criticism.   Thus, there will be both communal and in-dividual efforts, with the benefits of both.

The selections are brief enough to allow half a dozen readers to be heard in one class hour, but long enough to allow you and the teacher to discover whether you are able to apply the principles you have just studied.   The prose selections are thoughtful rather than flashy.   They demand, and will repay, close study.   They deal with problems of educa-tion and of life in general that concern all of us.   Some who have studied them testify that they have been a fruitful source of ideas and of phrases for public speaking, writing, and conversation, and even that they contain some of the germinal ideas of a liberal education.   Note incidentally that some of the selections in the next chapter deal with the problems of read-ing.   They should be considered as part of the text.

The poems offered in later chapters are some of the classics of English literature that should be a part of everyone's literary treasury.   I have added such modern poems as seem to be of comparable quality and suita-ble for reading aloud.   In choosing the poems as well as the selections of light verse, narrative, and drama, I have aimed to reject the transient and local and to offer what has proved, or what I hope *will* prove, dura-ble, memorable, and entertaining.

It may be that some students will have selections of their own choice that they prefer to read.   If so, they had better first have the teacher's approval, and they must consider three things.   First, the selection should be in every way suitable for reading in class and should be such as to al-low for demonstration of the principles being considered.   Second, if it is not familiar to the teacher, he should be provided in advance with a copy of it, for he cannot be expected to criticize effectively a reading of some-thing he has not studied, any more than the student can read effectively what *he* has not studied.   Third, the class cannot be expected to criticize intelligently what its members have never seen or heard and do not have in hand.   Bear in mind that class readings are meant not to entertain but to demonstrate skills.

We shall proceed in the next chapter to study how thoughts and feelings expressed in language may be apprehended and communicated orally to others. But first you may like to test your skill in understanding language on some of the exercises that follow.

Tests of Understanding

Do you accept and use uncritically the familiar phrases of everyday speech? Take, for instance, "The exception proves the rule." What does it mean? Just what does an exception in a series of similar events prove? And how? Does "proves the rule" mean proves to *be* the rule, proves the rule is valid, or proves that a rule exists? Do you understand this statement vaguely, wrongly, or not at all?

How well do you understand literary English? Take the second line of Mrs. Howe's familiar "Battle Hymn of the Republic": "He is trampling out the vintage where the grapes of wrath are stored." What does it mean? Experience with many students reveals that hardly one in a hundred can explain it. "Trampling out." We trample out things we want to get rid of—fires, anthills, weeds. It is a vintage that is being trampled out. What is a vintage? It has something to do with grapes and vineyards. Is it something to get rid of or something to be preserved? Is it the grapes, or the juice, or the residue after the juice is extracted? The metaphor will not be clear to you unless you have seen or heard of the primitive method of wine making still used in some vineyards where the gathered grapes are dumped into a vat and the juice is trampled out of them by the bare feet of the workmen—or their daughters; Tennyson speaks of girls whose legs are "red with the spurted purple of the vats." But these are "grapes of wrath." What does that mean? John Steinbeck made it the title of a novel. Is wrath to be found in the grapes, the wine, the laborers? Are these evil grapes that are to be destroyed? Or could it be that a vintage of wrath is being prepared for a righteous use? Consider the first line—"Mine eyes have seen the glory of the coming of the Lord"—and the third line—"He has loosed the fateful lightning of his terrible swift sword." This is surely a warlike gesture. Is God working up his wrath preparatory to fighting? This is a battle hymn, remember. What does the line mean?

Now try to explain the following familiar passages:

1. He prepareth a table before me in the presence of mine enemies.

Psalm 23.

2. The quality of mercy is not strained;
   It droppeth as the gentle rain from heaven.

WILLIAM SHAKESPEARE, *The Merchant of Venice.*

3. And thus the native hue of resolution
   is sicklied o'er with the pale cast of thought.
   WILLIAM SHAKESPEARE, *Hamlet.*

4. When I have fears that I may cease to be
   Before my pen has gleaned my teeming brain.
   JOHN KEATS, "When I Have Fears."

5. And join with thee calm Peace and Quiet,
   Spare Fast, that oft with gods doth diet.
   JOHN MILTON, *"Il Penseroso."*

Can you understand a long, complicated sentence with many modifying clauses, such as may be found in an insurance policy, and can you, after studying it, read it aloud, holding all its structure in mind so that it will be clear to a listener? Try your skill on one of the following sentences:

1. The Company, in consideration of the warranties herein contained, and of the cash premium and the policy fee, and subject to the limits, exceptions, exclusions, special provisions, general conditions and form of coverage elected by the insured as hereinafter set forth, does hereby insure the insured named and described in the schedule of warranties, which schedule is material and which the insured by the acceptance of this policy warrants to be true, against loss by reason of the liability imposed by law upon the named insured for damage on account of bodily injuries accidentally suffered or alleged to have been suffered, while this policy is in force, including death resulting at any time therefrom by any person or persons not employed by the named insured or his spouse by reason of the operation or use by the named insured or his spouse, of any private passenger motor vehicle loaned to or driven by such named insured or his spouse, but not owned, hired, or leased by the named insured or his spouse. (An accident insurance policy.)

2. I shall observe, in passing, that it seems not so much from any essential distinction in the faculty of the two poets, or in the nature of the objects contemplated by either, as in the more immediate adaptability of these objects to the distinct purpose of each, that the objective poet, in his appeal to the aggregate human mind, chooses to deal with the doings of men (the result of which dealing, in its pure form, when even description, as suggesting a describer, is dispensed with, is what we call dramatic poetry); while the subjective poet, whose study has been himself, appealing through himself to the absolute Divine mind, prefers to dwell upon those external scenic appearances which strike out most abundantly and uninterruptedly his inner light and power, selects that silence of the earth and sea in which he can best hear the beating of his individual heart, and leaves the noisy, complex, yet imperfect exhibitions of nature in the manifold experience of man around him, which serve only to distract and suppress the working of his brain. ROBERT BROWNING, *Essay on Shelley.*

2

EXPRESSION OF THOUGHT

The guiding aim throughout this book is *to develop adequate mental and emotional responsiveness to the meaning of literature and skill in communicating it orally to others.*

Mastering Our Medium

It might be exciting to plunge at once into the exercise of your emotional and impersonative powers, to explore the heights of poetry and drama, but we have first the more prosaic task of examining the conventional patterns of spoken English—our medium of communication. That is, as we have said, the foundation upon which all of our study must be built. You may say that you already know how to speak English, and, of course, you do, if it is your native language. You get along all right, are able to express yourself and communicate with others. But speaking is an art, so it is capable of endless improvement. What we seek is the highest possible proficiency in it. Having a line to speak, we should, like good actors, try to find the *best* way to speak it, not blurt it out spontaneously. We shall begin in this chapter by studying the language of meaningful expository prose and trying to find the most effective vocal expression of it.

How Do We Judge Good Speech?

What are the essential characteristics of effective speaking? Note first that speech for our purposes is not private self-expression like cries of pain or singing in the bath. It is social, intended to be heard, a means of communication with others. It should be judged not by how well it expresses the speaker but by how it impresses the hearer. In reading, especially, our concern is not with getting ourselves expressed but with getting our author expressed so as to create the proper response in our hearers. And the response we want is not admiration of our skill but appreciation of our message.

The first requirement of good speech is that it be clear—in voice, in articulation, and in the modulations that affect meaning. Second, it should be animated, vital, and vivid enough for the immediate situation— not cold, detached, colorless, or indifferent. Third, it should carry meaning with the greatest possible economy of the hearer's attention. It should, of course, be loud enough to be heard easily. Straining to understand discourages attention and weakens interest. Since English is a language of marked gradations of stress, it will be most easily understood when the essential idea-carrying words and syllables stand out clearly from those that are not important. A level monotony, whether shouted or merely murmured, puts an unneeded strain on the listener, which may, if long continued, put him to sleep. It is important also for easy listening that utterance be fluid and controlled, not marred by fumbling, hesitation, or uncertainty, or by distracting mannerisms in intonation and behavior.

Natural Expression

A fourth quality desirable in good speech is naturalness. We do not like what is affected, artificial, or pretentious in any aspect of behavior, but what we consider natural in speaking is what we have become accustomed to, since custom is a kind of second nature. Our natural manner of speaking cannot be defended merely because it *seems* natural to *us*. We should try to conform to what is normal, standard, and conventional with those who may be considered the conservers of the best traditions of our language, people whose pattern of speech reveals a cultural background of education and intelligence, who have lived or traveled in various English-speaking regions, and who are free from the localisms and provincialisms of single communities. This is, indeed, a slippery standard, but, since there are no cultural law givers for English as there are for French, it is the best we can devise. Examples of this kind of speech can readily be heard—from actors, professors, public lecturers, and our better radio and television announcers—but not from ballyhooing hucksters with their oily unction and forced jollity. Trying to conform to this standard may at first make you feel unnatural, but it should bring you closer to the norm of good speaking.

Conversational Quality

Finally, as naturalness implies, good reading of prose should sound conversational. The founders of the elocution movement in the late eighteenth century deplored the fact that reading in the churches, the law courts, and elsewhere was flat, colorless, and artificial, far inferior to utterance by the same persons in earnest talk. The same condition is found today. The common tendency in reading aloud is to report the words without enough attention to their import and to let the voice level off into a monotone. Recognizing words quickly, organizing them instantly into meaningful phrases, and speaking them as if they were our own are skills that are all too rare, but they can be developed by concentration and practice. Lowell was captivated by Emerson's skill in these matters when reading from manuscript: "How artfully does the deliberate utterance, that seems waiting for the fit word, appear to make the audience partners in the labors of thought and make us feel as if the glance of humor were a sudden suggestion, as if the perfect phrase lying written there on the desk were as unexpected to him as to us."

The problem is to train the eye to range ahead and identify the units of thought, to get a firm grasp on the meaning, and to hold it in the focus of attention while speaking it. This is one of the two essential characteristics the late James A. Winans found in conversational delivery.[1] The other was "a lively sense of communication," not something physical like what is called "eye contact" but a *sense* of contact with one's hearers. Since most of our attention must be on the page, we tend to ignore our audience, but we can learn to pay attention to it too. There may be reading occasions when mere mechanical reporting is called for ("The law states . . ." "These are the directions on the can"), but most occasions call for active sharing with the hearers of what is on the page, and the reader's attitude should indicate that he wants them to receive it and respond to it. The manner of a soliloquy or a private vocal exercise will not do; what should be revealed is a felt sense of communication.

These criteria will serve our present purpose, but do not assume that they will be adequate for all occasions. It may well be that, in reading some forms of poetry, drama, ritual, prayer, and the like, none of them are applicable.

Methods of Teaching Expression

How does one acquire clear, vivid, economical, natural, conversational expression in reading aloud, and how is it taught? Various methods of speech improvement have been in use since early times, and it will be well to review them here. Remember that in this chapter we are considering not bodily behavior, voice improvement, or articulation, but chiefly the expressive pattern of the voice.

---

[1] James A. Winans, *Speech Making* (New York: Appleton-Century-Crofts, Inc., 1938), Chapters 2, 20.

First, improvement may be made if one merely reads as he speaks, but with constant alert attention to the meaning of his text. This so-called natural method of reading or teaching may seem to be no method at all, but you will find that there is much to be learned about the discovery of meaning in print and the translation of it into vocal expression while following your natural habits of expression. What is chiefly required is a sharpening of your awareness of meaning. If, for instance, you are sharply aware of a contrast between two ideas, you will naturally stress the words that express the contrast.

Second, you may find or formulate rules of expression that tell what classes of words to stress or subordinate, when to pause, what intonation is called for, and so on, and keep the rules in mind while reading, or memorize what they prescribe. Such reading by rule will take your mind off the meaning, and it can never be foolproof. "Always pause at a comma" says an old rule, but we do not ordinarily pause at the comma in "Yes, sir."

Third, we can listen carefully to the speech patterns of good speakers and try to conform to them. We should all be sensitive to the speech of our environment and notice our deviations from the norm, but we differ widely from each other in our susceptibilities to this influence. Some of us after a month in England will come home with a quite unconscious British accent; others will remain unaffected. Some Georgia crackers may spend twenty years in the North and never lose their native speech pattern, while others may lose it completely within a few months. It is not easy to hear ourselves as others hear us, but some help can be got in this way.

Fourth, we may have a teacher tell us just how our voices should behave (pause here, let your voice fall there, prolong this word, etc.), a method used by some drama coaches. This leaves all the work to the teacher and reduces the student to a mere puppet, helpless when confronted by the next problem in reading, but it is often effective as a last resort.

Finally, one may merely imitate someone else's reading of a given passage, perhaps a phonograph recording by a famous actor. This method, sometimes used in teaching foreign languages, also leaves the reader uninstructed for his next attempt, though it may give him helpful suggestions.

These methods will serve our present purposes, and we will be using all of them, with chief emphasis on the first, but the careful student of acting, especially when reading Shakespeare, and the serious interpreter of fine poetry may wish to study and experiment with the *elements* of vocal expression: time, pitch, force, and quality of voice. These elements were first thoroughly analyzed and systematized in 1827 by James Rush in his ponderous and intricate *Philosophy of the Human Voice*, which, during the next hundred years, was the dominant influence in teaching elocution. It is true, as Rush pointed out, that every syllable we utter has a certain duration in time, a basic pitch with usually a slide up or down or both, a degree of force relative to neighboring syllables, and a certain quality of voice, and each of these may be managed in a better or a worse way to achieve the desired effect. But it is only on very special occasions that detailed analysis of each element in each syllable is justifiable. There is no doubt, however, that serious actors, comedians, and reciters are able to design their utterance by conscious use of these elements and can do so without sounding mechanical.

Words as Symbols

These refinements of vocal expression are important modifiers of meaning, but basically, of course, the meaning lies in the words themselves. We can and do convey meaning by means of cries, gestures, signs, bells, and whistles, but our chief symbols in communication are words. By definition a word is "an articulate sound or series of sounds which symbolizes and communicates an idea." That is to say, it is vocal, not printed; a symbol, not an object; for communication, not self expression. But it may have a written or printed symbol as well as a spoken one. In origin, the written or printed form is, in turn, a symbol of the spoken form, but its symbolization or reference is the same for us in all of these forms. What then is this "word" that can be symbolized in various ways. It is not the black characters we see on the page or the sound waves by which it travels to our ears. We can hardly do better than accept Plato's notion that it is something "graven on the soul," or Justice Holmes's that it is "the skin of a living thought." The important thing is that these word-symbols, during the centuries since their origins, have been conventionalized in spelling, pronunciation, and meaning so that they carry the same significance for the one who writes them, the one who translates them from written to spoken form, and the one who hears them spoken.

But here two warnings must be given. First, in this symbolical character of language lies a great danger for the reader—the danger that words may become merely symbols, divorced from meaning. As John Dewey said, if children in learning to read were taught

. . . to identify forms and to reproduce the sounds they stand for by methods which did not call for attention to meaning, a mechanical habit was established which makes it difficult to read subsequently with intelligence. The vocal organs have been trained to go their own way automatically in isolation; and meaning cannot be tied on at will.[2]

[2] John Dewey, *Democracy and Education* (New York: The Macmillan Co., 1916), p. 167.

And again,

Adults and children alike are capable of using even precise verbal formulae with only the vaguest and most confused sense of what they mean. Genuine ignorance is more profitable because likely to be accompanied by humility, curiosity and open-mindedness; while ability to repeat catch-phrases, cant terms, familiar propositions, gives the conceit of learning and coats the mind with a varnish waterproof to new ideas.[3]

Second, though, as noted earlier, our different personalities, backgrounds, and experiences may lead different persons to get different shades of meaning from the same symbol, these differences are generally not very important. Semanticists and some teachers of interpretation have made too much of the ambiguity of language, paying more attention to differences of impression than to similarities. Some teachers go so far as to urge each reader to choose from his text a meaning that suits him, though this would seem to defeat the very purpose of language. We can understand and communicate the thought and feeling of a writer only when the symbols he uses mean the same to us and to our hearers as to him. "Same" here means "similar in all relevant respects," as Ogden and Richards stated in their pioneering study of language and communication, *The Meaning of Meaning*.[4]

The Study of Words

Turn now to Ruskin's advice in the selection at the end of the chapter (page 41). We shall use this selection as our first practice exercise. Read it through carefully, studying the words as Ruskin directs. You will need, of course, a good dictionary, one that gives complete etymologies. Investigate the ancestry and family connections of "authoritatively," "intensely," "illiterate," "uneducated," "accuracy," "peerage," "canaille," "noblesse," "parliament," etc. If you look up the word "canaille," for instance, you will find that it means "rabble." But you will get a finer appreciation of it if you learn that it is a cousin of our word "canine," and that both come from a Latin root meaning "dog." "Canaille," then, is a pack of curs. If you investigate the family connections of "illiterate," you will learn its relationship here to the phrase "letter by letter," above it, and possibly discover why Ruskin incloses it in quotation marks. In reading this sentence, try to express vocally what Ruskin indicated to the eye by his quotation marks. And, if you will find out what the British Museum is, you will not, I hope, read the clause "but if you read ten pages of a good book" in such a way as to imply that this great British library is stocked only with *bad* books.

[3] John Dewey, *How We Think* (Boston: D. C. Heath & Co., 1910), p. 176.
[4] C. K. Ogden and I. A. Richards, *The Meaning of Meaning* (8th ed.; New York: Harcourt, Brace & World, Inc., 1946), p. 205.

You must make it a practice to stop at every word that is either new or stale and work your way back to the significant reality for which it stands. Only when you master verbal meanings can you begin to be truly educated, and only thus can you read with intelligent expression.

Note also Ruskin's statement that "a false accent . . . is enough, in the parliament of any civilized nation, to assign to a man a certain degree of inferior standing for ever." For college students, and especially for those studying oral reading, any carelessness in the pronunciation of words is beyond pardon. It is never safe to guess at pronunciations. You should make prompt and thorough investigation of every word about which there exists the least doubt, and, if you do not have doubts about words of which your pronunciation is irregular, you must be hopelessly unobservant. Note in this selection the number of syllables in "authoritatively," the sound of *u* in "accuracy," the third syllable of "difference," the accentuation of "entire" and "museum," the number of syllables in "parliament," and, of course, the pronunciation of "canaille" and "noblesse."

Grouping

It is likely that primitive man's first employment of speech was in sentence-words. He said "Go" or "Come" or "Beware," where we now use a phrase of several words with very little additional meaning. In the command "Please leave the room at once," we use six words to express a single idea that might be expressed by a gesture or by the single word "go." The same is true of such ideas as "Come to the window" or "Isn't it time we were going to dinner?" The units of thought as we find it expressed in conventional language are not the separate words of which phrases are composed. The units of thought are the phrases, or word groups, themselves. When we think of the meaning of the statement "A well-educated gentleman may not know many languages," we do not think of "a," then of "well," and then of "educated," etc. We think of "A-well-educated-gentleman," and then of the assertion that he "may-not-know-many-languages." Thought does not proceed by apprehension of separate successive words; it proceeds by word groups.

When we are creating thought as we go along, as in conversation, we generally make the grouping clear to our hearers, that is, make our ideas distinct. In reading from the printed page, our eyes must be trained to run quickly along the succession of words and organize them into proper groups before the voice attempts to utter them. If the voice fails to communicate this grouping to one's hearer's, it fails to communicate meaning, for meaning lies in the grouping. And, if we make a false grouping, we falsify or destroy meaning.

Serious ambiguities and misunderstandings may arise from faulty grouping of words. For instance, on the night before an important holiday, a bungling radio announcer gave the weather forecast as follows:

> Showers tonight, tomorrow—
> Clearing in the north—
> And central portion with occasional showers—
> And warmer in the south.

If you had been planning a picnic, would you have known for what to prepare? Try to read the announcement so that it means what it was intended to mean.

Each of the following sentences may have two meanings, depending on how the words are grouped, though each meaning is expressed by the same words in exactly the same order. Some of the groups make silly results, but they may easily be fallen into by a reader who is not alert.

1. a. "You hope," she said, "too much."
   b. You hope she said too much.

2. a. A man called, while you were out, to lunch with your wife.
   b. A man called, while you were out to lunch with your wife.

3. a. While we were eating, a child, the son of a chief, entered.
   b. While we were eating a child, the son of a chief entered.

4. a. The teacher says the principal is a fool.
   b. "The teacher," says the principal, "is a fool."

5. a. Moses was the daughter-of-Pharaoh's son.
   b. Moses was the daughter—of Pharaoh's son.

6. a. Woman! Without her, man would be a savage.
   b. Woman without her man—would be a savage.

7. a. A man going to sea—his wife requests the prayers of the church.
   b. A man going to see his wife—requests the prayers of the church.

8. a. What do you think! I will let you drive my new car!
   b. What! Do you think I will let you drive my new car!

By shifts in both grouping and stress the following sentence can be given a dozen or more meanings. See how many you can make:

> My friend Ralph has not yet married Celia.

As further evidence of the necessity of proper grouping, note the following sentences. Some of them are difficult, but their meaning will become clear when you discover the correct grouping. And it will not be clear *until* your grouping is right. In written sentences, the proper grouping is generally, but not always, indicated by punctuation. In these sentences the original punctuation marks have been omitted so as to provide a greater test of your powers of comprehension. Read the sentences aloud.

1. Mean men admire wealth great men glory. FRANCIS BACON.

2. Accuracy of diction means accuracy of sensation and precision of accent precision of feeling. JOHN RUSKIN.

3. For the good that I would I do not but the evil which I would not that I do. Rom.: 7, 19.

4. Get place and wealth if possible with grace
If not by any means get wealth and place.
ALEXANDER POPE.

5. Books are the best of things well used abused among the worst. RALPH WALDO EMERSON.

6. Dire was the tossing deep the groans despair
Tended the sick busiest from couch to couch.
JOHN MILTON.

7. We believe that to do is a greater evil than to suffer injustice and not to be punished than to be punished. PLATO.

8. That that is is that that is not is not.

9. Histories make men wise poets witty the mathematics subtle natural philosophy deep moral grave logic and rhetoric able to contend. FRANCIS BACON. (For Bacon, there were two kinds of philosophy—natural and moral.)

10. That that that that that man saw is this is obvious.

11. But when these words are taken as signifying what we have above defined and matter is understood as emotivity not aesthetically elaborated that is to say impressions and form elaboration intellectual activity and expression then our meaning cannot be doubtful. BENEDETTO CROCE. (Matter and form are being compared.)

12. John where Charles had had had had had had had had had had had the teacher's approval.

These examples should be enough to demonstrate that a reader cannot grasp meaning unless he sees it in true units of thought, and that he will not make it clear to his hearers if it is not clear in his own mind. It is a requisite of clearness, as Quintilian said,

that the phrases be distinct, that is, that the speaker begin and stop where he ought. He must observe where his words are to be reined in, as it were, and where suspended, . . . and where they are to be altogether brought to a stand. . . . The merit of making proper distinctions [groupings] may perhaps be little; but without it all other merit in speaking would be vain.[5]

[5] *Institutio Oratoria,* XI. iii, 35, 39.

Many have admired the skill with which Winston Churchill read his speeches, but without knowing the pains he took to facilitate the process. A British newspaper correspondent reported that his speeches were always typed out oversize, with plenty of space. They were written not in sentences and paragraphs, like ordinary copy, but phrase by phrase. On one line there might be only two or three words. Anyone who has an important reading assignment may well follow Churchill's example and type out the phrases on separate lines. Any method is worth trying that helps one to think, and to express himself, in true units of thought.

GROUPING IN VERSE. The problem of grouping in verse is essentially the same as in prose. Grouping must be governed by the thought, not by the line length. It would be convenient for the reader if the two agreed, but they seldom do. The following lines some readers have grouped as indicated. What corrections would you make?

> Or if Sion hill
> Delight thee more—and Siloa's brook that flowed
> Fast—by the oracle of God, [See page 250.]
>
> A dungeon—horrible on all sides—round
> As one great furnace—flamed. [See page 251.]
>
> Not to the sensual ear—but more endear'd—
> Pipe to the spirit ditties—of no tone. [See page 269.]

Some modern poets apparently believe that grouping should be made as difficult as possible for the reader, for they omit punctuation marks and terminate their lines at unexpected and irrational places. Try to read these extracts from two poems by Archibald MacLeish:

> Girl do you think ever
> Waking stretching your small
> Arms your back arched
> Your long legs straight
> Out your mouth red
> Round in a pout in a half
> Yawn half smile[6]

> Between the mutinous brave burning of the leaves
> And winter's covering of our hearts with his deep snow
> We are alone there are no evening birds we know
> The naked moon the tame stars circle at our eaves[7]

[6] From "Excavation of Troy," *Act Five and Other Poems,* by permission of Random House, Inc., publishers.

[7] From "Immortal Autumn," *Poems,* 1924–1933, by permission of Houghton Mifflin Company, publishers.

The unknown author of the following "Ambiguous Lines" intended them to be read with a comma in each line. Place the comma, and note what a difference this change in grouping makes.

> I saw a peacock with a fiery tail
> I saw a blazing comet pour down hail
> I saw a cloud all wrapt with ivy round
> I saw a lofty oak creep on the ground
> I saw a beetle swallow up a whale
> I saw a foaming sea brimful of ale
> I saw a pewter cup sixteen feet deep
> I saw a well full of men's tears that weep
> I saw wet eyes in flames of living fire
> I saw a house as high as the moon and higher
> I saw the glorious sun at deep midnight
> I saw the man who saw this wondrous sight.
> I saw a pack of cards gnawing a bone
> I saw a dog seated on Britain's throne
> I saw King George shut up within a box
> I saw an orange driving a fat ox
> I saw a butcher not a twelvemonth old
> I saw a great-coat all of solid gold
> I saw two buttons telling of their dreams
> I saw my friends who wished I'd quit these themes.

Or note Peter Quince's Prologue from Act V of *A Midsummer Night's Dream:*

> If we offend, it is with our good will.
> That you should think, we come not to offend,
> But with good will. To show our simple skill,
> That is the true beginning of our end.
> Consider then we come but in despite.
> We do not come as minding to content you,
> Our true intent is. All for your delight
> We are not here. That you should here repent you,
> The actors are at hand, and by their show
> You shall know all that you are like to know.

The punctuation indicates how Quince spoke it. As Lysander said, "He hath rid his prologue like a rough colt; he knows not the stop. A good moral, my Lord: it is not enough to speak, but to speak true."

VARIATION IN GROUPING. The limits of the groups within a given sentence are not fixed and constant but may vary with the occasion on which one reads, the intelligence of the listeners, and the purpose of the reader. If audibility is low, if the listeners are immature or dull-witted, or if the reader feels that he should be solemn or impressive, he will go slowly and make his grouping fine. That is, the attendant circumstances will determine whether you should read

You might read—all the books—in the British Museum—if you could live long enough,

or deliver this entire passage as two groups. This is not to imply, however, that there should always be pauses between groups. The essential thing is that the thought units be perceived by both speaker and hearer, and no mere mechanical pausing will ensure this. In the sentence

Whether there are sailors who sail without charts is doubtful.

the phrase "who sail without charts" is certainly a separate thought unit, but there is no need to pause before it. In all such matters, we have to depend on commonsense and the conventional idiom of the language. The one thing we must not do is to put together words that belong apart, or separate those that belong together.

GROUP RELATIONS. Besides noting the limits of separate word groups, we must, as is apparent from preceding examples, observe their relation to each other. The constituent units of a sentence are seldom merely strung together like beads; they are of different sizes and for different purposes, like the girders of a steel bridge, and bear various relationships to each other. These relationships are an integral part of meaning. Note how puzzling are the following groups when merely enumerated, thus:

A library may be very large—it is in disorder—it is not useful—one that is small —well arranged.

But when the proper connective words are inserted showing their relations to each other, their meaning becomes clear:

A library may be very large; but if it is in disorder, it is not so useful as one that is small but well arranged.

These interdependences among phrases are so various and so complicated that no rule can be formulated to cover them. If you wish them to be apparent in your voice, you must understand them and hold them in mind as you read.

The most common relationship between word groups is that of principal and subordinate. Most modifying phrases and clauses, and many conditional and parenthetical clauses, are subordinate in importance to main clauses, and so must be given less prominence in reading. Or two word groups may be of equal importance, as in parallelism and balance, or when they express a contrast, a restatement, a reinforcement, or an explanation. Sometimes a series of groups will mount to a climax as in Ruskin's first sentence. It breaks up into these groups:

I tell you earnestly and authoritatively
I know I am right in this
you must get into the habit of looking intensely at words
and assuring yourself of their meaning
syllable by syllable
nay, letter by letter.

In the first group, he announces that he is very much in earnest. In the second, he stops the continuity of his thought with a parenthetical but important statement that he is sure he is right. Then comes the message: We must (1) study words and (2) be sure of their meaning. Then he particularizes his statement by the phrase "syllable by syllable." Not satisfied with that, he particularizes and intensifies his meaning still further by specifying "letter by letter." Note that the connective "nay" does not mean here "no" or "less." Rather, it means "more." So whereas the chief logical importance is in the third and fourth groups, there is a steady increase in intensity from the beginning, through each successive group, to the end.

Sometimes the parts of one group will be separated from each other by intervening groups, as in this unusual sentence from Tennyson's "Launcelot and Elaine":

I, sometime call'd the maid of Astolat,
Come, for you left me taking no farewell,
Hither, to take my last farewell of you.

"I come hither" must be perceived and read as a single group, each of the first two words being held in suspense until the group is finished.

Often a series of word groups is built into a sentence much as stones of irregular shape and size are used to build a wall. And sometimes, as in forming an arch all the stones must be held in place until the keystone is added to bind them into unity, the elements of a sentence must be held suspended until a final phrase completes it. See, for instance, the final sentence of the Ruskin selection, or note these sentences:

Mathematics, even in its higher branches, when undue emphasis is put upon the technique of calculation, and science, when laboratory exercises are given for their own sake, suffer from the same evil.

Till the slow sea rise and sheer cliff crumble,
　Till terrace and meadow the deep gulfs drink,
Till the strength of the waves of the high tides humble
　The fields that lessen, the rocks that shrink,
Here now in his triumph where all things falter,
　Stretched out on the spoils that his own hand spread,
As a god self-slain on his own strange altar,
　Death lies dead.
ALGERNON CHARLES SWINBURNE.

High on a nightblack horse, in nightblack arms,
With white breast-bone, and barren ribs of Death,
And crown'd with fleshless laughter—some ten steps—
In the half-light—thro' the dim dawn—advanced
The monster, and then paused, and spake no word.
ALFRED, LORD TENNYSON.

CAUSE AND EFFECT. One relationship that calls for special attention is that between two units one of which expresses a cause, and the other a result of that cause. It is especially troublesome because authors frequently connect such units with an innocent-looking "and"—which does not indicate the relationship at all. When we say, "Close the door, and have a chair," the "and" indicates that you are to do two things. But, if we say, "Close the door, and you will suffocate us all," "and" indicates a result—in this case an unwanted result. Hence, "Close the door" in the second sentence must have a quite different expression. What it means is, "Do *not* close the door." Note these lines:

He batted his eyes, and the lightnings flashed;
He clapped his hands, and the thunders rolled.
JAMES WELDON JOHNSON

The two clauses which compose each line may be read as if they were parallel, as if one was merely added to the other; but a moment's study shows that the writer's intention was to make the lightnings a *result* of the batting of the eyes, and the thunders a *result* of the clapping of the hands. This cause-and-effect relationship is easily expressed by the voice if it is present in the mind, but it *must* be present. Try to express the cause-and-effect relationship between the parts of the following sentences:

1. Treat every man as he deserves, and who would escape hanging?
2. This grew; I gave commands; then all smiles stopped together. (See "My Last Duchess," page 368.)
3. Trust the people with the gravest questions, and in the end you educate the race.

4. Take from Washington the educated leaders, and you take from the country its moral mainspring.
5. You have had mental training, and instruction in various branches of learning; you ought to be full of intelligence.
6. Refuse to express a passion and it dies.
7. Count ten before venting your anger, and its occasion seems ridiculous.
8. I sift the snow on the mountains below, and the great pines groan aghast.
9. No uttered syllable, or, woe betide!
10. The hall door shuts again, and all the noise is gone.
11. The Christmas Spirit stood beside sick-beds, and they were cheerful; on foreign lands, and they were close at home; by struggling men, and they were patient in their greater hope; by poverty, and it was rich.

Ellipsis

Sometimes there is difficulty in grasping, and so expressing, the relationship between two words or phrases because a connective word or phrase has been omitted. In daily speech, we are accustomed to these ellipses, and they cause no trouble. We say, for instance, "The man I met," meaning "The man that I met." Or we say, "Take this book to the library, this to your room," without repeating in the second clause the words "take" and "book." But, in literature, such omissions are often troublesome. For instance, Whittier writes,

> The night is mother of the day,
> The winter of the spring.

meaning not that the night is the winter of the spring but that winter is the mother of the spring. Emerson, on one occasion, wished to say that books are the best of things when they are well used, but if they are abused, they are among the worst of things. This statement he compressed as follows:

Books are the best of things well used; abused, among the worst.

The meaning of such a passage is seldom difficult to discover; but the oral communication of it may, because of carelessness or haste, be quite inadequate. In oral reading, it is helpful to "think in" the omitted connective matter, or actually to speak it under your breath. The time required to supply these missing links will create pauses just where they are needed. Or, read aloud, inserting the appropriate "hence," "as," "therefore," "accordingly," "on the other hand," etc., and noting carefully your vocal inflections; then try to use the same inflections while omitting the connective. Practice the following passages.

1. Sweeter than any sung my songs that found no tongue;
   Nobler than any fact my wish that failed of act.

2. The race is to women more than the individual.

3. Men have a greater sense of justice, and women of mercy.

4. Self appears as what it is, an atom to a universe.

5. Suit the action to the word, the word to the action.

6. Is it ever hot in the square? There's a fountain to spout and splash!

7. [Let us] Consult how we may henceforth most offend
   Our Enemy, our own loss how repair,
   How overcome this dire calamity.

8. Teach me half the gladness
       That thy brain must know,
   Such harmonious madness
       From my lips would flow,
   The world should listen then, as I am listening now.

Emphasis

It is sometimes supposed that the meaning of a passage depends on "how you emphasize it." It depends on a good deal more than that, as we have just seen. It depends on the subtle shades of intonation, inflection, or cadence that reveal how one word or phrase is related to another. But it does also depend partly on which words are emphasized. To illustrate this fact, elocutionists used for a century or more (some still use it) this sentence:

Shall you ride to town today?

Perhaps they all borrowed it from John Mason's *Essay on Elocution* (London: 1748). At any rate it will be interesting to note his discussion of its ambiguity with its eighteenth-century flavor. He wrote,

This question is capable of being taken in four different senses, according to the different words on which you lay the emphasis. If it be laid on the word *you,* the answer may be, "No, but I intend to send my servant in my stead." If the emphasis be laid on the word *ride,* the proper answer might be, "No, I intend to walk it." If you place the emphasis on the word *town,* it is a different question, and the answer may be, "No, for I design to ride into the country." And if the emphasis be laid on the word *today,* the sense is still something different from all these, and the proper answer may be, "No, but I shall tomorrow."

In both speaking and reading, we may very easily convey a meaning we do not intend by stressing a wrong word, or failing to stress the right one. For many years, elocutionists complained that some preachers read the clause "He rose *again* from the dead" so as to imply that Christ had more than one Resurrection. They have pointed out also that many actors spoil the meaning of Macbeth's speech

> Will all great Neptune's ocean wash this blood
> Clean from my hand? No; this my hand will rather
> The multitudinous seas incarnadine,
> Making the green one red.

by linking "one" with "green," instead of with "red," and failing to stress it, so implying that the guilty blood would color, not all the seas, but only a green sea. A radio announcer, at the time an heir to the British throne was born, reported the child's mother as saying, "I'm going to be the *mother* of this child, not the *nurses.*" How should he have spoken the sentence? Similar examples of misplaced emphasis are heard every day.

THE NATURE OF EMPHASIS. In general, we emphasize a word as we accent a syllable, by giving it more force, longer duration, and higher pitch. Always, of course, it is the vowel that receives the stress, carries the pitch, and holds the duration of the syllable. Do not be afraid to dwell on the vowels of emphatic words. Little children know how to do it: "I want my ma-a-a-ma." In words of more than one syllable, it is the accented syllable, and usually it alone, that should receive emphasis: "*let*-ter," "con*sist*," even in polysyllables such as "*ac*curacy," "au*thor*itatively." But, if an emphatic words begins with a negative prefix, we commonly stress both the negative and the main syllable of the root word, as "*in*ac-curacy," "*un*educated," "*il*literate," "*un*conventional," "*un*economical." The important word may get special treatment in other ways also, such as by an abrupt attack or a slide of the pitch up or down. Always a word is emphasized by making it conspicuous. You can do this by pausing before it, or after it, or both, or, if it stands in a succession of loudly spoken words, by speaking it softly. Emphasis is as various as thought itself. It is best to think of it not as mere stressing of words but as giving prominence to important ideas, and bringing them into the focus of attention. Even when you emphasize the right words, you may give the wrong meaning. Archbishop Whately pointed out that the question "Is a candle brought to be put under a bushel, or under a bed?" might be so spoken as to imply that these were the only places where a candle could be put, and yet the right words would be accented. In emphasis, as in grouping, there is no substitute for thinking.

WHAT TO EMPHASIZE. We may, however, note three kinds of matter that generally receive emphasis. First are those words that carry the chief

freight of meaning. We have pointed out that primitive speech was probably made up of sentence words, and that we now express by cumbersome phrases what *could* be expressed, though less adequately, by single
words. Each phrase is generally dominated by a single idea, sometimes
expressed in a single word. "The weather is very cold today" can be reduced to the single word "Cold." Linguistic custom surrounds these key
words with grammatical baggage, much of which is not needed to convey
meaning. Obviously, then, in oral reading we should give emphasis to the
essential idea-carrying words and drop the less important ones into the
background. To attempt to emphasize all words is to emphasize none.
Meaning is clouded and obscured if we give strong value to every word,
like a schoolboy orator trying to make every syllable count. The words
that need attention are those that are indispensable, those we would use
if attempting to put the thought into a very economical telegram. Meaning will be clear when the thought-carrying words stand out in a bright
pattern against a background of less important words.

Second, prominence should be given to the new matter in each group
or sentence at the expense of the old. The important idea in one sentence
may, when repeated in the next sentence, become mere background material. For instance, in the third sentence of the Ruskin selection,

The entire difference between education and non-education . . . consists in
this accuracy.

"education and non-education" and "this accuracy" are repetitions of ideas
expressed in the preceding sentence. The new ideas are "entire difference" and "consists," and, hence, they should receive the highest prominence.

Third, we should give prominence to ideas that are compared or contrasted with each other. If the contrasted ideas are slightly obscure, or
somewhat removed from each other, or if two contrasts occur together, the
average reader has great difficulty in expressing them. How many will
note, for instance, that, in Ruskin's second sentence, "all the books in the
British Museum" is contrasted with "ten pages" and that it is not contrasted with "good books"? Or, in the fifth sentence, that "canaille" is
contrasted with "true descent" and "blood"? Most students see only the
contrast between "ancient" and "modern," and nearly all have difficulty in
expressing a contrast on both "modern" and "canaille." Still greater difficulty is sometimes experienced when emphasis must be spread over a
whole phrase, as in the second sentence on "all the books in the British Museum," or on "rosy lips and cheeks" in sentence number 5 below. Emphasis on "all" or on "books" at the expense of the other words will distort the
thought. It may be helpful to think of the phrase as meaning merely
"everything."

Underline in the following sentences the terms that stand in contrast to each other. To make perfectly sure that you know exactly what ideas stand in contrast to each other, tie these underlined terms together with a loose connecting line. Then speak the passages with exaggerated emphasis on the contrasts.

1. Ask not what your country can do for you—ask what you can do for your country. JOHN F. KENNEDY.

2. If a free society cannot help the many who are poor, it cannot save the few who are rich. JOHN F. KENNEDY.

3. Man's capacity for justice makes democracy possible; but man's inclination to injustice makes democracy necessary. REINHOLD NIEBUHR.

4. Man marks the earth with ruin—his control
   Stop with the shore;—upon the watery plain
   The wrecks are all thy deed.

   > LORD BYRON, addressing the ocean.

5. Love's not Time's fool, though rosy lips and cheeks
   Within his bending sickle's compass come.

   > WILLIAM SHAKESPEARE.

6. There is little doubt that in the great metropolitan centers there exists a disposition to live and let live, to give and take, to agree and to agree to differ, which is not to be found in simple homogeneous communities. WALTER LIPPMANN.

7. Mere liberty, though a very great thing to a bird, is the first and lowest and smallest condition of human society. J. S. BLACKIE.

8. There is more simplicity in the man who eats caviar on impulse than in the man who eats grape-nuts on principle. G. K. CHESTERTON.

9. Liberty is a wine which lifts a man for a moment into an imaginary heaven, only that it may plunge him into a real hell. (Three contrasts.) J. S. BLACKIE.

10. The misanthropes pretend that they despise humanity for its weakness. As a matter of fact they hate it for its strength. (Three contrasts.) G. K. CHESTERTON.

11. The world will little note nor long remember what we say here, but it can never forget what they did here. (Three contrasts.) ABRAHAM LINCOLN.

IMPLICATION. The words that do not receive emphasis, the words that should be pushed into the background, comprise, among others, two general classes: those whose meaning is implied and those that echo what has already been referred to.

If an idea is implied, it is a waste of the reader's energy and the hearer's attention to assert it with any vigor. We do not assert, for instance, that water *flows* under the bridge or that earth's last picture is *painted,* for it is a characteristic of water to flow and of pictures to be painted. In Ruskin's first sentence, "earnestly" and "authoritatively" should receive more weight than "I tell you," which we will probably understand whether we hear it or not. In the next group, "I know I am right in this," the words "in this" add nothing to the thought that is not implied without them, and could almost as well be omitted. So, also, the words "you must" that follow will be implied from the context, whether heard or not, and hence should be subordinated. When you say in the seventh sentence that an ordinary seaman "will be able to make his way," you mean, of course, that he will speak his wants; and so the word "speak" in the next clause expresses an idea that has already been implied. All such implications must be noted—and subordinated.

Spoken idiom prescribes also that many words such as auxiliary verbs, conjunctive adverbs, prepositions, and other particles receive no stress. Their meaning is not always implied, but, if not, it serves a merely auxiliary function in relation to the main ideas. For instance, in such a sentence as "*You* might have been *hurt* as well as *he*," we subordinate "might have been" and "as well as," though they are essential to the meaning. Such subordinations are so well established in English speech that no mention of them would seem to be needed. But mistakes continue to be made. Recently, an amateur radio announcer, in presenting a news report, was heard to say,

He hoped payment *could* start within a few days.

and

He promised to look into the *matter* as soon as possible.

and

The fate of the defendant *is* to be decided later.

There was nothing in the context of his script to justify these eccentric emphases. Such pitfalls await the speaker who is not giving thought to what he is saying.

Есно. A second class of words that must not be made prominent consists of those that echo ideas already expressed. They perform much the same function as pronouns. When we are aware of them, we habitually subordinate them, and little difficulty is experienced when the echo lies close to its antecedent. In Ruskin's fifth sentence, for instance,

Whatever language he knows, he knows precisely; whatever word he pronounces, he pronounces rightly.

no one will be tempted to stress the second "knows" or the second "pronounces." To do so would obviously confuse one's hearers. But some students will not notice that "language" in this sentence echoes the same word in the preceding sentence; and nearly all will lack sufficient mental span to remember that "illiterate" in the seventh sentence echoes "uneducated" in the sixth. If an echo is not the same word as its antecedent, but a synonym, it frequently escapes detection by all but the most vigilant. In the seventh sentence, "accent or turn of expression" is surely an echo of "speak a sentence" just above it and is, in turn, echoed in the next sentence by "false accent or a mistaken syllable."

In the following lines, there are echoes of this kind that are frequently missed. See if you can identify them and speak them with proper subordination, thus throwing emphasis on an important neighboring word.

> And if the freshening sea
> Made them a terror—'twas a pleasing fear. [See page 259.]
>
> She speaks, yet she says nothing; what of that?
> Her eye discourses. [See page 448.]
>
> Democracy is on trial, and no one knows how it will stand the ordeal. [See page 46.]

Of course, not all repeated material is mere echo. Some repetitions are for the sake of emphasis. You will probably decide that the phrase "letter by letter" in Ruskin's second sentence, though a repetition of the same phrase in the first sentence, is here repeated for the sake of emphasis, and that the same is true of "real accuracy" following it. But do not stumble into implying that you have earlier spoken of accuracy but not of *real* accuracy.

Nothing so conduces to clarity of meaning as the proper suppression of echoed and implied material. Clarity is achieved in reading, as in printing or in painting, when a bright pattern stands out against a dull background; and it is just as important that the background be dull as that the pattern be bright. The strong idea-carrying words cannot be brought into prominence unless the unimportant words are suppressed.

Read again the sentences above illustrating contrast, taking special pains to note and subordinate all echoed and implied material. Make these parts of the thought so weak as to be scarcely audible. By this means, you can make even sharper the focus of attention on the contrasted ideas.

Pause

One device for good expression, though mechanical in nature, is so important that it deserves a word. It is pause. Hiram Corson records that, when a boy in school, he was required to read aloud twice a day. The instruction imparted was "limited, but very good as far as it went, namely, 'Speak distinctly and mind your stops.'" Consequently he acquired a fluent utterance "properly sectioned off by minding the stops."

There are two principal reasons why readers fail to mind the stops. First, they lack confidence. The excitement of reading before others causes a nervous acceleration of what is normally a too rapid rate of utterance. Under such circumstances, the cessation of vocal activity for a fraction of a second seems an ominous silence full of dreadful possibilities. The reader feels that his audience will begin to wonder whether he has not broken down. To *deliberate* in the presence of an audience takes confidence. If you lack this confidence, there is not much that you can do about it except to keep as cool as possible, and hold your mind firmly on what you are saying. Confidence will come with experience.

A second reason why readers seldom pause is just that they do not *deliberate*. They skim. Their minds do not *dwell* on the ideas to be communicated. As surely as the mind begins to dwell on the ideas expressed, there will be a focusing on separate word groups (how else *can* one think?), and these word groups will generally be separated from each other by pauses.

A pause must not be thought of as a mere mechanical wait, a recess, a rest period. It must be packed with meaning if it is not to do more harm than good. It gives the reader a chance to take a breath, look ahead, and get a grip on the next thought, while it gives the hearer time to digest what has just been said and to become curious about what is coming. Pauses should be used by the reader to get clearly in mind the *relations* of phrases. Often they can be used to insert under the breath connective words and phrases that will help to make the expression of these relations clear.

In general, the places for pauses are easily discovered. Sometimes they are marked by punctuation. But it is not true, as many have been taught, that there must always be a pause at a comma. We do not, for instance, normally pause after "is" and after "and" in this sentence: "There is, first, the literature of knowledge, and, secondly, the literature of power." We do, however, pause at the other commas. Semicolons and periods are almost invariable indications of group endings, and there is no excuse for rushing breathlessly by them, and stopping only when breath is exhausted.

Pauses should, of course, be longer and more frequent when the thought is difficult or unfamiliar, or when the reader desires to be very impressive. Children understand the trick of increasing impressiveness, as when they say, "And then there came a great—big—bear!" Adults may have to return to childhood to discover so simple and obvious a device for expressiveness in reading.

As we have already noted, pauses may be effectively employed not only between phrases but also within a phrase. They may be used to isolate an unusual word so that it will be clearly heard, as "words of modern—canaille." Or they may be used for dramatic effect when suspense is allowed to accumulate before an idea that is to receive great prominence; as when Tennyson mourns "the sound of a voice—that is still"; or, in comedy, when Mrs. Malaprop bursts forth in astonishment, "I'm—*putrified!*" In any well-directed play, the location and duration of pauses become a very fine and very important study. Sometimes, if the play is a classic, the pauses are standardized and become part of the tradition of the acting of that play, which is passed down from generation to generation of actors.

It is impossible to list all the uses for pauses. The student must remember that they are an essential part of deliberation. "Speech is silvern; silence is golden," says the proverb, and silence is never more golden than in the midst of speech.

Précis Writing

In preparing a selection for reading, one of the best aids in getting at the essential thought is to reduce it to a précis. That is, you boil it down to about a third its original size; or, to change the figure, you squeeze the water out of it, retaining its original form and proportions. The parts discarded are details, figures, ornaments, repetitions, minor illustrations, and less important modifiers. The finished précis should say all that the original says but should say it much more briefly. Yet it should be coherent and readable. It should avoid, as far as possible, the wording of the original but should retain its attitude and point of view. That is, it should be not a comment on the selection but a restatement of the same material reduced to a concise summary. Nothing essential should be left out, and nothing should be added.

There is no surer test of your understanding of a selection (aside from reading it aloud to a competent teacher of reading) than reducing it to a précis. Wherever it has been tried, précis writing has been found to constitute an almost infallible test of intelligence. If approached in the spirit of a game, it becomes an absorbing exercise. You will be surprised to find how hard it is to summarize *all* of your author's thought, to keep it in correct proportion, and to avoid adding anything of your own. Here is a précis of Ruskin on words. See if you cannot make a better one.

Education Means Knowing Words—Ruskin

There is no doubt of it, you must learn to examine and understand words minutely. You might read everything and remain uneducated, but read a little well and you are somewhat educated. The difference is one of accuracy. The educated man knows thoroughly whatever he knows of language, and he is especially thoroughly acquainted with the etymologies of words. But the uneducated may speak many languages and really know none. A sailor can express himself in many languages, but his speech reveals his illiteracy, just as the scholar's speech reveals him. Hence, a verbal mistake will ruin one's reputation in any parliament.

Memorization

If you conscientiously study a selection according to these directions, you will probably find that you have almost, if not entirely, memorized it. But the worst thing you can possibly do in preparing a selection is to memorize merely the sounds of the words. What you should memorize is the *thought*. That is, memorize what goes into your précis. Then, by careful rereading and study of the selection, fix in mind the words in which your author clothes his thought. And remember Francis Bacon's discovery, corroborated by modern psychological studies: "If you read anything over twenty times, you will not learn it by heart so easily as if you were to read it only ten, trying to repeat it between whiles, and when memory failed looking at the book."

Whatever study you give a selection will have more enduring results if distributed over a long period of time. That is, it is better to study fifteen minutes a day for four days than to study for an hour at a time. The intervals between study are valuable because the mind assimilates material when not giving active attention to it.

Summary

The teachings of this chapter are applicable to all oral reading, whether of prose, poetry, or drama. We shall apply them first to passages chiefly of logical prose, beginning with Ruskin's advice on the study of words. We may summarize the directions of this chapter in a study plan:

PLAN OF STUDY

1. Read the selection through silently to get the drift of the thought. Close your book, and recall as completely as you can what you have just read.
2. Read it again, slowly, carefully, "suspiciously."
3. Look up immediately in a good dictionary all words you are not perfectly sure you can define and pronounce correctly. Investigate all allusions; be sure you understand not only their meaning but also the reasons for their use here.
4. Condense the thought of the whole into a précis approximately one-third the length of the original; that is, boil it down to a summary that retains all the essential parts of the thought. Avoid the wording of the

original. Keep all the parts in proportion. The parts discarded will be figures, repetitions, minor illustrations, and rhetorical flourishes. The finished précis should read smoothly and preserve the attitude or point of view of the original.

5. Note the word groups. It may be helpful to mark the limit of each by a vertical line, but do not allow this or any other mechanical device to interfere with re-creation of the thought while reading.

6. Note the relation of each group to its neighbors. Some possible relationships are cause and effect, contrast, repetition, restatement, amplification, development, subordination, parallelism, summary, parenthesis, climax, condition, reinforcement, modification, explanation.

7. Find the thought center in each group. That is, which words carry the chief weight of meaning? Note all contrasts, making sure that you see clearly which words contain the contrasted ideas. Which words are mere echoes of ideas already expressed, and which are new, adding something additional to the thought? Which ideas are implied and so do not need emphasis? Emphasis should take care of itself if your thinking is correct.

8. Where can you make clearer the relation between words or groups by inserting such connectives as "hence," "wherefore," "so," "as," "for," "besides," "furthermore," "since," "for example," "even," "thus," "on the contrary," or "then again"?

9. Where will your hearers need time to assimilate the thought or feeling, and where will a pause be valuable in separating elements not closely related, or in directing attention to an important idea? With what will your own mind be occupied during these pauses?

10. When you understand the content of the selection, practice reading it aloud, *rethinking the thought as you go.* Arrange to have several practice periods, separated from each other by several hours, or by a whole day. Read the selection several times at each period, always with close concentration on the thought as revealed by your analysis. Force your voice to expressiveness by vivid re-creation of the thought, and by sympathetic response to the spirit of the selection.

11. A great deal can be accomplished by self-criticism if you can hear yourself as others hear you. If a tape recorder is available, by all means use it. Record and listen to one sentence at a time, noticing your weaknesses and mistakes and trying to correct them in a second recording and as many more as are needed. Then record and judge the whole, listening *suspiciously,* and repeating the process as often as seems profitable.

12. All these steps will aid in case you decide to memorize the selection. Always memorize the *meaning,* rather than the sounds of the words, and by the whole, rather than by the part, method. After each reading of the selection, close your book and recall as much as you can of the thought. In this way, you will fix in mind the thought chain, and you can then readily substitute for your own the words of the author.

Criteria of Good Reading

As we proceed with our study, we shall, of course, gradually expect to increase our skill in reading. This should be accomplished by faithful adherence to the Plan of Study (which will be augmented as we proceed from chapter to chapter). But we need to have some check on our progress. We need criticism. And we need also to accumulate a body of criteria by which we can appraise reading or speaking wherever we hear them. Let us set down, then, a series of critical questions based on the teachings of this chapter, and to be increased in succeeding chapters, with which we may check the reading of our fellow students and others whom we hear. It will be found that many of them are applicable to social conversation, to the minister's sermon, to the political address, to the actor's interpretation of his lines, and to normal speech wherever heard. It is to be hoped that they will bring forth something more helpful and more intelligent than such lame comments as "Well, I thought he was pretty good," "Why, he spoke very well; in fact, I think he's a very good speaker," or "She has *marvelous* powers of interpretation! Her reading was positively *thrilling!*"

CRITERIA

1. Was the reader's utterance clear?
2. Was it sufficiently animated?
3. Was it easily understood, intelligently and conventionally modulated, not marred by fumbling, hesitation, uncertainty, or distracting eccentricities?
4. Did it seem natural, conform to our norm of natural speaking?
5. Did it resemble lively conversational speech, with the reader constantly aware of meaning and of its listeners?
6. Were word groups clearly marked and properly related?
7. Did the important thought-carrying words stand out sharply from those that were unimportant, echoed, or implied?
8. Was emphasis not merely mechanical but responsive to thought?
9. Was skilful use made of pause?

QUESTIONS FOR DISCUSSION

1. Discuss economy of the hearer's attention as an aim in good speaking.
2. When, and in what respects, is "be natural" good advice about speaking?
3. Is there a "conversational quality" present in all good speech, even when it doesn't sound conversational?
4. How can one revitalize words that have become stale?
5. Find additional examples of sentences that may, because of false grouping, be ambiguous or unclear.
6. Discuss the vocal means of indicating relationships between word groups.
7. Analyze and experiment with various forms of emphasis.
8. Discuss the relation of grouping, emphasis, implication, and echo to economy of the hearer's attention.

SELECTION FOR DRILL

The selection that follows is to be used as a drill selection in class. It can be made to illustrate all the teachings of this chapter, and it is excellent instruction for all students of reading. It should be read, studied, analyzed, reread, criticised, and read again until you can give a faithful rendering of all its logical content. Do not be discouraged if the drill becomes irksome. In the acquisition of any skill such as piano playing or tennis, there are likely to be periods of positive nausea. Your reward will come in the freedom and confidence that can be achieved only through periods of drudgery.

EDUCATION MEANS KNOWING WORDS

From SESAME AND LILIES I

John Ruskin

1. I tell you earnestly and authoritatively (I *know* I am right in this) you must get into the habit of looking intensely at words, and assuring yourself of their meaning, syllable by syllable—nay, letter by letter. 2. You might read all the books in the British Museum (if you could live long enough) and remain an utterly "illiterate," uneducated person; but if you read ten pages of a good book, letter by letter,—that is to say, with real accuracy,—you are for evermore in some measure an educated person. 3. The entire difference between education and non-education (as regards the merely intellectual part of it), consists in this accuracy. 4. A well educated gentleman may not know many languages,—may not be able to speak any but his own,—may have read very few books. 5. But whatever language he knows, he knows precisely; whatever word he pronounces, he pronounces rightly; above all, he is learned in the peerage of words; knows the words of true descent and ancient blood, at a glance, from words of modern canaille; remembers all their ancestry, their intermarriages, distant relationships, and the extent to which they were admitted, and offices they held, among the national noblesse of words at any time, and in any country. 6. But an uneducated person may know, by memory, many languages, and talk them all, and yet truly know not a word of any; —not a word even of his own. 7. An ordinarily clever and sensible seaman will be able to make his way ashore at most ports; yet he has only to speak a sentence of any language to be known for an illiterate person: so also the accent, or turn of expression of a single sentence, will at once mark the scholar. 8. And this is so strongly felt, so conclusively admitted, by educated persons, that a false accent or a mistaken syllable is enough, in the parliament of any civilized nation, to assign to a man a certain degree of inferior standing for ever.

SUGGESTIONS FOR ANALYSIS. (Numbers refer to sentences.) 1. Note the cumulative development of this sentence; it doesn't trail off, but mounts to a climax of intensity in the last phrase. "Nay" means "nay, more." The heart of the meaning is in "looking intensely at words"; bear down on "words." Don't imply by "in this" that you have been wrong in other things. 2. Supply a connective between 1 and 2. This is an astounding statement to those who have long been bludgeoned with the injunction to read widely. Ruskin says No; you are educated not by wide reading but by accurate reading. Don't speak "You might read" as if you really might, or you might choose not to. "All the books in the British Museum" should be treated as a unit, as if it were a single word. Spread your emphasis over all of it, and make it sound like a lot of books. This first clause is an exaggeration, with a touch of humor in it, as Ruskin implies by the parenthesis that follows. The thought is: *even* if you could read all these books, you might still be illiterate. In both occurrences of the word "person," the meaning is readily implied, and they don't need stress. It is probably best to stress both "real" and "accuracy." "Of a good book" is implied and doesn't need stress; above all, don't stress "good" so as to imply that the British Museum is full of *bad* books. Be sure to express the double contrast: "all the books," etc., vs. "ten pages" and "illiterate, uneducated" vs. "educated." These first two sentences are attention-spreading and mind-stretching; you must hold all of each in mind till you get to the end; there are places to pause, but no places to let down. 3. Note that "education," "non-education," and "accuracy" are echoes; the essence of the thought is "entire difference . . . consists." 4. Does "gentleman" here mean anything more than person? Make a distinction among "know," "speak," and "read." This sentence is a springboard for the next. 5. Watch the echoes here, and save your emphasis for what is important. Don't sing "above all"; make it mean what it says. Be aware of the unusual nature of this metaphor likening words to the nobility. Before "peerage" "think in" some such preparatory phrase as "what I may call." What connective will link this to the next clause? Express the double contrast in "knows the words . . . modern Canaille." "Words" occurs four times in this sentence; is it echo each time? Beware of wasting attention on it when it is already in our minds. The last phrase, "among the national. . . ." probably needs no sharp focus at any point. 6. "Uneducated" is contrast with what? If you feel the contrast, you will accent the first syllable. All the commas here call for pauses. 7. Watch your grouping; "make his way" is not in the same group as "ashore at most ports." It means he can make himself understood in various languages. "Illiterate person" is implied; by what? "Known" is the important idea. "Accent or turn of expression" is echo of what? This last clause says merely, "So also with the scholar." 8. There are so many elements in this sentence that it is difficult to find a peak or chief center of meaning. You may choose any of several. You can make "by educated persons" parenthetical. When analysis is complete, practice reading and rereading the selection, holding the meaning firmly in mind and trying to make your reading sound like direct, earnest, sincere conversation.

SELECTIONS FOR PRACTICE

Since our present concern is with "expression of thought," we provide here selections that *contain* thought and that require thinking by the reader. In general, they deal with problems of reading, learning, character, and social adjustment such as all will encounter in college. Some have proved so provocative that class meetings tend to become discussion sessions. This is an educational good, and not to be avoided if time permits, though chief attention should be given to how these ideas are best expressed orally. As a test of the reader's grasp of idea and development, I recommend that before reading he submit to his teacher a précis of his selection, and perhaps an analysis of the expressional problems it presents. I recommend also that assignments be so managed that all, or most, of the selections will be heard, though there is advantage too in having a selection presented by several readers so that performances may be compared.

THE FIRST RULE OF STUDY

From THE TEACHER[8]

George Herbert Palmer

The first rule shall be—*observe!* A simple matter—one, I dare say, which it will seem to you difficult not to follow. You have a pair of eyes; how can you fail to observe? Ah, but eyes can only look; that is not observing. You want to observe, not to look only. You want to penetrate into things, to find out what is there. There is nothing on earth which, when observed, is not of enormous interest. You cannot find anything so destitute of the principles of life, that, when you come to study it, it will not disclose those principles to you. But it makes all the difference whether you do thus observe, whether you are willing to hold your attention to the thing in hand and see what it contains. After puzzling long about the charm of Homer, I once applied to a learned friend and said to him, "Can you tell me why Homer is so interesting? Why can't you and I write as he wrote? Why is it that his art was lost with him, and that to-day it is impossible for us to quicken such interest as he?" "Well," said my friend, "I have meditated on that a great deal, but it seems to me it comes to about this: Homer looked long at a thing. Why," said he, "do you know that if you should hold up your thumb and look at it long enough, you would find it immensely interesting?" Homer looks a great while at his thumb; he sees precisely the thing he is dealing with. He does not confuse it with anything else. It is sharp to him; and because it is sharp to him it stands out sharply for us over all these thousands of years.

[8] By permission of, and by arrangement with, Houghton Mifflin Company.

43

HOW TO READ

From TWO VIEWS OF EDUCATION[9]

Lane Cooper

The process of making monotonous black characters on the page vividly stir the latent sense-perceptions is, however, relatively slow and irksome. Few people have ever learned to do it consistently; and hence, it is fair to say, few have ever truly learned to read. The moral is, read slowly. Take ample time. Pause where the punctuation bids one pause; note each and every comma; wait a moment between a period and the next capital letter. And pause when common sense bids you pause, that is, when you have not understood. As the line of sentences comes filing before the window of your soul, examine each individual expression with the animus, and more than the animus, you would maintain were you paying-teller in a bank; saying to yourself continually, "Do I know this word?" and, "What is this phrase worth?"

Read aloud; read slowly; read suspiciously. Re-read. What a busy man has time to read at all, he has time to read more than once. Was it not Emerson who held that he could not afford to own a book until it was ten years old—had at least to that extent proved its ability to survive? Jealous of his time, he let others sift the ashes. And was it not Schopenhauer who considered no book worth while that was not worth a third perusal? If we read a thing but once, that usually is but so much lost time. The most industrious student forgets a large part of what he tries to retain. The best-read man is the one who has oftenest read the best things.

OF STUDIES

Francis Bacon

Studies serve for delight, for ornament, and for ability. Their chief use for delight is in privateness and retiring; for ornament is in discourse; and for ability is in the judgement and disposition of business; for expert men can execute, and perhaps judge of particulars, one by one: but the general counsels, and the plots and marshalling of affairs come best from those that are learned. To spend too much time in studies is sloth; to use them too much for ornament is affectation; to make judgement wholly by their rules is the humour of the scholar: they perfect nature, and are perfected by experience: for natural abilities are like natural plants, that need proyning by study; and studies themselves do give forth directions too much at large, except they be bounded in by experience. Crafty men contemn studies, simple men admire them, and wise men use them; for

[9] By permission of the Yale University Press.

they teach not their own use; but that is a wisdom without them and above them, won by observation. Read not to contradict and confute, nor to believe and take for granted, nor to find talk and discourse, but to weigh and consider. Some books are to be tasted, others to be swallowed, and some few to be chewed and digested; that is, some books are to be read only in parts; others to be read but not curiously, and some few to be read wholly, and with diligence and attention. Some books also may be read by deputy, and extracts made of them by others; but that would be only in the less important arguments and the meaner sort of books; else distilled books are like common distilled waters, flashy things. Reading maketh a full man; conference a ready man; and writing an exact man; and therefore, if a man write little he had need have a great memory; if he confer little he had need have a present wit; and if he read little he had need have much cunning, to seem to know that he doth not.

WHAT IS A STUDENT?

From AEQUANIMITAS[10]

William Osler

Except it be a lover, no one is more interesting as an object of study than a student. Shakespeare might have made him a fourth in his immortal group. The lunatic with his fixed idea, the poet with his fine frenzy, the lover with his frantic idolatry, and the student aflame with the desire for knowledge are of "imagination all compact." To an absorbing passion, a whole-souled devotion, must be joined an enduring energy, if the student is to become a devotee of the gray-eyed goddess to whose law his services are bound. Like the quest of the Holy Grail, the quest of Minerva is not for all. For the one, the pure life; for the other, what Milton calls "a strong propensity of nature." Here again the student often resembles the poet—he is born, not made. While the resultant of two molding forces, the accidental, external conditions, and the hidden germinal energies, which produce in each one of us national, family, and individual traits, the true student possesses in some measure a divine spark which sets at naught their laws. Like the Snark, he defies definition, but there are three unmistakable signs by which you may recognize the genuine article from a Boojum—an absorbing desire to know the truth, an unswerving steadfastness in its pursuit, and an open, honest heart, free from suspicion, guile, and jealousy.

At the outset do not be worried about this big question—Truth. It is a very simple matter if each one of you starts with the desire to get as much as possible. No human being is constituted to know the truth, and nothing but the truth; and even the best of men must be content with fragments, with partial glimpses, never the full fruition. In this unsatis-

[10] By permission of P. Blakiston's Son & Co., Inc.

fied quest the attitude of mind, the desire, the thirst—a thirst that from the soul must rise!—the fervent longing, are the be-all and the end-all. What is the student but a lover courting a fickle mistress who ever eludes his grasp? In this very elusiveness is brought out his second great characteristic—steadfastness of purpose. Unless from the start the limitations incident to our frail human faculties are frankly accepted, nothing but disappointment awaits you. The truth is the best you can get with your best endeavor, the best that the best men accept—with this you must learn to be satisfied, retaining at the same time with due humility an earnest desire for an ever larger portion. Only by keeping the mind plastic and receptive does the student escape perdition. It is not, as Charles Lamb remarks, that some people do not know what to do with truth when it is offered them, but the tragic fate is to reach, after years of patient search, a condition of mindblindness in which the truth is not recognized, though it stares you in the face. This can never happen to a man who has followed step by step the growth of a truth, and who knows the painful phases of its evolution.

WHAT IS COLLEGE FOR?

From MEMORIES AND STUDIES[11]

William James

What the colleges should at least try to give us, is a general sense of what, under various disguises, superiority has always signified and may still signify. The feeling for a good human job anywhere, the admiration for the truly admirable, the disesteem of what is cheap and trashy and impermanent—this is what we call the critical sense, the sense for ideal values. It is the better part of what men know as wisdom. Some of us are wise in this way naturally and by genius; some of us never become so. But to have spent one's youth at college in contact with the choice and rare and precious, and yet still to be a blind prig or vulgarian, unable to scent out human excellence or to divine it among its accidents, to know it only when ticketed and labeled and forced on us by others, this indeed should be accounted the very calamity and shipwreck of a higher education.

The sense for human superiority ought, then, to be considered our line, as boring subways is the engineer's line and the surgeon's is appendicitis. Our colleges ought to have lit up in us a lasting relish for the better kind of man, a loss of appetite for mediocrities, and a disgust for cheap jacks. The best claim we can make for the higher education, the best single phrase in which we can tell what it ought to do for us, is, then, exactly what I said: it should enable us to know a good man when we see him.

Democracy is on trial, and no one knows how it will stand the ordeal.

---

[11] By permission of Longmans, Green & Co.

What its critics now affirm is that its preferences are inveterately for the inferior. So it was in the beginning, they say, and so it will be world without end. Vulgarity enthroned and institutionalized, elbowing everything superior from the highway, this, they tell us, is our irremediable destiny.

Now who can be absolutely certain that this may not be the career of democracy? Nothing future is quite secure; states enough have inwardly rotted; and democracy as a whole may undergo self-poisoning. But the best of us are filled with a contrary vision of a democracy stumbling through every error till its institutions glow with justice and its customs shine with beauty. Our better men shall show the way and we shall follow them; so we are brought round again to the mission of the higher education in helping us to know the better kind of man whenever we see him.

BOOKS ABOUT BOOKS

From ON READING SHAKESPEARE[12]

Logan Pearsall Smith

Whether there are sailors who sail without charts is doubtful, but there certainly are travellers who prefer to journey with no map to guide them, and readers who are contemptuous of books about books. They gain no profit, they say, by looking at things through the eyes of others. But this impromptu, uninstructed way of grasping at masterpieces in spantaneous leaps of feeling is but a poor way of learning how to enjoy them. The first surprise and flush of prompt delight is, of course, of great, perhaps the greatest, value; but a true appreciation is based on something more than feeling: it demands that we should not only enjoy, but understand our pleasure, and make it food for thought; should learn the esthetic reasons for it, and learn also all we can about the origins and environments of the monuments and masterpieces we gaze on. To understand them we must know their place in history, and their relative position among other masterpieces. And I at least find that my vision of the things I like is greatly enhanced and clarified by seeing them reflected in the luminous minds of other people. Esthetic appreciation is, luckily, a thing that can be communicated, can be learnt from others—the glow of it is a catching fire. How often an admiration spoken of by someone we admire —sometimes the mere mention of a preference—has opened for us the gate into a new world of beauty! And certainly the debt I owe to the great interpreters of literature is far too large to allow me to join in the common abuse of critics; they have given me ears, they have given me eyes, they have taught me—and have taught all of us really—the best way of appreciating excellence, and how and where to find it. How many sights unguided travellers pass by! how many beauties readers of great works will miss, if they refuse to read the books about them!

[12] By permission of Harcourt, Brace & Co.

THINKING FOR ONESELF

From THE ART OF LITERATURE[13]

Arthur Schopenhauer

A library may be very large, but if it is in disorder, it is not so useful as one that is small but well arranged. In the same way, a man may have a great mass of knowledge, but if he has not worked it up by thinking it over for himself, it has much less value than a far smaller amount which he has thoroughly pondered. For it is only when a man looks at his knowledge from all sides, and combines the things he knows by comparing truth with truth, that he obtains a complete hold over it and gets it into his power. A man cannot turn over anything in his mind unless he knows it; he should, therefore, learn something; but it is only when he has turned it over that he can be said to know it. . . .

It is incredible what a different effect is produced upon the mind by thinking for oneself, as compared with reading. It carries on and intensifies that original difference in the nature of two minds which leads the one to think and the other to read. What I mean is that reading forces alien thoughts upon the mind—thoughts which are as foreign to the drift and temper in which it may be for the moment, as the seal is to the wax on which it stamps its imprint. The mind is thus entirely under compulsion from without; it is driven to think this or that, though for the moment it may not have the slightest impulse or inclination to do so. . . .

Reading is nothing more than a substitute for thought of one's own. It means putting the mind into leading-strings. The multitude of books serves only to show how many false paths there are, and how widely astray a man may wander if he follows any of them. But he who is guided by his genius, he who thinks for himself, who thinks spontaneously and exactly, possesses the only compass by which he can steer aright. A man should read only when his own thoughts stagnate at their source, which will happen often enough even with the best of minds. On the other hand, to take up a book for the purpose of scaring away one's own original thoughts is sin against the Holy Spirit. It is like running away from Nature to look at a museum of dried plants or gaze at a landscape in copper-plate.

THE WORSHIP OF SELF-EXPRESSION

From THE CRISIS IN MORALS[14]

Gilbert Murray

Lastly, there has been the false theory: the theory which has already done a vast amount of harm in education and is still running riot in the

---

[13] By permission of The Macmillan Co.
[14] From *Harper's Magazine,* January, 1930, by permission of the editors.

field of art. I mean the worship of self-expression. I will leave art aside for the present, but in education I believe this vicious dogma is approaching its unlamented burial. No doubt it had some psychological excuse for coming into existence against an excessive authoritarianism which tried to turn out all pupils according to one pattern. It was right to consider each pupil's character and personality and train it in appropriate ways. But to suggest that the pupil's whole duty is to express himself, and the teacher's whole duty to help him to do so, seems to me the direct contrary of education. What I as a student have wanted to receive—and what as a teacher I have tried to give—has been always in different contexts the same thing: I wanted to get into contact with minds superior to my own, and thereby to become capable of seeing things which I could not now see, and appreciating and enjoying things that were now above me. We all start life with an extremely limited appreciation of the greatness and beauty by which we are surrounded, and also with a pretty confident opinion that a thing which does not happen to please us is not up to much. I cannot imagine an education which for me personally would have been more utterly damnable than to teach me to be contented with my existing beliefs and powers and just express them—to take the raw, untrained Australian boy called Gilbert Murray as the measure of the universe, and simply encourage him to go ahead. I trust however that this nightmare will pass.

THE WORLD OF BOOKS

From DREAMTHORP

Alexander Smith

In my garden I spend my days; in my library I spend my nights. My interests are divided between my geraniums and my books. With the flower I am in the present; with the book I am in the past. I go into my library, and all history unrolls before me. I breathe the morning air of the world while the scent of Eden's roses yet lingered in it, while it vibrated only to the world's first brood of nightingales, and to the laugh of Eve. I see the pyramids building; I hear the shoutings of the armies of Alexander; I feel the ground shake beneath the march of Cambyses. I sit as in a theatre,—the stage is time, the play is the play of the world. What a spectacle it is! What kingly pomp, what processions file past, what cities burn to heaven, what crowds of captives are dragged at the chariot-wheels of conquerors! I hear or cry "Bravo" when the great actors come on shaking the stage. I am a Roman emperor when I look at a Roman coin. I lift Homer, and I shout with Achilles in the trenches. The silence of the unpeopled Syrian plains, the out-comings and in-goings of the patriarchs, Abraham and Ishmael, Isaac in the fields at even-tide, Rebekah at the well, Jacob's guile, Esau's face reddened by desert sun-heat, Joseph's splendid funeral procession—all these things I find within the boards of my Old Testament. What a silence in those old books as of a half-peopled world—what bleating of flocks—what green pastoral rest—what indubitable human existence! Across brawling centuries of blood and war, I hear the bleating of Abraham's flocks, the tinkling of the bells of Rebekah's camels. O men and women, so far separated yet so near, so strange yet so well-known, by what miraculous power do I know ye all! Books are the true Elysian fields where the spirits of the dead converse, and into these fields a mortal may venture unappalled.

THE DUTY OF BEING HAPPY

From AN APOLOGY FOR IDLERS

Robert Louis Stevenson

Pleasures are more beneficial than duties because, like the quality of mercy, they are not strained, and they are twice blest. There must always be two to a kiss, and there may be a score in a jest; but wherever there is an element of sacrifice, the favor is conferred with pain, and, among generous people, received with confusion. There is no duty we so much underrate as the duty of being happy. . . . A happy man or woman is a better thing to find than a five-pound note. He or she is a radiating focus of good-will; and their entrance into a room is as though another candle had been lighted. We need not care whether they could prove the forty-seventh proposition; they do a better thing than that, they practically demonstrate the great Theorem of the Liveableness of Life. Consequently, if a person cannot be happy without remaining idle, idle he should remain. It is a revolutionary precept; but thanks to hunger and the workhouse, one not easily to be abused; and within practical limits, it is one of the most incontestable truths in the whole Body of Morality. Look at one of your industrious fellows for a moment, I beseech you. He sows hurry and reaps indigestion; he puts a vast deal of activity out to interest, and receives a large measure of nervous derangement in return. Either he absents himself entirely from all fellowship, and lives a recluse in a garret, with carpet slippers and a leaden inkpot; or he comes among people swiftly and bitterly, in a contraction of his whole nervous system, to discharge some temper before he returns to work. I do not care how much or how well he works, this fellow is an evil feature in other people's lives. They would be happier if he were dead. They could easier do without his services in the Circumlocution Office, than they can tolerate his fractious spirits. He poisons life at the well-head. It is better to be beggared out of hand by a scapegrace nephew, than daily hag-ridden by a peevish uncle.

SELF-EDUCATION

John Cardinal Newman

If I had to choose between a so-called University, which dispensed with residence and tutorial superintendence, and gave its degrees to any person who passed an examination in a wide range of subjects, and a University which had no professors or examinations at all, but merely brought a number of young men together for three or four years, and then sent them away as the University of Oxford is said to have done some sixty years since, if I were asked which of these two methods was the better discipline of the intellect,—mind, I do not say which is *morally* the better, for it is plain that compulsory study must be a good and idleness an intolerable mischief,—but if I must determine which of the two courses was the more successful in training, molding, enlarging the mind, which sent out men the more fitted for their secular duties, which produced better public men, men of the world, men whose names would descend to posterity, I have no hesitation in giving the preference to that University which did nothing, over that which exacted of its members an acquaintance with every science under the sun.

Self-education in any shape, in the most restricted sense, is preferable to a system of teaching which, professing so much, really does so little for the mind. Shut your College gates against the votary of knowledge, throw him back upon the searchings and the efforts of his own mind; he will gain by being spared an entrance into your Babel. Few indeed there are who can dispense with the stimulus and support of instructors, or will do anything at all, if left to themselves. And fewer still (though such great minds are to be found) who will not, from such unassisted attempts, contract a self-reliance and a self-esteem, which are not only moral evils, but serious hindrances to the attainment of truth. And next to none, perhaps, or none, who will not be reminded from time to time of the disadvantage under which they lie, by their imperfect grounding, by the breaks, deficiencies, and irregularities of their knowledge, by the eccentricity of opinion and the confusion of principle which they exhibit. They will be too often ignorant of what every one knows and takes for granted, of that multitude of small truths which fall upon the mind like dust, impalpable and ever accumulating; they may be unable to converse, they may argue perversely, they may pride themselves on their worst paradoxes or their grossest truisms, they may be full of their own mode of viewing things, unwilling to be put out of their way, slow to enter into the minds of others;—but, with these and whatever other liabilities upon their heads, they are likely to have more thought, more mind, more philosophy, more true enlargement, than those earnest but ill-used persons, who are forced to load their minds with a score of subjects against an examination, who have too much on their hands to indulge themselves in thinking or investigation, who devour premise and conclusion together with indiscriminate greediness, who hold whole sciences on faith, and commit demonstrations to memory, and who too often, as might be expected, when their period of education is passed, throw up all they have learned in disgust, having gained nothing really by their anxious labors, except perhaps the habit of application.

THE CHARACTER OF THE SOPHIST

From Two Views of Education[15]

Lane Cooper

To the Greeks—to Plato, for example—a Sophist was one who professed to have wisdom in general, and to be able to make other men wise, though he himself had no thorough knowledge of any one thing. For a substantial consideration, he would give you general culture with no special effort on his side, while you yourself were not under the painful necessity of learning anything in particular. He discoursed, or, as we would say, lectured; and you merely listened in delight to what he asserted. Yet to Plato the truly wise man was Socrates, who began operations by confessing his ignorance; who was swift to inquire, and reluctant to affirm; and who, when he taught, taught only the habit and method of investigation. . . . The primary trait of a Sophist is his unwillingness to admit his own ignorance. He simply lacks the courage to say "I do not know." He begins with a flat assertion, rather than a question or hypothesis; he has investigated no one subject from the bottom up, but deals in sounding generalities; and, through a show of wisdom, he deceives himself and imposes on the crowd, so that they pay him money and spread abroad his renown. . . .

Having mere scraps of classical lore, and an abysmal ignorance of the culture in the Middle Ages, he will use the words "old" and "mediaeval" as terms of censure, and "modern" as a term of unqualified praise. But his favorite word of commendation is "broad"; and his ideal man is "broad-minded," whatever that may mean—it seems to designate a person with a mind like a loose, ill-fitting shoe. He does not think that "broad" is the way that leadeth to destruction. . . . In his search for novelty of thought, he has acquired the habit of making the worse appear the better reason; he tells you that power gained by studying a subject that is hard, like Greek or mathematics, cannot be transferred to the acquisition of a subject that is easy. . . . In studies, he advocates the line of least resistance, which is the line of free choice from the kindergarten to the grave. He maintains that "culture" is to be had from every subject, and implies that it may be obtained as well from manual training or blacksmithing as from mathematics or Greek—or English. At all events, he will say these things so long as the crowd repeats them. . . . Finally, the Sophist cannot distinguish a man of real learning, save by a vague feeling of discomfort or apprehension when they meet, and a sense of being on his guard.

15 By permission of the Yale University Press.

THE VICE OF SNOBBERY

From SOLILOQUIES IN ENGLAND[16]

George Santayana

There is a philosophical principle implied in snobbery, a principle
which is certainly false if made absolute, but which fairly expresses the
moral relations of things in a certain perspective. If we all really stood
on different steps in a single ladder of progress, then to admire and imitate those above us and to identify ourselves with them by hook or by
crook would be simply to accelerate our natural development, to expand
into our higher self, and to avoid fatal abysses to the right and to the left
of the path marked out for us by our innate vocation. Life would then be
like the simple game which children call Follow the Leader; and this
scrupulous discipleship would be perfect freedom, since the soul of our
leader and our own soul that chooses him would be the same. This principle is precisely that of the transcendental philosophy where it maintains
that there is but one spirit in all men, and one logical moral evolution for
the world. In fact, it is the Germans rather than the English that are
solemn, convinced, and universal snobs . . .

On the whole, however, snobbish sentiment and transcendental philosophy do not express the facts of nature. Men and nations do not really
march in single file, as if they were being shepherded into some Noah's
Ark. They have perhaps a common root and similar beginnings, but they
branch out at every step into forms of life between which there is no
further interchange of sap, and no common destiny. Their several fruits
become incommensurable in beauty and in value, like the poetry of different languages, and more disparate the more each is perfected after its
kind. The whale is not a first sketch for the butterfly, nor its culmination;
the mind of an ox is not a fuller expression of that of a rabbit. The poet
does not evolve into the general, nor *vice versa;* nor does a man, in growing further, become a woman, superior as she may be in her own way.
That is why snobbery is really a vice; it tempts us to neglect and despise
our proper virtues in aping those of other people. If an angel appeared
to me displaying his iridescent wings and treble voice and heart fluttering
with eternal love, I should say, "Certainly, I congratulate you, but I do
not wish to resemble you." Snobbery haunts those who are not reconciled
with themselves; evolution is the hope of the immature. You cannot be
everything. Why not be what you are?

[16] By permission of Charles Scribner's Sons.

CAESAR'S ORIGINALITY

From notes to CAESAR AND CLEOPATRA[17]

George Bernard Shaw

Originality gives a man an air of frankness, generosity, and magnanimity by enabling him to estimate the value of truth, money, or success in any particular instance quite independently of convention and moral generalization. He therefore will not . . . tell a lie which everybody knows to be a lie (and consequently expects him as a matter of good taste to tell). His lies are not found out: they pass for candors. . . . He knows that the real moment of success is not the moment apparent to the crowd. Hence, in order to produce an impression of complete disinterestedness and magnanimity, he has only to act with entire selfishness; and this is perhaps the only sense in which a man can be said to be *naturally* great. It is in this sense that I have represented Caesar as great. Having virtue, he had no need of goodness. He is neither forgiving, frank, nor generous, because a man who is too great to resent has nothing to forgive; a man who says things that other people are afraid to say need be no more frank than Bismarck was; and there is no generosity in giving things you do not want to people of whom you intend to make use. This distinction between virtue and goodness is not understood in England: hence the poverty of our drama in heroes. Our stage attempts at them are mere goody-goodies. Goodness, in its popular British sense of self-denial, implies that man is vicious by nature, and that supreme goodness is supreme martyrdom. Not sharing that pious opinion, I have not given countenance to it in any of my plays. In this I follow the precedent of the ancient myths, which represent the hero as vanquishing his enemies, not in fair fight, but with enchanted sword, superequine horse and magical invulnerability, the possession of which, from the vulgar moralistic point of view, robs his exploits of any merit whatever.

MAN'S PREOCCUPATION WITH DEATH

From MAN AND SUPERMAN[18]

George Bernard Shaw

The Devil. Have you walked up and down upon the earth lately? I have; and I have examined Man's wonderful inventions. And I tell you that in the arts of life man invents nothing; but in the arts of death he outdoes Nature herself, and produces by chemistry and machinery all the slaughter of plague, pestilence, and famine. . . . In the arts of peace Man is a bungler. I have seen his cotton factories and the like, with machinery that a greedy dog could have invented if it had wanted money in-

---

[17] By permission of the Public Trustee and the Society of Authors.
[18] By permission of the Public Trustee and the Society of Authors.

stead of food. . . . There is nothing in Man's industrial machinery but his greed and sloth: his heart is in his weapons. . . .

Their imagination glows, their energies rise up at the idea of death, these people: they love it; and the more horrible it is the more they enjoy it. Hell is a place far above their comprehension: they derive their notion of it from two of the greatest fools that ever lived, an Italian and an Englishman. The Italian described it as a place of mud, frost, filth, fire, and venomous serpents: all torture. This ass, when he was not lying about me, was maundering about some woman whom he saw once in the street. The Englishman described me as being expelled from Heaven by cannons and gunpowder; and to this day every Briton believes that the whole of his silly story is in the Bible. What else he says I do not know; for it is all in a long poem which neither I nor anyone else ever succeeded in wading through.

It is the same in everything. . . . I could give you a thousand instances; but they all come to the same thing: the power that governs the earth is not the power of Life but of Death; and the inner need that has nerved Life to the effort of organizing itself into the human being is not the need for higher life but for a more efficient engine of destruction. The plague, the famine, the earthquake, the tempest were too spasmodic in their action; the tiger and crocodile were too easily satiated and not cruel enough: something more constantly, more ruthlessly, more ingeniously destructive was needed; and that something was Man, the inventor of the rack, the stake, the gallows, the electric chair; of sword and gun and poison gas; above all, of justice, duty, patriotism, and all the others isms by which even those who are clever enough to be humanely disposed are persuaded to become the most destructive of all the destroyers.

NO EASY WAY

From ADDRESS AT CHICAGO, SEPTEMBER 29, 1952

Adlai Stevenson

Long ago we asserted a great principle upon this continent, that men are, and of right out to be, free. Now we are called upon to defend that right against the mightiest forces of evil ever assembled under the sun. This is, therefore, a time to think. It is a time to feel. It is a time to pray. We shall need all the resources of the stubborn mind, the stout heart, the soul refreshed, in the task that confronts us. It is the most awesome task any people has ever faced, for we have become the leader and the mainstay of one of the great wings of humanity in conflict with another wing of humanity, and as such we must play the principal part in saving ourselves, our friends and our civilization.

Whose task is this? It is inescapably your task. You, and you alone, will decide the fate of your family and your country for decades to come. You will decide whether you are to be slaves or free, live gloriously or perish miserably. You may seek comfort at the feet of false leaders, who, like medicine doctors, beat drums to ward off evil spirits. You may listen to false leaders who tell you there is an easy way, that all you have to do is to elect them and thereafter relax in a tax-free paradise—the political equivalent of sending ten cents to cover the cost of postage. You may, fearing to face the facts squarely, be distracted by phony issues that have no bearing upon the life or death controversy of our time. But deluded you run the risk of being beguiled to destruction, for there is no easy way.

There is a lesson of history and of all human experience—struggle is the primary law of life. You struggle and you survive. You fail to struggle and you perish. The ways of the world are marked with the bones of people who hesitated.

Your salvation is in your own hands, in the stubbornness of your minds, in the tenacity of your hearts, and such blessings as God, sorely tried by his children, shall give us. Nature is indifferent to the survival of the human species, including Americans. I repeat, then, that the task is yours.

Yours is a democracy. Its government cannot be stronger or more tough-minded than its people. It cannot be more inflexibly committed to the task than they. It cannot be wiser than the people. As citizens of this democracy, you are the rulers and the ruled, the lawgivers and the law abiders, the beginning and the end. Democracy is a high privilege, but it is also a heavy responsibility whose shadow stalks, although you may ever walk in the sun.

I say these things to you, not only because I believe them to be true, but also because, as you love your country, I love my country, and I would see it endure and grow in light and become a living testament to all mankind—of goodness and of mercy and of wisdom.

THE INSTINCT FOR DOMINANCE[19]

From AFRICAN GENESIS

Robert Ardrey

Every organized animal society has its system of dominance. Whether it be a school of fish or a flock of birds or a herd of grazing wildebeest, there exists within that society some kind of status order in which individuals are ranked. Each individual knows all those whom he must fear and defer to, and all who must defer to him. Self-awareness in the limited sense of consciousness of rank seems to have appeared at some very early moment in the evolution of living things. . . .

One may conclude that in the eternal workings of natural selection an instinct for order has been found superior to an instinct for disorder. If nature abhors a vacuum, it likewise abhors anarchy. . . . Rank order of dominance may insure in one society strong leadership, in another lack of social friction, in another the genetic virtue that only the best will breed. . . . And what evolution has found wise in the past, wise in the generality, wise in all the ancient sortings, these things we must bear—whether we be lion, or trout or cow or cob. . . .

I walk the jungle path again—the wilderness not only of my long beginnings but of my own impenetrable nature—and images of dominance flit like bats through the void of my consciousness: the grinning face of a snaggle-toothed monarch; young lions dead; the drifting odour of a distant crematorium and the roasting flesh of Jews; a defeated rooster, dethroned and unsexed; a humiliated guest departing early from a Westchester dinner party; a lizzard bobbing his head four times in the presence of his master; a boasting schoolboy; a jackdaw fixing another jackdaw with a glittering stare; the trumpeting of a bull elephant in some nameless valley —or is it a sound of trumpets from hidden reaches of my own immemorial soul?

What in the primal nature of life has produced a force so pervasive, so agonizing, so precious? I do not know. I cannot guess. Somewhere in the dark wilderness of my ultimate beginnings lie moonlit pastures that I shall never see. But how precious is the force to life itself may be read in the death of individual creatures, as it may be read in the death of species.

NEGRO CHARACTER[20]

From THE FIRE NEXT TIME

James Baldwin

White Americans find it as difficult as white people elsewhere do to divest themselves of the notion that they are in possession of some intrinsic value that black people need, or want. And this assumption . . . makes the solution of the Negro problem depend on the speed with which Negroes accept and adopt white standards. How can one accept, let alone adopt, the values of a people who do not, on any level whatever, live the way they say they do, or the way they say they should? I cannot accept the proposition that the four-hundred-year travail of the American Negro should result merely in his attainment of the present level of American civilization. I am far from convinced that being released from the African witch doctor was worth while if I am now—in order to support the moral contradictions and the spiritual aridity of my life—expected to become dependent on the American psychiatrist. It is a bargain I refuse. The only thing white people have that black people need, or should want, is power—and no one holds power forever. White people cannot, in the

generality, be taken as models of how to live. . . . There is absolutely no
reason to suppose that white people are better equipped to frame the laws
by which I am to be governed than I am. It is entirely unacceptable that
I should have no voice in the political affairs of my own country, for I am
not a ward of America; I am one of the first Americans to arrive on these
shores.

The Negro's past, of rope, fire, torture, castration, infanticide, rape;
death and humiliation; fear by day and night, fear as deep as the marrow
of the bone; doubt that he was worthy of life, since everyone around him
denied it; sorrow for his women, for his kinsfolk, for his children, who
needed his protection, and whom he could not protect; rage, hatred, and
murder, hatred for white men so deep that it often turned against him and
his own, and made all love, all trust, all joy impossible—this past, this endless struggle to achieve and reveal and confirm a human identity, human
authority, yet contains, for all its horror, something very beautiful.

That man who is forced each day to snatch his manhood, his identity,
out of the fire of human cruelty that rages to destroy it knows, if he survives his effort, and even if he does not survive it, something about himself
and human life that no school on earth—and, indeed, no church—can
teach. He achieves his own authority, and that is unshakable. This is because, in order to save his life, he is forced to look beneath appearances,
to take nothing for granted, to hear the meaning behind the words. If
one is continually surviving the worst that life can bring, one eventually
ceases to be controlled by a fear of what life can bring; whatever it brings
must be borne. And at this level of experience one's bitterness begins to
be palatable, and hatred becomes too heavy a sack to carry. The apprehension of life here so briefly and inadequately sketched has been the experience of generations of Negroes, and it helps to explain how they have
endured and how they have been able to produce children of kindergarten
age who can walk through mobs to get to school. It demands great force
and great cunning continually to assault the mighty and indifferent fortress of white supremacy, as Negroes in this country have done so long.
It demands great spiritual resilience not to hate the hater whose foot is on
your neck, and an even greater miracle of perception and charity not to
teach your child to hate. The Negro boys and girls who are facing mobs
today come out of a long line of improbable aristocrats—the only genuine
aristocrats this country has produced.

3

EXPRESSION OF ATTITUDE AND INTENTION

"There are fifty ways of saying Yes," said George Bernard Shaw, "and five hundred of saying No, but only one way of writing them down." As playwright and drama coach, Shaw had to be constantly concerned with the inadequacy of print to represent the manifold meanings of speech, and we too, in translating printed into spoken symbols, must be aware of the many meanings a simple word may have in addition to its literal meaning, or "strict symbolization." "Yes" is a simple affirmative and "no" a simple negative, but when spoken each may carry the additional information that the speaker is doubtful, or reluctant, or impatient, or surly, or enthusiastic, or angry, or mournful, and so on to a total of possible meanings closer to five hundred than to fifty. Indeed, it is possible to speak "yes" and "no" so that their meanings are reversed, as when Ruskin's "nay, letter by letter" means "yes, even letter by letter," or when we say sarcastically, "Yes you will" meaning "No you won't." Think how many meanings can be expressed in speaking such single words as stop, don't, quick, look, run, silence, swine, angel, darling, chicken.

In all literary writing, whether essay, poem, narrative, or drama, there are, besides the literal meanings of the words and statements, additional meanings, explicit or potential, which derive from the attitudes, feelings, or intentions of the writer and the characters he creates. It is doubtful whether a writer ever achieves complete indifference in his expression, even if he wishes to achieve it. He may attempt merely to put on paper certain facts, events, and images and let them speak for themselves, but his very choice of these details and his manner of expressing them, his style, makes them speak for him and reveal his attitudes and intentions.

In spoken language, these are much more apparent, since, besides having the words themselves, the listener has the speaker's personality, voice, vocal modulation, facial expression, and gesture to aid his apprehension. The first task of the oral interpreter is to translate written into spoken language faithfully, without ignoring any of the aspects of meaning.

Various Attitudes in Speaking

The factors that influence our manner of speaking and so make an impression of some kind on our listeners and hence affect or contribute to meaning are so numerous and so various that it will be well to list the most important of them. There are, first, the more or less logical, or, rather, non-emotional, attitudes that one may take toward what he is saying—attitudes that are explanatory, thoughtful, critical, puzzled, questioning, or the like. Second, there are attitudes that have what psychologists call an "affective" tone—those that grow out of our interests and sentiments, such as aesthetic appreciation, patriotism, or a liking for nature, sports, children, or even study. Third, we are affected by simple sensory feelings of pleasantness or unpleasantness, pleasure or pain, either in what we read or in the reading situation. Watchers at President Kennedy's inauguration were more impressed by Robert Frost's frustrating struggle with the blinding sunlight than with the poem he tried to read. Fourth, our utterance is influenced by our more persistent organic experiences—appetites, aversions, physical flabbiness, drowsiness, and the like—and by their satisfaction. Fifth, it is obvious that our temperaments affect our speaking, whether apathetic, moody, cheerful, vivacious, depressed, suspicious, friendly, or what not. Sixth, our temporary current moods such as anxiety, resentment, amusement, and excitement color our speech. And seventh, those disturbed organic states marked by bodily changes in glands and muscles that we call emotions—rage, terror, shame, love, and the like—markedly affect our speech and are most readily apparent to our hearers.

This is a formidable catalog of emotions, feelings, attitudes, and states of mind, and any of them may carry to the listener an additional meaning beyond the mere words spoken, even in such simple statements as "It is going to rain," "Tell me where you live," or "We'll have to take a bus." Try expressing some of them.

A writer, moved by any of these mental, emotional, and physical states, or wishing to express them whether he feels them or not, may succeed in doing so, or he may fall short of his intention and fail to express them adequately. Also he may unconsciously allow some irrelevant irritation, irony, or enthusiasm to affect his composition and thus reveal attitudes, moods, and feelings that he does not intend to reveal.

The Interpreter's Relation to Attitude

What, then, is the interpreter's task with regard to this bewildering complex of possible meanings? Quite plainly it is a difficult task. Having only cold type to work from, except for the commentaries of others, he may very easily miss, slight, or falsify the writer's meaning. He is to set forth for his listeners the author's thought, feeling, and intention, yes. But in his delivery he may either minimize or accentuate any of these factors of meaning. It is well known that an actor may enhance the value and import of a playwright's lines, just as he may, on the other hand, fail to do them justice. And a reader of poetry may bring out a richness of word color, subtlety of rhythm, and depth of feeling that the poet himself was hardly aware of. All this is quite proper. But should he go further and try to read between the lines? Should he edit, as it were, the author's work, trying to divine his unrealized intentions, supplying omissions, and suppressing or eliminating irrelevancies? He can do this, without changing the author's words, by expressive techniques of voice and gesture.

Let us note, on the other hand, that, while an oral reader should faithfully represent his author's thoughts and sentiments, he need not share them. He is not merely a conduit through which a writer's sentiments flow to the hearer. Far from indorsing what he reads, he may heartily disapprove of it and may show that he disapproves; his very purpose in reading may be to show this disapproval. He can do this without misrepresenting what his author means. And, if he does approve, he may not expect that his readers will accept his sentiments. His attitude may be "I know you won't agree with me, but this expresses what I think, what I feel." The emotions of a poet are often personal and private, not meant to be transferred to, or duplicated in, his readers. He may describe his melancholy and despair, but Shelley's "Wail, for the world's wrong" is designed not to move us to wail with despair but rather to induce pleasant sympathy with his mood, so that we may feel a kind of pleasure in his pain. The interpreter, standing between poet and listener, will probably represent the feelings of both. When we hear Macbeth roar with brutal ferocity at a poor frightened messenger who has brought bad news, "The devil damn thee black, thou cream-faced loon! Where got'st thou that goose look?" we are not moved to share his rage. Our reaction is, rather, horror, or we may, in Aristotle's well-known words, experience a purgation of pity and fear. (We will let the literary scholars define the meaning of that puzzling phrase.) The actor who speaks Macbeth's lines may or may not feel his ferocity, depending on his histrionic method, but he will not frighten us, no matter how vividly he represents his character's passion.

In fiction or drama, a woman's grief will rarely move us to a like sorrow. We may feel pity and sympathy or, under some circumstances, annoyance, indignation, or amusement. Or, if we wish to take an example from light verse, Morris Bishop recounts a Father's gallant attempt to stimulate his daughter's appetite by describing the beauty and nutritive value of her food, and his angry frustration when she won't even drink her milk:

> Here, I said drink it, not blow in it! listen, Annie,
>   How would you like to have Father take that glass of milk and ram it
> Down your throat? How would you like a good swift whack on the fanny?
>   All right, go ahead and cry, damn it![1]

Though we may have had similar battles, we experience not his irritation but, rather, amusement. The point is that the emotions of poets, fictional characters, and others may not be intended to arouse like emotions in readers and audiences. The interpreter's function is to represent the emotions for his hearers and allow them to have their proper effect as the situation demands. On this and related matters, something more will be said in a later chapter.

It was implied above that an interpreter, standing between writer and audience, may express faithfully the writer's thought and feeling and at the same time respond to them as he expects his audience to respond. Or he may set forth the author's attitude while making clear his own attitude toward that attitude, which is generally the attitude he expects his audience to take too. This sort of double exposure may strike you as bewilderingly complicated and impossibly difficult, a juggling act that would baffle even a professional performer. But it is really not so difficult as it sounds, and you may accomplish it frequently without being aware how clever you are. Can you not, for instance, express the sugary sentimentality of some bit of pseudopoetry and at the same time your amusement and contempt at its banality—and without losing any of the sugar? Or can you not represent the sleepy indifference of some official toward your request for service while revealing with the same words your indignation at such treatment? It is likely that the emotions we express are more often mixed than pure.

The Functions of Language

We have made the business of interpretation seem very formidable indeed, and we had better reduce it to the simple formula in which Ogden and Richards set forth the "main functions of language as a means of communication," which they found in all utterance.[2] Besides literal meaning, "strict symbolization," there is, second, the speaker's attitude toward his

---

[1] Morris Bishop, *A Bowl of Bishop* (New York: Dial Press, Inc., 1954), p. 45.
[2] In *The Meaning of Meaning* (see note 6 in Chapter 1, above), Chapter 10.

audience: friendly, hostile, condescending, respectful, courteous, etc.; third, his attitude toward what he is saying: doubtful, confident, serious, ironic, facetious, enthusiastic, emotional, etc.; fourth, his intention, the effect he wishes to promote: to please, to mollify, to irritate, to arouse, or just to kill time, as sports announcers must often do. These, say Ogden and Richards, and you should note this carefully, are the functions "necessarily operative in all communication, the ways in which the work of speech is performed, the essential uses which speech serves." They constitute the meaning of what we say.

The key word here seems to be "attitude," and, though it does not cover emotion, except insofar as the third item includes it, we can use this formula as a guide for our further discussion.

Examples of Analysis

With this simple scheme of analysis in mind, let us look at some examples. First, we will take a brief passage from H. L. Mencken's *In Defense of Women* (see page 83) and see what we can make of it.

It takes no more actual sagacity to carry on the everyday hawking and haggling of the world, or to ladle out its normal doses of bad medicine and worse law, than it takes to operate a taxicab or fry a pan of fish.

The plain sense of this statement is clear enough, and the statement itself, as well as its extravagant language, indicates an attitude of disparagement and contempt. But he is sneering at our traditional pillars of society—businessmen, doctors, lawyers. Is he sincere in his contempt for them? Does he really mean what he says? Is he perhaps merely deprecating, facetious, ironic, disparaging, or is this bitter sarcasm, caustic satire, to be spoken with insolent arrogance? What is his attitude toward the reader? Is he ingratiating, confidential, or domineering? Does he respect us, or does he hold us too in contempt as members of the great American "booboisie"? Consider his intention. Does he mean to shock, irritate, amuse, or enlighten us, to cure our ignorance, or to explode a myth? Or perhaps in his arrogant way he is just having himself a good time, indifferent to our feelings and those of his victims.

What is to be *your* attitude toward all this as you present it to your audience? When you have determined Mencken's attitude and intention, do you approve of them? Are you shocked, troubled, indignant, or amused? Quick answers to these questions may be quite wrong. Study the passage carefully in its context.

A Dramatic Monolog. Now let us look at the last stanza of Browning's "Soliloquy of the Spanish Cloister." (See page 397.)

Or, there's Satan!—one might venture
Pledge one's soul to him, yet leave
Such a flaw in the indenture
As he'd miss till, past retrieve,
Blasted lay that rose-acacia
We're so proud of! *Hy, Zy, Hine* . . .
'St, there's Vespers! *Plena gratia,*
Ave, Virgo! Gr-r-r—you swine!

Here the literal meaning is not so plain, though the context clears up most of it. The speaker is an evil-minded monk who is filled with frenzied hatred of a brother monk, whom he has just come upon in the cloister garden, and whose inherent goodness, sweetness, and kindliness are a maddening rebuke to his own evil passions. He remains concealed, not daring to confront the object of his malice. In his wild frenzy, he wonders if he can, as in the old Faust legend, make a bargain with Satan, selling his soul to him if he will take his hated brother to hell—he doesn't say how, but leaving a flaw in the contract that Satan will miss until his brother monk is in hell, "past retrieve." Then he himself will escape from his bargain. Madness indeed! Apparently, there is much talk in the monastery of how proud they all are of their virtuous brother, here referred to with blistering sarcasm as "that rose-acacia" (a beautiful flowering plant). *Hy, Zy, Hine* are merely expletives of searing hate. In the midst of his wild passion, the speaker is startled by the vesper bell. *'St* seems to be a warning to himself to be careful. He shifts immediately to chanting with lugubrious, self-righteous piety the evening prayer, "Full of grace, hail, Virgin," then bursts out with one last savage snarl of hate. "Gr-r-r" is merely a conventional spelling of an inarticulate snarl, and the letters do not suggest the sound intended. Do *not* pronounce it as if it were the first syllable of "Gertrude." Just make it a prolonged guttural snarl.

With this explanation of the literal meaning of the stanza in mind, we can examine the attitudes involved. The first four lines suggest crafty, deliberate scheming, but the speaker's violent passion rules that out. Though he seems unrestrained in his madness, his superstition would make him aghast at his boldness in intriguing with the Devil, and his natural reflex would be to cross himself at the very thought of Satan. He would probably speak these lines rapidly, not thoughtfully, and his frenzy would explode on the word "blasted." Since this is a dramatic poem and a soliloquy, the readers are not being addressed; when he is not soliloquizing the monk's attitude toward his brother monk is what concerns us, and that is quite unmistakable. We may say that his intention is merely to vent his evil passion. He is not likely to do anything about it, and the object of his passion is probably quite unaware of his malevolence.

Now, what about the interpreter's attitude? He is not soliloquizing.

He shows this little scene to his audience and shares it with them. The passions represented here are so intense that they will need to be spoken intensely, but, remember, if you undertake to interpret them, they are not your passions. You are merely reporting them, but to some extent you feel them. Can you deliver an effective sneer without getting into the mood for it and distorting your face accordingly? Probably not. Give full vent to the bursts of hate, make the sarcasm on "that rose-acacia" as nasty as possible, but reserve your freedom as an interpreter to make your own response to them and make your audience feel that you are aware of how petty, small-minded, hypocritical, contemptible, and even pitiable and amusing this fellow is.

A BIT OF DRAMA. Now let us look at the opening lines of a play, Shaw's *The Man of Destiny*. The scene is a small inn in northern Italy; the characters, Napoleon and the innkeeper. Napoleon, as yet far from being emperor of France, is a young general on the make. He has just defeated the Austrians at Lodi and is waiting here for dispatches from Paris. The landlord, Giuseppe, says Shaw, is

. . . a swarthy vivacious shrewdly cheerful black-curled bullet-headed grinning little innkeeper of 40. Naturally an excellent host, he is in the highest spirits this evening at his good fortune in having as his guest the French commander to protect him against the license of the troops. . . . Napoleon is working hard, partly at his meal . . . and partly at a military map on which he from time to time marks the position of the forces by taking a grapeskin from his mouth and planting it on the map with his thumb . . . his long hair trails into the risotto [look it up] when he forgets it and leans more intently over the map.

The dialog begins:

Giuseppe. Will your excellency—
Napoleon (intent on his map, but cramming himself mechanically with his left hand). Dont talk. I'm busy.
Giuseppe (with perfect goodhumor). Excellency: I obey.
Napoleon. Some red ink.
Giuseppe. Alas! excellency, there is none.
Napoleon (with Corsican facetiousness). Kill something and bring me its blood.
Giuseppe (grinning). There is nothing but your excellency's horse, the sentinel, the lady upstairs, and my wife.
Napoleon. Kill your wife.
Giuseppe. Willingly, your excellency; but unhappily I am not strong enough. She would kill me.
Napoleon. That will do equally well.
Giuseppe. Your excellency does me too much honor.

How does one present a reading interpretation of a play? He does not act it, of course. Attempting to act the parts of successive speakers, jumping from one to the other, is sure to be ridiculous. The reader, lacking costume, make-up, and scenery, must let the scenes and actions be formed in his hearer's imaginations. He reads the lines, and there is no reason in the world why he should not read also the playwright's directions and explanations whenever they seem necessary or helpful in projecting the meaning. And, if it is necessary for clarity to announce the names of the alternating speakers, he should do so, but try not to do it mechanically.

Of course, he should represent the moods and attitudes of the characters. How will Giuseppe speak? Will he be awed by this strange French general? Napoleon is not presented as an awe-inspiring figure. You may well explain, as Shaw does, that Giuseppe is cheerful and vivacious. He is certainly not cringing or obnoxiously ingratiating, and he has intelligence enough to appreciate Napoleon's "Corsican" humor and to fall in with it. There is no indication of shock when he is told to kill something, even his wife. He seems free and at ease in bantering with this distinguished foreigner, almost as if they were old friends. Is his repeated use of "excellency" meant to be flattering, or is it merely the normal courtesy due an important guest? Does "She would kill me" indicate fear of his wife or merely an accustomed concession to her superior size and strength?

How does Napoleon speak? He is preoccupied, curt, but can be facetious, and he finds his dinner satisfactory. There is no indication that he is throwing his weight around. Is he so sure of his power and superiority that he doesn't feel any need to assert them? Shaw's directions are helpful. He wants his play to be well acted and takes pains to inform his actors how they are to speak and behave. Some fiction writers are not so helpful, and there is a current vogue among them of denying their readers all explanation of how their characters speak. All we are given is "he said" and "she said." But in this scene you will have no trouble with Napoleon's moods if you study what is given and are not too much influenced by what you know of his later character as emperor.

Your own attitude toward the scene should be what Shaw apparently intended his audience to feel—enjoyment and appreciation of the wit and interplay of the characters, and anticipation with interest of what will follow.

Expressing Attitude

These examples illustrate how attitudes in various forms of literature are to be analyzed, but they do not explain how an interpreter is to get himself to respond to them. This is the problem that troubles many students of interpretation, though it most often arises from a faulty or weak conception of what they wish to express. But we do not come to this problem without experience, as if it were analogous to learning how to pilot a jet plane. We have all experienced during our life histories countless mental states, sentiments, interests, sensory feelings, organic appetites, temperamental states, moods, and emotions, and we have expressed them. They are part of our natural heritage. Nobody has to teach a baby how to cry or a child how to sulk. And we have a good deal of control over these experiences. We can suppress or conceal them, and we can exaggerate them. It is safe to assume, though we must admit a wide range of difference between the phlegmatic and the mercurial person, that any norman person can express whatever attitudes he experiences. And, what is important for an interpreter, they are readily recognized and identified by those who observe them. Not infallibly, of course, for we often dispute among ourselves: "Was he offended?" "Didn't she seem to be showing her grief?" "I thought he looked tired," etc. And, what is still more important, we can *pretend* to feel them when we do not, and so express them as if they were real—but, again, not infallibly. There is no airtight formula for seeming bold when you are scared to death, patient when you are irritated to distraction, or solemn when you have the giggles. But we can generally smile, coo, growl, shriek with fear, shout for joy, or wrinkle our noses in distaste in *simulation* of emotions we don't feel at all. And, in general, we can go even further and represent the characters of other persons. To some extent we are all actors, all experienced in impersonation. We learned it in our childish games, and so are able to play parts even in formal stage plays.

You have had, then, a great deal of experience in interpretation and may need merely to give free rein to your natural and acquired abilities. But literature, especially poetry, often seems to present events, moods, and feelings that are foreign to your experiences in life. It is doubtful whether these fictitious experiences are really beyond your range. A poet's experiences are rarely unique. He deals with familiar things, though his expression of them may, indeed, be unique. What you probably lack chiefly is depth of impression, or perhaps inability to master subtle blends of mood or delicate shades of feeling, which call merely for more penetrating study.

Brightening the Pattern of Expression

The fault most commonly found in oral readers, when it is not wrong impression, is *weak* impression, resulting in colorless expression. We want our reading to be vivid and moving (not, of course, noisy or flamboyant), and for brightening the pattern of your expression you have various resources. To begin with, do not overlook the power of the words themselves. They will have some effect even if not well spoken. Thousands of silent private readers have wept or chuckled over mere fiction. Even bad oral reading can be very moving if the material read is moving. You have this foundation to build on, so see that your author's words are clearly spoken. But you want to add to them the power that can come from your vocal and physical resources, what Robert Louis Stevenson called a "responsive" voice, one that breaks and changes and speaks with winning inflection, a legible countenance, a lively play of facial expression, and speaking gestures. How can these faculties be stimulated?

First, you can *try* to be more expressive. Let yourself go. Avoid suppression or restraint of vocal and physical responses. Don't be afraid of enthusiasm. Try to feel the moods, sentiments, and feelings of your author.

Second, take time. Time is required for impressions to crystallize in your audience. Some readers seem to try to unload their material as quickly as possible and then hurry away from it. Try to relish what you are doing and linger over it. Pause after a serious statement to let it sink in; pause before a comic idea so that it will explode more sharply; and pause to create suspense as to what is coming, to let expectancy ripen. Cultivate a change of pace, skipping over unimportant and easily understood phrases but bearing down firmly on what is most important or difficult to grasp or charged with feeling. If your mind is actively discriminating the relative values of the various phrases as you utter them, you will not move at an even pace, you will avoid the pedestrian monotony that deadens so much of the oral reading we hear.

Third, cultivate a lively sense of communication. Keep asking yourself, "How will my audience receive this phrase (or this word)?" Keep watching them to see whether they *do* respond as you think they should. Try not to be afraid of them. Adjust yourself alertly to their responses, as a fencer or a boxer must adjust himself to the responses of his opponent. Try to develop a genuine desire to have what you read received and appreciated. Cultivate a kind of "double talk" by carrying on, while you read aloud to them, a separate silent colloquy with them, saying "Isn't this a beautiful line?" "Am I making you see this image?" "Am I projecting the full color of these vowels?" "Note this somber mood (or this witty suggestion)," etc. That is, keep thinking to yourself the things you would be saying if you were lecturing on appreciation of the selection. On some occasions, you can break your reading and interpolate such comments and explanations. If you can keep in eager contact with the minds of your listeners, you will greatly brighten and intensify the pattern of your expression.

Fourth, remember that emotions don't reside in cold type; they are inside us. They can arise from our sensations and sentiments, but, in literature, and especially in poetry, they arise chiefly from images. A writer, to make others feel, presents vivid images of things, and they will be more deeply felt when a reader visualizes them sharply as they are presented to him. You should dwell on the poet's descriptions until you really see them, and your audience sees from your behavior and facial expression that they are real to you. You can visualize them even if they are such sights as you have never actually seen; events narrated need not be such as you have had a part in; persons represented need not be be such as you have known. You have seen thousands of pictures, still or moving, of all sorts of scenes and places. You have witnessed all kinds of actions and met all kinds of characters on the stage, in motion pictures, and on television, from babies playing in the cradle to astronauts zooming off into space, and, from these observed experiences, you should be able to re-create vividly anything that an author can present to you. You have only to use the imagination with which all of us are endowed.

Fifth, you can enliven expression by keeping your muscles in tune. Lively interpretation never comes from a slack, sluggish, inert body. Take a lesson from the athletes. Those exercises they go through, running up the steps of the stadium or lying on their backs and pedaling an imaginary bicycle, are never used in the game. They are for physical conditioning. Such exercises would help you too, though I would recommend something less strenuous. Before a reading, try to work up appropriate body tension and a sense of aliveness. Breathe deeply, keep the chest up and the head erect.

Physical alertness will, first, affect sympathetically the intricate complex of small muscles that activate voice and articulation. It will also stimulate the heavy breathing muscles that support the voice. These muscles, like any others, reflect general body slackness or tonicity. You would probably read with better voice if the class hour opened with five minutes of calisthenics, provided, of course, you didn't come in exhausted by a long run from that previous class at the other end of the campus.

Second, body tension and readiness should stimulate the outward physical responsiveness that is the theme of Stevenson's little lecture at the end of this chapter. A reader communicates with his audience through two channels, the eye and the ear. While his voice is heard, his person is seen. Facial expression, movements of the hands and head, and general physical responses to mood and meaning should carry to the hearers' eyes the same message that his voice carries to their ears. Expression should be unified, involving all the channels of communication.

You need to recognize that our civilized environment has imposed upon us thousands of repressions and inhibitions that check our natural free responsiveness. From babyhood, we have been told to sit still, to stop wriggling, and to speak softly, if at all. During twelve years or so of schooling, we have sat rigidly in rows, suppressing the activity of body and face normal to young people. Our crowded, hurried, conventional society enforces further repressions. Natural enthusiasms are checked because we do not want to "make a scene," "make fools of ourselves," or "slop over." And some students cultivate an air of bored cynicism destructive of all enthusiasm. You need to counteract these deadening influences, to recover some of the natural spontaneity of childhood. You should cultivate the free facial and gestural vivacity exemplified by skilled actors, so that you will, as Stevenson says, have "looks to correspond with every feeling" and "never discredit speech with uncouth manners or become unconsciously our own burlesques." As you practice a selection, try to feel it in every muscle, not forgetting that most important muscle, the heart. Try to pantomime every suggested image and emotion. Don't be afraid to let yourself go. When you come to class, you can depend on the teacher and your classmates to check you if you become too wild.

Third, the control of bodily expression is an effective means of controlling emotion. During the past half-century a new contribution to elocutionary method has come to us through the James-Lange theory of emotion and the behavioristic view of psychology. Briefly, the James-Lange theory holds that the feelings, instead of being the cause of bodily expression, are the result of it. The emotion we feel is caused by some motion of the body. Perhaps we had better let Professor James develop the theory:

Everybody knows how panic is increased by flight, and how the giving away to the symptoms of grief or anger increases the passions themselves. . . . In rage, it is notorious how we "work ourselves up" to a climax by repeated outbursts of expression. Refuse to express the passion and it dies. Count ten before venting your anger, and its occasion seems ridiculous. Whistling to keep up courage is no mere figure of speech. On the other hand, sit all day in a moping posture, sigh, and reply to everything with a dismal voice, and your melancholy lingers. There is no more valuable precept in moral education than this, as all who have had experience know; if we wish to conquer undesirable emotional tendencies in ourselves, we must assiduously, and in the first instance cold-bloodedly, go through the outward movements of those contrary dispositions which we prefer to cultivate. The reward of persistency will infallibly come, in the fading out of the sullenness or depression, and the advent of real cheerfulness and kindliness in their stead. Smooth the brow, brighten the eye, contract the dorsal rather than the ventral aspect of the frame, and speak in a major key, pass the genial compliment and your heart must be frigid indeed if it do not gradually thaw.[3]

The behaviorist theory points in the same direction. According to the behaviorists, the physical response is the emotion. The response is partly evident in facial expression and other outward gesture, but it is also partly concealed in glandular and visceral disturbances. We can control the outer manifestations of emotion, and by this means exercise some con-

[3] William James, *Psychology: Briefer Course* (New York: Holt, Rinehart & Winston, Inc., 1907), p. 382.

trol over the inner responses. The same conclusion is supported by the more recent psychology of *Gestalt*, which teaches that outer and inner aspects of feeling are parts of a unified whole, or pattern, and that if the pattern is begun it tends to run its full course to completion.[4]

The moral from any of these psychological theories is plain. If you find your reading colorless and apathetic, *simulate* an interest in it, and this simulated interest will become genuine. The actor has more opportunity than the reader to put himself into the physical attitudes suitable for the various emotions, but the reader can at least give his muscles the *feel* of such attitudes; he can cultivate appropriate tensions and relaxations; he can, as Stevenson says, cultivate "a lively and not a stolid countenance."

The Mechanical Approach

But, if these natural responses do not produce the results you want, as they may not with more difficult passages, you may need to have someone with more experience and skill instruct you in mechanical terms on how to achieve desired effects. You may need to be told such things as to speak a given line staccato or with rising pitch, to hesitate here, to roll out this phrase with full voice, to whisper this word or blast that one, to turn your inflections up here or let them fall there, to hiss out your fricative consonants for this sentiment and prolong your liquid consonants for this other, to change your mood to boasting, despair, or cheerfulness, to make your vowels long and golden in this line, to make this statement ring with triumph, and so on and on and on. There can be no complete catalog of such devices, nor any dependable rule governing their use. Literature is too various for that. If your own intelligence does not tell you what to do and when, you may get help from your teacher. And you may get helpful suggestions by studying recordings of the speech of skilled readers and actors. And perhaps listening critically to a recording of your own effort will enable you to spot some weaknesses and design some method of correcting them.

Interpreting Questions

A group of attitudes that call for special attention are those that have the form of questions. It is often assumed that all questions have a uniform structure, either beginning with an interrogative pronoun or adverb or having the verb before the subject, that they are merely inquires, and that they are to be spoken with a rising inflection. But writers often put questions in the form of assertions, and assertions in the form of questions.

[4] See W. M. Parrish, "Implications of Gestalt Psychology," *Quarterly Journal of Speech*, XIV (1928), 8–29.

"Will you sit down?" and "You are going with me," though different in form, may each be either a simple inquiry or a firm command. There are also rhetorical questions, those that are asked merely for effect, with no expectation of an answer, such as Patrick Henry's "Why stand we here idle?"

VARIANTS IN INTONATION AND INFLECTION. Different kinds of questions call for different patterns of vocal expression. We generally ask questions that are to be answered by "Yes" or "No," such as "Do you want to come along?" differently from those that call for specific information, such as "When does the mailman come?" In general, "Did you like the show?" calls for a rising inflection on every word; "Why should I care?" on none; and Hamlet's question, "Why did you laugh then when I said Man delights not me?" on only the first four, or maybe five, words. British intonation pattern in making an inquiry typically differs from the American, the intonation falling instead of rising, though both will inflect the last word upward. These, however, are risky statements and not to be accepted as gospel. Any question may involve so many variable factors of meaning that there is no uniform way of speaking it. The simple-seeming inquiry "Why did you do that?" may have any of the meanings here listed:

1. I'm merely curious.
2. I don't understand.
3. I can't imagine why you should do such a thing.
4. Don't be so stupid.
5. You ought to know better.
6. You know what the consequences will be.
7. How awful! We are ruined.
8. That's dangerous.

Try to read the question expressing each of these meanings.

QUESTIONS IN LITERATURE. Literature abounds in passages that have the form of questions but express meanings, attitudes, and intentions quite other than mere requests for information. To ignore these is often to miss entirely the flavor of some of our finest literature. Think of the travesty of reading as mere inquiries these questions from Markham's "The Man with the Hoe" when they were intended as powerful condemnations of the "masters, lords, and rulers of all lands" (see page 334):

Who loosened and let down this brutal jaw?
Whose was the hand that slanted back this brow?
Whose breath blew out the light within this brain?

Here are some other questions from selections in this book. Study carefully the context of each on the page indicated; define the meaning; then try to speak them so as to express their true intention.

1. Neighbor, how stands the Union? (page 86)
2. "The night is fine," the Walrus said.
   "Do you admire the view?" (pages 142–47)
3. Hunger and only hunger changes worlds? (page 221)
4. Shall I, wasting in despair
   Die, because a woman's fair? (page 203)
5. Where are the songs of Spring? Ay, where are they? (page 213)
6.   O, wind,
   If Winter comes, can Spring be far behind? (page 261)
7. O Beauty, are you not enough?
   Why am I crying after love? (page 224)
8. My word! Where *does* that person come from? (page 443)

These examples should serve to illustrate the rich variety of sentiments that are expressed in the form of questions.

Comedy

We need also to take particular notice of those attitudes that we refer to by such terms as *comedy, humor, wit, satire, irony, sarcasm, raillery, drollery, ribaldry, facetiousness, ridicule, derision, amusement, the ludicrous, hilarity, jokes, jests, quips, wisecracks, witticisms, sport, buffoonery, clownishness,* and the like. The range here is enormous, and the very number of these terms indicates how common such attitudes are in literature and in daily talk. It would be futile to try here to distinguish the various forms of comedy from each other. Dictionaries are available for that. But perhaps we should try to find the underlying quality or impulse that activates all of them. Many critics throughout history have sought the unifying principle of comedy, some by searching for its origin and exploring its history.

Aristotle thought there was a form of wit suitable for an "honorable gentleman," a happy mean between the unrestrained buffoonery of the clown and the boorishness of the *agelast,* or "never-laugher." Stage comedy, he said, represents men of an "inferior moral bent," ludicrous because of some deformity (of body or character) that "does not strike us as painful, and causes no harm to others." In his great work on education,[5] Quintilian says the cause of laughter has not been sufficiently explained, and he does little to enlighten us in his twenty pages of Roman jokes, very few of which seem funny today. But he seems to be on the right track when he cites Cicero's theory that humor rises from "deceiving expectations," that is, from the unexpected.

[5] *Institutio Oratoria,* III.

It is encouraging to have the view of some modern critics that humor is fundamental in human nature and was present, though in a crude form, even in our primitive ancestors. Louis Untermeyer says, "In the broadest sense, the world's favorite humor has been a playful expression of primitive sensuality."[6] But, with civilization, some humor at least has been refined into perceptive wit. As John Ciardi says,

> . . . there are many orders of humor from the belly laugh to the wry and rueful chuckle at oneself, and not all of them become a man. I suspect in fact that the belly laugh was invented by the ape as an explosion of his own sense of superiority the day he knocked down another ape and felt good about it. . . . But what ape ever looked at himself, recognized that he is himself mildly ridiculous, and realized at the same time that what is ridiculous in him is not his own invention but something rooted in the nature of being? Between the belly laugh and the chuckle lies the whole range of primitive evolution. For only a man can chuckle the true chuckle.[7]

One of the most perceptive and most influential explanations of the nature of comedy was made nearly a hundred years ago by George Meredith. I quote from this lecture at some length:

> You may estimate your capacity for comic perception by being able to detect the ridicule of them you love without loving them less; and more by being able to see yourself somewhat ridiculous in dear eyes, and accepting the correction their image of you proposes.
> Each one of an affectionate couple may be willing, as we say, to die for the other, yet unwilling to utter the agreeable word at the right moment; but if the wits were sufficiently quick for them to perceive that they are in a comic situation, as affectionate couples must be when they quarrel, they would not wait for the moon or the almanac, . . . to bring back the flood-tide of tender feelings, that they should join hands and lips.
> If you detect the ridicule, and your kindliness is chilled by it, you are slipping into the grasp of Satire.
> If, instead of falling foul of the ridiculous person with a satiric rod, to make him writhe and shriek aloud, you prefer to sting him under a semi-caress, by which he shall in his anguish be rendered dubious whether indeed anything has hurt him, you are an engine of Irony.
> If you laugh all round him, tumble him, roll him about, deal him a smack, and drop a tear on him, own his likeness to you, and yours to your neighbor, spare him as little as you shun, pity him as much as you expose, it is a spirit of Humor that is moving you.
> The comic, which is the perceptive, is the governing spirit, awakening and giving aim to these powers of laughter, but it is not to be confounded with them; it enfolds a thinner form of them, differing from satire in not sharply driving into the quivering sensibilities, and from humor in not comforting them and tucking them up, or indicating a broader than the range of this bustling world to them. . . .

[6] Louis Untermeyer, *A Treasury of Ribaldry* (Garden City, N.Y.: Hanover House, 1956), p. xv.
[7] John Ciardi, *The Saturday Review*, June 15, 1963, p. 20.

The laughter of satire is a blow in the back or the face. The laughter of comedy is impersonal and of unrivaled politeness, nearer a smile—often no more than a smile. It laughs through the mind, for the mind directs it; and it might be called the humor of the mind.

One excellent test of the civilization of a country, as I have said, I take to be the flourishing of the comic idea and comedy; and the test of true comedy is that it shall awaken thoughtful laughter.

On the Idea of Comedy and of the Uses of the Comic Spirit.

Another extract from this lecture will be found among the readings at the end of this chapter. It defines an imaginary elf called "The Comic Spirit," identified by some critics with Puck in *A Midsummer Night's Dream,* or with Ariel in *The Tempest.*

THE READING OF COMEDY. How does one present humorous material to an audience? The formula is the same as for other attitudes: Present the content, but with unusually sharp perception; show the author's attitude toward it, which will be some variety of the comic; reflect his attitude toward the reader or hearer; and implement his intention, which will be to stimulate a response that may lie anywhere between a perceptive smile or rueful chuckle and a hilarious guffaw. As with other feelings, what is perceived and felt by the reader will probably be perceived and felt by the hearers. Hence, he must be sharply aware of witty turns of phrase, unexpected and incongruous words and ideas, thwarted expectations, absurd rhymes, puns and other plays on words, grotesque exaggerations, fantastic resemblances, irony, paradox, and all the other incongruities that constitute comedy. Skilful use of pauses is important, but no rule can tell you when to use them or how long to make them.

It is probably true that comedians are born, not made, but every normally intelligent person has something of the comedian in him, responds in some way to what he feels is funny, and can generally communicate his comic appreciations to others. But how widely we differ in comic perception! A bright young instructor once entered a faculty office, book in hand, read aloud the first sentence of Shaw's preface to *Saint Joan* and burst into hilarious laughter, continuing to chuckle to himself for some minutes. Here is the sentence. What is funny about it?

Joan of Arc, a village girl from the Vosges, was born about 1412; burnt for heresy, witchcraft, and sorcery in 1431; rehabilitated after a fashion in 1456; designated venerable in 1904; declared Blessed in 1908; and finally canonized in 1920.

A not very bright senior was asked to define the comic aspects of Ogden Nash's "The Porcupine." Instead, he wrote a solemn justification of feeling aggrieved and resentful when wronged by others. Here are the lines. Do you find them serious or comical?

Any hound a porcupine nudges
Can't be blamed for harboring grudges.
I know one hound that laughed all winter
At a porcupine that sat on a splinter.

Wits should be sharp enough to distinguish between real feeling and pretended feeling.

Comedians and tellers of tall tales often assume a grave air of solemnity and seem to make their humor sharper by delivering it straight-faced. Others abandon themselves to their own humor, sometimes to the point of becoming inarticulate, and move their hearers to a like hilarity. The fact that both methods may succeed indicates that there is no best way to be funny. One's choice of a method, if, indeed, he is able to choose, will depend on the situation, the nature of his material, and his personality.

Attempts have been made, of course, to explain how humor should be expressed, or how it *is* expressed. For instance, a modern Spanish writer defines "irony" as "that vague movement at the corner of the mouth." Let us look at a description by James Burgh in his *Art of Speaking*, first published in 1761.

Raillery, in sport, without real animosity, puts on the aspect of cheerfulness. The tone of the voice is sprightly. With contempt or disgust, it casts a look asquint, from time to time, to the object; and quits the cheerful aspect for one mixed between an affected grin and sourness. The upper lip is drawn up with an air of disdain. The arms are set akimbo on the hips; and the right hand now and then thrown out toward the object, as if one were going to strike another a slight back-handed blow. The pitch of the voice rather low, the tone arch and sneering; the sentences short; the expression satyrical, with mock-praise intermixed.

This is suggestive, but certainly not definitive. Other attempts have been little more helpful. Our best recourse is to depend on sharpness of appreciation and our natural responsiveness of body and voice.

A special difficulty arises in reading such material as the verses of Lewis Carroll (see pages 142–47), because the narrative seems so obvious and casual, so childlike and bland. Students not far removed from childhood, and those accustomed to reading to children, are prone to accept such extravagances at face value, for to a child there is nothing incongruous in oysters walking, or walruses talking with carpenters, or Father William balancing an eel on the end of his nose. Hence, such stories are often read with naïve innocence of the comic values that mature minds find in them. That is, the reading is on the kindergarten level, rather than the college level. A mature reader will be keenly alert to what is grotesque, farcical, and fantastic in these masterpieces of comedy, and will communicate his appreciation of it to his audience. The essence of their comedy is nonsense, a form of humor that seems to be growing in popularity, and, of course, only a person of good sense can recognize non-sense.

In more obvious forms of humor, there is a strong temptation for a reader to identify himself with the author, or his characters, and assume, more or less unconsciously, that he, and not the author, is furnishing the wit and cleverness. Instead of showing us the comedy his author has provided, serving merely as the interpreter of another's humor, he puts himself forward as the comedian and invites applause for himself. In the stronger forms of humor, this leads easily to clowning and the exhibitionist practices of the showoff. "That's villainous," says Hamlet, "and shows a most pitiful ambition in the Fool that uses it." "Pray you, avoid it."

SATIRE. Some of the world's greatest literature exposes and ridicules the vices and follies of mankind in the form called "satire." It generally involves an assumption of superiority on the part of the satirist, as is evident in the passage quoted from Mencken, and it may be that this is what has led some critics to conclude that *all* humor arises from this feeling of superiority over one's victim. But all humor is not arrogant gloating, and all satire is not cruel and cutting, "sharply driving into the quivering sensibilities," to use Meredith's phrase. It may be very gentle and humble, especially when the satirist is exposing his own follies and weaknesses, as is often the case with Ogden Nash. And it may be very sympathetic, very close to pity. So, before you interpret a piece of satirical writing, note carefully the quality of the satire, and don't give a nasty sarcastic tone to what is only a mild rebuke. Often you should laugh not *at* your victim but *with* him. In the selections for practice following this chapter and the chapter on verse, you will find many examples of satire, mostly of the gentler sort.

PLAN OF STUDY

1. In each sentence you read, note the bare logical thought, and restate it in words that leave out the color, mood, and intention.
2. Then note in the author's manner of expression all indications of mental attitude, sensory feeling, physical state, sentiment, temperament, mood, and emotion that affect or add to the basic thought expressed.
3. Does the author seem to have said successfully just what he intended, or more, or less?
4. Do you approve the author's sentiments and share them, and do you expect your hearers to approve and share them?
5. Discover the author's attitude toward his readers, and determine what your attitude toward your hearers should be.
6. Define his attitude toward what he is saying, and determine your proper attitude toward it in reading it to others.

7. Try to discover his intention concerning what he says, the effect he wishes to promote.

8. Try through imagination to enter into the mood and feeling of what you are to read. Visualize sharply. Think of examples that will intensify the feeling.

9. In practice, throw off restraint and let yourself go. Exaggerate expression.

10. Choose places for deliberate pauses. Vary your pace in accordance with thought and feeling. That is, decide where you can skip through a phrase and where you should linger and bear down.

11. Cultivate a lively sense of communication with your hearers. Think of this during preparation.

12. Dwell on descriptions, images, and figures of speech till they are sharp and clear.

13. Keep physically alive and responsive as you practice, and try to carry this vitality over into your public reading.

14. In difficult passages, deliberately design your expression.

15. If your selection contains questions, determine carefully the attitude and intention they imply.

16. In humorous material, define carefully the nature of the comedy. Adapt your expression to the nature of the comedy, the situation in which you will read, and your personality.

17. Record your reading, and listen critically to the playback to note where you can make improvements. Repeat.

CRITERIA

1. Did the reader seem to understand the mental states, sensory feelings, sentiments, physical condition, temperament, moods, and emotions expressed or implied by the author in the selection read?

2. Did he express them appropriately, at the same time revealing his approval, disapproval, doubts, relish, enthusiasm, or other attitude toward the author's thought and attitude?

3. Did he rouse in his hearers the appropriate attitudinal and emotional responses, these not being necessarily the attitudes and emotions expressed by the author?

4. Did he properly represent his author's attitude toward his readers and make clear his own response to this attitude?

5. Did he properly represent the author's attitude toward his thought and make clear his own response to this attitude?

6. Did he properly reveal his author's intention and his own attitude toward it?

7. Was he sufficiently responsive to moods and feelings, with a lively countenance, a flexible voice, and free bodily expression?

8. Was his tempo well managed, with effective pauses and changes of pace?

9. Did he have a lively sense of communication with his audience?

10. Was his imagination alive to scenes and images?

11. Did he seem physically alive, rather than inert and unresponsive?

12. Were questions in his text so spoken as to show their true intent?

13. Did he show sharp perception of the incongruities and thwarted expectations that are the cause of comedy, and did he express them effectively?
14. In reading comedy, did he preserve his own character and avoid objectionable clowning?

QUESTIONS FOR DISCUSSION

1. Try to find a piece of writing that has no indication whatever of the author's attitude, intention, interest, or feeling. Defend your choice of it as such.
2. Find one in which the writer has revealed attitudes you think he did not intend to reveal. Defend your choice.
3. Discuss the relation between an author's attitudes and those an interpreter of them should reveal to his audience.
4. Can any normal person express whatever attitudes he experiences? Can he always communicate them to others? What practices or devices will help him to express them and communicate them to others?
5. How is emotion communicated? What is its relation to physical action?
6. Is there an essential element that is common to all comedy and humor? If so, try to define it.

SELECTION FOR DRILL

TRUTH OF INTERCOURSE

Robert Louis Stevenson

1. [Language is not our only means of communication.] 2. We are subject to physical passions and contortions; the voice breaks and changes, and speaks by unconscious and winning inflections; we have legible countenances, like an open book; and the soul, not locked into the body as a dungeon, dwells ever on the threshold with appealing signals. 3. Groans and tears, looks and gestures, a flush or a paleness, are often the most clear reporters of the heart, and speak more directly to the hearts of others. 4. The message flies by these interpreters in the least space of time, and the misunderstanding is averted in the moment of its birth. 5. To explain in words takes time and a just and patient hearing, and in the critical epochs of a close relation, patience and justice are not qualities on which we can rely. 6. But the look or gesture explains things in a breath; they tell their message without ambiguity. . . .

7. Pitiful is the case of the blind, who cannot read the face; pitiful that of the deaf, who cannot follow the changes of the voice. 8. And there are others also to be pitied; for there are some of an inert, uneloquent nature, who have been denied all the symbols of communication, who have neither a lively play of facial expression, nor speaking gestures, nor a responsive voice, nor yet the gift of frank, explanatory speech: people truly made of clay, people tied for life into a bag which no one can undo. 9. Such people we must learn slowly by the tenor of their acts, or through yea and nay communication; or we take them on trust on the strength of a general air, and now and again, when we see the spirit breaking through in a flash, correct or change our estimate. 10. But these will be uphill intimacies, without charm or freedom to the end; and freedom is the chief ingredient in confidence.

11. Some minds, romantically dull, despise physical endowments. 12. That is a doctrine for a misanthrope; to those who like their fellow-creatures it must always be meaningless; and for my part, I can see few things more desirable, after the possession of such radical qualities as honor and humor and pathos, than to have a lively and not a stolid countenance; to have looks to correspond to every feeling; to be elegant and delightful in person, so that we shall please in the intervals of active pleasing, and may never discredit speech with uncouth manners or become unconsciously our own burlesques. 13. But of all unfortunates there is one creature (for I will not call him man) conspicuous in misfortune. 14. This is he who has forfeited his birthright of expression, who has cultivated artful intonations, who has taught his face tricks, like a pet monkey, and on every side perverted or cut off his means of communication with his fellow-men. 15. The body is a house of many windows; there we all sit, showing ourselves and crying on the passers-by to come and love us. 16. But this fellow has filled his windows with opaque glass, elegantly colored. 17.

His house may be admired for its design, the crowd may pause before the stained windows, but meanwhile the poor proprietor must lie languishing within, uncomforted, unchangeably alone.

SUGGESTIONS FOR ANALYSIS. This selection has been chosen for drill because it illustrates a considerable variety of attitudes, and because it is a unique treatment of the non-verbal means of expression that are so important to students of interpretation. A persuasive statement of a conviction about life and human intercourse, it has more depth and charm than a casual reading reveals. Almost obscured by Stevenson's deliberately unconventional style, his original, almost eccentric manner of expression, is a coherent development of thought and a clear logical structure. Don't miss them. The prevailing attitude may be defined as a pleasant, but earnest and pleading, exposition. There is sincere passion for honesty in our interpersonal relationships and deep pity for those who cannot, and indignation toward those who will not, practice such truth of intercourse.

This précis may be helpful in getting at the essential thought: Communication is not by words alone, but also by bodily, vocal, and facial expression, which reveals the soul within. These are the clearest and quickest carriers of messages from heart to heart. Words involve delay, and without patience and justice may fail us in a crisis, but looks and gestures convey meaning quickly and clearly. We pity the blind and the deaf, but should also pity the inert and unexpressive who have no means of revealing their inner selves. With them, acquaintance is slow, uncertain, and difficult; first impressions must be revised, and we never feel free with them. Some unromantic people dislike physical expressiveness, but, if we love our fellow men, we must value very highly vivacity and charm in appearance and expression. Most unfortunate is he who hides his real self by falsifying his expression. We all crave sympathy, but this fellow must always lack it because he will not permit himself to be known.

(Numbers refer to sentences.) 1. Supply a connective to show relation to the next sentence. 2. Isn't Stevenson implying that these means of expression are delightful, that we are fortunate in having them. Note the structure: He is saying that we can communicate through (a) emotional manifestations, (b) vocal inflections, (c) facial expression, (d) glances of the eye, and, in summary, through revealing body responses. Vitalize and dwell upon his images. Let your muscles respond to "passions and contortions"; recall examples of "winning inflections"; open your countenance on the next phrase; think of an occasion when only the eyes were eloquent; react against the gloom of "dungeon"; and brighten at the vision of appealing signals from a doorway. Continue this method throughout the selection. But none of this can be done if you hurry. 3. These details are colorful too, but they only repeat; the only new idea is "most clear." "Reporters of the heart" has been clearly implied. 4. "Flies" is a deceptively strong word for its use here; save your emphasis for "least space of time." The second clause suggests a feeling of relief. 5. Explaining in words requires two things; separate them. Both cause delay and annoyance. Think of examples. 6. This suggests a feeling of relief and freedom. "Look or gesture" is contrasted with what? The last clause has no obvious thought center. 7. Show your sympathy here. 8. "Nature" is important. These people have *no* way to communicate. "Symbols of communication" merely echoes what you have been talking about all along. "All" is the important word.

"Speaking gestures" means gestures that speak; the two words are equally important. What feeling is called for in "made of clay" and "tied . . . into a bag"? Pity? Annoyance? Contempt? Why "truly"? Do you recognize biblical phrases here and in "forfeit his birthright" in 12 and "the body is a house" in 15? 9. What attitude here, and continued in 10? "In a flash" is another phrase of unneeded vividness. Couldn't it be omitted without serious loss? "Estimate" is echo of what? Explain the last statement in 10. 11. Explain "romantically dull." Is there romance in freedom of intercourse? What attitude is called for here, and in the first clause of 12? "Like" stands in contrast with what? What are "radical qualities"? Reflect on this unusual list of desirable character traits, here stated parenthetically. What would you like to add to them? A pleasant reaction is called for toward the list of qualities that follow. What are "intervals of active pleasing"? The last part of 12 calls for an attitude of contempt and shame. 13. Is the feeling here merely pity? What about a pause before "creature"? "Misfortune" echoes "unfortunates." Need you be told? 14. How serious is forfeiting a birthright? Don't forget that "expression" is what this whole selection is about, though frequently referred to in other terms. What attitudes are called for here? Can you illustrate an "artful intonation" as you speak the words? Beware of overdoing the monkey tricks. 15. The first clause has two ideas; separate them. What attitude toward the rest? Yearning? 16. What attitude toward "this fellow"? 17. The first two clauses are concessive, but the last, on solitary confinement, is deep tragedy. Don't miss it.

SELECTIONS FOR PRACTICE

Some of the selections that follow illustrate various attitudes. Others deal with aspects of art, literary appreciation, and interpretation, and should be considered as part of the text.

THE COMIC SPIRIT

From On the Idea of Comedy and of the Uses of the Comic Spirit

George Meredith

If you believe that our civilization is founded in common sense (and it is the first condition of sanity to believe it), you will, when contemplating men, discern a Spirit overhead; not more heavenly than the light flashed upward from glassy surfaces, but luminous and watchful; never shooting beyond them, nor lagging in the rear; so closely attached to them that it may be taken for a slavish reflex, until its features are studied. It has the sage's brows, and the sunny malice of a faun lurks at the corners of the half-closed lips drawn in an idle wariness of half-tension. That slim feasting smile, shaped like the long-bow, was once a big round satyr's laugh, that flung up the brows like a fortress lifted by gunpowder. The laugh will come again, but it will be of the order of the smile, finely-tempered, showing sunlight of the mind, mental richness rather than noisy enormity. Its common aspect is one of unsolicitous observation, as if surveying a full field and having leisure to dart on its chosen morsels, without any fluttering eagerness. Men's future upon earth does not attract it; their honesty and shapeliness in the present does; and whenever they wax out of proportion, overblown, affected, pretentious, bombastical, hypocritical, pedantic, fantastically delicate; whenever it sees them self-deceived or hoodwinked, given to run riot in idolatries, drifting into vanities, congregating in absurdities, planning short-sightedly, plotting dementedly; whenever they are at variance with their professions, and violate the unwritten but perceptible laws binding them in consideration one to another; whenever they offend sound reason, fair justice; are false in humility or mined with conceit, individually, or in the bulk; the Spirit overhead will look humanely malign, and cast an oblique light on them, followed by volleys of slivery laughter. That is the Comic Spirit.

THE MASCULINE BAG OF TRICKS

From In Defense of Women[8]

H. L. Mencken

What men, in their egotism, constantly mistake for a deficiency of intelligence in woman is merely an incapacity for mastering that mass of

[8] By permission of Alfred A. Knopf, Inc.

small intellectual tricks, that complex of petty knowledges, that collection of cerebral rubber-stamps, which constitutes the chief mental equipment of the average male. A man thinks that he is more intelligent than his wife because he can add up a column of figures more accurately, and because he understands the imbecile jargon of the stock market, and because he is able to distinguish between the ideas of rival politicians, and because he is privy to the minutiae of some sordid and degrading business or profession, say soap-selling or the law. But these empty talents, of course, are not really signs of a profound intelligence; they are, in fact, merely superficial accomplishments, and their acquirement puts little more strain on the mental powers than a chimpanzee suffers in learning how to catch a penny or scratch a match. The whole bag of tricks of the average business man, or even of the average professional man, is inordinately childish. It takes no more actual sagacity to carry on the everyday hawking and haggling of the world, or to ladle out its normal doses of bad medicine and worse law, than it takes to operate a taxicab or fry a pan of fish. No observant person, indeed, can come into close contact with the general run of business and professional men—I confine myself to those who seem to get on in the world, and exclude the admitted failures —without marveling at their intellectual lethargy, their incurable ingenuousness, their appalling lack of ordinary sense. The late Charles Francis Adams, a grandson of one American President and a great-grandson of another, after a long lifetime in intimate association with some of the chief business "geniuses" of that paradise of traders and usurers, the United States, reported in his old age that he had never heard a single one of them say anything worth hearing. These were vigorous and masculine men, and in a man's world they were successful men, but intellectually they were all blank cartridges.

THE LOQUACIOUS MAN

From CHARACTERS[9]

Theophrastus (371–287 B.C.)

Loquacity, if one should wish to define it, would seem to be an incontinence of talk.

The Loquacious Man is one who will say to those whom he meets, if they speak a word to him, that they are quite wrong, and *he* knows all about it, and that, if they listen to him, they will learn; then, while one is answering him, he will put in, "Do you tell me so?—don't forget what you are going to say"; or "Thanks for reminding me"; or "How much one gets from a little talk, to be sure!"; or "By-the-bye"—; or "Yes! you have seen it in a moment"; or "I have been watching you all along to see if you would come to the same conclusion as I did"; and other such cues will he make for himself, so that his victim has not even breathing-time. Aye,

[9] The Jebb translation.

and when he has prostrated a few lonely stragglers, he is apt to march next upon large, compact bodies, and to rout them in the midst of their occupations. Indeed, he will go into the schools and the palaestras, and hinder the boys from getting on with their lessons, by chattering at this rate to the trainers and masters. When people say that they are going, he loves to escort them, and see them safe into their houses. On learning the news from Ecclesia, he hastens to report it; and to relate, in addition, the old story of the battle in Aristophon (the orator)'s year, and of the Lacedaemonian victory in Lysander's time; also of the speech for which he himself once got glory in the Assembly; and he will throw in some abuse of "the masses," too, in the course of his narrative; so that the hearers will either forget what it was about, or fall into a doze, or desert him in the middle and make their escape. Then, on a jury, he will hinder his fellows from coming to a verdict, at a theatre from seeing the play, at a dinner-party, from eating; saying that "it is hard for a chatterer to be silent," and that this tongue *will* run, and that he could not hold it, though he should be thought a greater chatterer than a swallow. Nay, he will endure to be the butt of his own children, when, drowsy at last, they make their request of him in these terms—"Papa, chatter to us, that we may fall asleep!"

FEAR OF NEIGHBORS

From HERETICS[10]

G. K. Chesterton

If we were tomorrow morning snowed up in the street in which we live, we should step suddenly into a much larger and much wilder world than we have ever known. And it is the whole effort of the typically modern person to escape from the street in which he lives. First he invents modern hygiene and goes to Margate. Then he invents modern imperialism and goes to Timbuctoo. He goes to the fantastic borders of the earth. He pretends to shoot tigers. He almost rides on a camel. And in all this he is still essentially fleeing from the street in which he was born; and of this flight he is always ready with his own explanation. He says he is fleeing from his street because it is dull; he is lying. He is really fleeing from his street because it is a great deal too exciting; it is exciting because it is exacting; it is exacting because it is alive. He can visit Venice because to him the Venetians are only Venetians; the people of his own street are men. He can stare at the Chinese because for him the Chinese are a passive thing to be stared at; if he stares at the old lady in the next garden, she becomes active. He is forced to flee in short from the too stimulating society of his equals—of free men, perverse, personal, deliberately different from himself. The street in Brixton is too glowing and overpowering. He has to soothe and quiet himself among tigers and vul-

[10] By permission of Dodd, Mead & Co., Inc., publishers of *Heretics*.

tures, camels and crocodiles. These creatures are indeed very different from himself. But they do not put their shape or color or custom into a decisive intellectual competition with his own. They do not seek to destroy his principles and assert their own; the stranger monsters of the suburban street do seek to do this. The camel does not contort his features into a fine sneer because Mr. Robinson has not got a hump; the cultured gentleman at No. 5 does exhibit a sneer because Robinson has not got a dado. The vulture will not roar with laughter because a man does not fly; but the major at No. 9 will roar with laughter because a man does not smoke. The complaint we commonly have to make of our neighbors is that they will not, as we express it, mind their own business. . . . What we really mean . . . is something much deeper. We do not dislike them because they have so little force and fire that they cannot be interested in themselves. We dislike them because they have so much force and fire that they can be interested in us as well. What we dread about our neighbors, in short, is not the narrowness of their horizon, but their superb tendency to broaden it. And all aversions to ordinary humanity have this general character. They are not aversions to its feebleness (as is pretended), but to its energy. The misanthropes pretend that they despise humanity for its weakness. As a matter of fact, they hate it for its strength.

DAN'L WEBSTER

From THE DEVIL AND DANIEL WEBSTER[11]

Stephen Vincent Benét

Yes, Dan'l Webster's dead—or at least, they buried him. But every time there's a thunderstorm around Marshfield, they say you can hear his rolling voice in the hollows of the sky. And they say that if you go to his grave and speak loud and clear, "Dan'l Webster—Dan'l Webster!" the ground'll begin to shiver and the trees begin to shake. And after a while you'll hear a deep voice saying, "Neighbor, how stands the Union?" Then you better answer the Union stands as she stood, rock-bottomed and copper-sheathed, one and indivisible, or he's liable to rear right out of the ground. At least, that's what I was told when I was a youngster.

You see, for a while, he was the biggest man in the country. He never got to be President, but he was the biggest man. There were thousands that trusted in him right next to God Almighty, and they told stories about him that were like the stories of patriarchs and such. They said, when he stood up to speak, stars and stripes came right out in the sky, and once he spoke against a river and made it sink into the ground. They said, when he walked the woods with his fishing rod, Killall, the trout would jump out of the streams right into his pockets, for they knew it was no use putting up a fight against him; and, when he argued a case, he could turn on the harps of the blessed and the shaking of the earth underground. That was the kind of man he was, and his big farm up at Marshfield was suitable to him. The chickens he raised were all white meat down through the drumsticks, the cows were tended like children, and the big ram he called Goliath had horns with a curl like a morning-glory vine and could butt through an iron door. But Dan'l wasn't one of your gentlemen farmers; he knew all the ways of the land, and he'd be up by candlelight to see that the chores got done. A man with a mouth like a mastiff, a brow like a mountain and eyes like burning anthracite—that was Dan'l Webster in his prime.

STEADY NERVES IN A CRISIS

From G. B. S., A Full Length Portrait[12]

George Bernard Shaw

In moments of crisis my nerves act in the most extraordinary way. When utter disaster seems imminent my whole being is instantaneously braced to avoid it. I size up the situation in a flash, set my teeth, contract my muscles, take a firm grip of myself, and, without a tremor, always do the wrong thing. . . .

I learned to drive in 1908 on a car that had its accelerator pedal between the clutch and the brake. That arrangement became automatic for me; and when I changed to cars with the accelerator to the right of the brake I became a deadly dangerous driver in an emergency when I had not my trusty chauffeur next me to turn off the spark when I mistook the pedals. He was unfortunately not with me in South Africa. Well, we were on our way to Port Elizabeth from a pleasant seaside place called Wilderness. I was at the wheel and had done a long drive over mountain passes, negotiating tracks and gorges in a masterly manner, when we came upon what looked like a half mile of straight safe smooth road; and I let the car rip. Suddenly she twisted violently to the left over a bump and made for the edge of the road. I was more than equal to the occasion: not for an instant did I lose my head: my body was rigid: my nerves were of steel. I turned the car's head the other way, and pressed down the wrong pedal as far as it would go. The car responded nobly: she dashed across the road, charged and cleared a bank, taking a barbed wire fence with her, and started off across the veldt. On we went, gathering speed, my foot hard on the accelerator, jerking and crashing over the uneven ground, plunging down a ravine and up the other side, and I should have been bumping over the veldt to this day if Commander Newton, who was in charge of me, hadn't said sternly, "Will you take your foot off the accelerator and put it on the brake." Well, I am always open to reason. I did as he suggested and brought the car to a standstill, the last

---

[12] Reprinted by permission of Hesketh Pearson.

strand of barbed wire still holding, though drawn out for miles. I was unhurt; but my wife had been rolled about with the luggage in the back seat and was seriously wounded.

THE FACES OF MANHATTAN[13]

Russell Baker

Where do New Yorkers get these faces that they wear in the streets of Manhattan? The variety is tonic, especially to anyone who has been drugged by the faces of Washington. Washington is basically a one-face town. The typical Washington face has been scrutinized by the security police and certified non-eccentric by the Federal Government. Coming into Manhattan from such a place is to rediscover the human face. People are walking the streets with the most startling confessions written from chin to hairline. For anyone starved for the face of humanity, it is wonderful.

If there is one common characteristic of the New York face, it is disengagement from all other faces. It will not look at you. You can stand on a street corner and stare it right in the eyes, and it will refuse to see you. A Washington face when stared into will check itself ostentatiously. You can watch it start to worry, to ask itself, "Is there ink on my nose?" or "Has the F.B.I. heard that my wife sneered at the Un-American Activities Committee last week?" New York faces, on the other hand, remain perfectly composed no matter how closely examined. They refuse to have their privacy disturbed.

One of the most interesting places to watch faces is Times Square. Times Square faces tend, on the whole, to be slightly desperate. In the early evening there are the young, taut faces bent on picking up the illusory trail of pleasure. The happy imbecile faces grinning at the neon arcades. The faces of life's losers studying the lewd movie posters. The strained hungry faces of the boys who think that tonight, this night, something exciting may happen at last. And there are the tourists' faces— harried, bland, intoxicated faces, in-from-Scarsdale faces, faces struggling to look like tough sophisticated New York faces, tired faces, betrayed faces.

For an antidote there is the East Side, lair of the successful face, a face that boldly commands respect. Doormen, with their cunning, hooded faces so clever at appraising the price of your necktie, nod to these successful East Side faces and whistle up taxicabs for them. They are faces that transmit vital, tantalizing messages. "I am off to merge Consolidated," they say, without moving a jaw muscle. Or, "My prima ballerina has already been waiting 45 minutes."

For famous faces, Fifth Avenue is unbeatable. "Look," these Fifth Avenue faces say, "I am famous, and its a great bore to be looked at all

[13] The New York Times, May 17, 1964; © 1964 by The New York Times Company. Reprinted by permission.

the time, but you see how unruffled I am by your stare." There are more —the Village faces (Ohio faces wearing beards), Mets-fan faces (lippy, sad), Yankee-fan faces (smug), Mafia faces, Harlem faces, faces running on benzedrine and faces unsafe to walk with on a lonely street.

It would be good for the country to ship a large assortment of them to Washington, but it probably isn't in the cards.

ROBERT FROST ON TECHNIQUE IN POETRY WRITING

From Dialogue with an Audience: The First Seven Years[14]

John Ciardi

One evening at Bread Loaf Mr. Frost was reading his poems and talking about them. He was often a sort of horse trader in ideas. He seemed to pull out a conceptual stick to whittle while he talked *around* the idea he was trading for, rambling off in what seemed to be indirection, only to turn and surprise the idea from behind. It could be a great performance, and that night's was one of his greatest.

His conceptual stick for the occasion was "technical tricks": he wanted to tell us about some of his. He read a poem, paused to ask the audience in what meter it was written, and then had fun scolding those who did not know it was in hendecasyllabics. A bit later he interrupted a reading to say he was "a synecdochist by profession," and went on to have his fun with those who did not know which trope a synecdoche is, or even that it is a trope. So he went on. He pointed out rhyme pairings in which he took special pleasure. He paused to underline some of what he called his "bright ideas" for the management of the poem. He had things to say about "the tune" of this poem and that. He was well cast in the role of the master craftsman and he was having a good time.

I had been watching a sweet elderly lady in the second row. She had been giving signs of increasing agitation as the talk went on. The applause had hardly died down when she was on her feet, waving her arm furiously for attention, and spilling out the question she had been repressing (if it could be called a question) even as she called for attention. "But, Mr. Frost," she cried, "*surely* when you are writing one of your *beautiful poems, surely* you can't be thinking about"—and here her voice slurred the dirty words—"about *technical tricks!*"

Mr. Frost put his hands together, the spread fingers touching tip to tip, looked owlish for a moment, and then leaned forward into the microphone and said in a playfully gravelly bass: "I *revel* in 'em!"

[14] *The Saturday Review*, September 14, 1963.

SCIENCE AND PHILOMELA

From THE ONLY WAY TO WRITE A MODERN POEM ABOUT A NIGHTINGALE[15]

Aldous Huxley

The contemporary man of letters finds himself confronted, as he pre-
pares to write about Nature, by a fascinating problem—the problem of
harmonizing, within a single work of art, the old, beloved raw materials,
handed down to him by the mythmakers of an earlier time, with the new
findings and hypotheses now pouring in upon him from the sciences of his
own day.

In this second half of the twentieth century what should a literary
artist, writing in the English language, do about nightingales? The first
thing to be remarked is that the spraying of English hedgerows with
chemical weed killers has wiped out most of their population of assorted
caterpillars, with the result that caterpillar-eating nightingales . . . have
now become rarities in a land where they were once the most widely distributed of poetical raw materials. . . . No weeds, no caterpillars. No
caterpillars, no Philomel with melody, no plaintive anthem or charming
of magic casements. The immortal bird still sings . . . where the caterpillars are sufficiently plentiful, its old immemorially moving song. Darkling we listen,

> While thou art pouring forth thy soul abroad
> In such an ecstasy!

listen in the moonlight, while

> . . . thick the bursts come crowding through the leaves!
> Again—thou hearest!
> Eternal Passion!
> Eternal pain!

But Philomel, it turns out, is not Philomel, but her mate. And when
the cock nightingale sings, it is not in pain, not in passion, not in ecstasy,
but simply to proclaim to other cock nightingales that he has staked out a
territory and is prepared to defend it against all comers. And what makes
him sing at night? A passion for the moon, a Baudelairean love of darkness? Not at all. If he sings at intervals during the night, it is because,
like all the other members of his species, he has the kind of digestive system that makes him want to feed every four or five hours throughout the
twenty-four. Between caterpillars, during these feeding times, he warns
his rivals ("Jug, Jug, Jug") to keep off his private property.

To the twentieth-century man of letters this new information about a
tradition-hallowed piece of poetic raw material is itself a piece of poten-
tially poetic raw material. To ignore it is an act of literary cowardice.
The new facts about nightingales are a challenge from which it would be
pusillanimous to shrink. And what a challenge! . . . Cheerfully accept-

[15] *Harper's Magazine*, August, 1963, pp. 62–66.

ing the fact, let us advance together, men of letters and men of science, further and further into the ever-expanding regions of the unknown.

THE POET'S EMOTION

From TRADITION AND THE INDIVIDUAL TALENT[16]

T. S. Eliot

It is not in his personal emotions, the emotions provoked by particular events in his life, that the poet is in any way remarkable or interesting. His particular emotions may be very simple, or crude, or flat. The emotion in his poetry will be a very complex thing, but not with the complexity of the emotions of people who have very complex or unusual emotions in life. One error, in fact, of eccentricity in poetry is to seek for new human emotions to express; and in this search for novelty in the wrong place it discovers the perverse. The business of the poet is not to find new emotions, but to use the ordinary ones and, in working them into poetry, to express feelings which are not in actual emotions at all. And emotions which he has never experienced will serve his turn as well as those familiar to him. Consequently, we must believe that "emotion recollected in tranquillity" is an inexact formula. For it is neither emotion, nor recollection, nor, without distortion of meaning, tranquillity. It is a concentration, and a new thing resulting from concentration, of a very great number of experiences which to the practical and active person would not seem to be experiences at all; it is a concentration which does not happen consciously or of deliberation. These experiences are not "recollected," and they finally unite in an atmosphere which is "tranquil" only in that it is a passive attending upon the event. Of course this is not quite the whole story. There is a great deal, in the writing of poetry, which must be conscious and deliberate. In fact, the bad poet is usually unconscious where he ought to be conscious, and conscious where he ought to be unconscious. Both errors tend to make him "personal." Poetry is not a turning loose of emotion, but an escape from emotion! it is not the expression of personality, but an escape from personality. But, of course, only those who have personality and emotions know what it means to want to escape from these things.

THE POET'S INSPIRATION

From A DEFENSE OF POETRY

Percy Bysshe Shelley

Poetry is the record of the best and happiest moments of the happiest and best minds. We are aware of evanescent visitations of thought and

---

[16] From *Selected Essays* New Edition, by T. S. Eliot, copyright, 1932, 1936, 1950, by Harcourt, Brace & World, Inc.; copyright 1960, 1964, by T. S. Eliot. Reprinted by permission of the publishers.

feeling sometimes associated with place or person, sometimes regarding our own mind alone, and always arising unforseen and departing unbidden, but elevating and delightful beyond all expression: so that even in the desire and the regret they leave, there cannot but be pleasure, participating as it does in the nature of its object. It is as it were the interpenetration of a diviner nature through our own; but its footsteps are like those of a wind over the sea, which the coming calm erases, and whose traces remain only, as on the wrinkled sands which pave it. These and corresponding conditions of being are experienced principally by those of the most delicate sensibility and the most enlarged imagination; and the state of mind produced by them is at war with every base desire. The enthusiasm of virtue, love, patriotism, and friendship is essentially linked with such emotions; and whilst they last, self appears as what it is, an atom to a universe. Poets are not only subject to these experiences as spirits of the most refined organization, but they can colour all that they combine with the evanescent hues of this ethereal world; a word, a trait in the representation of a scene or a passion will touch the enchanted chord, and reanimate, in those who have ever experienced these emotions, the sleeping, the cold, the buried image of the past. Poetry thus makes immortal all that is best and most beautiful in the world; it arrests the vanishing apparitions which haunt the interlunations of life, and veiling them, or in language or in form, sends them forth among mankind, bearing sweet news of kindred joy to those with whom their sisters abide—abide, because there is no portal of expression from the caverns of the spirit which they inhabit into the universe of things. Poetry redeems from decay the visitations of the divinity in man.

Poetry turns all things to loveliness; it exalts the beauty of that which is most beautiful, and it adds beauty to that which is most deformed; it marries exultation and horror, grief and pleasure, eternity and change; it subdues to union under its light yoke all irreconcilable things. It transmutes all that it touches, and every form moving within the radiance of its presence is changed by wondrous sympathy to an incarnation of the spirit which it breathes: its secret alchemy turns to potable gold the poisonous waters which flow from death through life; it strips the veil of familiarity from the world, and lays bare the naked and sleeping beauty, which is the spirit of its forms.

THE ARTIST AND SOCIETY

From MANNER OF SPEAKING[17]

John Ciardi

No good artist embraces wholeheartedly the values of the society in which he lives. Yet at the same time, he must recognize that it is society and only society that stores from the past and transmits to him his traditions, his forms, and even the world view and the sort of passion that will

[17] *The Saturday Review*, November 23, 1963, p. 15.

make his work possible. No genius has ever flowered apart from society —without a passionate immersion in the traditions society has stored up for him, and without a zealous joy in remaking what society has made possible.

Imagine that the enormous inherited gift that was Mozart was snatched up at birth by a time machine and transported to the Greek Golden Age. Can one doubt that, barring fantastic mischance, the transported Mozart would become a master musician of that other age? Who knows what he might have accomplished with lute, flute, reeds, drums, or as a rhapsode? Marvelous things, one must suppose.

But (leaving out the quartets, ensembles, operas) how many symphonies could he have composed? He could not have had even the dimmest concept of symphonic music. The very idea of the orchestra had yet to be formed by society. The individual instruments that would bit by bit blend together to form that idea had hardly begun their evolution. It is for these reasons that the natural genius of twenty Mozarts could not have composed a single symphony. Society had not yet made such a thing possible.

It is by the power of genius that men make essentially new connections, but the elements among which it has its connections to make are forever from society. We may think of ourselves as lucky in having artists who dare rebel. The fact is that their rebellion is never really from society. Rather they insist on holding up to all levels of society its own best levels. The health of that rebellion is the health of us all.

INTUITION AND EXPRESSION

From AESTHETICS[18]

Benedetto Croce

One often hears people say that they have many great thoughts in their minds, but that they are not able to express them. But if they really had them, they would have coined them into just so many beautiful, sounding words, and thus have expressed them. If these thoughts seem to vanish or to become few and meagre in the act of expressing them, the reason is that they did not exist or really were few and meagre. People think that all of us ordinary men imagine and intuit countries, figures and scenes like painters, and bodies like sculptors; save that painters and sculptors know how to paint and carve such images, while we bear them unexpressed in our souls. They believe that anyone could have imagined a Madonna of Raphael; but that Raphael was Raphael owing to his technical ability in putting the Madonna upon canvas. Nothing can be more false than this view. The world which as a rule we intuit is a small thing. It consists of little expressions, which gradually become greater and wider with the increasing spiritual concentration of certain moments. They are the words we say to ourselves, our silent judgments "Here is a man, here

[18] By permission of The Macmillan Co.

is a horse, this is heavy, this is sharp, this pleases me," etc. It is a medley
of light and color, with no greater pictorial value than would be expressed
by a haphazard splash of colours, from among which one could barely
make out a few special, distinctive traits. This and nothing else is what
we possess in our ordinary life; this is the basis of our ordinary action. . . .

It has been observed by those who have best studied the psychology
of artists that when, after having given a rapid glance at any one, they attempt to obtain a real intuition of him, in order, for example, to paint his
portrait, then this ordinary vision, that seems so precise, so lively, reveals
itself as little better than nothing. What remains is found to be at the
most some superficial trait, which would not even suffice for a caricature.
The person to be painted stands before the artist like a world to discover.
Michelangelo said, "One paints, not with the hands, but with the brain."
Leonardo shocked the prior of the Convent of the Graces by standing for
days together gazing at the "Last Supper" without touching it with the
brush. He remarked of this attitude: "The minds of men of lofty genius
are most active in invention when they are doing the least external work."
The painter is a painter, because he sees what others only feel or catch a
glimpse of, but do not see. We think we see a smile, but in reality we
have only a vague impression of it, we do not perceive all the characteristic traits of which it is the sum, as the painter discovers them after he has
worked upon them and is thus able to fix them on the canvas. We do not
intuitively possess more even of our intimate friend, who is with us every
day and at all hours, than at most certain traits of physiognomy which
enable us to distinguish him from others.

THE COLDNESS OF GENIUS

From The Paradox of Acting

Denis Diderot

Great poets, great actors, and, I may add, all great copyists of Nature,
in whatever art, beings gifted with fine imagination, with broad judgment,
with exquisite tact, with a sure touch of taste, are the least sensitive of all
creatures. They are too apt for too many things, too busy with observing,
considering, and reproducing, to have their inmost hearts affected with any
liveliness. To me such an one always has his portfolio spread before him
and his pencil in his fingers.

It is we who feel; it is they who watch, study, and give us the result.
And then . . . well, why should I not say it? Sensibility is by no means
the distinguishing mark of a great genius. He will have, let us say, an
abstract love of justice, but he will not be moved to temper it with mercy.
It is the head, not the heart, which works in and for him. Let some unforeseen opportunity arise, the man of sensibility will lose it; he will never
be a great king, a great minister, a great commander, a great advocate, a
great physician. Fill the front of a theatre with tearful creatures, but I
will none of them on the boards.

And pray, why should the actor be different from the poet, the painter, the orator, the musician? It is not in the stress of the first burst that characteristic traits come out. It is in moments of stillness and self-command; in moments entirely unexpected. Who can tell whence these traits have their being? They are a sort of inspiration. They come when the man of genius is hovering between nature and his sketch of it, and keeping a watchful eye on both. The beauty of inspiration, the chance hits of which his work is full, and of which the sudden appearance startles himself, have an importance, a success, a sureness very different from that belonging to the first fling. Cool reflection must bring the fury of enthusiasm to its bearings.

The extravagant creature who loses his self-control has no hold on us; this is gained by the man who is self-controlled. The great poets, especially the great dramatic poets, keep a keen watch on what is going on, both in the physical and the moral world.

REVELATION IN THE THEATRE[19]

Max Reinhardt

The theatre is deathless. It is the happiest loophole of escape for those who have secretly put their childhood in their pockets and have gone off with it to play to the end of their days. The art of the stage affords also liberation from the conventional drama of life, for it is not dissimulation that is the business of the play but revelation. Only the actor who cannot lie, who is himself undisguised, and who profoundly unlocks his heart deserves the laurel. The supreme goal of the theatre is truth, not the outward, naturalistic truth of every day, but the ultimate truth of the soul.

We can telegraph and telephone and wire pictures across the ocean; we can fly over it. But the way to the human being next us is still as far as to the stars. The actor takes us on this way. With the light of the poet he climbs the unexplored peaks of the human soul, his own soul, in order to transform it secretly there and to return with his hands, eyes, and voice full of wonders.

He is at once sculptor and sculpture; he is man at the farthest borderline between reality and dream, and he stands with both feet in both realms. The actor's power of self suggestion is so great that he can bring about in his body not only inner and psychological but even outer and physical changes. And when one ponders on the miracle of Konnersreuth, whereby a simple peasant girl experiences every Friday the Passion of Christ, with so strong an imaginative power that her hands and feet show wounds and she actually weeps tears of blood, one may judge to what wonders and to what mysterious world the art of acting may lead; for it is

[19] From *The Encyclopaedia Britannica*, vol. 22, p. 39, by permission of the publishers.

assuredly by the same process that the player, in Shakespeare's words, changes utterly his accustomed visage, his aspect and carriage, his whole being, and can weep for Hecuba and make others weep. Every night the actor bears the stigmata, which his imagination inflicts upon him, and bleeds from a thousand wounds.

ON UNPERFECT ACTORS[20]

Emile Capouya

The actor does his work in an atmosphere of crisis. He needs the nerves of a hero, and such purity of intent that the presence of the audience and his own pride and shame at standing before them are subdued to his purpose and turned to another kind of energy, the energy of art. All the time he is on stage, his calling is to do only the exactly right thing. Think of the predicament of the actor in the classic theatre, measuring himself night after night against a masterpiece. If he is a Shakespearean actor, and a man of sense, he must know that compared to his author he is a pygmy, as insignificant in the history of the play as Hillary crawling in the vast Himalayas. If he knows it, his artistic life is an honorable martyrdom, all selflessness and abnegation, with none of the businessman's or politician's cheerful ignorance about the state of his own soul. But how often does he know it? How often, rather, do we see the actor comport himself for three hours like a brutal, benighted, and besotted beast, and then come forward to his curtain call in the comfortable assurance of a job well botched? To be an actor and have artistic standards, one would first have to be a man and have human ones. Where is the actor to learn manhood nowadays? Whom shall he take for his pattern?

He is in a fix, all right, like the rest of us. It shows in the technical details of his performance, in his frequent inability, for example, to speak verse decently. Every actor knows by heart Hamlet's directions to the players: "Speak the speech, I pray you, as I pronounced it to you, trippingly on the tongue. . . . Nor do not saw the air too much with your hand, thus. . . ." But the actor has no faith in words—this is, after all, the age of the illustrated magazine, the comic strip, the motion picture, and television. He has no faith in words, and no modesty about the value of his own contribution, so that in speaking a great poet's verse he refuses to let the words do their proper work. Instead, he underlines, and winks, and smirks, and nudges the audience, as if he wanted to remind them of the unfortunate connection between the stage and the brothel. Do you remember that televised political convention opened by the Boy Orator of the Snake River, who, when he spoke of something low, bent at the knees, and when he mentioned something high, reached for the welkin? One expects that sort of thing in a politician, but an artist should be above it. The best course is to do as the French classic actors in speaking verse:

[20] *Saturday Review*, December 14, 1963, pp. 40–41.

with a weaker language and worse poets than ours, they have the modesty, in principle, to stand up straight, with their hands at their sides, open their mouths, and listen closely to the words.

HAMLET'S ADVICE TO THE PLAYERS

From HAMLET

William Shakespeare

Speak the speech, I pray you, as I pronounced it to you, trippingly on the tongue: but if you mouth it, as many of your players do, I had as lief the town-crier spoke my lines. Nor do not saw the air too much with your hand, thus; but use all gently: for in the very torrent, tempest, and, as I may say, whirlwind of your passion, you must acquire and beget a temperance that may give it smoothness. O, it offends me to the soul to hear a robustious periwig-pated fellow tear a passion to tatters, to very rags, to split the ears of the groundlings; who, for the most part, are capable of nothing but inexplicable dumbshows and noise. I would have such a fellow whipp'd for o'erdoing Termagant; it out-herods Herod: pray you, avoid it. . . .

Be not too tame neither, but let your own discretion be your tutor: suit the action to the word, the word to the action; with this special observance, that you o'erstep not the modesty of nature: for anything so overdone is from the purpose of playing, whose end, both at the first and now, was and is, to hold, as 'twere, the mirror up to Nature; to show virtue her own feature, scorn her own image, and the very age and body of the time his form and pressure. But this overdone, or come tardy of, though it make the unskilful laugh, cannot but make the judicious grieve; the censure of the which one must, in your allowance, o'erweigh a whole theatre of others. O, there be players that I have seen play, and heard others praise, and that highly, not to speak it profanely, that, neither having the accent of Christians nor the gait of Christian, pagan nor man, have so strutted and bellowed, that I have thought some of Nature's journeymen had made men, and not made them well, they imitated humanity so abominably. . . .

And let those that play your Clowns speak no more than is set down for them: for there be of them that will themselves laugh, to set on some quantity of barren spectators to laugh too; though, in the meantime, some necessary question of the play be then to be considered: that's villainous, and shows a most pitiful ambition in the Fool that uses it.

4

VOICE AND PRONUNCIATION

The Need for Voice Consciousness

It is remarkable that people who are careful to appear in public appropriately dressed and well groomed, who are deeply concerned about the face and figure they present to others, are yet so careless about the impression they make when they open their mouths to speak. Voice and pronunciation are such intimate and revealing aspects of personality that their improvement should be eagerly sought by all who care about their reputation and social acceptability. But few of us are speech-conscious. We have no handy voice reflectors, analogous to mirrors, to enable us to hear ourselves as others hear us and to keep reminding us of how we sound. Tape recorders are becoming more common and more compact and portable, but outside the laboratory they are not much used for self-examination. And, when we do hear our voices played back from a speech recorder, the almost inevitable reaction is "Do I really sound like that?" If there were some salable elixer or mechanical gadget that would improve the voice, as cosmetics, girdles, and electric vibrators are alleged to improve the face and figure, we should have hucksters bombarding us day and night with appeals to improve our speech, and we should doubtless become more conscious of our speech behavior. But many of us, unaware of our shortcomings, are quite content to live with them, and, as we have seen, some ideas, attitudes, and feelings can be expressed with any kind of voice, and even without articulate words.

But our special interest is the interpretation of literature, and, as we approach the study of poetry particularly, voice and pronunciation become very important, since much of the effect of poetry lies in its sounds. Only an instrument with a beautiful tone can adequately render beautiful music. It becomes our present task to define good voice and to discover if we can how it may be developed. The best way to voice improvement is through skilled individual supervision and long, patient practice, as anyone knows who has undertaken the cultivation of his singing voice. No book can supply infallible prescriptions for every person's vocal ills, since what will help one voice may harm another. I can only offer some general directions and hope that they will be helpful.

Isolating Voice Quality

We need first to separate basic voice quality from the other aspects of speech that are often confused with it. Employment in English speech of a Swedish or Spanish intonation pattern calls for criticism, but it is not a fault of voice proper. Neither are such deviant pronunciations as "erl" for "oil" or "tin" for "ten." When we describe a voice as surly, friendly, mournful, or the like, we are describing not its basic quality but, rather, its emotional color, the mood of the speaker, his temporary or habitual *use* of whatever voice he has. One may mourn effectively with any kind of voice and mumble with a good voice as well as with a poor one. In speaking, of course, one's voice always has a psychological component, but, if we are to treat vocal quality with a view to improving it, we must isolate it from other aspects of speech, as a musician thinks of the tone quality or timbre of his instrument quite apart from the technique employed in playing it.

What Is Good Voice Quality?

When we have isolated this basic physical quality of voice from the other aspects of speech, we must analyze it and consider which characteristics of it are satisfactory for the uses to which it will be put, and which are not. The elocutionists of the nineteenth century, following the pioneer teachings of James Rush in his *Philosophy of the Human Voice* (1827), divided voice into the four elements of pitch, volume, time, and quality (using "quality" not as the essence of voice but as one of its elements), and tried to improve each separately. Some present-day writers on speech continue the use of these rubrics and this method. Such a treatment is likely to lead to an artificiality divorced from the purposes of speech, as it did with the elocutionists, and we will make little use of it. Instead, let us look at some of the descriptive adjectives commonly applied to voice and note whether they describe its essential quality or something else, and whether they designate features that are desirable in ordinary (but not dramatic) speech or those that are not desirable.

animated	grating	mournful	slow
bitter	gruff	muddy	soft
bland	guttural	muffled	sonorous
brassy	hard	mumbling	strained
breathy	harsh	nasal	strident
broken	heavy	orotund	strong
cheerful	high pitched	penetrating	surly
clear	hoarse	pleasant	tense
colorful	husky	powerful	thin
colorless	lifeless	pure	throaty
deep	lively	raspy	tight
drawling	loud	reedy	treble
falsetto	low pitched	relaxed	tremulous
firm	melancholy	resonant	weak
flat	mellow	rough	weary
flexible	monotonous	shrill	wheezy

If this list seems to indicate that vocal faults are more common than virtues, that is probably the case. At least, we are more aware of faults than of virtues, since a good voice seldom calls attention to itself. The desirable attributes of voice were well stated by Quintilian the old Roman teacher of orators: "That delivery is elegant which is supported by a voice that is easy, powerful, fine, flexible, firm, sweet, well sustained, clear, pure, that cuts the air and penetrates the ear." A better statement would be hard to find.

Let us take his ideas and some others and combine them into a coherent and usable formula for good voice. We can agree, first, that we should like our voices to be pleasant and agreeable, with a happy balance of resonances and overtones, not irritating, offensive, obtrusive, or distracting. Hence, second, they should be clear, pure, and resonant, not breathy, raspy, hoarse, muddy, coarse, or rough. Third, they should be relaxed and easily produced, not tight, strained, shrill, strident, or tense. Fourth, they should be firm, controlled, and capable of speaking with authority, not wavering, weak, thin, faded, tremulous, spasmodic, or jumpy. Fifth, they should be flexible and responsive, each moving freely and appropriately through its characteristic range of pitch and volume, and varying easily in tempo and color. In summary, we want our voices to be pleasant, clear, relaxed but firm, and flexible. How are these attributes to be developed?

Control of the Breath

The first step in development of these vocal attributes is control of the breath. The function of breathing in voice production is generally known, and all that is called for here is a brief review of the process and some simple exercises for strengthening, firming, and controlling the voice. Voice is formed in the larynx when the vocal cords, or folds, are brought close to-gether and breath is exhaled through the narrow chink between them, causing their edges to vibrate. Breathing goes on automatically from birth till death, without our having to pay any attention to it—inhalation and exhalation being of approximately equal duration. But the process is subject to conscious control, and, in speaking, its pattern has to be modi-fied; in order for one to utter long phrases in continuous speech, inhala-tions must be taken in quick gasps and exhalations must be prolonged. The control of this exhaled breath is the key factor in developing all of the attributes of good voice mentioned above.

DIAPHRAGMATIC-ABDOMINAL BREATHING. Teachers of speech and sing-ing have found that the voice functions best when breathing is controlled through the diaphragmatic-abdominal system of muscles. In this process, inhalation is accomplished by contracting the diaphragm, the dome-shaped membranous partition that divides the chest from the abdomen. This enlarges the chest cavity and draws air into the lungs. But it also compresses the visceral organs in the abdomen below it and causes a no-ticeable bulge in the abdominal wall just above the belt line. When inhala-tion is complete, the process is reversed, the abdominal muscles contracting like a rubber girdle, compressing the viscera and causing them to push up against the diaphragm, thus driving air out of the lungs. This highly sim-plified account will serve our present ends.[1]

It is important to understand that control of the voice depends on con-trol of the contracting abdominal muscles in coordination with control of the relaxing diaphragm. Generally, we are not conscious of the action of these muscles, but we can readily test their operation by placing one hand firmly on the "diaphragmatic triangle" (formed by the belt line as a hypo-tenuse and the slanting lines of the lower ribs) and feeling the movement of the abdominal wall. It is also important to learn that tensing these antagonistic muscles, diaphragmatic against abdominal, and keeping them tense while phonating, will impart to the voice a firmness, fullness, and power of which you may not have supposed it to be capable.

This may properly be called the "natural" method of breathing; at least, it is the method generally used by the mammalian animals whose or-ganic structure is similar to man's. But many millenniums ago man de-cided to stand erect, and more recently he has spent a great deal of his time in a sitting position, and both of these innovations have interfered

---

[1] A detailed account of the mechanics of the whole speech process may be found in Virgil A. Anderson, *Training the Speaking Voice* (Fair Lawn, N.J.: Oxford Uni-versity Press, 1942); G. W. Gray and C. M. Wise, *The Bases of Speech* (New York: Harper & Row, 1946); and L. S. Judson and A. T. Weaver, *Voice Science* (New York: Appleton-Century-Crofts, Inc., 1942).

with the normal abdominal breathing process and encouraged him to breathe by lifting his ribs. There can be little doubt that the resultant chest breathing is less conducive to good vocal tone. Some teachers of singing will not allow their pupils to use it at any time. In oral reading too, one ought to take some pains to avoid it. The major secret of good voice in both speaking and singing is active control of the gradually relaxing diaphragm during vocalization. This muscle is so central in bodily functioning that it is hardly too much to say that diaphragmatic control means emotional control, self-control. Incidentally, it will be found helpful in controlling the nervous disturbance known as "stage fright." To a serious student of voice, no labor can be too great that is expended in acquiring and improving this form of breath control.

EXERCISES FOR BREATH CONTROL.

1. First, examine your breathing machinery to see how it is operating. Lie flat on your back on the floor; place one hand on the diaphragmatic triangle; and take a succession of deep regular breaths. Count mentally, not vocally, to three or four during each inhalation and each exhalation, so as to keep the breathing steady and even. The abdomen should expand as you inhale. You can strengthen the muscles by placing a heavy stack of books on the upper abdomen so that each inhalation will lift them.

2. Try to retain the same muscular action while standing comfortably erect. Try it also with arms stretched high above the head.

3. Try panting like a dog. Try it in various positions—while lying flat, on all fours, standing erect, and with arms extended above the head. Keep at it until you can notice a definite to-and-fro motion in the diaphragmatic triangle. Keep the chest still.

4. Speaking vigorously, count up to five at about the tempo soldiers use in marching; then catch a quick breath through the mouth and repeat the counting several times. As each breath is taken, you should be able to feel a sudden abdominal expansion.

5. Keeping the throat completely relaxed, and trying to use a vigorous abdominal stroke on each syllable, utter vigorously in marked rhythm,

Ha, ha, ha (breath)
Ha, ha, ha (breath), etc.

You should feel the abdomen contract sharply on each "ha," and expand quickly on each breath. The nearer you come to a natural laugh, the better.

6. Place your hands flat on the seat of a chair or on a low table; then move your feet back till your body is in a straight diagonal line, the weight supported on hands and toes. Arms should be perpendicular so that most of the weight will be on the hands. Keep your body in a straight line; don't let it sag or hump. Let your head fall forward, the

neck and jaw completely relaxed. Then lift your head to its normal position, taking a deep breath, and speak as directed in 4 and 5 above. You may be surprised at the fullness, firmness, and depth of your tones.

7. Rest a bit. Then take the same position and, with firm tones and marked rhythm, chant some such fluid lines as these from Kipling's "Dedication," taking a deep breath before each line:

Beyond the path of the outmost sun through utter darkness hurled—
Further than ever comet flared or vagrant star-dust swirled—
Live such as fought and sailed and ruled and loved and made our world.

8. Repeat the exercise while standing erect, trying to retain the feeling of the firmly tensed abdominal wall. These are the body conditions desirable in reading poetry of deep, sustained feeling.

Vocal Relaxation

A second requirement for good voice is relaxation of the muscles of the throat and jaw that hold the larynx in place but should not be involved in tone production. It is often their interference that causes a voice to be, and to sound, tight, pinched, and strained. The delicate muscles within the larynx that operate the vocal cords should be allowed to do their work without any pull or strain from outside muscles. For good voice, the throat should feel relaxed and comfortable, and voice production should seem to both speaker and listener to be effortless and free. If the cords of the neck stand out, if the face becomes flushed, if the jaw is tight and the tongue rigid, voice quality is sure to be affected. Our first tendency, when the voice is tired, when we must speak very loudly, or when we are under emotional strain, is to do just the wrong thing. We tend to tighten the muscles of the throat when the most helpful thing would be to relax them. Thus, we aggravate the condition we wish to remove. These causes, combined in some climates with the irritating effects of fog and smoke-laden air, have made many voices chronically hoarse, rough, and unpleasant. A *good* voice is one that seems to flow through the throat as if there were nothing there to impede it.

EXERCISES FOR VOICE RELAXATION.

1. In speaking or singing, try to throw all the labor upon the breathing muscles, and think of the throat as an open tube through which the tone flows. Do not allow any feeling of strain in any part of the throat. Relax the muscles that hold the head erect, and let it fall forward on the chest. Then roll it about slowly on the shoulders, trying to keep the neck muscles completely relaxed.

2. Let the jaw drop. Relax the muscles completely, and let it really drop. Then let the head fall forward after it. Then, with neck, jaw, and

tongue completely relaxed, shake the head briskly from side to side, until you can feel the jaw flop back and forth and the tongue waggle from side to side in the jaws. This is an excellent remedy for a tired, tight voice.

3. Simulate a yawn or, if possible, actually yawn—shamelessly. Try to retain the feeling of throat relaxation that follows.

4. With the throat in the relaxed condition induced by these exercises, and with breathing carefully controlled, chant slowly some such dreamy lines as these from Swinburne's "Garden of Proserpine":

> I am tired of tears and laughter,
> And men that laugh and weep;
> Of what may come hereafter
> For men that sow and reap:
> I am weary of days and hours,
> Blown buds and barren flowers,
> Desires and dreams and powers
> And everything but sleep.

Vocal Resonance

Besides requiring firm breath support and a relaxed throat, a good voice should have a pleasing balance of resonances and not sound tinny, nasal, throaty, or hollow. The part that resonance contributes to voice is difficult to explain and difficult to understand. But we know that a cavity of proper size and shape has power to amplify a pure tone, giving it richness, color, and volume. The effectiveness of a resonator depends on its size, the size of the openings into it, and the material of which its walls are constructed. The box of a violin is one kind of resonator; a brass horn is another. The voices of these instruments would be thin and colorless without their resonators, and so would yours.

The principal vocal resonators are the nasal cavities, the mouth, and the pharynx. The size and shape of these cavities, their relationship to each other, and the materials of their walls are the factors that help to make each voice what it is. While we cannot alter our natural physical structure, we can modify the size and shape of the openings into these cavities, we can keep our pharyngeal muscles relaxed, we can teach our tongues not to bulge back into the pharynx, and we can relax the jaw and open the mouth for sounds that do not require that it be closed. To many foreigners, the typical American voice is the one they hear from the tourist who clamps a cigar tightly in one corner of his mouth and emits his speech in a nasal snarl from the other corner. Speaking through a locked jaw is one of our worst habits. It is responsible for much of the shrillness and raspiness of our voices, as well as for our mumbled articulation. And it contributes to the excessive nasality that is so common among us. This fault is largely due to a rigid jaw that inhibits free mouth resonance and a lazy velum that allows too wide an opening into the nasal cavities.

Most teachers of voice agree that some nasal resonance is desirable as giving brilliance and color to the voice. The problem is to determine how much. None of us like either a tense nasal rasp in a voice nor a lazy nasal drawl. Nor, on the other hand, do we like the dead-sounding cold-in-the-head quality sometimes heard. In between, there is a desirable mean.

EXERCISES TO IMPROVE RESONANCE.

1. With breath firmly supported and throat relaxed, hum the sound of the consonant *m* briefly; then open the mouth slowly, trying to avoid any change in the placement or feel of the tone. Let the jaw open wide and the tongue drop with it till the tone becomes *a* as in "arm." Then gradually close the lips while the tone continues, trying not to make any change in the placement. Repeat this slow alternation of sounds until the breath supply is low. The result may be represented thus:

mmm-aaa-mmm-aaa-mmm-aaa

2. Beginning with a hum, change to an open *ah* and hold it as long as breath suffices, trying to keep the tone steady, rich, round, and full, feeling its reverberation through all the resonance cavities.

3. Try the same, increasing the volume of the tone toward the middle point of its duration, then letting it die away gradually. Try not to strain or alter the resonance as volume increases. Let the tone swell, don't force it, and keep jaw and throat relaxed.

4. Try the same exercises with other vowels, beginning always with a hum.

5. Maintaining the conditions recommended for breathing, relaxation, and tone production, begin again with a hum and open *ah*, then take another breath and chant slowly some such solemn lines as the following, trying to maintain throughout each line the resonance and placement of tone described above. Make the vowels full, rich, and golden. This is an exercise not in interpretation but in voice development.

> Fear no more the heat o' the sun,
>   Nor the furious winter's rages;
> Thou thy wordly task hast done,
>   Home art gone, and ta'en thy wages:
> Golden lads and girls all must,
>   As chimney-sweepers, come to dust.

Pronunciation

As the stream of voice, whatever its basic quality, flows through the articulatory area, it may be modified in additional ways to form the letter sounds we articulate into words and speech. Though the form and structure of the speech organs that cause these modifications—the lips, tongue, jaw, and velum—may differ somewhat from person to person, as may the habit of using them, the resulting sounds they make are remarkably uniform among all speakers of English. Otherwise we should not have coast-to-coast broadcasts.

Some speakers, however, deviate so far from the norm of articulation that their speech impresses others as unclear or unpleasant. Some are at times not sure how a certain sound should be made, or what sounds a word should contain. All of us are prone to carelessness in enunciation, and too few of us have a genuine respect for our language and take pride in speaking it well. So we take shortcuts, telescope sounds that ought to stand apart, substitute one sound for another, or let sounds escape half-formed. Perhaps these are natural tendencies in speakers of all languages, but in English they are notorious. In interpreting literature to others, we ought to speak English in its best and purest form.

But what is sometimes called carelessness in pronunciation is not always to be condemned and avoided. It may be one of the inevitable developments in a living language. Some of the careless pronunciations of our English-speaking ancestors have become firmly established in acceptable cultured speech. For example, they reduced such words as "moved," "hopped," and "pinned" from two syllables to one; they dropped the initial *k* or *g* from "knife," "know," "gnaw," "gnat"; they introduced the *sh* sound into such words as "social," "ancient," and "cautions"; and these "corruptions" are now standard in cultivated speech. Just what does it mean, then, to pronounce carefully?

MODERN SPELLING IS OBSOLETE. That spelling is no longer a dependable guide to pronunciation becomes apparent when one tries to pronounce letter by letter such words as "tongue," "Lincoln," "couple," "psalm," "carriage," "talk," "thorough," "debt," "knight," "guide," "sword," "women," and "righteous." Our present spellings were designed for the pronunciations of several centuries ago, and, in the meantime, there have been many changes in sounds without a corresponding change in spelling. Some consonants have become silent, or have changed their values, and our vowels have become so unreliable that often a letter gives no clue as to its sound. Note, for instance, these pairs of words with similar spellings that do not rhyme: "all," "shall"; "ever," "fever"; "power," "mower"; "wholly," "jolly"; "form," "worm"; "stove," "move." Perhaps the most remarkable divergence has developed in words spelled with *ough*, which now has nine different pronunciations, as in "bough," "bought," "through," "though," "cough," "tough," "hough," "borough," and "hiccough," and none of them are like the sound for which those letters originally stood. These irregularities are familiar to all of us, and yet, when we attempt to pronounce carefully, our first impulse is to pronounce according to spelling.

These historical changes have not been completely haphazard. Most of them may be included under three general patterns of development— the "great vowel shift," the gradation of vowel quality in unstressed syllables, and the assimilation of contiguous sounds to each other.

THE GREAT VOWEL SHIFT. Since the time of Chaucer (*circa* 1400), the main English vowels have changed their quality by each moving up to a higher tongue position. For instance, "bone" was formerly "bän," "to" was "tō," "sea" was pronounced as "say," and still earlier with the vowel of "sat," and "meet" was pronounced as "mate" now is. The two highest vowels, *ē* and *ōō*, became the diphthongs *i* and *ou*; that is, "ice" and "house" were formerly "ēes" and "hōōs," though some of the *ōō* sounds relaxed to to *ŏŏ* ("foot") or *ŭ* ("flood"). A few early vowels survive in Scotland, where one may still "lie doon and dee" for Annie Laurie. These shifts in quality have thrown our vowels out of line with those in such languages as French, German, and Italian, so we have difficulty in pronouncing foreign names like "Weser," "Hegel," "Rouen," "Milo," "Gide," "Proust," "Weber," and "Beethoven." These changes, being gradual, account for some of the puzzling rhymes we find in Shakespeare and other poets of his time "moan," "gone"; "over," "recover"; "come," "doom"; "love," "remove"; "feast," "rest"; "eye," "liberty"; "nature," "feature"; etc. In one stage of its development, "long *i*" was pronounced the same as *oi*, which accounts for such eighteenth-century rhymes as "joy" and "cry," "toil" and "smile," and "joined" and "find." A few words such as "route," "dour," "either," and "deaf" are apparently still in a state of transition.

GRADATION. Another historical tendency is that which reduces vowels when unaccented to an obscure neutral quality, generally the sound we give *a* in "ago," *e* in "moment," and *o* in "contain." Dictionaries formerly represented this sound merely by italicizing whatever vowel it was spelled with, but all the better recent dictionaries represent it with the schwa symbol /ə/. It is said to be the most common sound in spoken English. Sometimes, unaccented high front vowels are reduced to *i* instead of the schwa vowel, as when we pronounce "always" and "palace" as "alwiz" and "palis." And sometimes, when an unstressed vowel is followed by *l* or *n*, it is lost completely and the weight of the syllable is carried by *l* or *n*, as in "cat'l" and "Lat'n" for "cattle" and "Latin." This obscuring of unstressed vowels is quite common and proper in ordinary speech, otherwise our speech would sound stilted and pedantic, but it should be cautiously restrained in formal speech, as in reading serious poetry.

ASSIMILATION. Another development in the long history of English speech is the gradual assimilation of many consonant sounds to their neighbors. *Assimilation* means simply "becoming similar to." This, like many other developments in the language, is due to our tendency to take shortcuts, to ease over the rough places of articulation, to make one position of the speech organs serve where two are called for. For instance, the work "thank" seems to call for an *n* followed by a *k*, but it is easier to anticipate the position of the *k* by pronouncing the *n* as *ng*, since both *ng* and *k* are tongue-back velar sounds, so we say, "thangk." Such past-tense forms as "hoped," "washed," and "kicked" were formerly pronounced with two syllables, as the spelling indicates. But *e* ceased to be sounded, and thus a voiced *d* was brought next to a voiceless *p, sh,* or *k,* and this caused it to lose its voiced quality and become *t,* so these words are now pronounced "hopt," "washt," "kickt." After voiced sounds, however, as in "sag," "kill," "name," "love," and "hoe," we continue to pronounce *d.* Our plurals, possessives, and third-person-singular endings are affected in a similar way. We spell them all with *s,* and we pronounce *s* after voiceless sounds, as in "He takes Philip's cats." But, after voiced sounds, though we write, "He calls John's dogs," we pronounced it as "He callz Johnz dogz."

According to the same principle, "cupboard," "handkerchief," "raspberry," and "grandma," spelled as they were formerly pronounced, are now pronounced "kuberd," "hangkerchif," "razberry," and "gramma."

An assimilation that causes some uncertainty is that of *t, d, s,* or *z* with a following *y* before an unstressed vowel, resulting in *sh* or *zh,* as in "issue." Here *s* assimilates with the *y,* which is the first element in "long *u.*" In "mission," formerly with three syllables, as in similar words spelled with *i,* the *i* gradually weakened so that at about the time of Shakespeare the pronunciation was "miss-yun." Then *s* and *y* gradually assimilated to *sh.* This development may be clearer if we set down the descriptions of the sounds involved, with ditto marks to show the similarities:

s— voiceless	tongue-blade		alveolar		fricative
combines with y— voiced	"		—front	palatal	glide
to form sh— voiceless	"	"	"	"	fricative

Other examples are "sugar," "issue," "tissue," "pressure," "nauseous," "special," "ocean," "conscience," etc. In a similar manner, *z,* generally spelled with *s,* combines with *y* to form *zh,* as in "vision," "glazier," "confusion," "decision," "azure," "pleasure," "usual," etc.

In words where *t* or *d* was followed by *y,* or by a weak *i,* which later became *y,* a similar change occurred, as in "partial," "cordial," "feature," "verdure," "ratio," "question," "righteous," "soldier," "educate," "credulous," etc.

Though these assimilations are now standard and uniform in cultured speech, there are still some cautious purists, perhaps too conscious of spelling, who resist the normal easy pronunciation of "nature," "literature," "educate," and the like. The best authorities, however, sanction such shortcuts even in formal speech, though they are not likely to approve also the accompanying gradation of *u* to the schwa vowel, as in (*ĕj-ə-kăt*) for "educate," in situations where formality is desirable.

These examples of the disparity between spelling and pronunciation should not lead to the conclusion that spelling is of no value in determining pronunciation. For the great majority of words, it is still a helpful, if imperfect, guide. It may tell us little or nothing about the pronunciation of such words as "one," "eye," "who," "choir," "women," "righteous," "colonel," "tough," and "ewe," but it is of great help in such words as "medieval," "misanthrope," "ingenuousness," "statistics," "athletic," "authoritatively," "homogeneous," and "fatuous," all of which are frequently mispronounced because the reader does not look sharply at the spelling.

DICTIONARY AUTHORITY. In the midst of the uncertainties caused by a constantly developing language, with words varying in sound with their context, the formality of the occasion on which they are spoken, the regional background of the speaker, etc., we seek an authority that will tell us just how words *should* be pronounced, and we turn to a dictionary. Our search for authority may, however, be disappointing, not because good dictionaries are lacking but because no dictionary can give us a correct pronunciation of every word for every occasion and purpose for which it may be used. No dictionary attempts to do so, and no dictionary pretends (except in its advertising) to set a standard of usage for everyone to follow. It attempts merely to *record* the usage "that now prevails among educated and cultured" speakers, pronunciations that are "normally and unaffectedly used by cultivated people," "the actual speech . . . of the community of effective citizens," to quote from three of the leading dictionaries in current use. These statements leave wide latitude for choice and opinion, and, to quote again from one of them, "The lexicographer can not, if he would, avoid passing judgment on the facts of usage."

The only recently revised "complete" dictionary is the highly controversial *Webster's Third New International Dictionary of the English Language, Unabridged,* 1961. It was greeted by a storm of both praise and blame from both scholars and popular reviewers,[2] but it is the only place to turn for information about the hundred thousand or so new words that have recently come into the language. Because of its bulk and weight, it

[2] These criticisms are collected in James Sledd and Wilma R. Ebbitt, *Dictionaries and That Dictionary* (Chicago: Scott, Foresman & Co., 1962).

will be consulted chiefly in the library. Less formidable, but quite adequate for most purposes, are the so-called desk or college dictionaries, of which there are four intended for general use on college campuses. All have been carefully edited by reputable scholars and may be considered reliable. They are

1. *Webster's Seventh New Collegiate Dictionary*, 1963, based on *Webster's Third New International Dictionary.*
2. *The American College Dictionary*, 1947.
3. *Webster's New World Dictionary of the American Language, College Edition*, 1953.
4. *Funk and Wagnalls Standard College Dictionary*, 1963.

For the sake of brevity, these will be designated as Webster 7, ACD, World, and Standard.

To these we may add the Kenyon-Knott *Pronouncing Dictionary of American English* (1944), which gives only pronunciations and uses the International Phonetic Alphabet, and *Webster's Collegiate*, sixth edition, 1951, which will doubtless remain in use for some years. The latter has full explanations of how the various speech sounds are formed and how they are modified in use—explanations that are lacking or inadequate in the four listed above.

Since a student may find himself using now one of these dictionaries and now another, he needs to be aware of how they differ from each other in designating sounds. Devising symbols for designating speech sounds to the eye, and translating them back into speech, has always been a troublesome problem. The most accurate method of identifying sounds is by describing their organic formation, for instance, designating d as a voiced tongue-point alveolar stop and $\bar{o}$ as a mid-back lip-rounded vowel (if you understand these terms). But, of course, such cumbersome designations cannot be used every time we refer to a sound. The International Phonetic Alphabet (IPA) is used by linguistic scholars and by some speech teachers, and its symbols as defined in the Kenyon-Knott dictionary are a very accurate method of representing sounds. But they are not generally familiar, and regular dictionaries are slow to adopt them.

For many years, the "Webster Key" has been used by dictionaries and other reference books, and it is still largely employed by the four works we are considering. Most students are familiar with these diacritical markings, or think they are. They will get little help in understanding them from the four works we are discussing, since each symbol is generally listed merely as the sound used in one or two key words, which may or may not be familiar to the reader. For instance, in the guide to pronunciation, usually found on the inside cover, we are merely given a symbol such as "â," followed by the words "care, air," with no explanation, and in

Webster 7 we find "a" with the very puzzling notation "*father* as pronounced by speakers who do not rhyme it with bother."

COMPARISON OF SYMBOLS. Comparison of the uniformities and differences among the symbols used in these four dictionaries may well begin with their common treatment of the neutral vowel heard in the unaccented syllables of "ago," "recent," "easily," "connect," "circus," "famous," etc. Webster 7 and Standard have joined ACD and World in using the IPA schwa /ə/ for this, the most common sound in spoken English. It is helpful to have this reminder that all such weak syllables, however spelled, have the same sound. It occurs also, of course, in the flow of speech in weak monosyllables in such phrases as "I *can* go," "you *and* I," and "he w*a*s there" and is sometimes acceptable even in formal speech, nearly always for "of," "the," and "a." World and Webster 7 use the phonetic symbol /ŋ/ for *ng*, as in "sang," "ring," and "lung." The other two retain the spelling *ng*. These are the only IPA symbols used, excpet those that correspond to the letters of the regular alphabet.

The "long" vowels are uniformly represented by the familiar macron (ā, ē, ī, ō, ū), except that for ū Webster 7 has (yü), and Standard has (yōō). For the "short" vowels, ACD retains the conventional marking, ă, ĕ, ĭ, ŏ, ŭ, but World and Standard omit the diacritic, and Webster 7 omits it from *a, e,* and *i,* but writes "short" *o* as (ä), and "short" *u* as the schwa /ə/. This means that in Webster 7 the difference between the two vowels in "construct" (kən-'strəkt) is indicated only by the accent mark before the second syllable, the editors assuming, contrary to the views of many phoneticians, that the two sounds are identical. The same symbol is made to serve also for the two vowels in "further" ('fər-th̲ər), for which World writes ('fûr-th̲ēr), ACD has (fûr-t̷h̲ər), and Standard has (fûr-t̷h̲ər). None of the four explain or recognize that these are single *r*-colored vowels, not *u* or *e* followed by the consonant *r*. And, very oddly, none of the four give any consideration to the different vowels used in such words by the millions of "*r*-droppers" in the East and South, or to their substitution of the schwa for an *r* that follows a vowel when they do not omit the *r* altogether.

Note in "further" the four different treatments of the voiced *th.* Note also that, instead of using the customary slanted, dartlike accent mark after a stressed syllable, Webster 7 uses a small perpendicular rectangle *before* the syllable, placed high for primary accent and low for secondary accent ('pen-mən-,ship).

For the variable vowel in such words as "wear," "care," and "air," Webster 7 gives the two common pronunciations (wa(ə)r, we(ə)r), and always inserts as optional a schwa glide between all vowels and a following *r*. The other three have (âr), with no explanation of what it means. For words like "more," ACD has only (mōr); the other three record both (mōr) and (môr), but Webster 7 writes the latter as (mȯ(ə)r), and uses this new symbol also for all such words as "law," "all," and "gnaw," where the others retain the familiar (ô).

Pronunciation of the diphthong *ou*, as in "house," "out," and "down," has long been marked merely as (ou) without diacritics, indicating that it begins with "short" ŏ, which is equivalent to (*a*) as in "art." Webster 7 writes it (au̇), indicating that it begins with the (ă) of "at." Though this pronunciation is often heard, it has long been condemned as dialectal by many thousands of teachers. Another innovation of Webster 7 is the recording of both (*hw*) and (*w*) for words beginning with *wh*, thus indicating that "wile" and "while," "wet" and "whet," "watt" and "what" may be pronounced alike. This dropping of the *h* has also long been opposed by many thousands of teachers and is still regarded by many as careless or vulgar. The same is true of Webster 7's acceptance of (ü), (üm), and (üz) for "who," "whom," and "whose."

The new Webster's dictionaries have been severely criticised for not holding higher standards, or for not recognizing various levels of formality in usage. The editors' defense is that they have merely recorded the "standard speech of educated Americans," "actual educated speech," pronunciations "prevailing in the best present usage," and it is not their function to judge. But, of course, they *do* judge when they decide what is "best" or "prevailing," and who is "educated." Perhaps all a critic is entitled to say is that the editors of Webster 7 must have listened to speakers who were a little less educated than those heard by editors of the other dictionaries. Doubtless, we all lapse at times into such pronunciations as "yuzh-el," "des-pert," "ex-lent," "off-cer," "cum-ta-ble," all recorded in Webster 7, but few of us would defend them as the "best" usage, certainly not for formal speech. For our colloquial ease, "nach-er" and "arz" will serve well enough for "nature" and "ours," but they will not do for Wordsworth's line

Little we see in nature that is ours.

There are other differences in recorded usage and in the methods of indicating it in these four dictionaries, but these are enough to alert the student to the discrepancies he may find in consulting them. They suggest the need of a table of comparative pronunciations of representative words, and such a table is here provided. When you have examined it carefully and tried to pronounce the words as indicated, consider whether the differences are due (1) merely to use of different symbols, (2) to different judgments as to proper pronunciations, (3) to different levels of formality, (4) to changes in fashion during recent years, (5) to laxer standards in some than in other works, or (6) to editorial preference.

A Table of Pronunciation Transcriptions from Four Dictionaries*

Word	Webster 7	ACD	World	Standard
Usual	'yüzh-ə-wəl, 'yü-zhəl	ū' zhōō əl	ū' zhōō-əl ū' zhōōl	yōō' zhōō əl
Heretofore	'hirt-ə- ,fō(ə)r, fo(ə)r, ,hirt-ə-'	hĭr' tə fōr'	hêr' too-fôr, hêr' tə-fōr	hir' tə-fôr', -fōr'
Cultural	'kəĺch-(ə)-rəl	kŭl' cher əl	kul' chêr-əl	kul' chər-əl
Forequarter	'fōr ,kwȯ(r)t-ər, 'fȯr-	fōr' kwôr' tər	fôr'-kwor'-tĕr, fôr'-kwor'-tĕr	fôr' kwôr' tər, fōr'-
Earthenware	'ər-then- ,wa(ə)r, -thən-, '- ,we(ə)r	ûr' thən wâr'	ûr' thən-wâr'	ûr' thən-wâr'
Furthermore	'fər-tho(r)-,mō(ə)r, -,mȯ(ə)r	fûr' ĺĥər mōr'	fũr' thêr-môr', -mōr	fûr thər-môr', -mōr'
Thoroughfare	'thər-ə-, 'thə-rə-, -,fa(ə)r, ,fe(ə)r	thûr' ō fâr', thûr' ə-	thũr' ə-fâr'	thûr' ō-fâr, thûr'-ə-
Mature	mə-'(y)ủ(ə)r, also -'chủ(ə)r	mə tyōōr', -tōōr'	mə-tyoor', -toor'	mə-tyōōr', -tōōr', -chōōr'

* See page 110 in text for explanation of title abbreviations.

A Standard of Pronunciation. This discussion should make it clear that there is no absolute standard for the pronunciation of each English word. But there is a *general* standard that is constant enough to enable us to understand each other in spite of the individual twists we sometimes give our words, the variations that have developed in different geographical regions, the modifications we make in our speech because of different levels of formality, and even the outrageous corruptions found in our substandard dialects. It is notable that our better radio and television announcers and motion-picture actors have achieved a uniformity of pronunciation that enables them to be readily understood in all parts of America, in all the English-speaking countries, and in other countries by those who know English as a second language. This standard, so far as it *is* a standard, is well defined in both the sixth and seventh editions of *Webster's Collegiate* as "the usage that now prevails among the educated and cultured people to whom the language is vernacular."

All of us have abundant opportunity to hear such speech, and we should try to listen to it critically—not so much critizing the speaker's conformity to our standard as criticizing our conformity to his. Again we urge the need of speech consciousness, critical awareness of how we speak and how others speak, delicate sensitivity to our own speech habits and those of others. Our chief difficulty in trying to speak by the standard just defined is not so much uncertainty as to how words should be pronounced as slackness and carelessness in pronouncing them. Too often, we ignore the acoustical requirements of a formal situation and use the

relaxed manner of colloquial intimacy when the voice should be firm and
the articulation clear and precise. In interpreting a tender confidence intended for a private ear, the public reader must still be conscious that all
members of his audience have a right to hear. Young actors who quite
commendably wish to "seem natural" must still remember to speak for the
customers in the back seats.

THE SOUNDS OF POETRY. Interpretation of poetry poses additional
problems. The harmonious combinations of sounds that poets labor to
achieve should be clearly articulated, since appreciation of poetry depends, in part, on enjoyment of its sound effects. Fricative consonants
should have enough friction to make them clearly audible to all in your
audience, and stopped sounds should be definitely stopped. Do not omit
the final *d* in such words as "mind" and "sound" or weaken the inter-
vocalic *t* and *d* in such words as "matter," "better," "model," and "middle"
or turn the *t*'s in the first two into *d*'s. Liquid consonants, *m*, *n*, *ng*, *l*, and
r, should often be lingered over, as if relishing their flavor. Do not pervert "William" and "million" into "wi-yum" and "mi-yun." Give them
clear *l*'s. But, in prolonging words with postvowel *r*'s,—"far," "roar,"
"very"—it is better to dwell on the vowel rather than on the *r*. Wordsworth's fine line

> The winds that will be howling at all hours

should not be corrupted into something like

> The wins 't 'll be howlinga tall ares.

The repetition of *l* in "will," "howling," and "all" should be clearly heard,
as should the repetition of *w* in "winds" and "will."

Our habitual lip-lazy articulation is quite inadequate to interpret the
sparkle and color the poets have written into some of their finest passages.
Notice in these lines from Tennyson's "Morte d'Arthur" how, as a critic
has said, "the verse climbs over rough consonants and pants in monosyllables till the summit is reached, when the broad water opens suddenly
upon the sight":

> Dry clash'd his harness in the icy caves
> And barren chasms, and all to left and right
> The bare black cliff clanged round him, as he based
> His feet on juts of slippery crag that rang
> Sharp-smitten with the dint of armed heels—
> And on a sudden, lo! the level lake,
> And the long glories of the winter moon.

And notice the effect of liquid consonants and the avoidance of stops in
these lines from Tennyson's "Princess":

Myriads of rivulets hurrying through the lawn,
The moan of doves in immemorial elms,
And murmuring of innumerable bees.

And see what fun Alfred Noyes had playing with sounds in writing these lines from "A Song of Sherwood":

Oberon, Oberon, rake away the gold,
Rake away the red leaves, roll away the mould,
Rake away the gold leaves, roll away the red,
And wake Will Scarlet from his leafy forest bed.

Note also these skilfully wrought sound effects in Chesterton's "Lepanto":

Strong gongs groaning as the guns boom far,
Don John of Austria is going to the war,
Stiff flags straining in the night-blasts cold
In the gloom black purple, in the glint old-gold,
Torchlight crimson on the copper kettle-drums,
Then the tuckets, then the trumpets, then the cannon, and he comes.

VOWEL QUALITY. These passages make it plain that vowels as well as consonants need attention. In such passages as "roll away the mould" and "strong gongs groaning," there is obvious play with sound effects, and the vowels besides carry the pulse of the meter and the emotional continuity. Each strong vowel should be moulded carefully with lips and tongue so that its quality is distinct and individual. For ū, ō, and ô, the lips should be rounded. For the low vowels, ă and ä, the jaw should be well opened. Speech forced through a clenched jaw can never have good quality. Resist the lazy tendency to allow all vowels to drift in toward the neutral tongue position so that "meet," "met," "mate," "mat," "mote," "moot," and "might" all sound very much alike. A helpful exercise is to pronounce each vowel separately, following the directions for tone production in this chapter. Keeping the ear sharply focused on tone quality, sound each vowel firmly four times, then pronounce with the same quality several words containing that sound, thus:

ä, ä, ä, ä—arm, far, father, palm, lark
ō, ō, ō, ō—oat, hope, grow, stone, broke

There is also a lazy tendency to allow the velum to relax and so to nasalize vowels that occur next to nasal consonants, as in "man," "main," and "moan." You can correct this fault by practicing words in which the vowel is between stopped consonants (which require a closed velum), noting the quality of the vowel, then trying to retain it in similarly formed words containing homorganic nasals. That is, pronounce "bad"; then try to retain the same vowel quality in "man"; do the same with "bayed" and "main," "bode" and "moan," "bead" and "mean," and "big" and "Ming."

It is remarkable how much power, feeling, and beauty can be given to poetry by well-supported, well-molded vowels. The author recalls the performance of a none too talented student who really got his imagination aroused, his feelings stimulated, and his breathing controlled on the last two lines of the familiar Wordsworth sonnet:

> Have sight of Proteus rising from the sea,
> And hear old Triton blow his wreathed horn.

Rising was spoken with deliberate swelling power that made us visualize the ancient god emerging majestically from the waves, and the strong full tones of "blow," "wreathed," and "horn" made us hear the reverberations rolling sonorously down the beach. It was a memorable performance.

UNCONVENTIONAL COMBINATIONS. A reader of poetry needs to develop a kind of sixth sense for combinations of sounds that are not likely to be readily identified by his hearers—unconventional uses of words, variations from the normal word order, and accidental juxtapositions of sounds that may suggest something other than what is meant. For example, if Shakespeare's line

> When I have seen by time's fell hand defaced

is not clearly spoken, it may be heard as a mystifying remark about something that "fell handy-faced." Byron's lines about

> The oak leviathans, whose huge ribs make
> Their clay creator the vain title take
> Of lord of thee, [see page 258]

have an unexpected use of familiar words and an inverted order that may make the passage quite unintelligible if it is not clearly pronounced and phrased and stressed.

Lines with such unfamiliar words as the following contain may not be understood no matter how finely articulated.

> And all his greaves and cuisses dash'd with drops
> Of onset, [see page 271]   ALFRED LORD TENNYSON.

> A shielded scutcheon blush'd with blood of queens and kings,
> [see page 267]   JOHN KEATS.

> Clasp'd like a missal where swart Paynims pray, [see page 267]
>   JOHN KEATS.

If some of these words are strange to you, they may be equally strange to your hearers, and the least you can do is to pronounce them accurately and be able, if need be, to define them. You should leave no ground for your hearers to think that their failure to understand a word was due to your blurred pronunciation of it. The same is true of your pronunciation of proper names. They all *have* conventional pronunciations, and you are responsible for those that occur in your reading. Some of those in the selections in this book that may send you to the dictionary are "Pleiades," "Eurydice," "Maenad," "Lethe," "Persephone," "Medici," "Belial," "Baiae," "Lacedaemonian," "Telemachus," "Semiramis," "Sinai," "Hymeneal," "Bellerophon," and "Stygian." How many of these are you sure of?

THE POET'S PRONUNCIATION. It is sometimes supposed that one ought to pronounce a poet's words as he pronounced them, and as he expected others to pronounce them, that one cannot interpret his work faithfully unless one speaks as he did. This sounds plausible, but it is often quite impracticable. We modernize the pronunciation of all poetry written since about 1400. Some of Shakespeare's lines might sound quite unintelligible if pronounced as he intended. Milton rhymed "groves" with "loves" and "verse" with "pierce." In the eighteenth century, such rhymes as "starve" and "reserve," "art" and "desert," "guard" and "heard," and "toil" and "smile" were common. Shelley rhymed "thou," "low," "blow"; "thou," "below," "know"; "wert," "heart," "art"; "loud," "cloud," "flowed"; and "know," "flow," "now." How should they be pronounced today in situations in which the rhyme seems important to the harmony? Should we violate the rhyme, or violate modern usage? It is probably best in most cases to ignore the rhyme and give the words their modern sounds. Very rarely is it desirable to have the hearer's attention distracted from the meaning of a passage to the unconventionality of the reader's pronunciation. However, the modern British practice of rhyming "again" with "rain" and "been" with "seen" is common enough to be acceptable to literate Americans.

Fluidity of Utterance

Another matter, involving breath control as well as pronunciation and interpretation, needs attention. In normal speech, our words are not separated from each other as on the printed page but flow together without any breaks between them until we come to the end of a phrase. A unit of thought, a meaningful word group, is normally also a breath group. Words are as closely tied together as the syllables of a polysyllabic word, sometimes so closely that assimilation may occur between them, "got you" becoming "gochoo," just as "statue" become "stachoo." Only when very emphatic do we separate our words and articulate them as if with Pogo sticks.

In general, poetry calls for even greater smoothness and fluidity than prose. It is the expression of controlled emotion; its sounds are often deliberately designed to blend with each other; it is generally intended to be spoken legato rather than staccato; and its meter encourages continuity. It calls for well-sustained breath groups, even when the lines are made up of monosyllables, as in Mrs. Browning's

> I love thee with the love I seemed to lose
> With my lost saints.

Sometimes one encounters continuous phrases of a length to tax the lung capacity of even the deepest breathers, as in this passage from Arnold's "Dover Beach" (see page 273):

> But now I only hear
> Its melancholy, long, withdrawing roar,
> Retreating, to the breath
> Of the night-wind, down the vast edges drear
> And naked shingles of the world.

Here thought and feeling suggest a long continuous glide down into the depths of despair. Try reading this passage. Take a full breath, and try to make it carry your voice firmly and evenly to the end and leave you with still some breath in reserve.

The reader of poetry should learn to begin every unit of meaning with a full breath supply, whether he thinks he will need it or not. Or, he should in preparation, as a singer does, predesign the places where he will take breath. Then he will be able to make the lines flow, keep the vowels firm and sustained, and make the consonants sharp and distinct. Passages may be found that seem to call for a separate focus on each word, as in Wordsworth's grocery-list enumeration,

> Praise, blame, love, kisses, tears, and smiles,

but such passages are rare.

Articulatory Prestidigitation

The meaning of this formidable title can be boiled down to *deftness of tongue.* It should be apparent from the preceding discussion that in intelligible speech the tongue must make rapid and accurate shifts from one definite position to another. The tongue is a muscle, and, like other muscles, it can be trained by exercise. It is doubtful whether any better exercise is pronunciation can be found than the rapid articulation of some of the songs from the Gilbert and Sullivan operas. The catchy lines keep interest alive; the meter encourages a regular and rapid tempo; and the lines contain all the sounds and combinations of sounds on which drill is needed.

Choose one of the three passages that follow, and master it for rapid articulation. It should be memorized. Begin by speaking it slowly, enunciating every sound with exaggerated distinctness. Gradually increase your tempo until you reach, or exceed, the tempo prescribed by Sullivan's music, if you know his music, *but never sacrifice distinctness to speed.* Do not at any stage lapse into the shortcuts of ordinary conversation. See that *every syllable* receives a distinct pulse of the voice; make your utterance staccato. Do not say "inf'mation," "veg'table," or "hypot'nuse"; give such words four full syllables, but keep the syllables in proportion. It is well to accent normally weak syllables when the meter calls for an accent on them. Do not begin the second passage with "Fire not" instead of "If I were not." Take *very, very* great pains to sound clear *t*'s and *d*'s in such words as "model," "modern," "letter," "better," "hatter," and "matter." Make a clear *u* in "us," and do not omit the *v* in "of." Try to maintain clear vowels in such words as "am," "at," "and," "for," "you," "not," and "should." Note that "general" is intended to rhyme with "mineral."

In your labor to master the articulation, do not neglect the *spirit* of the verses. They represent the comic spirit at its best. Enjoy them, and try to make your hearers enjoy them too.

1. I am the very model of a modern Major-General,
   I've information vegetable, animal, and mineral,
   I know the kings of England, and I quote the fights historical,
   From Marathon to Waterloo, in order categorical;
   I'm very well acquainted too with matters mathematical;
   I understand equations, both the simple and quadratical;
   About binomial theorem I'm teeming with a lot of news—
   With many cheerful facts about the square of the hypotenuse; . . .
   I'm very good at integral and differential calculus;
   I know the scientific names of beings animalculous;
   In short, in matters vegetable, animal, and mineral
   I am the very model of a modern Major-general.
                                    The Pirates of Penzance.

2. If I were not a little mad and generally silly,
   I should give you my advice upon the subject, willy nilly;
   I should show you in a moment how to grapple with the question,
   And you'd really be astonished at the force of my suggestion.
   On the subject I shall write you a most valuable letter,
   Full of excellent suggestions when I feel a little better,
   But at present I'm afraid I am as mad as any hatter,
   So I'll keep 'em to myself, for my opinion doesn't matter!
                                    Ruddigore.

3. Now is not this ridiculous—and is not this preposterous?
A thorough-paced absurdity—explain it if you can.
Instead of rushing eagerly to cherish us and foster us,
They all prefer this melancholy literary man.
Instead of slyly peering at us,
Casting looks endearing at us,
Blushing at us, flushing at us—flirting with a fan;
They're actually sneering at us, fleering at us, jeering at us!
Pretty sort of treatment for a military man!

Patience.

PLAN OF STUDY

1. Try to hear a recording of your voice in both reading and speaking. Judge it objectively, and note faults you would like to get rid of.
2. Make it a point to inhale deeply and quickly at every convenient breathing place. Do not allow your breath supply to run low.
3. Try to keep the diaphragmatic-abdominal muscles firm while practicing and while reading to others, so that your voice will be firmly supported and evenly sustained.
4. Keep your voice free from strain. Think constantly of throat and jaw relaxation. When you have to speak loudly try to *open* the throat instead of contracting it.
5. Never pronounce by guess. Look up every word you have any doubt about, and be sure you know what the lexicographer means by his markings.
6. Practice forming your vowels clearly and accurately. Avoid the lazy tendency to let them drift toward the central schwa position. But don't give weak vowels a strong pronunciation.
7. Take pains to form consonant sounds precisely and accurately.
8. Make proper allowance for accepted gradations of vowels and assimilations of consonants, but in these matters it is generally best in public reading to lean toward formality. In doubtful cases, decide in advance what you will do.
9. Keep in mind that your pronunciations should be loud enough and precise enough to be clearly heard and understood by *all* your audience.
10. Plan to speak poetry with much more than normal formality.
11. Be alert for word combinations that may sound confusing, and take special pains with them.

CRITERIA

1. Was the reader's voice well supported and well sustained, pleasant in quality, clear, relaxed, and flexible?
2. Was breath supply well managed?
3. Was pronunciation accurate and clear?
4. Were vowels accurately shaped, with due allowance for legitimate gradations?
5. Were consonants distinct, with due allowance for legitimate assimilations?

6. Did formality of pronunciation suit the occasion?
7. Was reading of poetry smooth and fluid, and did it give due prominence to the sound effects peculiar to poetry?

QUESTIONS FOR DISCUSSION

1. Discuss the voices of your classmates, and try to discover why and in what respects they seem good or bad.
2. Can you separate basic voice quality from pronunciation, intonation pattern, pitch, volume, and emotional coloring?
3. Why is it that some foreigners who have learned English and live in an English-speaking environment retain all their lives a foreign accent, while others under like circumstances learn in a few months to speak conventional English?
4. Is the human voice capable of making sounds that do not occur in any language you are familiar with?
5. What sounds occur in other languages that are not used in English? Find examples.
6. Find words now undergoing a change in spelling to make them conform to their present pronunciation.
7. Find words that seem to be undergoing a change in pronunciation. Can you discover a reason for the change?

SELECTIONS FOR PRACTICE

For additional practice in pronunciation, here is, complete, one of the favorite patter songs from the Gilbert and Sullivan operas. Swinburne's "Nephelidia" is added because of the excellent material it affords for drill on individual consonant sounds.

THE DREAM SONG

From IOLANTHE

W. S. *Gilbert*

When you're lying awake with a dismal headache, and repose is tabooed by anxiety,
I conceive you may use any language you choose to indulge in without impropriety;
For your brain is on fire—the bedclothes conspire of usual slumber to plunder you:
First your counterpane goes and uncovers your toes, and your sheet slips demurely from under you;
Then the blanketing tickles—you feel like mixed pickles, so terribly sharp is the pricking,
And you're hot and you're cross, and you tumble and toss till there's nothing 'twixt you and the ticking;
Then your bedclothes all creep to the floor in a heap, and you pick 'em all up in a tangle,
Next your pillow resigns and politely declines to remain at its usual angle.
Well, you get some repose in the form of a doze, with hot eyeballs and head ever aching,
But your slumbering teems with such horrible dreams that you'd very much better be waking;
For you dream you are crossing the Channel, and tossing about in a steamer from Harwich—
Which is something between a large bathing machine and a very small second-class carriage—
And you're giving a treat (penny ice and cold meat) to a party of friends and relations—
They're a ravenous horde—and they all came on board at Sloan Square and South Kensington Stations.
And bound on that journey you find your attorney (who started that morning from Devon);
He's a bit undersized, and you don't feel surprised when he tells you he's only eleven.
Well, you're driving like mad with this singular lad (by the by, the ship's now a four-wheeler),

And you're playing round games, and he calls you bad names when
    you tell him that "ties pay the dealer";
But this you can't stand, so you throw up your hand, and you find
    you're as cold as an icicle,
In your shirt and your socks (the black silk with gold clocks), cross-
    ing Salisbury Plain on a bicycle:
And he and the crew are on bicycles too—which they've somehow or
    other invested in—
And he's telling the tars all the particulars of a company he's inter-
    ested in—
It's a scheme of devices, to get at low prices all goods from cough
    mixtures to cables
(Which tickled the sailors), by treating retailers as though they were
    all vegetables—
You get a good spadesman to plant a small tradesman (first take off
    his boots with a boot-tree),
And his legs will take root, and his fingers will shoot, and they'll
    blossom and bud like a fruit-tree—
From the greengrocer tree you get grapes and green pea, cauliflower,
    pineapple, and cranberries,
While the pastrycook plant cherry brandy will grant, apple puffs,
    and three-corners, and Banburys—
The shares are a penny, and ever so many are taken by Rothschild
    and Baring,
And just as a few are allotted to you, you awake with a shudder
    despairing—
You're a regular wreck, with a crick in your neck; and no wonder
    you snore for your head's on the floor, and you're needles and
    pins from your soles to your shins; and your flesh is a-creep, and
    your left leg's asleep; and you've cramps in your toes, and a fly
    on your nose, and some fluff in your lung, and a feverish tongue,
    and a thirst that's intense, and a general sense that you haven't
    been sleeping in clover;
But the darkness has passed, and it's daylight at last, and the night
    has been long—ditto, ditto, my song—and thank Goodness they're
    both of them over!

NEPHELIDIA

Algernon Charles Swinburne

From the depth of the dreamy decline of the dawn through a notable
    nimbus of nebulous moonshine,
    Pallid and pink as the palm of the flag-flower that flickers with
    fear of the flies as they float,
Are the looks of our lovers that lustrously lean from a marvel of
    mystic miraculous moonshine,

These that we feel in the blood of our blushes that thicken and
threaten with throbs through the throat?
Thicken and thrill as a theatre thronged at appeal of an actor's
appalled agitation,
Fainter with fear of the fires of the future than pale with the
promise of pride in the past;
Flushed with the famishing fulness of fever that reddens with radiance of rathe recreation,
Gaunt as the ghastliest of glimpses that gleam through the gloom
of the gloaming when ghosts go aghast?
Nay, for the nick of the tick of the time is a tremulous touch on the
temples of terror,
Strained as the sinews yet strenuous with strife of the dead who is
dumb as the dust-heaps of death;
Surely no soul is it, sweet as the spasm of erotic emotional equisite
error,
Bathed in the balms of beautified bliss, beatific itself by beati-
tude's breath.
Surely no spirit or sense of a soul that was soft to the spirit and soul
of our senses
Sweetens the stress of surprising suspicion that sobs in the semblance and sound of a sigh;
Only this oracle opens Olympian, in mystical moods and triangular
tenses,—
"Life is the lust of a lamp for the light that is dark till the dawn of
the day when we die."
Mild is the mirk and monotonous music of memory, melodiously
mute as it may be,
While the hope in the heart of a hero is bruised by the breach of
men's rapiers, resigned to the rod;
Made meek as a mother whose bosom-beats bound with the bliss-
bringing bulk of a balm-breathing baby,
As they grope through the grave-yard of creeds, under skies growing green at a groan for the grimness of God.
Blank is the book of his bounty beholden of old, and its binding is
blacker than bluer:
Out of blue into black is the scheme of the skies, and their dews
are the wine of the bloodshed of things:
Till the darkling desire of delight shall be free as a fawn that is freed
from the fangs that pursue her,
Till the heart-beats of hell shall be hushed by a hymn from the
hunt that has harried the kennel of kings.

5

VERSE

When Goethe first visited Italy, he found the atmosphere conducive to both making poetry and making love, and he managed to combine the two in one operation. With his arms around his inamorata, he found himself working out the meter of a new poem by drumming on her back with his fingers, an action she accepted happily as a form of caress. Some poets, it seems, can practice their trade under distracting circumstances; and one of their preoccupations is rhythm.

In the beginning [says Morris Bishop] was the Bard, singing the best words, words of the hunt and the fight, and pounding his rhythms on the cave wall with a tiger-bone. Immediately after was the clown, mocking the Bard in falsetto, mingling nasty words with the noble. And all the people made harsh glottal explosions, signifying pleasure. Thus light verse was born.[1]

Light verse, as we conceive it, is any metrical writing that does not have the seriousness and emotional appeal of poetry. It has only the form of poetry, and it usually adheres more strictly to metrical form than does serious poetry. It seems best to consider this formal aspect of poetry before getting involved with its content, and so, in this chapter, we will deal with the interpretation of metrical form, chiefly as illustrated by light verse.

Until modern times, rhythm was an indispensable element in poetry, and one of its most moving and delightful elements. But, a hundred years ago, Walt Whitman's genius, it is said, shattered the conventional bonds of meter and gave us free verse, a form that is now favored by many poets, though (dare we say it?) many of them lack Whitman's genius. His lines, it should be noted, are free not in the sense that they avoid meter but, rather, in that they are not uniform in length and not grouped into

---

[1] Morris Bishop, *A Bowl of Bishop* (New York: Dial Press, Inc., 1954), p. 3.

regular stanza patterns. It is natural for the emotions of poetry to find expression in rhythm. As Gilbert Highet has said, "Our love for rhythm is part of our subconscious and emotional endowment."[2] But we find rhythm delightful also when applied to very ordinary matter, or even to nonsense.

Verse and Prose

Is it necessary to define the difference between poetry and prose? Apparently it is, since recent investigations show that many students distinguish poetry from prose only by the way it is printed on the page. The definition of poetry I shall save for a later chapter. But the distinction between prose and meter also needs to be cleared up, since some identify meter also only by its typographical appearance, instead of by its sound. What follows may strike some readers as trivial and obvious, but it leads to implications and conclusions that may seem revolutionary. All depends on the reader's previous training. Although prose developed later than poetry, and is said to be free from the tyranny of meter, it looks more disciplined, because the printer stops each line when he comes to his established margin and trues it up so that all lines are of equal length. The length of a line of verse, however, is dictated not by the printer but by the number of accents the author has chosen to put into it, resulting in ragged edges on the page. It is by these ragged lines that many identify both poetry and verse.

Meter, however, whether in serious poetry or light verse, does not appear visibly on the page, or anywhere else. It is an audible element, perceivable only by the ear. Meter is a form of rhythm. The essence of rhythm, properly defined, is regularity in the recurrence of some unit of perception. There must be units, and they must recur at what seem to be regularly spaced intervals. There is no rhythm in a smoothly flowing stream, because there are no units, and none in a wild forest jumble, because the trees are not alike and not regularly arranged. Rhythms, of course, may be perceived by the eye, as in observing a row of evenly spaced trees or columns, or they may be perceived by the kinesthetic sense as in dancing, or through the sense of feeling, as in finger taps on a girl's back. It is thought that basically the perception of rhythm is kinesthetic. But the rhythm of meter can be perceived only through the auditory sense, since the units of which it is composed are accents or stresses, and these do not show in print. To write in meter, a versifier must select and arrange words in such a way that when his lines are pronounced in the normal manner there will be heard a regular recurrence of accented syllables.

[2] Gilbert Highet, *The Powers of Poetry* (Fair Lawn, N.J.: Oxford University Press, 1960), p. 12.

Foot Scansion

Our ideas about meter were derived from the practices of the ancient Greeks and Romans, in whose languages meter was measured by feet, a foot usually consisting of one long and one or more short syllables. Apparently, the ancients were conscious of these feet as constituents of a line of poetry, and they had names for each variety of foot, nearly thirty of them. We are familiar with only a few—iambus, trochee, anapaest, dactyl, spondee, and perhaps amphibrach. English scholars, trained for centuries in Greek and Latin, when they began to give attention to English poetry, assumed that it had the same characteristics as the ancient languages, but it does not. Our syllables do, of course, differ in length; it takes more time to pronounce "splurge" than "up." But it is not consciousness of this difference that constitutes our meter. English is an accented language. That is, some of our syllables have accent and some do not, and, instead of differentiating them as long or short, it would be better to use the terms *accented* and *unaccented, stressed* and *unstressed,* or *heavy* and *light.* Further, we are not conscious of the foot as a unit of meter. We perceive meter from a regular recurrence of accented syllables.

How do we know which syllables to stress? Stress is not imposed by the meter; on the contrary the meter is created by the stresses when we pronounce words in the accustomed way. Nearly every word of more than one syllable has a main stress and one or more syllables without stress. When we encounter a strange word such as "impious," "cerebral," "Belial," or "Persephone," we can find its stresses marked for us in a dictionary. But often we encounter strings of monosyllables, as

> The sea was wet as wet could be,
> The sands were dry as dry.

How are these to be treated? We simply speak them naturally. If we know English, we know that some of them are stressed and some are not, and we know which is which by virtue of knowing English. It would never occur to us to accent "the," "was," "as," and "could," though a foreigner just learning English might do so. The genius of the language and the sense of the line guide us. And so also when monosyllables are mixed with longer words.

Forms of Meter

If in a line of verse the accented syllables are separated by one unaccented syllable, we call the meter *iambic,* or, if the line begins with an accented syllable, it may be called *trochaic,* though such lines are commonly felt much the same as iambic lines, and there is seldom any point in distinguishing them. Some of the lines of Milton's *"L'Allegro"* begin with accented syllables and some do not, but this does not mean that the meter varies between iambic and trochaic. If two weak syllables occur between accents, the line is *dactylic* or *anapaestic,* though, again, there is seldom any point in distinguishing one from the other. The length of a line is measured by the number of accents it contains, and here again we use Greek terms—*trimeter, tetrameter, pentameter,* etc. The great Greek and Latin epics are in dactylic hexameter, a meter not well suited to English, though Longfellow did well with it in "Evangeline." The favorite English meter, used in *Paradise Lost* and Shakespeare's plays, and most other long poems, is iambic pentameter.

Irregularities in Meter

Once the pulse of a meter is established, both poet and reader can tolerate variations from strict regularity. An iambic line may have two, or even three, contiguous heavy syllables or several contiguous light ones without seriously violating the rhythm. *Paradise Lost* begins,

> Of Man's first disobedience, and the fruit . . .

Here surely we should stress "man's," "first," and "dis-," and there is no call for stress on "and," though strict meter would require it. If "-dience" is not reduced to one syllable, we will have four weak syllables in succession—"di-ence," "and," "the." Such lines occur often in both Milton and Shakespeare, and frequently there is nothing to suggest that a line is iambic pentameter except that it contains ten syllables. The reader of such lines will have to determine as best he can the relative importance of thought and rhythm and govern his stresses accordingly.

In more recent poetry, with the weakening of the classical traditions, iambic and anapaestic elements are mingled indiscriminately, and with no loss in rhythm, as in these lines from Shelley's "The Cloud":

> I wield the flail of the lashing hail,
> And whiten the green plains under,
> And then again I dissolve it in rain,
> And laugh as I pass in thunder.

The rhythm is not broken by having sometimes one and sometimes two weak syllables between the accented ones (and there is no doubt as to which are accented). Even the three successive stresses on "green plains under" do not seem to break the rhythm. Now note these lines from W. S. Gilbert's *Pinafore:*

> When I was a lad I served a term
> As office boy to an attorney's firm.

I cleaned the windows and I swept the floor,
And I polished up the handle of the big front door.

Here there are sometimes three weak syllables between the accents, and yet the lines are markedly rhythmical, with four strong beats in each. You might be tempted to scan the fourth as iambic, but not if you know it as set to Sullivan's music, which puts strong stresses on "pol-," "hand-," and "big front door." The lines range in length from nine to thirteen syllables, but the music allots the same quantity of time to each—four beats. "Front" does not receive one of the beats, though it is accented.

There is a similar pattern of rhythm in a song quoted in the preceding chapter:

I am the very model of a modern Major-General,
I've information vegetable, animal, and mineral, [etc.]

It is possible to scan these lines as iambic octameters, but again the music calls for four beats to the line. Did Sullivan understand the rhythm of speech as well as the rhythm of music and so make his music conform to the natural rhythm of speech? At any rate, one familiar with the music can hardly avoid reading the lines with four strong stresses, as

I ám the very módel of a módern Major-Géneral,

These examples may suggest that the rhythm of a line is not always definite and unmistakable, that it may be ambiguous, depending on how it is felt or perceived by different readers. Few poems illustrate this better than G. K. Chesterton's "Lepanto," a vigorous, clanging chant, full of battle cries, marching feet, and booming drums, describing the Christian crusade against the Turks in 1571 (see page 283). That it is highly rhythmical is unquestionable, but just try to analyze it! The poem begins,

White founts falling in the Courts of the sun,
And the Soldan of Byzantium is smiling as they run;
There is laughter like the fountains in that face of all men feared,
It stirs the forest darkness, the darkness of his beard;

Apparent throughout is a caesura, or pause, in the middle of each of its hundred and fifty lines (except where a line is broken into two shorter ones), and throughout the lines rhyme in pairs. A line may have as many as sixteen syllables, but the caesuras and end rhymes help to create clear, short units. How many stresses in each unit? Two? Three? Or more? And does it make any difference in the rhythm? The second and third lines *could* be scanned as trochaic octameters, but that would not represent the pulsing beat of the whole poem. Later, there are such lines as

Dim drums throbbing in the hills half heard, . . .
Strong gongs groaning as the guns boom far, . . .

> Stiff flags straining in the night blasts cold, . . .
> Where the gray seas glitter and the sharp tides shift.

which seem more representative of the basic rhythm. If you tried beating a bass drum to these lines you would probably have such a rhythm as

> Boom, boom, boom (rest), boom, boom, boom,

and this beat can be applied to the entire poem, but not rigidly. There will be many lines where you cannot find a strong syllable to fit some of the "booms," and there are many significant ideas and feelings and arresting images that will make you want to modify such a strict pattern. But the pattern is there, and few poems will suggest a more regular beat or yield greater pleasure from the pulse of their movement. You will find a similar rhythm in Vachel Lindsay's "The Congo." Compare also Browning's "Up at a Villa—Down in the City," (page 387).

The Effect of Rhythm

There are some reservations we must make about the pleasure of rhythm. First, quite obviously, the rhythm of sharp, disturbing sounds, as of a machine gun or a steel riveter, is not pleasant. Second, the units of rhythm must not be so close together as to form a blur, nor so far apart as not to be felt as repetitions. Rhyme words that are eight or ten lines apart will not be perceived as regular. Third, and this is the important point for us, a steadily regular rhythm soon becomes monotonous, and so, annoying; we complain of singsong. If it continues on and on, our ears automatically tune it out, and we cease to be aware of it. And, if it is still continued, though we may be unconscious of it, it tires us and becomes a soporific. There was sound psychology in the now obsolete practice of rocking babies to sleep. In reading verse, since the rhythm is created by the reader, he should use his freedom of accent and tempo, when he has it, to avoid monotony. We can stand long runs of blank verse (iambic pentameter) because the rhythm is usually weak and somewhat varied. But, with shorter lines and frequent rhymes, it is often desirable to deliberately break the meter by lingering on important words, lengthening pauses, and varying tempo.

Good poets and musicians avoid long-continued regularity, except when the effect they are representing is monotony. Robert Browning, in "Through the Medidja to Abd el Kadr," represents the weariness and monotony felt by a horseman plunging steadily through deep desert sands by using short two-accent lines and a single rhyme throughout the forty lines:

> As I ride, as I ride,
> With a full heart for my guide,

So its tide rocks my side,
As I ride, as I ride,
That, as I were double eyed,
He, in whom our tribes confide,
Is descried, ways untried,
As I ride, as I ride. [Etc.]

Here, reader and hearer will appreciate monotony without being tired by it. But sometimes a writer may use a very regular meter when he wishes to have the reader sharply alert to meaning. In such a case, the interpreter must try to suppress and obscure the rhythm so that the meaning may be kept sharp and clear. Such excessive regularity we will find in the story of "The Little Eohippus," later in this chapter.

Rhythm in moderation is pleasant. Its effect is to arouse or intensify emotion, and many emotions seem naturally to find expression in rhythm— not sharp, crackling, explosive emotions of rage, terror, and pain but, rather, feelings of resignation, sorrow, and love. And, as strong rhythm encourages emotion and is well suited to its expression, so it tends to discourage careful thinking and is not well suited to the expression of reasoned thought. If you yield to its soothing influence you do not want to think.

Imitative Rhythms

Many poets have used rhythms intended to imitate various actions and movements—storms at sea, burbling brooks, action in battle, a smooth-running motor car, men marching, dancing, horseback riding, and the like. Kipling's "Boots—boots—boots—boots—movin' up and down again" comes to mind. And, of course, every good poet tries to fit his meter to his mood. One of the favorite movements is galloping on horseback, and poets' horses seem to have various gaits. Notice, besides the Browning poem just quoted, his "How They Brought the Good News from Ghent to Aix," Benét's "Jesse James," Guiney's "The Wild Ride," Markham's "Joy of the Hills," Rice's "The Mystic," and Tennyson's "Sir Galahad," all to be found in the Index of this book. You might at some time arrange a whole program of "horseback" readings. Is the prevailing meter of these poems the anapaest? Is it well suited to their themes? Do the moods of these various gallopers suit the meter chosen? Rice's gallop in "The Mystic" is magnificent, but is such a movement appropriate for representing his quest for God?

Lines and Stanzas

Besides syllabic meter, there is a rhythm of lines and stanzas. If lines are of even length, or of alternating lengths, and if they conform to units of thought, they are felt as units and set up a pleasing expectation of, and satisfaction in, their regular repetition. The same is true, though to a lesser degree, of stanzas, when they are brief and simple in structure. If rhymes are used, they will, of course, strongly accentuate the regularity. But the repetition of such long ten-line stanzas as those in Keats's "Ode to a Nightingale" will be felt only dimly, if at all, and the oral reader can do little to impress their pattern on the hearer. However, the short four-line stanzas of "*La Belle Dame sans Merci*" give a very definite sense of regularity. If a poem's lines do not conform to thought units, if they are frequently "run-on," they will not be perceived as units, and it is seldom desirable for the reader to force them into a pattern.

In a great deal of blank verse, the line is a unit only on paper. Without artificial forcing, it cannot be made to register as pentameter, and, generally, there is no point in trying to make the line units distinct. They are commonly ignored by modern actors of Shakespeare—some of whom also ignore the meter. And those prosodists who find a caesura in every line of blank verse are probably merely imagining what they think ought to be there. The average reader, in speaking naturally the lines of such good metrists as Milton, Wordsworth, and Tennyson, will rarely feel or express such a division, and it need not be artificially introduced merely as a concession to classical laws of scansion.

QUATRAINS AND SPENSERIAN STANZAS. One of the commonest stanzas in English verse is the quatrain generally found in old folk ballads, a four-line stanza with alternating four- and three-accent lines, generally rhymed *abab*. Typical is this one from a Robin Hood ballad:

> There are twelve months in all the year
> As I hear many men say,
> But the merriest month in all the year
> Is the merry month of May.

The sense calls for a complete stop at the end of each stanza, and the repetition of this brief unit creates a movement that is pleasing and satisfying, and well adapted to long narrative, as in Coleridge's "The Ancient Mariner." Many variations and irregularities occur, such as lengthening of the second line to four beats or shortening of the fourth to two.

Another much favored narrative form is the Spenserian stanza, evolved by Spenser for his *Faerie Queene*, and copied in Byron's *Childe Harold*, Keats's *Eve of St. Agnes*, and many other poems. It consists of eight iambic pentameter lines, rhyming *ababbcbc*, followed by an "Alexandrine," or iambic hexameter, rhyming with the preceding line. This long final line rounds the stanza into a pleasing unit and affords the reader regular resting places such as are not found in blank verse.

The set forms of poetry developed by early Italian and French poets—villanelle, sestina, ballade, etc.—are seldom found in modern poetry. Their forms, though rigid, present no special problems for the oral reader. Many of the best-known, best-loved, and most quoted English poems are sonnets. This familiar pattern of fourteen iambic pentameters, usually expressing some moving philosophic reflection, is well adapted to many reading situations, and furnishes a good test of poetic appreciation. In general, it calls for sustained feeling and a smooth, even flow of voice, rather than for sprightliness, gaiety, or vigor. Traditionally, the young poet earned his wings by writing sonnets, but, in a recent collection of poems by some sixty new poets, only three are represented by this form.[3]

ECCENTRIC LINES AND STANZAS. Some modern writers, searching for the ultimate in freedom from the limitations of form, write what passes for verse but is either straight prose or a wild departure from any recognizable metric line or stanza. The fractured pattern frequently includes mutilated punctuation, deliberate misspellings, and deviate capitalization. The result can be simply typographical caprice or a private joke. Some catch the eye because of the pattern they form on the page—a diamond, an hourglass, an angel's wing. A newer twist is the action image, in which the typographical appearance resembles the action depicted in the poem. E. E. Cummings has created such eye-catchers in a poem about a falling leaf and one about a jumping grasshopper. Obviously, when the whole impact of a poem depends on its shape on the page, it is better left on the page not read aloud. Yet certain visually oriented poems contain enough traditional poetic values to provide an interesting though formidable challenge to the oral reader.

The Nature of Rhyme

As we have seen, the patterns of lines and stanzas are frequently marked by rhymes. Though rhyme is familiar to us from childhood, it needs, like other familiar concepts, to be examined in order for us to find out whether we really know what we mean by it. Dictionaries define it as correspondence in the terminal sounds of words. But "mints" and "wants" do not rhyme, though the last three sounds in each are alike; neither do "subject" and "object," which have the same final syllable; nor do "difference" and "reference," though the two terminal syllables in each are identical. What is the meaning, then, of "correspondence in terminal sounds"? To form a conventional rhyme, it is required that the accented vowels of two words, and all that follows them, should sound alike. It is

[3] Donald Hall and Robert Pack, *New Poets of England and America* (Cleveland: The World Publishing Co., 1962).

expected too that what precedes the vowels will be different; we do not accept "rite" and "right" as rhymes, since they are completely identical in sound. If the rhyming words contain two or more syllables, as do "ravel" and "travel" or "dutiful" and "beautiful," the similarity must begin with the last accented syllable and continue to the end of the word. The same is true when the rhyme carries through several words, as in "executioner" and "you shun her," "interpolate them" and "purple ate them," "Cyrano" and "here a No."

Rhyme has no value, of course, if it is unnoticed, and it is most effective when it occurs at expected intervals. Sometimes, writers use rhymes merely as a convention, constructing their phrases in such a way that rhyme words are not prominent. This is true of Robert Browning's "My Last Duchess," which a reader may study for some time without discovering that it is rhymed in couplets. But, in the similar rhymed couplets of Pope's "rocking-horse meter," the thought units nearly always conform to the lines, and so the rhymes are conspicuous. Always, the reader should be governed by the apparent intention of the author, making rhyme prominent only when it seems intended to be prominent.

Humor in Rhymes

Comic versifiers have shown the most astounding ingenuity in finding or creating rhymes, sometimes distorting a word grotesquely to make it rhyme with another. Ogden Nash distorts "pretty" to rhyme with "putty," "Memphis" to rhyme with "emphasis," and performs the impossible by constructing a rhyme for Koussevitsky:

> Lend me a ninety-piece orchestra tutored by Koussevitsky,
> I don't want the ownership of it, I just want the usevitsky.

When you read to others such rhymes as these, and other bits of word play intended to be funny, the proper thing to do is to enjoy them. Show that you appreciate them, and give them a focus that will make your hearers appreciate them. Merely cantering over the words indifferently, as many readers do, is shirking your duty. Bear down on odd rhymes, linger on them, or pause before or after them to let them have their proper effect. You need have no false modesty about displaying your wit, because it is not *your* wit.

Ogden Nash often uses unmetrical lines of varying length, often very long ones, that rhyme in pairs, and in which the rhymes at the ends of the lines are also the ends of thought groups. As Gilbert Highet says, he wanders off into the stratosphere through a long sentence and then reverts to the rhyme, "which everything but my subconscious ear has forgotten." In speaking these meandering lines, it is often effective to hurry rapidly through them, without careful phrasing of the meaning, and then come down hard on the rhyme word and pause after it, since it is generally the rhyme that contains the focus of humor.

Alliteration and Assonance

Akin to rhyme are alliteration, the recurrence of similar sounds at the beginnings of neighboring words, and assonance, the recurrence of similar vowels, generally within the syllables. We like these similarities in sounds and use them in our daily speech, as in such simple phrases as "dirty dog," "fine friend," and "damp, dark day." They seem to come naturally to poets, who readily turn out such phrases as

> The fair breeze blew, the white foam flew,
>   The furrow followed free.
>
> Beyond the loom of the last lone star.
>
> They rise in green robes roaring from the green hells of the sea.
>
> I fear the fickle freaks of fortune false.

These repetitions of sounds reinforce the rhythm, increase smoothness of movement, give phrases a feeling of unity and continuity, and generally have a beauty of their own that enhances the pleasure we feel in hearing poetry spoken. About all that the speaker of such passages needs to do is to be aware of such devices and keep them in mind while reading. If articulation is good, they will perform their function and have their proper effect. Sometimes they will need to be accentuated, and this can be done by dwelling on like vowels and like continuant consonants and releasing plosive consonants with more energy.

The comic poets delight in alliteration and other kinds of word play. Note this passage from Gilbert's *The Mikado:*

> To sit in solemn silence in a dull dark dock,
> In a pestilential prison with a life-long lock
> Awaiting the sensation of a short sharp shock
> From a cheap and chippy chopper on a big black block.

Apropos of nothing in particular, Morris Bishop turns out such lines as

> Chipper as a tripper on a southbound clipper.
> I'm glummer than a plumber in a slum all summer.
> At Easter every feaster loves the hoister of the oyster.

Turn back to the discussion of humor in Chapter 3 for some cautions about reading comic verse.

Our literature is particularly rich in works of wit, satire, and nonsense, in which the humor is reinforced by meter, rhyme, alliteration, assonance, and extravagant word play for the delectation of all those who delight in the *sound* of language. Some of the best of these works are collected at the end of this chapter, to be used in the study and management of metrical form in oral reading.

Light verse is not less worthy of study for being light. As the great Dutch scholar Erasmus said, "Trifles may be a whet to more serious thoughts, and comical matters may be so treated of as that a reader of ordinary sense may possibly thence reap more advantage than from some more big and stately argument." Humor and satire are often more effective weapons against evil than rhetoric and invective.

The selections that follow, however, are not serious satires. In "The Little Eohippus," for instance, the moral that human nature changes gets lost in hilarious paleontological grotesqueries. Most of the selections are merely highly intelligent nonsense. Have fun with them, but keep in mind Meredith's paradox that comedy should awaken "thoughtful laughter."

PLAN OF STUDY

1. After you have read the selection and, it is assumed, enjoyed it, begin your study by paraphrasing the thought. Don't let the verse blind you to what it is all about.
2. Analyze and define the meter. Is it pure, mixed, or irregular?
3. Note where metrical stresses may conflict with sense stresses. Decide in all cases which should have right of way.
4. Study the adaptation of the meter to the meaning and mood of the poem. Does it need to be intensified or obscured? Is there danger of monotony?
5. If it is too regular, where can you weaken it by pauses, changes of tempo, varying the weight of accents, dwelling on important syllables, etc.
6. Analyze line and stanza patterns. Are they meant to be felt as units?
7. Analyze the rhyme scheme, and consider how prominent the rhymes should be made. Give special attention to any that seem designed to please, to astonish, or to amuse.
8. Look for alliteration, assonance, and other sound effects. Assess their value and function, and plan to give them effective expression.
9. Consider carefully the appropriate attitude to take toward comic verse. Plan to give it effective expression through voice and pronunciation, but see that the comedy is neither underdone nor overdone. It may be best to let it speak for itself. Beware of self-exploitation.

CRITERIA

1. Was the reader aware of, and responsive to, the meter of the poem?
2. Did he keep a proper balance between sense stress and metrical stress?
3. Did he prevent unwanted monotony in meter, stanza, and rhyme?

4. Were line and stanza units made distinct when they had logical or rhythmical significance?
5. Were rhymes appreciated and given their proper value?
6. Was the reader responsive to other sound effects that contribute to the pleasure of verse?
7. In reading comic verse, did he exploit the comedy without exploiting himself?

QUESTIONS FOR DISCUSSION

1. How close together in time do units of rhythm have to be in order to be *felt* as rhythmical—a second, a minute, an hour, a day? Do men confined to perpetual darkness or light feel the rhythm of recurring days?
2. How do various persons differ in their susceptibility to rhythm? Can a sense of rhythm be cultivated?
3. Discuss the relation of rhythm to emotion.
4. Compare English and classical scansion.
5. How important is rhythm in poetry? Does dispensing with it result in a gain or a loss?
6. Does prose ever contain unintentional rhythm? If so, what is its effect?
7. Does hearing light verse in childhood prepare one to appreciate poetry?

SELECTION FOR DRILL

THE LITTLE EOHIPPUS

From SIMILAR CASES[4]

Charlotte Perkins Gilman

There was once a little animal,
  No bigger than a fox,
And on five toes he scampered
  Over Tertiary rocks.
They called him Eohippus,   5
  And they called him very small,
And they thought him of no value—
  When they thought of him at all;
For the lumpish old Dinoceras
  And Coryphodon so slow   10
Were the heavy aristocracy
  In days of long ago.

Said the little Eohippus,
  "I am going to be a horse!
And on my middle finger-nails   15
  To run my earthly course;
I am going to have a flowing tail;
  I'm going to have a mane!
I'm going to stand fourteen hands high
  On the psychozoic plain!"   20

The Coryphodon was horrified,
  The Dinoceras was shocked;
And they chased young Eohippus,
  But he skipped away and mocked.
And they laughed enormous laughter,   25
  And they groaned enormous groans,
And they bade young Eohippus
  Go view his father's bones.
Said they, "You always were as small
  And mean as now we see,   30
And that's conclusive evidence
  That you're always going to be."
"What! Be a great, tall, handsome beast,
  With hoofs to gallop on?
Why! You'd have to change your nature!"   35
  Said the Loxolophodon.
They considered him disposed of,
  And retired with gait serene;

[4] This and the two following selections are reprinted from *In This Our World*, by permission of the author.

That was the way they argued
In "the early Eocene."

40

SUGGESTIONS FOR ANALYSIS. For many years, both paleontologists and lovers of light verse have known and quoted these lines. Their appeal does not wear off. The basic facts are probably familiar—our modern horse proves to be a descendant of this small, five-toed (more likely four-toed) animal. First, paraphrase the selection. This, and the two following selections, three *Similar Cases*, parody the typical animal story for children. In reading it, try to suggest the flavor of a child's story, but look out! With the fifth line, you get into deep scientific waters. Better have dictionary and encyclopedia handy. Children will readily accept the notion that such an animal could talk and prophesy his future over many million years. Doesn't Peter Rabbit talk? But you must appreciate its fantastic absurdity and its comedy.

Note that the metrical unit is the quatrain of old ballad form, the second and fourth lines rhyming. The meter is very regular and will obscure the meaning if you don't break it up. In line 1, you can make a slight pause after "once" to allow suspense to accumulate. Bear down on "five toes" and "Tertiary." 5: Pause after "him," again for suspense. Learn to make use of such simple devices for clarity, attention, and suspense. 5–8: Moderate the meter by intensifying the meaning. 9–12: In this quatrain, the meaning ends with the third line; suppress the fourth one. "Heavy aristocracy" formerly meant "very important people." These heavy monsters are represented as talking like VIP's today. Don't miss their attitude of ponderous superiority and withering contempt. Slow down, and make the attitude mock importance. 13–16: Make "said" prominent; it carries new and unexpected information. The attitude is that of a boastful child. The chief point is in "middle finger-nails," which have developed into hooves on the modern horse. Line 16 is negligible. 17–20: The boasting continues, climaxing on "fourteen hands high." "Psychozoic" (when animals had minds) must be strongly distinguished from "Tertiary" in line 4. Many millions of years intervened between these periods. "Plain" is merely a rhyme word, as was "rocks" in line 4. Don't let them steal the emphasis. 21–36: What is wanted here is *mock* horror and shock, but make the laughter and groans really enormous. These ponderous members of the contemporary ruling class were, of course, completely confident and self-satisfied. "Change your nature" should be uttered as something every fool knows is impossible.

The last two lines may be made to imply various things. Are they merely a statement of fact? Who are "they"? Does the statement imply that we may congratulate ourselves on having a more sensible view? Or is there a suggestion that some of us have *not* liberalized our attitudes? Compare this with the two following *Similar Cases*. Is it all just good-natured fun, or biting satire directed at us, now?

SELECTIONS FOR PRACTICE

THE ANTHROPOIDAL APE

From SIMILAR CASES

Charlotte Perkins Gilman

There was once an Anthropoidal Ape,
    Far smarter than the rest,
And everything that they could do
    He always did the best;
So they naturally disliked him,
    And they gave him shoulders cool,
And when they had to mention him
    They said he was a fool.
Cried this pretentious Ape one day,
    "I'm going to be a Man!
And stand upright, and hunt, and fight,
    And conquer all I can!
I'm going to cut down forest trees,
    To make my houses higher!
I'm going to kill the Mastodon!
    I'm going to make a fire!"

Loud screamed the Anthropoidal Apes
    With laughter wild and gay;
They tried to catch that boastful one,
    But he always got away.
So they yelled at him in chorus,
    Which he minded not a whit;
And they pelted him with coconuts,
    Which didn't seem to hit.
And then they gave him reasons
    Which they thought of much avail,
To prove how his preposterous
    Attempt was sure to fail.
Said the sages, "In the first place,
    The thing cannot be done!
And, second, if it could be,
    It would not be any fun!
And, third, and most conclusive,
    And admitting no reply,
You would have to change your nature!
    We should like to see you try!"
They chuckled then triumphantly,
    These lean and hairy shapes,
For these things passed as arguments
    With the Anthropoidal Apes.

THE NEOLITHIC MAN

From Similar Cases

Charlotte Perkins Gilman

There was once a Neolithic Man,
　An enterprising wight,
Who made his chopping implements
　Unusually bright.
Unusually clever he,
　Unusually brave,
And he drew delightful Mammoths
　On the borders of his cave.
To his Neolithic neighbors,
　Who were startled and surprised,
Said he, "My friends, in course of time,
　We shall be civilized!
We are going to live in cities!
　We are going to fight in wars!
We are going to eat three times a day
　Without the natural cause!
We are going to turn life upside down
　About a thing called gold!
We are going to want the earth, and take
　As much as we can hold!
We are going to wear great piles of stuff
　Outside our proper skins!
We are going to have diseases!
　And Accomplishments!! And Sins!!!"

Then they all rose up in fury
　Against their boastful friend,
For prehistoric patience
　Cometh quickly to an end.
Said one, "This is chimerical!
　Utopian! Absurd!"
Said another, "What a stupid life!
　Too dull, upon my word!"
Cried all, "Before such things can come,
　You idiotic child,
You must alter Human Nature!"
　And they all sat back and smiled.
Thought they, "An answer to that last
　It will be hard to find!"
It was a clinching argument
　To the Neolithic Mind!

THE RURAL DANCE ABOUT THE MAYPOLE

Early English Ballad, Anonymous

Come lasses and lads, take leave of your dads,
  And away to the Maypole hey;
For every he has got a she
  With a Minstrel standing by:
  For Willy has gotten his Jill,
  And Johnny has got his Joan,
To jig it, jig it, jig it, jig it, jig it up and down.

"Y'are out," says Dick, " 'Tis a lie," says Nick,
  "The fiddler played it false";
" 'Tis true," says Hugh, and so says Sue,
  And so says nimble Alice.
    The fiddler then began
    To play the tune again,
And every girl did trip it, trip it, trip it to the men.

Yet there they sat, until it was late
  And tired the fiddler quite,
With singing and playing, without any paying
  From morning until night.
    They told the fiddler then
    They'd pay him for his play,
And each a twopence, twopence, twopence, gave him and went away.

"Good night," says Tom, and so says John,
  "Good night," says Dick to Will,
"Good night" says Sis, "Good night" says Pris,
  "Good night," says Peg to Nell.
    Some run, some went, some stayed
    Some dallied by the way,
And bound themselves by kisses twelve to meet next holiday.

THE BAKER'S TALE

From THE HUNTING OF THE SNARK

Lewis Carroll

They roused him with muffins—they roused him with ice—
  They roused him with mustard and cress—
They roused him with jam and judicious advice—
  They set him conundrums to guess.

When at length he sat up and was able to speak,
  His sad story he offered to tell;

And the Bellman cried "Silence! Not even a shriek!"
And excitedly tingled his bell.

There was silence supreme! Not a shriek, not a scream,
Scarcely even a howl or a groan,
As the man they called "Ho!" told his story of woe
In an antediluvian tone.

"My father and mother were honest, though poor—"
"Skip all that!" cried the Bellman in haste.
"If it once becomes dark, there's no chance of a Snark—
We have hardly a minute to waste!"

"I skip forty years," said the Baker, in tears,
"And proceed without further remark
To the day when you took me aboard of your ship
To help you in hunting the Snark.

"A dear uncle of mine (after whom I was named)
Remarked when I bade him farewell—"
"Oh, skip your dear uncle!" the Bellman exclaimed,
As he angrily tingled his bell.

"He remarked to me then," said that mildest of men,—
" 'If your Snark be a Snark that is right,
Fetch it home by all means—you may serve it with greens,
And it's handy for striking a light.

" 'You may seek it with thimbles—and seek it with care;
You may hunt it with forks and hope;
You may threaten its life with a railway share;
You may charm it with smiles and soap—' "

("That's exactly the method," the Bellman bold
In a hasty parenthesis cried:—
"That's exactly the way I have always been told
That the capture of Snarks should be tried!")

" 'But oh, beamish nephew! beware of the day
If your Snark be a Boojum! For then
You will softly and suddenly vanish away,
And never be met with again!'

"It is this, it is this that oppresses my soul
When I think of my uncle's last words;
And my heart is like nothing so much as a bowl
Brimming over with quivering curds!

"It is this, it is this"—"We have had that before!"
The Bellman indignantly said.
And the Baker replied: "Let me say it once more;
It is this, it is this that I dread!

"I engage with the Snark—every night after dark—
    In a dreamy delirious fight;
I serve it with greens in those shadowy scenes,
    And I use it for striking a light:

"But if ever I meet with a Boojum, that day,
    In a moment (of this I am sure),
I shall softly and silently vanish away—
    And the notion I cannot endure!"

FATHER WILLIAM

Lewis Carroll

"You are old, Father William" the young man said,
    "And your hair has become very white;
And yet you incessantly stand on your head—
    Do you think, at your age, it is right?"

"In my youth," Father William replied to his son,
    "I feared it might injure the brain;
But, now that I'm perfectly sure I have none,
    Why, I do it again and again."

"You are old," said the youth, "as I mentioned before,
    And have grown most uncommonly fat;
Yet you turned a back-somersault in at the door—
    Pray, what is the reason of that?"

"In my youth," said the sage, as he shook his grey locks,
    "I kept all my limbs very supple
By the use of this ointment—one shilling the box—
    Allow me to sell you a couple?"

"You are old," said the youth, "and your jaws are too weak
    For anything tougher than suet;
Yet you finished the goose, with the bones and the beak—
    Pray, how did you manage to do it?"

"In my youth," said his father, "I took to the law,
    And argued each case with my wife;
And the muscular strength which it gave to my jaw
    Has lasted the rest of my life."

"You are old," said the youth, "one would hardly suppose
    That your eye was as steady as ever;
Yet you balanced an eel on the end of your nose—
    What made you so awfully clever?"

"I have answered three questions, and that is enough,"
Said his father. "Don't give yourself airs!
Do you think I can listen all day to such stuff?
Be off, or I'll kick you down-stairs!"

THE WALRUS AND THE CARPENTER

Lewis Carroll

The sun was shining on the sea,
Shining with all his might:
He did his very best to make
The billows smooth and bright—
And this was odd, because it was
The middle of the night.

The moon was shining sulkily,
Because she thought the sun
Had got no business to be there
After the day was done—
"It's very rude of him," she said,
"To come and spoil the fun!"

The sea was wet as wet could be.
The sands were dry as dry.
You could not see a cloud, because
No cloud was in the sky:
No birds were flying overhead—
There were no birds to fly.

The Walrus and the Carpenter
Were walking close at hand:
They wept like anything to see
Such quantities of sand:
"If this were only cleared away,"
They said, "it *would* be grand!"

"If seven maids with seven mops
Swept it for half a year,
Do you suppose," the Walrus said,
"That they could get it clear?"
"I doubt it," said the Carpenter,
And shed a bitter tear.

"O Oysters, come and walk with us!"
The Walrus did beseech.
"A pleasant walk, a pleasant talk,
Along the briny beach:
We cannot do with more than four,
To give a hand to each."

The eldest Oyster looked at him,
But never a word he said:
The eldest Oyster winked his eye
And shook his heavy head—
Meaning to say he did not choose
To leave the oyster-bed.

But four young Oysters hurried up,
All eager for the treat:
Their coats were brushed, their faces washed,
Their shoes were clean and neat—
And this was odd, because, you know,
They hadn't any feet.

Four other Oysters followed them,
And yet another four;
And thick and fast they came at last,
And more, and more, and more—
All hopping through the frothy waves,
And scrambling to the shore.

The Walrus and the Carpenter
Walked on a mile or so,
And then they rested on a rock
Conveniently low:
And all the little Oysters stood
And waited in a row.

"The time has come," the Walrus said,
"To talk of many things:
Of shoes—and ships—and sealing-wax—
Of cabbages—and kings—
And why the sea is boiling hot—
And whether pigs have wings."

"But wait a bit," the Oysters cried,
"Before we have our chat;
For some of us are out of breath,
And all of us are fat!"
"No hurry!" said the Carpenter.
They thanked him much for that.

"A loaf of bread," the Walrus said,
"Is what we chiefly need:
Pepper and vinegar besides
Are very good indeed—
Now, if you're ready, Oysters dear,
We can begin to feed."

"But not on us!" the Oysters cried,
 Turning a little blue.
"After such kindness, that would be
 A dismal thing to do!"
"The night is fine," the Walrus said.
 "Do you admire the view?

"It was so kind of you to come!
 And you are very nice!"
The Carpenter said nothing but
 "Cut us another slice:
I wish you were not quite so deaf—
 I've had to ask you twice!"

"It seems a shame," the Walrus said,
 "To play them such a trick,
After we've brought them out so far,
 And made them trot so quick!"
The Carpenter said nothing but
 "The butter's spread too thick!"

"I weep for you," the Walrus said:
 "I deeply sympathize."
With sobs and tears he sorted out
 Those of the largest size,
Holding his pocket-handkerchief
 Before his streaming eyes.

"O Oysters," said the Carpenter,
 "You've had a pleasant run!
Shall we be trotting home again?"
 But answer came there none—
And this was scarcely odd, because
 They'd eaten every one.

MORNING

Charles Stuart Calverly

'Tis the hour when white-horsed Day
Chases Night her mares away;
When the Gates of Dawn (they say)
 Phoebus opes:
And I gather that the Queen
May be uniformly seen,
Should the weather be serene,
 On the slopes.

When the ploughman, as he goes
Leathern-gaitered o'er the snows,
From his hat and from his nose
   Knocks the ice;
And the panes are frosted o'er,
And the lawn is crisp and hoar,
As has been observed before
   Once or twice.

When, arrayed in breastplate red,
Sings the robin for his bread,
On the elmtree that hath shed
   Every leaf;
While, within, the frost benumbs
The still sleepy schoolboy's thumbs,
And in consequence his sums
   Come to grief.

But when breakfast-time hath come,
And he's crunching crust and crumb,
He'll no longer look a glum
   Little dunce;
But be brisk as bees that settle
On a summer rose's petal:
Wherefore, Polly, put the kettle
   On at once.

ODE TO TOBACCO

Charles Stuart Calverly

Thou who, when fears attack,
Bidst them avaunt, and Black
Care, at the horseman's back
   Perching, unseatest;
Sweet, when the morn is gray;
Sweet, when they've cleared away
Lunch; and at close of day
   Possibly sweetest:

I have a liking old
For thee, though manifold
Stories, I know, are told,
   Not to thy credit;
How one (or two at most)
Drops make a cat a ghost—
Useless, except to roast—
   Doctors have said it:

How they who use fusees
All grow by slow degrees
Brainless as chimpanzees,
   Meagre as lizards:
Go mad, and beat their wives;
Plunge (after shocking lives)
Razors and carving knives
   Into their gizzards.

Confound such knavish tricks!
Yet know I five or six
Smokers who freely mix
   Still with their neighbours;
Jones—(who, I'm glad to say,
Asked leave of Mrs. J.)—
Daily absorbs a clay
   After his labours.

Cats may have had their goose
Cooked by tobacco-juice;
Still why deny its use
   Thoughtfully taken?
We're not as tabbies are:
Smith, take a fresh cigar!
Jones, the tobacco-jar!
   Here's to thee, Bacon!

THE YARN OF THE NANCY BELL

W. S. Gilbert

'Twas on the shores that round our coast
   From Deal to Ramsgate span,
That I found alone on a piece of stone
   An elderly naval man.

His hair was weedy, his beard was long,
   And weedy and long was he;
And I heard this wight on the shore recite,
   In a singular minor key:—

"Oh, I am a cook, and a captain bold,
   And the mate of the Nancy brig,
And a bo'sun tight, and a midshipmite,
   And the crew of the captain's gig."

And he shook his fists and he tore his hair,
   Till I really felt afraid,
For I couldn't help thinking the man had been drinking,
   And so I simply said:

"O elderly man, it's little I know
Of the duties of men of the sea,
And I'll eat my hand if I understand
However you can be

"At once a cook, and a captain bold,
And the mate of the Nancy brig,
And a bo'sun tight, and a midshipmite,
And the crew of the captain's gig."

And he gave a hitch to his trousers, which
Is a trick all seamen larn,
And having got rid of a thumping quid,
He spun his painful yarn:—

" 'Twas in the good ship Nancy Bell
That we sailed to the Indian Sea,
And there on a reef we come to grief,
Which has often occurred to me.

"And pretty nigh all the crew was drowned
(There was seventy-seven o' soul),
And only ten of the Nancy's men
Said 'Here!' to the muster-roll.

"There was me and the cook and the captain bold,
And the mate of the Nancy brig,
And the bo'sun tight, and a midshipmite,
And the crew of the captain's gig.

"For a month we'd neither wittles nor drink,
Till a-hungry we did feel;
So we drawed a lot, and accordin', shot
The captain for our meal.

"The next lot fell to the Nancy's mate,
And a delicate dish he made;
Then our appetite with the midshipmite
We seven survivors stayed.

"And then we murdered the bo'sun tight,
And he much resembled pig;
Then we wittled free, did the cook and me,
On the crew of the captain's gig.

"Then only the cook and me was left,
And the delicate question, 'Which
Of us two goes to the kettle?' arose,
And we argued it out as sich.

"For I loved that cook as a brother, I did,
  And the cook he worshiped me;
But we'd both be blowed if we'd either be stowed
  In the other chap's hold, you see.

" 'I'll be eat if you dines off me,' says Tom;
  'Yes, that,' says I, 'you'll be:
I'm boiled if I die, my friend,' quoth I;
  And 'Exactly so,' quoth he.

"Says he, 'Dear James, to murder me
  Were a foolish thing to do,
For don't you see that you can't cook *me*,
  While I can—and will—cook *you?*'

"So he boils the water, and takes the salt
  And the pepper in portions true
(Which he never forgot), and some chopped shalot,
  And some sage and parsley too.

" 'Come here,' says he, with a proper pride,
  Which his smiling features tell;
' 'Twill soothing be if I let you see
  How extremely nice you'll smell.'

"And he stirred it round and round and round,
  And he sniffed at the foaming froth;
When I ups with his heels, and smothers his squeals
  In the scum of the boiling broth.

"And I eat that cook in a week or less,
  And—as I eating be
The last of his chops, why, I almost drops,
  For a wessel in sight I see!

                    .   .   .   .   .

"And I never larf, and I never smile,
  And I never lark nor play,
But sit and croak, and a single joke
  I have—which is to say:—

" 'Oh, I am a cook, and a captain bold,
  And the mate of the Nancy brig,
And a bo'sun tight, and a midshipmite,
  And the crew of the captain's gig!' "

HOW JACK FOUND THAT BEANS MAY GO BACK ON A CHAP

Guy Wetmore Carryl

Without the slightest basis
For hypochondriasis,
   A widow had forebodings which a cloud around her flung,
And with expression cynical
For half the day a clinical
   Thermometer she held beneath her tongue.

Whene'er she read the papers
She suffered from the vapors,
   At every tale of malady or accident she'd groan;
In every new and smart disease,
From housemaid's knee to heart disease,
   She recognized the symptoms as her own!

She had a yearning chronic
To try each novel tonic,
   Elixir, panacea, lotion, opiate, and balm;
And from a homeopathist
Would change to an hydropathist,
   And back again, with stupefying calm!

She was nervous, cataleptic,
And anemic, and dyspeptic:
   Though not convinced of apoplexy, yet she had fears.
She dwelt with force fanatical,
Upon a twinge rheumatical,
   And said she had a buzzing in her ears!

Now all of this bemoaning
And this grumbling and this groaning
   The mind of Jack, her son and heir, unconscionably bored.
His heart completely hardening,
He gave his time to gardening,
   For raising beans was something he adored.

Each hour in accents morbid
This limp maternal bore bid
   Her callous son affectionate and lachrymose good-bys.
She never granted Jack a day
Without some long "Alackaday!"
   Accompanied by rolling of the eyes.

But Jack, no panic showing,
Just watched his beanstalk growing,
   And twined with tender fingers the tendrils up the pole.
At all her words funereal
He smiled a smile ethereal,
   Or sighed an absent-minded "Bless my soul!"

That hollow-hearted creature
Would never change a feature:
   No tear bedimmed his eye, however touching was her talk.
She never fussed or flurried him,
The only thing that worried him
   Was when no bean-pods grew upon the stalk!

But then he wabbled loosely
His head, and wept profusely,
   And, taking out his handkerchief to mop away his tears,
Exclaimed: "It hasn't got any!"
He found this blow to botany
   Was sadder than were all his mother's fears.

The Moral is that gardeners pine
Whene'er no pods adorn the vine.
Of all sad words experience gleans
The saddest are "It might have beans."
   (I did not make this up myself:
   'Twas in a book upon my shelf.
   It's witty, but I don't deny
   It's rather Whittier than I.)

THE SYCOPHANTIC FOX AND THE
GULLIBLE RAVEN

Guy Wetmore Carryl

A raven sat upon a tree,
   And not a word he spoke, for
His beak contained a piece of Brie,
   Or, maybe it was Roquefort.
      We'll make it any kind you please—
      At all events it was a cheese.

Beneath the tree's umbrageous limb
   A hungry fox sat smiling;
He saw the raven watching him,
   And spoke in words beguiling:
      "J'admire," said he, "ton beau plumage,"
      (The which was simply persiflage).

Two things there are, no doubt you know,
To which a fox is used:
A rooster that is bound to crow,
A crow that's bound to roost;
And whichsoever he espies
He tells the most unblushing lies.

"Sweet fowl," he said, "I understand
You're more than merely natty,
I hear you sing to beat the band
And Adelina Patti.
Pray render with your liquid tongue
A bit from 'Götterdämmerung.' "

This subtle speech was aimed to please
The crow, and it succeeded;
He thought no bird in all the trees
Could sing as well as he did.
In flattery completely doused,
He gave the "Jewel Song" from "Faust."

But gravitation's law, of course,
As Isaac Newton showed it,
Exerted on the cheese its force,
And elsewhere soon bestowed it.
In fact, there is no need no tell
What happened when to earth it fell.

I blush to add that when the bird
Took in the situation
He said one brief, emphatic word,
Unfit for publication.
The fox was greatly startled, but
He only sighed and answered "Tut."

The Moral is: A fox is bound
To be a shameless sinner.
And also: When the cheese comes round
You know it's after dinner.
But (what is only known to few)
The fox is after dinner, too.

JESSE JAMES[5]

(A Design in Red and Yellow for a Nickel Library)
William Rose Benét

Jesse James was a two-gun man,
(Roll on, Missouri!)

[5] Used by permission of Dodd, Mead and Co., Inc. From *Golden Fleece*, copyright 1935

Strong-arm chief of an outlaw clan,
  (*From Kansas to Illinois!*)
He twirled an old Colt forty-five;
  (*Roll on, Missouri!*)
They never took Jesse James alive.
  (*Roll, Missouri, roll!*)

Jesse James was King of the Wes';
  (*Cataracts in the Missouri!*)
He'd a di'mon' heart in his lef' breas';
  (*Brown Missouri rolls!*)
He'd a fire in his heart no hurt could stifle;
  (*Thunder, Missouri!*)
Lion eyes an' a Winchester rifle.
  (*Missouri, roll down!*)

Jesse James rode a pinto hawse;
Come at night to a water-cawse;
Tetched with the rowel that pinto's flank;
She sprung the torrent from bank to bank.

Jesse rode through a sleepin' town;
Looked the moonlit street both up an' down;
Crack-crack-crack, the street ran flames
An' a great voice cried, "I'm Jesse James!"

Hawse an' afoot they're after Jess!
  (*Roll on, Missouri!*)
Spurrin' an' spurrin'—but he's gone Wes'.
  (*Brown Missouri rolls!*)
He was ten foot tall when he stood in his boots;
  (*Lightnin' like the Missouri!*)
More'n a match fer sich galoots.
  (*Roll, Missouri, roll!*)

Jesse James rode outa the sage;
Roun' the rocks come the swayin' stage;
Straddlin' the road a giant stan's
An' a great voice bellers, "Throw up yer han's!"

Jesse raked in the di'mon' rings,
The big gold watches an' the yuther things;
Jesse divvied 'em then an' thar
With a cryin' child had lost her mar.

They're creepin'; they're crawlin'; they're stalkin' Jess;
  (*Roll on, Missouri!*)
They's a rumor he's gone much further Wes';
  (*Roll, Missouri, roll!*)
They's word of a cayuse hitched to the bars
  (*Ruddy clouds on Missouri!*)

Of a golden sunset that bursts into stars.
(*Missouri, roll down!*)

Jesse James rode hell fer leather;
He was a hawse an' a man together;
In a cave in a mountain high up in air
He lived with a rattlesnake, a wolf, an' a bear.

Jesse's heart was as sof' as a woman;
Fer guts an' stren'th he was sooper-human;
He could put six shots through a woodpecker's eye
And take in one swaller a gallon o' rye.

They sought him here an' they sought him there,
    (*Roll on, Missouri!*)
But he strides by night through the ways of the air;
    (*Brown Missouri rolls!*)
They say he was took an' they say he is dead,
    (*Thunder, Missouri!*)
But he ain't—he's a sunset overhead!
    (*Missouri down to the sea!*)

Jesse James was a Hercules.
When he went through the woods he tore up the trees,
When he went on the plains he smoked the groun'
An' the hull lan' shuddered fer miles aroun'.

Jesse James wore a red bandanner
That waved on the breeze like the Star Spangled Banner;
In seven states he cut up dadoes.
He's gone with the buffler an' the desperadoes.

Yes, Jesse James was a two-gun man
    (*Roll on, Missouri!*)
The same as when this song began;
    (*From Kansas to Illinois!*)
An' when you see a sunset burst into flames
    (*Lightnin' like the Missouri!*)
Or a thunderstorm blaze—that's Jesse James!
    (*Hear that Missouri roll!*)

SALES TALK FOR ANNIE[6]

Morris Bishop

Eat your banana, Annie dear;
    It's from a tropic tree

[6] From *A Bowl of Bishop*, Dial Press, New York, 1954.

In lands where lurked the buccaneer
  By the Río Tilirí,
Or where the Cockscomb Mountains rise
  Above the Monkey River,
And lonely men with fevered eyes
  By turns perspire and shiver.
The parrot and the kinkajou
  And the armor-clad iguana
Have spared this golden fruit for you—
  But no, she won't even touch the lovely banana!

Eat your tapioca, please.
  In forests of Brazil
The Tupis and the Guaranis
  Have cooked it on a grill.
The poison of cassava roots
  Is thereby circumvented,
And flour and bread it constitutes.
  (It often is fermented.)
From Urubú and Urucú
  To distant Yanaoca
Indians grew this food for you,
  So for gosh sakes get going on your tapioca.

Drink your milk, my little lass.
  Oh, does it not look yummy!
A moo-cow ate the sun-lit grass
  And made it in her tummy.
The moo-cow's milk is free from faults,
  It's good for every human
(Containing sugar, fats, and salts,
  And casein and albumin.)
Here, I said to drink it, not blow in it! Listen, Annie,
  How would you like to have Father take that glass of milk and
    ram it
Down your throat? How would you like a good swift whack on the
    fanny?
  All right, go ahead and cry, damn it!

WHO'D BE A HERO (FICTIONAL)?[7]

Morris Bishop

When, in my effervescent youth,
  I first read "David Copperfield,"
I felt the demonstrated truth
  That I had found my proper field.

[7] From *A Bowl of Bishop*, Dial Press, New York, 1954.

As David, simple, gallant, proud,
Affronted each catastrophe,
Involuntarily I vowed,
"That's me!"

In Sherlock Holmes and Rastignac
Much of myself was realized;
In Cyrano de Bergerac
I found myself idealized.
Where dauntless hardihood defied
The wrong in doughty derring-do,
I periodically cried,
"That's me too!"

The lads of Bennett, Wells, and Co.
Confronted many a thwarting thing,
But well-intentioned, fumbling, slow,
They tried to do the sporting thing;
And some would nurse a carking shame,
Hiding the smart from other men.
They often caused me to exclaim,
"That's me again!"

The fiction of the present day
I view with some dubiety;
The hero is a castaway,
A misfit to society,
A drunkard or a mental case,
A pervert or a debauchee.
I murmur with a sour grimace,
"Where's me?"

LISTEN HERE, CAPITAL AND LABOR[8]

Morris Bishop

Hearken to me, O Capital and Labor!
This is no time for quarrels and scraps.
Let's all get together like one big neighbor—
Capital and Labor, you deaf perhaps?

Now bushelmen, bushel, and bakers, bake;
Sturdily cast, ye casters on slush;
Stripper-opaquers, strip, opaque;
Ye offset tuschers, tusch, tusch!

Let the ideal of production illumine
The soul of director, mechanic, clerk.

[8] From *A Bowl of Bishop,* Dial Press, New York, 1954.

Let us heed the word of ex-President Truman
And dedicate all of our strength to work.

So pullers and wringermen, speed your wringers;
Octopus fishers, catch octopus;
And fingerwavers, wave your fingers;
Bus boys, bus girls, buss, buss.

Be earnest! Be firm!, Be enthusiastic!
Till a hundred million cars are loose
On the roads, till we're up to our waists in plastic.
Never you mind. Produce! Produce!

Address, addressograph operators;
Jolly recappers, recap, recap;
And cure curates; curate, curators;
Purse, pursers; lappers, lap.

THE PIRATE DON DURKE OF DOWDEE[9]

Mildred Plew Meigs

Ho, for the Pirate Don Durke of Dowdee!
He was as wicked as wicked could be,
But oh, he was perfectly gorgeous to see!
The Pirate Don Durke of Dowdee.

His conscience, of course, was as black as a bat,
But he had a floppety plume on his hat,
And when he went walking it jiggled—like that!
The plume of the Pirate Dowdee.

His coat it was crimson and cut with a slash,
And often as ever he twirled his mustache,
Deep down in the ocean the mermaids went splash,
Because of Don Durke of Dowdee.

Moreover, Dowdee had a purple tattoo,
And stuck in his belt where he buckled it through
Were a dagger, a dirk and a squizzamaroo,
For fierce was the prirate Dowdee.

So fearful he was he would shoot at a puff,
And always at sea when the weather grew rough,
He drank from a bottle and wrote on his cuff,
Did Pirate Don Durke of Dowdee.

Oh, he had a cutlass that swung at his thigh,
And he had a parrot called Pepperkin Pye,

---

[9] By permission of the author.

And a zigzaggy scar at the end of his eye,
Had Pirate Don Durke of Dowdee.

He kept in a cavern, this buccaneer bold,
A curious chest that was covered with mould,
And all of his pockets were jingly with gold!
Oh jing! went the gold of Dowdee.

His conscience, of course, it was crook'd like a squash,
But both of his boots made a slickery slosh
And he went through the world with a wonderful swash,
Did Pirate Don Durke of Dowdee.

It's true he was wicked as wicked could be,
His sins they outnumbered a hundred and three,
But oh, he was perfectly gorgeous to see,
The Pirate Don Durke of Dowdee.

WHO DID WHICH?
OR
WHO INDEED?[10]

Ogden Nash

Oft in the stilly night,
When the mind is fumbling fuzzily,
I brood about how little I know,
And know that little so muzzily.
Ere slumber's chains have bound me,
I think it would suit me nicely,
If I knew one tenth of the little I know,
But knew that tenth precisely.

O Delius, Sibelius,
And What's-his-name Aurelius,
O Manet, O Monet,
Mrs. Siddons and the Cid!
I know each name
Has an oriflamme of fame,
I'm sure they all did something,
But I can't think what they did.

Oft in the sleepless dawn
I feel my brain is hominy
When I try to identify famous men,
Their countries and anno Domini.
Potemkin, Pushkin, Ruskin,

Velásquez, Pulaski, Laski;
They are locked together in one gray cell,
And I seem to have lost the passkey.

O Tasso, Picasso,
O Talleyrand and Sally Rand,
Elijah, Elisha,
Eugene Aram, Eugène Sue,
Don Quixote, Donn Byrne,
Rosencrantz and Guildenstern,
Humperdinck and Rumpelstiltskin,
They taunt me, two by two.

At last, in the stilly night,
When the mind is bubbling vaguely,
I grasp my history by the horns
And face it Haig and Haigly.
O, Austerlitz fought at Metternich,
And Omar Khayyam wrote *Moby Dick*,
Blücher invented a kind of shoe,
And Kohler of Kohler, the Waterloo;
Croesus was turned to gold by Minos,
And Thomas à Kempis was Thomas Aquinas.
Two Irish Saints were Patti and Micah,
The Light Brigade rode at Balalaika,
If you seek a roué to irk your aunt,
Kubla Khan but Immanuel Kant,
And no one has ever been transmogrified
Until by me he has been biogrified.

Gently my eyelids close;
I'd rather be good than clever;
And I'd rather have my facts all wrong
Than have no facts whatever.

PARSLEY FOR VICE-PRESIDENT![11]

Ogden Nash

I'd like to be able to say a good word for parsley, but I can't,
And after all what can you find to say for something that even the
    dictionary dismisses as a biennial umbelliferous plant?
I will not venture to deny that it is umbelliferous,
I will only add that it is of a nasty green color, and faintly odoriferous.
Now, there is one sin for which a lot of cooks and hostesses are
    someday going to have to atone,

[11] From *I'm a Stranger Here Myself*, copyright, 1938, by Ogden Nash, and re-printed by permission of Little, Brown & Co.

Which is that they can't bear to cook anything and leave it alone.
No, they see food as something to base a lot of beautiful dreams and
    romance on,
Which explains lamb chops with pink and blue pants on.
Everything has to be all decorated and garnished
So the guests will be amazed and astarnished,
And whatever you get to eat, it's sprinkled with a lot of good old
    umbelliferous parsley looking as limp and wistful as Lillian Gish,
And it is limpest, and wistfullest, and also thickest, on fish.
Indeed, I think maybe one reason for the disappearance of Enoch
    Arden
Was that his wife had an idea that mackerel tasted better if instead
    of looking like mackerel it looked like a garden.
Well, anyhow, there's the parsley cluttering up your food,
And the problem is to get it off without being rude,
And first of all you try to scrape it off with your fork,
And you might as well try to shave with a cork,
And then you surreptitiously try your fingers,
And you get covered with butter and gravy, but the parsley lingers,
And you turn red and smile at your hostess and compliment her on
    the recipe and ask her where she found it,
And then you return to the parsley and as a last resort you try to eat
    around it,
And the hostess says, Oh you are just picking at it, is there something
    wrong with it?
So all you can do is eat it all up, and the parsley along with it,
And now is the time for all good parsleyphobes to come to the aid of
    the menu and exhibit their gumption,
And proclaim that any dish that has either a taste or an appearance
    that can be improved by parsley is ipso facto a dish unfit for
    human consumption.

VERY LIKE A WHALE[12]

Ogden Nash

One thing that literature would be greatly the better for
Would be a more restricted employment by authors of simile and
    metaphor.
Authors of all races, be they Greeks, Romans, Teutons or Celts,
Can't seem to say that anything is the thing it is but have to go out
    of their way to say that it is like something else.
What does it mean when we are told
That the Assyrian came down like a wolf on the fold?
In the first place, George Gordon Byron had had enough experience

---

[12] From *Many Long Years Ago*, copyright, 1935, by Ogden Nash, and reprinted
by permission of Little, Brown & Co.

To know that it probably wasn't just one Assyrian, it was a lot of
Assyrians.

However, as too many arguments are apt to induce apoplexy and
thus hinder longevity,

We'll let it pass as one Assyrian for the sake of brevity.

Now then, this particular Assyrian, the one whose cohorts were
gleaming in purple and gold,

Just what does the poet mean when he says he came down like a
wolf on the fold?

In heaven and earth more than is dreamed of in our philosophy
there are a great many things,

But I don't imagine that among them there is a wolf with purple and
gold cohorts or purple and gold anythings.

No, no, Lord Byron, before I'll believe that this Assyrian was actually like a wolf I must have some kind of proof;

Did he run on all fours and did he have a hairy tail and a big red
mouth and big white teeth and did he say Woof woof woof?

Frankly I think it very unlikely, and all you were entitled to say, at
the very most,

Was that the Assyrian cohorts came down like a lot of Assyrian cohorts about to destroy the Hebrew host.

But that wasn't fancy enough for Lord Byron, oh dear me no, he had
to invent a lot of figures of speech and then interpolate them,

With the result that whenever you mention Old Testament soldiers
to people they say Oh yes, they're the ones that a lot of wolves
dressed up in gold and purple ate them.

That's the kind of thing that's being done all the time by poets, from
Homer to Tennyson;

They're always comparing ladies to lilies and veal to venison,

And they always say things like that the snow is a white blanket
after a winter storm.

Oh it is, is it, all right then, you sleep under a six-inch blanket of
snow and I'll sleep under a half-inch blanket of unpoetical
blanket material and we'll see which one keeps warm,

And after that maybe you'll begin to comprehend dimly

What I mean by too much metaphor and simile.

HUNTER TRIALS[13]

John Betjeman

It's awf'lly bad luck on Dianna,
　　Her ponies have swallowed their bits;
She fished down their throats with a spanner
　　And frightened them all into fits.

[13] From *Collected Poems* (Boston: Houghton Mifflin Co., 1959). Reprinted by
permission of John Murray, Publishers, Ltd.

So now she's attempting to borrow.
Do lend her some bits, Mummy, *do;*
I'll lend her my own for tomorrow,
But to-day I'll be wanting them too.

Just look at Prunella on Guzzle,
The wizardest pony on earth;
Why doesn't she slacken his muzzle
And tighten the breech in his girth?

I say, Mummy, there's Mrs. Geyser
And doesn't she look pretty sick?
I bet it's because Mona Lisa
Was hit on the hock with a brick.

Miss Blewitt says Monica threw it,
But Monica says it was Joan,
And Joan's very thick with Miss Blewitt
So Monica's sulking alone.

And Margaret failed in her paces,
Her withers got tied in a noose,
So her coronets caught in the traces
And now all her fetlocks are loose.

Oh, it's me now. I'm terribly nervous.
I wonder if Smudges will shy.
She's practically certain to swerve as
Her Pelham is over one eye.

❉   ❉   ❉   ❉   ❉   ❉

Oh wasn't it naughty of Smudges?
Oh, Mummy, I'm sick with disgust.
She threw me in front of the judges,
And my silly old collarbone's bust.

THE OLYMPIC GIRL[14]

John Betjeman

The sort of girl I like to see
Smiles down from her great height at me.
She stands in strong, athletic pose
And wrinkles her *retroussé* nose.
Is it distaste that makes her frown,
So furious and freckled, down
On an unhealthy worm like me?
Or am I what she likes to see?

[14] From *Collected Poems* (Boston: Houghton Mifflin Co., 1959). Reprinted by permission of John Murray, Publishers, Ltd.

I do not know, though much I care.
εἰθε γενοιμην[15] . . . would I were
(Forgive me, shade of Rupert Brooke)
An object fit to claim her look.
Oh! would I were her racket press'd
With hard excitement to her breast
And swished into the sunlit air
Arm-high above her tousled hair,
And banged against the bounding ball
"Oh! Plung!" my tauten'd strings would call
"Oh! Plung! my darling, break my strings.
For you I will do brilliant things."
And when the match is over, I
Would flop beside you, hear you sigh;
And then, with what supreme caress,
You'ld tuck me up into my press.
Fair tigress of the tennis courts,
So short in sleeve and strong in shorts,
Little, alas, to you I mean,
For I am old and bald and green.

SMALL BENN[16]

John Ciardi

Look outside. Do you see Small Benn
Digging a cave to be his den?
He doesn't want to live with us.
He says he's tired of Mummy's fuss.
He says he's tired of Daddy's ways
Of being *reasonable.* He says
Daddy's reasons are much too long
And they always end with *Benn is wrong.*
He says maybe he's not too bright
But he'd like some reasons why *Benn is right.*
He says he's tired of Miss Myra Priss.
He says he certainly will not miss
John L.—that he's just a noisy tease.
So he asked for a shovel. He *did* say please.
And he's out there now—has been all day.
And he *has* been digging, I must say.
He says no, he's not going to run away.

---

[15] The pronunciation of this phrase is approximately "ā'-thĕh gĕ-noi'-main," and the meaning is roughly "Would it might be!" The entire line is quoted from Rupert Brooke's poem "The Old Vicarage, Grantchester." In reading, it may be best to omit the Greek phrase and the credit to Brooke and read merely, "would I were an object fit to claim her look."

[16] From *Saturday Review,* December 14, 1963.

He wants his allowance. He wants his food.
But he's moving into his cave for good.
Except, that is, for snacks, TV,
And maybe when there's company,
Or to get a drink.
        —Well, good luck, Benn.
Come in and see us now and then.
At least, I hope, to wash your face.
For a cave is a sort of smudgy place.
And you know the rule—you have to be
Washed and neat to watch TV.
Better yet—for it looks like rain—
Why not come back in again
And rest a while? Its getting late.
You must be tired. The cave can wait.
You could sleep here just one more night.
And I could come and tuck you tight,
And kiss you, and put out the light.
That's *reasonable.* And it could be *right.*
There—right *and* reasonable. No? Well, then,
Whenever you're ready—you say when.
But don't forget—we'll miss you, Benn.

THOSE THREE[17]

John Ciardi

Miss Myra and Small Benn and John L.—those three
Grew tired of Mummy, grew tired of me,
Grew tired of manners, of baths, and of bed,
And of having to mind us whatever we said
(Which they never did, where they always went late,
Which they never took, which were bad when they ate.)

Which is to say, they meant to be rid
Of a lot of things they never did
(Or never on time, or never right)—
And so they ran away one night.

They left us a note and in it they said:
"Minding and manners and baths and bed
Have ruined our lives. We are running away.
Goodbye. There is nothing more to say."

And they signed it and left. And so they were rid
Of all those things they never did
(Or never right, or never on time).
Small Benn took a quarter, Miss Myra a dime,

[17] From *Saturday Review,* December 26, 1963.

And John L. (who never *could* save) one cent.
And they bought their tickets and off they went.

They wrote us from Spain, but they sent no news.
They wrote us from Egypt and asked for shoes
(Which we sent them at once, for well we knew
How the hot sand burns when your shoes wear through).
They wrote us from India, next, to say
How happy they were they had run away.
"We are seeing the world! It is good to be rid
Of all those things we never did—
Minding and manners and baths and bed.
Small Benn has warts. Miss Myra's head
Is gorgeously caked. John L. just said
All the bad words he was never allowed
To use at home. My he looks proud!
And none of us ever mind anymore.
And we drop our things all over the floor.
And we never ever go to bed.
Well, thanks for the shoes." That's what they said
In the note from India.
                    Their last note
(The very last one they ever wrote
As far as we know) was marked "At Sea."
And what is said was: "Since we're free,
We're bound for Australia. That's where we'll be
By the time this letter gets to you.
We're going to catch us a Kangaroo.
Please send us at once a Kangaroo Trap,
Some Pretzels and Pickles, and maybe a Map
With the Kangaroo Places marked in red,
And a Ball of Twine, and a Spool of Thread
(John L. has a rip, and Small Benn's kite
Is out of string.) We are all right.
I hope you are sorry we ran away."
It was signed "Miss Myra," and dated "May."

We sent the Twine for Small Benn's kite
Air-parcel-post that very night,
With a spool of thread (and a needle, too)
For John L's rip. But the best I could do
With the Kangaroo Map was a bit of a mess.
I didn't know, so I had to guess
Where the Kangaroo Places were likely to be,
And *all* of Australia looked likely to me,
And even some parts of Alaska and Texas.
Before I was through, there were so many X's
They covered the map so, that no one could tell

What it was a map *of*.   I did do quite well
With the pretzels and pickles (one tub and barrel)
Which I wrapped in odd bits of Miss Myra's apparel.
(She had left things behind—in her hurry perhaps.)
So that much went well.   But the Kangaroo Traps!—
Oh, those Kangaroo Traps!   Have any of *you*
Tried shopping for things that might possibly do
For catching and holding a live Kangaroo?
I finally bought a large cage from the zoo.
At least that would *hold* one, though I couldn't guess
How it might *trap* it—and couldn't care less.
We wrapped it all up.   It made quite a pack,
So we sent *that* by ship.
                              In three years it came back
With a letter that read: "Dear Mr. and Mrs.:
By official report (and that is what this is)
Miss Myra and Small Benn and John L.—those three—
Have been here and gone.   As it seems now to me
They will not be back, as I think you'll agree.
The details are as follows:
                              Small Benn: lost at sea.
Sailed off in a tantrum, split up on a reef.
Some think he attacked it.   We share your great grief.

The one called Miss Myra (as far as we know):
Lies buried in ninety-nine inches of snow.
Report states that though it was starting to blow
She went out to buy pickles at forty-below.
We repeat our condolences.
                              That leaves—let's see—
The one called John L.   As sworn before me
By rumor and hearsay and witnesses, he
Did say his bad words to a King Kangaroo
That replied with a kick that would certainly do
To put him in orbit, and certainly did.
Once more our regrets.   Postage due, seven quid.
I am, sir, and madam, John Jasper MacNeice,
House Painter, Gents' Tailor, and Chief of Police."

We read it straight through, and again, and again
(Once backwards, and once in a mirror) and then,
I looked at Mummy and she looked at me.
And that's when we knew that at last we were free
Of Miss Myra and Small Benn and John L.—those three.
But we fought back our tears and our sorrow, we did.
I counted my money, and sent seven quid
(That's twenty-one dollars) to J. J. MacNeice,
House Painter, Gents' Tailor, and Chief of Police.

And Mummy replied with a courteous note,
Taking pains (for politeness) to say that he wrote
A most elegant hand, and she thanked him for that.
And when she was finished, I put on my hat.
And she put on hers. And in silence we two
Walked out through the park, down those paths we both knew,
And—still silent—we paused half a day at the zoo,
For it brought back fond memories—to her and to me—
Of Miss Myra and Small Benn and John L.—those three.

SUPERMAN[18]

John Updike

I drive my car to supermarket,
  The way I take is superhigh,
A superlot is where I park it,
  And Super Suds are what I buy.

Supersalesmen sell me tonic—
  Super-Tone-O, for Relief.
The planes I ride are supersonic.
  In trains, I like the Super Chief.

Supercilious men and women
  Call me superficial—me,
Who so superbly learned to swim in
  Supercolossality.

Superphosphate-fed foods feed me;
  Superservice keeps me new.
Who would dare to supersede me,
  Super-super-superwho?

SIGHT UNSEEN[19]

Kingsley Amis

As I was waiting for the bus
  A girl came up the street,
Delectable as double-plus
  At seven hundred feet.

[18] "Superman" from *The Carpentered Hen and other Tame Creatures* by John
Updike. Copyright © 1955 by John Updike. Reprinted with the permission of
Harper & Row, Publishers.
[19] Reprinted by permission of the author and the publishers, Victor Gollancz, Ltd.

Her head was high, her step was free,
  Her face a lyric blur,
Her waist was narrow, I could see,
  But not the rest of her.

At fifty feet I watched her stop,
  Bite at a glove, then veer
Aside into some pointless shop,
  Never to reappear.

This happens every bloody day:
  They about-turn, they duck
Into their car and belt away,
  They hide behind a truck.

Look, if they knew me—understood,
  There might be cause to run;
Or if they saw me, well and good;
  And yet they don't, not one.

Love at first sight: by this we mean
  A stellar entrant thrown
Clear on the psyche's radar-screen,
  Recognised before known.

All right—things work the opposite
  Way with the poles reversed;
It's galling, though, when girls omit
  To switch the set on first.

6

REVIEW

If interpretation is a teachable art, it must have a well-defined method. There must be a place to begin, a first step, and a coherent technique built upon this foundation. The first task of an interpreter of literature is to gain a clear understanding of what he would read, an understanding derived from careful analysis of linguistic structure. Words must be understood, both singly and in their combinations into meaningful groups. Those that are important in conveying meaning must be distinguished from those that are not. The function of each word group in its relation to other groups must be studied. When this literal meaning of a passage is clearly grasped, the reader must consider how the author intends it to be received, what mood and attitude accompany and modify the meaning. Then some steps must be taken to intensify the author's thought and intention so that they will vividly impress the hearers. Suitable voice for the occasion must be considered, and for each word a pronunciation must be determined that will be appropriate for its occurrence in the given context. And in reading verse all of this must be harmonized with the demands of meter and rhyme.

We need now an exercise in which we can draw together all the precepts and principles so far presented. We shall find almost an ideal opportunity to embody them all in that superbly ironic bit of verse by Edwin Arlington Robinson called "Miniver Cheevy." In it we shall find a challenge to our keenest insight, a trial of our finest techniques. All that we have learned of grouping, of emphasis, of pausing, of attitude, will be needed, and all the devices for increasing vividness. These seemingly simple stanzas must be carefully analyzed if we are to prevent the words from flowing past our lips so rhythmically that their sense is lost. And how much meaning they carry! Here is a whole life history in thirty-two lines. Theodore Dreiser couldn't have told it in less than a thousand pages!

MINIVER CHEEVY[1]

Edwin Arlington Robinson

Miniver Cheevy, child of scorn,
    Grew lean while he assailed the seasons;
He wept that he was ever born,
    And he had reasons.

Miniver loved the days of old
    When swords were bright and steeds were prancing;
The vision of a warrior bold
    Would set him dancing.

Miniver sighed for what was not,
    And dreamed and rested from his labors;
He dreamed of Thebes and Camelot,
    And Priam's neighbors.

Miniver mourned the ripe renown
    That made so many a name so fragrant;
He mourned Romance, now on the town,
    And Art, a vagrant.

Miniver loved the Medici,
    Albeit he had never seen one;
He would have sinned incessantly
    Could he have been one.

Miniver cursed the commonplace
    And eyed a khaki suit with loathing;
He missed the mediaeval grace
    Of iron clothing.

Miniver scorned the gold he sought,
    But sore annoyed was he without it;
Miniver thought, and thought, and thought,
    And thought about it.

Miniver Cheevy, born too late,
    Scratched his head and kept on thinking;
Miniver coughed and called it fate,
    And kept on drinking.

[1] From *Town Down the River*, by permission of Charles Scribner's Sons.

Finding the Meaning

This story is already so highly condensed, it is revealed so largely by means of suggestion, that an attempt further to condense it into a précis is almost futile. You will find it more profitable to expand it into a complete life history. Try, then, writing in detail a Life of Miniver Cheevy. Include every detail that is suggested by these lines, but *only* what is suggested.

But first, of course, you must make a careful analysis of the poem, line by line. Miniver is first characterized as a "child of scorn." This is apparently the keynote of his character. The phrase means not that he suffered from the scorn of others, but that he looked upon everything in his environment with contempt and loathing. His assailing the seasons was not mere complaining about the weather, but a lament that he had been born too late. Does line 4 mean that he really had reasons for weeping, or that he *thought* he had, or that he could *give* you reasons? What the reasons were is explained in the stanzas that follow.

What does Miniver's love of bright swords and prancing steeds tell you of his disposition? Was he dull or lively? sour or sanguine? Note that these visions set him dancing. But note also that he dreamed and rested. Explain "Priam's neighbors." What did Miniver find so attractive in Thebes, Camelot, and Troy? You must understand the allurements of these cities.

Note that "mourned" in the fourth stanza echoes "sighed for" in the third. This fourth stanza needs especially close study. What does it mean to be "on the town"? This idiom has changed its meaning completely since Robinson's day. It means here not "out for a good time," but "on relief," as we say; dependent on the town for support. There was no Federal social security then; each town was expected to take care of its own derelicts. Now, who, or what, was on the town? Who was a vagrant? Does it make sense to say that Romance was on the town, and that Art was a vagrant wanderer? Miniver's mourning Romance and Art obviously means that he mourned the lack of them.

Why did Miniver love the Medici? And why are you told that he had never seen one? *Might* he have seen one? When did he live? and where? He was familiar with khaki uniforms, which places him in the present. How, then, do you account for this line? Why would he have sinned incessantly if he could have belonged to this famous family? Was he evil by nature? Does his scorn of the commonplace imply that he was really superior in his tastes, and would have been happy and at home in the gorgeous menage of Lorenzo the Magnificent? He might have lived there, as did many others, on the support of his patron, and would not have been afflicted with the uncomfortable necessity of providing himself with gold, which he both scorned and needed.

This problem of subsistence seems to have baffled him, and reduced him to futile philosophizing. Or how do you interpret lines 27 and 28? Has the discouragement and disintegration suggested in the last stanza been foreshadowed above? Miniver keeps on thinking of what? Why does he cough? What does he attribute to fate? Be very specific about all these points. There is much more here than meets the eye.

Attitude

With the thought mastered, we are ready to consider that all-important aspect of interpretation—*attitude*. The essential question to answer is, How do you, the interpreter, *feel* about the story you are telling? How do you feel toward Miniver Cheevy? You should feel, perhaps, as the author feels, but you will find that he is curiously impersonal. Comb the story as you will, you will find not a single word that expresses his personal attitude toward the man whose story he is telling. Cannot you, then, merely tell the story also without giving it any color or mood? That would be to dodge your responsibility as an interpreter. You must reveal to your hearers, as the cold page cannot, just how the story is to be received. The oral interpreter may never be as impersonal as an author. The function of an interpreter is to interpret.

If you will read carefully between the lines, you will discover several suggestions from which you should be able to construct a sound and defensible conception of the author's mood. Do you find any evidence of strong condemnation, scorn, or disgust, or, on the other hand, of sympathy, pity, or justification? You will probably agree that none of these is strongly suggested. Neither is there any strong suggestion of either gayety or gravity. Surely you will not find here the mood of tragedy. The last stanza presents a drab picture, but even it is lightened by the comic detail of scratching the head. Is it possible to conceive of scratching one's head as a tragic gesture? If you observe carefully (and our first rule is *observe*) you will find other comic touches: Look again at the fourth line, and at the tenth; and consider again who was "on the town" while mourning the lack of Romance in modern life. And is there nothing comic in a vagrant dreamer bemoaning the decay of art? Note again line 18, and the rest of that fifth stanza, and all of the seventh stanza. Do you not find here a wise and tolerant and benign spirit of Comedy, which looks upon Miniver's weaknesses and absurdities, not with annoyance, scorn, or contempt, but with amused and kindly appreciation of their ridiculousness? Read again the selection from Meredith's Essay on Comedy in Chapter 3, and the other selection from this essay among the readings at the end of Chapter 3. Or better, read, if it is available, the entire essay. See whether it does not define the appropriate mood for the reading of "Miniver Cheevy." Then see whether you cannot read it with this highly civilized comic appreciation, with a "finely-tempered smile, showing sunlight of the mind, mental richness rather than noisy enormity."

Vividness of Expression

None of the methods discussed in Chapter 3 will be so helpful in interpreting Miniver Cheevy's story as the use of imagination in thinking your way into the meaning of the lines. If thought and feeling are really present in consciousness as you read, they will emerge somewhere visibly —perhaps in a lifted eyebrow, or in wrinkles around the mouth, or a lengthened jaw, or a depressed shoulder. Labor to re-create the thought so vividly that you feel it in your muscles.

In line 4 can you suggest visibly the exaggerated plausibility with which Miniver would probably give his reasons? In the next stanza, let your own eye brighten sympathetically to the vision of a warrior bold. Reflect Miniver's enthusiasm, but don't attempt to impersonate him. Then you may sigh with gentle mock sympathy as Miniver sighed for what was not. Beware of maintaining a constant mood. Vary your expression as the pattern changes in successive stanzas.

The absurdly obvious statement in line 18 needs special attention. How do you say absurdly obvious things? How would you say, for instance, that you greatly admired Julius Caesar, although, of course, you had never known him personally? Do not attempt to moralize in your statement of Miniver's sinning in the next two lines; retain your comic appreciation. You might appropriately continue with the exclamation "The gay old rogue!" Something swanking is suggested by the "mediaeval grace of iron clothing." And do not miss the contrast in the paradox that Miniver scorned the gold he sought. Try to suggest his comic puzzlement in wrestling with the situation—by merely thinking about it.

The last stanza is rich in suggestions: maladjustment, futility, rationalization, despair, disintegration, tuberculosis (?), dissipation, death. Can you get them all expressed? You will need a vivid imagination and alert vocal and physical responsiveness to every shade of meaning.

Metrical Variation

These stanzas are so very regular in form that you will have to watch carefully to guard against singsong. Note that every stanza begins with "Miniver." The rhymes are frequent and conspicuous. Don't accentuate them, but rather minimize them wherever you can. That is, when you have a choice between a rhyme word and another word near it, put your emphasis on the neighboring word. And whenever a sense accent or a logical pause conflicts with the metrical accent or verse pause, make the most of it. In the second line, for instance, you can break the regularity by stressing the two successive strong syllables "grew lean." In the third line the scansion calls for a stress on "he," but the sense does not. Hurry lightly past the word. And so with others. There is little danger that you will completely obscure the rhythm. There is much more danger of creating a singsong that will obscure the sense.

Conclusion

This may seem a too elaborate study for so brief a poem, but experience shows that it demands and repays such study. When the analysis has been completed, the poem should be read aloud again and again, until all its subtleties are revealed in your voice and face. But in this, as in any finished artistic creation, the marks of the artist's labor should be erased. "What one takes the greatest pains to do," said Michelangelo, "should look as if it had been thrown off quickly, almost without effort—nay, in despite of the truth, as though it cost one no trouble. The great precept is: Take infinite pains, and make something that looks effortless."

7

POETRY

> The crown of literature is poetry. It is its end and aim. It is the sublimest activity of the human mind. It is the achievement of beauty. The writer of prose can only step aside when the poet passes.
>
> W. SOMERSET MAUGHAM

What *is* poetry, "this sublimest activity of the human mind?" In a literal sense it is of course the collective body of poems. And what are poems? Poems are what poets write. What, then, is a poet? We can define him as one who writes poetry, and we are back where we started from.

This is not an artificially contrived predicament. It is the kind of rotary buck-passing one may find in dictionaries. Is there any way to break out of the circle, to get off the merry-go-round?

In the long tradition of literary criticism many attempts have been made to discover the essential nature of poetic activity, often by starting with one or another of these three factors. Most critics have accepted Aristotle's theory that a poet, or any artist, is a workman, a maker, who produces a product in imitation of nature by working in conscious accordance with accepted rules of art. But some have despaired of understanding the poet and his method and agreed with Socrates that he is "a light and winged and holy thing," a seer or madman, who speaks only by divine inspiration from the Muses. Modern critics have developed the theory that poetry is merely self-expression, an overflow of the poet's emotions. Some can define the nature of poetry only by describing its effect on the reader. They say that if your reading causes goose flesh, a lump in the throat, bristling of the skin, a feeling like taking off the top of the head, shivers down the spine, a sensation in the pit of the stomach, or some other such sensation, then you know you are reading authentic poetry. And there has been much speculation about the function of poetry, whether it is to express beauty, to reveal truth, to give pleasure, to arouse emotion, to relieve the poet's feeling, to reveal his character and inner experience (providing material for his biography), or whether a poem has no purpose but to be itself, a little cosmos that is because it is.

In spite of all the confusion in critical theory, poetry still lives. Thousands attempt to compose it, millions find pleasure in reading it, and many will pay an admission fee to hear it read. Why does it survive in this age of science and technology?

The Fragrance of Experience

Poetry survives because poets say something that accords with our experience, say it skilfully, and in words that please us because of their sounds and associations. "Always in poetry," said the philosopher, Alfred North Whitehead, "is a fragrance of experience which the poet alone has been able to capture, though we recognize it also as our own."[1] Aristotle called it the pleasure of recognition. "I think," said Keats, "poetry should surprise with a fine excess and not by singularity—it should strike the reader as a wording of its own highest thoughts, and appear almost a remembrance."[2] Thornton Wilder, the playwright, says, "The response we make when we 'believe' a work of the imagination is that of saying, 'This is the way things are. I have always known it without being fully aware that I knew it. Now in the presence of this play or novel or poem (or picture or piece of music) I know that I know it.' It is this form of knowledge that Plato called 'recollection.' We have all murdered. We have all seen the ridiculous in estimable persons and in ourselves. We have all known terror as well as enchantment. Imaginative literature has nothing to say to those who do not recognize—who cannot be *reminded*—of such conditions."[3]

T. S. Eliot said that, so far as a poet expresses in his poetry "what other people feel, he is also affecting that feeling by making it more conscious: in giving people words for their feelings, he is teaching them something about themselves."[4] As another writer puts it, in reading a poem "we hardly separate our recognition that the feeling is, or has been, our feeling

---

[1] See Lucien Price, *Dialogues of Alfred North Whitehead* (New York: The New American Library of World Literature, Inc., 1954), p. 160.

[2] Maurice Buxton Forman (ed.), *The Letters of John Keats* (Fair Lawn, N.J.: Oxford University Press, 1935), p. 108.

[3] Thornton Wilder, "A Platform and a Passion or Two," *Harper's Magazine,* October 1957, p. 48.

[4] T. S. Eliot, "The Social Function of Poetry," in R. W. Stallman (ed.), *Critiques and Essays in Criticism* (New York: The Ronald Press Co., 1949), p. 113.

too from recognition that our own feeling is more precious now that it has an expression adequate for it."[5]

These statements define the characteristic effect that poetry has on those who are susceptible to its appeal. Let us test them by applying them to some notable lines of poetry. Doubtless you have been impressed by the sight of a bright full moon in an otherwise empty sky, felt something you could not express until Wordsworth articulated it for you:

> The Moon doth with delight
> Look round her when the heavens are bare.

Doubtless you have felt that more credit should go to those who stand ready but are never called to participate in great events. Milton expresses it for you:

> They also serve who only stand and wait.

Or perhaps you have felt a disturbing sadness when you are aware that beautiful summer days cannot continue forever, and you find your mood aptly described by Shakespeare:

> O! how shall summer's honey breath hold out
> Against the wreckful siege of battering days?

Touchstones of Poetry

Here are some other memorable lines from standard poetry that may stir within you a kind of pleasure of remembrance, and enhance the value of your familiar feelings and impressions. All are taken from poems in this book.

> The mind is its own place, and in itself
> Can make a Heaven of Hell, a Hell of Heaven.
>
> JOHN MILTON.

> Stone walls do not a prison make,
> Nor iron bars a cage.
>
> RICHARD LOVELACE.

> Come, and trip it as you go,
> On the light fantastic toe.
>
> JOHN MILTON.

> His little, nameless, unremembered acts
> Of kindness and of love.
>
> WILLIAM WORDSWORTH.

> Boughs which shake against the cold,
> Bare ruin'd choirs, where late the sweet birds sang.
>
> WILLIAM SHAKESPEARE.

[5] N. F. Doubleday, *Studies in Poetry* (New York: Harper & Row, 1949), p. 19.

Come lovely and soothing death,
Undulate round the world, serenely arriving, arriving.
                                        WALT WHITMAN.

                    O, wind,
If Winter comes, can Spring be far behind?
                                PERCY BYSSHE SHELLEY.

A creature not too bright or good
For human nature's daily food.
                                WILLIAM WORDSWORTH.

Season of mists and mellow fruitfulness,
    Close bosom-friend of the maturing sun.
                                        JOHN KEATS.

The old order changeth, yielding place to new,
And God fulfils Himself in many ways.
                            ALFRED, LORD TENNYSON.

And we are here as on a darkling plain
Swept with confused alarms of struggle and flight,
Where ignorant armies clash by night.
                                MATTHEW ARNOLD.

What's in a name? that which we call a rose
By any other name would smell as sweet.
                                WILLIAM SHAKESPEARE.

And so we might go on. Such passages—Matthew Arnold called them "touchstones of poetry"—are samples by which we may test the quality of poetry in general. It would be well for every student to have a collection of his own against which to judge the new poems he encounters.

An Over-all Theory Needed

But we still need a comprehensive explanation of the nature of poetry, a definition of its necessary quality, a theory of its composition and its essence. There are three reasons why oral interpreters should be concerned with poetic theory. First, if we are to interpret poetry intelligently to others, we should know what it is. Second, in order to select poems to read to others we should be able to identify authentic poetry when we see it, to be able to separate the wheat from chaff. Third, we need a theory of art, and of poetry in particular, to help us formulate an art of interpretation.

There are two principal artistic theories that are current in our day. The first is the Classical theory formulated by Aristotle, which dominated art criticism for more than two thousand years and is still valid and operative. The second is the Romantic or Expressive theory that got its impetus from the writings of Wordsworth and Coleridge beginning about 1800. They are not mutually exclusive, as we shall see. The first is concerned mainly with the nature of the product and with its effect; the second, with the artist and his emotions. Both have developed ramifications too extensive to be treated here. We can only explain them briefly and try to apply them to our problems as interpreters. Those who want a fuller explanation and comparison of them may find it in M. H. Abrams' highly influential book, *The Mirror and the Lamp*.[6]

The Classical Theory

All the arts, said Aristotle, are forms of imitation. They differ from each other in the mediums, the manners, and the objects of their imitation. Some imitate with color and form, others with rhythm, harmony, or language. The object of artistic imitation is nature, including human nature. In epic and drama the objects imitated are men in action; in lyric poetry the principal objects of imitation are men's moods, feelings, and impressions. Art, then, is essentially *imitation of nature*. As Shakespeare put it in Hamlet's advice to the players, the object of acting is, "to hold . . . the mirror up to nature; to show virtue her own feature, scorn her own image, and the very age and body of the time [its] form and pressure."

But art did not mean to Aristotle a servile copying, a photographic reproduction, of nature. Poetry, he said, represents not what has happened, but what *might* happen, what a certain kind of person is likely or is bound to do or say on a given occasion, how he would speak or act according to the law of probability or necessity. As S. H. Butcher explained:

> Poetry is an expression of the universal element in human life. . . . Fine are eliminates what is transient and particular and reveals the permanent and essential features of the original. It discovers the form toward which an object tends, the result which nature strives to attain, but rarely or never can attain. Beneath the individual it finds the universal. It passes beyond the bare reality given by nature, and expresses a purified form of reality disengaged from accident, and freed from conditions which thwart its development. The real and ideal from this point of view are not opposites, as they are sometimes conceived to be. The ideal is the real, but rid of contradictions, unfolding itself according to the laws of its own being, apart from alien influences and the disturbances of chance. [The artist] aims at something better than the actual. He reproduces a new thing, not the actual thing of experience, not a copy of reality, but a higher reality.[7]

A work of art, then, is "an idealized representation of human life." The peculiar function of the artist is to "to divine nature's unfulfilled inten-

---

[6] M. H. Abrams, *The Mirror and the Lamp: Romantic Theory and the Critical Tradition* (New York: The Norton Library, 1958).

[7] S. H. Butcher, *Aristotle's Theory of Poetry and Fine Art* (London: Macmillan & Co., Ltd., 1895), pp. 151–25. Available also from Dover Publications, Inc., New York, 1951, with an Introduction by John Gassner.

tion," and reveal her ideal in a product apparent to the senses of the beholders. "The end of the fine arts is to give pleasure or rational enjoyment," not to the artist but to the spectator, who is conceived as "a man of sound aesthetic instincts," "a man of educated taste." In the development of this theory by Horace, the Roman poet-critic, and Sir Philip Sydney, the English poet-critic, and many others, the aim of poetry was defined as "delightful teaching," or "to profit and delight."

The Romantic Theory

Perhaps the clearest and most striking statement of the romantic or expressive theory is that of Wordsworth, "Poetry is the spontaneous overflow of powerful feelings." It was echoed by Byron when he said, "Thus to their extreme verge the passions brought/Dash into poetry, which is but a passion." Wordsworth modified his statement by saying further that poetry is "emotion recollected in tranquility." His own poems were carefully meditated both before and after composition, and it was long and deep contemplation that prepared him to speak spontaneously. And the carefully constructed and highly regular stanzas of Byron's "Childe Harold" and "Don Juan" are anything but spontaneous blurts of raw passion. However, Wordsworth's influential writings mark a turning-point in literary theory, shifting the focus of study from fidelity to truth and nature and the demands of the audience to the emotions of the poet. The definition of poetry as "expression of emotion" became firmly established and is still current.

With some writers the criterion became sincerity: Did the poet represent his feelings truly? Was he true to himself? This shifted attention to the poet's biography and sociological background—a congenial study in a society that has an almost pathological itch to know the private lives of its prominent members. The questions asked by modern criticism, says Stanley E. Hyman, are "What is the significance of the work in relation to the artist's life, his childhood, his family, his deepest needs and desires? What is its relation to his social group, his class, his economic livelihood, the larger patterns of his society?"[8]

With other writers a criterion of art that flourished for a time, and may still be employed, was merely to ask whether the artist did well what he attempted to do. There was little consideration of whether the thing he attempted was worth doing. If he set out merely to make a mud pie, he was to be judged by how well he made it, and if he made it well he was an artist, and his pie was a worthy object of art. By this theory, one who reads well an ordinary news report deserves as much credit as one who reads successfully a difficult poem by T. S. Eliot.

[8] Stanley Edgar Hyman, *The Armed Vision* (New York: Alfred A. Knopf, Inc., 1948), p. 6.

Then came a group of critics who, says Louis Untermeyer, propounded the notion:

. . . that poetry was written not so much for delight as for the covert expression of multiple meanings. Being such, poetry obviously required dissection and thus this school became so busy searching for devious meanings, remote associations, and levels of irony and ambiguity that . . . it took the life out of narratives, dismembered sonnets, and twisted twelve-line lyrics through twenty paragraphs of tortured prose.[9]

Often their devious tracing of associations, conscious or unconscious, and ingenious ferreting out of "symbolist suggestions" are merely exercises of their own imaginations.

In reaction to this theory there developed another, and quite different, concept of poetry which has become, says Abrams, "the central position of present-day critics," the concept that "a poem should not mean but be," that it is "an object in itself, a self-contained universe of discourse, of which we cannot demand that it be true to nature, but only, that it be true to itself."[10]

Chaos in Modern Art

Whether because of these conflicting theories or in spite of them, or because of the loss of traditional standards in a changing world, we cannot say, but there is no doubt that a great deal of modern poetry has become so chaotic that it is no longer appealing or intelligible to the general reader. The same chaotic condition prevails also in the other arts—music, painting, sculpture, and drama. Current criticism and comment abound in such disparaging terms as headless and footless writing, shredded prose, tiresome exhibitionism, sterile intellectualism, infantile barbarism, systematic confusion, mad mouthfuls of language, verbal anarchy, fractured grammar, studied obscurity. T. S. Eliot's lines in "The Hollow Men" are applicable:

> Shape without form, shade without colour,
> Paralysed force, gesture without motion.

DEFENCE OF CHAOS. Some modern critics earnestly attempt to explain and defend this chaos, only to be condemned and ridiculed by other critics. One poet-critic declares, "Poetry reviews are the worst written, sloppiest, silliest critical pieces published anywhere today," and cites this example from a review in a distinguished quarterly: "An utopian and oral poetry like his refuses to be an object to be pointed at as I am now doing;

[9] Louis Untermeyer, *Modern British Poetry* (New York: Harcourt, Brace & World, Inc., 1962), p. 21.

[10] *Op. cit.*, pp. 282, 272.

it tries to be speech that does not know the negative, therefore adds instead of subtracts, and subsumes contraries in its affirmative sweep."[11] Too often we find in modern criticism a fog of professional jargon that only confuses and obfuscates. As David Daiches has said, "The gap between the experience of the ordinary educated reader and the pretentious analyses of the professional critics is already so great that serious criticism of poetry has ceased to serve any social function at all."[12] Bernard Berenson, acknowledged the greatest authority on painting in our times, wrote at the age of ninety, "None of my young contemporaries write as if they enjoyed a work of art. They attack it with questions, with problems, with psychoanalysis, with recondite learning, with didactical acumen, with metaphysical conumdrum, with logic absolute. . . . For the 'youngs' one artifact is as good as another, because they are interested in events and not what works of art do to us."[13] He might have been speaking of *literary* critics.

Some critics read into a poem dark and subtle meanings, Freudian implications, and esoteric philosophies that the poet himself never dreamed of. "Nothing is easier," says David Daiches, "for a critic with any skill at analysis than to maintain that no poem can be good unless it is complex and paradoxical and then proceed to demonstrate the qualities of complexity and paradox in the poems he likes and to show their absence in those he dislikes."[14]

UNCRITICAL CRITICS. There are also uncritical critics who lavish on new poems an extravagance of praise which cannot possibly be deserved. Standards of literary judgment have always been slippery since they must be largely subjective, but they seem lately to have slipped beyond all reason. Anything labeled "poem" may get respectful attention and may be solemnly pronounced "great." This is why we need "touchstones" of excellence. And those young poets who haven't yet been able to get their lives or their art adjusted to the realities of modern existence and can only scream in revolt are often regarded with pity and sympathy as tragic victims of a changing world (hasn't it *always* been changing?) living under the awful shadow of the impending bomb. Beethoven, Shelley, and Keats also lived in a time of crisis, the aftermath of the French Revolution, and amid the destructive conquests of Napoleon, and they also suffered personal torments and tragedies, yet in their works they achieved tranquility and beauty. What we expect of genius is that it will create order in the midst of disorder. As John Gassner says, "Art creates an idea of order

[11] William Jay Smith, "The New Poetry," *Harper's Magazine*, September, 1963.
[12] David Daiches, *A Study of Literature* (Ithaca, N.Y.: Cornell University Press, 1948), p. 167.
[13] Quoted in *The Reporter*, July 18, 1963, p. 55.
[14] *Op. cit.*, pp. 160–61.

where, to the inartistic or unphilosophical observer, life is only a whirl of action and a chaos of emotion. . . . The crude matter of life assumes significance from the shaping hand of the artist."[15]   Our best poets understand this.   Reginald L. Cook observes, "When Blake says, 'Nature has no Outline, but Imagination has,' he is saying what Frost also knows, that art orders chaos—makes, as it were, little bits of radio-active clarity."[16]

ECCENTRICITY IS NOT GENIUS.   Of the many aspiring young poets writing today, not all are geniuses, though some may pose as such.   Some have no better claim to distinction than rebellion against convention.   It has become a current vogue to attempt to create poetry by repudiating all its traditional forms.   Rhyme, rhythm, meter, stanza form, assonance, alliteration, harmony, even punctuation and grammar are thrown overboard, apparently to achieve novelty and originality.   In music and painting this trend is even more prevalent.   Obscurity is sought as a virtue.   There are those, said Donald Stauffer, "who construct puzzles from their unique experiences which only an omniscient God can unriddle," or which can be understood only when they "float upon a bottomless quagmire of annotation."[17]   As Peter Viereck said, their cult of obscurity is stifling the growth of poetry; they "forbid anybody except crossword-puzzle decoders to get fun out of poetry, not to mention beauty."[18]   And when this chaos fails to attract an audience, the defence is made that since at times an occasional genius was not appreciated in his own day, *they* fail to win appreciation because they are geniuses, too advanced for their time.   Even T. S. Eliot, who himself requires some decoding, has felt the need to protest against this preposterous view.   There is a difference, he says, "between the writer who is merely eccentric and grotesque, and the genuine poet: the former may have feelings that are unique, but which cannot be shared, or are not worth sharing, and which are therefore socially useless; while the genuine poet discovers new shades and variations of sensibility in which others can participate."[19]

We should not assume that all self-expression is art, and all eccentricity genius.   Any child can express himself by daubing a paper with paint, beating a keyboard with his rag doll, or linking syllables into meaningless nonsense, but in so doing he does not become an artist, deserving of our

[15] "Aristotelean Literary Criticism," *Aristotle's Theory of Poetry and Fine Art* (New York: Dover Publications, Inc., 1951), p. xli.
[16] Reginald L. Cook, *The Dimensions of Robert Frost* (New York: Holt, Rinehart & Winston, Inc.), p. 115.
[17] Donald Stauffer, *The Golden Nightingale* (New York: The Macmillan Co., 1949), p. 27.
[18] See John Ciardi's *Mid-Century American Poets* (New York: Twain Publishers, Inc., 1950), p. 29.
[19] *Op. cit.*, p. 113.

study and respect. Society has always been burdened with would-be geniuses, many of them properly consigned to asylums. We are too easily taken in by writers who affect a superior air and solemnly assert their own importance. Our gullibility in the presence of such creatures was appropriately satirized by W. S. Gilbert in his opera, *Patience:*

> And every one will say,
> As you walk your mystic way
> "If this young man expresses himself in terms too deep for *me,*
> Why, what a very singularly deep young man this deep young man
> must be!"

MADNESS IN POETS. There is some warrant for believing that poets are partly mad. Plato seemed to think so, and Shakespeare grouped them with lunatics and lovers. Many artists have been so negligent of social conventions that they were regarded by their contemporaries as more than a little queer. But madness in an artist's behavior does not necessarily mean madness in his work. Indeed, there is abundant reason to believe that real artists, as revealed by their works, are the sanest and most normal of men. Their madness is a kind of inspiration which enables them to see more deeply into the heart of things than ordinary mortals can. The highest tribute we can pay an artist is not to declare that he is so eccentric or "original" that nobody understands him, but to regard him as so sane and normal that his appeal is universal. Poetry, said Shelley, "is the record of the best and happiest moments of the happiest and best minds." And note well T. S. Eliot's statement that "the greatest poets are those who have given the most pleasure to the greatest number, and the greatest *variety,* of human beings, throughout the period of time since they wrote."[20] That is the test of their greatness.

Universality

Such a test implies a universal quality in poetry, something basic that appeals to all human beings, and draws from all the same response. Poets write for an audience, not merely to express themselves. Wordsworth, says Professor Abrams, had "a basic standard for establishing validity, whether in the aims of the poet or the criteria of the critic—the common nature of man, always and everywhere. . . . This way of thinking depends on the assumption that human nature in its passions and sensibilities no less than its reason is everywhere fundamentally the same."[21] The words and voice-tones of Robert Frost, says Professor Reginald L. Cook,

[20] *Op. cit.,* p. 111.
[21] *Op. cit.,* p. 104.

"are simply words and tones common to man. . . . Anyone can read them, determining the pitch, volume and tempo for himself."[22] John Ciardi would be a little more selective. The proper language for criticism, he thinks, and also presumably the proper language for poetry, is not that of the man on the street but "the language that would be spoken on the street if every man on it spoke his mother tongue with love and pride."[23]

These statements reinforce the implication of those quoted earlier about poetry as remembrance—the implication that in general poetry has a common appeal for all normal people and can be understood and appreciated by them. We can ignore those few poets who cultivate obscurity, or write for a private coterie of their own kind, since our readings will be prepared for a general audience who will, we hope, respond normally to the meaning of a poem.

OUR DIFFERENCES. The general public, however, is made up of individuals who in many respects are not alike, and certainly, as many writers maintain, they differ in their susceptibility to poetry. Some teachers go so far as to encourage each reader to take from a poem whatever meaning he likes. And of course a student who delights in rebellion against mental discipline, or who has a deep conceit of the superiority of his own mind, greets such freedom with glee. "No one has a right to tell me what I must like," he declares, with self-satisfied misstatement of the problem, and will not allow anyone to point out meanings and values in a poem that he does not see if left to himself. That we differ from each other in many respects is obvious to all, and modern psychologists have had a field day in discovering and pointing out these differences. They find that since our response to any new stimulus is conditioned by our past experiences we therefore differ in our responses, our habits, our emotions, our thoughts, and our personalities. They have found also that we differ in our muscular, nervous, and glandular structures, and so cannot be expected to respond in the same way or in the same degree to outer stimuli. Some of us are sluggish and inert; others are emotional and dynamic. Some are sensitive and easily moved; others are calloused and indifferent. And they have discovered remarkable variations in our imaginative susceptibilities.

Now all this is important in the appreciation of poetry and in the interpretation of it for others. If Andrew Marvell's line, "Ripe apples drop about my head," recalls to one person an occasion when he was painfully

---

[22] Reginald L. Cook, *Op. cit.*, p. 211.
[23] John Ciardi, "Dialogue with an Audience," *The Saturday Review*, September 14, 1963, p. 27.

injured by a falling apple, and to another, only the lush abundance of autumn; if Thomas Gray's line, "The ploughman homeward plods his weary way," suggests to one a dirty and bedraggled farmer, reeking with sweat and the smell of horses, and to another, an idealized rustic, contented with a day's work well done, how can we talk of unversality or uniformity of response and appreciation?

OUR SIMILARITIES.   The answer would seem to be that though in a particular case our responses may differ, we are yet basically alike in our susceptibilities and impulses.   This is the view of I. A. Richards in his highly influential *Principles of Literary Criticism*, the book, says Stanley Hyman, with which modern criticism began.   "Within racial boundaries," says Richards, "and perhaps within the limits of certain very general types, *many impulses are common to all men.*   Their stimuli and the courses which they take seem to be uniform."   He continues, "Some impulses remain the same, taking the same course on the same occasions, from age to age, from prehistoric times until today."   He finds that for every art there is "a type of impulse which is extraordinarily uniform."[24]   This should explain why the poems of Homer, Sappho, and Theocritus still have charms for us after all the intervening centuries.

As to the fact that we do not all see images in the same way, Richards says, "The sensory qualities of images, their vivacity, clearness, fullness of detail and so on, do not bear any constant relation to their effects."   Some people, he says, seem to enjoy poetry without experiencing any imagery at all.   "Something takes the place of vivid images in these people."   The effects of a poem may be the same on two people though they do not see the same images at all, for "images which are different in their sensory qualities may have the same effects."[25]

This topic of uniformity has been treated with some fullness because the preoccupation of many writers and teachers with our individual differences has very harmful results in oral interpretation.   It encourages the student to be satisfied with a superficial impression of a poem and to give it a purely personal interpretation.   It absolves him from responsibility to seek out its *essential* meaning and to keep it dominant while not neglecting the various lower layers of meaning that may be found in its images, its suggestions, its sound effects, its rhythms, etc.   It harms those who doubt their ability to appreciate literature—who wonder whether nature has not deprived them of some gift that others have.   And it encourages the bumptious and the egotistical to regard their opinions and reactions as entirely satisfactory and beyond any need of improvement.

[24] I. A. Richards, *Principles of Literary Criticism* (New York: Harcourt, Brace & World, Inc., 1948), pp. 190–93.
[25] *Ibid.*, pp. 119, 120, 123.

Some Conclusions

We have wandered far in the briar patch of criticism. Have we emerged at last into open air and a clear view? No. *But we have seen the patch,* and that is important. One who is aware of the wide divergence of views among the analysts of poetry will not be inclined to accept as gospel whatever opinions he may stumble upon in his reading.

If any firm conclusions can be drawn from this discussion, they will be about as follows: Every normal person can understand poetry and is in some degree susceptible to its appeal. Granted that a poem may have more than one meaning, may be appreciated on several levels, and that various readers may react to it in various ways, yet it has at its core an *essential* experience that should be the same for all properly susceptible readers. This meaning is best defined in terms of the poem's effect on a properly qualified reader, or rather on a considerable number of qualified readers. The reactions of these qualified readers will not vary materially from their norm. That is, there is a *core* of meaning, and a *norm* of response to it. Some readers will come closer to this center than others. But one who gets too far away from it fails in full appreciation, though he may respond to some peripheral aspects of the poem.

How do we identify the "qualified reader" of poetry—the ideal critic, we may call him? Three traits are indispensable, and perhaps they will suffice. First, he must be sensitive to the values that are characteristic of poetry, not merely a cold scientific analyst. He must be gifted with imagination and capable of feeling. Second, he must be a man of educated taste, one familiar with the poetic tradition from Homer to Robert Frost, his mind well stocked with the best examples of literature, so that he can use them as a basis of comparison in judging the value of a poem. Third, he must be a person of good judgment, level-headed, cautious in forming opinions, not given to snap decisions or impulsive thinking.

In general, the meaning of a poem is not factual, but emotive. It will sharpen our imaginative awareness of experience and will give pleasure. To say that a poem expresses emotion does not necessarily mean that the poet talks about his emotions. Rather he sets forth the symbols, objects, situations, events, images that evoke emotion in the reader, together with such formal elements as meter, rhyme, assonance, word music, stanza pattern, etc.

This is about as close as we can come to a definition of what poetry is and how it is to be evaluated. The wide range of opinions cited should protect these conclusions from any charge of prejudice or dogmatism. And the looseness of these formulations allows the interpreter to do a great deal of thinking for himself. Indeed, it requires him to do so.

Oral Interpretation as an Art

Is there an art of interpreting poetry vocally which corresponds to the art of the poet, the painter, and the sculptor? May an interpreter be a creative artist, imitating nature and expressing emotion as do other artists?

Interpretation is an ambiguous word. In language translation it means transferring meaning from the symbols of one language to the symbols of another without any change or loss. Similarly, in the interpretation of classical music the conductor or soloist is expected to present Beethoven and Brahms as pure Beethoven and Brahms, with no intrusion of his personal idiosyncrasies. He will win praise from the critics by being faithful to the established text and tradition, not by innovations; although there are, of course, minor variations among conductors and performers. But in popular music, interpreting seems to mean embellishing or modifying a composition to conform to the personal style of the performer, sometimes transforming it so completely that it is hardly recognizable. Each performer is expected to have a personal style which distinguishes his interpretations from those of other performers of the same music.

It is plain enough that an interpreter of literature or music is not a creator, but rather a re-creator, producing not something of his own but re-producing what has already been composed. The interpreter of literature will do best to follow the example of the interpreter of classical music and concentrate on faithful reproduction of his text. But in translating from the medium of printed words to the medium of speech he has a great deal more freedom of expression than a musician. The musician's score prescribes melodies, harmonies, tempos, changes in volume, crescendos, retards, accents, etc., which are not in the printed text of a poem. These elements the oral reader must supply for himself, as well as discovering various attitudes, feelings, implications, suggestions, overtones, levels of meaning, etc., which may be only dimly intimated in the text of a poem. In expressing these elements he has considerable scope for invention, for creative artistry.

Traditionally, of course, the spoken word came first. In early times poetry was composed orally and not written down at all. It lived on men's tongues and was generally sung, often with instrumental accompaniment. When writing was invented, the written symbols could represent only the words of a poem. They were incapable of representing the tones and inflections and bodily behavior of the reciter on which so much of a poem's value depends, and modern printing still omits such elements. Reading aloud, then, does not present poetry in a new light; it restores to it elements which it once had, but which print fails to represent.

Poets and critics are generally aware of this lack. "As a substitute for the classic lyre or romantic harp," Wordsworth required for his poetry "an

animated or impassioned recitation." Lane Cooper, a cautious and author-
itative scholar, once stated dogmatically, "Every bit of literature properly
so called that history has to show is intended, not for the eye primarily,
but for the ear. Every line of Shakespeare, every line of Milton, is meant
to be pronounced, cannot be duly appreciated until it is pronounced."[26]

So it is in pronouncing poetry that a reader may qualify in some sense
as a creative artist. Students of drama often say that an actor may create
a part, though his lines are already prescribed for him. In the same sense
an oral reader of poetry may create by revealing meanings that seem to
lie beneath the cold type. In descriptions and in the speeches of various
persons in a poem his insight and imagination may not only reproduce
what the poet has said, but amplify and even improve upon it. Thus he
may be, like other artists, an imitator of nature and an expresser of emotion. There will be further discussion of this matter in later chapters.

Qualifications for Appreciation

But artists are people with special endowments, or rather, as we have
seen, with certain endowments more highly developed than in ordinary
people. If you are to be an artist in interpretation, you need to consider
what endowments are most needed. Chiefly they are those mentioned
above as desirable in a "qualified reader" of poetry.

First, there is the need for sensitivity to poetic effects. The language
of poetry is not the language of science, or history, or the morning newspaper. It speaks to the imagination and the emotions, rather than to reason, and requires for its appreciation what Chesterton called "the virginity
of the spirit which enjoys with astonishment and fear." Preoccupation
with modern science and mechanics will unfit us for such enjoyment.
Against their contrary pull we should try to win back some of our childhood acceptance of mystery and fancy and ambiguity, our early delight in
the sounds of words and the flow of rhythm, our susceptibility to images
and symbols, for this is the stuff of which poetry is made. If we are so
literal-minded that we dispute as untrue such a statement as Richard
Lovelace's:

> Stone walls do not a prison make,
> Nor iron bars a cage;

if we do not relish the sounds of the words and their suggestions in such a
passage as Tennyson's:

> The moan of doves in immemorial elms
> And murmuring of innumerable bees;

[26] Lane Cooper, *Two Views of Education* (New Haven: Yale University Press,
1922), p. 115.

we are not properly attuned for appreciation of poetry. (Note the pretended ridicule of poetic language in Ogden Nash's "Very Like a Whale," page 162.)

Our susceptibility to poetry will depend largely upon how extensively we have been exposed to it, how familiar we have become with its language and idiom. Robert Frost once said, "A poem is best read in the light of all the other poems ever written." Poetry confronts the reader with such phrases as mournful numbers, weeds of peace, a brow of Egypt, casting the body's vest aside, trampling out the vintage, reeking tube and iron shard, flowing cups with no allaying Thames, shuffle off this mortal coil, etc. Such language is likely to be understood only by one who has read a great deal of poetry. As Wordsworth said, "An *accurate* taste in poetry, and in all the other arts, as Joshua Reynolds has observed, is an *acquired* talent, which can only be produced by thought and a long continued intercourse with the best models of composition."[27]

Poetic language may be highly figurative, its sentences are often inverted or elliptical, its vocabulary may contain many rare or obsolete words. Poets are fond of double meanings, of paradox, and irony. Their allusions to persons, places, events, myths, legends, and to other literary works are often so rich and various that we can follow them only with the aid of reference books. But we can, by the method Wordsworth described, "by thought and long-continued intercourse with the best models," come to appreciate and enjoy what they write.

The Need and the Rewards of Thorough Study

Fortunately many of our best poems are simple and easily understood, and there is no point in torturing them to extract meanings that are not there. But there are many also which can only be appreciated after long and careful study, and which will reward such pains by profit and delight. Few students realize how completely it is possible for a judicious and sympathetic critic to know a poem. By study of the poet's work, his methods and habits of production, he may come to know the poet's intentions better than the poet himself knows them. He might even be able to correct the poet's less successful passages, bring them up to the level of the best ones, and thus make them more typical of the poet than what was originally written. The artist, we have found, tries to represent nature in its ideal form, to do so by eliminating what is transient and temporary and accidental and revealing what is essential and typical. As Joshua Reynolds said, "he corrects nature by herself, her imperfect state by her more perfect." And just so the critic may then correct the poet by himself, his imperfect work by his more perfect. Denis Diderot, the eighteenth cen-

---

[27] "Preface" to the *Lyrical Ballads,* 1815.

tury philosopher, thought that an actor might go even further and *enhance* the ideal type created by the poet. "Sometimes," he said, "the poet feels more deeply than the actor; sometimes, and perhaps oftener, the actor's conception is stronger than the poet's." He cites Voltaire's astonished exclamation when he heard a brilliant actress in a part that he had written: "Did I really write that?" At that moment, Diderot says, "the ideal type in the speaking of the part went well beyond the poet's ideal in the writing of it."[28] Similar examples can be found in the modern theatre.

A modern composer of music has declared that he never understood his own work until he heard it conducted by Dimitri Metropoulos. "A composer's idea of his own work is not necessarily the correct one," said Morton Gould, and "he understands my work better than I do." He tells of his difficulty in conducting one of his own works, his inability to "make it come off," his feeling that he had written it wrong. Then he went to hear Metropoulos conduct it, and he said, "Here he was conducting my own work, . . . and suddenly I heard it the way I had intended it."[29]

Note that this penetrating interpretation was based not upon a Freudian analysis of the composer but upon study of his composition. A real work of art exists quite apart from the artist who created it. A poem's value does not depend upon who wrote it. A good poem is still a good poem if its author is unknown. If it should suddenly be discovered that the sonnets attributed to Shakespeare were written by someone else, their value as sonnets would not be decreased. A poem lives by its own inherent merit, and it is the work itself that we should study. We should go back of the poet's words, *through* his words, to the thoughts, feelings, and impressions that apparently moved him to creation to discover, if we can, his intentions, and try to express *them*. And with our added resources of voice and action we may produce a work even better than the one on the page.

Preparation for Reading Poetry

How shall we proceed in preparing a poem for reading aloud? The first steps have been explained in previous chapters. You must analyze the sentences to determine what they mean, noting which words are important to the thought and which are subordinate, how they are grouped in units of meaning and the relation of these groups to each other, taking special notice of ellipses and inverted word order. Very important is the poet's attitude or intention concerning the statements he makes and the mood, feeling, or emotion both of the parts and the whole—melancholy,

---

[28] Denis Diderot, *The Paradox of Acting*, trans. by W. H. Pollock (London: Chatto and Windus, 1883), p. 55.

[29] See Richard Boyer, "Maestro on a Mountaintop," *The New Yorker*, April 15, 1950, p. 45.

delight, wonder, alarm, sorrow, contentment, cheerfulness, hope, courage, desire, satiety, love, benevolence, pride, pity, indignation, innocence, piety, reverence, and the like. A later chapter will discuss more fully the emotional quality of poetry. You must work out some method of making your oral reading vivid and moving for your hearers. You must consider the demands of the poem for a full-sustained voicing of its lines. You must analyze the words, letter by letter, to determine their sound values and plan to pronounce them so that all these values will be realized. You must study the formal elements of the verse, its rhyme, meter, and stanza pattern, and consider whether these metrical effects will need to be amplified or minimized when you read the poem aloud.

The first thing to do, however, is to read the poem through attentively, letting it do its work upon you, and getting all you can of the pleasure of first acquaintance. On most occasions this first impression will be the only one your hearers will get, though they will *hear* the poem and you are only *seeing* it on paper. Investigate at once all unfamiliar words and allusions and master their meaning and pronunciation. Then examine the thought content of the poem to discover its "plain sense." Just what does the poem say in literal prose? Reduce it to a brief paraphrase.

Analysis of "The Solitary Reaper"

Let us illustrate with Wordsworth's "The Solitary Reaper," which you will find at the end of this chapter. Your paraphrase will read something like this:

Look at that hill girl harvesting grain all alone and singing a sad song. Either stop, or go by quietly. Listen! The valley is full of her song.

It is more welcome than a nightingale's song to tired travelers in some oasis in the Arabian desert. It is more thrilling than a cuckoo's song in the quiet Hebrides islands.

What is she singing about? Maybe for some long past troubles, or maybe for some recent difficulty that might occur again.

Anyhow she sang as if she would never stop. I saw her, and I listened without moving. And as I went on up the hill I remembered her song.

This seems unpromising stuff for poetry, but Wordsworth has made of it a poem that has delighted thousands of readers for a hundred years and more. What values can be found in it that will delight you, and that can be communicated to your hearers?

The incident related is simple enough, though you may never have had a comparable experience. Perhaps Wordsworth hadn't either. He may have invented it all. But the incident and the scene can easily be imagined. Take all the details he has given you and try to re-create the scene as vividly as he did. The language too is simple, as is the sentence form. There are no troublesome ellipses, inversions, or condensations, and the phrases are so clear and uncomplicated that a child can grasp them. The meter flows along smoothly and the rhymes are frequent and regular, so much so that an uncritical reader may yield too much to them and create mere singsong. There are no brilliant metaphors—none at all except such threadbare ones as have long since lost their metaphorical meaning—the vale "overflowing" with sound, the bird's song "breaking" the silence, the numbers "flowing." The language is remarkably literal for a poem so moving. There are not even any vivid descriptions, either of the girl or of her song, though the poet does give attention to the effect of the song.

That is, we seem to have here a poem that is lacking in all the usual characteristics of poetry. Of what, then, does its effectiveness consist? What are the poetic values that we must try to communicate to our hearers as we read it?

INDEFINITENESS OF THE POET'S IMPRESSION. Let us note first what it is about this Highland girl that impresses the poet as he comes upon her suddenly in this isolated valley. It is apparent that he is deeply moved, but with what feeling? Is he delighted? Startled? Awestruck? Surprised? If he had put his feeling into one adjective, what would it be? Behold her! Isn't she—what? Beautiful? Charming? Odd? Industrious? Courageous? Graceful? Romantic? The adjective is not there. You will not find it anywhere in the poem. If you will note in the title the word "solitary," and in the first stanza the words, "single," "solitary," "by herself," and "alone," it will be apparent that he is impressed by her aloneness. Traditionally harvesting was a communal activity, the entire community working together, and often singing and dancing together in the ceremonies that developed around this annual chore. Was it this departure from ancient custom that impressed the poet? He doesn't say. Here is one of the vaguenesses or ambiguities characteristic of much good poetry. We are given the essential details of the scene—the Highland girl, alone, reaping and singing, cutting and binding the grain as she sings a melancholy song—and we form our own impression. In your interpretation of the poem, then, give your hearers the details in a clear sympathetic voice and trust them to be moved as the poet intended.

The rest of the poem is mostly about the song, but there too a specific description is lacking. The poet deals chiefly with the effect of the song. We are told only that it is "melancholy" and "plaintive," and that he finds it "welcome" and "thrilling." He compares it to the songs of birds, and speculates as to its theme.

Since this poem can hardly be said to contain any deep philosophical thought, any penetrating insight into nature, any brilliant flights of imagination, or even any vivid descriptions of persons or things, we must look elsewhere for the sources of its poetic effects. Certainly a large part of its effectiveness depends upon the choice and arrangements of the words, upon their sounds and their connotations, both singly and in combination. Though the language is simple and familiar, the wording is distinctive and somehow right. To test this, try to alter the wording without destroying the poetic quality of the lines. Instead of "Behold her, single in the field," try this wording: "Regard her in the field alone." Instead of "Breaking the silence of the seas/Among the farthest Hebrides," try "Disturbing the ocean quiet in remote northern islands." Or in what is probably the best-known and best-loved line of the poem, "For old, unhappy, far-off things," try the effect of merely changing the word order: "For far-off, old, un-happy things," or "For unhappy, far-off, old things."

Is it not apparent that any alteration in the language destroys the poetry? The tone and feel of the lines, their essential meaning, is lost if the wording is changed. Here is a demonstration that good poetry cannot be translated, for the essential poetry of the lines lies in the sounds of the words, in their arrangement and their relation to each other. What they suggest to us depends partly, perhaps largely, upon the pattern they form. A part of this pattern is the rhythm which their arrangement creates, and the rhymes.

In your oral reading of the poem you must give careful attention to these subtle "sound effects" and the more or less vague suggestions of meaning and feeling that arise from them. These suggestions will vary among your hearers, and none may feel the poem in quite the same way that you do. Some will be more susceptible to the literal ideas, some to the emotions, some to the images, and some to the sounds of the words and the meter; but there should be a universal effect which is substan-tially the same for all. The fact of individual differences and sus-ceptibilities should not encourage you to give the poem an individual interpretation which expresses merely your personal reactions to the stimuli. It should rather encourage you to give full value to all the stimuli the poem contains so that each individual listener can respond according to his own natural bent.

THE MOOD OF THE POEM. Though Wordsworth does not define his feeling as he recalls this incident of his travels, he does not leave us in any serious doubt about it: The sight of this girl and the sound of her song formed a "welcome" interlude in his journey, and he cherished the experi-ence long after he has passed on up the hill. It was, of course, a pleasant experience. It would be absurd to interpret the poem as criticism of a social system that requires women to labor in the fields. Prevailing through it is a kind of wonder, not sharply defined. But that sort of experience is common to all of us. We are struck by something we see and we exclaim, "Just look at that. Isn't that a picture!" without defining, or being able to define, just how we are impressed. Such vague moods in poetry are not the less moving; indeed they may be more moving because they are not sharply delineated. Quite naturally we ask what a poem means in order that we may know how we ought to feel about it. But here the "meaning," whatever it is, will not help us. We might note a statement by T. S. Eliot that the chief use of "meaning" in some poetry is "to satisfy one habit of the reader, to keep his mind diverted and quiet, while the poem does its work upon him: much as the imaginary burglar is always provided with a bit of nice meat for the house-dog." A poem of this kind may be said to burglarize the reader through its mood. Or, to put it another way, the mood is in large part the meaning.

In a short lyric poem the mood is nearly always constant and continuous from beginning to end. In "The Solitary Reaper," the mood, which we may characterize as a kind of pleasant contemplative wonder, must be established at the very beginning of the poem and maintained consistently to the end. And do not suppose that the melancholy of the girl's song must induce a like melancholy in the poet. The contemplation of melancholy can be pleasant. As Shelley said, "Our sweetest songs are those that tell of saddest thought." The mood should be established on the very first word "Behold."

TEMPO. One of the most important elements in the effect of a poem on those who hear it read is its tempo, the rate at which it moves. Some verses are intended to gallop, others to move along as slowly as a funeral procession. It will not do to give one the tempo of the other. A great deal of our best poetry is characterized by a mood of resigned romantic melancholy, often a melancholy that seems to be enjoyed for its own sake. Such poetry must be read with measured deliberation. To hurry it is to destroy it. Time is needed for the images to take form and the mood to establish itself, for images, mood, and meaning are all one and cannot be isolated from each other. Such lines must be lingered over, caressed lovingly with the voice, and uttered with an almost level intonation. To speak them with the crisp tones of sprightly conversation is to destroy them utterly. Avoid also making the lines choppy by cutting them up into separate phrases with pauses between. Such poetry should have the sustained even fluidity of song, what musicians call a *sostenuto* quality, all the syllables held full length and tied together by a continuous unbroken flow of voice. In such reading you run the risk of monotony, but a certain amount of monotony may be desirable and will not be a *dull* monotony if your imagination is alert, if images are sharply visualized, and if your feeling is strong and genuine.

Summary

Needless to say, you can make this whole process come off successfully only when you reflect in your voice and behavior the feeling that moved the poet. And for both you and your audience the proper feeling can be generated only from the images of the poem and from its movement and meter and the sounds of the words. You must, then, both during preparation and while you are reading, keep your imagination active and alert so that the images are vividly realized.

Since listeners differ in their susceptibility to poetry, some being affected more by one element in it and some by another, the interpreter must take pains to present fully and adequately all of the elements of which it is composed, and not merely those to which he personally is most susceptible. To represent adequately the "plain sense" of a poem, to harmonize this with the demands of rhythm and rhyme without neglecting either, to give full value to the sounds of the words so that both their identity and their emotional overtones are clear, to make the images sharp and distinct and to allow oneself to be appropriately moved by them, and while doing this to create a harmonious whole, a unified work of art, demands a very high order of intelligence and a constant alertness of mind during the process of reading. If you possess these intellectual qualities, and if besides you are one of those persons whom Shelley described as "of the most delicate sensibility and the most enlarged imagination," and if you utter the poem with a voice that has good quality and is flexible and responsive to all shades of meaning and feeling, you should be able to create, or re-create, a genuine work of art that will profit and delight your hearers.

PLAN OF STUDY

1. In relaxed leisure read the poem through silently and thoughtfully, noting especially any fragrance it contains of your own past experience.
2. Read it aloud trying to give full expression to all the rhythms and harmonies of which you are aware.
3. After investigating unfamiliar words, references, and allusions, and unraveling any tangled grammatical constructions, translate the poem into a prose paraphrase, then read it again with special attention to what it says, its thought element, as explained in Chapter 2.
4. Analyze the attitude, intention, mood, and feeling expressed in the poem. Be alert for paradox and irony. Read it aloud again with sympathetic reflection of these elements.
5. Analyze its rhythm, rhyme, and stanza pattern. Consider whether for best effect these need to be accentuated or obscured when you read aloud.

6. Note striking examples of word music, alliteration, assonance, etc. and any phrases that seem particularly beautiful or apt.
7. Analyze the poem's truth to nature in its descriptions, metaphors, moods, and emotions.
8. Discover the symbols, images, situations, and events that evoke emotion and define what emotion they evoke.
9. Try to penetrate behind the poet's words to the experiences and emotions that stimulated him to write, and let them color your speaking of the poem.
10. With all these elements held firmly in mind, practice reading the poem again and again, but not all at one sitting; practice at intervals. If a recording of the poem is available, by all means make use of it, but only after you have made your own analysis.

CRITERIA

1. Did the reader seem to find in the poem an expression of his own thought and feeling and take pleasure in communicating them?
2. Did he understand the poem and express accurately its thought, mood, and feeling?
3. Was he appropriately moved by it?
4. Was he responsive to its rhythm, tempo, word music, beauty of phrase? Did he achieve a proper mean between monotonous singsong and prose?
5. Was his interpretation normal and appropriate, free from personal bias or distortion?
6. Did his insight penetrate to the essential meaning of the poem, and did he achieve an effective and unified expression of it?

QUESTIONS FOR DISCUSSION

1. How do you reconcile the theory that poetry is expression of impulses welling up from within with the theory that it is deliberate representation of what the poet has observed as significant in life and nature?
2. Discuss the Webster's dictionary definition of poetry as "writing that formulates a concentrated imaginative awareness of experience in language chosen and arranged to create a specific emotional response through meaning, sound, and rhythm."
3. Discuss "Poetry is an expression of the universal element in life."
4. Discuss "An accurate taste in poetry is an acquired talent."
5. Discuss uniformity in appreciation and in interpretation. To what extent is a reader bound by his text, and to what extent is he free for individual expression.
6. What qualifications are needed for appreciation of poetry? For its interpretation?
7. Discuss the relation of a poem's mood and tempo to its meaning.

SELECTION FOR DRILL

THE SOLITARY REAPER

William Wordsworth

Behold her, single in the field,
Yon solitary Highland Lass!
Reaping and singing by herself;
Stop here, or gently pass!
Alone she cuts and binds the grain   5
And sings a melancholy strain;
O listen! for the Vale profound
Is overflowing with the sound.

No Nightingale did ever chaunt
More welcome notes to weary bands   10
Of travellers in some shady haunt
Among Arabian sands:
A voice so thrilling ne'er was heard
In spring-time from the Cuckoo-bird
Breaking the silence of the seas   15
Among the farthest Hebrides.

Will no one tell me what she sings?—
Perhaps the plaintive numbers flow
For old, unhappy, far-off things,
And Battles long ago: 20
Or is it some more humble lay,
Familiar matter of today?
Some natural sorrow, loss, or pain,
That has been, and may be again?

Whate'er the theme, the maiden sang   25
As if her song could have no ending;
I saw her singing at her work,
And o'er the sickle bending;—
I listened, motionless and still;
And as I mounted up the hill   30
The music in my heart I bore,
Long after it was heard no more.

SUGGESTIONS FOR ANALYSIS. (Numbers refer to lines.)
1. The first word, "behold," is very important. It should set the tone for the whole reading. Speak it firmly with full voice, and in a mood of wonder and admiration. "Single" is a significant word, its sense repeated in "solitary," "by herself," and "alone," but don't overstress the idea. 2. Do not stress "lass"; it is implied by "her." 3. "Reaping" and "singing" are separate ideas. 4. Don't make "stop here" a command. The line means, "Let us pause and take in the scene or else go by quietly so as not to disturb her." "Gently" is more impor-

tant than "pass." 6, 7. Better use even stress on "melancholy strain" and "vale profound." Linger on "O," and make it sound real. Each line 1–6 is a thought unit; don't run them together. But don't separate them completely. 9. Since the nightingale and cuckoo are not American birds, you can probably only imagine their songs, but try. 9, 11. We have kept Wordsworth's pronunciation of "chaunt" but changed his spelling; but for "haunt" we have kept his spelling but changed his pronunciation. Forcing them to rhyme would probably be unwise. 9–12. Can you carry these lines on one breath? The Hebrides are barren islands off the northwest coast of Scotland. To an Englishman they carry a connotation of remoteness. 17. This is not a request for information, or a complaint. The speaker merely wonders what the song was about, since it was probably in a local dialect that he did not understand. All the questions in this stanza mean "I wonder," rather than "I want to know." In 19 and 20 especially give full expression to imagination and feeling. 18. What are "numbers?" 23, 24. "Pain" and "again" might better be left unrhymed, unless it is your habit to rhyme them. 27. This is about as prosy a line as you will find in good poetry, but do not let it sound like prose; sustain the mood and feeling of the context.

The mood should be continuous throughout the poem. How do you define it? Pleasant contemplative wonder? The tempo should be deliberate and evenly sustained, neither hurried nor dragging.

SELECTIONS FOR PRACTICE

In this and the following chapters I have aimed to provide representative examples of the best English poetry from Elizabethan times down to the present. The arrangement is roughly chronological. I recommend that each student of interpretation try one or more of the established classics of our literature before attempting more recent poems. He should get the feel of what our poetic tradition has been, and still is, before undertaking to judge and interpret modern poetry. That is, his education should begin at A instead of at Z.

ROSALIND'S MADRIGAL

Thomas Lodge

Love in my bosom like a bee,
    Doth suck his sweet;
Now with his wings he plays with me,
    Now with his feet.
Within mine eyes he makes his nest,
His bed amidst my tender breast;
My kisses are his daily feast,
And yet he robs me of my rest.
    Ah, wanton, will ye?

And if I sleep, then percheth he,
    With pretty flight,
And makes his pillow of my knee,
    The livelong night.
Strike I my lute, he tunes the string;
He music plays if so I sing;
He lends me every lovely thing;
Yet cruel he my heart doth sting—
    Whist, wanton, still ye!

Else I wish roses every day
    Will ship you hence,
And bind you, when you long to play,
    For your offence.
I'll shut my eyes to keep you in,
I'll make you fast it for your sin,
I'll count your power not worth a pin;
Alas! what hereby shall I win
    If he gainsay me?

What if I beat the wanton boy
    With many a rod?
He will repay me with annoy,
    Because a god.

Then sit thou safely on my knee,
And let thy bower my bosom be;
Lurk in mine eyes, I like of thee.
O Cupid, so thou pity me,
 Spare not, but play thee!

SHALL I, WASTING IN DESPAIR

George Wither

Shall I, wasting in despair,
Die, because a woman's fair?
Or make pale my cheeks with care,
'Cause another's rosy are?
Be she fairer than the day,
Or the flowery meads in May!
 If she be not so to me,
  What care I how fair she be?

Shall my heart be grieved or pined,
'Cause I see a woman kind?
Or a well disposèd nature
Joinèd with a lovely feature?
Be she meeker, kinder than
Turtle dove, or pelican!
 If she be not so to me,
  What care I how kind she be?

Shall a woman's virtues move
Me to perish for her love?
Or her well deserving known,
Make me quite forget mine own?
Be she with that goodness blest
Which may gain her name of best;
 If she be not such to me,
  What care I how good she be?

'Cause her fortune seems too high,
Shall I play the fool, and die?
Those that bear a noble mind,
Where they want of riches find,
Think what, with them they would do
That without them dare to woo;
 And unless that mind I see,
  What care I how great she be?

Great, or good, or kind, or fair,
I will ne'er the more despair!
If she love me, this believe,

I will die ere she shall grieve!
If she slight me, when I woo,
I can scorn, and let her go!
    For if she be not for me,
    What care I for whom she be?

From L'ALLEGRO

John Milton

Haste thee, nymph, and bring with thee
Jest, and youthful Jollity,
Quips and Cranks and wanton Wiles,
Nods and Becks and Wreathèd Smiles,
Such as hang on Hebe's cheek,
And love to live in dimple sleek;
Sport that wrinkled Care derides,
And Laughter holding both his sides.
Come, and trip it as you go,
On the light fantastic toe;
And in thy right hand lead with thee
The Mountain Nymph, sweet Liberty;
And if I give thee honour due,
Mirth, admit me of thy crew,
To live with her, and live with thee,
In unreprovèd pleasures free:
To hear the Lark begin his flight,
And singing, startle the dull night,
From his watch-tower in the skies,
Till the dappled dawn doth rise;
Then to come in spite of sorrow,
And at my window bid good-morrow,
Through the Sweet-Briar or the Vine,
Or the twisted Eglantine;
While the Cock, with lively din,
Scatters the rear of darkness thin,
And to the stack, or the barn-door,
Stoutly struts his Dames before:
Oft listening how the Hounds and horn
Cheerly rouse the slumbering morn,
From the side of some hoar hill,
Through the high wood echoing shrill:
Sometime walking, not unseen,
By Hedge-row Elms, on Hillocks green,
Right against the Eastern gate
Where the great Sun begins his state,

Robed in flames and Amber light,
The clouds in thousand Liveries dight;
While the Ploughman, near at hand,
Whistles o'er the Furrowed Land,
And the Milkmaid singeth blithe,
And the Mower whets his scythe,
And every Shepherd tells his tale
Under the Hawthorn in the dale.

. . . . .

Towered Cities please us then,
And the busy hum of men,
Where throngs of Knights and Barons bold,
In weeds of Peace high triumphs hold,
With store of Ladies, whose bright eyes
Rain influence, and judge the prize
Of Wit or Arms, while both contend
To win her Grace whom all commend.
There let Hymen oft appear
In Saffron robe, with Taper clear,
And pomp and feast and revelry,
With mask and antique Pageantry;
Such sights as youthful Poets dream
On Summer eves by haunted stream.
Then to the well-trod stage anon,
If Jonson's learnèd Sock be on,
Or sweetest Shakespear, Fancy's child,
Warble his native Wood-notes wild.
And ever, against eating Cares,
Lap me in soft Lydian Airs,
Married to immortal verse,
Such as the meeting soul may pierce,
In notes with many a winding bout
Of linkèd sweetness long drawn out,
With wanton heed and giddy cunning,
The melting voice through mazes running,
Untwisting all the chains that tie
The hidden soul of harmony;
That Orpheus' self may heave his head
From golden slumber on a bed
Of heaped Elysian flowers, and hear
Such strains as would have won the ear
Of Pluto to have quite set free
His half-regained Eurydice.
    These delights if thou canst give,
    Mirth, with thee I mean to live.

From IL PENSEROSO

John Milton

—Sweet Bird, that shunn'st the noise of folly,
Most musical, most melancholy!
Thee, Chauntress, oft the Woods among
I woo, to hear thy even-song;
And, missing thee, I walk unseen
On the dry smooth-shaven Green,
To behold the wandering Moon,
Riding near her highest noon,
Like one that had been led astray
Through the Heaven's wide pathless way,
And oft, as if her head she bowed,
Stooping through a fleecy cloud.
    Oft, on a Plat of rising ground,
I hear the far-off Curfew sound
Over some wide-watered shore,
Swinging slow with sullen roar;
Or, if the Air will not permit,
Some still removèd place will fit,
Where glowing Embers through the room
Teach light to counterfeit a gloom,
Far from all resort of mirth,
Save the Cricket on the hearth,
Or the Bellman's drowsy charm
To bless the doors from nightly harm.
    Or let my Lamp, at midnight hour,
Be seen in some high lonely Tower,
Where I may oft out-watch the Bear,
With thrice-great Hermes, or unsphere
The spirit of Plato, to unfold
What Worlds or what vast regions hold
Th' immortal mind that hath forsook
Her mansion in this fleshly nook;
And of those Dæmons that are found
In fire, air, flood, or under ground,
Whose power hath a true consent
With Planet or with Element.
Sometime let Gorgeous Tragedy
In Sceptred Pall come sweeping by,
Presenting Thebes, or Pelops' line,
Or the tale of Troy divine,
Or what (though rare) of later age
Ennobled hath the Buskined stage. . . .
    Thus, Night oft see me in thy pale career,

Till civil-suited Morn appear,
Not tricked and frounced, as she was wont
With the Attic Boy to hunt,
But Kerchieft in a comely Cloud,
While rocking winds are Piping loud,
Or ushered with a shower still,
When the gust hath blown his fill,
Ending on the rustling Leaves,
With minute drops from off the Eaves.
And, when the Sun begins to fling
His flaring beams, me, Goddess, bring
To archèd walks of twilight groves,
And shadows brown, that Sylvan loves,
Of Pine, or monumental Oak,
Where the rude Axe with heavèd stroke
Was never heard the Nymphs to daunt,
Or fright them from their hallowed haunt.
There, in close covert, by some Brook,
Where no profaner eye may look,
Hide me from Day's garish eye,
While the Bee with Honeyed thigh,
That at her flowery work doth sing,
And the Waters murmuring,
With such consort as they keep,
Entice the dewy-feathered Sleep.
And let some strange mysterious dream,
Wave at his Wings in Airy stream,
Of lively portraiture displayed,
Softly on my eyelids laid.
And as I wake, sweet music breathe
Above, about, or underneath,
Sent by some Spirit to mortals good,
Or th' unseen Genius of the Wood.
    But let my due feet never fail
To walk the studious Cloister's pale,
And love the high-embowèd roof,
With antic Pillars massy proof,
And storied Windows richly dight,
Casting a dim religious light.
There let the pealing Organ blow,
To the full-voiced Quire below,
In Service high and Anthems clear,
As may with sweetness, through mine ear,
Dissolve me into ecstasies,
And bring all Heaven before mine eyes.
    And may at last my weary age
Find out the peaceful hermitage,

The Hairy Gown and Mossy Cell,
Where I may sit and rightly spell,
Of every Star that Heaven doth shew,
And every Herb that sips the dew;
Till old experience do attain
To something like Prophetic strain.
   These pleasures, Melancholy, give,
And I with thee will choose to live.

TO ALTHEA, FROM PRISON

Richard Lovelace

When Love with unconfinèd wings
   Hovers within my gates,
And my divine Althea brings
   To whisper at the grates;
When I lie tangled in her hair
   And fetter'd to her eye,
The gods that wanton in the air
   Know no such liberty.

When flowing cups run swiftly round
   With no allaying Thames,
Our careless heads with roses bound,
   Our hearts with loyal flames;
When thirsty grief in wine we steep,
   When healths and draughts go free—
Fishes that tipple in the deep
   Know no such liberty.

When, like committed linnets, I
   With shriller throat shall sing
The sweetness, mercy, majesty,
   And glories of my King;
When I shall voice aloud how good
   He is, how great should be,
Enlargèd winds, that curl the flood,
   Know no such liberty.

Stone walls do not a prison make,
   Nor iron bars a cage;
Minds innocent and quiet take
   That for an hermitage;
If I have freedom in my love
   And in my soul am free,
Angels alone, that soar above,
   Enjoy such liberty.

THE GARDEN

Andrew Marvell

How vainly men themselves amaze,
To win the palm, the oak, or bays,
And their uncessant labours see
Crowned from some single herb or tree
Whose short and narrow-vergèd shade
Does prudently their toils upbraid,
While all flowers and all trees do close
To weave the garlands of repose!

Fair quiet, have I found thee here,
And innocence, thy sister dear?
Mistaken long, I sought you then
In busy companies of men.
Your sacred plants, if here below,
Only among the plants will grow;
Society is all but rude
To this delicious solitude.

No white nor red was ever seen
So am'rous as this lovely green.
Fond lovers, cruel as their flame,
Cut in these trees their mistress' name;
Little, alas, they know or heed,
How far these beauties hers exceed!
Fair trees! wheres'e'er your barks I wound
No name shall but your own be found.

When we have run our passion's heat,
Love hither makes his best retreat.
The gods that mortal beauty chase,
Still in a tree did end their race:
Apollo hunted Daphne so,
Only that she might laurel grow;
And Pan did after Syrinx speed,
Not as a nymph, but for a reed.

What wond'rous life is this I lead!
Ripe apples drop about my head;
The luscious clusters of the vine
Upon my mouth do crush their wine;
The nectarine, and curious peach,
Into my hands themselves do reach;
Stumbling on melons, as I pass,
Ensnared with flowers, I fall on grass.

Meanwhile the mind, from pleasure less,
Withdraws into its happiness;—
The mind, that ocean where each kind
Does straight its own resemblance find;
Yet it creates, transcending these,
Far other worlds, and other seas,
Annihilating all that's made
To a green thought in a green shade.

Here at the fountain's sliding foot,
Or at some fruit-tree's mossy root,
Casting the body's vest aside,
My soul into the boughs does glide:
There, like a bird, it sits and sings,
Then whets, then combs its silver wings,
And till prepared for longer flight,
Waves in its plumes the various light.

Such was that happy garden-state,
While man there walked without a mate:
After a place so pure and sweet,
What other help could yet be meet!
But 'twas beyond a mortal's share
To wander solitary there:
Two paradises 'twere in one,
To live in paradise alone.

How well the skilful gard'ner drew
Of flowers and herbs this dial new,
Where, from above, the milder sun
Does through a fragrant zodiac run,
And, as it works, the industrious bee
Computes its time as well as we!
How could such sweet and wholesome hours
Be reckoned but with herbs and flowers?

SHE WAS A PHANTOM OF DELIGHT

William Wordsworth

She was a Phantom of delight
When first she gleamed upon my sight:
A lovely Apparition, sent
To be a moment's ornament;
Her eyes as stars of twilight fair;
Like Twilight's, too, her dusky hair;
But all things else about her drawn
From May-time and the cheerful Dawn;

A dancing Shape, an Image gay,
To haunt, to startle, and way-lay.

I saw her upon nearer view,
A Spirit, yet a Woman too!
Her household motions light and free,
And steps of virgin-liberty;
A countenance in which did meet
Sweet records, promises as sweet;
A Creature not too bright or good
For human nature's daily food;
For transient sorrows, simple wiles,
Praise, blame, love, kisses, tears, and smiles.

And now I see with eye serene
The very pulse of the machine;
A Being breathing thoughtful breath,
A Traveller between life and death;
The reason firm, the temperate will,
Endurance, foresight, strength, and skill;
A perfect Woman, nobly planned,
To warn, to comfort, and command;
And yet a Spirit still, and bright
With something of angelic light.

THREE YEARS SHE GREW

William Wordsworth

Three years she grew in sun and shower,
Then Nature said, "A lovelier flower
On earth was never sown;
This Child I to myself will take;
She shall be mine, and I will make
A Lady of my own.

"Myself will to my darling be
Both law and impulse: and with me
The Girl, in rock and plain,
In earth and heaven, in glade and bower,
Shall feel an overseeing power
To kindle or restrain.

"She shall be sportive as the fawn
That wild with glee across the lawn
Or up the mountain springs;
And hers shall be the breathing balm,
And hers the silence and the calm
Of mute insensate things.

"The floating clouds their state shall lend
To her; for her the willow bend;
Nor shall she fail to see
Even in the motions of the Storm
Grace that shall mould the Maiden's form
By silent sympathy.

"The stars of midnight shall be dear
To her; and she shall lean her ear
In many a secret place
Where rivulets dance their wayward round,
And beauty born of murmuring sound
Shall pass into her face.

"And vital feelings of delight
Shall rear her form to stately height,
Her virgin bosom swell;
Such thoughts to Lucy I will give
While she and I together live
Here in this happy dell."

Thus Nature spake—The work was done—
How soon my Lucy's race was run!
She died, and left to me
This heath, this calm, and quiet scene;
The memory of what has been,
And never more will be.

TO AUTUMN

John Keats

Season of mists and mellow fruitfulness,
    Close bosom-friend of the maturing sun;
Conspiring with him how to load and bless
    With fruit the vines that round the thatch-eaves run;
To bend with apples the moss'd cottage-trees,
    And fill all fruit with ripeness to the core;
        To swell the gourd, and plump the hazel shells
With a sweet kernel; to set budding more,
    And still more, later flowers for the bees,
    Until they think warm days will never cease,
        For Summer has o'er-brimm'd their clammy cells.

Who hath not seen thee oft amid thy store?
    Sometimes whoever seeks abroad may find
Thee sitting careless on a granary floor,
    Thy hair soft-lifted by the winnowing wind;

Or on a half-reap'd furrow sound asleep,
　Drows'd with the fume of poppies, while thy hook
　　Spares the next swath and all its twinèd flowers:
And sometimes like a gleaner thou dost keep
　Steady thy laden head across a brook;
　Or by a cider-press, with patient look,
　　Thou watchest the last oozings hours by hours.

Where are the songs of Spring? Ay, where are they?
　Think not of them, thou hast thy music too,—
While barrèd clouds bloom the soft-dying day,
　And touch the stubble-plains with rosy hue;
Then in a wailful choir the small gnats mourn
　Among the river sallows, borne aloft
　　Or sinking as the light wind lives or dies;
And full-grown lambs loud bleat from hilly bourn;
　Hedge-crickets sing; and now with treble soft
　The red-breast whistles from a garden-croft;
　　And gathering swallows twitter in the skies.

THE LEADEN ECHO[1]

Gerard Manley Hopkins

How to keep—is there any, any, is there none such, nowhere known,
　some bow or brooch or braid or brace, lace, latch or catch or
　key to keep
Back beauty, keep it, beauty, beauty, beauty, . . . from vanishing
　away?
Oh, is there no frowning of these wrinkles, ranked wrinkles deep,
Down? no waving-off of these most mournful messengers, still mes-
　sengers, sad and stealing messengers of gray?
No, there's none, there's none—oh, no, there's none!
Nor can you long be, what you now are, called fair—
Do what you may do, do what you may,
And wisdom is early to despair:

Be beginning; since, no, nothing can be done
To keep at bay
Age and age's evils—hoar hair,
Ruck and wrinkle, drooping, dying, death's worst, winding sheets,
　tombs and worms, and tumbling to decay;
So be beginning, be beginning to despair.
Oh, there's none—no, no, no, there's none:
　Be beginning to despair, to despair,
　Despair, despair, despair, despair.

THE GOLDEN ECHO[2]
Gerard Manley Hopkins

Spare!
There is one, yes, I have one (Hush there!);
Only not within seeing of the sun,
Not within the singeing of the strong sun,
Tall sun's tingeing, or treacherous the tainting of the earth's air,
Somewhere elsewhere there is ah, well, where! one,
One. Yes, I can tell such a key, I do know such a place,
Where whatever's prized and passed of us, everything that's fresh
    and fast-flying of us, seems to us sweet of us and swiftly away
    with, done away with, undone,
Undone, done with, soon done with, and yet dearly and dangerously
    sweet
Of us, the wimpled-water-dimpled, not-by-morning-matchèd face,
The flower of beauty, fleece of beauty, too too apt to, ah! to fleet,
Never fleets more, fastened with the tenderest truth
To its own best being and its loveliness of youth: it is an everlasting-
    ness of, O it is an all youth!
Come then, your ways and airs and looks, locks, maiden gear, gal-
    lantry and gayety and grace,
Winning ways, airs innocent, maiden manners, sweet looks, loose
    locks, long locks, lovelocks, gaygear, going gallant, girlgrace—
Resign them, sign them, seal them, send them, motion them with
    breath,
And with sighs soaring, soaring sighs deliver
Them; beauty-in-the-ghost, deliver it, early now, long before death
Give beauty back, beauty, beauty, beauty, back to God, beauty's
    self and beauty's giver.
See; not a hair is, not an eyelash, not the least lash lost; every hair
Is, hair of the head, numbered.
Nay, what we had lighthanded left in surely the mere mold
Will have waked and have waxed and have walked with the wind
    whatwhile we slept,
This side, that side hurling a heavyheaded hundredfold
What while we, while we slumbered.
O then, weary then why should we tread? O why are we so haggard
    at the heart, so care-coiled, care-killed, so fagged, so fashed, so
    cogged, so cumbered,
When the thing we freely forfeit is kept with fonder a care,
Fonder a care kept than we could have kept it, kept
Far with fonder a care (and we, we should have lost it) finer, fonder
A care kept.—Where kept? Do but tell us where kept, where.—

[2] From *Poems of Gerard Manley Hopkins*, Third Edition, edited by W. H. Gard-
ner. Copyright 1948 by Oxford University Press, Inc. Reprinted by permission.

Yonder.—What high as that! We follow, now we follow.—Yonder,
  yes, yonder, yonder,
Yonder.

THE INVISIBLE BRIDE[3]

Edwin Markham

The low-voiced girls that go
  In gardens of the Lord,
Like flowers of the field they grow
  In sisterly accord.

Their whispering feet are white
  Along the leafy ways;
They go in whirls of light
  Too beautiful for praise.

And in their band forsooth
  Is one to set me free—
The one that touched my youth—
  The one God gave to me.

She kindles the desire
  Whereby the gods survive—
The white ideal fire
  That keeps my soul alive.

Now at the wondrous hour,
  She leaves her star supreme,
And comes in the night's still power,
  To touch me with a dream.

Sibyl of mystery
  On roads unknown to men,
Softly she comes to me,
  And goes to God again.

THE JOY OF THE HILLS[4]

Edwin Markham

I ride on the mountain tops, I ride;
I have found my life and am satisfied.
Onward I ride in the blowing oats,
Checking the field-lark's rippling notes—
  Lightly I sweep
  From steep to steep:

[3] Copyrighted by the author and used by his permission.
[4] Copyrighted by the author and used by his permission.

Over my head through the branches high
Come glimpses of a rushing sky;
The tall oats brush my horse's flanks;
Wild poppies crowd on the sunny banks;
A bee booms out of the scented grass;
A jay laughs with me as I pass.

I ride on the hills, I forgive, I forget
    Life's hoard of regret—
    All the terror and pain
    Of the chafing chain.
    Grind on, O cities, grind:
    I leave you a blur behind.
I am lifted elate—the skies expand:
Here the world's heaped gold is a pile of sand.
Let them weary and work in their narrow walls:
I ride with the voices of waterfalls!

I swing on as one in a dream—I swing
Down the airy hollows, I shout, I sing!
The world is gone like an empty word:
My body's a bough in the wind, my heart a bird!

ACROSS THE FIELDS TO ANNE[5]

Richard Burton

How often in the summer-tide,
His graver business set aside,
Has stripling Will, the thoughtful-eyed,
As to the pipe of Pan,
Stepped blithesomely with lover's pride
Across the fields to Anne.

It must have been a merry mile,
This summer stroll by hedge and stile,
With sweet foreknowledge all the while
How sure the pathway ran
To dear delights of kiss and smile,
Across the fields to Anne.

The silly sheep that graze to-day,
I wot, they let him go his way,
Nor once looked up, as who should say:
"It is a seemly man."
For many lads went wooing aye
Across the fields to Anne.

[5] By permission of Lothrop, Lee and Shepard Co., Inc.

The oaks, they have a wiser look;
Mayhap they whispered to the brook:
"The world by him shall yet be shook,
It is in nature's plan;
Though now he fleets like any rook
Across the fields to Anne."

And I am sure, that on some hour
Coquetting soft 'twixt sun and shower,
He stooped and broke a daisy-flower
With heart of tiny span,
And bore it as a lover's dower
Across the fields to Anne.

While from her cottage garden-bed
She plucked a jasmine's goodlihede,
To scent his jerkin's brown instead;
Now since that love began,
What luckier swain than he who sped
Across the fields to Anne?

The winding path whereon I pace,
The hedgerow's green, the summer's grace,
Are still before me face to face;
Methinks I almost can
Turn poet and join the singing race
Across the fields to Anne!

WHEN EARTH'S LAST PICTURE IS PAINTED[6]

Rudyard Kipling

When Earth's last picture is painted and the tubes are twisted and
   dried,
When the oldest colours have faded, and the youngest critic has died,
We shall rest, and, faith, we shall need it—lie down for an aeon or
   two,
Till the Master of All Good Workmen shall put us to work anew.

And those that were good shall be happy: they shall sit in a golden
   chair;
They shall splash at a ten-league canvas with brushes of comets' hair;
They shall find real saints to draw from—Magdalene, Peter, and Paul;
They shall work for an age at a sitting and never be tired at all!

And only the Master shall praise us, and only the Master shall blame;
And no one shall work for money, and no one shall work for fame,
But each for the joy of the working, and each, in his separate star,
Shall draw the Thing as he sees It for the God of Things as They are!

[6] From *The Seven Seas.* Reprinted by permission of Mrs. George Bambridge and
Doubleday & Co., Inc.

THE WILD SWANS AT COOLE[7]

W. B. Yeats

The trees are in their autumn beauty,
The woodland paths are dry,
Under the October twilight the water
Mirrors a still sky;
Upon the brimming water among the stones
Are nine-and-fifty swans.

The nineteenth autumn has come upon me
Since I first made my count;
I saw, before I had well finished,
All suddenly mount
And scatter wheeling in great broken rings
Upon their clamorous wings.

I have looked upon those brilliant creatures,
And now my heart is sore.
All's changed since I, hearing at twilight,
The first time on this shore,
The bell-beat of their wings above my head,
Trod with a lighter tread.

Unwearied still, lover by lover,
They paddle in the cold
Companionable streams or climb the air;
Their hearts have not grown old;
Passion or conquest, wander where they will,
Attend upon them still.

But now they drift on the still water,
Mysterious, beautiful;
Among what rushes will they build,
By what lake's edge or pool
Delight men's eyes when I awake some day
To find they have flown away?

EVE[8]

Ralph Hodgson

Eve, with her basket, was
Deep in the bells and grass,

---

[7] From *Collected Poems*, copyright, 1933, by The Macmillan Co. and used with their permission.

[8] From *Poems*, copyright by The Macmillan Co., and used with their permission.

Wading in bells and grass
Up to her knees.
Picking a dish of sweet
Berries and plums to eat,
Down in the bells and grass
Under the trees.

Mute as a mouse in a
Corner the cobra lay,
Curled round a bough of the
Cinnamon tall. . . .
Now to get even and
Humble proud heaven and
Now was the moment or
Never at all.

"Eva!" Each syllable
Light as a flower fell,
"Eva!" he whispered the
Wondering maid,
Soft as a bubble sung
Out of a linnet's lung,
Soft and most silverly
"Eva!" he said.

Picture that orchard sprite;
Eve, with her body white,
Supple and smooth to her
Slim finger tips;
Wondering, listening,
Listening, wondering,
Eve with a berry
Half-way to her lips.

Oh, had our simple Eve
Seen through the make-believe!
Had she but known the
Pretender he was!
Out of the boughs he came,
Whispering still her name,
Tumbling in twenty rings
Into the grass.

Here was the strangest pair
In the world anywhere,
Eve in the bells and grass
Kneeling, and he
Telling his story low. . . .
Singing birds saw them go

Down the dark path to
The Blasphemous Tree.

Oh, what a clatter when
Titmouse and Jenny Wren
Saw him successful and
Taking his leave!
How the birds rated him,
How they all hated him!
How they all pitied
Poor motherless Eve!

Picture her crying
Outside in the lane,
Eve, with no dish of sweet
Berries and plums to eat,
Haunting the gate of the
Orchard in vain. . . .
Picture the lewd delight
Under the hill tonight—
"Eva!" the toast goes round,
"Eva!" again.

A CONSIDERABLE SPECK[9]

Robert Frost

A speck that would have been beneath my sight
On any but a paper sheet so white
Set off across what I had written there,
And I had idly poised my pen in air
To stop it with a period of ink,
When something strange about it made me think
This was no dust speck by my breathing blown,
But unmistakably a living mite
With inclinations it could call its own.
It paused as with suspicion of my pen,
And then came racing wildly on again
To where my manuscript was not yet dry,
Then pause again and either drank or smelt—
With horror, for again it turned to fly.
Plainly with an intelligence I dealt.
It seemed too tiny to have room for feet,
Yet must have had a set of them complete
To express how much it didn't want to die.
It ran with terror and with cunning crept.

It faltered! I could see it hesitate—
Then in the middle of the open sheet
Cower down in desperation to accept
Whatever I accorded it of fate.
I have none of the tenderer-than-thou
Political collectivistic love
With which the modern world is being swept—
But this poor microscopic item now!
Since it was nothing I knew evil of
I let it lie there till I hope it slept.
I have a mind myself, and recognize
Mind where I meet with it in any guise.
No one can know how glad I am to find
On any sheet the least display of mind.

THE DEATHLESS DREAM

From THE PEOPLE, YES, No. 75[10]

Carl Sandburg

Hunger and only hunger changes worlds?
The dictate of the belly
that gnawing under the navel,
this alone is the builder and the pathfinder
sending man into danger and fire
and death by struggle?
    Yes and no, no and yes.
    The strong win against the weak.
    The strong lose against the stronger.
And across the bitter years and the howling winters
    the deathless dream will be the stronger,
    the dream of equity will win.
There are shadows and bones shot with lights
    too strong to be lost.
    Can the wilderness be put behind?
    Shall man always go on dog-eat-dog?
    Who says so?
    The stronger?
    And who is the stronger?
And how long shall the stronger hold on
    as the stronger?
    What will tomorrow write?
    "Of the people by the people for the people?"

[10] From *The People, Yes* by Carl Sandburg, copyright, 1936, by Harcourt, Brace & Co., Inc.; renewed, 1964, by Carl Sandburg. Reprinted by permission of the publishers.

What mockers ever wrung a crop from a waiting soil
Or when did cold logic bring forth a child?
"What use is it?" they asked a kite-flying sky gazer
And he wished in return to know, "What use is a baby?"
The dreaming scholars who quested the useless,
who wanted to know merely for the sake of knowing,
they sought and harnessed electrodynamic volts
becoming in time thirty billion horses in one country
hauling with thirty-billion-horse-power
and this is an early glimpse, a dim beginning,
the first hill of a series of hills.

What comes after the spectrum?
With what will the test-tubes be shaken tomorrow?
For what will the acetylene torch and pneumatic chisel be scrapped?
What will the international partnerships of the world laboratories
   track down next, what new fuels, amalgams, alloys, seeds, cross-
   breeds, unforeseen short cuts to power?
Whose guess is better than anybody else's on whether the breed of
   fire-bringers is run out, whether light rays, death rays, laugh rays,
   are now for us only in a dim beginning?
Across the bitter years and the howling winters
   the deathless dream will be the stronger
   the dream of equity will win.

AND IN THE HANGING GARDENS—[11]

Conrad Aiken

And in the hanging gardens there is rain
From midnight until one, striking the leaves
And bells of flowers, and stroking boles of planes,
And drawing slow arpeggios over pools
And stretching strings of sound from eaves to ferns.
The princess reads. The knave of diamonds sleeps.
The king is drunk, and flings a golden goblet
Down from the turret window (curtained with rain)
Into the lilacs.
                    And at one o'clock
The vulcan under the garden wakes and beats
The gong upon his anvil. Then the rain
Ceases, but gently ceases, dripping still,
And sound of falling water fills the dark
As leaves grow bold and upright, and as eaves
Part with water. The princess turns the page

[11] From *Selected Poems* by Conrad Aiken. Copyright © 1961 by Conrad Aiken.
Reprinted by permission of Oxford University Press, Inc.

Beside the candle, and between two braids
Of golden hair. And reads: "From there I went
Northward a journey of four days, and came
To a wild village in the hills, where none
Was living save the vulture and the rat
And one old man who laughed but could not speak.
The roofs were fallen in, the well grown over
With weed. And it was here my father died.
Then eight days further, bearing slightly west,
The cold wind blowing sand against our faces,
The food tasting of sand. And as we stood
By the dry rock that marks the highest point
My brother said: 'Not too late is it yet
To turn, remembering home.' And we were silent
Thinking of home." The princess shuts her eyes
And feels the tears forming beneath her eyelids
And opens them, and tears fall on the page.
The knave of diamonds in the darkened room
Throws off his covers, sleeps, and snores again.
The king goes slowly down the turret stairs
To find the goblet.
                    And at two o'clock
The vulcan in his smithy underground
Under the hanging gardens, where the drip
Of rain among the clematis and ivy
Still falls from sipping flower to purple flower
Smites twice his anvil, and the murmur comes
Among the roots and vines. The princess reads:
"As I am sick, and cannot write you more,
And have not long to live, I give this letter
To him, my brother, who will bear it south
And tell you how I died. Ask how it was,
There in the northern desert, where the grass
Was withered, and the horses, all but one,
Perished . . ." The princess drops her golden head
Upon the page between her two white arms
And golden braids. The knave of diamonds wakes
And at his window in the darkened room
Watches the lilacs tossing, where the king
Seeks for the goblet.
                     And at three o'clock
The moon inflames the lilac heads, and thrice
The vulcan, in his root-bound smithy, clangs
His anvil; and the sounds creep softly up
Among the vines and walls. The moon is round,
Round as a shield above the turret top.
The princess blows her candle out, and weeps

In the pale room, where scent of lilacs comes,
Weeping, with hands across her eyelids, thinking
Of withered grass, withered by sandy wind.
The knave of diamonds, in his darkened room,
Holds in his hands a key, and softly steps
Along the corridor, and slides the key
Into the door that guards her. Meanwhile, slowly,
The king, with raindrops on his beard and hands,
And dripping sleeves, climbs up the turret stairs,
Holding the goblet upright in one hand;
And pauses on the midmost step to taste
One drop of wine wherewith wild rain has mixed.

THINGS[12]

Aline Kilmer

Sometimes when I am at tea with you,
    I catch my breath
At a thought that is old as the world is old
    And more bitter than death.

It is that the spoon that you just laid down
    And the cup that you hold
May be here shining and insolent
    When you are still and cold.

Your careless note that I laid away
    May leap to my eyes like flame,
When the world has almost forgotten your voice
    Or the sound of your name.

The golden Virgin da Vinci drew
    May smile on over my head,
And daffodils nod in the silver vase
    When you are dead.

So let moth and dust corrupt and thieves
    Break through and I shall be glad,
Because of the hatred I bear to things
    Instead of the love I had.

For life seems only a shuddering breath,
    A smothered, desperate cry;
And things have a terrible permanence
    When people die.

MAP OF MY COUNTRY[13]

John Holmes

A map of my native country is all edges,
The shore touching sea, the easy impartial rivers
Splitting the local boundary lines, round hills in two townships,
Blue ponds interrupting the careful county shapes.
The Mississippi runs down the middle. Cape Cod. The Gulf.
Nebraska is on latitude forty. Kansas is west of Missouri.

When I was a child, I drew it, from memory,
A game in the schoolroom, naming the big cities right.

Cloud shadows were not shown, nor where winter whitens,
Nor the wide road the day's wind takes.

None of the tall letters told my grandfather's name.
Nothing said, Here they see in clear air a hundred miles.
Here they go to bed early. They fear snow here.
Oak trees and maple boughs I had seen on the long hillsides
Changing color, and laurel, and bayberry, were never mapped.
Geography told only capitals and state lines.

I have come a long way using other men's maps for the turnings.
I have a long way to go.
It is time I drew the map again,
Spread with the broad colors of life, and words of my own
Saying, Here the people worked hard, and died for the wrong reasons.
Here wild strawberries tell the time of year.
I could not sleep, here, while bell-buoys beyond the surf rang.
Here trains passed in the night, crying of distance,
Calling to cities far away, listening for an answer.

On my own map of my own country
I shall show where there were never wars,
And plot the changed way I hear men speak in the west,
Words in the south slower, and food different.
Not the court-houses seen floodlighted at night from trains,
But the local stone built into housewalls,
And barns telling the traveler where he is
By the slant of the roof, the color of the paint.
Not monuments. Not the battlefields famous in school.
But Thoreau's pond, and Huckleberry Finn's island.
I shall name an unhistorical hill three boys climbed one morning.
Lines indicate my few journeys,
And the long way letters come from absent friends.

Forest is where green fern cooled me under the big trees.
Ocean is where I ran in the white drag of waves on white sand.
Music is what I heard in a country house while hearts broke,
Not knowing they were breaking, and Brahms wrote it.
All that I remember happened to me here.
This is the known world.
I shall make a star here for a man who died too young.
Here, and here, in gold, I shall mark two towns
Famous for nothing, except that I have been happy in them.

THE EXPRESS[14]

Stephen Spender

After the first powerful plain manifesto
The black statement of pistons, without more fuss
But gliding like a queen, she leaves the station.
Without bowing and with restrained unconcern
She passes the houses which humbly crowd outside,
The gasworks and at last the heavy page
Of death, printed by gravestones in the cemetery.
Beyond the town there lies the open country
Where, gathering speed, she acquires mystery,
The luminous self-possession of ships on ocean.
It is now she begins to sing—at first quite low
Then loud, and at last with a jazzy madness—
The song of her whistle screaming at curves,
Of deafening tunnels, brakes, innumerable bolts.
And always light, aerial, underneath
Goes the elate meter of her wheels.
Steaming through metal landscape on her lines
She plunges new eras of wild happiness
Where speed throws up strange shapes, broad curves
And parallels clean like the steel of guns.
At last, farther than Edinburgh or Rome,
Beyond the crest of the world, she reaches night
Where only a low streamline brightness
Of phosphorus on the tossing hills is white.
Ah, like a comet through flames she moves entranced
Wrapt in her music no bird song, no, nor bough
Breaking with honey buds, shall ever equal.

BUICK[15]

Karl Shapiro

As a sloop with a sweep of immaculate wing on her delicate spine
And a keel as steel as a root that holds in the sea as she leans,
Leaning and laughing, my warm-hearted beauty, you ride, you ride,
You tack on the curves with parabola speed and a kiss of goodbye,
Like a thoroughbred sloop, my new high-spirited spirit, my kiss.

As my foot suggests that you leap in the air with your hips of a girl,
My finger that praises your wheel and announces your voices of song,
Flouncing your skirts, you blueness of joy, you flirt of politeness,
You leap, you intelligence, essence of wheelness with silvery nose,
And your platinum clocks of excitement stir like the hairs of a fern.

But now with your eyes that enter the future of roads you forget; the smoke
Where you turned on the stinging lathes of Detroit and Lansing at night
And shrieked at the torch in your secret parts and the amorous tests,
But now with your eyes that enter the future of roads you forget;
You are all instinct with your phosphorous glow and your streaking hair.

And now when we stop it is not as the bird from the shell that I leave
Or the leathery pilot who steps from his bird with a sneer of delight,
And not as the ignorant beast do you squat and watch me depart,
But with exquisite breathing you smile, with satisfaction of love,
And I touch you again as you tick in the silence and settle in sleep.

HOLLYHOCKS[16]

Lew Sarett

I have a garden, but, oh, dear me!
What a ribald and hysterical company:
Incorrigible mustard, militant corn,
Frivolous lettuce, and celery forlorn;
Beets apoplectic and fatuous potatoes,
Voluptuous pumpkins and palpitant tomatoes;
Philandering pickles, trysting at the gate,
Onions acrimonious, and peppers irate;

[15] From *Person, Place and Thing*, copyright, 1942, by Karl Jay Shapiro. Reprinted by permission of Harcourt, Brace & Co., Inc.
[16] From *Wings Against the Moon*, by permission of Holt, Rinehart & Winston, Inc., publishers.

And a regiment of hollyhocks marching around them
To curb their mischief, to discipline and bound them.

Hollyhocks! Hollyhocks! What should I do
Without the morale of a troop like you!

Some lackadaisically yawn and nod;
Others, hypochondriac, droop on the sod:
Cabbage apathetic, parsnips sullen,
Peas downtrodden by the lancing mullein;
Boorish rutabagas, dill exotic,
The wan wax-bean, bilious and neurotic;
Dropsical melons, varicose chard,
And cauliflowers fainting all over the yard.
Thank heaven for the hollyhocks! Till day is done
They prod them to labor in the rain and the sun.

Hollyhocks! Hollyhocks! Stiff as starch!
Fix your bayonets! Forward! March!

BLINDMAN'S BUFF[17]

Peter Viereck

Night-watchmen think of dawn and things auroral.
Clerks wistful for Bermudas think of coral.
The poet in New York still thinks of laurel.
(But lovers think of death and touch each other
As if to prove that love is still alive.)

The Martian space-crew, in an Earthward dive,
Think of their sweet unearthly earth Up There,
Where darling monsters romp in airless air.
(Two lovers think of death and touch each other,
Fearing that day when only one's alive.)

We think of cash, but cash does not arrive.
We think of fun, but fate will not connive.
We never mention death. Do we survive?
(The lovers think of death and touch each other
To live their love while love is yet alive.)

Prize-winners are so avid when they strive;
They race so far; they pile their toys so high
Only a cad would trip them. Yet they die.
(The lovers think of death and touch each other;
Of all who live, these are the most alive.)

Plump creatures smack their lips and think they thrive;
The hibernating bear, but half alive,
Dreams of free honey in a stingless hive.
He thinks of life at every lifeless breath.
(The lovers think of death.)

FERN HILL[18]

Dylan Thomas

Now as I was young and easy under the apple boughs
About the lilting house and happy as the grass was green,
    The night above the dingle starry,
        Time let me hail and climb
    Golden in the heydays of his eyes,
And honored among wagons I was prince of the apple towns
And once below a time I lordly had the trees and leaves
        Trail with daisies and barley
    Down the rivers of the windfall light.

And as I was green and carefree, famous among the barns
About the happy yard and singing as the farm was home,
    In the sun that is young once only,
        Time let me play and be
    Golden in the mercy of his means,
And green and golden I was huntsman and herdsman, the calves
Sang to my horn, the foxes on the hills barked clear and cold,
        And the sabbath rang slowly
    In the pebbles of the holy streams.

All the sun long it was running, it was lovely, the hay-
Fields high as the house, the tunes from the chimneys, it was air
    And playing, lovely and watery
        And fire green as grass.
    And nightly under the simple stars
As I rode to sleep the owls were bearing the farm away,
All the moon long I heard, blessed among stables, the nightjars
        Flying with the ricks, and horses
    Flashing into the dark

And then to awake, and the farm, like a wanderer white
With the dew, come back, the cock on his shoulder: it was all
    Shining, it was Adam and maiden,
        The sky gathered again
    And the sun grew round that very day.

So it must have been after the birth of the simple light
In the first, spinning place, the spellbound horses walking warm
   Out of the whinnying green stable
     On to the fields of praise,

And honored among foxes and pheasants by the gay house
Under the new-made clouds and happy as the heart was long
   In the sun born over and over,
     I ran my heedless ways,
     My wishes raced through the house-high hay
And nothing I cared, at my sky blue trades, that time allows
In all his tuneful turning so few and such morning songs
   Before the children green and golden
     Follow him out of grace.

Nothing I cared, in the lamb white days, that time would take me
Up to the swallow-thronged loft by the shadow of my hand,
   In the moon that is always rising,
     Nor that riding to sleep
     I should hear him fly with the high fields
And wake to the farm forever fled from the childless land.
Oh as I was young and easy in the mercy of his means,
     Time held me green and dying
     Though I sang in my chains like the sea.

L'INGLESE[19]

John Ciardi

Walpole, travelling in the Alps,
talked of goat trails and abysses.
Powdered wigs make prickly scalps
in a chaise above a crisis.

"The *least* slip," so he wrote to West,
would have tumbled wig and all
into such fog and sudden rest
that— Well, he had no wish to fall.

"But is it possible," he thought,
"the next step is not one too many?,"
while the sweating peasants sought
footholds for their daily penny.

One man's terror, one man's trade.
With milord upon their shoulders

[19] From *The New Yorker*, January 18, 1964; © 1964 The New Yorker Magazine, Inc.

and a long way back to bed,
the porters edged around the boulders.

Came "a cruel accident."
Next day Walpole still bemoans:
When the trail at last had bent
to an almost-road of stones,

he let his little spaniel out
("the prettiest, fattest, dearest creature!")
for its creature needs, no doubt,
or to admire some Alpine feature.

"When from a wood," he wept and wrote,
"a young wolf sprang at once and seized
poor, dear Tory by the throat!"—
and vanished, one must guess, well pleased.

"I saw it but I screamed in vain!"
The prey was seized, the wolf was gone.
What seemed above all else to pain
Walpole, once the thing was done,

was that it happened in full day,
"but two o'clock and broad sunshine."
His "Alpine savages"—for pay,
and full, he wrote, "of sour wine"—

made such commotion as seemed due,
but had their Englishman to bear.
In three leagues Turin came in view
and they could rest once they were there.

Envoi

Sensibility better suits
the man inside the chaise
than the bearers—ugly brutes—
of those Alpine ways.

Yet the weight falls on all mankind
the day the wolf attacks;
milord had things upon his mind,
they milord upon their backs.

. . . AND MR FERRITT

Judith Wright

But now Mr Ferritt
with his troublesome nose,

with his shaven chin
and his voice like a grief
that grates in dark corners,
moves in his house
and scrapes his dry skin
and sees it is morning.

O day, you sly thief,
now what have you taken
of all the small things
I tie on my life?
The radio serial
whines in the kitchen,
caught in a box,
and cannot get out.
The finch in his cage,
the border of phlox
as straight as a string
drawn up in my garden,
the potted geranium,
all are there.
But day from his cranium
twitches one hair;
and never again
will a hair grow there.
—O day, you sly thief,
how you pluck at my life,
frets Mr Ferritt;
but there, he must bear it.

Outside the fence
the wattle-tree grows.
It tosses; it shines;
it speaks its one word.
Beware, beware!
Mr Ferritt has heard.
—What are axes for?
What are fences for?
Who planted that wattle-tree
right at my door?
God only knows.
All over the garden
its dust is shaken.
No wonder I sneeze
as soon as I waken.

O world, you sly thief;
my youth you have taken,

and what have you given
who promised me heaven,
but a nagging wife
and a chronic catarrh,
and a blonde on the pictures
as far as a star?
And wild and gold
as a film-star's hair
that tree stands there,
blocking the view
from my twenty-perch block.
What are axes for,
what are fences for
but to keep this tree
away from my door?

And down came the tree.
But poor Mr Ferritt
still has hay-fever.
Nothing will cure it.

THE GRIESLY WIFE[20]

John Manifold

"Lie still, my newly married wife,
  Lie easy as you can.
You're young and ill accustomed yet
  To sleeping with a man."

The snow lay thick, the moon was full
  And shone across the floor.
The young wife went with never a word
  Barefooted to the door.

He up and followed sure and fast,
  The moon shone clear and white.
But before his coat was on his back
  His wife was out of sight.

He trod the trail wherever it turned
  By many a mound and scree,
And still the barefoot track led on,
  And an angry man was he.

He followed fast, he followed slow,
  And still he called her name,

But only the dingoes of the hills
　　Yowled back at him again.

His hair stood up along his neck,
　　His angry mind was gone,
For the track of the two bare feet gave out
　　And a four-foot track went on.

Her nightgown lay upon the snow
　　As it might upon the sheet,
But the track that led from where it lay
　　Was never of human feet.

His heart turned over in his chest,
　　He looked from side to side,
And he thought more of his gumwood fire
　　Than he did of his griesly bride.

And first he started walking back
　　And then begun to run,
And his quarry wheeled at the end of her track
　　And hunted him in turn.

Oh, long the fire may burn for him
　　And open stand the door,
And long the bed may wait empty:
　　He'll not be back any more.

8

IMAGINATION IN POETRY

> The lunatic, the lover and the poet
> Are of imagination all compact;
> One sees more devils than vast hell can hold,
> That is, the madman: the lover, all as frantic,
> Sees Helen's beauty in a brow of Egypt:
> The poet's eye, in a fine frenzy rolling,
> Doth glance from heaven to earth, from earth to heaven;
> And as imagination bodies forth
> The forms of things unknown, the poet's pen
> Turns them to shapes and gives to airy nothing
> A local habitation and a name.
>> WILLIAM SHAKESPEARE, A *Midsummer-Night's Dream*, V, i.

Thus does Shakespeare have Duke Theseus expound the psychology of imagination as employed by the poet.

Wordsworth had in mind a different form of imagination when he proposed in his *Lyrical Ballads* "to choose incidents and situations from common life, and to relate or describe them, throughout, as far as was possible, in a selection of language really used by men, and, at the same time, to throw over them a certain colouring of imagination, whereby ordinary things should be presented to the mind in an unusual aspect." Whatever the form which the imagination may take, there can be no doubt that it is an essential element in poetry. Shelley, indeed, defined poetry as the "expression of the imagination." He had also a clear conception of the very great value of the imaginative faculty in matters outside the field of poetry, for he said further, "A man, to be greatly good, must imagine intensely and comprehensively; he must put himself in the place of another

235

and of many others; the pains and pleasures of his species must become his own. The great instrument of moral good is the imagination; and poetry administers to the effect by acting upon the cause."[1]

It is not, however, only in morals that the gift of imagination is of value. There are many situations outside the province of ethics in which "one must put himself in the place of another." In all our social relations, in teaching, in politics, in business, a sympathetic insight into the "pains and pleasures" of others, their tastes and desires, likes and dislikes, is indispensable for the highest success. And imagination, though of a different kind, is essential also in the activity of the scientist and the inventor. If imagination serves these useful functions, it is surely worth cultivating; and if, as Shelley says, "poetry enlarges the circumference of the imagination," this is an additional inducement to the study of poetry.

How the Imagination Works in Poetry

If we accept Wordsworth's statement that the composition of a poem begins with "emotion recollected in tranquillity," and becomes a "spontaneous overflow of powerful feeling," and T. S. Eliot's doctrine that the proper emotion is evoked in the reader when an "objective correlative," that is, a set of objects, a situation, a chain of events which shall be the formula of that *particular* emotion, is presented, it would seem that emotion in poetry depends entirely upon imaginative activity. The language of poetry consists largely of images and symbols. In them the poet expresses his thoughts and feelings and impressions, and through these symbols and images we readers re-create in ourselves thoughts and feelings and impressions similar to those of the poet.

There are various ways in which the imagination is appealed to in poetry. First, there are descriptions of things and events and persons and moods, often in very simple and seemingly unimaginative language. This is, in general, the method employed in "The Solitary Reaper," though the poem consists less of objective description than of imaginative suggestions of how the scene impresses the poet. Turn to de la Mare's "The Listeners" at the end of this chapter. Here there is little that is not literal description, granting, of course, the existence of the phantoms. There are no poetic flights, no striking metaphors, no figures of speech at all, one may say, except the *surging backward* of the silence when the plunging hoofs are gone. It is by the skillful choice of meaningful details and the careful selection of descriptive words that this mysterious incident is created and drenched in its supernatural atmosphere.

Secondly, sometimes a single, apt word or phrase will create an image that the poet wishes us to see:

[1] "A Defence of Poetry," in *Complete Works of Percy Bysshe Shelley* (New York: Charles Scribner's Sons, 1930), Chap. 7, p. 136.

Death lays his *icy hand* on kings
She was a *phantom* of delight
Boughs which *shake against* the cold
Full of sorrow and *leaden-eyed* despairs

Sometimes the image is more extended, and often it is a comparison, in the form of a simile or metaphor, which reveals some striking or hitherto unappreciated likeness between two objects, as when Shakespeare calls leafless boughs

> Bare ruin'd choirs where late the sweet birds sang;

or when he has Macbeth compare conscience to a bed of torture:

> Better be with the dead . . .
> Than on the torture of the mind to lie
> In restless ecstasy;

or when Matthew Arnold likens the world to

> a darkling plain
> Swept with confused alarms of struggle and flight,
> Where ignorant armies clash by night.

Third, there are personifications—of animals, birds, snakes, even cockroaches; of trees, clouds, flowers, rocks, valleys, and other inanimate things; and of abstractions such as time, grief, liberty, truth, hope, and all the vices and virtues. Besides, the poets have created a host of fabulous creatures such as dragons, satyrs, centaurs, monsters, gods, demons, fairies, cupids, angels, and furies. All of these may be represented as behaving and speaking like human beings. And all have been at times blended into countless fables, myths, allegories, hyperboles, and fanciful fictions far removed from scientific fact and literal truth. Some rationalists of the eighteenth century, concerned about making language a precise symbolization of literal fact, thought that these lies and fictions were "fatal to peace and good manners" and went so far as to propose that wild tales and even "specious metaphors" be prohibited by law. But we, brought up in a more liberal age, readily accept even the wildest fantasies, and it is well that we do, since otherwise we should not be capable of appreciating many of the delights of poetry. We should, however, be able to distinguish fact from fancy.

The Analysis of Images

In examining a poetic figure you should note just what is being compared with what, and the nature of the similarities. In "Death lays his icy hand on kings" it is clear enough that death is being likened to a person with cold hands. In Shakespeare's sonnet quoted above, bare boughs are likened to empty choir-stalls in a ruined cathedral. In these examples the points of similarity are readily found. Sometimes, however, the similarities are only vaguely suggested. If you try to define the ways in which this world is like a confused battlefield, as suggested in Arnold's figure in "Dover Beach," you will have considerable difficulty, you will encounter endless ambiguities, and you will probably destroy both the beauty and the "meaning" of the figure.

Poetry, as has often been said, is untranslatable. If we find a poet "difficult," it may be because we are looking for literal statements of fact such as we find in a news story, instead of accepting poetry for what it is—a complex of statement, image, and sound, which is meant to appeal more to the emotions and the imagination than to the intellect. Poets are often obscure, sometimes quite unnecessarily so, and if you fail to understand a poet's figures and images the fault may be his. If he does not employ material that ought to be familiar to a qualified reader, if his constructions are tortured anl his references obscure, "if he permits himself to become the auto-intoxicated victim of his private verbal games," he may justly be considered at fault. But if you fail to appreciate a figure because you don't examine it attentively, because you are not receptive and open-minded toward it, or because your present education does not cover some of the words and references that a reasonably cultured reader should understand, then the fault cannot be attributed to the poet.

You may ask, Why doesn't the poet say what he means instead of clouding his intention in a lot of figures? What we must understand is that often the figure *is* the meaning, and not merely an ornament used to decorate the meaning. In this respect poetic language is not essentially different from our daily speech. We seldom realize how much our ordinary talk consists of metaphors, and how untranslatable they often are. Try, for instance, to put into literal terms these common figures of everyday speech, to explain what they mean in nonfigurative language:

> He put something over on me.
> We patched up our quarrel.
> This makes a hit with me.
> Don't jump to conclusions.
> We can't make the grade.

If you find it difficult to reduce these expressions to literal terms without sacrificing something of their economy, vividness, and clarity, do not expect to have less difficulty with poetic figures. "A symbol cannot be expressed in any other terms," says a modern critic. "The expression is the symbol." And he quotes the poet Yeats as saying, "It is not possible to separate an emotion or a spiritual state from the image that calls it up and gives it expression."[2]

Neither is it possible to separate the essential meaning of a poetic passage from its *sound.* In studying the images and figures and descriptions of which poetry largely consists, and in interpreting them to our audience, we must be constantly aware of the sounds of the words in which they are presented and of the movement of the rhythm. It is essential in reading poetry, says I. A. Richards, "to give the words their full imagined sound and body. . . . Even before the words have been intellectually understood and the thoughts they occasion formed and followed, the movement and sound of the words is playing deeply and intimately upon the interests."[3]

The Ambiguity of Symbols

The precise effects of the sounds, and of the images themselves, will not be the same upon all hearers, because, as I have noted, hearers differ in their susceptibilities, and images are ambiguous in their suggestions. William Empson, in analyzing the line, "Bare ruin'd choirs where late the sweet birds sang," has pointed out the great number of ways in which we may feel a similarity between boughs and choirs. Both are places in which to sing, places where the singers sit in rows; both are made of wood; the architectural detail of the church was derived from the forest; the stained glass windows may have the images of leaves and flowers; the walls of the abandoned building are grey like the winter sky; etc., and so "there is a kind of ambiguity" in not knowing which of these likenesses to hold most clearly in mind.[4] Empson regards ambiguity not as the defect, but as the virtue, of poetry, since it affords richness of suggestion to the reader. (Ambiguity here means not that the meaning is doubtful or uncertain, but that there is more than one legitimate meaning.)

It follows that some readers may be more influenced by one of these meanings, and some by another, but this fact need not throw us into confusion. The poet's medium of expression is words, and as was pointed out in an earlier chapter, words mean to us only what we have come to associate with them from our previous experience. Perhaps we never get from a poet's, or anyone else's, words the full and exact meaning of the one who speaks them, because no two people have had exactly the same experiences. We may indeed find that we have had no previous experi-

---

[2] Donald Stauffer, *The Golden Nightingale* (New York: The Macmillan Co., 1949), pp. 29, 31.

[3] I. A. Richards, *Science and Poetry* (New York: W. W. Norton & Co., Inc., 1926), p. 31.

[4] See William Empson, *Seven Types of Ambiguity* (2d ed.; New York: New Directions, 1947), pp. 2–3.

ence whatever with the poet's words. For instance, when Tennyson wrote, "The callow throstle lispeth," he had doubtless seen and heard young throstles and they seemed to him to lisp. But if to us, as in probable, *callow* and *throstle* are not familiar words, our imaginations will make scarcely any response to Tennyson's line.

But in general a poet's words and images do have meaning for us because we have had previous experience with them; and they arouse in us substantially the same associations and connotations that they arouse in others. All the best poetry speaks a universal language. We respond to Wordsworth's sonnet (see page 318) because we too have felt at times that worldly considerations are "too much with us," and that we neglect the beauties of nature. If we have not seen, we can at least imagine, a sea that "bares her bosom to the moon," and can even conceive some sort of image of "Proteus rising from the sea," and "hear old Triton blow his wreathèd horn." The fact that one of us may think of the moon on Long Island Sound, and another on San Francisco Bay, or only of a lithograph of the moonlit sea, does not make any essential difference.

For the appreciation of such passages we are greatly aided by the photographs and paintings we have seen, the plays we have witnessed, and the sights and sounds with which we are familiarized through phonograph, radio, television, and motion picture. Dwellers on inland plains who have never seen any large body of water may nevertheless visualize the restless to and fro of the waves, and even feel the mysterious power of the "unplumbed, salt, estranging sea."

Imagination Works through Suggestion

The poet in presenting a scene to us works by means of suggestion. He does not give us a complete and detailed description, a photographic representation of a mood or scene or incident. Rather he seizes upon some salient detail, some essential characteristic, some typical form of an object, and by suggestion causes us to fill in the details with our own imaginations. "His lines," says Professor Winchester, "bring to our imagination . . . only those details in which the emotional power of the scene resides."[5] He does this by selecting from the manifold elements of his subject those details which reveal it in its most typical form. He gives us the heart of a scene, the essence of an emotion. The poet's genius as a poet lies precisely in this ability to reveal to us the essential form or pattern or "Gestalt" of an object. It is in this respect that he shows his skill as an imitator of nature.

[5] Caleb Thomas Winchester, *Principles of Literary Criticism* (New York: The Macmillan Co., 1899), p. 134.

UNFAMILIAR TERMS HINDER IMAGINATION. This discussion of the nature and the materials of the poetic imagination suggests three major reasons why we may fail to respond to the poet's imagery. First, the words and phrases he uses may be so unfamiliar as to create no response in our minds. We must know his language. We cannot, of course, get much stimulation from German poetry unless we understand German. The best poets are often so widely read and so deeply experienced with life that their language has a richness beyond our experience. They refer to places and persons and things which we may never have heard of, or which, if we have heard their names, bring no clear image to our minds. When Keats, for instance, says in "The Eve of St. Agnes" that:

A shielded scutcheon blush'd with blood of queens and kings.

and again, that Madeline slept:

Clasp'd like a missal where swart Paynims pray.

he is using images to which only the most erudite of his readers will respond. And when Shelley says that the Mediterranean lay dreaming:

Beside a pumice isle in Baiæ's bay.

he is carrying the average reader somewhat beyond his depth in geology and geography. If such passages are to give us more than the vague pleasure we can derive from the mere sounds of the words, we must take some pains to discover their meaning.

It is a curious fact that many even of those that pretend to enjoy poetry are not willing to take the pains necessary to understand it. Content to ladle off a few vague emotional impressions, they miss entirely that higher pleasure which comes from the discovery and the contemplation of its deep philosophical truths. In poetry, even more than in prose, you must acquire the habit of looking intensely at words, and assuring yourself of their meaning. You must allow no image to pass without a serious and earnest endeavor to re-create it in your own mind. Nothing short of this deserves the name of reading. If you merely pronounce the poet's words to your hearers, allowing them to gather from such a performance whatever meaning they can, you throw upon them a burden which is properly yours. You do not stir their imaginations or move them to any proper emotional response. Pronouncing words is not interpreting literature. The business of the interpreter is to interpret. Only as he catches the emotional and imaginative content (as well, of course, as the thought content) of his selection, only as his mind expands to contain its content, as his body warms to its emotion, and as his eye brightens to its imagery, will he succeed in stirring in his hearers those responses which constitute what I call appreciation of poetry.

STALENESS AND FAMILIARITY HINDER IMAGINATION. A second reason why we often fail to respond to the poet's imagery is that it may be so trite and familiar as to stifle our response. This *may* be the fault of the poet, or it may be due merely to much repetition of very good poetry. Good poetry is full of surprises, even if it surprises us oftenest, as Max Eastman said, by telling us most exactly what we know. But this element of surprise is dulled and blurred if we have become too familiar with a poem. Then our problem is to win back the thrill of the first reading. To many persons brought up in the church the Bible has become meaningless from much repetition. It would be a wonderful experience for one of mature taste and sharp perception to come upon these beautiful passages for the first time. But, familiar to us from childhood, they pass over us without making the slightest impression, except like music to stir a few vague feelings. We even allow our hymn writers to compose of religious stereotypes such a mixed metaphor as this:

> Crown him with many crowns,
> The Lamb upon his throne!

and we sing it in utter oblivion of its incongruousness.

The cure for such insensibility to meaning is to attempt to recapture the thrill that comes from a first reading of such passages. We must penetrate through the callus formed by endless repetition and get back to the meaning of the figure, the emotional significance of the scene. And at times we must resist the siren lure of mere rhythm and assonance, and examine a figure or a description with the critical eye of a bank cashier, and then, when the heart of the passage is understood, bring back the emotional significance by putting it again in its setting of verse and meter. Good interpretation demands the kind of plasticity which in a much higher degree must be possessed by actors. To feel and to communicate night after night the same passion of grief or rage or fear or love require a quickness of imaginative response and a plasticity of mood that only the most gifted possess. Lacking such plasticity the only alternative is the less certain method of cold technique.

Test your ability to real-ize and vitalize such passages as these:

> Along the cool sequestered vale of life
> They kept the noiseless tenor of their way.
>
> THOMAS GRAY.

> Tell me not in mournful numbers
> Life is but an empty dream.
>
> HENRY WADSWORTH LONGFELLOW.

> He maketh me to lie down in green pastures: he leadeth
> me beside the still waters.
>
> Psalm 23.

DISTRACTION AND HURRY HINDER IMAGINATION. A third reason why we may miss the imaginative splendors of good poetry lies in the extravagant tempo of modern life. Bombarded constantly with a veritable hailstorm of sensations, our attention distracted continually from one thing to another, hurried at an ever accelerating pace from babyhood till old age, we become less and less suited for critical contemplation and philosophical calm. For the appreciation as well as for the creation of art there is needed, besides quiet and leisure, a constant and long-continued environment, a milieu of settled and habitual surroundings, a warp of familiar custom and habit. Poetry must not be read in snatches. It is not, like billboard slogans, for him who runs to read. It has depths which no such cursory examination will reveal. It can best be appreciated in "that serene and blessed mood" which Wordsworth describes:

> In which the affections gently lead us on,—
> Until, the breath of this corporeal frame
> And even the motion of our human blood
> Almost suspended, we are laid asleep
> In body, and become a living soul:
> While with an eye made quiet by the power
> Of harmony, and the deep power of joy,
> We see into the life of things.

Or the reader may well take the advice of Milton's Thoughtful Man, Il Penseroso:

> And join with thee calm Peace, and Quiet,
> Spare Fast, that oft with gods doth diet,
> And hear the Muses in a ring
> Aye round about Jove's altar sing;
> And add to these retirèd leisure
> That in trim gardens takes his pleasure;
> But, first and chiefest, with thee bring
> Him that yon soars on golden wing,
> Guiding the fiery-wheelèd throne,
> The Cherub Contemplation.

In such a mood the reader should study his selection and prepare it for public rendition. First, of course, there must be painstaking examination of its thought, rhythm, and imagery. In de la Mare's "The Listeners," assigned for study at the end of this chapter, you must create a picture of a building, and do it from a very few details: a moonlit door, a turret, a leaf-fringed sill, a dark stair, and an empty hall. That is all you have to work with. If you are not careful you will miss some of these details, and if you hurry you will not get them integrated into a picture. The imagination works from mere suggestions, but it will not create the picture the poet intended unless it first gets hold of all the suggestions he offers. Then again, you must create from a very few details the traveler's appearance, mood, and mission: He has just arrived on horseback, his horse eats hungrily of the forest grasses, he stands perplexed and still, he has grey eyes, he knocks on the door, then *smites* it a second time, then suddenly smites even louder, lifts his head, shouts his message, mounts, and plunges off into the silence. These details are meaningless until through long study you find a meaning for them. And so with the mysterious listeners, and the other elements of the poem.

When the picture is once formed, it should be dwelt upon until the re-creative power of the imagination suffuses all your avenues of expression with an emotional glow—manifest in your eye, your facial expression, your bodily tensions, and in the vibrations of your voice. You should be *possessed* by the spirit of the poem. The poet by inspiration or by long contemplation penetrates to the heart of life, and reveals to us a permanent and ideal truth. The interpreter of poetry, as well as the interpreter of life—that is, the interpretative reader, as well as the poet himself—must have the ability to detach himself from the distractions of his environment, and dwell in rapt contemplation upon the object of his study. Then he can appear before his audience with that imaginative responsiveness which makes his reading seem as real as if it were his own creation.

Our Resources

Let us review the resources we have to work with in the communication of poetic values. We have first the words, the language, of the author. Second, we have our voices, our vocal expression. Third, we have visible action, facial expression, gesture. Each of these may alone be an effective instrument in moving an audience. Think of the thousands of persons who, sitting alone with a book, reading silently to themselves, have been thrilled by the adventures in Scott's novels, or moved to tears by the pathos of Dickens. Ivanhoe and David Copperfield are vividly re-created and excite as much feeling as if they were actual. Shakespeare's Macbeth and Hamlet, Portia, and Rosalind are discussed and argued over as if they were real persons, and often by those who have never seen them on the stage. Indeed, the sight of these characters on the stage is often disappointing and irritating to those who have already formed their conception of them by reading the plays. Shakespeare's fairies can be clearly imagined as real when we only read about them, but when we see them represented by a group of hundred-and-twenty-pound girls bouncing about on a plank stage, they lose their identity as fairies and become merely performers.

Consider also the powerful effect of drama as presented only to the ear, with no stimulus to the eye, as in radio plays. By his radio drama of an invasion from Mars, Orson Welles threw many hearers into a state of actual terror. It is not likely that any such panic could have been created by a motion picture or television or stage play in which the characters were visible. And it is questionable whether television is as powerful a dramatic medium as the radio alone. Scenes that we visualize for ourselves are often more moving than those presented to us ready-made.

Visible Expression

Besides being moved by a reader's words and voice we are affected also by his visible behavior. From this largely comes our impression of any speaker's mood, attitude, and purpose, the nature and intensity of his feeling, as well as his character and personality. Expression, as prompted by a reader's imagination, is a manifestation to the observer's eye and ear of what he is experiencing. It is sometimes said that "expression is always perfect," that is, the reader's vocal and bodily behavior is an accurate reflection of what he feels and means while reading. These manifestations are often too elusive to be clearly described in elocutionary terms, but they are readily perceived and understood. They are a dependable index of an interpreter's appreciation of what he is reading—more dependable than what he could write on an examination paper. These evidences of imaginative aliveness are the chief marks of excellence in interpretation, and are the criteria by which the reader's performance should be judged. They can seldom, if ever, be achieved by mechanical methods of managing voice and gesture. They must come from within.

The lack of a specific technique for the expression of imaginative and emotional values is, to some students, disappointing and baffling. "I see clearly what the poet is describing," they may say. "I understand his emotion, and I feel it myself. The trouble is that I can't express it. I try to let myself go, but somehow I *don't* go. I don't have the necessary technique of expression. That's what I want to get from this course."

This desire is understandable and, to some extent, commendable. Look again at what was said in Chapter 3 about the mechanical method of interpretation. At times you, or your teacher, may be able to discover devices of voice or gesture that will promote the right effect, and if these are practiced until they are perfected and made to seem spontaneous, they may be effectively employed in public performance. But in general your best recourse, and always your first recourse, should be to trust imagination and feeling to prompt the right expression, as you must trust the hearer's imagination to create the right impression.

There is ground for believing that technique in teaching all the arts is much overemphasized, and that what is needed for artistic expression is sharper vision, deeper feeling, and keener intuition. Benedetto Croce, the Italian philosopher, said, "Feelings or impressions . . . pass by means of words from the obscure region of the soul into the clarity of the contemplative spirit. *It is impossible to distinguish intuition from expression in this cognitive process.* The one appears with the other at the same instant, because they are not two, but one."[6] See a fuller development of Croce's idea in the selection on page 93.

Appreciation of poetry, and the vocal and visible expression of appreciation, will come from penetrating insight into meaning and mood, and will be evidenced by vivid realization of them while we are reading. We ordinary mortals, of course, can seldom, if ever, see as sharply as poets see, for we must allow, on the testimony of Plato, Aristotle, Shakespeare, and others of lesser note, that the poet has within him a supernatural sensitiveness, a kind of divine madness, that he is a seer, a prophet, an inspired being. He sees into things more deeply than ordinary folk, but only perhaps because he examines more minutely the outward forms of things. "Homer looks a great while at his thumb." (See page 43.) But if we do our best to visualize what the poet has revealed, we may expect to be moved in the appropriate way, and we may expect that our vision and our emotion will be communicated to our hearers.

Cicero stated the matter well:

For every emotion of the mind has from nature its own peculiar look, tone, and gesture; and the whole frame of man, and his whole countenance, and the variations of his voice, sound like strings in a musical instrument, just as they are moved by the affections of the mind. . . . For all the powers of action proceed from the mind, and the countenance is the image of the mind, and the eyes are its interpreters.[7]

PLAN OF STUDY

1. Take time to examine carefully every imaginative suggestion the poet gives you, every description, every picture, every figure. Fill in the details of these suggestions until they are complete, real, and vivid.
2. Draw upon all your past experience and reading for the enrichment of these pictures; try to re-create vividly all sense impressions suggested—sight, sound, touch, smell, taste.
3. Investigate immediately and thoroughly all unfamiliar terms and references. Do not be satisfied until you get as clear a picture as seems possible of every object mentioned, and try to understand the significance of every image, what it contributes to the poem. Do the same with the sound effects.

[6] Benedetto Croce, *The Essence of Aesthetics,* trans. Douglas Ainslie (London: W. Heinemann, Ltd., 1921), p. 21.
[7] Cicero, *De oratore* iii. 57, 59.

4. In every figure of speech note exactly the points of likeness in the objects compared. There may be several in each figure.
5. If after your analysis some ambiguity remains, be sure that the fault, if it is a fault, is the poet's, not yours.
6. Take pains to revivify any trite or overfamiliar terms and images. How would they impress you if seen for the first time?
7. When the poem is thoroughly understood seek a quiet place and surrender yourself to its spirit. Integrate all details into a coherent whole, a unity of mood and feeling and movement. Chant the poem aloud, giving full value to the sounds of the words and the movement of the rhythm, and abandon yourself to its emotion. In this private rehearsal don't be afraid to let yourself go. In public recitation recall as much as you can of this abandon while observing the restraints of good sense and good taste.

CRITERIA

1. Did the reader while he was reading seem to see the scenes and objects described or suggested by the poet?
2. Did he pass over unfamiliar or difficult images without seeming to visualize them?
3. Did he revitalize trite and familiar images?
4. Was there evidence in his voice and visible expression of complete absorption in the imaginative content of the poem? Was he possessed by the poet's vision? That is, was there clear indication of his imaginative response to what he was reading?

QUESTIONS FOR DISCUSSION

1. To what extent are a poet's imaginings duplicated by his readers?
2. Discuss the relative effect of a complete detailed description of a scene or experience as compared with a mere suggestion of it.
3. What is the relation of imagination to insight?
4. Discuss: "Excellence in oral interpretation should be judged by the evidences the reader reveals of his imaginative response to the readings."
5. Discuss imaginative activity in terms of the theory, first, that poetry is imitation of nature; second, that it is expression of emotion; third, that it is revelation of the poet's life, character, and sincerity; fourth, that a poem is a self-contained universe of discourse and need be true only to itself.

SELECTION FOR DRILL

THE LISTENERS[8]

Walter de la Mare

"Is there anybody there?" said the Traveller,
    Knocking on the moonlit door;
And his horse in the silence champed the grasses
    Of the forest's ferny floor.
And a bird flew up out of the turret,   5
    Above the Traveller's head:
And he smote upon the door again a second time;
    "Is there anybody there?" he said.
But no one descended to the Traveller;
    No head from the leaf-fringed sill   10
Leaned over and looked into his grey eyes,
    Where he stood perplexed and still.
But only a host of phantom listeners
    That dwelt in the lone house then
Stood listening in the quiet of the moonlight   15
    To that voice from the world of men:
Stood thronging the faint moonbeams on the dark stair,
    That goes down to the empty hall,
Hearkening in an air stirred and shaken
    By the lonely Traveller's call.   20
And he felt in his heart their strangeness,
    Their stillness answering his cry,
While his horse moved, cropping the dark turf,
    'Neath the starred and leafy sky;
For he suddenly smote on the door, even   25
    Louder, and lifted his head:—
"Tell them I came, and no one answered,
    That I kept my word," he said.
Never the least stir made the listeners,
    Though every word he spake   30
Fell echoing through the shadowiness of the still house,
    From the one man left awake:
Ay, they heard his foot upon the stirrup,
    And the sound of iron on stone,
And how the silence surged softly backward,   35
    When the plunging hoofs were gone.

SUGGESTIONS FOR ANALYSIS. Be sure of the meaning of *champed, turret, cropping*. Make sure of the pronunciation of *forest, spake, ay, stirrup, hoofs*. Note carefully which are main details and which are subordinate. The main thread of the poem is in the narration of the traveler's actions and their results. Statements about the horse, the bird, various descriptive touches, etc., are sub-

[8] By permission of Holt, Rinehart & Winston, Inc.

ordinate. Don't be tricked by the verse or rhyme into emphasizing matter which is echoed or implied; such as "to the Traveller," in line 9; "where he stood," in line 12; all of line 14; "their strangeness, their stillness . . . leafy sky," lines 21–24.

Construct a clear picture of the scene. Visualize the building and its setting. How is the traveler dressed? in clothes of what period? How are the phantoms dressed? Visualize their grouping on the stair. Through what kind of window does the moonlight stream? Stained glass? Visualize the dark stair and empty hall. How do the phantoms react to the traveler's summons? What has brought him here? What is his relation to those within? Has he been here before? What is the promise he has made and kept? Interpret the gesture: "and lifted his head." Note that "suddenly" he "smote" the door. Why? He "plunged" off into the darkness. Why? In what mood did he speak? Gently, pleadingly, angrily, defiantly, sadly? After all these questions are solved there will remain a good deal of mystery—as the poet intended.

You will not be able to analyze the meter by conventional scansion. You should, however, be able to feel the recurrence of three surges of emphasis in each line, a surge sometimes spread over several syllables. You will add a delightful quality to the beauty of the verse if you articulate with deftness and precision all the light syllables sprinkled between these peaks of emphasis. Do not weaken the vowels too much in such lines as the 31st. The numerous syllables if delicately articulated suggest the re-echoing of the rider's knocking through the deserted halls. Make the most of the long vowels in such lines as the 17th.

The prevailing mood is of mystery. There is no point in trying to read into the poem an allegory. Give us the picture drenched in mysterious moonlight, and leave it with us. The picture is enjoyable for its own sake, without being tagged with a moral. Compare the poem with Browning's "Childe Roland to the Dark Tower Came."

SELECTIONS FOR PRACTICE

From PARADISE LOST

John Milton

Of Man's first disobedience, and the fruit
Of that forbidden tree, whose mortal taste
Brought death into the world, and all our woe,
With loss of Eden, till one greater Man
Restore us, and regain the blissful seat,
Sing, Heavenly Muse, that on the secret top
Of Oreb, or of Sinai, didst inspire
That shepherd who first taught the chosen seed
In the beginning how the heavens and earth
Rose out of Chaos: or, if Sion hill
Delight thee more, and Siloa's brook that flowed
Fast by the oracle of God, I thence
Invoke thy aid to my adventurous song,
That with no middle flight intends to soar
Above th' Aonian mount, while it pursues
Things unattempted yet in prose or rime.
And chiefly Thou, O Spirit, that dost prefer
Before all temples th' upright heart and pure,
Instruct me, for Thou know'st; Thou from the first
Wast present, and, with mighty wings outspread,
Dove-like sat'st brooding on the vast Abyss,
And mad'st it pregnant; what in me is dark
Illumine, what is low raise and support;
That, to the height of this great argument,
I may assert Eternal Providence,
And justify the ways of God to men.
　　Say first—for Heaven hides nothing from thy view,
Nor the deep tract of Hell—say first what cause
Moved our grand Parents, in that happy state,
Favoured of Heaven so highly, to fall off
From their Creator, and transgress his will
For one restraint, lords of the world besides?
Who first seduced them to that foul revolt?
Th' infernal Serpent; he it was whose guile,
Stirred up with envy and revenge, deceived
The mother of mankind, what time his pride
Had cast him out from Heaven, with all his host
Of rebel Angels, by whose aid, aspiring
To set himself in glory above his peers,
He trusted to have equalled the Most High,
If he opposed; and, with ambitious aim
Against the throne and monarchy of God

Raised impious war in Heaven, and battle proud,
With vain attempt. Him the Almighty Power
Hurled headlong flaming from the ethereal sky,
With hideous ruin and combustion, down
To bottomless perdition; there to dwell
In adamantine chains and penal fire,
Who durst defy the Omnipotent to arms.
 Nine times the space that measures day and night
To mortal men, he with his horrid crew
Lay vanquished, rolling in the fiery gulf,
Confounded, though immortal. But his doom
Reserved him to more wrath; for now the thought
Both of lost happiness and lasting pain
Torments him; round he throws his baleful eyes,
That witnessed huge affliction and dismay,
Mixed with obdurate pride and steadfast hate.
At once, as far as Angels ken, he views
The dismal situation waste and wild:
A dungeon horrible on all sides round
As one great furnace flamed; yet from those flames
No light; but rather darkness visible
Served only to discover sights of woe,
Regions of sorrow, doleful shades, where peace
And rest can never dwell, hope never comes
That comes to all; but torture without end
Still urges, and a fiery deluge, fed
With ever-burning sulphur unconsumed.
Such place Eternal Justice had prepared
For those rebellious; here their prison ordained
In utter darkness, and their portion set,
As far removed from God and light of Heaven
As from the centre thrice to the utmost pole.

From TINTERN ABBEY

William Wordsworth

Five years have past; five summers, with the length
Of five long winters! and again I hear
These waters, rolling from their mountain-springs
With a soft inland murmur.—Once again
Do I behold these steep and lofty cliffs,
That on a wild secluded scene impress
Thoughts of more deep seclusion; and connect
The landscape with the quiet of the sky.
The day is come when I again repose
Here, under this dark sycamore, and view

These plots of cottage-ground, these orchard-tufts,
Which at this season, with their unripe fruits,
Are clad in one green hue, and lose themselves
'Mid groves and copses. Once again I see
These hedgerows, hardly hedgerows, little lines
Of sportive wood run wild: these pastoral farms,
Green to the very door; and wreaths of smoke
Sent up, in silence, from among the trees!
With some uncertain notice, as might seem
Of vagrant dwellers in the houseless woods,
Or of some Hermit's cave, where by his fire
The Hermit sits alone.
                              These beauteous forms,
Through a long absence, have not been to me
As is a landscape to a blind man's eye:
But oft, in lonely rooms, and 'mid the din
Of towns and cities, I have owed to them
In hours of weariness, sensations sweet,
Felt in the blood, and felt along the heart;
And passing even into my purer mind,
With tranquil restoration:—feelings too
Of unremembered pleasure: such, perhaps,
As have no slight or trivial influence
On that best portion of a good man's life,
His little, nameless, unremembered acts
Of kindness and of love. Nor less, I trust,
To them I may have owed another gift,
Of aspect more sublime; that blessed mood,
In which the burthen of the mystery,
In which the heavy and the weary weight
Of all this unintelligible world,
Is lightened:—that serene and blessèd mood
In which the affections gently lead us on,—
Until, the breath of this corporeal frame
And even the motion of our human blood
Almost suspended, we are laid asleep
In body, and become a living soul:
While with an eye made quiet by the power
Of harmony, and the deep power of joy,
We see into the life of things.
                              If this
Be but a vain belief, yet, oh! how oft—
In darkness and amid the many shapes
Of joyless daylight; when the fretful stir
Unprofitable, and the fever of the world,
Have hung upon the beatings of my heart—

How oft, in spirit, have I turned to thee,
O sylvan Wye! thou wanderer thro' the woods,
How often has my spirit turned to thee!

And now, with gleams of half-extinguished thought,
With many recognitions dim and faint,
And somewhat of a sad perplexity,
The picture of the mind revives again:
While here I stand, not only with the sense
Of present pleasure, but with pleasing thoughts
That in this moment there is life and food
For future years. And so I dare to hope,
Though changed, no doubt, from what I was when first
I came among these hills; when like a roe
I bounded o'er the mountains, by the sides
Of the deep rivers, and the lonely streams,
Wherever nature led: more like a man
Flying from something that he dreads, than one
Who sought the thing he loved. For nature then
(The coarser pleasures of my boyish days,
And their glad animal movements all gone by)
To me was all in all.—I cannot paint
What then I was. The sounding cataract
Haunted me like a passion; the tall rock,
The mountain, and the deep and gloomy wood,
Their colours and their forms, were then to me
An appetite; a feeling and a love,
That had no need of a remoter charm,
By thought supplied, nor any interest
Unborrowed from the eye.—That time is past,
And all its aching joys are now no more,
And all its dizzy raptures. Not for this
Faint I, nor mourn, nor murmur; other gifts
Have followed; for such loss, I would believe,
Abundant recompense. For I have learned
To look on nature, not as in the hour
Of thoughtless youth; but hearing oftentimes
The still, sad music of humanity,
Nor harsh nor grating, though of ample power
To chasten and subdue. And I have felt
A presence that disturbs me with the joy
Of elevated thoughts; a sense sublime,
Of something far more deeply interfused,
Whose dwelling is the light of setting suns,
And the round ocean and the living air,
And the blue sky, and in the mind of man;
A motion and a spirit, that impels

All thinking things, all objects of all thought,
And rolls through all things. Therefore am I still
A lover of the meadows and the woods,
And mountains; and of all that we behold
From this green earth; of all the mighty world
Of eye, and ear,—both what they half create,
And what perceive; well pleased to recognise
In nature and the language of the sense,
The anchor of my purest thoughts, the nurse,
The guide, the guardian of my heart, and soul
Of all my moral being.

From INTIMATIONS OF IMMORTALITY

William Wordsworth

I

There was a time when meadow, grove and stream,
The earth, and every common sight,
        To me did seem
        Apparelled in celestial light,
The glory and the freshness of a dream.
It is not now as it hath been of yore;—
        Turn wheresoe'er I may,
        By night or day,
The things which I have seen I now can see no more.

II

The Rainbow comes and goes,
And lovely is the Rose;
The Moon doth with delight
Look round her when the heavens are bare;
        Waters on a starry night
        Are beautiful and fair;
The sunshine is a glorious birth;
But yet I know, where'er I go,
That there hath past away a glory from the earth.

III

Now, while the birds thus sing a joyous song,
        And while the young lambs bound
        As to the tabor's sound,
To me alone there came a thought of grief;
A timely utterance gave that thought relief,
        And I again am strong:
The cataracts blow their trumpets from the steep;

No more shall grief of mine the season wrong;
I hear the echoes through the mountains throng,
The winds come to me from the fields of sleep,
    And all the earth is gay;
      Land and sea
    Give themselves up to jollity,
      And with the heart of May
    Doth every Beast keep holiday;—
      Thou Child of joy,
Shout round me, let me hear thy shouts, thou happy shepherd-boy!

IV

Ye blessèd Creatures, I have heard the call
    Ye to each other make; I see
The heavens laugh with you in your jubilee:
    My heart is at your festival,
    My head hath its coronal,
The fullness of your bliss, I feel—I feel it all.
    Oh evil day! if I were sullen
    While Earth herself is adorning,
      This sweet May-morning,
    And the Children are culling
      On every side,
    In a thousand valleys far and wide,
    Fresh flowers; while the sun shines warm,
And the Babe leaps up on his Mother's arm:—
    I hear, I hear, with joy I hear!
    —But there's a Tree, of many, one,
A single Field which I have looked upon,
Both of them speak of something that is gone:
    The Pansy at my feet
    Doth the same tale repeat:
Whither is fled the visionary gleam?
Where is it now, the glory and the dream?

V

Our birth is but a sleep and a forgetting:
The Soul that rises with us, our life's Star,
    Hath had elsewhere its setting,
      And cometh from afar:
Not in entire forgetfulness,
    And not in utter nakedness,
But trailing clouds of glory do we come
    From God, who is our home:
Heaven lies about us in our infancy!
Shades of the prison-house begin to close
    Upon the growing Boy,

But He beholds the light, and whence it flows,
He sees it in his joy;
The Youth, who daily farther from the east
Must travel, still is Nature's priest,
And by the vision splendid
Is on his way attended;
At length the Man perceives it die away,
And fade into the light of common day.

KUBLA KHAN: OR, A VISION IN A DREAM

A FRAGMENT

Samuel Taylor Coleridge

In Xanadu did Kubla Khan
A stately pleasure-dome decree:
Where Alph, the sacred river, ran
Through caverns measureless to man
Down to a sunless sea.

So twice five miles of fertile ground
With walls and towers were girdled round:
And there were gardens bright with sinuous rills,
Where blossom'd many an incense-bearing tree;
And here were forests ancient as the hills,
Enfolding sunny spots of greenery.

But oh! that deep romantic chasm which slanted
Down the green hill athwart a cedarn cover!
A savage place! as holy and enchanted
As e'er beneath a waning moon was haunted
By woman wailing for her demon-lover!
And from this chasm, with ceaseless turmoil seething,
As if this earth in fast thick pants were breathing,
A mighty fountain momently was forced:
Amid whose swift half-intermitted burst
Huge fragments vaulted like rebounding hail,
Or chaffy grain beneath the thresher's flail:
And 'mid these dancing rocks at once and ever
It flung up momently the sacred river.
Five miles meandering with a mazy motion
Through wood and dale the sacred river ran,
Then reach'd the caverns measureless to man,
And sank in tumult to a lifeless ocean:
And 'mid this tumult Kubla heard from far
Ancestral voices prophesying war!

The shadow of the dome of pleasure
Floated midway on the waves;
Where was heard the mingled measure
From the fountain and the caves.
It was a miracle of rare device,
A sunny pleasure-dome with caves of ice!

A damsel with a dulcimer
In a vision once I saw:
It was an Abyssinian maid,
And on her dulcimer she play'd,
Singing of Mount Abora.
Could I revive within me
Her symphony and song,
To such a deep delight 'twould win me,
That with music loud and long,
I would build that dome in air,
That sunny dome! those caves of ice!
And all who heard should see them there,—
And all should cry, Beware! Beware!—
His flashing eyes, his floating hair!
Weave a circle round him thrice,
And close your eyes with holy dread,
For he on honey-dew hath fed,
And drunk the milk of Paradise.

APOSTROPHE TO THE OCEAN

CHILDE HAROLD'S PILGRIMAGE, IV

Lord Byron

There is a pleasure in the pathless woods,
There is a rapture on the lonely shore,
There is society where none intrudes,
By the deep Sea, and music in its roar:
I love not man the less, but Nature more,
From these our interviews, in which I steal
From all I may be, or have been before,
To mingle with the Universe, and feel
What I can ne'er express, yet cannot all conceal.

Roll on, thou deep and dark blue Ocean—roll!
Ten thousand fleets sweep over thee in vain;
Man marks the earth with ruin—his control
Stops with the shore;—upon the watery plain
The wrecks are all thy deed, nor doth remain
A shadow of man's ravage, save his own,

When for a moment, like a drop of rain,
He sinks into thy depths with bubbling groan,
Without a grave, unknell'd, uncoffin'd and unknown.

His steps are not upon thy paths—thy fields
Are not a spoil for him—thou dost arise
And shake him from thee; the vile strength he wields
For earth's destruction thou dost all despise,
Spurning him from thy bosom to the skies,
And send'st him, shivering in thy playful spray,
And howling, to his Gods, where haply lies
His petty hope in some near port or bay,
And dashest him again to earth—there let him lay.

The armaments which thunderstrike the walls
Of rock-built cities, bidding nations quake,
And monarchs tremble in their capitals,
The oak leviathans, whose huge ribs make
Their clay creator the vain title take
Of lord of thee, and arbiter of war—
These are thy toys, and, as the snowy flake,
They melt into thy yeast of waves, which mar
Alike the Armada's pride, or spoils of Trafalgar.

Thy shores are empires, changed in all save thee—
Assyria, Greece, Rome, Carthage, what are they?
Thy waters washed them power while they were free,
And many a tyrant since: their shores obey
The stranger, slave, or savage; their decay
Has dried up realms to deserts:—not so thou,
Unchangeable save to thy wild waves' play—
Time writes no wrinkle on thine azure brow—
Such as creation's dawn beheld, thou rollest now.

Thou glorious mirror, where the Almighty's form
Glasses itself in tempests: in all time,
Calm or convulsed—in breeze, or gale, or storm,
Icing the pole, or in the torrid clime
Dark-heaving;—boundless, endless, and sublime—
The image of Eternity—the throne
Of the Invisible; even from out thy slime
The monsters of the deep are made; each zone
Obeys thee; thou goest forth, dread, fathomless, alone.

And I have loved thee, Ocean! and my joy
Of youthful sports was on thy breast to be
Borne, like thy bubbles, onward: from a boy
I wanton'd with thy breakers—they to me
Were a delight; and if the freshening sea

Made them a terror—'twas a pleasing fear,
For I was as it were a child of thee,
And trusted to thy billows far and near,
And laid my hand upon thy mane—as I do here.

ODE TO THE WEST WIND

Percy Bysshe Shelley

I

O, wild West Wind, thou breath of Autumn's being,
Thou, from whose unseen presence the leaves dead
Are driven, like ghosts from an enchanter fleeing,

Yellow, and black, and pale, and hectic red,
Pestilence-stricken multitudes: O, thou,
Who chariotest to their dark wintry bed

The wingèd seeds, where they lie cold and low,
Each like a corpse within its grave, until
Thine azure sister of the spring shall blow

Her clarion o'er the dreaming earth, and fill
(Driving sweet buds like flocks to feed in air)
With living hues and odours plain and hill:

Wild Spirit, which art moving everywhere;
Destroyer and preserver; hear, O, hear!

II

Thou on whose stream, 'mid the steep sky's commotion,
Loose clouds like earth's decaying leaves are shed,
Shook from the tangled boughs of Heaven and Ocean,

Angels of rain and lightning: there are spread
On the blue surface of thine airy surge,
Like the bright hair uplifted from the head

Of some fierce Mænad, even from the dim verge
Of the horizon to the zenith's height
The locks of the approaching storm. Thou dirge

Of the dying year, to which this closing night
Will be the dome of a vast sepulchre,
Vaulted with all thy congregated might

Of vapours, from whose solid atmosphere
Black rain, and fire, and hail will burst: O, hear!

III

Thou who didst waken from his summer dreams
The blue Mediterranean, where he lay,
Lulled by the coil of his crystalline streams,

Beside a pumice isle in Baiæ's bay,
And saw in sleep old palaces and towers
Quivering within the wave's intenser day,

All overgrown with azure moss and flowers
So sweet, the sense faints picturing them!   Thou
For whose path the Atlantic's level powers

Cleave themselves into chasms, while far below
The sea-blooms and the oozy woods which wear
The sapless foliage of the ocean, know

Thy voice, and suddenly grow gray with fear,
And tremble and despoil themselves: O, hear!

IV

If I were a dead leaf thou mightest bear;
If I were a swift cloud to fly with thee;
A wave to pant beneath thy power, and share

The impulse of thy strength, only less free
Than thou, O, uncontrollable!   If even
I were as in my boyhood, and could be

The comrade of thy wanderings over heaven,
As then, when to outstrip thy skiey speed
Scarce seemed a vision; I would ne'er have striven

As thus with thee in prayer in my sore need.
Oh lift me as a wave, a leaf, a cloud!
I fall upon the thorns of life!   I bleed!

A heavy weight of hours has chained and bowed
One too like thee: tameless, and swift, and proud.

V

Make me thy lyre, even as the forest is:
What if my leaves are falling like its own!
The tumult of thy mighty harmonies

Will take from both a deep, autumnal tone,
Sweet though in sadness.   Be thou, spirit fierce,
My spirit!   Be thou me, impetuous one!

Drive my dead thoughts over the universe
Like withered leaves to quicken a new birth!
And, by the incantation of this verse,

Scatter, as from an unextinguished hearth
Ashes and sparks, my words among mankind!
Be through my lips to unawakened earth

The trumpet of a prophecy! O, wind,
If Winter comes, can Spring be far behind?

TO NIGHT

Percy Bysshe Shelley

Swiftly walk over the western wave,
      Spirit of Night!
Out of thy misty eastern cave,
Where all the long and lone daylight
Thou wovest dreams of joy and fear,
Which make thee terrible and dear,—
      Swift be thy flight!

Wrap thy form in a mantle gray,
      Star-inwrought!
Blind with thine hair the eyes of Day;
Kiss her until she be wearied out,
Then wander o'er city, and sea, and land,
Touching all with thine opiate wand—
      Come, long sought!

When I arose and saw the dawn,
      I sighed for thee;
When light rode high, and the dew was gone,
And noon lay heavy on flower and tree,
And the weary Day turned to his rest,
Lingering like an unloved guest,
      I sighed for thee.

Thy brother Death came, and cried,
      Wouldst thou me?
Thy sweet child Sleep, the filmy-eyed,
Murmured like a noontide bee,
Shall I nestle near thy side?
Wouldst thou me?—And I replied,
      No, not thee!

Death will come when thou art dead,
      Soon, too soon—
Sleep will come when thou art fled;
Of neither would I ask the boon
I ask of thee, belovèd Night—
Swift be thine approaching flight,
      Come soon, soon!

TO A SKYLARK

Percy   Bysshe   Shelley

Hail to thee, blithe spirit!
  Bird thou never wert,
That from heaven, or near it,
  Pourest thy full heart
In profuse strains of unpremeditated art.

Higher still and higher
  From the earth thou springest
Like a cloud of fire;
  The blue deep thou wingest,
And singing still dost soar, and soaring ever singest.

In the golden lightning
  Of the sunken sun,
O'er which clouds are bright'ning,
  Thou dost float and run;
Like an unbodied joy whose race is just begun.

The pale purple even
  Melts around thy flight;
Like a star of heaven,
  In the broad daylight
Thou art unseen, but yet I hear thy shrill delight,

Keen as are the arrows
  Of that silver sphere,
Whose intense lamp narrows
  In the white dawn clear,
Until we hardly see, we feel that it is there.

All the earth and air
  With thy voice is loud,
As, when night is bare,
  From one lonely cloud
The moon rains out her beams, and heaven is overflowed.

What thou art we know not;
  What is most like thee?
From rainbow clouds there flow not
  Drops so bright to see,
As from thy presence showers a rain of melody.

Like a poet hidden
  In the light of thought,

Singing hymns unbidden,
    Till the world is wrought
To sympathy with hopes and fears it heeded not:

Like a high-born maiden
    In a palace-tower,
Soothing her love-laden
    Soul in secret hour
With music sweet as love, which overflows her bower:

Like a glow-worm golden
    In a dell of dew,
Scattering unbeholden
    Its aërial hue
Among the flowers and grass, which screen it from the view:

Like a rose embowered
    In its own green leaves,
By warm winds deflowered,
    Till the scent it gives
Makes faint with too much sweet these heavy-wingèd thieves:

Sound of vernal showers
    On the twinkling grass,
Rain-awakened flowers,
    All that ever was
Joyous, and clear, and fresh, thy music doth surpass:

Teach us, sprite or bird,
    What sweet thoughts are thine:
I have never heard
    Praise of love or wine
That panted forth a flood of rapture so divine.

Chorus Hymeneal,
    Or triumphal chaunt,
Matched with thine would be all
    But an empty vaunt,
A thing wherein we feel there is some hidden want.

What objects are the fountains
    Of thy happy strain?
What fields, or waves, or mountains?
    What shapes of sky or plain?
What love of thine own kind? what ignorance of pain?

With thy clear keen joyance
    Languor cannot be:

Shadow of annoyance
  Never came near thee:
Thou lovest; but ne'er knew love's sad satiety.

Waking or asleep,
  Thou of death must deem
Things more true and deep
  Than we mortals dream,
Or how could thy notes flow in such a crystal stream?

We look before and after,
  And pine for what is not:
Our sincerest laughter
  With some pain is fraught;
Our sweetest songs are those that tell of saddest thought.

Yet if we could scorn
  Hate, and pride, and fear;
If we were things born
  Not to shed a tear,
I know not how thy joy we ever should come near.

Better than all measures
  Of delightful sound,
Better than all treasures
  That in books are found,
Thy skill to poet were, thou scorner of the ground!

Teach me half the gladness
  That thy brain must know,
Such harmonious madness
  From my lips would flow,
The world should listen then, as I am listening now.

ODE TO A NIGHTINGALE

John Keats

My heart aches, and a drowsy numbness pains
  My sense, as though of hemlock I had drunk,
Or emptied some dull opiate to the drains
  One minute past, and Lethe-wards had sunk;
'Tis not through envy of thy happy lot,
  But being too happy in thine happiness,—
    That thou, light-winged Dryad of the trees,
      In some melodious plot
Of beechen green, and shadows numberless,
  Singest of summer in full-throated ease.

O, for a draught of vintage! that hath been
　Cool'd a long age in the deep-delved earth,
Tasting of Flora and the country green,
　Dance, and Provençal song, and sunburnt mirth!
O, for a beaker full of the warm South,
　Full of the true, the blushful Hippocrene,
　　With beaded bubbles winking at the brim,
　　And purple-stained mouth;
　That I might drink, and leave the world unseen,
　　And with thee fade away into the forest dim:

Fade far away, dissolve, and quite forget
　What thou among the leaves has never known,
The weariness, the fever, and the fret
　Here, where men sit and hear each other groan;
Where palsy shakes a few, sad, last gray hairs,
　Where youth grows pale, and spectre-thin, and dies;
　　Where but to think is to be full of sorrow
　　And leaden-eyed despairs,
　Where Beauty cannot keep her lustrous eyes,
　　Or new Love pine at them beyond to-morrow.

Away! away! for I will fly to thee,
　Not charioted by Bacchus and his pards,
But on the viewless wings of Poesy,
　Though the dull brain perplexes and retards;
Already with thee! tender is the night,
　And haply the Queen-Moon is on her throne.
　　Cluster'd around by all her starry Fays;
　　But here there is no light,
　Save what from heaven is with the breezes blown
　　Through verdurous glooms and winding mossy ways.

I cannot see what flowers are at my feet,
　Nor what soft incense hangs upon the boughs,
But, in embalmed darkness, guess each sweet
　Wherewith the seasonable month endows
The grass, the thicket, and the fruit-tree wild;
　White hawthorn, and the pastoral eglantine;
　　Fast fading violets cover'd up in leaves;
　　And mid-May's eldest child,
　The coming musk-rose, full of dewy wine,
　　The murmurous haunt of flies on summer eves.

Darkling I listen; and, for many a time
　I have been half in love with easeful Death,
Call'd him soft names in many a mused rhyme,
　To take into the air my quiet breath;

Now more than ever seems it rich to die,
   To cease upon the midnight with no pain,
      While thou art pouring forth thy soul abroad
         In such an ecstasy!
      Still wouldst thou sing, and I have ears in vain—
      To thy high requiem become a sod.

Thou wast not born for death, immortal Bird!
   No hungry generations tread thee down;
      The voice I hear this passing night was heard
         In ancient days by emperor and clown:
      Perhaps the self-same song that found a path
         Through the sad heart of Ruth, when, sick for home,
            She stood in tears amid the alien corn;
               The same that oft-times hath
         Charm'd magic casements, opening on the foam
         Of perilous seas, in faery lands forlorn.

Forlorn! the very word is like a bell
   To toll me back from thee to my sole self!
      Adieu! the fancy cannot cheat so well
         As she is fam'd to do, deceiving elf.
      Adieu adieu! thy plaintive anthem fades
         Past the near meadows, over the still stream,
            Up the hill-side; and now 'tis buried deep
               In the next valley-glades:
         Was it a vision, or a waking dream?
         Fled is that music:—Do I wake or sleep?

From THE EVE OF ST. AGNES

John Keats

Out went the taper as she hurried in;
   Its little smoke, in pallid moonshine, died:
She clos'd the door, she panted, all akin
   To spirits of the air, and visions wide:
No uttered syllable, or, woe betide!
   But to her heart, her heart was voluble,
      Paining with eloquence her balmy side;
   As though a tongueless nightingale should swell
Her throat in vain, and die, heart-stifled, in her dell.

A casement high and triple arch'd there was,
   All garlanded with carven imag'ries
Of fruits, and flowers, and bunches of knot-grass.
   And diamonded with panes of quaint device,
   Innumerable of stains and splendid dyes,

As are the tiger-moth's deep-damask'd wings;
And in the midst, 'mong thousand heraldries,
And twilight saints, and dim emblazonings,
A shielded scutcheon blush'd with blood of queens and kings.

Full on this casement shone the wintry moon,
And threw warm gules on Madeline's fair breast,
As down she knelt for heaven's grace and boon;
Rose-bloom fell on her hands, together prest,
And on her silver cross soft amethyst,
And on her hair a glory, like a saint:
She seem'd a splendid angel, newly drest,
Save wings, for heaven:—Porphyro grew faint:
She knelt, so pure a thing, so free from mortal taint.

Anon his heart revives: her vespers done,
Of all its wreathèd pearls her hair she frees;
Unclasps her warmèd jewels one by one;
Loosens her fragrant bodice; by degrees
Her rich attire creeps rustling to her knees:
Half-hidden, like a mermaid in sea-weed,
Pensive awhile she dreams awake, and sees,
In fancy, fair St. Agnes in her bed,
But dares not look behind, or all the charm is fled.

Soon, trembling in her soft and chilly nest,
In sort of wakeful swoon, perplex'd she lay,
Until the poppied warmth of sleep oppress'd
Her soothèd limbs, and soul fatigued away;
Flown, like a thought, until the morrow-day;
Blissfully haven'd both from joy and pain;
Clasp'd like a missal where swart Paynims pray;
Blinded alike from sunshine and from rain,
As though a rose should shut, and be a bud again.

Stol'n to this paradise, and so entranced,
Porphyro gazed upon her empty dress,
And listen'd to her breathing, if it chanced
To wake into a slumberous tenderness;
Which when he heard, that minute did he bless,
And breath'd himself: then from the closet crept.
Noiseless as fear in a wide wilderness,
And over the hush'd carpet, silent, stept,
And 'tween the curtains peep'd, where, lo!—how fast she slept.

Then by the bedside, where the faded moon
Made a dim, silver twilight, soft he set
A table, and, half anguish'd, threw thereon
A cloth of woven crimson, gold, and jet:—

O for some drowsy Morphean amulet!
The boisterous, midnight, festive clarion,
The kettle-drum, and far-heard clarionet,
Affray his ears, though but in dying tone:—
The hall door shuts again, and all the noise is gone.

And still she slept an azure-lidded sleep,
In blanchèd linen, smooth, and lavender'd,
While he from forth the closet brought a heap
Of candied apple, quince, and plum, and gourd;
With jellies soother than the creamy curd,
And lucent syrups, tinct with cinnamon;
Manna and dates, in argosy transferr'd
From Fez; and spicèd dainties, every one,
From silken Samarcand to cedared Lebanon.

These delicates he heap'd with glowing hand
On golden dishes and in baskets bright
Of wreathèd silver: sumptuous they stand
In the retirèd quiet of the night,
Filling the chilly room with perfume light.—
"And now, my love, my seraph fair, awake!
Thou art my heaven, and I thine eremite:
Open thine eyes, for meek St. Agnes' sake,
Or I shall drowse beside thee, so my soul doth ache." . . .

She hurried at his words, beset with fears,
For there were sleeping dragons all around,
At glaring watch, perhaps, with ready spears—
Down the wide stairs a darkling way they found.—
In all the house was heard no human sound.
A chain-drooped lamp was flickering by each door;
The arras, rich with horseman, hawk, and hound,
Flutter'd in the besieging wind's uproar;
And the long carpets rose along the gusty floor.

They glide, like phantoms, into the wide hall;
Like phantoms, to the iron porch they glide;
Where lay the Porter, in uneasy sprawl,
With a huge empty flagon by his side:
The wakeful bloodhound rose, and shook his hide,
But his sagacious eye an inmate owns:
By one, and one, the bolts full easy slide:—
The chains lie silent on the footworn stones;—
The key turns, and the door upon its hinges groans.

And they are gone: ay, ages long ago
These lovers fled away into the storm. . . .

ODE ON A GRECIAN URN

John Keats

Thou still unravish'd bride of quietness,
  Thou foster-child of silence and slow time,
Sylvan historian, who canst thus express
  A flowery tale more sweetly than our rhyme:
What leaf-fring'd legend haunts about thy shape
  Of deities or mortals, or of both,
    In Tempe or the dales of Arcady?
What men or gods are these? What maidens loth?
What mad pursuit? What struggle to escape?
    What pipes and timbrels? What wild ecstasy?

Heard melodies are sweet, but those unheard
  Are sweeter; therefore, ye soft pipes, play on;
Not to the sensual ear, but, more endear'd,
  Pipe to the spirit ditties of no tone:
Fair youth, beneath the trees, thou canst not leave
  Thy song, nor ever can those trees be bare;
    Bold Lover, never, never canst thou kiss
Though winning near the goal—yet, do not grieve;
  She cannot fade, though thou hast not thy bliss,
    For ever wilt thou love, and she be fair!

Ah, happy, happy boughs! that cannot shed
  Your leaves, nor ever bid the Spring adieu;
And, happy melodist, unwearièd,
  For ever piping songs for ever new;
More happy love! more happy, happy love!
  For ever warm and still to be enjoy'd,
    For ever panting, and for ever young:
All breathing human passion far above,
  That leaves a heart high-sorrowful and cloy'd,
    A burning forehead, and a parching tongue.

Who are these coming to the sacrifice?
  To what green altar, O mysterious priest,
Lead'st thou that heifer lowing at the skies,
  And all her silken flanks with garlands dressed?
What little town by river or sea shore,
  Or mountain-built with peaceful citadel,
    Is emptied of this folk, this pious morn?
And, little town, thy streets for evermore
  Will silent be: and not a soul to tell
    Why thou art desolate, can e'er return.

O Attic shape!   Fair attitude! with brede
　　Of marble men and maidens overwrought,
With forest branches and the trodden weed;
　　Thou, silent form, dost tease us out of thought
As doth eternity: Cold Pastoral!
　　When old age shall this generation waste,
　　　Thou shalt remain, in midst of other woe
Than ours, a friend to man, to whom thou say'st,
　　"Beauty is truth, truth beauty,"—that is all
Ye know on earth and all ye need to know.

MORTE D'ARTHUR

Alfred, Lord Tennyson

So all day long the noise of battle roll'd
Among the mountains by the winter sea;
Until King Arthur's table, man by man,
Had fallen in Lyonness about their Lord,
King Arthur: then, because his wound was deep,
The bold Sir Bedivere uplifted him,
Sir Bedivere, the last of all his knights,
And bore him to a chapel nigh the field,
A broken chancel with a broken cross,
That stood on a dark strait of barren land.
On one side lay the Ocean, and on one
Lay a great water, and the moon was full.
　　Then spake King Arthur to Sir Bedivere:
"The sequel of to-day unsolders all
The goodliest fellowship of famous knights
Whereof this world holds record. Such a sleep
They sleep—the men I loved. I think that we
Shall nevermore, at any future time,
Delight our souls with talk of knightly deeds,
Walking about the gardens and the halls
Of Camelot, as in the days that were.
I perish by this people which I made,—
Tho' Merlin sware that I should come again
To rule once more—but let what will be, be,
I am so deeply smitten thro' the helm
That without help I cannot last till morn." . . .
　　But, as he walk'd, King Arthur panted hard,
Like one that feels a nightmare on his bed
When all the house is mute. So sigh'd the King,
Muttering and murmuring at his ear, "Quick, quick!

I fear it is too late, and I shall die."
But the other swiftly strode from ridge to ridge,
Clothed with his breath, and looking, as he walk'd,
Larger than human on the frozen hills.
He heard the deep behind him, and a cry
Before. His own thought drove him, like a goad.
Dry clash'd his harness in the icy caves
And barren chasms, and all to left and right
The bare black cliff clang'd round him, as he based
His feet on juts of slippery crag that rang
Sharp-smitten with the dint of armèd heels—
And on a sudden, lo! the level lake,
And the long glories of the winter moon.
    Then saw they how there hove a dusky barge,
Dark as a funeral scarf from stem to stern,
Beneath them; and descending they were ware
That all the decks were dense with stately forms
Black-stoled, black-hooded, like a dream—by these
Three Queens with crowns of gold—and from them rose
A cry that shiver'd to the tingling stars,
And, as it were one voice, an agony
Of lamentation, like a wind, that shrills
All night in a waste land, where no one comes,
Or hath come, since the making of the world.
    Then murmur'd Arthur, "Place me in the barge,"
And to the barge they came. There those three Queens
Put forth their hands, and took the King, and wept.
But she, that rose the tallest of them all
And fairest, laid his head upon her lap,
And loosed the shatter'd casque, and chafed his hands,
And call'd him by his name, complaining loud,
And dropping bitter tears against his brow
Striped with dark blood: for all his face was white
And colourless, and like the wither'd moon
Smote by the fresh beam of the springing east;
And all his greaves and cuisses dash'd with drops
Of onset; and the light and lustrous curls—
That made his forehead like a rising sun
High from the dais-throne—were parch'd with dust;
Or, clotted into points and hanging loose,
Mix'd with the knightly growth that fringed his lips.
So like a shatter'd column lay the King;
Not like that Arthur who, with lance in rest,
From spur to plume a star of tournament,
Shot thro' the lists at Camelot, and charged
Before the eyes of ladies and of kings.

Then loudly cried the bold Sir Bedivere,
"Ah! my Lord Arthur, whither shall I go?
Where shall I hide my forehead and my eyes?
For now I see the true old times are dead,
When every morning brought a noble chance,
And every chance brought out a noble knight.
Such times have been not since the light that led
The holy Elders with the gift of myrrh.
But now the whole Round Table is dissolved
Which was an image of the mighty world;
And I, the last, go forth companionless,
And the days darken round me, and the years,
Among new men, strange faces, other minds."

And slowly answered Arthur from the barge:
"The old order changeth, yielding place to new,
And God fulfils Himself in many ways,
Lest one good custom should corrupt the world.
Comfort thyself: what comfort is in me?
I have lived my life, and that which I have done
May He within Himself make pure! but thou,
If thou shouldst never see my face again,
Pray for my soul. More things are wrought by prayer
Than this world dreams of. Wherefore, let thy voice
Rise like a fountain for me night and day.
For what are men better than sheep or goats
That nourish a blind life within the brain,
If, knowing God, they lift not hands of prayer
Both for themselves and those who call them friend?
For so the whole round earth is every way
Bound by gold chains about the feet of God.
But now farewell. I am going a long way
With these thou seest—if indeed I go—
(For all my mind is clouded with a doubt)
To the island-valley of Avilion;
Where falls not hail, or rain, or any snow,
Nor ever wind blows loudly; but it lies
Deep-meadow'd, happy, fair with orchard-lawns
And bowery hollows crown'd with summer sea,
Where I will heal me of my grievous wound."

So said he, and the barge with oar and sail
Moved from the brink, like some full-breasted swan
That, fluting a wild carol ere her death,
Ruffles her pure cold plume, and takes the flood
With swarthy webs. Long stood Sir Bedivere
Revolving many memories, till the hull
Look'd one black dot against the verge of dawn,
And on the mere the wailing died away.

DOVER BEACH

Matthew Arnold

The sea is calm to-night,
The tide is full, the moon lies fair
Upon the straits;—on the French coast the light
Gleams and is gone; the cliffs of England stand,
Glimmering and vast, out in the tranquil bay.
Come to the window, sweet is the night-air!
Only, from the long line of spray
Where the sea meets the moon-blanch'd land,
Listen! you hear the grating roar
Of pebbles which the waves draw back, and fling,
At their return, up the high strand,
Begin, and cease, and then again begin,
With tremulous cadence slow, and bring
The eternal note of sadness in.
Sophocles long ago
Heard it on the Ægean, and it brought
Into his mind the turbid ebb and flow
Of human misery; we
Find also in the sound a thought,
Hearing it by this distant northern sea.

The Sea of Faith
Was once, too, at the full, and round earth's shore
Lay like the folds of a bright girdle furl'd.
But now I only hear
Its melancholy, long, withdrawing roar,
Retreating, to the breath
Of the night-wind, down the vast edges drear
And naked shingles of the world.

Ah, love, let us be true
To one another! for the world, which seems
To lie before us like a land of dreams,
So various, so beautiful, so new,
Hath really neither joy, nor love, nor light,
Nor certitude, nor peace, nor help for pain;
And we are here as on a darkling plain
Swept with confused alarms of struggle and flight,
Where ignorant armies clash by night.

Chorus from ATALANTA IN CALYDON

Algernon Charles Swinburne

When the hounds of spring are on winter's traces,
   The mother of months in meadow or plain
Fills the shadows and windy places
   With lisp of leaves and ripple of rain;
And the brown bright nightingale amorous
Is half assuaged for Itylus,
For the Thracian ships and the foreign faces,
   The tongueless vigil, and all the pain.

Come with bows bent and with emptying of quivers,
   Maiden most perfect, lady of light,
With a noise of winds and many rivers,
   With a clamour of waters, and with might;
Bind on thy sandals, O thou most fleet,
Over the splendour and speed of thy feet;
For the faint east quickens, the wan west shivers,
   Round the feet of the day and the feet of the night.

Where shall we find her, how shall we sing to her,
   Fold our hands round her knees, and cling?
O that man's heart were as fire and could spring to her,
   Fire, or the strength of the streams that spring!
For the stars and the winds are unto her
As raiment, as songs of the harp-player;
For the risen stars and the fallen cling to her,
   And the southwest-wind and the west-wind sing.

For winter's rains and ruins are over,
   And all the season of snows and sins;
The days dividing lover and lover,
   The light that loses, the night that wins;
And time remember'd is grief forgotten,
And frosts are slain and flowers begotten,
And in green underwood and cover
   Blossom by blossom the spring begins.

The full streams feed on flower of rushes,
   Ripe grasses trammel a travelling foot,
The faint fresh flame of the young year flushes
   From leaf to flower and flower to fruit;
And fruit and leaf are as gold and fire,
And the oat is heard above the lyre,
And the hoofèd heel of a satyr crushes
   The chestnut-husk at the chestnut-root.

And Pan by noon and Bacchus by night,
  Fleeter of foot than the fleet-foot kid,
Follows with dancing and fills with delight
  The Mænad and the Bassarid;
And soft as lips that laugh and hide,
The laughing leaves of the trees divide,
And screen from seeing and leave in sight
  The god pursuing, the maiden hid.

The ivy falls with the Bacchanal's hair
  Over her eyebrows hiding her eyes;
The wild vine slipping down leaves bare
  Her bright breast shortening into sighs;
The wild vine slips with the weight of its leaves,
But the berried ivy catches and cleaves
To the limbs that glitter, the feet that scare
  The wolf that follows, the fawn that flies.

THE GARDEN OF PROSERPINE

Algernon Charles Swinburne

Here, where the world is quiet;
  Here, where all trouble seems
Dead winds' and spent waves' riot
  In doubtful dreams of dreams;
I watch the green field growing
For reaping folk and sowing,
For harvest-time and mowing,
  A sleepy world of streams.

I am tired of tears and laughter,
  And men that laugh and weep;
Of what may come hereafter
  For men that sow to reap:
I am weary of days and hours,
Blown buds of barren flowers,
Desires and dreams and powers
  And everything but sleep.

Here life has death for neighbour,
  And far from eye or ear
Wan waves and wet winds labour,
  Weak ships and spirits steer;
They drive adrift, and whither
They wot not who make thither,
But no such winds blow hither,
  And no such things grow here.

No growth of moor or coppice,
  No heather-flower or vine,
But bloomless buds of poppies,
  Green grapes of Proserpine,
Pale beds of blowing rushes,
Where no leaf blooms or blushes
Save this whereout she crushes
  For dead men deadly wine.

Pale, without name or number,
  In fruitless fields of corn,
They bow themselves and slumber
  All night till light is born;
And like a soul belated,
In hell and heaven unmated,
By cloud and mist abated
  Comes out of darkness morn.

Though one were strong as seven,
  He too with death shall dwell,
Nor wake with wings in heaven,
  Nor weep for pains in hell;
Though one were fair as roses,
His beauty clouds and closes;
And well though love reposes,
  In the end it is not well.

Pale, beyond porch and portal,
  Crowned with calm leaves, she stands
Who gathers all things mortal
  With cold immortal hands;
Her languid lips are sweeter
Than love's who fears to greet her
To men that mix and meet her
  From many times and lands.

She waits for each and other,
  She waits for all men born;
Forgets the earth her mother,
  The life of fruits and corn;
And spring and seed and swallow
Take wing for her and follow
Where summer song rings hollow
  And flowers are put to scorn.

There go the loves that wither,
  The old loves with wearier wings;
And all dead years draw thither,
  And all disastrous things;

Dead dreams of days forsaken,
Blind buds that snows have shaken,
Wild leaves that winds have taken,
    Red strays of ruined springs.

We are not sure of sorrow,
    And joy was never sure;
To-day will die to-morrow;
    Time stoops to no man's lure;
And love, grown faint and fretful
With lips but half regretful
Sighs, and with eyes forgetful
    Weeps that no loves endure.

From too much love of living,
    From hope and fear set free,
We thank with brief thanksgiving
    Whatever gods may be
That no life lives forever;
That dead men rise up never;
That even the weariest river
    Winds somewhere safe to sea.

Then star nor sun shall waken,
    Nor any change of light:
Nor sound of waters shaken,
    Nor any sound or sight:
Nor wintry leaves nor vernal,
Nor days nor things diurnal;
Only the sleep eternal
    In an eternal night.

DEDICATION[9]

Rudyard Kipling

Beyond the path of the outmost sun through utter darkness hurled—
Further than ever comet flared or vagrant star-dust swirled—
Live such as fought and sailed and ruled and loved and made our
    world.

They are purged of pride because they died, they know the worth of
    their bays;
They sit at wine with the Maidens Nine and the Gods of the Elder
    Day—
It is their will to serve or be still as fitteth Our Father's praise.

[9] From *Departmental Ditties and Ballads and Barrack-Room Ballads,* reprinted by permission of Mrs. George Bambridge and Doubleday & Co., Inc.

'Tis theirs to sweep through the ringing deep where Azrael's outposts are,
Or buffet a path through the Pit's red wrath when God goes out to
   war,
Or hang with the reckless Seraphim on the rein of a red-maned star.

They take their mirth in the joy of the Earth—they dare not grieve
   for her pain—
They know of toil and the end of toil, they know God's Law is plain,
So they whistle the Devil to make them sport who know that Sin is
   vain.

And ofttimes cometh our wise Lord God, master of every trade,
And tells them tales of His daily toil, of Edens newly made;
And they rise to their feet as He passes by, gentlemen unafraid.

To these who are cleansed of base Desire, Sorrow and Lust and
   Shame—
Gods for they knew the hearts of men, men for they stooped to
   Fame—
Borne on the breath that men call Death, my brother's spirit came.

He scarce had need to doff his pride or slough the dross of Earth—
E'en as he trod that day to God so walked he from his birth,
In simpleness and gentleness and honour and clean mirth.

So cup to lip in fellowship they gave him welcome high
And made him place at the banquet board—the Strong Men ranged
   thereby,
Who had done his work and held his peace and had no fear to die.

Beyond the loom of the last lone star, through open darkness hurled,
Further than rebel comet dared or hiving star-swarm swirled,
Sits he with those that praise our God for that they served His world.

SAILING TO BYZANTIUM[10]

W. B. Yeats

I

That is no country for old men. The young
In one another's arms, birds in the trees,
—Those dying generations—at their song,
The salmon-falls, the mackerel-crowded seas,
Fish, flesh, or fowl, commend all summer long
Whatever is begotten, born, and dies.
Caught in that sensual music all neglect
Monuments of unageing intellect.

II

An aged man is but a paltry thing,
A tattered coat upon a stick, unless
Soul clap its hands and sing, and louder sing
For every tatter in its mortal dress,
Nor is there singing school but studying
Monuments of its own magnificence;
And therefore I have sailed the seas and come
To the holy city of Byzantium.

III

O sages standing in God's holy fire
As in the gold mosaic of a wall,
Come from the holy fire, perne in a gyre,
And be the singing-masters of my soul.
Consume my heart away; sick with desire
And fastened to a dying animal
It knows not what it is; and gather me
Into the artifice of eternity.

IV

Once out of nature I shall never take
My bodily form from any natural thing,
But such a form as Grecian goldsmiths make
Of hammered gold and gold enamelling
To keep a drowsy Emperor awake;
Or set upon a golden bough to sing
To lords and ladies of Byzantium
Of what is past, or passing, or to come.

MR. FLOOD'S PARTY[11]

Edwin Arlington Robinson

Old Eben Flood, climbing alone one night
Over the hill between the town below
And the forsaken upland hermitage
That held as much as he should ever know
On earth again of home, paused warily.
The road was his with not a native near;
And Eben, having leisure, said aloud,
For no man else in Tilbury Town to hear:

"Well, Mr. Flood, we have the harvest moon
Again, and we may not have many more;
The bird is on the wing, the poet says,
And you and I have said it here before.

[11] From *Collected Poems*. By permission of The Macmillan Co.

Drink to the bird." He raised up to the light
The jug that he had gone so far to fill,
And answered huskily: "Well, Mr. Flood,
Since you propose it, I believe I will."

Alone, as if enduring to the end
A valiant armor of scarred hopes outworn,
He stood there in the middle of the road
Like Roland's ghost winding a silent horn.
Below him, in the town among the trees,
Where friends of other days had honored him,
A phantom salutation of the dead
Rang thinly till old Eben's eyes were dim.

Then, as a mother lays her sleeping child
Down tenderly, fearing it may awake,
He set the jug down slowly at his feet
With trembling care, knowing that most things break;
And only when assured that on firm earth
It stood, as the uncertain lives of men
Assuredly did not, he paced away,
And with his hand extended paused again:

"Well, Mr. Flood, we have not met like this
In a long time; and many a change has come
To both of us, I fear, since last it was
We had a drop together. Welcome home!"
Convivially returning with himself,
Again he raised the jug up to the light;
And with an acquiescent quaver said:
"Well, Mr. Flood, if you insist, I might.

"Only a very little, Mr. Flood—
For auld lang syne. No more, sir; that will do."
So, for the time, apparently it did,
And Eben evidently thought so too;
For soon amid the silver loneliness
Of night he lifted up his voice and sang,
Secure, with only two moons listening,
Until the whole harmonious landscape rang—

"For auld lang syne." The weary throat gave out,
The last word wavered; and the song being done,
He raised again the jug regretfully
And shook his head, and was again alone.
There was not much that was ahead of him,
And there was nothing in the town below—
Where strangers would have shut the many doors
That many friends had opened long ago.

THE TUFT OF FLOWERS[12]

Robert Frost

I went to turn the grass once after one
Who mowed it in the dew before the sun.

The dew was gone that made his blade so keen
Before I came to view the leveled scene.

I looked for him behind an isle of trees;
I listened for his whetstone on the breeze.

But he had gone his way, the grass all mown,
And I must be, as he had been,—alone,

"As all must be," I said within my heart,
"Whether they work together or apart."

But as I said it, swift there passed me by
On noiseless wing a bewildered butterfly,

Seeking with memories grown dim over night
Some resting flower of yesterday's delight.

And once I marked his flight go round and round,
As where some flower lay withering on the ground.

And then he flew as far as eye could see,
And then on tremulous wing came back to me.

I thought of questions that have no reply,
And would have turned to toss the grass to dry;

But he turned first, and led my eye to look
At a tall tuft of flowers beside a brook,

A leaping tongue of bloom the scythe had spared
Beside a reedy brook the scythe had bared.

I left my place to know them by their name,
Finding them butterfly-weed when I came.

The mower in the dew had loved them thus,
By leaving them to flourish, not for us,

Nor yet to draw one thought of ours to him,
But from sheer morning gladness at the brim.

The butterfly and I had lit upon,
Nevertheless, a message from the dawn,

[12] From *Boy's Will*, by permission of Holt, Rinehart & Winston, Inc.

That made me hear the wakening birds around,
And hear his long scythe whispering to the ground,

And feel a spirit kindred to my own;
So that henceforth I worked no more alone;

But glad with him, I worked as with his aid,
And weary, sought at noon with him the shade;

And dreaming, as it were, held brotherly speech
With one whose thought I had not hoped to reach.

"Men work together," I told him from the heart,
"Whether they work together or apart."

THE BEAR[13]

Robert Frost

The bear puts both arms around the tree above her
And draws it down as if it were a lover
And its choke-cherries lips to kiss good-by,
Then lets it snap back upright in the sky.
Her next step rocks a bowlder on the wall
(She's making her cross-country in the fall.)
Her great weight creaks the barbed-wire in its staples
As she flings over and off down through the maples,
Leaving on one wire tooth a lock of hair.
Such is the uncaged progress of the bear.
The world has room to make a bear feel free;
The universe seems cramped to you and me.
Man acts more like a poor bear in a cage
That all day fights a nervous inward rage,
His mood rejecting all his mind suggests.
He paces back and forth and never rests
The toe-nail click and shuffle of his feet,
The telescope at one end of his beat,
And at the other end the microscope,
Two instruments of nearly equal hope,
And in conjunction giving quite a spread.
Or if he rests from scientific tread,
'Tis only to sit back and sway his head
Through ninety odd degrees of arc, it seems,
Between two metaphysical extremes.
He sits back on his fundamental butt
With lifted snout and eyes (if any) shut,
(He almost looks religious but he's not),
And back and forth he sways from cheek to cheek,

[13] From *West Running Brook,* by permission of Holt, Rinehart & Winston.

At one extreme agreeing with one Greek,
At the other agreeing with another Greek
Which may be thought, but only so to speak.
A baggy figure, equally pathetic
When sedentary and when peripatetic.

LEPANTO[14]

G. K. Chesterton

White founts falling in the Courts of the sun,
And the Soldan of Byzantium is smiling as they run;
There is laughter like the fountains in that face of all men feared,
It stirs the forest darkness, the darkness of his beard;
It curls the blood-red crescent, the crescent of his lips;
For the inmost sea of all the earth is shaken with his ships.
They have dared the white republics up the capes of Italy,
They have dashed the Adriatic round the Lion of the Sea,
And the Pope has cast his arms abroad for agony and loss,
And called the kings of Christendom for swords about the Cross.
The cold queen of England is looking in the glass;
The shadow of the Valois is yawning at the Mass;
From evening isles fantastical rings faint the Spanish gun,
And the Lord upon the Golden Horn is laughing in the sun.

Dim drums throbbing, in the hills half heard,
Where only on a nameless throne a crownless prince has stirred,
Where, risen from a doubtful seat and half-attainted stall,
The last knight of Europe takes weapons from the wall,
The last and lingering troubadour to whom the bird has sung,
That once went singing southward when all the world was young.
In that enormous silence, tiny and unafraid,
Comes up along a winding road the noise of the Crusade.
Strong gongs groaning as the guns boom far,
Don John of Austria is going to the war;
Stiff flags straining in the night-blasts cold
In the gloom black-purple, in the glint old-gold,
Torchlight crimson on the copper kettle-drums,
Then the tuckets, then the trumpets, then the cannon, and he comes.
Don John laughing in the brave beard curled,
Spurning of his stirrups like the thrones of all the world,
Holding his head up for a flag of all the free.
Love-light of Spain—hurrah!
Death-light of Africa!
Don John of Austria
Is riding to the sea.

[14] Used by permission of Dodd, Mead & Co., Inc. From *Poems*, copyright, 1915.

Mahound is in his paradise above the evening star,
(*Don John of Austria is going to the war.*)
He moves a mighty turban on the timeless houri's knees,
His turban that is woven of the sunsets and the seas.
He shakes the peacock gardens as he rises from his ease,
And he strides among the tree-tops and is taller than the trees;
And his voice through all the garden is a thunder sent to bring
Black Azrael and Ariel and Ammon on the wing.
Giants and the Genii,
Multiplex of wing and eye,
Whose strong obedience broke the sky
When Solomon was king.

They rush in red and purple from the red clouds of the morn,
From the temples where the yellow gods shut up their eyes in scorn;
They rise in green robes roaring from the green hells of the sea
Where fallen skies and evil hues and eyeless creatures be,
On them the sea-valves cluster and the gray sea-forests curl,
Splashed with a splendid sickness, the sickness of the pearl;
They swell in sapphire smoke out of the blue cracks of the ground,—
They gather and they wonder and give worship to Mahound.
And he saith, "Break up the mountains where the hermit-folk can
          hide,
And sift the red and silver sands lest bone of saint abide,
And chase the Giaours flying night and day, not giving rest,
For that which was our trouble comes again out of the west.
We have set the seal of Solomon on all things under sun,
Of knowledge and of sorrow and endurance of things done.
But a noise is in the mountains, in the mountains; and I know
That voice that shook our palaces—four hundred years ago:
It is he that saith not 'Kismet'; it is he that knows not Fate;
It is Richard, it is Raymond, it is Godfrey at the gate!
It is he whose loss is laughter when he counts the wager worth,
Put down your feet upon him, that our peace be on the earth."
For he heard drums groaning and he heard guns jar,
(*Don John of Austria is going to the war.*)
Sudden and still—hurrah!
Bolt from Iberia!
Don John of Austria
Is gone by Alcalar.

St. Michael's on his Mountain in the sea-roads of the north
(*Don John of Austria is girt and going forth.*)
Where the gray seas glitter and the sharp tides shift
And the sea-folk labor and the red sails lift.
He shakes his lance of iron and he claps his wings of stone;
The noise is gone through Normandy; the noise is gone alone;
The North is full of tangled things and texts and aching eyes,

And dead is all the innocence of anger and surprise,
And Christian killeth Christian in a narrow dusty room,
And Christian dreadeth Christ that hath a newer face of doom,
And Christian hateth Mary that God kissed in Galilee,—
But Don John of Austria is riding to the sea.
Don John calling through the blast and the eclipse,
Crying with the trumpet, with the trumpet of his lips,
Trumpet that sayeth *ha!*
Domino Gloria!
Don John of Austria
Is shouting to the ships.

King Philip's in his closet with the Fleece about his neck
(*Don John of Austria is armed upon the deck.*)
The walls are hung with velvet that is black and soft as sin,
And little dwarfs creep out of it and little dwarfs creep in.
He holds a crystal phial that has colors like the moon,
He touches, and it tingles, and he trembles very soon,
And his face is as a fungus of a leprous white and gray
Like plants in the high houses that are shuttered from the day,
And death is in the phial and the end of noble work,
But Don John of Austria has fired upon the Turk.
Don John's hunting, and his hounds have bayed—
Booms away past Italy the rumor of his raid.
Gun upon gun, ha! ha!
Gun upon gun, hurrah!
Don John of Austria
Has loosed the cannonade.

The Pope was in his chapel before day or battle broke,
(*Don John of Austria is hidden in the smoke.*)
The hidden room in man's house where God sits all the year,
The secret window whence the world looks small and very dear.
He sees as in a mirror on the monstrous twilight sea
The crescent of his cruel ships whose name is mystery;
They fling great shadows foe-wards, making Cross and Castle dark,
They veil the plumèd lions on the galleys of St. Marks;
And above the ships are palaces of brown, black-bearded chiefs,
And below the ships are prisons, where with multitudinous griefs,
Christian captives, sick and sunless, all a laboring race repines
Like a race in sunken cities, like a nation in the mines.
They are lost like slaves that swat, and in the skies of morning hung
The stair-ways of the tallest gods when tyranny was young.
They are countless, voiceless, hopeless as those fallen or fleeing on
Before the high Kings' horses in the granite of Babylon.
And many a one grows witless in his quiet room in hell
Where a yellow face looks inward through the lattice of his cell,
And he finds his God forgotten, and he seeks no more a sign—

(*But Don John of Austria has burst the battle-line!*)
Don John pounding from the slaughter-painted poop,
Purpling all the ocean like a bloody pirate's sloop,
Scarlet running over on the silvers and the golds,
Breaking of the hatches up and bursting of the holds,
Thronging of the thousands up that labor under sea
White for bliss and blind for sun and stunned for liberty.
Vivat Hispania!
Domino Gloria!
Don John of Austria
Has set his people free!

Cervantes on his galley sets the sword back in the sheath
(*Don John of Austria rides homeward with a wreath.*)
And he sees across a weary land a straggling road in Spain,
Up which a lean and foolish knight for ever rides in vain,
And he smiles, but not as Sultans smile, and settles back the blade . . .
(*But Don John of Austria rides home from the Crusade.*)

THE MYSTIC[15]

Cale Young Rice

There is a quest that calls me,
    In nights when I am lone,
The need to ride where the ways divide
    The Known from the Unknown.
I mount what thought is near me
    And soon I reach the place,
The tenuous rim where the Seen grows dim
    And the Sightless hides its face.

I have ridden the wind,
I have ridden the sea,
I have ridden the moon and stars.
I have set my feet in the stirrup seat
Of a comet coursing Mars.
And everywhere
Thro' the earth and air
My thought speeds, lightning-shod,
It comes to a place where checking pace
It cries, "Beyond lies God!"

It calls me out of the darkness,
    It calls me out of sleep,
"Ride! ride! for you must, to the end of Dust!"
    It bids—and on I sweep

[15] By permission of the author.

To the wide outposts of Being,
 Where there is Gulf alone—
And thro' a Vast that was never passed
 I listen for Life's tone.

I have ridden the wind,
I have ridden the night,
I have ridden the ghosts that flee
From the vaults of death like a chilling breath
Over eternity.
And everywhere
Is the world laid bare—
Ether and star and clod—
Until I wind to its brink and find
But the cry, "Beyond lies God!"

It calls me and ever calls me!
 And vainly I reply,
"Fools only ride where the ways divide
 What Is from the Whence and Why"!
I'm lifted into the saddle
 Of thoughts too strong to tame
And down the deeps and over the steeps
 I find—ever the same.

I have ridden the wind,
I have ridden the stars,
I have ridden the force that flies
With far intent thro' the firmament
And each to each allies.
And everywhere
That a thought may dare
To gallop, mine has trod—
Only to stand at last on the strand
Where just beyond lies God.

FOUR PRELUDES ON PLAYTHINGS OF THE WIND[16]

"The past is a bucket of ashes."

Carl Sandburg

1

The woman named Tomorrow
sits with a hairpin in her teeth
and takes her time

and does her hair the way she wants it
and fastens at last the last braid and coil
and puts the hairpin where it belongs
and turns and drawls: Well, what of it?
My grandmother, Yesterday, is gone.
What of it? Let the dead be dead.

2

The doors were cedar
and the panels strips of gold
and the girls were golden girls
and the panels read and the girls chanted:
     We are the greatest city,
     the greatest nation:
     nothing like us ever was.
The doors are twisted on broken hinges.
Sheets of rain swish through on the wind
     where the golden girls ran and the panels read:
     We are the greatest city,
     the greatest nation,
     nothing like us ever was.

3

It has happened before.
Strong men put up a city and got
     a nation together,
And paid singers to sing and women
     to warble: We are the greatest city,
          the greatest nation,
          nothing like us ever was.
And while the singers sang
and the strong men listened
and paid the singers well
and felt good about it all,
     there were rats and lizards who listened
     . . . and the only listeners left now
     . . . are . . . the rats . . . and the lizards.

And there are black crows
crying, "Caw, caw,"
bringing mud and sticks
building a nest
over the words carved
on the doors where the panels were cedar
and the strips on the panels were gold
and the golden girls came singing:

We are the greatest city,
the greatest nation:
nothing like us ever was.

The only singers now are crows crying, "Caw, caw,"
And the sheets of rain whine in the wind and doorways.
And the only listeners now are . . . the rats . . . and the lizards.

4

The feet of the rats
scribble on the doorsills;
the hieroglyphs of the rat footprints
chatter the pedigrees of the rats
and babble of the blood
and gabble of the breed
of the grandfathers and the great-grandfathers
of the rats.

And the wind shifts
and the dust on a doorsill shifts
and even the writing of the rat footprints
tells us nothing, nothing at all
about the greatest city, the greatest nation
where the strong men listened
and the women warbled: Nothing like us ever was.

LANDSCAPE AS A NUDE[17]

Archibald MacLeish

She lies on her left side her flank golden:
Her hair is burned black with the strong sun:
The scent of her hair is of rain in the dust on her shoulders:
She has brown breasts and the mouth of no other country:

Ah she is beautiful here in the sun where she lies:
She is not like the soft girls naked in vineyards
Nor the soft naked girls of the English islands
Where the rain comes in with the surf on an east wind:

Hers is the west wind and the sunlight: the west
Wind is the long clean wind of the continents—
The wind turning with earth: the wind descending
Steadily out of the evening and following on:

The wind here where she lies is west: the trees
Oak ironwood cottonwood hickory: standing in

[17] From *Frescoes for Mr. Rockefeller's City*, by permission of Houghton Mifflin Co.

Great groves they roll on the wind as the sea would:
The grasses of Iowa Illinois Indiana

Run with the plunge of the wind as a wave tumbling:
Under her knees there is no green lawn of the Florentines:
Under her dusty knees is the corn stubble:
Her belly is flecked with the flickering light of the corn:

She lies on her left side her flank golden:
Her hair is burned black with the strong sun:
The scent of her hair is of dust and of smoke on her shoulders:
She has brown breasts and the mouth of no other country.

HERITAGE[18]

Countee Cullen

What is Africa to me:
Copper sun or scarlet sea,
Jungle star or jungle track,
Strong bronzed men, or regal black
Women from whose loins I sprang
When the birds of Eden sang?
One three centuries removed
From the scenes his fathers loved,
Spicy grove, cinnamon tree,
What is Africa to me?

So I lie, who all day long
Want no sound except the song
Sung by wild barbaric birds
Goading massive jungle herds,
Juggernauts of flesh that pass
Trampling tall defiant grass
Where young forest lovers lie,
Plighting troth beneath the sky.
So I lie, who always hear,
Though I cram against my ear
Both my thumbs and keep them there,
Great drums throbbing through the air.
So I lie, whose fount of pride,
Dear distress, and joy allied,
Is my somber flesh and skin,
With the dark blood dammed within
Like great pulsing tides of wine
That, I fear, must burst the fine
Channels of the chafing net
Where they surge and foam and fret.

[18] From *Color,* by permission of Harper & Row, Inc.

Africa? A book one thumbs
Listlessly, till slumber comes.
Unremembered are her bats
Circling through the night, her cats
Crouching in the river reeds,
Stalking gentle flesh that feeds
By the river brink; no more
Does the bugle-throated roar
Cry that monarch claws have leapt
From the scabbards where they slept.
Silver snakes that once a year
Doff the lovely coats you wear,
Seek no covert in your fear
Lest a mortal eye should see;
What's your nakedness to me?
Here no leprous flowers rear
Fierce corollas in the air;
Here no bodies sleek and wet,
Dripping mingled rain and sweat,
Tread the savage measures of
Jungle boys and girls in love.

What is last year's snow to me,
Last year's anything? The tree
Budding yearly must forget
How its past arose or set—
Bough and blossom, flower, fruit,
Even what shy bird with mute
Wonder at her travail there,
Meekly labored in its hair.
One three centuries removed
From the scenes his fathers loved,
Spicy grove, cinnamon tree,
What is Africa to me?

So I lie, who find no peace
Night or day, no slight release
From the unremittent beat
Made by cruel padded feet
Walking through my body's street.
Up and down they go, and back,
Treading out a jungle track.
So I lie, who never quite
Safely sleep from rain at night—
I can never rest at all
When the rain begins to fall;
Like a soul gone mad with pain
I must match its weird refrain;

Ever must I twist and squirm,
Writhing like a baited worm,
While its primal measures drip
Through my body, crying, "Strip!
Doff this new exuberance.
Come and dance the Lover's Dance!"
In an old remembered way
Rain works on me night and day.

Quaint, outlandish heathen gods
Black men fashion out of rods,
Clay and brittle bits of stone,
In a likeness of their own,
My conversion came high-priced;
I belong to Jesus Christ,
Preacher of humility;
Heathen gods are naught to me.
Father, Son and Holy Ghost,
So I make an idle boast;
Jesus of the twice-turned cheek,
Lamb of God, although I speak
With my mouth thus, in my heart
Do I play a double part.
Even at Thy glowing altar
Must my heart grow sick and falter,
Wishing He I served were black,
Thinking then it would not lack
Precedent of pain to guide it,
Let who would or might deride it;
Surely then this flesh would know
Yours had borne a kindred woe.
Lord, I fashion dark gods, too,
Daring even to give You
Dark despairing features where,
Crowned with dark rebellious hair,
Patience wavers just so much as
Mortal grief compels, while touches
Quick and hot, of anger, rise
To smitten cheek and weary eyes.
Lord forgive me if my need
Sometimes shapes a human creed.

All day long and all night through,
One thing only must I do:
Quench my pride and cool my blood,
Lest I perish in the flood.
Lest a hidden ember set
Timber that I thought was wet

Burning like the dryest flax,
Melting like the merest wax,
Lest the grave restore its dead.
Not yet has my heart or head
In the least way realized
They and I are civilized.

JUST A SMACK AT AUDEN[19]

William Empson

Waiting for the end, boys, waiting for the end.
What is there to be or do?
What's become of me or you?
Are we kind or are we true?
Sitting two and two, boys, waiting for the end.

Shall I build a tower, boys, knowing it will rend
Crack upon the hour, boys, waiting for the end?
Shall I pluck a flower, boys, shall I save or spend?
All turns sour, boys, waiting for the end.

Shall I send a wire, boys? Where is there to send?
All are under fire, boys, waiting for the end.
Shall I turn a sire, boys? Shall I choose a friend?
The fat is in the pyre, boys, waiting for the end.

Shall I make it clear, boys, for all to apprehend,
Those that will not hear, boys, waiting for the end,
Knowing it is near, boys, trying to pretend,
Sitting in cold fear, boys, waiting for the end?

Shall we send a cable, boys, accurately penned,
Knowing we are able, boys, waiting for the end,
Via the Tower of Babel, boys? Christ will not ascend.
He's hiding in his stable, boys, waiting for the end.

Shall we blow a bubble, boys, glittering to distend,
Hiding from our trouble, boys, waiting for the end?
When you build on rubble, boys, Nature will append
Double and re-double, boys, waiting for the end.

Shall we make a tale, boys, that things are sure to mend,
Playing bluff and hale, boys, waiting for the end?
It will be born stale, boys, stinking to offend,
Dying ere it fail, boys, waiting for the end.

[19] From *Collected Poems of William Empson,* copyright, 1949, by William Empson. Reprinted by permission of Harcourt, Brace & World, Inc.

Shall we go all wild, boys, waste and make them lend,
Playing at the child, boys, waiting for the end?
It has all been filed, boys, history has a trend,
Each of us enisled, boys, waiting for the end.

What was said by Marx, boys, what did he perpend?
No good being sparks, boys, waiting for the end.
Treason of the clerks, boys, curtains that descend,
Lights becoming darks, boys, waiting for the end.

Waiting for the end, boys, waiting for the end.
Not a chance of blend, boys, things have got to tend.
Think of those who vend, boys, think of how we wend,
Waiting for the end, boys, waiting for the end.

THE COTTAGE HOSPITAL[20]

John Betjeman

At the end of a long-walled garden
      in a red provincial town,
A brick path led to a mulberry—
      scanty grass at its feet.
I lay under blackening branches
      where the mulbery leaves hung down
Sheltering ruby fruit globes
      from a Sunday-tea-time heat.
Apple and plum espaliers
      basked upon bricks of brown;
The air was swimming with insects,
      and children played in the street.

Out of this bright intentness
      into the mulberry shade
Musca domestica (housefly)
      swung from the August light
Slap into slithery rigging
      by the waiting spider made
Which spun the lithe elastic
      till the fly was shrouded tight.
Down came the hairy talons
      and horrible poison blade
And none of the garden noticed
      that fizzing, hopeless fight.

---

[20] From *Collected Poems* (Boston: Houghton Mifflin Co., 1959). Reprinted by permission of John Murray, Publishers, Ltd.

Say in what Cottage Hospital
   whose pale green walls resound
With the tap upon polished parquet
   of inflexible nurses' feet
Shall I myself be lying
   when they range the screens around?
And say shall I groan in dying,
   as I twist the sweaty sheet?
Or gasp for breath uncrying,
   as I feel my senses drown'd
While the air is swimming with insects
   and children play in the street?

HEARING OF HARVESTS ROTTING IN THE VALLEYS[21]

W. H. Auden

Hearing of harvests rotting in the valleys,
Seeing at end of street the barren mountains,
Round corners coming suddenly on water,
Knowing them shipwrecked who were launched for islands,
We honor founders of these starving cities,
Whose honor is the image of our sorrow.

Which cannot see its likeness in their sorrow
That brought them desperate to the brink of valleys;
Dreaming of evening walks through learned cities,
They reined their violent horses on the mountains,
Those fields like ships to castaways on islands,
Visions of green to them that craved for water.

They built by rivers and at night the water
Running past windows comforted their sorrow;
Each in his little bed conceived of islands
Where every day was dancing in the valleys,
And all the year trees blossomed on the mountains,
Where love was innocent, being far from cities.

But dawn came back and they were still in cities;
No marvellous creature rose up from the water,
There was still gold and silver in the mountains,
And hunger was a more immediate sorrow;
Although to moping villagers in valleys
Some waving pilgrims were describing islands.

"The gods," they promised, "visit us from islands,
Are stalking head-up, lovely through the cities;
Now is the time to leave your wretched valleys

And sail with them across the lime-green water;
Sitting at their white sides, forget their sorrow,
The shadow cast across your lives by mountains."

So many, doubtful, perished in the mountains
Climbing up crags to get a view of islands;
So many, fearful, took with them their sorrow
Which stayed them when they reached unhappy cities;
So many, careless, dived and drowned in water;
So many, wretched, would not leave their valleys.

It is the sorrow; shall it melt?   Ah, water
Would gush, flush, green these mountains and these valleys
And we rebuild our cities, not dream of islands.

THE FORCE THAT THROUGH THE GREEN
FUSE DRIVES THE FLOWER[22]

Dylan Thomas

The force that through the green fuse drives the flower
Drives my green age; that blasts the roots of trees
Is my destroyer.
And I am dumb to tell the crooked rose
My youth is bent by the same wintry fever.

The force that drives the water through the rocks
Drives my red blood; that dries the mouthing streams
Turns mine to wax.
And I am dumb to mouth unto my veins
How at the mountain spring the same mouth sucks.

The hand that whirls the water in the pool
Stirs the quicksand; that ropes the blowing wind
Hauls my shroud sail.
And I am dumb to tell the hanging man
How of my clay is made the hangman's lime.

The lips of time leech to the fountain head;
Love drips and gathers, but the fallen blood
Shall calm her sores.
And I am dumb to tell a weather's wind
How time has ticked a heaven round the stars.

And I am dumb to tell the lover's tomb
How at my sheet goes the same crooked worm.

AN OWL FOR A NIGHTINGALE[23]

Peter Viereck

1

One tawny paw is all it takes to squash
This owl who nests in brows his grounded stare.
And I am both what anchors and what flies,
The sheltering eyelids and the straining eyes.
What ailed me from the arsenals of shape
To wear so armorless a pilgrim's-cape?
And who am, who is "I"? If soul, I'd flash
Through this poor pelt—through, off, no matter where,
Just to wrench free one instant. Or else I'd shout
In midnight ululations—"let me out"—
    Straight up at Such as cooped me here:
"How did you get me into such a scrape?"

2

But "I" being less than soul, of dustier plume:
If I escape it is myself I lose.
Big hooting flapping earth-bound ego, close
Your hopeless wings at last and bless aloud—
Seeing only song flits through—this slandered home,
This warm sweet roost built from such stinking trash.
Sing out its theme (there never was but one),
Throw back your head and sing it all again,
Sing the bewildered honor of the flesh.
I say the honor of our flesh is love;
I say no soul, no god could love as we—
A forepaw stalking us from every cloud—
Who loved while sentenced to mortality.
    Never to be won by shields, love fell
O only to the wholly vulnerable.

3

What hubbub rocks the nest? What panic-freighted
Invasion—when he tried to sing—dilated
The big eyes of my blinking, hooting fowl?
A cartilaginous, most rheumatic squeak
Portends (half mocks) the change; the wrenched bones creak;
Unself descends, invoked or uninvited;

[23] An earlier version, entitled "Some Lines in Three Parts," appeared in Mr. Viereck's *The First Morning*, Charles Scribner's Sons, 1952. This revision is to be used in Peter Viereck's *New and Selected Poems*, Bobbs-Merrill, 1966. Published here by permission of the author.

Self ousts itself, consumed and consummated;
An inward-facing mask is what must break.
The magic feverish fun of chirping, all
That professorial squints and squawks indicted,
Is here—descends, descends—till wisdom, hoarse
From bawling beauty out, at last adores,
Possessed by metamorphosis so strong.
Then, with a final flutter, philomel—
How mud-splashed, what a mangy miracle!—
Writhes out of owl and stands with drooping wing.
Just stands there. Moulted, naked, two-thirds dead.
From shock and pain (and dread of holy dread)
    Suddenly vomiting.
Look away quick, you are watching the birth of song.

LOCAL PLACES[24]

Howard Moss

The song you sang you will not sing again,
Floating in the spring to all your local places,
Lured by archaic senses to the wood
To watch the frog jump from the mossy rock,
To listen to the stream's small talk at dark,
Or to feel the springy pine-floor where you walk—
If your green secrecies were such as these,
The mystery is now in other trees.

If, in the desert, where the cactus dryly,
Leniently allows its classic bloom
To perfume aridness, you searched for water,
And saw, at night, the scalp of sand begin
To ripple like the sea, as though the moon
Had tides to time those waves of light's illusion,
The rock that spilled so softly from your hand
Is now ten thousand other grains of sand.

If you lay down beside the breathing ocean,
Whose lung is never still, whose motion pulls
A night-net over sleep, you knew the way
It lulled the dreamer toward his vision, how
Drowned mariners turned over in its slough,
Green-eyed among the weeds. You see it now
A less than visionary sea, and feel
Only its blue surfaces were ever real.

Or if you were born to naked flatness
Of rock, or rock that twisted up in mountains,
The jagged risers stonily ascending,
And bent down once to see the mica's tight,
Flat scales of silver, layered in the granite,
And kept one scale to be your jewel at night,
Another sliver now breaks light; its gleam
Is similar to yours, yet not the same.

Once history has used your single name,
Your face is one, time will not see again.
Into such a din is every singer born,
The general music mutes the single horn.
The lights in the small houses, one by one,
Go out, foundations topple slowly down—
The tree, the sand, the water, and the stone,
What songs they sing they always sing again.

A NORTHERN SPRING[25]

Gene Baro

Across the greening lawn,
blankets and pillows lie
with daffodil and crocus
in the new sun's eye.

Storm windows have come down:
the house now drinks its fill
of the brimming Maytime wind
at the swept window sill;

but, like old winds, indeed,
like branches at the pane,
stiff brush and broom are making
a wintery refrain,

a music that will die
upon the well-scrubbed air
when, hands on hips in her doorway,
my mother stands there

and dreams her August roses
have flowered pink and red
and sees the harvest making
and the fresh season's bread,

sees smoke again from the chimneys,
sees seasons that are past,

new leaves and snowflakes falling
in the kindred northwind's blast.

This is a winter country,
its spring just a cleaning day,
though my mother will stand in her doorway
and pass half an hour away.

WALT WHITMAN AT BEAR MOUNTAIN[26]

Louis Simpson

"... life which does not give the preference to any other life, of any previous
period, which therefore prefers its own existence . . ."

ORTEGA Y GASSET

Neither on horseback nor seated,
But like himself, squarely on two feet,
The poet of death and lilacs
Loafs by the footpath. Even the bronze looks alive
Where it is folded like cloth. And he seems friendly.

"Where is the Mississippi panorama
And the girl who played the piano?
Where are you, Walt?
The Open Road goes to the used-car lot.

"Where is the nation you promised?
These houses built of wood sustain
Colossal snows,
And the light above the street is sick to death.

"As for the people—see how they neglect you!
Only a poet pauses to read the inscription."

"I am here," he answered.
"It seems you have found me out.
Yet, did I not warn you that it was Myself
I advertised? Were my words not sufficiently plain?

"I gave no prescriptions,
And those who have taken my moods for prophecies
Mistake the matter."
Then, vastly amused—"Why do you reproach me?
I freely confess I am wholly disreputable.
Yet I am happy, because you have found me out."

A crocodile in wrinkled metal loafing . . .

[26] Copyright © 1960 by Louis Simpson. Reprinted from *At the End of the
Open Road* by Louis Simpson by permission of Wesleyan University Press.

Then all the realtors,
Pickpockets, salesmen, and the actors performing
Official scenarios,
Turned a deaf ear, for they had contracted
American dreams.

But the man who keeps a store on a lonely road,
And the housewife who knows she's dumb,
And the earth, are relieved.

All that grave weight of America
Cancelled! Like Greece and Rome.
The future in ruins!
The castles, the prisons, the cathedrals
Unbuilding, and roses
Blossoming from the stones that are not there . . .

The clouds are lifting from the high Sierras,
The Bay mists clearing.
And the angel in the gate, the flowering plum
Dances like Italy, imagining red.

9

EMOTION IN POETRY

> Thus to their extreme verge the passions brought
> Dash into poetry, which is but a passion.
> LORD BYRON, *Don Juan.*

Do not be misled by the word "passions" as Byron uses it. In current speech it connotes a violent disturbance, generally sexual, but in his day it was just another word for feeling or emotion. The same was true of "affection," which with us generally means a tender feeling of attachment. But by whatever name we call this familiar human experience it has since earliest times been regarded as an essential quality, if not the very essence, of poetry. A review of some statements about it will refresh our memories.

Aristotle taught that all works of art give pleasure because of our natural delight in objects of imitation. He held also that the function of tragedy was to relieve the audience's emotions of pity and fear. And he recommended that the poet, in order to depict the emotions of his characters, should while composing assume the very attitudes and gestures appropriate to the several emotions. According to Horace one of the chief ends of poetry was to give pleasure. Milton characterized poetry as "sensuous and passionate," and the judicious Samuel Johnson believed that a poet's feeling should evoke a corresponding feeling in the reader, and said that in reading Shakespeare an "unresisted passion stormed the breast."

The conception of poetry as a welling up of emotion within the poet and its overflow or expression in words, strongly influenced by the writings of Coleridge and Wordsworth, has pretty well dominated poetic theory since their day. This doctrine shifted the center of critical theory from imitation of nature and its effect upon the reader, to the poet himself, making his emotions the source of poetry, although it did not ignore the reader entirely. Poe, for instance, said that "a poem deserves its title only inasmuch as it excites, by elevating the soul." John Stuart Mill called poetry "the expression or uttering forth of feeling," and Bliss Perry said it "begins in excitement, in some body-and-mind experience." John Masefield, Poet Laureate of England, says enchantment is the main function of poetry, and that "it has always to come from the excitement of the poet, . . . the effect of the poem will always depend upon the measure of excitement he can maintain." In these statements excitement seems to be equivalent to emotion.

Recent critics are just as specific as older ones in identifying poetry with emotion. Yvor Winters calls a poem a statement "in which special pains are taken with the expression of feeling." Kenneth Burke says that literature as art is "designed for the express purpose of arousing emotion." I. A. Richards says that poetry is "the supreme form of emotive language," and Eliseo Vivas says the vast majority of his contemporaries accept the modern dogma that the artist is primarily concerned with emotion. We have already noticed T. S. Eliot's doctrine of an "objective correlative" as a formula which evokes emotion in the reader. We should note also his statement that "Poetry is not a turning loose of emotion, but an escape from emotion."

For more than two thousand years, then, critics have held that poetry is closely involved with emotion. But as oral interpreters of poetry there are a number of things we need to know about this involvement. We need to know what emotion is. Like many familiar concepts—truth, beauty, art, justice—it is not easily defined. When we are about to put our fingers on it, it slips away. Is it synonymous with pleasure, excitement, enchantment, disturbance? We need to know what a poet experiences, and by what means he expresses his experience. When we look at a page of poetry we find only words, just as when we look at a page of cold scientific writing. By what process do the poetic words affect us? How do they arouse our emotions, if they do arouse them? Just what are we supposed to communicate to our hearers, and how? What is our audience supposed to experience? The common view is that a poet has an emotion; he puts it on paper; we read what he has written and feel the same emotion; if we read it aloud we convey to our hearers the same emotion that the poet felt. But this "bucket brigade" theory of the transference of emotion from one person to another cannot survive careful scrutiny. It does not fit the facts of literary appreciation, and it leaves too many things to be explained.

The Nature of Emotion

It is generally accepted that an emotion is a widespread bodily and mental (i.e. psychosomatic) reaction or disturbance that upsets our normal relaxed calm, with resulting pleasure or pain. It is evidenced largely by change in the rate of breathing and heartbeat, and it is accompanied by an impulse to action of some sort—to strike at what causes anger, to run from what causes fear. This response generally relieves the emotion and it passes away. Typically, emotion is transient; it will not endure for long unless its cause is renewed. Emotion may be caused by almost anything—a word, a thought, a sight, an event, an image recalled, a physical state—but the one who experiences it must be in an appropriate receptive attitude. A loud explosion will not startle or frighten us if we are expecting it. A painful blow will seldom anger us if we know it is delivered in sport.

The Poet's Emotion

The emotion a poet tries to put into his poem is not likely to be actually felt as he composes. It will be rather, as Wordsworth said, an "emotion recollected in tranquility." The normal instinctive impulse to physical action which accompanies an emotion is not an impulse to write. Indeed, words are not the most suitable medium for expressing emotion. We are often aware of powerful feelings that we cannot put into language. We are, as we say, dumb with fear, speechless with indignation, inarticulate with grief, and when thus frozen into dumbness if any communication takes place it will likely be through visible and vocal, but not verbal, signs. Since emotion is a total bodily disturbance, it has a better medium of expression in the dance.

If the poet does feel emotion as he writes, it is bound to be modified and transformed during the process of translating it into words. It may be diffused, rationalized, sublimated. When his expression has to be trimmed to suit the demands of some precise pattern such as the sonnet, what gets expressed may not be the original feeling at all. And in a long poem such as *Paradise Lost*, or *The Idylls of the King*, requiring several years for its composition, the original emotion, if there was one, cannot be made to glow over so long a period.

Then, too, poets generally do not attempt to express such primitive primary emotions as fear and rage. (Note, however, John Betjeman's "Slough," page 345.) More often what is expressed is a mild generalized feeling of pleasure, excitement, restlessness, or dejection that is not accompanied by a strong impulse to action.

Poetry, then, is not literally a "spontaneous overflow of powerful feeling." Some scholars now question whether emotion is the dominant element in poetry, whether indeed it is a necessary element for either the poet or his readers. D. G. James, while allowing the presence of intellectual and emotional elements in poetry, insists that the central element is "imaginative prehension." "The primary fact about poetry," he says, "is that in and through it an imaginative object is conveyed," and "the weight of emphasis must always be on the vividness with which we grasp an imaginative object or situation."[1] Perhaps the fact is that a poet *may* be stimulated by some excitement, as Masefield says, or he may not. He may just "get an idea" for a poem and proceed in a calm workmanlike way to put it into poetic form, imitating some significant scene, or mood, or experience, or event, or developing some significant thought. If he does represent emotion, T. S. Eliot says, "emotions which he has never experienced will serve his turn as well as those familiar to him."

With such poets as Stephen Spender and Robert Frost emotion seems to develop after composition has begun, not before. In his essay, "The Making of a Poem," Spender has no suggestion that emotion is what stimulates him to write, although he says the successful composition of a poem through sweat and toil "*results* in an intense physical excitement."[2] More recently he has written of the poet as a "critically aware, objective carpenter with words."[3] Robert Frost said that his poems did not start with an idea, or an intuitive impulse, or with external observation. Rather they began with a vague mood, a kind of verbal readiness that picked up an idea or emotion and developed from "ecstasy at some surprise in the mind" that the idea or emotion was already present.[4] Eliseo Vivas says, "It is not necessary to assume that the actual emotion that is worked up by the poet into the poem is the actual occasion of the creative act."[5]

If you find this somewhat baffling it is because there are no final answers about the nature of poetical emotion. The discussion, however, should make you more intelligent about the problems involved and furnish some grounding for your own speculations on them and your attempts to interpret poetical emotion to others. In these attempts you will need to distinguish between a poet's emotion, if any, his expression of that emotion, its effect on his readers, the response an oral reader should wish to arouse in his hearers, and the means by which he attempts to arouse it. You need to be aware also of the various ways in which poets express

---

[1] D. G. James, "I. A. Richards," in R. W. Stallman (ed), *Critiques and Essays in Criticism* (New York: The Ronald Press Co., 1949), p. 478.

[2] Stephen Spender, "The Making of a Poem," in Stallman, *op. cit.*, p. 28.

[3] Stephen Spender, in *The Saturday Review*, August 8, 1964, p. 16.

[4] Reginald L. Cook, *The Dimensions of Robert Frost* (New York: Holt, Rinehart & Winston, Inc., 1958), p. 53.

[5] Eliseo Vivas, "The Objective Correlative of T. S. Eliot," in Stallman, *op. cit.*, p. 399.

emotion and the different kinds of response they intend to stimulate. Sometimes the reader's feeling and the audience's feeling should be quite different from the poet's.

Kinds of Emotional Expression in Poetry

A poet's emotion, when clearly identifiable, may take various forms. It may be a direct expression of a personal private feeling caused by an immediate experience: "But she is in her grave, and oh the difference to me." Second, it may be a general feeling that all normal people can be expected to share, as Wordsworth's shame and sorrow that England has allowed love of commerce to replace love of nature: "The world is too much with us; . . . getting and spending, we lay waste our powers." Third, the poet may say nothing about his feeling, may not even mention himself, but merely present a picture, an incident, a situation for the reader's imagination to seize upon, as does Markham in "The Man with the Hoe": "Bowed by the weight of centuries he leans upon his hoe and gazes at the ground." Fourth, he may represent someone else as speaking and expressing emotions that are not the poet's at all, perhaps emotions he would not wish to share: "If hate killed men, Brother Lawrence, God's blood, would not mine kill you!" And there are vaguer and more delicate shades of feeling that may find other and more elusive forms of expression.

The Reader's Emotion

The reader of a poem, as we have said, may not be expected to feel as the poet felt in composing it. (Review of Chapter 3 will be helpful here.) He does not have the direct stimulus which moved the poet; he reacts only to the stimulus which the poet presents, its images, ideas, figures of speech, word-color, rhythms, etc. He may experience only what I. A. Richards calls an imaginal and incipient response. Richards says that it is in terms of these "incipient promptings, lightly stimulated tendencies to acts of one kind and another, faint preliminary preparations for doing this and that," and in the resolution and balancing of these impulses, "that all the most valuable effects of poetry may be described."[6]

A great deal depends upon the nature of the poet's stimulus and his way of expressing his response to it. If he is moved by some private personal experience, the reader's response may be quite different from the poet's. Robert Burns's expression of his love for various Nells, Peggys, Jeans, Megs, and Marys will not stimulate us to love them since we don't know them. Wordsworth's sonnet "To Sleep" is a moving description of his weariness and yearning for rest, but it does not move us to insomnia and

---

[6] I. A. Richards, *Principles of Literary Criticism* (New York: Harcourt, Brace & World, Inc., 1948), p. 113.

set us to counting sheep. Keats's depression when he fears he may not live to write down all the poems that fill his teeming brain is not a sentiment that we will feel as he does. Our feeling in such cases is rather sympathy with the poet's emotion. It is as if we came upon an intimate friend who was mourning the loss of some dear one whom we had never met. He grieves from a sharp sense of personal loss, but we feel no personal loss; we grieve merely in sympathy with his grief.

If, on the other hand, the poet expresses such a feeling as all may share, as does Keats in "To Autumn," our feelings will be very much like his own. And so with most descriptive and narrative poems. But if the poem is dramatic, that is, represents other persons as speaking, the difference between their emotions and the reader's may be very great. A painful emotion in the character may arouse a pleasant one in the reader, and vice versa. The distress and frustration of the gentleman in Browning's "Up at a Villa—Down in the City" we find amusing. Macbeth's murderous rage moves us to horror. And so with other characters.

The Interpreter's Function

Against this background let us consider the obligations of a reader who undertakes to interpret poetry orally to others. John Masefield points out that poets today have less stimulus than in earlier times to make their poems exciting. The primitive poet, he says, was a man of the tribe, living as the tribe lived, sharing its interests and delights. He spoke or sang his verses to assemblies of his fellow tribesmen, frequently composing as he sang; and he had the direct, instant criticism of an audience that might grow cold with disapproval or indifference as he sang, or that might catch his excitement and carry him beyond himself with enthusiasm.[7] He was a public entertainer. The early epics were composed for audiences and lived only, or chiefly, on the tongues of public reciters. Only in later times were they written down and so preserved for posterity. In ancient Greece contests in reciting poetry were established by law. A poet who recited his own works, or a professional reader who recited the works of some poet, was called a *rhapsode,* and the impassioned style of his recitation has given us the modern words *rhapsodist* and *rhapsodic.* The young rhapsode, Ion, in Plato's dialogue of that name (see Appendix, *Ion*), confesses that when reading Homer, "at the tale of pity my eyes are filled with tears, and when I speak of horrors, my hair stands on end and my heart throbs." Roman poets "published" their verses by bawling them in the public baths, often to the annoyance of the customers. And during the Middle Ages high-born ladies in France and Italy thrilled from their

[7] John Masefield, *With the Living Voice* (New York: The Macmillan Co., 1925), pp. 12–14.

balconies to the love lyrics composed and sung to them by wandering troubadours.

One function of the modern interpreter might be to restore to poetry some of the values of direct contact with an audience which poets had in earlier societies. Masefield believes that the public recitation of poetry, besides acquainting people again with its enchantments, may stimulate poets to recover the vitality that once enabled them to thrill and move their hearers. Significantly, another modern poet, John Holmes, related that by listening to recordings of his own readings, and by his experiences in reading his poems to audiences, he "discovered the need of much wilder and wider rhythms—a poem ought to be a good fat part for an actor." He learned "not only to speak poetry to be heard, but to write poems to be spoken to be heard."[8]

Poetry Is Meant To Be Communicated

We will digress here to note the theory sometimes propounded that poetry is meant for the closet and has no concern with an audience. Some artists scorn, or pretend to scorn, communication. An artist may say that communication is irrelevant or unimportant, that he is making something that satisfies him personally, something expressive of himself or of his feelings, something individual and private. This view has found encouragement from modern critics.

But I. A. Richards points out that the artist does not realize how completely his activity is controlled by the necessity for communication. "The very structure of our minds," he says, "is largely determined by the fact that man has been engaged in communicating for so many hundreds of thousands of years. . . . An experience has to be formed, no doubt, before it is communicated, but it takes the form it does largely because it may have to be communicated. . . . The arts are the supreme form of the communicative activity." True enough, the artist may not deliberately and consciously aim at an audience. He may feel that direct concern over how his work will be received would dissipate his attention from his creative activity and cheapen the result. "But this conscious neglect of communication," says Professor Richards, "does not in the least diminish the communicative aspect. . . . The very process of getting the work 'right' has itself, as far as the artist is normal, immense communicative consequences. . . . The degree to which it accords with the relevant experience of the artist is a measure of the degree to which it will arouse similar experiences in others."[9]

This closet theory of poetry ignores not only the history of poetry and

---

[8] John Holmes, in John Ciardi, *Mid-Century American Poets* (New York: Twayne Publishers, Inc., 1950), p. 204.
[9] I. A. Richards, *op. cit.*, pp. 25–27.

its essential communicative aspect; it ignores also the vocal values which are a part of its very essence. As Bliss Perry said, "A poem is not primarily a series of printed word-signs addressed to the eye; it is a series of sounds addressed to the ear, and the arbitrary symbols for these sounds do not convey the poem unless they are audibly rendered."[10]

Applications

After this digression we return to the oral interpreter's emotional activity. We are trying to consider separately the poet's feeling, the silent reader's feeling, the interpreter's feeling, and the feeling he wishes to arouse in his audience, and this unavoidably leads to a good deal of repetition. Let us examine some poems and try to determine what emotional treatment they call for. All may be found through the index and will not be quoted in the text. Wordsworth's sonnet, "The World is too much with us," to be used for drill at the end of this chapter, expresses a communal emotion that all can feel, and the hearers are more likely to be moved if the reader too seems to feel it. Poet, interpreter, and audience all agree in their response, though few may wish to go so far as to reject Christianity, as the poet suggests. So also with Wilfred Owen's "Anthem for Doomed Youth" and Markham's "The Man with the Hoe."

But Michael Drayton's "Since there's no help, come let us kiss and part" is personal, though in a sense dramatic too. Perhaps Drayton never experienced this situation but only imagined it. As we regard his relief over his renunciation, or pretended renunciation, of love, we do not feel relief, but rather amusement. How should the interpreter be affected? Does he side with the poet, or with the audience? or with both? He may *assume* the feeling of the poet without really sharing it. That is, he may act the part. Or he may, while presenting the feeling, show at the same time that he is amused by it, or sympathizes with it, or in similar situations that he disapproves of it. And so Mrs. Browning's sonnet of deep personal feeling, "How do I love thee?" can be interpreted by a man, acting the part of the author, and by a man who is not in love at all. Any emotion he may feel is not personal and real, for a specific emotion always has a cause and an object. We are not just angry in general; we are angry *at* something. We do not experience love in general; we love some one or some thing. Mrs. Browning's love is *her* love and will not be experienced by interpreter or audience, though both may sympathize with it and find pleasure in it.

In a similar manner a girl, reading Keats's sonnet, "Bright star! Would I were steadfast as thou art," may imagine the emotions of a man pillowed upon his fair love's ripening breast, sympathize with them, and move her

[10] Bliss Perry, *A Study of Poetry* (Boston: Houghton Mifflin Co., 1920), p. 100.

audience to sympathy with them, but neither she nor the women in her audience will feel quite what Keats felt—a yearning to rest forever on his beloved's bosom.

An interpreter, then, should distinguish between a poet's impersonal description of events, scenes, experiences, etc., that cause emotion, his expression of a general emotion such as all can share, and expression of a personal private emotion rising from a specific experience, and relate and identify himself toward the situation accordingly.

When a poem is definitely dramatic, when a character other than the poet is represented as speaking, and when the audience is not expected to experience the same emotion as this character, a different problem arises. Should an interpreter identify his feeling with that of the character, or with that of the audience? Or should he be emotionally neutral? Any one of these three choices may in different situations be best. In reading Browning's "Soliloquy of the Spanish Cloister," for instance, an interpreter may, in portraying the cheap malignant hatred of this odd character, work up in himself, in greater or lesser degree, the passions he is representing. He may, on the other hand, be able to present the character vividly without experiencing any feeling of hate, just as we all may feign anger without being angry, or pretend to be cheerful when we are not. Or he may while presenting the poem identify himself with the audience, contemplate with them the scene he is presenting, and feel with them the contempt and amusement the poem is intended to arouse. In informal situations he may even interpolate comments that reveal the identity of his feeling with that of the audience, as do many teachers of literature in reading dramatic scenes to their classes.

On Feeling Emotion

Something further needs to be said on whether an interpreter should feel the emotions he tries to arouse in others. Differences of temperament and method indicate that there can be no answer that is universally valid, but we need to consider some factors that have a bearing on the matter. As we know from our silent reading, words alone can be very moving. For his audience, an interpreter takes the place of the printed text, but very rarely can he be as impassive as cold print, merely presenting the vocal symbols of what he reads and allowing them to have what effect they may. Even in presenting bare narrative or description he can hardly avoid coloring it by his voice and gesture. That audiences can be, and often are, moved by a cold performer is obvious enough, just as they are moved by inanimate puppets or animated cartoons. Many effective actors go through their parts cold, though they seldom *seem* cold; they have mastered moving techniques which they can use without being themselves moved. An oral reader also, if he does not feel, and visibly or audibly reveal his feeling, will need to acquire a technique that creates the illusion of feeling.

Remember too that if an emotion is assumed it tends to become real. It may be felt when the speaker doesn't intend to feel it. And note also that emotion is contagious. A hearty laugher makes others merry; an apostle of gloom depresses all around him; a display of courage makes others more brave. By feeling what he speaks an interpreter may help greatly to stimulate feeling in his hearers. He has a great advantage over the poet since his vocal and visible action may enhance the effect of the poet's words and make them much more moving.

The Means of Emotional Expression

When an interpreter does feel emotion, he will make it evident chiefly by the tone of his voice, but he should use also the visible means of communication—bodily movement and facial expression. Gilbert Murray said that the Greek lyric "was derived directly from the religious dance; that is, not merely the pattering of the feet, but the *yearning movement of the whole body*, the ultimate expression of emotion that cannot be pressed into articulate speech, compact of intense rhythm and intense feeling."[11] Such "all-over" response, so effective in enlivening expression, can be practiced without being unduly conspicuous.

Though it is normal and natural for any real emotion to express itself in some overt physical movement—that is, in gesture—the current convention of good taste, in recitation as in singing, requires that such responses be carefully schooled. In public performances these "bodily yearnings" must find visible outlet chiefly in facial expression. For a reader of Shelley's salute to the skylark, "Hail to thee, blithe spirit," to greet the bird with a wave of the hand would be as inappropriate as for a concert singer of Schubert's "Hark, hark! the lark" to do the same. Emotional intensity and imaginative alertness in both cases should be expressed chiefly through voice and face. In Milton's "L'Allegro" there is a fine description of a singer's voice running through the intricate mazes of a song "with wanton heed and giddy cunning." A reader, like a singer, may wish to give an impression of wantonness and giddiness, but he should control it with a due exercise of heed and cunning. Abandon must be disciplined; passion must be properly schooled. One may, by an excess of emotion, excite a different and unwanted feeling in his audience. We do not sympathize with those who too easily give way to mirth, or indignation, or grief, and tearing a passion to tatters offends us to the soul. It is question-

[11] Gilbert Murray, "What English Poetry May Still Learn from Greek," *Atlantic Monthly*, Nov. 1912, p. 669.

able whether Anglo-Saxon audiences would relish the extravagant emo-
tionalism of the Russian poet, Evgeny Evtushenko, who has on a recent
reading tour thrilled European audiences.

EMOTION AND POETIC FORM. Since a part of the pleasure of poetry
comes from its formal elements, its word-color, rhythm, and rhyme, some
students of literature feel that the sounds alone of certain words, and even
of certain letters, have power to arouse specific feelings. Some sounds, no
doubt, are pleasanter and more beautiful than others, but whether specific
word-sounds can excite specific emotions is another matter. Do the mere
sounds of "home" and "love" arouse tender feelings? If so, should not the
same tender feelings be evoked by "comb" and "shove?" Tennyson's line

> And murmuring of innumerable bees,

is often quoted as one of the most beautiful and moving in English poetry.
But by altering just one consonant and adding one you get the parody,

> And murdering of innumerable beeves,

with its slaughter-house suggestion. Thomas Gray's line

> The short and simple annals of the poor.

is pleasantly melancholy and evocative, but it can be made ridiculous by
adding just two consonant sounds:

> The short and simple flannels of the poor.

Plainly it is the change in meaning, not in sound, that alters our feeling for
these lines.

Yet there are critics who believe that even single consonants have
power to suggest particular moods and feelings. One of the latest of them
is Gilbert Highet. The letter *s*, he says, shows hatred, and is "the letter of
disgust and sinister cunning, the letter which begins the words *snake* and
serpent and *Satan*." But it also begins the words *sweet, syrup, saint, soul,
sorrow, sob*, and *sigh!* And he goes on, "The letter *f* is quiet, almost mute,
like a tiny breeze blowing; so it can echo the soft activities of nature in
springtime."[12] But it can also echo the threat of a "frightful, frantic, furious frown."

The effect of a letter as sound cannot be dissociated from the situation
in which it occurs, the sounds of neighboring letters, the meanings of
words, the mood and expectancy developing in the listener, etc. "There
are no gloomy or gay vowels," says I. A. Richards, "and the army of critics

[12] Gilbert Highet, *The Powers of Poetry* (Fair Lawn, N.J.: Oxford University Press,
1960), pp. 5–7.

who have attempted to analyse the effects of passages into vowel and consonant collocations have, in fact, merely been amusing themselves." But if not singly, then in combinations, letter sounds may help to give an affective color to words. We can test this by comparing the sounds of place-names that are not associated with common word-meanings. That is, compare the effect of Oshkosh, Keokuk, Sopchoppy with that of such liquid and enticing names as Menominee, Winnebago, Apalachicola. Do you suppose that the hearts of the local residents beat with the same tender feeling when they think or sing of good old Oshkosh as when they think or sing of good old Menominee?

Poets certainly make use of certain letter combinations to give added stimulus to the effects they seek. In Tennyson's description of the Lotos-eaters the dreamy effect desired is promoted by open vowels and liquid consonants:

> A land where all things always seemed the same!
> And round the keel with faces pale,
> Dark faces pale against that rosy flame,
> The mild-eyed melancholy Lotos-eaters came.

Compare it with the abrupt force and splintering effect he achieves by a different combination in his song of the knights of King Arthur:

> Flash brand and lance, fall battleaxe upon helm,
> Fall battleaxe, and flash brand! Let the King reign.

EMOTION AND METER. Word-sounds combine with rhythm in stimulating moods and emotions. Herbert Spencer said that meter is "an idealization of the natural language of strong emotion, which is known to be more or less metrical if the emotion be not too violent." Another critic has said that "in rhythm the noblest emotions find their noblest expression." Meter and sound combined are the vehicle that carries many of the most moving passages of poetry. Readers should be alert for them and give them their full value. With little or no help from meaningful words they are capable of expressing quite different and easily identifiable feelings. Even a child feels the difference between a lullaby and a gallop. This can be illustrated by comparing two passages in which meaning is at a minimum and the effect depends chiefly upon sound and meter. Compare the pure nonsense of Lewis Carroll's Jabberwocky:

> 'Twas brillig, and the slithy toves
> Did gyre and gimble in the Wabe;
> All mimsy were the borogoves,
> And the mome raths outgrabe.

with Swinburne's *almost* nonsensical parody on himself:

Surely no spirit or sense of a soul that was soft to the spirit and soul of
our senses
Sweetens the stress of surprising suspicion that sobs in the semblance and
sound of a sigh.

The point is that even without clear meaning the two passages are different in mood and feeling.

Morris Bishop, in "Sing a Song of the Cities,"[13] has strung together
some place names so as to suggest several moods and emotions, and even
a situation, a narrative, a dialogue. True, sound and meter are aided by
names which are, or imply, meaningful words, as Gowanda suggests, "Go
on," but sound and meter carry the chief burden. Consider whether the
last line can be made to mean that there is a bad odor in repetition of certain experiences, or in returning home. Read it aloud, trying to express
meaning and feeling in its suggested dialogue:

> "Towanda Winooski? Gowanda!"
> Rahway Setauket Eugene.
> "Watseka? Ware! Tonawanda!"
> Flushing Modesto De Queene.
>
> "Wantagh Malone Petaluma!
> Pontiac! Rye! Champaign!
> Kissimmee Smackover! Yuma!"
> Ossining, Waverly Kane.
>
> "Rockaway! Homestead Tacoma!
> Neenah Metuchen Peru!
> Owego Moberly Homer!
> Dover Andover Depew!"

Should Poetry Sound Formal or Natural?

There is difference of opinion as to how far the formal element in
poetry—meter, rhyme, line length, etc.—should be allowed to dominate in
oral reading. Some say that since all speech is basically conversational,
intended to communicate meaning, poetry should have the normally varied
tones of ordinary talk. On the other hand, the theory and practice of
many critics and poets calls for a leveling out of the conversational pattern
into a monotonous chant, with meter and feeling dominating the utterance. The first method emphasizes grammatical structure and meaning,
and makes poetry sound very much like prose. The second emphasizes
fluidity and feeling, and tends toward song. It is a very old problem, one

[13] Morris Bishop, *A Bowl of Bishop* (New York: Dial Press, Inc., 1954), p. 102.

which concerned Quintilian, the great teacher of Roman youth, and he suggests a solution for it:

Let not his (the Roman boy's) reading of the poets be like that of prose . . . for it is verse, and the poets say that they sing; yet let it not degenerate into sing-song, or be rendered effeminate with unnatural softness, as is now the practice among most readers; on which sort of reading we hear that Caius [Julius] Caesar, while he has still under age, observed happily of someone that was practicing it, "If you are singing, you sing badly; if you pretend to read, you nevertheless sing."

It is likely that Wordsworth would have agreed with this compromise. For his lyrical poems he wanted "an animated or impassioned recitation," but made the reservation that the formal and emotional elements should not be allowed to dominate. "The law of long and short syllable," he said, "must not be so inflexible . . . as to deprive the Reader of all voluntary power to modulate, in subordination to the sense, the music of the poem."

There are, of course, many kinds of poetry, and so there must be many proper ways of pronouncing it. Of the three elements we find in it—thought, feeling, and form—any one of them may in a given poem seem more important than the others. All poems are not metrical, or musical. Some are sprightly, or conversational, or dramatic, or even choppy, or are meant to sound more or less like ordinary talk. Some of Whitman, Browning, and Sandburg have such qualities. Robert Frost always sought deliberately to achieve what he called the "tones" of everyday speech, though he was far from negligent of meter. Though there must be in all poetry, as in prose, a basic structure of logic and syntax, even in the deeply emotional poetry of the great English odes and sonnets, often rigidly metrical, it should be possible to find a golden mean between the conversational manner and the smooth-flowing, sustained, emotional manner of utterance, a mean that will do justice to both prose-sense and meter, both thought and feeling. This would seem to be especially desirable in reading Shakespeare's plays, but rare is the actor who achieves it.

Deliberation

Finally, poems of deep and serious feeling should not be hurried. To rush through, or over, them is as inappropriate as to play a funeral march in jig time. Poetry contains such emotions as we love to experience for their own sake, images which require time for their realization, melodies which should dwell long in our ears. "Realization," says Max Eastman, "is a flower of leisure and does not blossom quickly." He goes on to say that a prime requisite in appreciation of poetry is the power to linger, "the power of lingering with energy." It is a good phrase for the oral reader to keep in mind.

PLAN OF STUDY

1. Define carefully the emotions expressed in the poem. Are they private and individual, such as may be shared by all normal readers, or emotions of someone other than the poet?
2. Consider what attitude you should show toward these emotions—whether to share them, to merely sympathize with them, or to join the audience in observing them. This attitude will be chiefly mental, but it should be apparent in your delivery.
3. Consider how you want your audience to react, and how you can obtain the desired reaction.
4. Note all the emotional effects that may be enhanced by the sounds of the words and their rhythm, and plan to give them full value.
5. Plan to read with a vitality and intensity that will command attention and move your hearers in the desired way. But rather than try to work up a high pitch of emotion concentrate on how you can present vividly the events, scenes, experiences, sounds, and rhythms that evoke emotion.
6. In rehearsal allow these stimuli to affect freely your bodily responses, but in public be more reserved, remembering that strong emotional displays may offend and repel instead of pleasing.
7. In poems of deep sustained feeling keep your utterance smooth and even, avoiding the sudden modulations of sprightly conversation, but don't sing. Plan to speak deliberately.
8. Through all your study and practice try to keep thought, feeling, imagination, and form integrated into a coherent whole.

CRITERIA

1. Did the reader maintain an appropriate glow of excitement?
2. Did he make an intelligent choice as to whether to share the poet's emotion, merely report on it, sympathize with it, react against it?
3. Did he stimulate his audience to the appropriate reaction?
4. Did he capitalize on all effects of sound and rhythm that could help to stimulate emotional response?
5. Were his visible responses effective, but appropriately disciplined?
6. Was his utterance sustained, fluid, and deliberate, and his intonation sufficiently level?
7. Did he present the poem as a coherent whole, unified in thought and feeling?

QUESTIONS FOR DISCUSSION

1. How and to what extent is poetry involved with emotion?
2. Do modern poets seem less concerned with emotion than older poets? If so, do they have something to substitute for it? images? irony? idea? narrative? exposition?

3. If a poet does not intend to arouse feeling, what reaction does he expect from his readers? If readers are not to be moved, what appeal is poetry supposed to have for them?
4. Discuss the difference between expressing an emotion and communicating it.
5. Discuss the relation of the oral reader's feeling to that of the poet and the audience.
6. What are the limitations of speech as a medium of communicating emotion?
7. Discuss the relative effectiveness of words, statements, images, rhythms, sound effects, and gesture in arousing emotion.
8. Explain how poetry is essentially communicative, whether or not the poet means it to be.
9. In terms of what the audience hears, how does a rhythmical, emotional reading of a poem differ from a conversational or merely rational one?

SELECTION FOR DRILL

THE WORLD IS TOO MUCH WITH US

William Wordsworth

The world is too much with us; late and soon,
Getting and spending, we lay waste our powers;
Little we see in Nature that is ours;
We have given our hearts away, a sordid boon!
The sea that bares her bosom to the moon;   5
The winds that will be howling at all hours,
And are up-gathered now like sleeping flowers;
For this, for everything, we are out of tune;
It moves us not.—Great God! I'd rather be
A Pagan suckled in a creed outworn;   10
So might I, standing on this pleasant lea,
Have glimpses that would make me less forlorn;
Have sight of Proteus rising from the sea;
Or hear old Triton blow his wreathèd horn.

SUGGESTIONS FOR ANALYSIS. Take great pains with the pronunciation of *world, with, soon, our, powers, little, nature, ours, bosom, winds, will be, howling, flowers, not, God, outworn, standing, Proteus, Triton.* Note the grammatical construction of "late and soon"; it belongs with the second line, and is subordinate to "getting and spending." In lines 5–8 keep the thought suspended until the main clause: "we are out of tune." The ejaculation "Great God!" had better be attached to the clause that follows it, if it is not to sound profane. The word-group will be: "Great God! I'd rather be a Pagan." In general, give the lines the full value of the slow iambic meter, but in several places you will need to break its regularity. You can increase the impression of profound sadness by bearing down evenly on the successions of heavy monosyllables: "It moves us not" and "we lay waste our powers." Keep the lungs full of air, and support every word-group steadily and continuously with firm abdominal pressure. Give full value to all the strong syllables, especially on the open vowels. Avoid such colloquial readings as, "We'v giv'n 'r hearts away" and "The win's th't wi' be howling 't all ares." Feeling should be deep and genuine and evenly sustained. Make your hearers feel that you actually see the ocean before you, that you hear the winds, and that you catch a vision of old Triton and Proteus, and that you are profoundly moved by our indifference to Nature's beauties. This dejection reaches a climax in line 9: "It moves us not," then changes to something like despair, from which it reacts to a brighter mood in the last three lines.

SELECTIONS FOR PRACTICE

All the sonnets provided for practice in reading are grouped together on the following pages. They are, I believe, representative of the best the language affords. They are followed by a variety of other poems illustrating various kinds of emotional expression. These, like the sonnets, are arranged in a rough chronological order.

Sir Philip Sidney

With how sad steps, O Moon, thou climb'st the skies!
How silently, and with how wan a face!
What! may it be that even in heav'nly place
That busy archer his sharp arrows tries?
Sure, if that long-with-love-acquainted eyes
Can judge of love, thou feel'st a lover's case,
I read it in thy looks,—thy languished grace,
To me, that feel the like, thy state descries.
Then, ev'n of fellowship, O Moon, tell me,
Is constant love deem'd there but want of wit?
Are beauties there as proud as here they be?
Do they above love to be lov'd, and yet
Those lovers scorn whom that love doth possess?
Do they call virtue there ungratefulness?

Michael Drayton

Since there's no help, come, let us kiss and part!
Nay, I have done; you get no more of me!
And I am glad, yea, glad, with all my heart,
That thus so cleanly I myself can free.
Shake hands for ever!   Cancel all our vows!
And when we meet at any time again,
Be it not seen in either of our brows,
That we one jot of former love retain!
Now at the last gasp of Love's latest breath,
When, his pulse failing, Passion speechless lies;
When Faith is kneeling by his bed of death,
And Innocence is closing up his eyes,—
Now, if thou wouldst, when all have given him over,
From death to life thou might'st him yet recover!

William Shakespeare

Shall I compare thee to a summer's day?
Thou art more lovely and more temperate:

Rough winds do shake the darling buds of May,
And summer's lease hath all too short a date:
Sometime too hot the eye of heaven shines,
And often is his gold complexion dimm'd;
And every fair from fair sometime declines,
By chance or nature's changing course untrimm'd;
But thy eternal summer shall not fade
Nor lose possession of that fair thou owest;
Nor shall Death brag thou wander'st in his shade,
When in eternal lines to time thou growest:
    So long as men can breathe or eyes can see,
    So long lives this and this gives life to thee.

William Shakespeare

When, in disgrace with fortune and men's eyes,
I all alone beweep my outcast state
And trouble deaf heaven with my bootless cries
And look upon myself and curse my fate,
Wishing me like to one more rich in hope,
Featured like him, like him with friends possess'd,
Desiring this man's art and that man's scope,
With what I most enjoy contented least;
Yet in these thoughts myself almost despising,
Haply I think on thee,—and then my state,
Like to the lark at break of day arising
From sullen earth, sings hymns at heaven's gate;
    For thy sweet love remember'd such wealth brings
    That then I scorn to change my state with kings.

William Shakespeare

When to the sessions of sweet silent thought
I summon up remembrance of things past,
I sigh the lack of many a thing I sought,
And with old woes new wail my dear time's waste;
Then can I down an eye, unused to flow,
For precious friends hid in death's dateless night,
And weep afresh love's long-since-cancell'd woe,
And moan the expense of many a vanish'd sight.
Then can I grieve at grievances foregone,
And heavily from woe to woe tell o'er
The sad account of fore-bemoanèd moan,
Which I new pay as if not paid before.
    But if the while I think on thee, dear Friend,
    All losses are restored, and sorrows end.

William Shakespeare

Since brass, nor stone, nor earth, nor boundless sea,
But sad mortality o'ersways their power,
How with this rage shall beauty hold a plea,
Whose action is no stronger than a flower?
O! how shall summer's honey breath hold out
Against the wreckful siege of battering days,
When rocks impregnable are not so stout
Nor gates of steel so strong, but Time decays?
O fearful meditation! where, alack!
Shall Time's best jewel from Time's chest lie hid?
Or what strong hand can hold his swift foot back?
Or who his spoil of beauty can forbid?
   O! none, unless this miracle have might,
   That in black ink my love may still shine bright.

William Shakespeare

When I have seen by Time's fell hand defaced
The rich proud cost of outworn buried age;
When sometime lofty towers I see down-razed
And brass eternal slave to mortal rage;
When I have seen the hungry ocean gain
Advantage on the kingdom of the shore,
And the firm soil win of the watery main,
Increasing store with loss, and loss with store;
When I have seen such interchange of state,
Or state itself confounded to decay;
Ruin hath taught me thus to ruminate—
That time will come and take my love away.
   This thought is as a death, which cannot choose
   But weep to have that which it fears to lose.

William Shakespeare

No longer mourn for me when I am dead
Than you shall hear the surly sullen bell
Give warning to the world that I am fled
From this vile world, with vilest worms to dwell:
Nay, if you read this line, remember not
The hand that writ it; for I love you so
That I in your sweet thoughts would be forgot
If thinking on me then should make you woe.
O! if,—I say, you look upon this verse,
When I perhaps compounded am with clay,

Do not so much as my poor name rehearse,
But let your love even with my life decay;
Lest the wise world should look into your moan
And mock you with me after I am gone.

William Shakespeare

That time of year thou mayst in me behold
When yellow leaves, or none, or few, do hang
Upon those boughs which shake against the cold,
Bare ruin'd choirs, where late the sweet birds sang.
In me thou see'st the twilight of such day
As after sunset fadeth in the west,
Which by and by black night doth take away,
Death's second self, that seals up all in rest.
In me thou see'st the glowing of such fire
That on the ashes of his youth doth lie,
As the death-bed whereon it must expire,
Consumed with that which it was nourish'd by.
This thou perceiv'st, which makes thy love more strong,
To love that well which thou must leave ere long.

William Shakespeare

Let me not to the marriage of true minds
Admit impediments. Love is not love
Which alters when it alteration finds,
Or bends with the remover to remove:
O, no! it is an ever-fixèd mark
That looks on tempests, and is never shaken;
It is the star to every wand'ring bark,
Whose worth's unknown, although his height be taken.
Love's not Time's fool, though rosy lips and cheeks
Within his bending sickle's compass come;
Love alters not with his brief hours and weeks,
But bears it out even to the edge of doom:
If this be error, and upon me proved,
I never writ, nor no man ever loved.

ON HIS BLINDNESS

John Milton

When I consider how my light is spent
Ere half my days, in this dark world and wide,
And that one Talent which is death to hide
Lodged with me useless, though my Soul more bent
To serve therewith my Maker, and present

My true account, lest he returning chide,
Doth God exact day-labour, light denied?
I fondly ask; But patience, to prevent
That murmur, soon replies, God doth not need
Either man's work, or his own gifts: who best
Bear his mild yoke, they serve him best: his State
Is Kingly. Thousands at his bidding speed
And post o'er Land and Ocean without rest:
They also serve who only stand and wait.

TO SLEEP

William Wordsworth

A flock of sheep that leisurely pass by,
One after one; the sound of rain, and bees
Murmuring; the fall of rivers, winds and seas,
Smooth fields, white sheets of water, and pure sky:
I've thought of all by turns, and yet do lie
Sleepless! and soon the small birds' melodies
Must hear, first utter'd from my orchard trees,
And the first cuckoo's melancholy cry.
Even thus last night, and two nights more I lay,
And could not win thee, Sleep! by any stealth:
So do not let me wear to-night away:
Without Thee what is all the morning's wealth?
Come, blessèd barrier between day and day
Dear mother of fresh thoughts and joyous health!

LONDON, 1802

William Wordsworth

Milton! thou shouldst be living at this hour:
England has need of thee: she is a fen
Of stagnant waters: altar, sword, and pen,
Fireside, the heroic wealth of hall and bower,
Have forfeited their ancient English dower
Of inward happiness. We are selfish men:
Oh! raise us up, return to us again;
And give us manners, virtue, freedom, power.
Thy soul was like a Star, and dwelt apart:
Thou hadst a voice whose sound was like the sea,
Pure as the naked heavens, majestic, free;
So didst thou travel on life's common way
In cheerful godliness; and yet thy heart
The lowliest duties on herself did lay.

WHEN I HAVE BORNE IN MEMORY WHAT HAS TAMED

William Wordsworth

When I have borne in memory what has tamed
Great Nations; how ennobling thoughts depart
When men change swords for ledgers, and desert
The student's bower for gold,—some fears unnamed
I had, my Country!—am I to be blamed?
Now, when I think of thee, and what thou art,
Verily, in the bottom of my heart
Of those unfilial fears I am ashamed.
For dearly must we prize thee; we who find
In thee a bulwark for the cause of men;
And I by my affection was beguiled:
What wonder if a Poet now and then,
Among the many movements of his mind,
Felt for thee as a lover or a child!

ON THE CASTLE OF CHILLON

Lord Byron

Eternal Spirit of the chainless Mind!
Brightest in dungeons, Liberty! thou art,
For there thy habitation is the heart—
The heart which love of Thee alone can bind;
And when thy sons to fetters are consign'd,
To fetters, and the damp vault's dayless gloom,
Their country conquers with their martyrdom,
And Freedom's fame finds wings on every wind.
Chillon! thy prison is a holy place
And thy sad floor an altar, for 'twas trod,
Until his very steps have left a trace
Worn as if thy cold pavement were a sod,
By Bonnivard! May none those marks efface!
For they appeal from tyranny to God.

OZYMANDIAS OF EGYPT

Percy Bysshe Shelley

I met a traveller from an antique land
Who said: Two vast and trunkless legs of stone
Stand in the desert. Near them on the sand,
Half sunk, a shatter'd visage lies, whose frown
And wrinkled lip and sneer of cold command

Tell that its sculptor well those passions read
Which yet survive, stamp'd on these lifeless things,
The hand that mock'd them and the heart that fed;
And on the pedestal these words appear:
"My name is Ozymandias, king of kings:
Look on my works, ye Mighty, and despair!"
Nothing beside remains. Round the decay
Of that colossal wreck, boundless and bare,
The lone and level sands stretch far away.

WHEN I HAVE FEARS

John Keats

When I have fears that I may cease to be
Before my pen has glean'd my teeming brain,
Before high-pilèd books, in charact'ry
Hold like rich garners the full-ripen'd grain;
When I behold, upon the night's starr'd face,
Huge cloudy symbols of a high romance,
And think that I may never live to trace
Their shadows, with the magic hand of chance;
And when I feel, fair creature of an hour!
That I shall never look upon thee more,
Never have relish in the faery power
Of unreflecting love:—then on the shore
Of the wide world I stand alone, and think
Till love and fame to nothingness do sink.

BRIGHT STAR! WOULD I WERE STEADFAST AS THOU ART

John Keats

Bright Star! would I were steadfast as thou art—
Not in lone splendour hung aloft the night,
And watching, with eternal lids apart,
Like Nature's patient, sleepless Eremite,
The moving waters at their priestlike task
Of pure ablution round earth's human shores,
Or gazing on the new soft-fallen mask
Of snow upon the mountains and the moors:—
No—yet still steadfast, still unchangeable,
Pillow'd upon my fair love's ripening breast,
To feel for ever its soft fall and swell,
Awake for ever in a sweet unrest;
Still, still to hear her tender-taken breath,
And so live ever,—or else swoon to death.

HOW DO I LOVE THEE?

Elizabeth Barrett Browning

How do I love thee? Let me count the ways.
I love thee to the depth and breadth and height
My soul can reach, when feeling out of sight
For the ends of Being and Ideal Grace.
I love thee to the level of everyday's
Most quiet need, by sun and candlelight.
I love thee freely, as men strive for Right;
I love thee purely, as they turn from Praise;
I love thee with the passion put to use
In my old griefs, and with my childhood's faith;
I love thee with a love I seemed to lose
With my lost saints,—I love thee with the breath,
Smiles, tears, of all my life!—and, if God choose,
I shall but love thee better after death.

THE NEW COLOSSUS[14]

Emma Lazarus

Not like the brazen giant of Greek fame,
With conquering limbs astride from land to land;
Here at our sea-washed, sunset gates shall stand
A mighty woman with a torch, whose flame
Is the imprisoned lightning, and her name
Mother of Exiles. From her beacon hand
Glows world-wide welcome; her mild eyes command
The air-bridged harbor that twin cities frame.
"Keep, ancient lands, your storied pomp!" cries she
With silent lips. "Give me your tired, your poor,
Your huddled masses yearning to breathe free,
The wretched refuse of your teeming shore.
Send these, the homeless, tempest-tost to me,
I lift my lamp beside the golden door!"

BE STILL. THE HANGING GARDENS WERE A DREAM[15]

Trumbull Stickney

Be still. The Hanging Gardens were a dream
That over Persian roses flew to kiss

[14] This sonnet is engraved on a tablet on the base of the Statue of Liberty on Bedloe's Island in New York Harbor.
[15] By permission of Henry A. Stickney.

The curlèd lashes of Semiramis.
Troy never was, nor green Skamander stream.
Provence and Troubadour are merest lies,
The glorious hair of Venice was a beam
Made within Titian's eye. The sunsets seem,
The world is very old and nothing is.
Be still. Thou foolish thing, thou canst not wake,
Nor thy tears wedge thy soldered lids apart,
But patter in the darkness of thy heart.
Thy brain is plagued. Thou art a frighted owl
Blind with the light of life thou'ldst not forsake,
And Error loves and nourishes thy soul.

ANTHEM FOR DOOMED YOUTH[16]

Wilfred Owen

What passing-bells for these who die as cattle?
Only the monstrous anger of the guns.
Only the stuttering rifles' rapid rattle
Can patter out their hasty orisons.
No mockeries for them; no prayers nor bells,
Nor any voice of mourning save the choirs,—
The shrill, demented choirs of wailing shells;
And bugles calling for them from sad shires.

What candles may be held to speed them all?
Not in the hands of boys, but in their eyes
Shall shine the holy glimmers of good-bys.
The pallor of girls' brows shall be their pall;
Their flowers the tenderness of patient minds,
And each slow dusk a drawing-down of blinds.

AS IN THE MIDST OF BATTLE THERE IS ROOM[17]

George Santayana

As in the midst of battle there is room
    For thoughts of love, and in foul sin for mirth;
    As gossips whisper of a trinket's worth
Spied by the death-bed's flickering candle-gloom;
As in the crevices of Caesar's tomb
    The sweet herbs flourish on a little earth:
    So in this great disaster of our birth
We can be happy, and forget our doom.

[16] From *Poems* by Wilfred Owen, © 1963 by Chatto & Windus. Reprinted by permission of the publisher, New Directions Publishing Corp.
[17] By permission of Charles Scribner's Sons.

For morning, with a ray of tenderest joy
   Gilding the iron heaven, hides the truth,
And evening gently woos us to employ
   Our grief in idle catches. Such is youth;
Till from that summer's trance we wake, to find
Despair before us, vanity behind.

SONG

John Donne

Go and catch a falling star,
   Get with child a mandrake[18] root,
Tell me where all times past are,
   Or who cleft the Devil's foot;
Teach me to hear mermaids singing,
Or to keep off envy's stinging,
     And find
     What wind
Serves to advance an honest mind.

If thou be'st born to strange sights,
   Things invisible go see,
Ride ten thousand days and nights
   Till age snow white hairs on thee;
Thou, when thou return'st, wilt tell me
All strange wonders that befell thee,
     And swear
     No where
Lives a woman true and fair.

If thou find'st one let me know,
   Such a pilgrimage were sweet;
Yet do not, I would not go,
   Though at next door we might meet;
Though she were true when you met her,
And last till you write your letter,
     Yet she
     Will be
False, ere I come, to two or three.

THE CANONIZATION

John Donne

For God's sake hold your tongue, and let me love;
   Or chide my palsy, or my gout;
   My five gray hairs, or ruined fortune flout;

---

[18] The mandragora, a root to which many superstitions were attached.

With wealth your state, your mind with arts improve;
    Take you a course, get you a place,
    Observe his Honor, or his Grace;
Or the king's real, or his stamped face
    Contemplate; what you will, approve,
    So you will let me love.

Alas! alas! who's injured by my love?
    What merchant's ships have my sighs drowned?
    Who says my tears have overflowed his ground?
When did my colds a forward spring remove?
    When did the heats which my veins fill
    Add one more to the plaguy bill?
Soldiers find wars, and lawyers find out still
    Litigious men, which quarrels move,
    Though she and I do love.

Call us what you will, we are made such by love;
    Call her one, me another fly;
    We're tapers too, and at our own cost die,
And we in us find th 'eagle and the dove.
    The phœnix[19] riddle hath more wit
    By us; we two being one, are it;
So, to one neutral thing both sexes fit.
    We die and rise the same, and prove
    Mysterious by this love.

We can die by it, if not live by love,
    And if unfit for tomb or hearse,
    Our legend be, it will be fit for verse;
And if no piece of chronicle we prove,
    We'll build in sonnets pretty rooms;
    As well a well-wrought urn becomes
The greatest ashes, as half-acre tombs,
    And by these hymns all shall approve
    Us canonized for love;

And thus invoke us. "You, whom reverend love
    Made one another's hermitage;
    You, to whom love was peace, that now is rage;
Who did the whole world's soul contract, and drove
    Into the glasses of your eyes;
    So made such mirrors, and such spies,
That they did all to you epitomize,
    Countries, towns, courts, beg from above
    A pattern of your love."

---

[19] The Phœnix, symbol of immortality, was supposed, after living centuries, to burn itself in a nest of spices, and then to rise from the ashes.

SONG OF THE OPEN ROAD[20]

Walt Whitman

1

Afoot and light-hearted I take to the open road,
Healthy, free, the world before me,
The long brown path before me leading wherever I choose.

Henceforth I ask not good-fortune, I myself am good-fortune,
Henceforth I whimper no more, postpone no more, need nothing,
Done with indoor complaints, libraries, querulous criticisms,
Strong and content I travel the open road.

The earth, that is sufficient,
I do not want the constellations any nearer,
I know they are very well where they are,
I know they suffice for those who belong to them.

(Still here I carry my old delicious burdens,
I carry them, men and women, I carry them with me wherever I go,
I swear it is impossible for me to get rid of them,
I am fill'd with them, and I will fill them in return.)

. . .

5

From this hour I ordain myself loos'd of limits and imaginary lines,
Going where I list, my own master total and absolute,
Listening to others, considering well what they say,
Pausing, searching, receiving, contemplating,
Gently, but with undeniable will, divesting myself of the holds that
    would hold me.

I inhale great draughts of space,
The east and the west are mine, and the north and the south are mine.
I am larger, better than I thought,
I did not know I held so much goodness.

All seems beautiful to me,
I can repeat over to men and women, You have done such good to me
    I would do the same to you,
I will recruit for myself and you as I go,
I will scatter myself among men and women as I go,
I will toss a new gladness and roughness among them,
Whoever denies me it shall not trouble me,
Whoever accepts me he or she shall be blessed and shall bless me.

. . .

---

[20] From *Leaves of Grass* (New York: Doubleday & Co., Inc., 1924).

9

Allons! whoever you are come travel with me!
Travelling with me you find what never tires.
The earth never tires,
The earth is rude, silent, incomprehensible at first, Nature is rude
　　and incomprehensible at first,
Be not discouraged, keep on, there are divine things well envelop'd.
I swear to you there are divine things more beautiful than words
　　can tell.

.　.　.

15

Allons! the road is before us!
It is safe—I have tried it—my own feet have tried it well—be not
　　detain'd!
Let the paper remain on the desk unwritten, and the book on the
　　shelf unopen'd!
Let the tools remain in the workshop! let the money remain unearn'd!
Let the school stand! mind not the cry of the teacher!
Let the preacher preach in his pulpit! let the lawyer plead in the
　　court, and the judge expound the law.

Camerado, I give you my hand!
I give you my love more precious than money,
I give you myself before preaching or law;
Will you give me yourself? will you come travel with me?
Shall we stick by each other as long as we live?

DEATH CAROL[21]

From WHEN LILACS LAST IN THE DOORYARD BLOOM'D

Walt Whitman

Come lovely and soothing death,
Undulate round the world, serenely arriving, arriving,
In the day, in the night, to all, to each,
Sooner or later delicate death.

Prais'd be the fathomless universe,
For life and joy, and for objects and knowledge curious,
And for love, sweet love—but praise! praise! praise!
For the sure-enwinding arms of cool-enfolding death.

Dark mother always gliding near with soft feet,
Have none chanted for thee a chant of fullest welcome?
Then I chant it for thee, I glorify thee above all,

21 From *Leaves of Grass* (New York: Doubleday & Co., Inc., 1924).

I bring thee a song that when thou must indeed come, come
unfalteringly.

Approach strong deliveress,
When it is so, when thou hast taken them I joyously sing the dead,
Lost in the loving floating ocean of thee,
Laved in the flood of thy bliss, O death.

From me to thee glad serenades,
Dances for thee I propose saluting thee, adornments and feastings
for thee,
And the sights of the open landscape and the high-spread sky are
fitting,
And life and the fields, and the huge and thoughtful night.

The night in silence under many a star,
The ocean shore and the husky whispering wave whose voice I know,
And the soul turning to thee, O vast and well-veil'd death,
And the body gratefully nestling close to thee.

Over the tree-tops I float thee a song,
Over the rising and sinking waves, over the myriad fields and the
prairies wide,
Over the dense-pack'd cities all and the teeming wharves and ways,
I float this carol with joy, with joy to thee, O death.

A BIRD'S LAMENT FOR HIS MATE[22]

From OUT OF THE CRADLE ENDLESSLY ROCKING

Walt Whitman

Soothe! soothe! soothe!
Close on its waves soothes the wave behind,
And again another behind embracing and lapping, every one close,
But my love soothes not me, not me.

Low hangs the moon, it rose late,
It is lagging—O I think it is heavy with love, with love.
O madly the sea pushes upon the land,
With love, with love.

O night! do I not see my love fluttering out among the breakers?
What is that little black thing I see there in the white?

Loud! loud! loud!
Loud I call to you, my love!
High and clear I shoot my voice over the waves,

[22] From *Leaves of Grass* (New York: Doubleday & Co., Inc., 1924).

Surely you must know who is here, is here,
You must know who I am, my love.

Low-hanging moon!
What is that dusky spot in your brown yellow?
O it is the shape, the shape of my mate!
O moon, do not keep her from me any longer.

Land! land! O land!
Whichever way I turn, O I think you could give me my mate back
    again if you only would,
For I am almost sure I see her dimly whichever way I look.
O rising stars!
Perhaps the one I want so much will rise, will rise with some of you.

O throat! O trembling throat!
Sound clearer through the atmosphere!
Pierce the woods, the earth,
Somewhere listening to catch you must be the one I want.
Shake out carols!
Solitary here, the night's carols!
Carols of lonesome love! death's carols!
Carols under that lagging, yellow, waning moon!
O under that moon where she droops almost down into the sea!
O reckless despairing carols.
But soft! sink low!
Soft! let me just murmur,
And do you wait a moment you husky-nois'd sea,
For somewhere I believe I heard my mate responding to me,
So faint, I must be still, be still to listen,
But not altogether still, for then she might not come immediately
    to me.

Hither my love!
Here I am! here!
With this just-sustain'd note I announce myself to you,
This gentle call is for you my love, for you.

Do not be decoy'd elsewhere,
That is the whistle of the wind, it is not my voice,
That is the fluttering, the fluttering of the spray,
Those are the shadows of leaves.

O darkness! O in vain!
O I am very sick and sorrowful.

O brown halo in the sky near the moon, drooping upon the sea!
O troubled reflection in the sea!
O throat! O throbbing heart!
And I singing uselessly, uselessly all the night.

O past! O happy life! O songs of joy!
In the air, in the woods, over fields,
Loved! loved! loved! loved! loved!
But my mate no more, no more with me!
We two together no more.

THE MAN WITH THE HOE[23]

(Written after seeing Millet's world-famous painting)
Edwin Markham

Bowed by the weight of centuries he leans
Upon his hoe and gazes on the ground,
The emptiness of ages in his face,
And on his back the burden of the world.
Who made him dead to rapture and despair,
A thing that grieves not and that never hopes,
Stolid and stunned, a brother to the ox?
Who loosened and let down this brutal jaw?
Whose was the hand that slanted back this brow?
Whose breath blew out the light within this brain?

Is this the Thing the Lord God made and gave
To have dominion over sea and land;
To trace the stars and search the heavens for power;
To feel the passion of Eternity?
Is this the dream He dreamed who shaped the suns
And marked their ways upon the ancient deep?
Down all the caverns of Hell to their last gulf
There is no shape more terrible than this—
More tongued with censure of the world's blind greed—
More filled with signs and portents for the soul—
More packt with danger to the universe.

What gulfs between him and the seraphim!
Slave of the wheel of labor, what to him
Are Plato and the swing of Pleiades?
What the long reaches of the peaks of song,
The rift of dawn, the reddening of the rose?
Through this dread shape the suffering ages look;
Time's tragedy is in that aching stoop;
Through this dread shape humanity betrayed,
Plundered, profaned, and disinherited,
Cries protest to the Judges of the World,
A protest that is also prophecy.

O masters, lords and rulers in all lands,
Is this the handiwork you give to God,

[23] Copyrighted by the author, and used by his permission.

This monstrous thing distorted and soul-quenched?
How will you ever straighten up this shape;
Touch it again with immortality;
Give back the upward looking and the light;
Rebuild in it the music and the dream;
Make right the immemorial infamies,
Perfidious wrongs, immedicable woes?

O masters, lords and rulers in all lands,
How will the Future reckon with this man?
How answer his brute question in that hour
When whirlwinds of rebellion shake all shores?
How will it be with kingdoms and with kings—
With those who shaped him to the thing he is—
When this dumb terror shall rise to judge the world,
After the silence of the centuries?

BREDON HILL[24]

A. E. Housman

In summertime on Bredon
     The bells they sound so clear;
Round both the shires they ring them
     In steeples far and near,
     A happy noise to hear.

Here of a Sunday morning
     My love and I would lie
And see the colored counties
     And hear the larks so high
     About us in the sky.

The bells would ring to call her
     In valleys miles away:
"Come all to church, good people;
     Good people, come and pray."
     But here my love would stay.

And I would turn and answer
     Among the springing thyme,
"Oh, peal upon our wedding,
     And we will hear the chime,
     And come to church in time."

But when the snows at Christmas
     On Bredon top were strown,

[24] From *A Shropshire Lad,* by permission of Holt, Rinehart & Winston, Inc.

My love rose up so early
  And stole out unbeknown
  And went to church alone.

They tolled the one bell only,
  Groom there was none to see,
The mourners followed after,
  And so to church went she,
  And would not wait for me.

The bells they sound on Bredon,
  And still the steeples hum.
"Come all to church, good people,—"
  Oh, noisy bells, be dumb;
  I hear you, I will come.

SPRING NIGHT[25]

Sara Teasdale

The park is filled with night and fog,
  The veils are drawn about the world,
The drowsy lights along the paths
  Are dim and pearled.

Gold and gleaming the empty streets,
  Gold and gleaming the misty lake,
The mirrored lights like sunken swords,
  Glimmer and shake.

Oh, is it not enough to be
Here with this beauty over me?
My throat should ache with praise, and I
Should kneel in joy beneath the sky.

O Beauty, are you not enough?
Why am I crying after love
With youth, a singing voice, and eyes
To take earth's wonder with surprise?
Why have I put off my pride,
Why am I unsatisfied,—
I, for whom the pensive night
Binds her cloudy hair with light,—
I, for whom all beauty burns
Like incense in a million urns?
O Beauty, are you not enough?
Why am I crying after love?

[25] From *Collected Poems,* by permission of The Macmillan Co.

FULFILLMENT[26]

Robert Nichols

Was there love once? I have forgotten her.
　Was there grief once? Grief still is mine.
Other loves I have; men rough, but men who stir
　More joy, more grief than love of thee and thine.

Faces cheerful, full of whimsical mirth,
　Lined by the wind, burned by the sun;
Bodies enraptured by the abounding earth,
　As whose children, brothers we are and one.

And any moment may descend hot death
　To shatter limbs! pulp, tear, and blast
Belovèd soldiers who love rude life and breath
　Not less for dying faithful to the last.

O the fading eyes, the grimèd face turned bony,
　Open, black, gushing mouth, fallen head,
Failing pressure of a held hand shrunk and stony,
　O sudden spasm, release of the dead!

Was there love once? I have forgotten her.
　Was there grief once? Grief still is mine.
O loved, living, dying, heroic soldier,
　All, all my joy, my grief, my love are thine!

A CONSECRATION[27]

John Masefield

Not of the princes and prelates with periwigged charioteers
Riding triumphantly laureled to lap the fat of the years,—
Rather the scorned—the rejected—the men hemmed in with the
　spears;

The men of the tattered battalion which fights till it dies,
Dazed with the dust of the battle, the din and the cries,
The men with the broken heads and the blood running into their eyes.

Not the be-medaled Commander, beloved of the throne,
Riding cock-horse to parade when the bugles are blown,
But the lads who carried the koppie and cannot be known.

---

[26] From *Ardours and Endurances* (New York: Frederick A. Stokes Co., 1918).
[27] From *Poems,* copyright by The Macmillan Co., and used with their permission.

Not the ruler for me, but the ranker, the tramp of the road,
The slave with the sack on his shoulders pricked on with the goad,
The man with too weighty a burden, too weary a load.

The sailor, the stoker of steamers, the man with the clout,
The chantyman bent at the halliards putting a tune to the shout,
The drowsy man at the wheel and the tired look-out.

Others may sing of the wine and the wealth and the mirth,
The portly presence of potentates goodly in girth;—
Mine be the dirt and the dross, the dust and scum of the earth!

Theirs be the music, the color, the glory, the gold;
Mine be a handful of ashes, a mouthful of mold.
Of the maimed, of the halt and the blind in the rain and the cold—
Of these shall my songs be fashioned, my tales be told.

Amen.

THE PURIFICATION[28]

Richard Church

They have gone over, the god, the
    friend, the lover,
They have gone over.
It is growing gray now;
There comes the end of day now.

They were signs then, the stars were
    a glory for men,
They were signs then.
Those lights flare unseen now,
Things paltry and mean now.

They were true pleasure, the friendly
    trust, the praise without measure.
They were true pleasure.
Praise is an empty sound now.
Trust treads no firm ground now.

They were music, joy, and truth, the
    kisses she gave him in youth.
They were music, joy, and truth.
They are less beautiful now;
They are but dutiful now.

Aye, they have come to an end, the
    god, the lover, the friend;
They have come to an end.

---

[28] By permission of the author.

The soul is alone now:
Strong, naked, full-grown now.

DUST[29]

Rupert Brooke

When the white flame in us is gone,
    And we that lost the world's delight
Stiffen in darkness, left alone
    To crumble in our separate night;

When your swift hair is quiet in death,
    And through the lips corruption thrust
Has stilled the labor of my breath—
    When we are dust, when we are dust!—

Not dead, not undesirous yet,
    Still sentient, still unsatisfied,
We'll ride the air, and shine and flit,
    Around the places where we died,

And dance as dust before the sun,
    And light of foot, and unconfined,
Hurry from road to road, and run
    About the errands of the wind.

And every mote, on earth or air,
    Will speed and gleam down later days,
And like a secret pilgrim fare
    By eager and invisible ways,

Nor ever rest, nor ever lie,
    Till, beyond thinking, out of view,
One mote of all the dust that's I
    Shall meet one atom that was you.

Then in some garden hushed from wind,
    Warm in a sunset's afterglow,
The lovers in the flowers will find
    A sweet and strange unquiet grow

Upon the peace; and past desiring,
    So high a beauty in the air,
And such a light, and such a quiring,
    And such a radiant ecstasy there,

They'll know not if it's fire, or dew,
    Or out of earth, or in the height,

[29] Used by permission of Dodd, Mead & Co., Inc. From *Collected Poems*, copyright, 1915.

Singing, or flame, or scent, or hue,
  Or two that pass, in light, to light,

Out of the garden higher, higher . . .
  But in that instant they shall learn
The shattering fury of our fire,
  And the weak passionless hearts will burn

And faint in that amazing glow,
  Until the darkness close above;
And they will know—poor fools, they'll know!—
  One moment, what it is to love.

FEUD[30]

Lew Sarett

Poor wayworn creature! Oh, sorely harried deer,
  What drove you, quivering like a poplar-blade,
To refuge with my herd? What holds you here
  Within my meadow, broken and afraid?

Tilting your nose to tainted air, you thrill
  And freeze to wailing wolves! Fear you the sound
Of the coyotes eager for a tender kill?
  Or yet the baying of the hunter's hound?

Let fall your anguish, harried one, and rest;
  Bed yourself down among your kin, my cattle;
Sleep unperturbed. No spoiler shall molest
  You here this night, for I shall wage your battle.

There was a day when coyotes in a pack,
  Wolves of another hue, another breed,
With Christ upon their lips, set out to track
  Me down and drop me, for my blood, my creed.

Oh, hunted creature, once I knew the thud
  Of padded feet that put you into flight,
The bugle-cry, suffused with lust for blood,
  That trembled in the silver bell of night.

I knew your frenzied rocky run, the burst
  Of lungs, the rivers of fire in every vein;
I knew your foaming lip, your boundless thirst,
  The rain of molten-hammering in your brain.

Abide with me, then, against the wolves' return,
  For I shall carry on the feud for you;

[30] From *Slow Smoke,* by permission of Holt, Rinehart & Winston, Inc.

And it shall be, to me, of small concern
If the wolf-hearts walk on four soft feet or two.

Oh, let them come! And I shall burn their flanks
With a blast of hell to end their revelry,
And whistle molten silver through their ranks,
Laughing—one round for you, and one for me.

BRAVE NEW WORLD[31]

Archibald MacLeish

But you, Thomas Jefferson,
You could not lie so still,
You could not bear the weight of stone
On the quiet hill,

You could not keep your green grown peace
Nor hold your folded hand
If you could see your new world now,
Your new sweet land.

There was a time, Tom Jefferson,
When freedom made free men.
The new found earth and the new freed mind
Were brothers then.

There was a time when tyrants feared
The new world of the free.
Now freedom is afraid and shrieks
At tyranny.

Words have not changed their sense so soon
Nor tyranny grown new.
The truths you held, Tom Jefferson,
Will still hold true.

What's changed is freedom in this age.
What great men dared to choose
Small men now dare neither win
Nor lose.

Freedom, when men fear freedom's use
But love its useful name,
Has cause and cause enough for fear
And cause for shame.

We fought a war in freedom's name
And won it in our own.

[31] Copyright 1946 by Archibald MacLeish. Reprinted from *Act Five and Other Poems*, by Archibald MacLeish, by permission of Random House, Inc.

We fought to free a world and raised
A wall of stone.

Your countrymen who could have built
The hill fires of the free
To set the dry world all ablaze
With liberty—

To burn the brutal thorn in Spain
Of bigotry and hate
And the dead lie and the brittle weed
Beyond the Plate:

Who could have heaped the bloody straw,
The dung of time, to light
The Danube in a sudden flame
Of hope by night—

Your countrymen who could have hurled
Their freedom like a brand
Have cupped it to a candle spark
In a frightened hand.

Freedom that was a thing to use
They've made a thing to save
And staked it in and fenced it round
Like a dead man's grave.

You, Thomas Jefferson,
You could not lie so still,
You could not bear the weight of stone
On your green hill,

You could not hold your angry tongue
If you could see how bold
The old stale bitter world plays new—
And the new world old.

ESCAPE[32]

Robert Graves

(*August 6, 1916. Officer Previously Reported Died of Wounds, Now
Reported Wounded: Graves, Capt. R., Royal Welch Fusiliers*)

. . . But I *was* dead, an hour or more:
I woke when I'd already passed the door
That Cerberus guards and half-way down the road
To Lethe, as an old Greek sign-post showed.

[32] From *Fairies and Fusiliers,* reprinted by permission of International Authors N.V.

Above me, on my stretcher swinging by,
I saw new stars in the sub-terrene sky,
A Cross, a Rose in Bloom, a Cage with Bars,
And a barbed Arrow feathered with fine stars.
I felt the vapors of forgetfulness
Float in my nostrils: Oh, may Heaven bless
Dear Lady Proserpine, who saw me wake
And, stooping over me, for Henna's sake
Cleared my poor buzzing head and sent me back
Breathless, with leaping heart along the track.
After me roared and clattered angry hosts
Of demons, heroes, and policemen-ghosts.
"Life, life! I can't be dead, I won't be dead:
Damned if I'll die for anyone," I said . . .
Cerberus stands and grins above me now,
Wearing three heads, lion and lynx and sow.
"Quick, a revolver! but my Webley's gone,
Stolen . . . no bombs . . . no knife . . . (the crowd swarms on,
Bellows, hurls stones) . . . not even a honeyed sop . . .
Nothing . . . Good Cerberus . . . Good dog . . . But stop!
Stay! . . . A great luminous thought . . . I do believe
There's still some morphia that I bought on leave."
Then swiftly Cerberus' wide mouths I cram
With Army biscuit smeared with Tickler's jam;
And Sleep lurks in the luscious plum and apple.
He crunches, swallows, stiffens, seems to grapple
With the all-powerful poppy . . . then a snore,
A crash; the beast blocks up the corridor
With monstrous hairy carcase, red and dun—
Too late: for I've sped through.
                    O Life! O Sun!

EVENING MEAL IN THE TWENTIETH CENTURY[33]

John Holmes

How is it I can eat bread here and cut meat,
And in quiet shake salt, speak of the meal,
Pour water, serve my son's small plate?
Here now I love well my wife's gold hair combed,
Her voice, her violin, our books on shelves in another room,
The tall chest shining darkly in supper-light.
I have read tonight
The sudden meaningless foreign violent death
Of a nation we both loved, hope

[33] Reprinted by permission of the publisher, Duell, Sloan, & Pearce, Inc. Copyright, 1943, by John Holmes.

For a country not ours killed. But blacker than print:
For the million people no hope now. For me
A new hurt to the old health of the heart once more:
That sore, that heavy, that dull and I think now incurable
Pain:
Seeing love hated, seeing real death,
Knowing evil alive I was taught was conquered.
How shall I cut this bread gladly, unless more share
The day's meals I earn?
Or offer my wife meat from our fire, our fortune?
It should not have taken me so long to learn.
But how can I speak aloud at my own table tonight
And not curse my own food, not cry out death,
And not frighten my young son?

THE IRISH UNIONIST'S FAREWELL TO
GRETA HELLSTROM IN 1922[34]

John Betjeman

Golden haired and golden hearted
    I would ever have you be,
As you were when last we parted
    Smiling slow and sad at me.
Oh! the fighting down of passion!
    Oh! the century-seeming pain—
Parting in this off-hand fashion
    In Dungarvan in the rain.

Slanting eyes of blue, unweeping,
    Stands my Swedish beauty where
Gusts of Irish rain are sweeping
    Round the statue in the square;
Corner boys against the walling
    Watch us furtively in vain,
And the Angelus is calling
    Through Dungarvan in the rain.

Gales along the Commeragh Mountains,
    Beating sleet on creaking signs,
Iron gutters turned to fountains,
    And the windscreen laced with lines.
And the evening getting later,
    And the ache—increased again,
As the distance grows the greater

[34] From *Collected Poems* (Boston: Houghton Mifflin Co., 1959). Reprinted by permission of John Murray, Publishers, Ltd.

From Dungarvan in the rain.

There is no one now to wonder
What eccentric sits in state
While the beech trees rock and thunder
Round his gate-lodge and his gate.
Gone—the ornamental plaster,
Gone—the overgrown demesne
And the car goes fast, and faster,
From Dungarvan in the rain.

Had I kissed and drawn you to me,
Had you yielded warm for cold,
What a power had pounded through me
As I stroked your streaming gold!
You were right to keep us parted:
Bound and parted we remain,
Aching, if unbroken hearted—
Oh! Dungarvan in the rain!

SLOUGH[35]

John Betjeman

Come, friendly bombs, and fall on Slough
It isn't fit for humans now,
There isn't grass to graze a cow
Swarm over, Death!

Come, bombs, and blow to smithereens
Those air-conditioned, bright canteens,
Tinned fruit, tinned meat, tinned milk, tinned beans
Tinned minds, tinned breath.

Mess up the mess they call a town—
A house for ninety-seven down
And once a week a half-a-crown
For twenty years,

And get that man with double chin
Who'll always cheat and always win,
Who washes his repulsive skin
In women's tears,

And smash his desk of polished oak
And smash his hands so used to stroke
And stop his boring dirty joke
And make him yell.

But spare the bald young clerks who add
The profits of the stinking cad;
It's not their fault that they are mad,
 They've tasted Hell.

It's not their fault they do not know
The birdsong from the radio,
It's not their fault they often go
 To Maidenhead

And talk of sports and makes of cars
In various bogus Tudor bars
And daren't look up and see the stars
 But belch instead.

In labour-saving homes, with care
Their wives frizz out peroxide hair
And dry it in synthetic air
 And paint their nails.

Come, friendly bombs, and fall on Slough
To get it ready for the plough.
The cabbages are coming now:
 The earth exhales.

THE HEAVY BEAR WHO GOES WITH ME[36]

"the withness of the body"—WHITEHEAD

Delmore Schwartz

The heavy bear who goes with me,
A manifold honey to smear his face,
Clumsy and lumbering here and there,
The central ton of every place,
The hungry beating brutish one
In love with candy, anger, and sleep,
Crazy factotum, dishevelling all,
Climbs the building, kicks the football,
Boxes his brother in the hate-ridden city.

Breathing at my side, that heavy animal,
That heavy bear who sleeps with me,
Howls in his sleep for a world of sugar,
A sweetness intimate as the water's clasp,
Howls in his sleep because the tight-rope

[36] By permission of the author.

Trembles and shows the darkness beneath.
—The strutting show-off is terrified,
Dressed in his dress-suit, bulging his pants,
Trembles to think that his quivering meat
Must finally wince to nothing at all.
That inescapable animal walks with me,
Has followed me since the black womb held,
Moves where I move, distorting my gesture,
A caricature, a swollen shadow,
A stupid clown of the spirit's motive,
Perplexes and affronts with his own darkness,
The secret life of belly and bone,
Opaque, too near, my private, yet unknown,
Stretches to embrace the very dear
With whom I would talk without him near,
Touches her grossly, although a word
Would bare my heart and make me clear,
Stumbles, flounders, and strives to be fed
Dragging me with him in his mouthing care,
Amid the hundred million of his kind,
The scrimmage of appetite everywhere.

TRAVELOGUE FOR EXILES[37]

Karl Shapiro

Look and remember. Look upon this sky;
Look deep and deep into the sea-clean air,
The unconfined, the terminus of prayer.
Speak now and speak into the hallowed dome.
What do you hear? What does the sky reply?
The heavens are taken: this is not your home.

Look and remember. Look upon this sea;
Look down and down into the tireless tide.
What of a life below, a life inside,
A tomb, a cradle in the curly foam?
The waves arise; sea-wind and sea agree
The waters are taken: this is not your home.

Look and remember. Look upon this land,
Far, far across the factories and the grass.
Surely, there, surely, they will let you pass.
Speak then and ask the forest and the loam.
What do you hear? What does the land command?
The earth is taken: this is not your home.

DO NOT GO GENTLE INTO THAT GOOD NIGHT[38]

Dylan Thomas

Do not go gentle into that good night,
Old age should burn and rave at close of day;
Rage, rage against the dying of the light.

Though wise men at their end know dark is right,
Because their words had forked no lightning they
Do not go gentle into that good night.

Good men, the last wave by, crying how bright
Their frail deeds might have danced in a green bay,
Rage, rage against the dying of the light.

Wild men who caught and sang the sun in flight
And learn, too late, they grieved it on its way,
Do not go gentle into that good night.

Grave men, near death, who see with blinding sight
Blind eyes could blaze like meteors and be gay.
Rage, rage against the dying of the light.

And you, my father, there on the sad height,
Curse, bless, me now with your fierce tears, I pray.
Do not go gentle into that good night,
Rage, rage, against the dying of the light.

ELEGY JUST IN CASE[39]

John Ciardi

Here lie Ciardi's pearly bones
In their ripe organic mess.
Jungle blown, his chromosomes
Breed to a new address.

Progenies of orchids seek
The fracture's white spilled lymph.
And his heart's red valve will leak
Fountains for a protein nymph.

Was it bullets or a wind
Or a rip-cord fouled on Chance?
Artifacts the natives find
Decorate them when they dance.

[38] From *The Collected Poems of Dylan Thomas.* Copyright 1953 by Dylan Thomas. © 1957 by New Directions. Reprinted by permission of the publishers, New Directions, New York.

[39] From *Mid-Century American Poets,* copyright, 1950, by John Ciardi; reprinted by permission of Twayne Publishers, Inc.

Here lies the sgt.'s mortal wreck
Lily spiked and termite kissed,
Spiders pendant from his neck,
Beetles shining on his wrist.

Bring the tic and southern flies
Where the land crabs run unmourning
Through a night of jungle skies
To a climeless morning.

And bring the chalked eraser here
Fresh from rubbing out his name.
Burn the crew-board for a bier.
(Also Colonel what's-his-name.)

Let no dice be stored and still.
Let no poker deck be torn.
But pour the smuggled rye until
The barracks threshold is outworn.

File the papers, pack the clothes,
Send the coded word through air:
"We regret and no one knows
Where the sgt. goes from here."

"Missing as of inst. oblige,
Deepest sorrow and remain . . ."
Shall I grin at persiflage?
Could I have my skin again

Would I choose a business form
Stilted mute as a giraffe,
Or a pinstripe unicorn
On a cashier's epitaph?

Darling, darling, just in case
Rivets fail or engines burn,
I forget the time and place
But your flesh was sweet to learn.

In the grammar of not yet
Let me name one verb for chance,
Scholarly to one regret:
That I leave your mood and tense.

Swift and single as a shark
I have seen you churn my sleep.
Now if beetles hunt my dark
What will beetles find to keep?

Fractured meat and open bone—
Nothing single or surprised.
Fragments of a written stone
Undeciphered but surmised.

FOR A VERY OLD MAN, ON THE DEATH
OF HIS WIFE[40]

Jane Cooper

So near to death yourself
You cannot justly mourn
For one who was beautiful
Before these children were born.
You only remember her
Poised by the edge of the sea
As you stalked heron-legged,
Chairing the baby high
(Red-capped, hilarious)
Through the ecstatic surf,
And all the boardwalk flags
Clapped to her seaward laugh.

Or perhaps she would pretend
To lose you over the edge
Of that great curve of blue
Distinct as a cliffy ledge,
And cry and wave and cry
Until with a little breath
She spied the red-capped head
Of the pledge both flung at death;
Then she would swing her hat
With her graceful arm held high
As if she would top the flags
And the flags could sweep the sky.

Now it is she who is gone
And you wait on the sand:
The place itself has changed,
The boardwalks are torn down.
For places curve with time
Over the horizon's rim;
Only a seabird flies
Lower and seems to skim
All that has been or is. . . .
No one is left to share
Those windless flags you see,
Alone in the dying glare.

[40] By permission of the author.

10

IMPERSONATION

When Shakespeare wanted to give the illusion that his two lovers, standing on the bare boards of a theatre in the glare of an afternoon sun, were in an orchard at night, he turned like the excellent technician he was to the magic and power of his poetry; and his audience, who were the best-trained listeners in the world, saw the moonlight silver the tops of the fruit trees as they listened to Romeo's voice. MARCHETTE CHUTE, *Shakespeare of London.*

We have been considering meaning, attitude, imagination, and emotion as they are found in such written discourse as exposition and lyric poetry, and how the author's total meaning may be interpreted orally to listeners. But there are types of literature that require a different treatment of these factors of meaning, types in which the author seems to disappear and we are confronted with the speeches of persons whom he has created. Such types are epic poetry, prose fiction, drama, and dramatic poetry. In these kinds of writing, we are called upon to represent the thoughts, attitudes, imaginings, and feelings of these fictitious persons, not of the author. Browning said of his dramatic lyrics that they were "so many utterances of so many imaginary persons, not mine." In reading such a lyric poem as Wordsworth's "The World Is too Much with Us," we assume that the author is expressing his own feelings, and they are generally such as we can share. He speaks for us, as we speak for him. We feel called upon to reflect his emotions, to re-create his images, to reveal his attitude toward what he is saying and toward the reader of the poem, as well as his intention in saying what he says.

In dramatic writing, these factors of meaning must still be dealt with, but they have changed their reference. The speeches of the characters reveal not an attitude toward the reader but rather an attitude toward other characters. The intention of the speakers also is not directed toward a reader or an audience but toward other characters in the play or story. In addition, an interpreter must discover and reveal to his listeners the situation in which these imaginary persons are represented as speaking and acting. Sometimes, but rarely, this is necessary also in interpreting lyric poetry, but in dramatic writing it is nearly always important. Then, too, an interpreter must reveal the character of each person represented, the complex of mental, emotional, and ethical traits that distinguishes one person from another, and besides, each person's physical behavior while speaking and his vocal mannerisms.

In epic poetry (which consists largely of speeches), and in prose fiction, the author often explains to us the situation in which the action takes place, the relations of the speakers to each other, their moods and attitudes, their appearance and behavior, and also their characteristic traits. A dramatist is likely to give us less of such information, and sometimes none at all. But in dramatic poems, and with these we shall be chiefly concerned, we must usually gather from what the speaker says all these factors so necessary to effective interpretation.

Lyrics Sometimes Dramatic

The line between lyric and dramatic is not a sharp one. Some would say that all lyric poetry has an element of the dramatic in it, that however much a poet may wish to set down with truth and fidelity his own inner thoughts and feelings he can hardly avoid a certain amount of posing. He may not be able to exclude all consideration of the impression of himself he hopes his poem will give. He may consciously or unconsciously desire to represent himself as a certain kind of person, and so dramatize himself. Or he may yield to an idea or a mood that fits a particular time and place, but is not typical of his customary thought and feeling. Is Milton strictly himself in both "L'Allegro" and "Il Penseroso"? Could he be? In each poem isn't he playing a part? It may be only in strictly descriptive poems, such as Auden's "The Express" or Keat's "To Autumn," that a poet can avoid completely such slight insincerities. In love poems especially it must be very difficult for the poet to avoid representing himself as more ardent than he really is, or at least as somewhat different. In interpreting lyrics, then, it may be that we have been doubly dramatic—posing as a poet in our reading and perhaps as a poet who is himself not free from pose.

At present, however, we are concerned with poems which are speeches that do not pretend to express the poet's sentiments, but are spoken by characters whom he has created, or are feigned speeches of real persons. These poetic inventions are, of course, highly various. First, they may not be persons at all but objects, birds, or beasts personified. Carl Sandberg represents grass as speaking, Sidney Lanier the Chattahoochee River, Shelly a cloud, and A. A. Milne a group of stuffed toy animals. How does one impersonate grass, a river, a cloud, a toy? In reading such poems is there any need to represent the character or mannerisms of the presumed speaker?

Second, sometimes the speaker is not an individual but a group. In Hovey's "At the End of the Day" a group of soldiers speaks. In Louise Guiney's "The Wild Ride" it is a galloping troup of Knights of the Grail. In Richard Burton's "The Song of the Unsuccessful" it is all the failures in the world, in T. S. Eliot's "Hollow Men" all the empty men of his time, or of all time. Kipling's "Gentlemen-Rankers" are British officers overseas who for various misdemeanors have been demoted to privates. And Archibald MacLeish's "Burial Ground by the Ties" represents the speech of hundreds of dead and buried railroad laborers. Can a single reader impersonate a group? We may say that one member speaks for a group all of whom have a common character, but it is still that group character which is personified.

Other dramatic poems represent the utterance of a single individual, or of two or more, each with a distinct personality and his own moods and emotions and reactions. Some are pure soliloquy, as Browning's "The Patriot." Others are monologues addressed to another person, whose character and whose reactions to the speech may be made manifest. Some are dialogues with two speakers alternating, as in the old folk ballad "Edward." And some are little dramas in which several persons take part, such as Delmore Schwartz's "Starlight like Intuition Pierced the Twelve," or that amazingly modern movie scenario of Theocritus, "The Women at the Adonis Festival."

In all these kinds of dramatic poetry, and in epic poetry, prose fiction, and drama, an interpreter should understand the personalities of the persons speaking, their moods, feelings, attitudes, and intentions, and try to reveal these qualities as he speaks their lines. How this can be done was explained and illustrated briefly in Chapter 3. A fuller treatment will be attempted here.

The Problem of the Actor

What we are concerned with is essentially the problem an actor faces when he undertakes to analyze a part, to reproduce the vocal and physical behavior in a given situation of a character assigned to him. His art and that of the interpretative reader have a good deal in common. This art of impersonation, like all the other arts, has been long studied and much written about. Let us learn what we can from those who have recorded their ideas about it. Even Plato philosophized about it in a dialogue be-

tween Socrates and the rhapsode, Ion, a flashy young professional elocu-
tionist who specialized in reciting Homer. (See "Ion" in the Appendix.)
Socrates tried to learn from Ion the nature of his art, the rules by which
it was governed, for he assumed that all the arts had rules comparable to
those that governed a charioteer, a pilot, or a physician. But Ion's mental
processes were all emotional and imaginative, and he could not define the
rationale of the art that had given him a reputation throughout Greece,
and a good living, so they concluded that his great gifts came merely from
inspiration of the muses.

Socrates' probing questions, however, are still pertinent, and we need
to look at them. He asked, "Will the rhapsode know better than the
physician what the ruler of a sick man ought to say? Will he know better
than a cowherd what ought to be said to soothe infuriated cows?" The
form of these questions suits more the poet or dramatist than the interpreter. Let us adapt them to our use and ask, Will an actor or other interpreter know better than a physician or a cowboy how a physician or
cowboy will speak and act? If you were casting a play that had a part
for a doctor or a cowboy, would you try to find a real doctor, a real cowboy, or would you prefer to have a well-trained actor? Doubtless we
would all prefer an actor. We would probably say that while the doctor
or cowboy might look the part, he wouldn't know how to act. What is it,
then, that an actor knows? What is the nature of his art, and how does
he learn it? We are not primarily concerned with the stage, but we need
to learn what we can from it, since many of the principles and techniques
of impersonation are the same for the solo reader as for the actor.

Suggestions from Literary Critical Theories

Instead of examining the techniques of various schools of acting, let
us see what help we can get from the theories of literary critics as they
were outlined in the chapter on poetry. If the theory that poetry is spontaneous emotion is applied to impersonative reading, the results can be
pretty dreadful. When an actor or reader merely emotes, without study
or design, he may bring down the house, but he will not bring illumination
to his part. There is something in the notion of spontaneity, however,
that is important. His speeches and his emotions should *seem* to be
created at the moment of utterance, and not sound rehearsed. The audience finds them more real and moving when they seem fresh and spontaneous. Even professional actors often lose their freshness after weary
weeks of rehearsal and repetition. Edith Oliver remarked recently in a
New Yorker review, "Surely one of the feats in a Shakespearean performance is to make the audience feel that a familiar line is being spoken for

the first time, having just leaped from brain to tongue."[1] A good place to notice and to practice this assumed leap from brain to tongue is Phoebe's speech in *As You Like It* (page 447). It is a spontaneous, or only slightly delayed, overflow of two conflicting emotions wherein the comical floundering of her flustered mind affords an excellent test of a reader's perceptiveness and skill in transitions of mood and attitude. Try it—but after studying the context, so that your responses will not *be* spontaneous, but only *seem* so.

The biographical theory of literary analysis, when translated into terms of interpretation, will likely result in a reading too heavily weighted with character analysis, to the neglect of such factors as situation and present attitude. But we *are* concerned with the characters and life histories of the persons we represent, and at times something significant from the character's past can be revealed by the skillful reading of a line. See examples in the analysis of "My Last Duchess" at the end of this chapter.

If an interpreter acquires his method from those critics of poetry who specialize in analyzing and decoding complexities, searching for hidden meanings and perhaps inventing them when they are not present, he may go far astray. He may seek an eccentric reading instead of a normal one, devising freakish and surprising tones and gestures which attract attention to his method and divert it from essential meaning. Such diversions are not unknown on the professional stage.

If one follows the "objective" theory that a poem is a little cosmos in itself, unrelated to other reality, with no cause or purpose outside itself, he is likely to evolve an interpretation that ignores responsiveness to conventional meaning, and lacks respect for both author and audience. It can become mere art for art's sake, without responsibility for subject matter or anything else, the kind of irresponsibility that has run riot in modern painting, sculpture, and music.

THE IMITATIVE THEORY. If we believe, as I think we should, that an artist owes fidelity to truth and actuality, we will not find much help in these approaches to the meaning of literature, but we *can* find help in the ancient classical theory of art as imitation. It will help us both to understand literature and to understand the art of interpreting it to others. Read again the brief review of this theory in Chapter 7. This, let us note carefully, is not a theory that artists produce by imitating other artists. In Aristotle's view all the arts are forms of imitation of nature, and the "primary objects of artistic imitation are human beings in action." In impersonation, these are not merely the primary, but the exclusive objects, counting personified things, of course, as persons.

Let us remember that interpretation is not strictly a creative but rather

---

[1] Edith Oliver, *The New Yorker*, October 24, 1964.

a re-creative activity, like singing, or playing the piano, or conducting an orchestra. Our text is prescribed for us and we are limited by it. We cannot push the author off the page and substitute a composition of our own. But an actor, or other interpreter, should do more than pronounce words. He should penetrate through the words to the ideal type which the author tried to put upon paper, and using the author's words, together with his own media of voice and gesture, he too can be an imitator of human nature, create, or re-create, a new and distinctive art product. In this re-creation it is possible for him to intensify, illuminate, and improve upon what the poet or dramatist has created.

Many students have difficulty with the notion of art as "imitation," not understanding how the word is used in this theory and what its relation is to such concepts as the real and the ideal. This is not surprising. All the arts in our time are in a chaotic state and undergoing endless experimentation, in which old standards are abandoned and authority scorned. But it is worth noting that sometimes when an authentic work of art appears and is commonly recognized as such, a critic's attempt to assess it may fall into agreement with the ancient concept, even though he is quite ignorant of its long tradition and assumes that he himself has just invented it. But the fact that it has been understood and accepted by philosophers, artists, and critics through the many centuries since its promulgation indicates that modern students should find it helpful in interpreting literature.

There are three aspects of the theory that need to be examined although they impinge on each other and it is difficult to keep them apart: first, the relation of art to actuality; second, the need to idealize the artist's product, which, in impersonation, is the characters he represents; third, the artist's function in relation to his product, and audience.

REALITY. Professor Butcher says in his commentary on Aristotle's Poetics,[2] that a work of art reproduces its original not as it actually is, but as it appears to the senses. It is concerned with outward appearances, it employs illusions, it does not attempt to embody the objective reality of things, but only their sensible appearances. It is not an attempt to create a literal likeness that will be taken for nature's original. A sculptor, for instance, does not try to deceive us into believing that his stone lion is a real lion. Even less does a painter attempt such deception.

But in the theatre many people do look for reality. The actor's medium of expression is identical with the product he creates; his medium is himself—his own body, voice, action, and emotion. And with this medium he creates another person with body, voice, action, and emotion.

[2] S. H. Butcher, *Aristotle's Theory of Poetry and Fine Art* (London: The Macmillan Co., Ltd., 1895), pp. 126–27.

Hence it is that persons who do not expect to be startled by a stone lion, and are not tempted to smell a rose painted on canvas, do expect to feel that action on the stage is real life, and not merely an imitation of life.

Stark Young said of such unschooled theatregoers, "They think that an actor's greatest triumph consists in making us think him some other person than himself. They prefer sometimes when he has died on the stage to have an actor remain out of sight and not return to bow before them with a smile on his face. People who insist on such deception and identity should frequent the dog and pony show. There they would see perfect naturalness, perfect illusion. Rover does not indeed act dog. He *is* dog. It is by just this exactly that critics of acting show what mere babies they are so far as art goes."[3]

In the movies, however, there is often a different expectation of naturalness, and no deception at all. The expectation of reality is encouraged by the settings, which, if not actual, are a very realistic duplication of actuality. And it is not the characters represented that are looked upon as real, but the actors. The more simple-minded patrons come not to see a drama or a display of competent acting, but to watch their favorite stars, in their own persons, move about in these various settings, generally making love to various other stars. In radio and television dramas, on the other hand, where the actors are not so well known, naive fans accept the fictional characters as real, and sometimes address them letters of advice, and even send money and other gifts to help them out of their fictional difficulties.

If the stage did give us real life instead of an imitation of life, we might not like it. Diderot, the French philosopher and critic, said:

An unhappy, a really unhappy woman, may weep and fail to touch you; worse yet, some trivial disfigurement in her may incline you to laughter; the accent which is apt to her is to your ear dissonant and vexatious; a movement which is habitual to her makes her grief show ignobly and sulkily to you; almost all the violent passions lend themselves to grimaces which a tasteless artist will copy but too faithfully, and which a great actor will avoid.

Let Diderot continue:

Reflect a little as to what, in the language of the theatre, is *being true.* Is it showing things as they are in nature? Certainly not. Were it so, the true would be the commonplace. What, then, is truth for stage purposes? It is the conforming of action, diction, face, voice, movement, and gesture, to an ideal type invented by the poet, and frequently enhanced by the player. . . . This type not only influences the tone, it alters the actor's very walk and bearing.

We would have this heroine fall with a becoming grace, that hero die like a gladiator of old in the midst of the arena to the applause of the circus, with a noble grace, with a fine and picturesque attitude. And who will execute this design of ours? The athlete who is mastered by pain, shattered by his own

[3] Stark Young, *Theatre Practice* (New York: Charles Scribner's Sons, 1926), p. 7.

sensibility, or the athlete who is trained, who has self-control, who as he breathes his last sigh, remembers the lessons of the gymnasium? Neither the gladiator of old nor the great actor dies as people die in their beds; it is for them to show us another sort of death, a death to move us; and the critical spectator will feel that the bare truth, the unadorned fact, would seem despicable and out of harmony with the poetry of the rest.[4]

IDEALIZATION. These quotations explain the artist's need to idealize his material, and, in some measure, how he does it. As Butcher said, "He seizes and reproduces a concrete fact, but transfigures it so that the higher truth, the idea of the universal shines through it." He "eliminates what is transient and particular and reveals the permanent and essential features of the original." Joshua Reynolds, writing of painting, said, "the great ideal perfection and beauty of art" were not to be sought in the heavens, that is, in inspiration, but upon the earth, and that the only way to find them was by "a long habit of observing what any set of objects of the same kind have in common," resulting in "an abstract idea of their forms more perfect than any one original." A photographer can give you an exact likeness of your actual appearance at the instant his shutter snapped, but a portrait painter who is a real artist will want to study your appearance and behavior under various conditions and blend these appearances into a picture that is typically and essentially you.

If on the stage you are called upon to play a part very much like yourself, it will not do to just be natural, to let yourself go. You must abstract and refine from your habitual behavior those features which are typical of you, eliminating what is trivial, accidental, or nonsignificant. Since every intonation and gesture becomes a part of your artistic product as perceived by the audience, you must exercise a rigorous censorship over them to see that only those are retained which are meaningful and necessary in communicating character, feeling, and incident. Above all, you must avoid the vague watery movement characteristic of real life. On the stage it would be not merely wasteful of attention, but distracting and confusing, since in the limelight every gesture and intonation has for the audience a highly intensified significance. By this idealization of yourself you should reveal your real self.

If you have to play a part very different from yourself, such as the Prince of Denmark or the King of Scotland, the same principles apply, but instead of studying yourself you study the data your author has provided; the speeches, of course, and the moods, emotions, attitudes, and traits of character they suggest. Beyond these, and whatever stage directions and analyses are provided, you have to depend largely on your imagination, activated by your memory of what you have seen in stage,

---

[4] Denis Diderot, *The Paradox of Acting*, trans. W. H. Pollock (London: Chatto and Windus, Ltd., 1883), pp. 22, 23.

motion picture, and television dramas, and what you can read of such unfamiliar characters and the social environment in which they lived. For this, the analysis of "My Last Duchess" at the end of this chapter may give you some guidelines.

An excellent summary of the whole process was made by Percy Fitzgerald, a popular and studious American actor of the late nineteenth century:

We must generalize and abstract, and not mistake the accident for the essence. . . . We must follow the method of men of science who compare and observe a great number of specimens until they discover one note. It is long, patient, minute observation that will discover for us what points are common to every specimen. This, then, is the method that all our great actors, consciously or unconsciously, follow, and it is the only method.[5]

When an artist thus "corrects nature by herself," studies the outward appearances of objects, emotions, behavior patterns in order to discover an ideal form, the real becomes the ideal. What then happens to our distinction between the real and the ideal? Can it be that what is called realism on the stage, in fiction, in interpretation, is merely a failure to study an object until its essential nature becomes clear?

The Impersonator's Function

We cannot, however, escape the fact that when an impersonator is presenting his conception of a character to an audience, his only medium is his own voice and body. How much should they be allowed to affect the character he portrays?

In school reading contests the performers often come to the platform with an air that says, "Here am I. Watch me do my piece." And the audience of parents and friends do just that, with no desire to see representation of a character other than the speaker's. In the movies too, as was remarked above, this attitude is very common, and it is not unknown on the professional stage. But what a sophisticated audience has a right to expect from an impersonator is that he will neither try to be himself nor be the character, but that he will *show* them the character, just as a painter may show his picture. If an impersonator obtrudes his own personality upon us, the purpose and meaning of art are lost. Here, as in painting, or poetry, or fiction, the artist should educate us by revealing the true forms of objects and people, showing us aspects of them and revealing depths that our untrained and uninspired faculties do not discover.

The obtrusion of the artist's personality into his product, though too

[5] Percy Fitzgerald, *The Art of Acting* (New York: The Macmillan Co., 1892), pp. 70, 90.

common in all the arts—think of the piano exhibitionists you have seen—is particularly obnoxious in impersonation. On the stage, Gordon Craig found the evil so bad that he wanted to get rid of the actor altogether, and put in his place an inanimate puppet, an *Ueber-manionette*. It is bad art, he said, "to make so personal, so emotional an appeal that the beholder forgets the thing itself while swamped by the personality, the emotion, of its maker." He quotes Napoleon as saying that we should see the hero as:

. . . a statue in which the weakness and the tremors of the flesh are no longer perceptible. Do away with the real tree, do away with the reality of delivery, and you tend to do away with the actor. This is what must come to pass in time. . . . Do away with the actor, and you do away with the means by which a debased stage-realism is produced and flourishes. No longer would there be a living figure to confuse us into connecting actuality and art; no longer a living figure in which the weakness and tremors of the flesh were perceptible.[6]

Inspiration

Such debased realism is generally found in a performer who neglects study and depends for his effects upon inspiration. Since our world is not peopled by a host of gods, each presiding over a separate department of life, we cannot readily follow Ion in his happy dependence on the muses. Nevertheless, we are conscious of something that at times seems to give us an unexpected lift in our endeavors, whether in invention, in writing, in athletics, or in interpretation. Whence it comes is a question. It may be a mere hunch, a flash of insight, a sudden heightening of our powers, a lucky strike, or a bubbling up of something from the subconscious which Stanislavsky called our "emotion-memory." He, however, warned that "our subconscious cannot function without its own engineer—our conscious technique."

But no real artist depends solely upon inspiration for his work. Instead of looking to heaven for some divine afflatus, always he looks closely at the earth, at the natural objects he seeks to imitate, striving always to "hold the mirror up to nature." If, for instance, he has the part of an old man to play, he will not look within himself and ask, "Now how would I act and speak if I were an old man?" Rather, he will go perhaps to a home for the aged and observe the behavior of the inmates. And the method by which he discovers the characteristic walk of an old man, the essential form of a tree, the typical grief of a girl, or the ideal voice and gesture of a cowherder, a king, or a gladiator, is just the method with which we began our study of reading—long, patient observation.

In his *Art of Poetry* Horace stated the matter well:

[6] Gordon Craig, *On the Art of the Theatre* (Chicago: Browne's Bookstore, 1911), p. 81

Whether by genius or by art an excellent poem is produced has long been a question: but I do not see what can be done by study without a rich vein of intellect, nor by genius when uncultivated: so true is it that either requires the help of either, and that the two combine in friendly union. He who passionately desires to reach in the race the goal, must first endure and do much as a boy, suffer from cold and toil, abstain from love and wine; he who at the Pythian games sings to the flute, has first been to school and feared a master.[7]

The eminent Talma, favorite actor of Napoleon, made an interesting contribution to the actor's method:

In the first place, by repeated exercises, he enters deeply into the emotions, and his speech acquires the accent proper to the situation of the personages he has to represent. This done, he goes to the theatre [presumably for rehearsal] not only to give theatrical effect to his studies, but also to yield himself to spontaneous flashes of his sensibility and all the emotions which it involuntarily produces in him. What does he then do? In order that his inspiration may not be lost, his memory, in the silence of repose, recalls the accent of his voice, the expression of his features, his action,—in a word, the spontaneous workings of his mind, which he had suffered to have free course, and in effect, everything which in the movements of his exaltation contributed to the effect he had produced. His intelligence then passes all these means in review, correcting them and fixing them in his memory, to reemploy them in succeeding representations. By this kind of labor the intelligence accumulates and preserves all the creations of sensibility.[8]

The Relation of Reading to Acting

The foregoing discussion draws largely from treatises on acting because that is the kind of impersonation that has been most written about. Character analysis is pretty much the same, whether for a part in a play or a solo reading of a monologue before a few friends. Methods of presentation, however, will differ. They depend partly on convention, partly on good taste, partly on the occasion, and partly on the nature of the material read. But there is no sharp division. We cannot say, This work must be *acted*, because it is labeled "drama"; and this one must be *read*, because it is labeled "poem," or "story." A monologue, such as "My Last Duchess," can be acted as if it were part of a play, with free movement, costume, makeup, lights, complete stage setting, and even the presence of the person being addressed. On the other hand, a scene meant to be staged, say a scene from *As You Like It*, can be read by a teacher at her desk, with none of the appurtenances of the theatre. And either performance may stir the beholder's imagination and be deeply moving; or it may not. The essential thing is to reveal the truth of idea, incident, character, and emotion set down by the poet or playwright.

[7] Horace, *Ars Poetica*, lines 408–15.
[8] Francois Joseph Talma, *Reflexions on the Actor's Art* (New York: Dramatic Museum of Columbia University, 1915), pp. 22–23.

The essential difference between acting and reading is that on the stage, actors visibly embody the characters, moving about, gesturing, and speaking as the characters, and thus dictating the audience's visual and vocal images of the scenes, while a reader is not in the scene he presents but stands apart from it and merely *shows* it to his hearers, allowing them to construct scene, action, and characters in their imaginations. If this seems obvious, it yet needs to be stated and insisted upon because so many interpreters try to act a scene that should merely be read.

No sensible interpreter will try to *act* a scene in which several persons are to be represented as speaking and reacting to each other. The old elocutionists of the turn of the century tried it and evolved set rules for dramatizing dialogue. For the first speech you drew your right foot back and turned slightly to the right; for the second, you stepped forward with the right foot, turning slightly to the left. This footwork often gave the spectator a picture of two persons not facing each other, but trying to turn their backs to each other. And all was done with appropriate gestures and changes of voice. If a third person appeared, you were really up against it. It was better not to allow a third person to appear.

Such parodies of acting persist and even today one can find badly taught schoolgirls in reading contests who contort themselves into a crouch supposedly representative of Shylock and snarl, "You spit upon my Jewish gaberdine," then stand erect and dignified for Antonio's reply, and then again the crouch and snarl. The absurdity of such attempts is better illustrated when a solo actor tries to render the balcony scene from *Romeo and Juliet.* It is easy enough to act Romeo looking up at Juliet, but how is one to get up into that balcony, which isn't there, to represent Juliet looking down at Romeo. Such a split-level scene just cannot be acted by a single performer. But it can be *read,* if the reader keeps himself out of it and merely *shows* the scene as taking place in the Capulet's garden. He must trust the spectators' imagination, allowing them to create the scene in their own minds, and not building it around himself, exhibiting himself as first one character and then the other.

READING RAPID DIALOGUE. Scenes in which there is rapid dialogue with short speeches are particularly difficult to handle. Look, for instance at the opening scene of *Hamlet,* or some of the scenes in Dylan Thomas' *Under Milk Wood.* Solo *acting* is out of the question; such scenes demand a cast of actors. And a reader will have difficulty with them. How can he make clear the rapid shift from speaker to speaker? Announcing who utters each speech will impede the flow of talk and may become annoying to the listener, but there is no other way. And there should be no objection to the reader interpolating comments of his own, and certainly none to reading the comments and directions provided by the playwright or story-teller. There is a curious objection among some interpreters to reading anything but speeches. The assumption seems to be that a good reader should be able to make all action clear without telling about it, so he tries to translate narrative into drama. The practice makes us suspect a thwarted would-be Thespian who wants to exhibit his skill in acting, instead of communicating a work of literature and making the narrative clear. Even in reading a Browning monologue a reader may properly announce at the beginning who is speaking and what the situation is, or even stop in the middle of the piece for needed comment or explanation.

As Don Geiger has said, the interpreter is "a member of the author's audience, is not only critic but also sympathetic sharer. That is, he will sometimes express attitudes which are not attitudes of the speakers within a piece, but the different attitudes of the audience which are caused by the literary action." He might have added attitudes of his own, shared neither by author nor audience. He continues, "Interpretation is an unformulable amalgam of acting, public speaking, critical reaction, and sympathetic sharing."[9]

EXAMPLES OF PERFORMANCE. Something can be learned about effective interpretation from the performances recently presented to the public by some of our most eminent actors.[10] All of these were well received by New York's dramatic critics and drew large audiences both in New York and some of them in extensive tours of the country. Hal Hollbrook impersonated Mark Twain reading from his own works, and Emlyn Williams did the same for Dickens. Both used costume and makeup and a reading stand, but not formal stage settings. Each read, or pretended to read, from a book, and each maintained constantly the character he was impersonating, never stepping out of it to speak as himself, not even to introduce himself. Each performance was strictly acting, but acting of a single character, though each impersonated the characters in the stories read as Twain and Dickens impersonated them.

Charles Laughton's reading from Dickens had a different pattern. Mr. Laughton bumbled onto the platform in his informal manner with a great pile of books under one arm, dumped them on the reading stand, fussed about a little, then looked at his audience, grinned boyishly, and blurted out a bashful "Hullo." It was a carefully designed piece of acting but without makeup or costume, that *seemed* to be just natural spontaneous Laughton. He maintained this impersonation of himself, if that is what it was, throughout the performance, commenting freely on the text, reading

[9] Don Geiger, *Oral Interpretation and Literary Study* (South San Francisco: Pieter Van Vlaten, 1958), pp. 40, 41.

[10] These are listed and examined by Keith Brooks and John E. Bielenberg in *The Southern Speech Journal* (Summer, 1964), pp. 288–302.

with a minimum of impersonation of the characters depicted and keeping the focus of attention on the stories.

His now famous Drama Quartet, reading "Don Juan in Hell" from Shaw's *Man and Superman,* had a still different pattern. Here he was assisted by three other famous actors, all mounted on high stools in a row across the front of the stage, each with the text of the play on a stand beside him, and each reading only one part, though without costume, makeup, or noticeable acting techniques. Always Shaw's ideas were kept in the foreground. There was, however, some surreptitious acting—it could hardly be otherwise with a group so steeped in the theatre—but it was probably not identified as such by the audience. For instance, at one point Mr. Laughton punctuated a speech by one of the other readers by letting his foot slip off the rung of his stool. It seemed an accident, but he confided privately that it happened just so in every performance.

We might consider also the lessons from Thornton Wilder's very popular play, *Our Town,* in which theatre conventions are almost completely ignored and the performance resembles a rehearsal by small-town amateurs. Properties are makeshift, and when lacking the action is carried on in pantomine. One actor shifts back and forth between acting and addressing the audience as narrator and commentator. It is all highly unorthodox, but highly successful as serious drama.

How Much Impersonation? These examples of successful professional performances reinforce what was said above—that there is no sharp distinction between reading and acting. The question we confront in deciding how to handle impersonative material is not a question of which of two methods to use, a strict either-or. It is rather a question of finding the appropriate place on a continuum between acting and plain reading. Sometimes, but rarely, all that is needed in impersonation is a mere report of the speaker's words, and sometimes it is appropriate to make a complete identification with the characters portrayed, short of veritable acting. The question is how far in a particular case an interpreter should go in identifying himself with the characters, how much he should modify his attitudes, intonations, pronunciation, facial expression, and gesture to conform to his conception of them. His choice should depend upon the situation, the social conventions that surround him, the dictates of good taste, and the nature of the material he is presenting. There are many occasions that call for moderation and restraint, where the show-off and the exhibitionist are not to be tolerated. The appropriate manner of relating an anecdote at a dinner party may depend upon how formal the party is. When a minister reads from the pulpit. "And God said, 'Let there be light,' " we do not expect him to try to act God, nor in reading the Sermon on the Mount to try to impersonate Jesus.

GROUP READING. The success of the Drama Quartet may have encouraged amateurs to imitate this form of presentation, for group readings have recently become popular. The readers try to capture some of the glamour of the stage by calling their performances Readers Theatre or Interpreters Theatre. In general, they have the form of a line-reading rehearsal for a play. The readers may stand in a row, or sit in chairs behind a table or scattered about the platform. They usually avoid costume and makeup. Action is, of course, limited, as is characterization, and the readers may or may not indicate the attitudes of the characters toward each other. Practically always they read from a book or script. The material read is usually a play, and each reader is assigned a part, but it may be a story, a scene from a novel, a long poem, or bits and pieces on a common theme. One service claimed for this kind of performance is that it acquaints dwellers in the hinterland with plays they have no opportunity to see acted, while saving the performers the trouble and expense of formal staging. Another is that compared with solo reading it gives more people a chance to get into the act. But it has limitations. It does not require that the participants make a careful study of their text, and it does not allow the observer to get a clear realization of scene and character, since he cannot readily create them in his own mind as he may when a single reader presents them, nor have them visibly set before him as in a conventionally acted play.

Envoi

In impersonation we try to represent not ourselves, nor some author, but the persons an author reports on or creates. Through study of the author's text we try to discover their characteristic traits, their attitudes, moods, emotions, responses, and the particular setting and circumstances in which they speak. This impression we translate, through our media of voice and action, into a pattern of expression that will give our auditors a true conception of the characters and their behavior. We derive this interpretation partly from our own natural responses, partly from what we have observed of life, read in literature, seen and heard on stage, screen, radio, television, disk and tape recordings, and other sources ranging from the masterpieces of art to cartoons and comic strips, and with the aid of our imaginations we work these materials into a conscious design of speech and gesture, which is our interpretation of the author's work.

This would seem to be a valuable discipline of both mind and expression. But it may have an additional value. We are told that the proper study of mankind is man, and surely the study of impersonation is a study of human nature. It is a humane discipline. But the human animal of our time is thought by many serious thinkers to have fallen into a sorry state. He has lost his way. He is, it is said, bewildered by the goalless dynamism of modern science and technology, which takes away his labor with automation and his brains with computers, and threatens his life with thermonuclear and napalm bombs. He finds that art and literature, which should be the interpreters of his culture, either dodge reality by abstractionism and surrealism, or represent mankind as fragmented, distorted, psychotic, perverted, or self-destructive, and he seeks to escape from boredom, despair, and disillusionment by excessive indulgence in sex, and alcohol, in sedatives, tranquillizers, and narcotics, or in the latest mass hysteria. A gloomy picture, surely, and, let us hope, not a true one.

Philosophers and other observers of our present culture fear that it is disintegrating, that it has lost its continuity with our past, and some think that the only way to save it is by recovering that connection. Lewis Mumford says, "It is only with reference to the full span of human existence that we can distinguish what is genuinely creative in the work of our time from what is just crazily 'original.' Without that connection with man's continuing life, all value and significance disappear."[11] Life's values, if they cannot be found in our present chaotic age, must be sought in man's long heritage as preserved in art and literature, extending from the remarkable drawings by Stone Age man of thirty thousand years ago in the caves of France and Spain, through the literary and artistic monuments of Mesopotamian, Egyptian, Greek, Roman, Medieval, and later cultures, down to the present. Perhaps a student of impersonation, by studying the portion of this heritage represented in the great characters created and preserved by literary geniuses, may come to understand something of man's essential nature, and so achieve a better understanding of himself and learn how to adjust himself to his destiny. And perhaps, just perhaps, he can stimulate some of the same understanding and adjustment in his auditors.

PLAN OF STUDY

1. Review the directions for study in earlier chapters.
2. Note whether your subject for impersonation is really a person or only a personification of some thing, or a group of persons, or someone speaking for a group.
3. Discover every indication of character, attitude, emotion, action, and situation furnished by the text. Is the speaker alone or are others present. If he is not soliloquizing, to whom is he speaking?
4. Try to create the speaker's past history, searching for causes that may make him speak and act as he does. Write out an analysis and exposition of his character. For instance, is he a person of strong feelings who shows them openly? Are his words meant to express his emotions or to conceal them? By what means in voice and gesture can you reveal these things?

[11] *The New Yorker*, March 6, 1965, p. 162.

5. Don't plan to depend on inspiration, or the impulse of the moment. Both may fail you and cause humiliation.
6. Don't read into the text things that are not there. Instead of trying to be original, be faithful to your author's intensions, follow the conventional pattern of expression, and avoid eccentricity.
7. Don't expect to merely be yourself, and don't attempt to *be* the character you represent. Rather *show* us the essential outward appearances that indicate his inner character.
8. Don't hesitate to interpolate into your impersonation comments and explanations of your own, if they seem needed.
9. Decide very carefully how far it seems best to identify yourself with the character you impersonate. Find the right mean between *being* the character and merely telling what he says.
10. In summary, you should integrate all you have learned from your study of the selection, and all you know about human behavior, into a deliberately designed and imagined performance that will effectively reveal your author's conception to your auditors.

CRITERIA

1. Had the reader adequately studied his selection? Did he understand it and effectively reflect its spirit and meaning?
2. Did his vocal expression, action, and gesture adequately portray the characters represented, without intrusion of his own personality?
3. Was the extent of his identification with the characters suitable to the selection, the occasion, and the audience, and within the limits of good taste?
4. Was his performance properly disciplined, free from irrelevancies of voice and gesture, and giving prominence to essentials?
5. Did he avoid both being himself and being the character, trying rather to show his audience the character and scene created by the author?
6. In dialogue, did he present a single unified picture to his audience's imagination, without requiring them to shift and readjust their picture for the various speakers.

QUESTIONS FOR DISCUSSION

1. In what respects are the methods of artists and scientists alike?
2. Discuss the relation of the real to the ideal in artistic production. How does an artist idealize concrete facts?
3. May inspiration ever be a help in interpretation?
4. Discuss the differences between acting and solo reading of a play.
5. May a reader impersonate himself as a reader? See the account of Charles Laughton's readings of Dickens.
6. Discuss "art is the expression of emotion" with reference to impersonation.
7. Discuss "art is imitation of men in action" with relation to impersonation.
8. How can an artist imitating nature "correct nature by herself?" Does this apply to impersonation?
9. What problems and limitations must be faced in solo reading of dialogue?

MY LAST DUCHESS

Ferrara

Robert Browning

That's my last Duchess painted on the wall,
Looking as if she were alive. I call
That piece a wonder, now: Frà Pandolf's hands
Worked busily a day, and there she stands.
Will't please you sit and look at her? I said   5
"Frà Pandolf" by design, for never read
Strangers like you that pictured countenance,
The depth and passion of its earnest glance,
But to myself they turned (since none puts by
The curtain I have drawn for you, but I)   10
And semed as they would ask me, if they durst,
How such a glance came there; so, not the first
Are you to turn and ask thus. Sir, 'twas not
Her husband's presence only, called that spot
Of joy into the Duchess' cheek: perhaps   15
Frà Pandolf chanced to say, "Her mantle laps
Over my lady's wrist too much," or "Paint
Must never hope to reproduce the faint
Half-flush that dies along her throat:" such stuff
Was courtesy, she thought, and cause enough   20
For calling up that spot of joy. She had
A heart—how shall I say?—too soon made glad,
Too easily impressed: she liked whate'er
She looked on, and her looks went everywhere.
Sir, 'twas all one! My favour at her breast,   25
The dropping of the daylight in the West,
The bough of cherries some officious fool
Broke in the orchard for her, the white mule
She rode with round the terrace—all and each
Would draw from her alike the approving speech,   30
Or blush, at least. She thanked men,—good! but thanked
Somehow—I know not how—as if she ranked
My gift of a nine-hundred-years-old name
With anybody's gift. Who'd stoop to blame
This sort of trifling? Even had you skill   35
In speech—(which I have not)—to make your will
Quite clear to such an one, and say, "Just this
Or that in you disgusts me; here you miss,
Or there exceed the mark"—and if she let
Herself be lessoned so, nor plainly set   40

Her wits to yours, forsooth, and made excuse,
—E'en then would be some stooping; and I choose
Never to stoop. Oh sir, she smiled, no doubt,
Whene'er I passed her; but who passed without
Much the same smile? This grew; I gave commands;   45
Then all smiles stopped together. There she stands
As if alive. Will't please you rise? We'll meet
The company below, then. I repeat,
The Count your master's known munificence
Is ample warrant that no just pretence   50
Of mine for dowry will be disallowed;
Though his fair daughter's self, as I avowed
At starting, is my object. Nay, we'll go
Together down, sir. Notice Neptune, though,
Taming a sea-horse, thought a rarity,   55
Which Claus of Innsbruck cast in bronze for me!

SUGGESTIONS FOR ANALYSIS. This poem is a favorite of oral readers though
few take the trouble to find out what it is all about. The chief difficulty is understanding the character of the Duke, who does the speaking. The average
modern schoolgirl who reads the poem has so little in common with his character
that she makes of him a ludicrous caricature. Your first and most important
task in preparing the poem is to analyze his character. What manner of man
is he?

Note the sub-title "Ferrara." Look it up in a good encyclopedia and read
the complete story of that romantic city. Browning's first title for the poem was
"Italy." The place, then, is clear enough, but what about the time? When did
this happen? There are no definite clues, but Ferrara was a dukedom only between 1470 and 1597, and other indications in the poem help to place the incident in the period of the Italian Renaissance. Unless you are familiar with that
great period in our civilization you are not likely to understand the Duke or his
attitude toward his last Duchess. He was a man of the Renaissance with all the
deep love of art, the pride, and the cruelty of the men of that period. You
might begin your study by reading Julia Cartwright's *Beatrice d'Este*, a charming biography of the daughter of a Duke of Ferrara.

The situation in the poem is clear enough if you read it attentively. The
Duke is showing a portrait of his last Duchess to an emissary who has come to
arrange the details of his next marriage. Why does he show the portrait? Because he admires it as a work of art, or because showing it affords him an opportunity to make sure that his next wife will be properly instructed in her
duties? Don't assume that he had to excuse his conduct toward his last wife.
His name and position are secure. If he would not stoop to correct his wife's
behavior why would he stoop to defend himself to a mere messenger? The
language used is deceiving. "Will't please you" and "Oh sir," etc., suggest to
us deference, and even pleading, when he is merely polite. Some of his courteous questions are really commands, and should be read as such. His statement about the dowry is a polite way of saying, "Your master will pay whatever
I ask." His willingness to "go together down" to the company below is gracious
condescension, as the messenger well knows. Perhaps he has more "skill in
speech" than he pretends.

What does he mean by "I gave commands; then all smiles stopped together."? Our notions of romantic love, derived from Hollywood and current fiction, are outraged by his cold brutal treatment of his wife. But you must try to see the situation from his point of view. His pride in his name and rank and position may seem offensive, but is it not well founded? What may such a man legitimately expect from his wife? You must consider the social customs of the times and his place in society. You might remember that recently England in effect deposed a king because the woman he wished to marry was not suited for the office of queen. You cannot understand the Duke's reactions merely by imagining your own in a comparable situation. Since the man and his feelings lie outside the range of your experience you must study the people and customs of the time in which he lived.

If you can grasp the character of the Duke you need not have much trouble with his mood. As he talks of his last Duchess is he moved by guilt, regret, admiration, annoyance, disgust, indignation, contempt, or something else? How is his avowal of interest in the "fair daughter's self," instead of her dowry, to be taken? Is the concluding reference to the bronze statue merely casual, or is it a device to change the subject and indicate that the bargain is closed?

You may read the poem several times before you discover that it is in rhymed couplets. The style is purely conversational and prosy, and so rhyme and meter can be ignored.

THE PATRIOT

An Old Story

Robert Browning

It was roses, roses, all the way,
    With myrtle mixed in my path like mad;
The house-roofs seemed to heave and sway,
    The church-spires flamed, such flags they had,
A year ago on this very day.   5

The air broke into a mist with bells,
    The old walls rocked with the crowd and cries.
Had I said, "Good folk, mere noise repels—
    But give me your sun from yonder skies!"
They had answered "And afterward, what else?"   10

Alack, it was I who leaped at the sun
    To give it my loving friends to keep!
Naught man could do, have I left undone:
    And you see my harvest, what I reap
This very day, now a year is run.   15

There's nobody on the house-tops now—
    Just a palsied few at the windows set;
For the best of the sight is, all allow,
    At the Shambles' Gate—or, better yet,
By the very scaffold's foot, I trow.   20

I go in the rain, and, more than needs,
    A rope cuts both my wrists behind;
And I think, by the feel, my forehead bleeds,
    For they fling, whoever has a mind,
Stones at me for my year's misdeeds.   25

Thus I entered, and thus I go!
    In triumphs, people have dropped down dead.
"Paid by the world, what dost thou owe
    Me?"—God might question; now instead,
'Tis God shall repay: I am safer so.   30

SUGGESTIONS FOR ANALYSIS. Who is speaking? Under what circumstances? To whom? In what mood?

What manner of man is he? Able, or a visionary; a strong man or a weakling; ambitious or unselfish; generous or close; a man of words, or of actions? Was he sincerely devoted to the public good? Browning calls him a patriot. What is the essence of patriotism? How can it be expressed in voice and bearing?

What is his present mood? Is he bitter, cynical, disillusioned, disappointed, resentful, defiant, confident, indifferent, courageous, resigned, puzzled, heroic, rebellious? Does his mood change during this monologue? With what feeling does he remember the joyous celebration a year ago? Is he physically weak, exhausted? How does he walk? With head up, or bowed? Or *is* he walking?

There were "roses all the way" where? Why the myrtle? What made the roofs heave and sway? What is the relation of the flaming spires to the flags? Was he the kind of inflated egotist who would frown on mere noise, and ask for the sun? Who were his "loving friends"? Political hangers-on? Where are they now? Did he give the people just cause to turn against him? What were his "year's misdeeds"? Can you find in history, ancient or current, any parallel for this sudden reverse of popular opinion? What is about to happen? Is the last stanza the expression of a calm reasoned faith, or merely an anxious hope, or a vague rationalization? The meaning is troublesome. Presumably he is consoling himself with two reflections: "I might have died even in a triumph"; and "If I had been richly rewarded in life God would expect a richer return to him. It is better to be in a position to expect a reward from God."

To give an adequate picture of the scene and character it is not necessary to hold your hands as though they were tied behind you, but it would be best not to attempt to gesticulate with them. Neither will your forehead need greasepaint to represent blood-stains and rain-streaks, but you had best not wear too cheerful a brow.

SELECTIONS FOR PRACTICE

SATAN ENCOURAGES BEELZEBUB

From PARADISE LOST, I

John Milton

. . . Satan . . .
Breaking the horrid silence, thus began:—
  "If thou beest he—but oh, how fall'n! how changed
From him who, in the happy realms of light,
Clothed with transcendent brightness, didst outshine
Myriads, though bright!—if he whom mutual league,
United thoughts and counsels, equal hope
And hazard in the glorious enterprise,
Joined with me once, now misery hath joined
In equal ruin; into what pit thou seest
From what height fallen: so much the stronger proved
He with his thunder: and till then who knew
The force of those dire arms? Yet not for those,
Nor what the potent Victor in his rage
Can else inflict, do I repent, or change,
Though changed in outward lustre; that fixed mind,
And high disdain from sense of injured merit,
That with the Mightiest raised me to contend,
And to the fierce contention brought along
Innumerable force of Spirits armed,
That durst dislike his reign, and, me preferring,
His utmost power with adverse power opposed
In dubious battle on the plains of Heaven,
And shook his throne. What though the field be lost?
All is not lost—the unconquerable will,
And study of revenge, immortal hate,
And courage never to submit or yield:
And what is else not to be overcome?
That glory never shall his wrath or might
Extort from me. To bow and sue for grace
With suppliant knee, and deify his power
Who, from the terror of this arm, so late
Doubted his empire—that were low indeed;
That were an ignominy and shame beneath
This downfall; since by fate the strength of gods,
And this empyreal substance, cannot fail;
Since, through experience of this great event,
In arms not worse, in foresight much advanced,
We may with more successful hope resolve
To wage by force or guile eternal war,

Irreconcilable to our grand Foe,
Who now triumphs, and in th' excess of joy
Sole reigning holds the tyranny of Heaven."
   So spake the apostate Angel, though in pain,
Vaunting aloud, but racked with deep despair;
And him thus answered soon his bold compeer:—
   "O Prince! O Chief of many thronèd powers,
That led the embattled Seraphim to war
Under thy conduct, and, in dreadful deeds
Fearless, endangered Heaven's perpetual King,
And put to proof his high supremacy,
Whether upheld by strength, or chance, or fate,
Too well I see and rue the dire event
That with sad overthrow and foul defeat
Hath lost us Heaven, and all this mighty host
In horrible destruction laid thus low,
As far as gods and Heavenly essences
Can perish: for the mind and spirit remains
Invincible, and vigor soon returns,
Though all our glory extinct, and happy state
Here swallowed up in endless misery.
But what if he our Conqueror (whom I now
Of force believe almighty, since no less
Than such could have o'erpowered such force as ours)
Have left us this our spirit and strength entire,
Strongly to suffer and support our pains,
That we may so suffice his vengeful ire;
Or do him mightier service, as his thralls
By right of war, whate'er his business be,
Here in the heart of Hell to work in fire,
Or do his errands in the gloomy Deep?
What can it then avail, though yet we feel
Strength undiminished, or eternal being
To undergo eternal punishment?"
   Whereto with speedy words the Arch-Fiend replied:—
"Fallen Cherub, to be weak is miserable,
Doing or suffering: but of this be sure—
To do aught good never will be our task,
But ever to do ill our sole delight,
As being the contrary to his high will
Whom we resist. If then his providence
Out of our evil seek to bring forth good,
Our labour must be to pervert that end,
And out of good still to find means of evil;
Which ofttimes may succeed so as perhaps
Shall grieve him, if I fail not, and disturb
His inmost counsels from their destined aim.

But see the angry Victor hath recalled
His ministers of vengeance and pursuit
Back to the gates of Heaven; the sulphurous hail,
Shot after us in storm, o'erblown hath laid
The fiery surge that from the precipice
Of Heaven received us falling; and the thunder,
Winged with red lightning and impetuous rage,
Perhaps hath spent his shafts, and ceases now
To bellow through the vast and boundless Deep.
Let us not slip the occasion, whether scorn
Or satiate fury yield it from our Foe.
Seest thou yon dreary plain, forlorn and wild,
The seat of desolation, void of light,
Save what the glimmering of these livid flames
Casts pale and dreadful? Thither let us tend
From off the tossing of these fiery waves;
There rest, if any rest can harbour there;
And, reassembling our afflicted powers,
Consult how we may henceforth most offend
Our Enemy, our own loss how repair,
How overcome this dire calamity,
What reinforcement we may gain from hope,
If not, what resolution from despair."

SATAN'S AMBITION

From PARADISE LOST, I

John Milton

So stretched out huge in length the Arch-Fiend lay,
Chained on the burning lake; nor ever thence
Had risen, or heaved his head, but that the will
And high permission of all-ruling Heaven
Left him at large to his own dark designs,
That with reiterated crimes he might
Heap on himself damnation, while he sought
Evil to others, and enraged might see
How all his malice served but to bring forth
Infinite goodness, grace, and mercy, shown
On Man by him seduced; but on himself
Treble confusion, wrath, and vengeance poured.
  Forthwith upright he rears from off the pool
His mighty stature; on each hand the flames
Driven backward slope their pointing spires, and, rolled
In billows, leave in the midst a horrid vale.

Then with expanded wings he steers his flight
Aloft, incumbent on the dusky air,
That felt unusual weight; till on dry land
He lights—if it were land that ever burned
With solid, as the lake with liquid fire,
And such appeared in hue, as when the force
Of subterranean wind transports a hill
Torn from Pelorus, or the shattered side
Of thundering Ætna, whose combustible
And fuelled entrails thence conceiving fire,
Sublimed with mineral fury, aid the winds,
And leave a singèd bottom all involved
With stench and smoke: such resting found the sole
Of unblest feet. Him followed his next mate,
Both glorying to have 'scaped the Stygian flood
As gods, and by their own recovered strength,
Not by the sufferance of supernal power.
    "Is this the region, this the soil, the clime,"
Said then the lost Archangel, "this the seat
That we must change for Heaven! this mournful gloom
For that celestial light? Be it so, since he
Who now is sovran can dispose and bid
What shall be right: farthest from him is best,
Whom reason hath equalled, force hath made supreme
Above his equals. Farewell, happy fields,
Where joy forever dwells! Hail, horrors! hail,
Infernal world! and thou, profoundest Hell,
Receive thy new possessor: one who brings
A mind not to be changed by place or time.
The mind is its own place, and in itself
Can make a Heaven of Hell, a Hell of Heaven.
What matter where, if I be still the same,
And what I should be, all but less than he
Whom thunder hath made greater? Here at least
We shall be free; the Almighty hath not built
Here for his envy, will not drive us hence:
Here we may reign secure, and in my choice
To reign is worth ambition, though in Hell:
Better to reign in Hell, than serve in Heaven.
But wherefore let we then our faithful friends,
The associates and co-partners of our loss,
Lie thus astonished on the oblivious pool,
And call them not to share with us their part
In this unhappy mansion, or once more
With rallied arms to try what may be yet
Regained in Heaven, or what more lost in Hell?"

THE CLOUD

Percy Bysshe Shelley

I bring fresh showers for the thirsting flowers,
    From the seas and the streams;
I bear light shade for the leaves when laid
    In their noonday dreams.
From my wings are shaken the dews that waken
    The sweet buds every one,
When rocked to rest on their mother's breast
    As she dances about the sun.
I wield the flail of the lashing hail,
    And whiten the green plains under,
And then again I dissolve it in rain,
    And laugh as I pass in thunder.

I sift the snow on the mountains below,
    And their great pines groan aghast;
And all the night 'tis my pillow white,
    While I sleep in the arms of the blast.
Sublime on the towers of my skiey bowers,
    Lightning my pilot sits;
In a cavern under is fettered the thunder,
    It struggles and howls at fits;
Over earth and ocean, with gentle motion,
    This pilot is guiding me,
Lured by the love of the genii that move
    In the depths of the purple sea;
Over the rills, and the crags, and the hills,
    Over the lakes and the plains,
Wherever he dream, under mountain or stream,
    The Spirit he loves remains;
And I all the while bask in heaven's blue smile,
    Whilst he is dissolving in rains.

The sanguine sunrise, with his meteor eyes,
    And his burning plumes outspread,
Leaps on the back of my sailing rack,
    When the morning star shines dead,
As on the jag of a mountain crag,
    Which an earthquake rocks and swings,
An eagle alit one moment may sit
    In the light of its golden wings.
And when sunset may breathe, from the lit sea beneath,
    Its ardours of rest and of love,

And the crimson pall of eve may fall
  From the depth of heaven above,
With wings folded I rest, on mine airy nest,
  As still as a brooding dove.

That orbèd maiden with white fire laden,
  Whom mortals call the moon,
Glides glimmering o'er my fleece-like floor,
  By the midnight breezes strewn;
And wherever the beat of her unseen feet,
  Which only the angels hear,
May have broken the woof of my tent's thin roof,
  The stars peep behind her and peer;
And I laugh to see them whirl and flee,
  Like a swarm of golden bees,
When I widen the rent in my wind-built tent,
  Till the calm rivers, lakes, and seas,
Like strips of the sky fallen through me on high,
  Are each paved with the moon and these.

I bind the sun's throne with a burning zone,
  And the moon's with a girdle of pearl;
The volcanoes are dim, and the stars reel and swim,
  When the whirlwinds my banner unfurl.
From cape to cape, with a bridge-like shape,
  Over a torrent sea,
Sunbeam-proof, I hang like a roof,—
  The mountains its columns be.
The triumphal arch through which I march
  With hurricane, fire and snow,
When the powers of the air are chained to my chair,
  Is the million-colored bow;
The sphere-fire above its soft colors wove,
  While the moist earth was laughing below.

I am the daughter of earth and water,
  And the nursling of the sky;
I pass through the pores of the ocean and shores;
  I change, but I cannot die.
For after the rain when with never a stain
  The pavilion of heaven is bare,
And the winds and sunbeams with their convex gleams
  Build up the blue dome of air,
I silently laugh at my own cenotaph,
  And out of the caverns of rain,
Like a child from the womb, like a ghost from the tomb,
  I arise and unbuild it again.

LA BELLE DAME SANS MERCI

John Keats

O what can ail thee, knight-at-arms,
    Alone and palely loitering?
The sedge has wither'd from the lake,
    And no birds sing.

O what can ail thee, knight-at-arms,
    So haggard and so woe-begone?
The squirrel's granary is full,
    And the harvest's done.

I see a lily on thy brow
    With anguish moist and fever dew,
And on thy cheeks a fading rose
    Fast withereth too.

"I met a lady in the meads,
    Full beautiful—a faery's child;
Her hair was long, her foot was light,
    And her eyes were wild.

"I made a garland for her head,
    And bracelets too, and fragrant zone;
She look'd at me as she did love,
    And made sweet moan.

"I set her on my pacing steed,
    And nothing else saw all day long,
For sideways would she lean, and sing
    A faery's song.

"She found me roots of relish sweet,
    And honey wild, and manna-dew,
And sure in language strange she said—
    'I love thee true.'

"She took me to her elfin grot,
    And there she wept and sigh'd full sore,
And there I shut her wild, wild eyes,
    With kisses four.

"And there she lullèd me asleep,
    And there I dream'd—ah! woe betide!—
The latest dream I ever dream'd
    On the cold hill's side.

"I saw pale kings and princes too,
   Pale warriors, death-pale were they all;
They cried—'La Belle Dame sans Merci
   Hath thee in thrall!'

"I saw their starved lips in the gloam,
   With horrid warning gapèd wide;
And I awoke, and found me here
   On the cold hill's side.

"And this is why I sojourn here,
   Alone and palely loitering,
Though the sedge is wither'd from the lake,
   And no birds sing."

SIR GALAHAD

Alfred, Lord Tennyson

My good blade carves the casques of men,
   My tough lance thrusteth sure,
My strength is as the strength of ten,
   Because my heart is pure.
The shattering trumpet shrilleth high,
   The hard brands shiver on the steel,
The splinter'd spear-shafts crack and fly,
   The horse and rider reel:
They reel, they roll in clanging lists,
   And when the tide of combat stands,
Perfume and flowers fall in showers,
   That lightly rain from ladies' hands.

How sweet are looks that ladies bend
   On whom their favours fall!
For them I battle till the end,
   To save from shame and thrall:
But all my heart is drawn above,
   My knees are bow'd in crypt and shrine:
I never felt the kiss of love,
   Nor maiden's hand in mine.
More bounteous aspects on me beam,
   Me mightier transports move and thrill;
So keep I fair thro' faith and prayer
   A virgin heart in work and will.

When down the stormy crescent goes,
   A light before me swims,

Between dark stems the forest glows,
   I hear a noise of hymns:
Then by some secret shrine I ride;
   I hear a voice but none are there;
The stalls are void, the doors are wide,
   The tapers burning fair.
Fair gleams the snowy altar-cloth,
   The silver vessels sparkle clean,
The shrill bell rings, the censer swings,
   And solemn chants resound between.

Sometimes on lonely mountain-meres
   I find a magic bark;
I leap on board: no helmsman steers:
   I float till all is dark.
A gentle sound, an awful light!
   Three angels bear the holy Grail:
With folded feet, in stoles of white,
   On sleeping wings they sail.
Ah, blessed vision! blood of God!
   My spirit beats her mortal bars,
As down dark tides the glory slides,
   And star-like mingles with the stars.

When on my goodly charger borne
   Thro' dreaming towns I go,
The cock crows ere the Christmas morn,
   The streets are dumb with snow.
The tempest crackles on the leads,
   And, ringing, springs from brand and mail;
But o'er the dark a glory spreads,
   And gilds the driving hail.
I leave the plain, I climb the height;
   No branchy thicket shelter yields;
But blessed forms in whistling storms
   Fly o'er waste fens and windy fields.

A maiden knight—to me is given
   Such hope, I know not fear;
I yearn to breathe the airs of heaven
   That often meet me here.
I muse on joy that will not cease,
   Pure spaces clothed in living beams,
Pure lilies of eternal peace,
   Whose odours haunt my dreams;
And, stricken by an angel's hand,
   This mortal armour that I wear,

This weight and size, this heart and eyes,
 Are touch'd, are turn'd to finest air.

The clouds are broken in the sky,
 And thro' the mountain-walls
A rolling organ-harmony
 Swells up, and shakes and falls.
Then move the trees, the copses nod,
 Wings flutter, voices hover clear:
"O just and faithful knight of God!
 Ride on! the prize is near."
So pass I hostel, hall, and grange;
 By bridge, and ford, by park and pale,
All-arm'd I ride, whate'er betide,
 Until I find the holy Grail.

ULYSSES

Alfred, Lord Tennyson

It little profits that an idle king,
By this still hearth, among these barren crags,
Match'd with an agèd wife, I mete and dole
Unequal laws unto a savage race,
That hoard, and sleep, and feed, and know not me.
I cannot rest from travel: I will drink
Life to the lees: all times I have enjoy'd
Greatly, have suffer'd greatly, both with those
That loved me, and alone; on shore, and when
Thro' scudding drifts the rainy Hyades
Vext the dim sea; I am become a name;
For always roaming with a hungry heart
Much have I seen and known,—cities of men,
And manners, climates, councils, governments,
Myself not least, but honour'd of them all,—
And drunk delight of battle with my peers,
Far on the ringing plains of windy Troy.
I am a part of all that I have met.
Yet all experience is an arch where-thro'
Gleams that untravell'd world, whose margin fades
Forever and forever when I move.
How dull it is to pause, to make an end,
To rust unburnish'd, not to shine in use!
As tho' to breath were life! Life piled on life
Were all too little, and of one to me

Little remains: but every hour is saved
From that eternal silence, something more,
A bringer of new things; and vile it were
For some three suns to store and hoard myself,
And this grey spirit yearning in desire
To follow knowledge like a sinking star,
Beyond the utmost bound of human thought.
　　This is my son, mine own Telemachus,
To whom I leave the sceptre and the isle—
Well-loved of me, discerning to fulfil
This labour, by slow prudence to make mild
A rugged people, and thro' soft degrees
Subdue them to the useful and the good.
Most blameless is he, centred in the sphere
Of common duties, decent not to fail
In offices of tenderness, and pay
Meet adoration to my household gods,
When I am gone.   He works his work, I mine.
　　There lies the port; the vessel puffs her sail:
There gloom the dark broad seas.   My mariners,
Souls that have toil'd, and wrought, and thought with me—
That ever with a frolic welcome took
The thunder and the sunshine, and opposed
Free hearts, free foreheads—you and I are old;
Old age hath yet his honour and his toil;
Death closes all: but something ere the end,
Some work of noble note, may yet be done,
Not unbecoming men that strove with Gods.
The lights begin to twinkle from the rocks:
The long day wanes: the slow moon climbs: the deep
Moans round with many voices.   Come, my friends,
'Tis not too late to seek a newer world.
Push off, and sitting well in order smite
The sounding furrows; for my purpose holds
To sail beyond the sunset, and the baths
Of all the western stars, until I die.
It may be that the gulfs will wash us down:
It may be we shall touch the Happy Isles,
And see the great Achilles, whom we knew.
Tho' much is taken, much abides; and tho'
We are not now that strength which in old days
Moved earth and heaven; that which we are, we are,
One equal temper of heroic hearts,
Made weak by time and fate, but strong in will
To strive, to seek, to find, and not to yield.

COME INTO THE GARDEN, MAUD

Alfred, Lord Tennyson

Come into the garden, Maud,
   For the black bat, night, has flown,
Come into the garden, Maud,
   I am here at the gate alone;
And the woodbine spices are wafted abroad,
   And the musk of the rose is blown.

For a breeze of morning moves,
   And the planet of love is on high,
Beginning to faint in the light that she loves
   On a bed of daffodil sky,
To faint in the light of the sun she loves,
   To faint in his light, and to die.

All night have the roses heard
   The flute, violin, bassoon;
All night has the casement jassamine stirr'd
   To the dancers dancing in tune;
Till a silence fell with the waking bird,
   And a hush with the setting moon.

I said to the lily, "There is but one,
   With whom she has heart to be gay.
When will the dancers leave her alone?
   She is weary of dance and play."
Now half to the setting moon are gone,
   And half to the rising day;
Low on the sand and loud on the stone
   The last wheel echoes away.

I said to the rose, "The brief night goes
   In babble and revel and wine.
O young lord-lover, what sighs are those,
   For one that will never be thine?
But mine, but mine," so I sware to the rose,
   "For ever and ever, mine."

And the soul of the rose went into my blood,
   As the music clash'd in the Hall;
And long by the garden lake I stood,
   For I heard your rivulet fall
From the lake to the meadow and on to the wood,
   Our wood, that is dearer than all;

From the meadow your walks have left so sweet
   That whenever a March-wind sighs
He set the jewel-print of your feet
   In violets blue as your eyes,
To the woody hollows in which we meet
   And the valleys of Paradise.

The slender acacia would not shake
   One long milk-bloom on the tree;
The white lake-blossom fell into the lake
   As the pimpernel dozed on the lea;
But the rose was awake all night for your sake,
   Knowing your promise to me;
The lilies and roses were all awake,
   They sigh'd for the dawn and thee.

Queen rose of the rosebud garden of girls,
   Come hither, the dances are done,
In gloss of satin and glimmer of pearls,
   Queen lily and rose in one;
Shine out, little head, sunning over with curls,
   To the flowers and be their sun.

There has fallen a splendid tear
   From the passion-flower at the gate.
She is coming, my dove, my dear;
   She is coming, my life, my fate.
The red rose cries, "She is near, she is near;"
   And the white rose weeps, "She is late;"
The larkspur listens, "I hear, I hear;"
   And the lily whispers, "I wait."

She is coming, my own, my sweet;
   Were it ever so airy a tread,
My heart would hear her and beat,
   Were it earth in an earthy bed;
My dust would hear her and beat,
   Had I lain for a century dead,—
Would start and tremble under her feet,
   And blossom in purple and red.

EVELYN HOPE

Robert Browning

Beautiful Evelyn Hope is dead!
   Sit and watch by her side an hour.
That is her book-shelf, this her bed;
   She plucked the piece of geranium-flower,

Beginning to die too, in the glass;
　　Little has yet been changed, I think:
The shutters are shut, no light may pass
　　Save two long rays through the hinge's chink.

Sixteen years old when she died!
　　Perhaps she had scarcely heard my name;
It was not her time to love; beside,
　　Her life had many a hope and aim,
Duties enough and little cares,
　　And now was quiet, now astir,
Till God's hand beckoned unawares,—
　　And the sweet white brow is all of her.

Is it too late then, Evelyn Hope?
　　What, your soul was pure and true,
The good stars met in your horoscope,
　　Made you of spirit, fire and dew—
And, just because I was thrice as old
　　And our paths in the world diverged so wide,
Each was naught to each, must I be told?
　　We were fellow mortals, naught beside?

No, indeed! for God above
　　Is great to grant, as mighty to make,
And creates the love to reward the love:
　　I claim you still, for my own love's sake!
Delayed it may be for more lives yet,
　　Through worlds I shall traverse, not a few:
Much is to learn, much to forget
　　Ere the time be come for taking you.

But the time will come,—at last it will,
　　When, Evelyn Hope, what meant (I shall say)
In the lower earth, in the years long still,
　　That body and soul so pure and gay?
Why your hair was amber, I shall divine,
　　And your mouth of your own geranium's red—
And what you would do with me, in fine,
　　In the new life come in the old one's stead.

I have lived (I shall say) so much since then,
　　Given up myself so many times,
Gained me the gains of various men,
　　Ransacked the ages, spoiled the climes;
Yet one thing, one, in my soul's full scope,
　　Either I missed or itself missed me:
And I want and find you, Evelyn Hope!
　　What is the issue? let us see!

I loved you, Evelyn, all the while!
  My heart seemed full as it could hold;
There was place and to spare for the frank young smile,
  And the red young mouth, and the hair's young gold.
So, hush,—I will give you this leaf to keep:
  See, I shut it inside the sweet cold hand!
There, that is our secret: go to sleep!
  You will wake, and remember, and understand.

HOW THEY BROUGHT THE GOOD NEWS FROM GHENT TO AIX

Robert Browning

I sprang to the stirrup, and Joris, and he;
I galloped, Dirck galloped, we galloped all three;
"Good speed!" cried the watch as the gate-bolts undrew,
"Speed!" echoed the wall to us galloping through;
Behind shut the postern, the lights sank to rest,
And into the midnight we galloped abreast.

Not a word to each other; we kept the great pace
Neck by neck, stride by stride, never changing our place;
I turned in my saddle and made its girths tight,
Then shortened each stirrup, and set the pique right,
Rebuckled the cheek-strap, chained slacker the bit,
Nor galloped less steadily Roland a whit.

'Twas moonset at starting; but while we drew near
Lokeren, the cocks crew and twilight dawned clear;
At Boom, a great yellow star came out to see;
At Düffeld, 'twas morning as plain as could be;
And from Mecheln church-steeple we heard the half-chime,
So Joris broke silence with, "Yet there is time!"

At Aershot, up leaped of a sudden the sun,
And against him the cattle stood black every one,
To stare through the mist at us galloping past,
And I saw my stout galloper Roland at last,
With resolute shoulders, each butting away
The haze, as some bluff river headland its spray:

And his low head and crest, just one sharp ear bent back
For my voice, and the other pricked out on his track;
And one eye's black intelligence,—ever that glance
O'er its white edge at me, his own master, askance!
And the thick heavy spume-flakes, which aye and anon
His fierce lips shook upwards in galloping on.

By Hasselt, Dirck groaned; and cried Joris, "Stay spur!
Your Roos galloped bravely, the fault's not in her,
We'll remember at Aix"—for one heard the quick wheeze
Of her chest, saw the stretched neck and staggering knees,
And sunk tail, and horrible heave of the flank,
As down on her haunches she shuddered and sank.

So, we were left galloping, Joris and I,
Past Looz and past Tongres, no cloud in the sky;
The broad sun above laughed a pitiless laugh,
'Neath our feet broke the brittle bright stubble like chaff;
Till over by Dalhem a dome-spire sprang white,
And "Gallop," gasped Joris, "for Aix is in sight!"

"How they'll greet us!"—and all in a moment his roan
Rolled neck and croup over, lay dead as a stone;
And there was my Roland to bear the whole weight
Of the news which alone could save Aix from her fate,
With his nostrils like pits full of blood to the brim,
And with circles of red for his eye-sockets' rim.

Then I cast loose my buffcoat, each holster let fall,
Shook off both my jack-boots, let go belt and all,
Stood up in the stirrup, leaned, patted his ear,
Called my Roland his pet-name, my horse without peer;
Clapped my hands, laughed and sang, any noise, bad or good,
Till at length into Aix Roland galloped and stood.

And all I remember is—friends flocking round
As I sat with his head 'twixt my knees on the ground;
And no voice but was praising this Roland of mine,
As I poured down his throat our last measure of wine,
Which (the burgesses voted by common consent)
Was no more than his due who brought good news from Ghent.

UP AT A VILLA—DOWN IN THE CITY

(As distinguished by an Italian person of quality)

Robert Browning

Had I but plenty of money, money enough and to spare,
The house for me, no doubt, were a house in the city-square.
Ah, such a life, such a life, as one leads at the window there!

Something to see, by Bacchus, something to hear, at least!
There, the whole day long, one's life is a perfect feast;
While up at a villa one lives, I maintain it, no more than a beast.

Well now, look at our villa! stuck like the horn of a bull
Just on a mountain's edge as bare as the creature's skull,
Save a mere shag of a bush with hardly a leaf to pull!
—I scratch my own, sometimes, to see if the hair's turned wool.

But the city, oh the city—the square with the houses!   Why?
They are stone-faced, white as a curd, there's something to take the
     eye!
Houses in four straight lines, not a single front awry!
You watch who crosses and gossips, who saunters, who hurries by:
Green blinds, as a matter of course, to draw when the sun gets high;
And the shops with fanciful signs which are painted properly.

What of a villa?   Though winter be over in March by rights,
'Tis May perhaps ere the snow shall have withered well off the
     heights:
You've the brown ploughed land before, where the oxen steam and
     wheeze,
And the hills over-smoked behind by the faint gray olive trees.

Is it better in May, I ask you?   You've summer all at once;
In a day he leaps complete with a few strong April suns.
'Mid the sharp short emerald wheat, scarce risen three fingers well,
The wild tulip, at end of its tube, blows out its great red bell
Like a thin clear bubble of blood, for the children to pick and sell.

Is it ever hot in the square?   There's a fountain to spout and splash!
In the shade it sings and springs; in the shine such foam-bows flash
On the horses with curling fish-tails, that prance and paddle and
     pash
Round the lady atop in her conch—fifty gazers do not abash,
Tho' all that she wears is some weeds round her waist in a sort of
     sash.

All the year long at the villa, nothing to see though you linger,
Except yon cypress that points like death's lean lifted forefinger.
Some think fireflies pretty, when they mix i' the corn and mingle,
Or thrid the stinking hemp till the stalks of it seem a-tingle.
Late August or early September, the stunning cicala is shrill,
And the bees keep their tiresome whine round the resinous firs on
     the hill.
Enough of the seasons,—I spare you the months of the fever and chill.

Ere you open your eyes in the city, the blessed church-bells begin:
No sooner the bells leave off, than the diligence rattles in;
You get the pick of the news, and it costs you never a pin.
By and by there's the travelling doctor gives pills, lets blood, draws
     teeth;
Or the Pulcinello-trumpet breaks up the market beneath.

At the post-office such a scene-picture—the new play piping hot!
And a notice how, only this morning, three liberal thieves were shot.
Above it, behold the archbishop's most fatherly of rebukes,
And beneath, with his crown and his lion, some little new law of the
    Duke's!
Or a sonnet with flowery marge, to the Reverend Don So-and-so
Who is Dante, Boccaccio, Petrarca, St. Jerome, and Cicero,
"And moreover," (the sonnet goes rhyming), "the skirts of St. Paul
    has reached,
Having preached us those six Lent-lectures more unctuous than ever
    he preached."
Noon strikes,—here sweeps the procession! our lady borne smiling
    and smart
With a pink gauze gown all spangles, and seven swords stuck in her
    heart!
Bang—whang—whang, goes the drum, *tootle-te-tootle* the fife;
No keeping one's haunches still: it's the greatest pleasure in life.

But bless you, it's dear—it's dear! fowls, wine, at double the rate.
They have clapped a new tax upon salt, and what oil pays passing
    the gate
It's a horror to think of.   And so, the villa for me, not the city!
Beggars can scarcely be choosers: but still—ah, the pity, the pity!
Look, two and two go the priests, then the monks with cowls and
    sandals,
And the penitents dressed in white skirts, a-holding the yellow
    candles.
One, he carries a flag up straight, and another a cross with handles,
And the Duke's guard brings up the rear, for the better prevention
    of scandals.
Bang—whang—whang, goes the drum, *tootle-te-tootle* the fife.
Oh, a day in the city-square, there is no such pleasure in life!

THE BISHOP ORDERS HIS TOMB AT
SAINT PRAXED'S CHURCH

ROME, 15—

Robert Browning

Vanity, saith the preacher, vanity!
Draw round my bed: is Anselm keeping back?
Nephews—sons mine . . . ah God, I know not!   Well—
She, men would have to be your mother once,
Old Gandolf envied me, so fair she was!
What's done is done, and she is dead beside,
Dead long ago, and I am Bishop since,

And as she died so must we die ourselves,
And thence ye may perceive the world's a dream.
Life, how and what is it? As here I lie
In this state-chamber, dying by degrees,
Hours and long hours in the dead night, I ask
"Do I live, am I dead?" Peace, peace seems all.
Saint Praxed's ever was the church for peace;
And so, about this tomb of mine. I fought
With tooth and nail to save my niche, ye know:
—Old Gandolf cozened me, despite my care;
Shrewd was that snatch from out the corner South
He graced his carrion with, God curse the same!
Yet still my niche is not so cramped but thence
One sees the pulpit o' the epistle-side,
And somewhat of the choir, those silent seats,
And up into the aëry dome where live
The angels, and a sunbeam's sure to lurk:
And I shall fill my slab of basalt there,
And 'neath my tabernacle take my rest,
With those nine columns round me, two and two,
The odd one at my feet where Anselm stands:
Peach-blossom marble all, the rare, the ripe
As fresh-poured red wine of a mighty pulse.
—Old Gandolf with his paltry onion-stone,
Put me where I may look at him! True peach,
Rosy and flawless: how I earned the prize!
Draw close: that conflagration of my church
—What then? So much was saved if aught were missed!
My sons, ye would not be my death? Go dig
The white-grape vineyard where the oil-press stood,
Drop water gently till the surface sink,
And if ye find . . . Ah God, I know not, I! . . .
Bedded in store of rotten fig-leaves soft,
And corded up in a tight olive-frail,
Some lump, ah God, of *lapis lazuli,*
Big as a Jew's head cut off at the nape,
Blue as a vein o'er the Madonna's breast . . .
Sons, all have I bequeathed you, villas, all,
That brave Frascati villa with its bath,
So, let the blue lump poise between my knees,
Like God the Father's globe on both his hands
Ye worship in the Jesu Church so gay,
For Gandolf shall not choose but see and burst!
Swift as a weaver's shuttle fleet our years:
Man goeth to the grave, and where is he?
Did I say basalt for my slab, sons? Black—
'Twas ever antique-black I meant! How else

Shall ye contrast my frieze to come beneath?
The bas-relief in bronze ye promised me,
Those Pans and Nymphs ye wot of, and perchance
Some tripod, thyrsus, with a vase or so,
The Saviour at his sermon on the mount,
Saint Praxed in a glory, and one Pan
Ready to twitch the Nymph's last garment off,
And Moses with the tables . . . but I know
Ye mark me not! What do they whisper thee,
Child of my bowels, Anselm? Ah, ye hope
To revel down my villas while I gasp
Bricked o'er with beggar's mouldy travertine
Which Gandolf from his tomb-top chuckles at!
Nay, boys, ye love me—all of jasper, then!
'Tis jasper ye stand pledged to, lest I grieve
My bath must needs be left behind, alas!
One block, pure green as a pistachio-nut,
There's plenty jasper somewhere in the world—
And have I not Saint Praxed's ear to pray
Horses for ye, and brown Greek manuscripts,
And mistresses with great smooth marbly limbs?
—That's if ye carve my epitaph aright,
Choice Latin, picked phrase, Tully's every word,
No gaudy ware like Gandolf's second line—
Tully, my masters? Ulpian serves his need!
And then how I shall lie through centuries,
And hear the blessed mutter of the mass,
And see God made and eaten all day long,
And feel the steady candle-flame, and taste
Good strong, thick, stupefying incense-smoke!
For as I lie here, hours of the dead night,
Dying in state and by such slow degrees,
I fold my arms as if they clasped a crook,
And stretch my feet forth straight as stone can point.
And let the bedclothes, for a mortcloth, drop
Into great laps and folds of sculptor's-work:
And as yon tapers dwindle, and strange thoughts
Grow, with a certain humming in my ears,
About the life before I lived this life,
And this life, too, popes, cardinals and priests,
Saint Praxed at his sermon on the mount,
Your tall pale mother with her talking eyes,
And new-found agate urns as fresh as day,
And marble's language, Latin pure, discreet,
—Aha, ELUCESCEBAT quoth our friend?
No Tully, said I, Ulpian at the best!
Evil and brief hath been my pilgrimage.

All *lapis*, all, sons! Else I give the Pope
My villas! Will ye ever eat my heart?
Ever your eyes were as a lizard's quick,
They glitter like your mother's for my soul,
Or ye would heighten my impoverished frieze,
Piece out its starved design, and fill my vase
With grapes, and add a visor and a Term,
And to the tripod ye would tie a lynx
That in his struggle throws the thyrsus down,
To comfort me on my entablature
Whereon I am to lie till I must ask
"Do I live, am I dead?" There, leave me, there!
For ye have stabbed me with ingratitude
To death—ye wish it—God, ye wish it! Stone—
Gritstone, a-crumble! Clammy squares which sweat
As if the corpse they keep were oozing through—
And no more *lapis* to delight the world!
Well, go! I bless ye. Fewer tapers there,
But in a row: and, going, turn your backs
—Ay, like departing altar-ministrants,
And leave me in my church, the church for peace,
That I may watch at leisure if he leers—
Old Gandolf—at me, from his onion-stone,
As still he envied me, so fair she was!

YOUTH AND ART

Robert Browning

It once might have been, once only:
  We lodged in a street together,
You, a sparrow on the housetop lonely,
  I, a lone she-bird of his feather.

Your trade was with sticks and clay,
  You thumbed, thrust, patted, and polished,
Then laughed "They will see some day,
  Smith made, and Gibson demolished."

My business was song, song, song;
  I chirped, cheeped, trilled, and twittered,
"Kate Brown's on the boards ere long,
  And Grisi's existence embittered!"

I earned no more by a warble
  Than you by a sketch in plaster;
You wanted a piece of marble,
  I needed a music-master.

We studied hard in our styles,
  Chipped each at a crust like Hindoos,
For air, looked out on the tiles,
  For fun, watched each other's windows.

You lounged, like a boy of the South,
  Cap and blouse—nay, a bit of beard too;
Or you got it, rubbing your mouth
  With fingers the clay adhered to.

And I—soon managed to find
  Weak points in the flower-fence facing,
Was forced to put up a blind
  And be safe in my corset-lacing.

No harm! It was not my fault
  If you never turned your eye's tail up
As I shook upon E *in alt.*,
  Or ran the chromatic scale up;

For spring bade the sparrows pair,
  And the boys and girls gave guesses,
And stalls in our street looked rare
  With bulrush and watercresses.

Why did not you pinch a flower
  In a pellet of clay and fling it?
Why did not I put a power
  Of thanks in a look, or sing it?

I did look, sharp as a lynx
  (And yet the memory rankles)
When models arrived, some minx
  Tripped up stairs, she and her ankles.

But I think I gave you as good!
  "That foreign fellow—who can know
How she pays, in a playful mood,
  For his tuning her that piano?"

Could you say so, and never say
  "Suppose we join hands and fortunes,
And I fetch her from over the way,
  Her, piano, and long tunes and short tunes?"

No, no; you would not be rash,
  Nor I rasher and something over:
You've to settle yet Gibson's hash,
  And Grisi yet lives in clover.

But you meet the Prince at the Board,
   I'm queen myself at *bals-paré*,
I've married a rich old lord,
   And you're dubbed knight and an R.A.

Each life's unfulfilled, you see;
   It hangs still, patchy and scrappy:
We have not sighed deep, laughed free,
   Starved, feasted, despaired,—been happy.

And nobody calls you a dunce,
   And people suppose me clever;
This could but have happened once,
   And we missed it, lost it forever.

A TALE

(*Epilogue to* The Two Poets of Croisic)

Robert Browning

What a pretty tale you told me
   Once upon a time
—Said you found it somewhere (scold me!)
   Was it prose or was it rhyme,
Greek or Latin? Greek, you said,
While your shoulder propped my head.

Anyhow there's no forgetting
   This much if no more,
That a poet (pray, no petting!)
   Yes, a bard, sir, famed of yore,
Went where suchlike used to go,
Singing for a prize, you know.

Well, he had to sing, not merely
   Sing but play the lyre;
Playing was important clearly
   Quite as singing: I desire,
Sir, you keep the fact in mind
For a purpose that's behind.

There stood he, while deep attention
   Held the judges round,
—Judges able, I should mention,
   To detect the slightest sound
Sung or played amiss: such ears
Had old judges, it appears!

None the less he sang out boldly,
    Played in time and tune,
Till the judges, weighing coldly
    Each note's worth, seemed, late or soon,
Sure to smile "In vain one tries
Picking faults out: take the prize!"

When, a mischief! Were they seven
    Strings the lyre possessed?
Oh, and afterwards eleven,
    Thank you! Well, sir—who had guessed
Such ill luck in store?—it happed
One of those same seven strings snapped.

All was lost, then! No! a cricket
    (What "cicada"? Pooh!)
—Some mad thing that left its thicket
    For mere love of music—flew
With its little heart on fire,
Lighted on the crippled lyre.

So that when (Ah joy!) our singer
    For his truant string
Feels with disconcerted finger,
    What does cricket else but fling
Fiery heart forth, sound the note
Wanted by the throbbing throat?

Ay and, ever to the ending,
    Cricket chirps at need,
Executes the hand's intending,
    Promptly, perfectly,—indeed
Saves the singer from defeat
With her chirrup low and sweet.

Till, at ending, all the judges
    Cry with one assent
"Take the prize—a prise who grudges
    Such a voice and instrument?
Why, we took your lyre for harp,
So it shrilled us forth F sharp!"

Did the conqueror spurn the creature,
    Once its service done?
That's no such uncommon feature
    In the case when Music's son
Finds his Lotte's power too spent
For aiding soul-development.

No! This other, on returning
   Homeward, prize in hand,
Satisfied his bosom's yearning:
   (Sir, I hope you understand!)
—Said "Some record there must be
Of this cricket's help to me!"

So, he made himself a statue:
   Marble stood, life-size;
'On the lyre, he pointed at you,
   Perched his partner in the prize;
Never more apart you found
Her, he throned, from him, she crowned.

That's the tale: its application?
   Somebody I know
Hopes one day for reputation
   Thro' his poetry that's—Oh,
All so learned and so wise
And deserving of a prize!

If he gains one, will some ticket
   When his statue's built,
Tell the gazer " 'Twas a cricket
   Helped my crippled lyre, whose lilt
Sweet and low, when strength usurped
Softness' place i' the scale, she chirped?

"For as victory was nighest,
   While I sang and played,—
With my lyre at lowest, highest,
   Right alike,—one string that made
'Love' sound soft was snapt in twain
Never to be heard again,—

"Had not a kind cricket fluttered,
   Perched upon the place
Vacant left, and duly uttered
   'Love, Love, Love,' whene'er the bass
Asked the treble to atone
For its somewhat sombre drone."

But you don't know music! Wherefore
   Keep on casting pearls
To a—poet? All I care for
   Is—to tell him that a girl's
"Love" comes aptly in when gruff
Grows his singing. (There, enough!)

SOLILOQUY OF THE SPANISH CLOISTER

Robert Browning

Gr-r-r—there go, my heart's abhorrence!
  Water your damned flower-pots, do!
If hate killed men, Brother Lawrence,
  God's blood, would not mine kill you!
What? your myrtle-bush wants trimming?
  Oh, that rose has prior claims—
Needs its leaden vase filled brimming?
  Hell dry you up with its flames!

At the meal we sit together:
  Salve tibi! I must hear
Wise talk of the kind of weather,
  Sort of season, time of year:
Not a plenteous cork-crop: scarcely
  Dare we hope oak-galls, I doubt:
What's the Latin name for "parsley"?
  What's the Greek name for Swine's Snout?

Whew! We'll have our platter burnished,
  Laid with care on our own shelf!
With a fire-new spoon we're furnished,
  And a goblet for ourself,
Rinsed like something sacrificial
  Ere 't is fit to touch our chaps—
Marked with L for our initial!
  (He-he! There his lily snaps!)

Saint, forsooth! While brown Dolores
  Squats outside the Convent bank
With Sanchicha, telling stories,
  Steeping tresses in the tank,
Blue-black, lustrous, thick like horsehairs,
  —Can't I see his dead eye glow,
Bright as 't were a Barbary corsair's?
  (That is, if he'd let it show!)

When he finishes refection,
  Knife and fork he never lays
Cross-wise, to my recollection,
  As do I, in Jesu's praise.
I the Trinity illustrate,
  Drinking watered orange-pulp—
In three sips the Arian frustrate;
  While he drains his at one gulp.

Oh, those melons? If he's able
  We're to have a feast: so nice!
One goes to the Abbot's table,
  All of us get each a slice.
How go on your flowers? None double?
  Not one fruit-sort can you spy?
Strange!—And I, too, at such trouble
  Keep them close-nipped on the sly!

There's a great text in Galatians,
  Once you trip on it, entails
Twenty-nine distinct damnations,
  One sure, if another fails:
If I trip him just a-dying,
  Sure of heaven as sure can be,
Spin him round and send him flying
  Off to hell, a Manichee?

Or, my scrofulous French novel
  On gray paper with blunt type!
Simply glance at it, you grovel
  Hand and foot in Belial's gripe:
If I double down its pages
  At the woeful sixteenth print,
When he gathers his greengages,
  Ope a sieve and slip it in 't?

Or, there's Satan!—one might venture
  Pledge one's soul to him, yet leave
Such a flaw in the indenture
  As he'd miss till, past retrieve,
Blasted lay that rose-acacia
  We're so proud of! *Hy, Zy, Hine* . . .
'St, there's Vespers! *Plena gratia,*
  Ave, Virgo! Gr-r-r—you swine!

THE CHESTNUT CASTS HIS FLAMBEAUX[12]

A. E. Housman

The chestnut casts his flambeaux, and the flowers
  Stream from the hawthorn on the wind away,
The doors clap to, the pane is blind with showers.
  Pass me the can, lad; there's an end of May.

There's one spoilt spring to scant our mortal lot,
  One season ruined of our little store.

[12] From *Last Poems,* by permission of Holt, Rinehart & Winston, Inc.

May will be fine next year as like as not:
　Oh, aye, but then we shall be twenty-four.

We for a certainty are not the first
　Have sat in taverns while the tempest hurled
Their hopeful plans to emptiness, and cursed
　Whatever brute and blackguard made the world.

It is in truth iniquity on high
　To cheat our sentenced souls of aught they crave,
And mar the merriment as you and I
　Fare on our long fool's errand to the grave.

Iniquity it is; but pass the can.
　My lad, no pair of kings our mothers bore;
Our only portion is the estate of man:
　We want the moon, but we shall get no more.

If here today the cloud of thunder lours
　Tomorrow it will hie on far behests;
The flesh will grieve on other bones than ours
　Soon, and the soul will mourn in other breasts.

The troubles of our proud and angry dust
　Are from eternity, and shall not fail.
Bear them we can, and if we can we must.
　Shoulder the sky, my lad, and drink your ale.

THE SONG OF THE UNSUCCESSFUL[13]

Richard Burton

We are the toilers from whom God barred
　The gifts that are good to hold.
We meant full well and we tried full hard,
　And our failures were manifold.

And we are the clan of those whose kin
　Were a millstone dragging them down.
Yea, we had to sweat for our brother's sin,
　And lose the victor's crown.

The seeming-able, who all but scored,
　From their teeming tribe we come:
What was there wrong with us, O Lord,
　That our lives were dark and dumb?

[13] By permission of Lothrop, Lee & Shepard Co.

The men ten-talented, who still
  Strangely missed of the goal,
Of them we are: it seems Thy will
  To harrow some in soul.

We are the sinners, too, whose lust
  Conquered the higher claims,
We sat us prone in the common dust,
  And played at the devil's games.

We are the hard-luck folk, who strove
  Zealously, but in vain;
We lost and lost, while our comrades throve,
  And still we lost again.

We are the doubles of those whose way
  Was festal with fruits and flowers;
Body and brain we were sound as they,
  But the prizes were not ours.

A mighty army our full ranks make,
  We shake the graves as we go;
The sudden stroke and the slow heartbreak,
  They both have brought us low.

And while we are laying life's sword aside,
  Spent and dishonored and sad,
Our epitaph this, when once we have died:
  "The weak lie here, and the bad."

We wonder if this can be really the close,
  Life's fever cooled by death's trance;
And we cry, though it seem to our dearest of foes,
  "God, give us another chance!"

AT THE END OF THE DAY[14]

Richard Hovey

There is no escape by the river,
There is no flight left by the fen;
We are compassed about by the shiver
Of the night of their marching men.
Give a cheer!
For our hearts shall not give way.
Here's to a dark to-morrow
And here's to a brave to-day!

[14] Used by permission of the publishers, Dodd, Mead & Co., Inc.

The tale of their hosts is countless,
And the tale of ours a score;
But the palm is naught to the dauntless,
And the cause is more and more.
Give a cheer!
We may die, but not give way.
Here's to a silent morrow,
And here's to a stout to-day!

God has said: "Ye shall fail and perish;
But the thrill ye have felt to-night
I shall keep in my heart and cherish
When the worlds have passed in night."
Give a cheer!
For the soul shall not give way.
Here's to the greater to-morrow
That is born of a great to-day!

Now shame on the craven truckler
And the puling things that mope!
We've a rapture for our buckler
That outwears the wings of hope.
Give a cheer!
For our joy shall not give way.
Here's in the teeth of to-morrow
To the glory of to-day!

THE WILD RIDE[15]

Louise Imogen Guiney

I hear in my heart, I hear in its ominous pulses,
All day, on the road, the hoofs of invisible horses,
All night, from their stalls, the importunate pawing and neighing.

Let cowards and laggards fall back! But alert to the saddle
Weatherworn and abreast, go men of our galloping legion,
With a stirrup-cup each to the lily of women that loves him.

The trail is through dolor and dread, over crags and morasses;
There are shapes by the way, there are things that appal or entice us;
What odds? We are Knights of the Grail, we are vowed to the riding.

Thought's self is a vanishing wing, and joy is a cobweb,
And friendship a flower in the dust, and glory a sunbeam:
Not here is our prize, nor, alas! after these our pursuing.

---

[15] By permission of Houghton Mifflin Co.

A dipping of plumes, a tear, a shake of the bridle,
A passing salute to this world and her pitiful beauty;
We hurry with never a word in the track of our fathers.

I hear in my heart, I hear in its ominous pulses,
All day, on the road, the hoofs of invisible horses,
All night, from their stalls, the importunate pawing and neighing.

We spur to a land of no name, outracing the storm-wind;
We leap to the infinite dark like sparks from the anvil.
Thou leadest, O God! All's well with Thy troopers that follow.

GENTLEMEN-RANKERS[16]

Rudyard Kipling

To the legion of the lost ones, to the cohort of the damned,
     To my brethren in their sorrow overseas,
Sings a gentleman of England cleanly bred, machinely crammed,
     And a trooper of the Empress, if you please.
Yea, a trooper of the forces who has run his own six horses,
     And faith he went the pace and went it blind,
And the world was more than kin while he held the ready tin,
     But to-day the Sergeant's something less than kind.
         We're poor little lambs who've lost our way,
           Baa! Baa! Baa!
         We're little black sheep who've gone astray,
           Baa—aa—aa!
         Gentlemen-rankers out on the spree,
         Damned from here to Eternity,
         God ha' mercy on such as we,
           Baa! Yah! Bah!

Oh, it's sweet to sweat through stables, sweet to empty kitchen slops,
     And it's sweet to hear the tales the troopers tell,
To dance with blowzy housemaids at the regimental hops
     And thrash the cad who says you waltz too well.
Yes, it makes you cock-a-hoop to be "Rider" to your troop,
     And branded with a blasted worsted spur,
When you envy, O how keenly, one poor Tommy being cleanly
     Who blacks your boots and sometimes calls you "Sir."

If the home we never write to, and the oaths we never keep,
     And all we know most distant and most dear,

---

[16] From *Departmental Ditties and Ballads and Barrack-Room Ballads,* reprinted by permission of Mrs. George Bambridge and Doubleday & Co., Inc.

Across the snoring barrack-room return to break our sleep,
　Can you blame us if we soak ourselves in beer?
When the drunken comrade mutters and the great guard-lantern
　　gutters
　And the horror of our fall is written plain,
Every secret, self-revealing on the aching whitewashed ceiling,
　Do you wonder that we drug ourselves from pain?

We have done with Hope and Honour, we are lost to Love and Truth,
　We are dropping down the ladder rung by rung,
And the measure of our torment is the measure of our youth.
　God help us, for we knew the worst too young!
Our shame is clean repentance for the crime that brought the sen-
　　tence,
　Our pride it is to know no spur of pride,
And the Curse of Reuben holds us till an alien turf enfolds us
　And we die, and none can tell Them where we died.
　　　　We're poor little lambs who've lost our way,
　　　　　Baa! Baa! Baa!
　　　　We're little black sheep who've gone astray,
　　　　　Baa—aa—aa!
　　　　Gentlemen-rankers out on the spree,
　　　　Damned from here to Eternity,
　　　　God ha' mercy on such as we,
　　　　　Baa! Yah! Bah!

"GRANDMITHER, THINK NOT I FORGET"[17]

Willa Sibert Cather

Grandmither, think not I forget, when I come back to town,
An' wander the old ways again, an' tread them up and down.
I never smell the clover bloom, nor see the swallows pass,
Wi'out I mind how good ye were unto a little lass;
I never hear the winter rain a-pelting all night through
Wi'out I think and mind me of how cold it falls on you.
An' if I come not often to your bed beneath the thyme,
Mayhap 'tis that I'd change wi' ye, and gie my bed for thine,
　Would like to sleep in thine.

I never hear the summer winds among the roses blow
Wi'out I wonder why it was ye loved the lassie so.
Ye gave me cakes and lollipops and pretty toys a score—
I never thought I should come back and ask ye now for more.
Grandmither, gie me your still white hands that lie upon your breast,

[17] From *April Twilights* (Boston: Richard G. Badger, 1903).

For mine do beat the dark all night and never find me rest;
They grope among the shadows an' they beat the cold black air,
They go seekin' in the darkness, an' they never find him there,
    They never find him there.

Grandmither, gie me your sightless eyes, that I may never see
His own a-burnin' full o' love that must not shine for me.
Grandmither, gie me your peaceful lips, white as the kirkyard snow,
For mine be tremblin' wi' the wish that he must never know.
Grandmither, gie me your clay-stopped ears, that I may never hear
My lad a-singin' in the night when I am sick wi' fear;
A-singin' when the moonlight over a' the land is white—
Ah, God! I'll up and go to him, a-singin' in the night,
    A-callin' in the night.

Grandmither, gie me your clay-cold heart, that has forgot to ache,
For mine be fire wi'in my breast an' yet it cannot break.
Wi' every beat it's callin' for things that must not be,—
So can ye not let me creep in an' rest awhile by ye?
A little lass afeard o' dark slept by ye years agone—
An' she has found what night can hold 'twixt sunset an' the dawn:
So when I plant the rose an' rue above your grave for ye,
Ye'll know it's under rue an' rose that I would like to be,
    That I would like to be.

GENERAL WILLIAM BOOTH ENTERS INTO HEAVEN[18]

To be sung to the tune of THE BLOOD OF THE LAMB
with indicated instruments.

Vachel Lindsay

Booth led boldly with his big bass drum.
    Are you washed in the blood of the Lamb?
The saints smiled gravely, and they said, "He's come."
    Are you washed in the blood of the Lamb?   *Bass drums*
Walking lepers followed, rank on rank,
Lurching bravos from the ditches dank,
Drabs from the alleyways and drug-fiends pale—
Minds still passion-ridden, soul-powers frail!
Vermin-eaten saints with mouldy breath
Unwashed legions with the ways of death—
    Are you washed in the blood of the Lamb?

Every slum had sent its half-a-score
The round world over—Booth had groaned for more.

[18] From *Collected Poems.* By permission of The Macmillan Co.

Every banner that the wide world flies
Bloomed with glory and transcendent dyes.
Big-voiced lasses made their banjos bang!   *Banjos*
Tranced, fanatical, they shrieked and sang,
    Are you washed in the blood of the Lamb?

Hallelujah! It was queer to see
Bull-necked convicts with that land make free!
Loons with bazoos blowing blare, blare, blare—
On, on, upward through the golden air.
    Are you washed in the blood of the Lamb?

Booth died blind, and still by faith he trod,
Eyes still dazzled by the ways of God.   *Bass drums slower*
Booth led boldly and he looked the chief: *and softer*
Eagle countenance in sharp relief,
Beard a-flying, air of high command
Unabated in that holy land.

Jesus came from out the Court-House door,
Stretched his hands above the passing poor.
Booth saw not, but led his queer ones there   *Flutes*
Round and round the mighty Court-House square.
Yet in an instant all that blear review
Marched on spotless, clad in raiment new.
The lame were straightened, withered limbs uncurled
And blind eyes opened on a new sweet world.

Drabs and vixens in a flash made whole!
Gone was the weasel-head, the snout, the jowl;   *Bass drums louder*
Sages and sibyls now, and athletes clean,   *and faster*
Rulers of empires, and of forests green!
The hosts were sandalled and the wings were fire—
    Are you washed in the blood of the Lamb?

But their noise played havoc with the angel-choir.   *Grand chorus tam-*
    Are you washed in the blood of the Lamb?   *bourines—all instru-*
Oh, shout Salvation! It was good to see   *ments in full blast*
Kings and princes by the Lamb set free.
The banjos rattled and the tambourines
Jing-jing-jingled in the hands of queens!

And when Booth halted by the curb for prayer
He saw his Master through the flag-filled air.
Christ came gently with a robe and crown   *Reverently sung—*
For Booth the soldier while the throng knelt down. *no instruments*
He saw King Jesus—they were face to face,
And he knelt a-weeping in that holy place.
    Are you washed in the blood of the Lamb?

THE RED-HAIRED MAN'S WIFE[19]

James Stephens

I have taken that vow—
   And you were my friend
But yesterday—now
   All that's at an end,
And you are my husband, and claim me, and I must depend.

Yesterday I was free,
   Now you, as I stand
Walk over to me
   And take hold of my hand.
You look at my lips, your eyes are too bold, your smile is too bland.

My old name is lost,
   My distinction of race:
Now the line has been crossed,
   Must I step to your pace?
Must I walk as you list, and obey and smile up in your face?

All the white and the red
   Of my cheeks you have won;
All the hair of my head,
   And my feet, tho' they run,
Are yours, and you own me and end me just as I begun.

Must I bow when you speak,
   Be silent and hear,
Inclining my cheek
   And incredulous ear
To your voice, and command, and behest, hold your lightest wish
     dear?

I am woman, but still
   Am alive, and can feel
Every intimate thrill
   That is woe or is weal.
I, aloof, and divided, apart, standing far, can I kneel?

If not, I shall know,
   I shall surely find out,
And your world will throw
   In disaster and rout;
I am woman and glory and beauty, I mystery, terror, and doubt.

I am separate still,
   I am I and not you:
And my mind and my will,
   As in secret they grew,
Still are secret, unreached and untouched and not subject to you.

BALLAD OF THE GOODLY FERE[20]

Simon Zelotes speaketh it somewhile after the Crucifixion.

Ezra Pound

Ha' we lost the goodliest fere o' all
For the priests and the gallows tree?
Aye lover he was of brawny men,
O' ships and the open sea.

When they came wi' a host to take Our Man
His smile was good to see,
"First let these go!" quo' our Goodly Fere,
"Or I'll see ye damned," says he.

Aye he sent us out through the crossed high spears
And the scorn of his laugh rang free,
"Why took ye not me when I walked about
Alone in the town?" says he.

Oh we drank his "Hale" in the good red wine
When we last made company.
No capon priest was the Goodly Fere,
But a man o' men was he.

I ha' seen him drive a hundred men
Wi' a bundle o' cords swung free,
That they took the high and holy house
For their pawn and treasury.

They'll no' get him a' in a book, I think,
Though they write it cunningly;
No mouse of the scrolls was the Goodly Fere
But aye loved the open sea.

If they think they ha' snared our Goodly Fere
They are fools to the last degree.
"I'll go to the feast," quo' our Goodly Fere,
"Though I go to the gallows tree."

"Ye ha' seen me heal the lame and blind,
And wake the dead," says he.

20 From *Personae* (New York: Liveright Publishing Corp., 1926).

"Ye shall see one thing to master all:
'Tis how a brave man dies on the tree."

A son of God was the Goodly Fere
That bade us his brothers be.
I ha' seen him cow a thousand men.
I have seen him upon the tree.

He cried no cry when they drave the nails
And the blood gushed hot and free.
The hounds of the crimson sky gave tongue,
But never a cry cried he.

I ha' seen him cow a thousand men
On the hills o' Galilee.
They whined as he walked out calm between,
Wi' his eyes like the gray o' the sea.

Like the sea that brooks no voyaging,
With the winds unleashed and free,
Like the sea that he cowed at Genseret
Wi' twey words spoke, suddenly.

A master of men was the Goodly Fere,
A mate of the wind and sea.
If they think they ha' slain our Goodly Fere
They are fools eternally.

I ha' seen him eat o' the honey-comb
Sin' they nailed him to the tree.

THE HOLLOW MEN[21]

Mistah Kurtz—he dead.
A penny for the Old Guy

T. S. Eliot

i

We are the hollow men
We are the stuffed men
Leaning together
Headpiece filled with straw.   Alas!
Our dried voices, when
We whisper together
Are quiet and meaningless
As wind in dry grass

---

[21] From *Collected Poems 1909–1962*, copyright, 1936, by Harcourt, Brace & World, Inc.; copyright, © 1963, 1964, by T. S. Eliot. Reprinted by permission of the publishers.

Or rats' feet over broken glass
In our dry cellar

Shape without form, shade without colour,
Paralysed force, gesture without motion;

Those who have crossed
With direct eyes, to death's other Kingdom
Remember us—if at all—not as lost
Violent souls, but only
As the hollow men
The stuffed men.

ii

Eyes I dare not meet in dreams
In death's dream kingdom
These do not appear:
There, the eyes are
Sunlight on a broken column
There, is a tree swinging
And voices are
In the wind's singing
More distant and more solemn
Than a fading star.

Let me be no nearer
In death's dream kingdom
Let me also wear
Such deliberate disguises
Rat's coat, crowskin, crossed staves
In a field
Behaving as the wind behaves
No nearer—

Not that final meeting
In the twilight kingdom

iii

This is the dead land
This is cactus land
Here the stone images
Are raised, here they receive
The supplication of a dead man's hand
Under the twinkle of a fading star.

Is it like this
In death's other kingdom
Waking alone
At the hour when we are

Trembling with tenderness
Lips that would kiss
Form prayers to broken stone.

iv

The eyes are not here
There are no eyes here
In this valley of dying stars
In this hollow valley
This broken jaw of our lost kingdoms

In this last of meeting places
We grope together
And avoid speech
Gathered on this beach of the tumid river

Sightless, unless
The eyes reappear
As the perpetual star
Multifoliate rose
Of death's twilight kingdom
The hope only
Of empty men.

v

Here we go round the prickly pear
Prickly pear prickly pear
Here we go round the prickly pear
At five o'clock in the morning.

Between the idea
And the reality
Between the motion
And the act
Falls the Shadow

For Thine is the Kingdom

Between the conception
And the creation
Between the emotion
And the response
Falls the Shadow

Life is very long

Between the desire
And the spasm
Between the potency
And the existence

Between the essence
And the descent
Falls the Shadow

For Thine is the Kingdom

For Thine is
Life is
For Thine is the

This is the way the world ends
This is the way the world ends
This is the way the world ends
Not with a bang but a whimper.

SPEECH TO A CROWD[22]

Archibald MacLeish

Tell me, my patient friends—awaiters of messages—
From what other shore: from what stranger:
Whence was the word to come?   Who was to lesson you?

Listeners under a child's crib in a manger—
Listeners once by the oracles: now by the transoms—
Whom are you waiting for?   Who do you think will explain?

Listeners thousands of years and still no answer—
Writers at night to Miss Lonely-Hearts: awkward spellers—
Open your eyes!   There is only earth and the man!

There is only you: there is no one else on the telephone:
No one else is on the air to whisper:
No one else but you will push the bell.

No one knows if you don't: neither ships
Nor landing-fields decode the dark between:
You have your eyes and what your eyes see *is.*

The earth you see is really the earth you are seeing:
The sun is truly excellent: truly warm:
Women are beautiful as you have seen them—

Their breasts (believe it) like cooing of doves in a portico:
They bear at their breasts tenderness softly.   Look at them!
Look at yourselves.   You are strong.   You are well formed.

Look at the world—the world you never took!
It is really true you may live in the world heedlessly:
Why do you wait to read it in a book then?

Write it yourselves!   Write to yourselves if you need to!
Tell yourselves there is sun and the sun will rise:
Tell yourselves the earth has food to feed you:—

Let the dead men say that men must die!
Who better than you can know what death is?
How can a bone or a broken body surmise it?

Let the dead shriek with their whispering breath:
Laugh at them!   Say the murdered gods may wake
But we who work have end of work together:

Tell yourselves the earth is yours to take!

Waiting for messages out of the dark you were poor.
The world was always yours: you will not take it.

BURYING GROUND BY THE TIES[23]

Archibald MacLeish

Ayee! Ai! This is heavy earth on our shoulders:
There were none of us born to be buried in this earth:
Niggers we were Portuguese Magyars Polacks:

We were born to another look of the sky certainly:
Now we lie here in the river pastures:
We lie in the mowings under the thick turf:

We hear the earth and the all-day rasp of the grasshoppers:
It was we laid the steel on this land from ocean to ocean:
It was we (if you know) put the U.P. through the passes

Bringing her down into Laramie full load
Eighteen mile on the granite anticlinal
Forty-three foot to the mile and the grade holding:

It was we did it: hunkies of our kind:
It was we dug the caved-in holes for the cold water:
It was we built the gully spurs and the freight sidings:

Who would do it but we and the Irishmen bossing us?
It was all foreign-born men there were in this country:
It was Scotsmen Englishmen Chinese Squareheads Austrians . . .

Ayee! but there's weight to the earth under it:
Nor for this did we come out—to be lying here
Nameless under the ties in the clay cuts:

---

[23] From *Frescoes for Mr. Rockefeller's City*, by permission of Houghton Mifflin Co.

There's nothing good in the world but the rich will buy it:
Everything sticks to the grease of a gold note—
Even a continent—even a new sky!

Do not pity us much for the strange grass over us:
We laid the steel to the stone stock of these mountains:
The place of our graves is marked by the telegraph poles!

It was not to lie in the bottoms we came out
And the trains going over us here in the dry hollows . . .

LAW LIKE LOVE[24]

W. H. Auden

Law, say the gardeners, is the sun,
Law is the one
All gardeners obey
Tomorrow, yesterday, today.

Law is the wisdom of the old
The impotent grandfathers shrilly scold;
The grandchildren put out a treble tongue,
Law is the senses of the young.

Law, says the priest with a priestly look,
Expounding to an unpriestly people,
Law is the words in my priestly book,
Law is my pulpit and my steeple.

Law, says the judge as he looks down his nose,
Speaking clearly and most severely,
Law is as I've told you before,
Law is as you know I suppose,
Law is but let me explain it once more,
Law is The Law.

Yet law-abiding scholars write;
Law is neither wrong nor right,
Law is only crimes
Punished by places and by times,
Law is the clothes men wear
Anytime, anywhere,
Law is Good-morning and Good-night.

Others say, Law is our Fate;
Others say, Law is our State;

Others say, others say
Law is no more,
Law is gone away.

And always the loud angry crowd
Very angry and very loud
Law is We,
And always the soft idiot softly Me.

If we, dear, know we know no more
Than they about the law,
If I no more than you
Know what we should and should not do
Except that all agree
Gladly or miserably
That the law is
And that all know this,
If therefore thinking it absurd
To identify Law with some other word,
Unlike so many men
I cannot say Law is again,
No more than they can we suppress
The universal wish to guess
Or slip out of our own position
Into an unconcerned condition.

Although I can at least confine
Your vanity and mine
To stating timidly
A timid similarity,
We shall boast anyway:
Like love I say.

Like love we don't know where or why
Like love we can't compel or fly
Like love we often weep
Like love we seldom keep.

STARLIGHT LIKE INTUITION PIERCED THE TWELVE[25]

Delmore Schwartz

Like intuition, starlight pierced the twelve,
The brittle night sky sparkled like a tune
Tapped and tinkled upon the xylophone:
Empty and vain, a glittering dune, the moon
Arose too big, and, in the mood which ruled,

[25] By permission of the author.

Looked like a useless beauty in a pit:
And then one said, after he carefully spat:
"No matter what we do, he looks at it!"

"I cannot see a child or find a girl
Beyond his smile which glows like that spring moon."
"—Nothing no more the same," the second said,
"Though all may be forgiven, never quite healed
The wound I bear as witness, standing by;
No ceremony surely appropriate,
Nor secret love, escape or sleep because
No matter what I do, he looks at it—"

"Now," said the third, "no thing will be the same:
I am as one who never shuts his eyes,
The sea and sky no more are marvellous,
And I no longer understand surprise!"
"Now," said the fourth, "nothing will be enough,
—I heard his word accomplishing all wit:
No word can be unsaid, no deed withdrawn;
No matter what is said, he measures it!"

"Vision, imagination, hope, or dream
Believed, denied, the scene we wished to see?
It does not matter in the least: for what
Is altered if it is not true?   That we
Saw goodness as it is—*this* is the awe
And the abyss which we will not forget,
His story now the skull which holds all thought:
No matter what I think, I think of it!"

"And I will never be what once I was,"
Said one for long as single as a knife,
"And we will never be as once we were;
We have died once, this is a second life."
"My mind is spilled in moral chaos," one
Righteous as Job exclaimed, "now infinite
Suspicion of my heart rots what I will,
—No matter what I choose, he stares at it!"

"I am as one native in summer places,
—Ten weeks' excitement paid for by the rich;
Debauched by that, and then all winter bored,"
The sixth declared, "his peak left us a ditch."
"He came to make this life more difficult,"
The seventh said, "No one will ever fit
His measures' heights, all is inadequate:
No matter what we have, what good is it?"

"He gave forgiveness to us: what a gift!"
The eighth chimed in. "But now we know *how much*
Must be forgiven. But if forgiven, what?
The crime which was will be, and the least touch
Revives the memory: what is forgiveness worth?"
The ninth spoke thus: "Who now will ever sit
At ease in Zion at the Easter feast?
No matter what the place he touches it!"

"And I will always stammer, since he spoke,"
One who had been most eloquent said, stammering.
"I looked too long at the sun: like too much light,
Too much of goodness is a boomerang,"
Laughed the eleventh of the troop. "I must
Try what he tried: I saw the infinite
Who walked the lake and raised the hopeless dead:
No matter what the feat, he has accomplished it!"

So spoke the twelfth; and then the twelve in chorus:
"Unspeakable unnatural goodness is
Risen and shines and never will ignore us;
He glows forever in all consciousness;
Forgiveness, love, and hope possess the pit
And bring our endless guilt, like shadow's bars:
No matter what we do, he stares at it!
What pity then deny? what debt defer?
We know he looks at us like all the stars,
And we shall never be what once we were,
This life will never be what once it was!"

STILL, CITIZEN SPARROW[26]

Richard Wilbur

Still, citizen sparrow, this vulture which you call
Unnatural, let him but lumber again to air
Over the rotten office, let him bear
The carrion ballast up, and at the tall

Tip of the sky lie cruising. Then you'll see
That no more beautiful bird is in heaven's height,
No wider more placid wings, no watchfuller flight;
He shoulders nature there, the frightfully free,

The naked-headed one. Pardon him, you
Who dart in the orchard aisles, for it is he

[26] From *Ceremony and Other Poems*, copyright, 1950, by Richard Wilbur. Reprinted by permission of Harcourt, Brace & World, Inc.

Devours death, mocks mutability,
Has heart to make an end, keeps nature new.

Thinking of Noah, childheart, try to forget
How for so many bedlam hours his saw
Soured the song of birds with its wheezy gnaw,
And the slam of his hammer all the day beset

The people's ears. Forget that he could bear
To see the towns like coral under the keel,
And the fields so dismal deep. Try rather to feel
How high and weary it was, on the waters where

He rocked his only world, and everyone's.
Forgive the hero, you who would have died
Gladly with all you knew; he rode that tide
To Ararat; all men are Noah's sons.

11

PROSE RHYTHM

No civilized age could be more indifferent than ours to the harmonies of beautiful prose, the highly wrought, carefully polished, figurative style cultivated by many writers of earlier centuries. Style has followed the arts in their aversion to ornament and indifference to beauty. Conspicuously plain are the slabs of glass and aluminum that cover our high office buildings, and no modern painter or sculptor would think of decorating his work with cupids, scrolls, cinque-foils, or acanthus leaves. We create no windows, high and triple arched,

> All garlanded with carven imag'ries
> Of fruits, and flowers, and bunches of knot-grass.

Nor do we compose descriptions of them so lush and beautiful as Keats's. (See page 266.) "No fine writing, please," admonishes *The New Yorker,* and many modern writers cultivate the simple lucidity of that well-written magazine, while others take for their model the haphazard, undisciplined, stream-of-consciousness style affected by James Joyce. Since most modern writing makes its appeal to the eye, rather than the ear, the harmonies of beautiful sounds are neglected, both in prose and in poetry.

Have we gained or lost by this aversion to ornate style? Fashions change, and the new quickly becomes the old—and trite. Perhaps in time we may tire of the styles of modern literature and turn again to the traditional interest in beautiful writing. Whether we do or not, the tradition is there, with its many opportunities for the oral interpreter, and we ought to know something about it, particularly as it flourished in prose composition.

The Harmonies of Prose

The form of poetry has sometimes been thought the chief element in its beauty, and the distinguishing characteristic which separates it from prose. But acquaintance with the history of English prose makes it evident that prose has harmonies as glorious as those of verse and, many feel, a good deal finer, because more various and more subtle. Indeed their very subtlety as compared with the rhythms of verse has been a fruitful source of controversy, and a less fruitful source of research. Prose harmonies have been analyzed by scholars, critics, and literati, and even by psychologists and physicists, in an attempt to ferret out their mystery, and trace their development.

Highly ornamented prose (Amy Lowell called it "polyphonic"—many sounding) is supposed to have been originated by the Greek rhetorician Isocrates, and to have been further developed by the Roman orator Cicero, whose style was taken as a model by the Latin writers of the Middle Ages, and remained for ten centuries the dominant influence on the style of civilized Europe. Indelibly stamped upon the literature of the Roman Church, it passed into modern English by means of the King James Bible and the Book of Common Prayer, and thence has affected all our great prose writers from Milton and Taylor and Browne down to the present.

Let us not assume that harmonious, or "polyphonic," prose is necessarily the best prose. Like poetry (or automobiles, or houses, or apples) prose is best when it best fulfills its function, and it is not always the function of prose to be beautiful. Often it has hard work to do—it is the medium of logic, of reasoned argument, of criticism and analysis, or of irony, satire, humor, and fantasy. It may achieve distinction in any of these manners. The kind of writing we are concerned with at present is primarily "literary" prose, the kind which in all times and in all languages spoken by civilized peoples has been admired by literary critics, the kind which pleases the aesthetic sense of the well trained and judicious reader, and which, like poetry, is beautiful in and of itself, almost regardless of what it may say. In our language, as I have already suggested, it has generally the sonorous harmonies of the English Bible and the Book of Common Prayer. Let us see if we can discover wherein its beauties lie, and so attune our ears to their appreciation.

WHEREIN LIES THE CHARM OF BEAUTIFUL PROSE? Let us take the passage from De Quincey whose charm for Professor Saintsbury not even fifty years of familiarity with its text could lessen, and which he considers a magazine of the secrets of prose rhythm.[1]

And her eyes,/ if they were e/ver seen,/ would be nei/ther

sweet/ nor subtle;/ no man/ could read/ their story;/

they would be found/filled/ with perishing/ dreams,/

and with wrecks/ of forgotten/ delirium.

[1] George Saintsbury, *A History of English Prose Rhythm* (London: The Macmillan Co., 1922), p. 308.

This is Professor Saintsbury's scansion, and it seems, as Quiller-Couch says,[2] to please no one but the author, and, we might add, to be intelligible to no one but the author. Of the beauty of the passage there can be no doubt. Let us put aside for the moment the question of scansion, and see if there are not other elements present which may help to account for its charm.

Professor Saintsbury points out that there are beautiful letters and beautiful syllables, and that though the vocabulary is quite ordinary, "the vowel music, assisted and qualified by the consonants and the word lengths, is unerring." He might have mentioned also the alliteration in "sweet nor subtle" and "found filled," and the abundance of liquid as compared with stopt consonants. In his analysis of other passages he refers to vowel music, contrast, balance, apt epithets, adaptation of sound to sense, etc. That these devices do serve to give distinction and harmony to language is readily apparent. Any device that may be included in what we call loosely "poetic diction," when employed, as such devices often are, in prose, seems to lift the writing into a higher realm approaching poetry. Note the following passages, all taken from oratory:

The next gale that sweeps from the north will bring to our ears the clash of resounding arms.

Bending his face to catch the words that tremble on the stricken lips.

Let their last feeble and lingering glance rather behold the gorgeous ensign of the republic . . . its arms and trophies streaming in their original lustre.

"Sublimity" is the term used by an ancient Greek writer[3] to describe such an elevated style. For sublimity of style he found five principal sources: grandeur of thought, vigorous and spirited treatment of the passions, a certain artifice in the employment of figures, dignified expression, and majesty and elevation of structure. To Longinus (?) sublimity was a quality of both prose and poetry, and we also will recognize these, and the other devices mentioned above, as characteristic of poetry as well as of prose. Most of them we have examined in previous chapters. The question arises then as to the difference between poetry and this "polyphonic" or "sublime" prose, and this brings us again to the problem of rhythm.

The Nature of Prose Rhythm

Most critics hold that prose has its own peculiar rhythm which, many feel, is distinct from the rhythm of poetry. Aristotle, for instance, said, "Metrical prose has an artificial air and distracts the attention. . . . Prose must therefore have rhythm but not meter, for then it will be poetry."[4]

---

[2] Sir Arthur Quiller-Couch, *On the Art of Writing* (New York: G. P. Putnam's Sons, Inc., 1919), p. 152.

[3] Supposed to have been Longinus.

[4] Aristotle *Rhetoric* iii. 8.

Cicero thought it worthy of remark "that if a verse is formed by the composition of words in prose it is a fault."[5]   Quintilian said, "Prose will not stoop to be measured by taps of the finger. . . . We must avoid what is metrical. . . . Versification produces weariness and satiety."[6]   Robert Louis Stevenson said:

> Each phrase of each sentence, like an air or a recitative in music, should be so artfully compounded out of long and short, out of accented and unaccented, as to gratify the sensual ear. And of this the ear is the sole judge. It is impossible to lay down laws. Even in our accentual and rhythmic language no analysis can find the secret of the beauty of a verse; how much less, then, of those phrases, such as prose is built of, which obey no law but to be lawless and yet to please?[7]

And Professor Saintsbury believes that "the great principle of foot arrangement in prose, and of Prose Rhythm, is *Variety*."[8]

Such opinion is entitled to the highest respect. It would be easy to conclude that harmonious prose is merely poetry without meter, did not all these writers, and a host of others, insist that prose has rhythm. Most of them assume that the rhythm of prose, like that of poetry, lies in some combination of light and heavy syllables. Professor Saintsbury, for instance, groups syllables into twenty-nine varieties of feet, but his arrangement is purely arbitrary, and has no law but his own caprice, as the sample quoted above will indicate. Some writers have counted the number of accents per phrase, but this device seems to yield no helpful results. Others have abandoned the attempt to discover rhythm in the arrangement of heavy and light syllables, and have attempted to find it elsewhere. One discovers a more or less subconscious throbbing underneath the flow of syllables. Another feels in each sentence a rushing, surging, gliding movement which, starting at some minimum of force, rapidity, pitch, or suspense, rises to a climax in one or all of these particulars, and then falls away again.

The trouble with all of these explanations is that they seldom satisfy anyone but their inventors. If we are to find any pleasure in prose rhythm which we can communicate to others we must have a more exact definition of it.

Some writers agree with Stevenson that prose phrases obey no law but to be lawless, and yet to please. Sir Arthur Quiller-Couch, for instance, says the rhythms of prose are so lax and various that he doubts if any explanation of them is possible. After reading Saintsbury's *History of Prose*

---

[5] Cicero *De oratore* iii. 44.

[6] Quintilian, *Institutio oratoria* IX. iv, 55, 77, 143.

[7] Robert Louis Stevenson, "On Some Technical Elements of Style in Literature," in Lane Cooper (ed.), *Theories of Style* (New York: The Macmillan Co., 1912), pp. 373–74.

[8] *Op. cit.*, p. 478.

Rhythm he still doubts. "What madman," he exclaims, "will say, 'Thus, or thus far shalt thou go' to a prose thus invented and thus with its free rhythms, after three hundred years working on the imagination of Englishmen? Or who shall determine its range, whether of thought or of music?"[9]

Several "madmen," however, have pointed out, if not how far it should go, at least how far it has gone in the direction of meter. An industrious German scholar[10] took the pains to analyze the clause endings in Cicero's orations, 17,000 of them (in Latin, of course), and found that in ninety-two per cent of them there was a definite metrical pattern, probably more or less consciously present in the orator's mind. Another German scholar[11] found from a careful study of English prose that it frequently contained iambic and dactylic periods alternating with nonrhythmical periods. A British investigator[12] suggests that Cicero and Quintilian probably failed to understand the principles by which their own utterances were governed, and states that the essence of rhythm, both in prose and poetry, is regularity of beat. Another[13] concludes that "a little investigation will prove that a great deal of prose is written in short stretches of meter."

But let us leave the investigators and critics and see what we can discover for ourselves. First, look at the following passages:

> And hence no force, however great,
>   Can draw a cord, however fine,
>   Into a horizontal line
> That shall be absolutely straight.

> Fondly do we hope,
>   Fervently do we pray,
> That this mighty scourge of war
>   May speedily pass away.

> Then ensued a scene of woe
>   The like of which no eye had seen,
> No heart conceived, and which no tongue
>   Can adequately tell.

>   Not that we
> Who drink thereof shall not grow old. We would
> Not have it so. But there is an ever
> Rushing, ever growing stream of youth

---

[9] Sir Arthur Quiller-Couch, *On the Art of Writing* (New York: G. P. Putnam's Sons, Inc., 1916), p. 66.

[10] T. Zielinski, *Das Clauselgesetz in Ciceros Reden* (Leipzig: 1904).

[11] P. Fijn Dratt, *Rhythm in English Prose* (Heidelberg: 1910).

[12] A. C. Clark, *Prose Rhythm in English* (Fair Lawn, N.J.: Oxford University Press, 1913).

[13] D. S. MacColl, *Essays and Studies of the English Association*, V. (1914).

That in these halls comes upward to the light.
It never ceases. Always
Bright with youthful hope it flows away
To gladden and enrich our commonwealth.

These "verses" will readily be classified as poetry, but not one of them was written as poetry, or even as verse. They are all taken from prose. The first, a true freak, occurred quite by accident in a work of science. The second you will recognize as coming from Lincoln's Second Inaugural. The other two are from public speeches, the one by Edmund Burke, the other by Abbot Lawrence Lowell.

These are extreme cases, but they demonstrate that verses do occur in prose. Perhaps they go even further and demonstrate that the formation of a verse in prose is obtrusive and unpleasing. We can agree with Aristotle that such metrical prose has an artificial air and distracts the attention. But we need not conclude therefore that meter is always objectionable in prose. We shall find it even in those passages that critics agree are the finest in our language. Let us look again at Saintsbury's prize passage:

And her eyes, if they were ever seen, would be neither sweet nor subtle; no man could read their story; they would be found filled with perishing dreams, and with wrecks of forgotten delirium.

Here, it is true, "there is not so much as a blank verse," but there is meter.

her eyes/ if they/ were ev/ er seen

would pass as acceptable iambic tetrameter;

would be nei/ ther sweet/ nor sub/tle

would serve as the next line of the same stanza;

and with wrecks/ of forgot/ten delir/ium

contains three successive anapests. With scansion thus suggested, these rhythms are plainly evident—too plainly perhaps for full enjoyment of the beauty of the passage. But to one who has not had the patterns pointed out, may not their presence, dimly felt but not clearly apprehended, bring a teasing sense of haunting elusiveness?[14]

Psychologists have discovered that our greatest pleasure in the perception of any rhythm comes just at the moment when we feel that a rhythm has been established and identified, and that any rhythm if long continued becomes tiresome, and even annoying. The best prose adapts itself to

[14] Here, as in some other parts of this chapter, I am borrowing from my paper "The Rhythm of Oratorical Prose" in A. M. Drummond (ed.), *Studies in Rhetoric and Public Speaking* (New York: The Century Co., 1925).

these principles.   In the best prose metrical runs seldom continue long, but change from iambic to anapest, from anapest to trochee, or are broken by phrases without rhythm.   Prose rhythm occurs in snatches.   Not often will be found such continuous runs as the one from Burke quoted above. Much more typical of the best prose is the De Quincey passage just quoted.

TIME-BEAT RHYTHM.   But there is, I believe, another kind of rhythm generally present in beautiful prose, and perceptible by anyone with a sensitive ear.   Leigh Hunt showed how Coleridge, in his "Christabel," broke the monotonous singsong of iambic tetrameter by "calling to mind the liberties allowed its old musical professors, the minstrels, and dividing it by time instead of by syllables—by the beat of four into which you might get as many syllables as you could, instead of alloting eight syllables to the poor line whatever it might have to say."[15]   In this case "as many syllables as you could" means either two or three for each time-beat.   That is, the feet of "Christabel" are iambics and anapests indiscriminately mixed, as in this typical passage:

> She had dreams all yesternight
> Of her own betrothed knight;
> And she in the midnight wood will pray
> For the weal of her lover that's far away.

If, as is quite evident, this irregularity does not interfere with the rhythm, may we not go further and try occasionally crowding four syllables into a foot?   Vachel Lindsay did it in "The Congo" and yet maintained the regularity of beat of a tom-tom:

> Béat an empty bárrel with the hándle of a bróom,
> Hárd as they were áble,
> Bóom, boom, bóom,
> With a sílk umbrélla and the hándle of a bróom.

May we carry this principle still further?   In these lines from Robert Bridges' "London Snow":

> In lárge white flákes fálling on the cíty brówn
> Steálthily and perpétually séttling and lóosely lýing.

some of the feet have five syllables, and some have only one.   That is, the number of light syllables between the heavy ones may be four, or none. In some of the lines of de la Mare's "The Listeners" there are as many as five light syllables between the surges of emphasis that make the rhythm of the line:

> Fell échoing through the shádowiness of the stíll hóuse.

[15] A. S. Cook (ed.), *What Is Poetry?* (Boston: Ginn & Co., 1893), p. 58.

Yet the rhythm is there, and plainly felt. It is there not because of any given number of syllables to the foot, but because the accents are at equal intervals of time apart. Verse rhythm is aided by line length and by rhyme. If we eliminate these, there remains a rhythm of "time-beats," of heavy syllables at equal intervals of time, separated by varying numbers of light syllables. Such rhythm is perceivable in high-sounding prose. Note, for instance, this passage from De Quincey's *English Mail Coach:*

From the silence and deep peace of this saintly summer night—from the pathetic blending of this sweet moonlight, dawnlight, dreamlight—from the manly tenderness of this flattering, whispering, murmuring love—suddenly as from the woods and fields—suddenly as from the chambers of the air opening in revelation—suddenly as from the ground yawning at her feet, leaped upon her, with the flashing of cataracts, Death the crowned phantom with all the equipage of his terrors, and the tiger roar of his voice.

Here there are snatches of meter, sometimes too marked, as:

> moonlight, dawnlight, dreamlight.
> flattering, whispering, murmuring love.
> suddenly as from the woods and fields. (blank verse)

But can you not also feel in any expressive reading of the passage a recurrence of heavy time-beats at equal intervals, as I have marked them in these sections?

> súddenly as from the chámbers of the áir ópening in revelátion.
> súddenly as from the g9round yáwning at her feét.
> Deáth the crówned phántom, with áll the équipage of his
> térrors, and the tíger róar of his vóice.

Note that at times two heavy syllables come together. Sometimes these are felt as a kind of compound stress crowning a surge of emphasis, as in "crowned phantom," or in this line from "The Listeners":

> Stoód thrónging the fáint móonbeams on the dárk stáir.

in the combination "stood throng-," and "faint moon-," and "dark stair." At other times two contiguous heavy syllables will be felt as separate accents or beats, perhaps with a pause between, as in "groúnd yáwning" and "aír ópening." This device, says Mr. A. C. Clark, peculiar to English prose, is responsible for some of its sublimest effects.[16]

Time-beats need not necessarily be separated from each other by unaccented syllables even in fairly long successions. Remarkable effects are sometimes secured by a run of strong heavy syllables. In the opening sentence of the finale of Browne's *Urne Buriall:*

---

[16] *Op. cit.*, p. 12.

Nów sínce thése déad bónes have already outlasted the living ones of Methuselah, etc.

Professor Saintsbury says that the first five words are "monosyllabic feet-
thuds, as of earth dropping on the coffin-lid or the urn." A similar succession of monosyllables in Bertrand Russell's "A Free Man's Worship," a
part of which is quoted at the end of this chapter:

> The slów, súre dóom fálls pítiless and dárk.

suggests the overpowering inevitability of the onward march of fate.

Unanalyzable Cadence Patterns

These two kinds of rhythm certainly help to account for the pleasure
derived from prose music. But let us not be too sure that we have definitely and completely trapped and ticketed the charm of harmonious
prose. Rhythm is so interwoven with neatness of phrase, harmony of
sound, and beauty of thought, that we cannot assume that it alone is responsible for the pleasure derived from a beautiful passage. In both
poetry and prose there is often a blending of regularity and variety into a
cadence pattern of syllables, which, like the successive strains of a Brahms
symphony, seems indeed to obey no law, and yet cannot be changed without a distinct loss. In this passage from Keats's "La Belle Dame sans
Merci":

> The sedge has withered from the lake,
> And no birds sing.

none of us, I think, would find the second line so satisfying if it read,
"And not a bird does sing." Nor in another stanza would we wish to
change:

> And on thy cheeks a fading rose
> Fast withereth too.—

so that the last line would read, "Fast is withering too." Yet the lines I
have supplied are, if anything, a little more regular than the original ones.
It is hard to say why Keats's rhythm seems just right.

And the same is often true in prose. The "King James" translators of
the Bible gave the world (in 1611) one of its finest monuments of English
prose. Later scholars, in attempting to bring this translation into nearer
conformity to the original Hebrew and Greek texts, have almost invariably
destroyed its music. Note, for instance, what they did to the thirteenth
chapter of I. Corinthians. I quote first the Authorized, or King James,
Version:

1 Though I speak with the tongues of men and of angels, and have not charity, I am become as sounding brass, or a tinkling cymbal.

8 Charity never faileth: but whether there be prophecies, they shall fail; whether there be tongues, they shall cease; whether there be knowledge, it shall vanish away.

12 For now we see through a glass, darkly; but then face to face: now I know in part; but then shall I know even as also I am known.

Now notice how these passages stand in the American Revised Version:

1 If I speak with the tongues of men and of angels, but have no love, I am become sounding brass, or a clanging cymbal.

8 Love never faileth: but whether there be prophecies, they shall be done away; whether there be tongues, they shall cease; whether there be knowledge, it shall be done away.

12 For now we see in a mirror, darkly; but then face to face: now I know in part; but then shall I know fully even as also I was fully known.

The mess which the Revisers made of this passage, says Professor Saintsbury, is notorious. "Being utterly ignorant of English literature they altered 'glass' to 'mirror,' because, I suppose, they were clever enough to know that 'glass' was not used for mirrors in the Apostle's days, and not clever enough to have heard of Gascoigne's 'Steel Glass' in the days of the 'Authorized' translators themselves. By recurring to 'love' instead of 'charity' . . . they have at one blow cut the whole rhythm of the passage to pieces, and submitted ugly jolting thuds for undulating spring-work. Because they thought a cymbal did not 'tinkle' but did 'clang,' they spoilt the sound of a whole phrase, and very doubtfully improved its sense, by altering to 'clanging' (they had not even the sense to try 'clashing,' and I wonder why they did not use 'bang'). Because of the absurd objection to synonyms . . . they spoilt the euphony by making both the 'prophecies' and the 'knowledge' be 'done away.' "[17]

Why is "charity" a better word than "love" here? It is hard to say, but most of us feel that it is. The superiority may lie in the cadence pattern of the syllables, or in the sounds of the letters, or in the connotations of the word. Just so the charm of any passage of beautiful prose may lie chiefly in these characteristics, or it may depend chiefly upon its rhythm of meter or time-beat, or it may be due to poetic diction, figures of speech, grandeur of thought, strong emotion, variety of rhetorical pattern, proportion, balance, or to alliteration, assonance, and euphony. The reader who would communicate its beauty to others must study the passage carefully for all of these devices and give them full value. As in reading poetry, he has the power to accentuate or diminish all of these effects.

[17] *Op. cit.*, p. 152. One wonders what Saintsbury would think of the change to "I am a noisy gong or a clanging cymbal," and "Love never ends; as for prophecy, it will pass away; as for tongues, they will cease; as for knowledge, it will pass away" in the revision of 1946.

His responsibility in prose is even greater because the harmonies of prose are often more subtle than those of poetry, and so may more easily be abused or lost.

Summary

Prose as well as poetry has harmonies, but they are more subtle and elusive. They lie partly in beautiful sound combinations, poetic diction, rhetorical structure, and other adjuncts of poetry, but they lie also partly in rhythm. Many deny or object to the presence of meter in prose, but have no other satisfactory explanation of prose rhythm. There is no doubt that slight runs of meter are perceptible in fine prose. They give pleasure only if varied and never long continued. There is also a rhythm of heavy syllables at equal intervals in time with varying numbers of light syllables between. Contiguous heavy syllables often contribute remarkable effects. There is also sometimes a pleasure in unanalyzable cadence patterns. All these devices should be understood by anyone who would communicate to others the harmonies of prose.

PLAN OF STUDY

(We are on very uncertain ground here, and only general directions can be given. All the instructions in previous chapters will be needed. Review especially the instructions in the chapters on Verse, Voice, and Pronunciation. After the thought is mastered do not neglect to read the selection aloud again and again with great deliberation, surrendering yourself to the sound and the swing of the words.)

1. Take special pains to give proper value to every consonant and vowel sound. Note the contribution which each makes to the total harmony. Round out the strong vowels fully.
2. See that every syllable falls accurately into its appointed place in the phrase, and contributes its proper value to the tone harmony of the whole.
3. Look particularly for snatches of meter, and mark their scansion. So far as you can govern them in reading, aim to break off metric runs almost as soon as started, remembering that meter in prose can easily become obtrusive and offensive.
4. Mark the syllables that seem to constitute a time-beat rhythm. In reading beware of letting such rhythms continue too long unless the weak syllables between are highly varied in number.
5. Watch for compound stress, and for successions of heavy monosyllables.
6. Note both uniformity and variety in the patterns of phrases, and try to keep the two in proper balance.

CRITERIA

1. Was utterance deliberate and carefully designed, so that every vowel and consonant sound, and every syllable, filled its proper place in the symphony of the whole?
2. Was too much or too little made of occasional sections of verse?
3. Were time-beat rhythms appreciated and properly capitalized?
4. In rendering both forms of rhythm was the pattern broken as soon as formed, or even before, so as to avoid the regularity which "produces weariness and satiety"?
5. Were the balance, proportion, and variety of phrase-groups properly appreciated and justly rendered?

QUESTIONS FOR DISCUSSION

1. What is supposed to have been the origin of English prose harmony?
2. Is harmonious prose better than plain prose?
3. What are some of the elements that may contribute to beautiful prose?
4. What characteristics of poetry, aside from rhythm, are found in prose?
5. Is prose rhythm different from poetic rhythm?
6. What is the evidence for and against the presence of meter in prose?
7. Under what circumstances is rhythm tiresome, and when is it pleasurable?
8. Define and illustrate time-beat rhythm.
9. To what other factors may the charm of beautiful prose be due?

SELECTION FOR DRILL

A FREE MAN'S WORSHIP

From Mysticism and Logic[18]

Bertrand Russell

Brief and powerless is Man's life; on him and all his race the slow, sure doom falls pitiless and dark. Blind to good and evil, reckless of destruction, omnipotent matter rolls on its relentless way; for man, condemned to-day to lose his dearest, to-morrow himself to pass through the gate of darkness, it remains only to cherish, ere yet the blow falls, the lofty thoughts that ennoble his little day; disdaining the coward terrors of the slave of Fate, to worship at the shrine that his own hands have built; undismayed by the empire of chance, to preserve a mind free from the wanton tyranny that rules his outward life; proudly defiant of the irresistible forces that tolerate, for a moment, his knowledge and his condemnation, to sustain alone, a weary but unyielding Atlas, the world that his own ideals have fashioned despite the trampling march of unconscious power.

Suggestions for Analysis. This selection is remarkable not so much for gorgeous poetic imagery as for its balance and variety of phrase and "elevation of structure." Nevertheless it contains some splendid imagery. Note the figures of falling doom, rolling matter, of the gate of darkness, the slave of fate, the empire of chance, etc. You will find examples of alliteration and assonance also. The long second sentence is beautifully balanced and proportioned. You will need all your powers of attention and comprehension to hold its elements in place in your mind as you read. Note that the main clause is "it remains," and that it is followed by four infinitive clauses, beginning "to cherish," "to worship," "to preserve," and "to sustain," each with appropriate modifiers. Keep this framework of the sentence clearly in mind.

Note these short stretches of meter:

> on hím and áll his ráce the slów
> blínd to góod and évil,
> réckless óf destrúction
> for mán condémned to-dáy to lóse his déarest
> the lófty thóughts that ennóble his líttle dáy
> despíte the trámpling márch of uncónscious pówer.

You will find also some rather emphatic time-beat rhythms. The paragraph opens with a suggestion of a strong time-beat given by the two strong stresses on "brief" and "pow-." This hint is not carried out, the potential rhythm being frustrated by the division of stress on "Man's life." This interrupted rhythm is taken up again, however, in the next clause, where the heavy monosyllables "slow, sure doom falls pit-," like the slow descending chords of a Tschaikowsky symphony, give a powerful emotional heightening to the impression of inevitability and pitilessness expressed by the words. There is a slight conflict be-

[18] By permission of W. W. Norton & Co., Inc.

tween the metrical pattern and the time-beat in the phrase "reckless of destruction." The metrical rhythm would give it three stresses, the time-beat calls for only two. Anyone familiar with reading poetry knows, however, that such superpositions are a means to variety and beauty. A slightly different time-beat rhythm is set up in the clauses "it remáins ónly to chérish ere yét the blów fálls." Here are three strong stresses followed by a rest, and then three more strong stresses at practically the same time intervals. There follows a splendid run of well marked time-beat rhythm:

> próudly defíant of the irresístible fórces that
> tólerate, for a móment, his knówledge and his con-
> demnátion, to sustáin alóne, a wéary but unyíelding
> Átlas, the wórld that his ówn idéals have fáshioned.

The passage must be broken, of course, by rests, and by accelerations and retardations, but the strong pulsing beat should never be completely lost until it finally resolves itself into the metric run which closes the paragraph:

> despíte the trámpling márch of uncónscious pówer.

Because of the profuse rhythm, it would be possible for this paragraph to seem monotonous and singsong; but the reader is helped to avoid monotony by the varied length of the rhythmical units, by the obvious demands for rests, by the apparent accelerations and retardations of certain phrases, and by frequent changes in the nature of the rhythm.

Note how the long drive of regularly stressed words in the time-beat passage just quoted heightens the suggestion of courage and firmness which the author is making.[19]

[19] For both the discovery and the analysis of this passage I am deeply indebted to Professor Hoyt H. Hudson.

SELECTIONS FOR PRACTICE

ECCLESIASTES, XII[20]

1 Remember now thy Creator in the days of thy youth, while the evil days come not, nor the years draw nigh, when thou shalt say, I have no pleasure in them;

2 While the sun, or the light, or the moon, or the stars, be not darkened; nor the clouds return after the rain:

3 In the day when the keepers of the house shall tremble, and the strong men shall bow themselves, and the grinders cease because they are few, and those that look out of the windows be darkened,

4 And the doors shall be shut in the streets, when the sound of the grinding is low, and he shall rise up at the voice of the bird, and all the daughters of music shall be brought low:

5 Also when they shall be afraid of that which is high, and fears shall be in the way, and the almond tree shall flourish, and the grasshopper shall be a burden, and desire shall fail; because man goeth to his long home, and the mourners go about the streets:

6 Or ever the silver cord be loosed, or the golden bowl be broken, or the pitcher be broken at the fountain, or the wheel broken at the cistern.

7 Then shall the dust return to the earth as it was; and the spirit shall return unto God who gave it.

ISAIAH, LX

1 Arise, shine; for thy light is come, and the glory of the Lord is risen upon thee.

2 For, behold, the darkness shall cover the earth, and gross darkness the people: but the Lord shall arise upon thee, and his glory shall be seen upon thee.

3 And the Gentiles shall come to thy light, and kings to the brightness of thy rising.

4 Lift up thine eyes round about, and see: all they gather themselves together, they come to thee: thy sons shall come from far, and thy daughters shall be nursed at thy side.

5 Then thou shalt see, and flow together, and thine heart shall fear, and be enlarged; because the abundance of the sea shall be converted unto thee, the forces of the Gentiles shall come unto thee.

18 Violence shall no more be heard in thy land, wasting nor destruction within thy borders; but thou shalt call thy walls Salvation, and thy gates Praise.

19 The sun shall be no more thy light by day; neither for brightness shall the moon give light unto thee: but the Lord shall be unto thee an everlasting light, and thy God thy glory.

[20] This and the following two selections are from the King James Version of the Bible.

20 Thy sun shall no more go down; neither shall thy moon withdraw itself: for the Lord shall be thine everlasting light, and the days of thy mourning shall be ended.

I. CORINTHIANS, XIII

1 Though I speak with the tongues of men and of angels, and have not charity, I am become as sounding brass, or a tinkling cymbal.

2 And though I have the gift of prophecy, and understand all mysteries, and all knowledge; and though I have all faith, so that I could remove mountains, and have not charity, I am nothing.

3 And though I bestow all my goods to feed the poor, and though I give my body to be burned, and have not charity, it profiteth me nothing.

4 Charity suffereth long, and is kind; charity envieth not; charity vaunteth not itself, is not puffed up,

5 Doth not behave itself unseemly, seeketh not her own, is not easily provoked, thinketh no evil;

6 Rejoiceth not in iniquity, but rejoiceth in the truth;

7 Beareth all things, believeth all things, hopeth all things, endureth all things.

8 Charity never faileth: but whether there be prophecies, they shall fail; whether there be tongues, they shall cease; whether there be knowledge, it shall vanish away.

9 For we know in part, and we prophesy in part.

10 But when that which is perfect is come, then that which is in part shall be done away.

11 When I was a child, I spake as a child, I understood as a child, I thought as a child: but when I became a man, I put away childish things.

12 For now we see through a glass, darkly; but then face to face: now I know in part; but then shall I know even as also I am known.

13 And now abideth faith, hope, charity, these three; but the greatest of these is charity.

THE VANITY OF AMBITION

From URNE BURIALL

Sir Thomas Browne

Now since these dead bones have already out-lasted the living ones of *Methuselah*, and in a yard under ground, and thin walls of clay, outworn all the strong and specious buildings above it; and quietly rested under the drums and tramplings of three conquests; what Prince can promise such diuturnity unto his Reliques, or might not gladly say,

Sic ego componi versus in ossa velim.

Time which antiquates Antiquities, and hath an art to make dust of all things, hath yet spared these *minor* Monuments.

In vain we hope to be known by open and visible conservatories, when to be unknown was the means of their continuation and obscurity their protection: If they dyed by violent hands, and were thrust into their Urnes, these bones become considerable, and some old Philosophers would honour them, whose souls they conceived most pure, which were thus snatched from their bodies; and to retain a stranger propension unto them: whereas they weariedly left a languishing corps, and with faint desires of reunion. If they fell by long and aged decay, yet wrapt up in the bundle of time, they fall into indistinction, and make but one blot with Infants. If we begin to die when we live, and long life be but a prolongation of death; our life is a sad composition; We live with death, and die not in a moment. How many pulses made up the life of *Methuselah,* were work for *Archimedes:* Common Counters summe up the life of *Moses* his man. Our dayes become considerable like petty sums by minute accumulations; where numerous fractions make up but small round numbers; and our dayes of a span long make not one little finger.

SLEEP

From THE GARDEN OF CYRUS

Sir Thomas Browne

But the quincunx of heaven runs low, and 'tis time to close the five ports of knowledge. We are unwilling to spin out our awaking thoughts into the phantasms of sleep, which often continueth precogitations; making cables of cobwebs, and wildernesses of handsome groves. Beside Hippocrates hath spoke so little, and the oneirocritical masters have left such frigid interpretations from plants, that there is little encouragement to dream of Paradise itself. Nor will the sweetest delight of gardens afford much comfort in sleep; wherein the dulness of that sense shakes hands with delectable odours; and though in the bed of Cleopatra, can hardly with any delight raise up the ghost of a rose.

Night, which Pagan theology could make the daughter of Chaos, affords no advantage to the description of order; although no lower than that mass can we derive its genealogy. All things began in order, so shall they end, and so shall they begin again; according to the ordainer of order and mystical mathematicks of the city of heaven.

Though Somnus in Homer be sent to rouse up Agamemnon, I find no such effects in these drowsy approaches of sleep. To keep our eyes open longer, were but to act our Antipodes. The huntsmen are up in America, and they are already past their first sleep in Persia. But who can be drowsy at that hour which freed us from everlasting sleep? or have slumbering thoughts at that time, when sleep itself must end, and, as some conjecture, all shall awake again?

THE QUEEN OF FRANCE AND THE SPIRIT OF CHIVALRY

Edmund Burke

I hear, and I rejoice to hear, that the great lady, the other object of the triumph, has borne that day (one is interested that beings made for suffering should suffer well), and that she bears all the succeeding days—that she bears the imprisonment of her husband, and her own captivity, and the exile of her friends, and the insulting adulation of addresses, and the whole weight of her accumulated wrongs, with a serene patience, in a manner suited to her rank and race, and becoming the offspring of a sovereign distinguished for her piety and her courage; that, like her, she has lofty sentiments; that she feels with the dignity of a Roman matron; that in the last extremity she will save herself from the last disgrace; and that, if she must fall, she will fall by no ignoble hand.

It is now sixteen or seventeen years since I saw the Queen of France, then the dauphiness, at Versailles; and surely never lighted on this orb, which she hardly seemed to touch, a more delightful vision. I saw her just above the horizon, decorating and cheering the elevated sphere she just began to move in, glittering like the morning star, full of life, and splendor, and joy. Oh! what a revolution! and what a heart must I have, to contemplate, without emotion, that elevation and that fall! Little did I dream, when she added titles of veneration to those of enthusiastic, distant, respectful love, that she should ever be obliged to carry the sharp antidote against disgrace concealed in that bosom; little did I dream that I should have lived to see such disasters fallen upon her in a nation of gallant men, in a nation of men of honor and of cavaliers. I thought ten thousand swords must have leaped from their scabbards to avenge even a look that threatened her with insult. But the age of chivalry is gone; that of sophisters, economists, and calculators has succeeded; and the glory of Europe is extinguished forever. Never, never more shall we behold that generous loyalty to rank and sex, that proud submission, that dignified obedience, that subordination of the heart, which kept alive, even in servitude itself, the spirit of an exalted freedom. The unbought grace of life, the cheap defense of nations, the nurse of manly sentiment and heroic enterprise is gone! It is gone, that sensibility of principle, that chastity of honor, which felt a stain like a wound, which inspired courage while it mitigated ferocity, which ennobled whatever it touched, and under which vice itself lost half its evil by losing all its grossness.

DREAM-FUGUE

(Tumultuosissimamente)

From The English Mail-Coach

Thomas De Quincey

Passion of sudden death! that once in youth I read and interpreted by the shadows of thy averted signs! rapture of panic taking the shape (which among tombs in churches I have seen) of woman bursting her sepulchral bonds—of woman's Ionic form bending forward from the ruins of her grave with arching foot, with eyes upraised, with clasped adoring hands— waiting, watching, trembling, praying for the trumpet's call to rise from dust forever! Ah, vision too fearful of shuddering humanity on the brink of almighty abysses!—vision that didst start back, that didst reel away, like a shrivelling scroll from before the wrath of fire racing on the wings of the wind! Epilepsy so brief of horror, wherefore is it that thou canst not die? Passing so suddenly into darkness, wherefore is it that still thou sheddest thy sad funeral blights upon the gorgeous mosaics of dreams? Fragment of music too passionate, heard once, and heard no more, what aileth thee, that thy deep rolling chords come up at intervals through all the worlds of sleep, and after forty years, have lost no element of horror?

DREAM-FUGUE, V

From The English Mail-Coach

Thomas De Quincey

Then was completed the passion of the mighty fugue. The golden tubes of the organ, which as yet had but muttered at intervals—gleaming among clouds and surges of incense—threw up, as from fountains un- fathomable, columns of heart-shattering music. Choir and anti-choir were filling fast with unknown voices. Thou also, Dying Trumpeter, with thy love that was victorious, didst enter the tumult; trumpet and echo—fare- well love, and farewell anguish—rang through the dreadful *sanctus*. Oh, darkness of the grave! that from the crimson altar and from the fiery font wert visited and searched by the effulgence in the angel's eye—were these indeed thy children? Pomps of life, that, from the burials of centuries, rose again to the voice of perfect joy, did ye indeed mingle with the festivals of death? Lo! as I looked back for seventy leagues through the mighty cathedral, I saw the quick and the dead that sang together to God, together that sang to the generations of man. All the hosts of jubilation, like armies that ride in pursuit, moved with one step. Us, that, with laureled heads, were passing from the cathedral, they overtook, and, as with a garment, they wrapped around with thunders greater than our own. As brothers we moved together; to the dawn that advanced, to the stars that fled; rendering thanks to God in the highest—that, having hid His face through one generation behind thick clouds of War, once again was ascending, from the Campo Santo of Waterloo was ascending, in the visions of Peace; rendering thanks for thee, young girl! whom having overshadowed with His ineffable passion of death, suddenly did God relent, suffered thy angel to turn aside His arm, and even in thee, sister unknown! shown to me for a moment only to be hidden for ever, found an occasion to glorify His goodness. A thousand times, amongst the phantoms of sleep, have I seen thee entering the gates of the golden dawn, with the secret word riding before thee, with the armies of the grave behind thee, —seen thee sinking, rising, raving, despairing; a thousand times in the worlds of sleep have I seen thee followed by God's angel through storms, through desert seas, through the darkness of quicksands, through dreams and the dreadful revelations that are in dreams; only that at the last, with one sling of His victorious arm, He might snatch thee back from ruin, and might emblazon in thy deliverance the endless resurrections of His love!

THE SECOND INAUGURAL ADDRESS

Abraham Lincoln

Neither party expected for the war the magnitude or the duration which it has already attained. Neither anticipated that the cause of the conflict might cease when, or even before, the conflict itself should cease. Each looked for an easier triumph, and a result less fundamental and astounding. Both read the same Bible, and pray to the same God, and each invokes his aid against the other. It may seem strange that any men should dare to ask a just God's assistance in wringing their bread from the sweat of other men's faces; but let us judge not, that we be not judged. The prayer of both could not be answered. That of neither has been answered fully. The Almighty has His own purposes. Woe unto the world because of offenses, for it must needs be that offenses come, but woe to that man by whom the offense cometh. If we shall suppose that American slavery is one of those offenses which, in the providence of God, must needs come, but which having continued through His appointed time, He now wills to remove, and that He gives to both North and South this terrible war as the woe due to those by whom the offense came, shall we discern therein any departure from those divine attributes which the believers in a living God always ascribe to Him? Fondly do we hope, fervently do we pray, that this mighty scourge of war may speedily pass away. Yet if God wills that it continue until all the wealth piled by the bondsman's two hundred and fifty years of unrequited toil shall be sunk, and until every drop of blood drawn with the lash shall be repaid by another drawn with the sword, as was said three thousand years ago, so still it must be said, that the judgments of the Lord are true and righteous altogether.

With malice toward none; with charity for all; with firmness in the right, as God gives us to see the right, let us strive on to finish the work we are in; to bind up the nation's wounds; to care for him who shall have borne the battle, and for his widow, and his orphan—to do all which may achieve and cherish a just and lasting peace among ourselves, and with all nations.

THE FRONT OF ST. MARK'S

From THE STONES OF VENICE

John Ruskin

And well may they fall back, for beyond those troops of ordered arches there rises a vision out of the earth, and all the great square seems to have opened from it in a kind of awe, that we may see it far away;—a multitude of pillars and white domes, clustered into a long low pyramid of coloured light; a treasure-heap, it seems, partly of gold, and partly of opal and mother-of-pearl, hollowed beneath into five great vaulted porches, ceiled with fair mosaic, and beset with sculpture of alabaster, clear as amber, and delicate as ivory, sculpture fantastic and involved, of palm leaves and lilies, and grapes and pomegranates, and birds clinging and fluttering among the branches, all twined together into an endless network of buds and plumes; and, in the midst of it, the solemn forms of angels, sceptred, and robed to the feet, and leaning to each other across the gates, their figures indistinct among the gleaming of the golden ground through the leaves beside them, interrupted and dim, like the morning light as it faded back among the branches of Eden, when first its gates were angel-guarded long ago. And round the walls of the porches there are set pillars of variegated stones, jasper and porphyry, and deep-green serpentine spotted with flakes of snow, and marbles, that half refuse and half yield to the sunshine, Cleopatra-like, "their bluest veins to kiss"—the shadow, as it steals back from them, revealing line after line of azure undulation, as a receding tide leaves the waved sand; their capitals rich with interwoven tracery, rooted knots of herbage, and drifting leaves of acanthus and vine, and mystical signs, all beginning and ending in the Cross; and above them, in the broad archivolts, a continuous chain of language and of life—angels, and the signs of heaven and the labours of men, each in its appointed season upon the earth; and above these another range of glittering pinnacles, mixed with white arches edged with scarlet flowers,—a confusion of delight, amidst which the breasts of the Greek horses are seen blazing in their breadth of golden strength, and the St. Mark's Lion, lifted on a blue field covered with stars, until at last, as if in ecstasy, the crests of the arches break into a marble foam, and toss themselves far into the blue sky in flashes and wreaths of sculptured spray, as if the breakers of the Lido shore had been frost-bound before they fell, and the sea-nymphs had inlaid them with coral and amethyst.

THE TAPESTRY OF NATURE

From MYTH AND MIRACLE

Robert G. Ingersoll

The rise and set of sun, the birth and death of day, the dawns of silver and the dusks of gold, the wonders of the rain and snow, the shroud of Winter and the many colored robe of Spring, the lonely moon with nightly loss or gain, the serpent lightning and the thunder's voice, the tempest's fury and the zephyr's sigh, the threat of storm and promise of the bow, cathedral clouds with dome and spire, earthquake and strange eclipse, frost and fire, the snow-crowned mountains with their tongues of flame, the fields of space sown thick with stars, the wandering comets hurrying past the fixed and sleepless sentinels of night, the marvels of the earth and air, the perfumed flower, the painted wing, the waveless pool that held within its magic breast the image of the startled face, the mimic echo that made a record in the viewless air, the pathless forests and the boundless seas, the ebb and flow of tides—the slow, deep breathing of some vague and monstrous life—the miracle of birth, the mystery of dream and death, and over all the silent and immeasurable dome. These were the warp and woof, and at the loom sat Love and Fancy, Hope and Fear, and wove the wondrous tapestries whereon we find the pictures of gods and fairy lands and all the legends that were told when Nature rocked the cradle of the infant world.

THE POETRY OF ANCIENT MYTHS

From MYTH AND MIRACLE

Robert G. Ingersoll

In all these myths and legends of the past we find philosophies and dreams and efforts, stained with tears, of great and tender souls who tried to pierce the mysteries of life and death, to answer the questions of the whence and whither, and who vainly sought with bits of shattered glass to make a mirror that would in very truth reflect the face and form of Nature's perfect self. These myths were born of hopes and fears, of tears and smiles, and they were touched and colored by all there is of joy and grief between the rosy dawn of birth and death's sad night. They clothed even the stars with passion, and gave to gods the faults and frailties of the sons of men. In them the winds and waves were music, and all the springs, the mountains, woods and perfumed dells were haunted by a thousand fairy forms. They thrilled the veins of Spring with tremulous desire, made tawny Summer's billowy breast the throne and home of love, filled Autumn's arms with sun-kissed grapes and gathered sheaves, and pictured Winter as a weak old king, who felt, like Lear, upon his withered face, Cordelia's tears.

MISCELLANEOUS SELECTIONS

THE WOMEN AT THE ADONIS FESTIVAL

IDYLL XV (TRANSLATION BY J. M. EDMONDS

Theocritus

[The scene of this mime is Alexandria, and the chief characters are two fellow-countrywomen of the author. Gorgo, paying a morning call, finds Praxinoa, with her two-year-old child, superintending the spinning of her maids, and asks her to come with her to the Festival of Adonis at the palace of Ptolemy II. Praxinoa makes some demur, but at last washes and dresses and sallies forth with her visitor and their two maids. After sundry encounters in the crowded streets, they enter the palace, and soon after the prima donna begins the Dirge—which is really a wedding-song containing a forecast of a dirge—with an address to the bride Aphrodite and a reference to the deification of the queen of Ptolemy I. The song describes the scene—the offerings displayed about the marriage-bed, the two canopies of greenery above it, the bedstead with its representation of the Rape of Ganymede, the coverlets which enwrap the effigies of Adonis and Aphrodite, the image of the holy bridegroom himself—and ends with an anticipation of the choral dirge to be sung on the morrow at the funeral of Adonis.]

Gorgo (with her maid Eutychis at the door, as the maid Eunoa opens it): Praxinoa at home?

Praxinoa (running forward): Dear Gorgo! at last! she *is* at home. I quite thought you'd forgotten me. (*to the maid*) Here, Eunoa, a chair for the lady, and a cushion in it.

Gorgo (refusing the cushion): No, thank you, really.

Praxinoa: Do sit down.

Gorgo (sitting): O what a silly I was to come! What with the crush and the horses, Praxinoa, I've scarcely got here alive. It's all big boots and people in uniform. And the street was never-ending, and you can't think how far your house is along it.

Praxinoa: That's my lunatic; came and took one at the end of the world, and more an animal's den, too, than a place for a human being to live in, just to prevent you and me being neighbours, out of sheer spite, the jealous old wretch! He's always the same.

Gorgo: My dear, pray don't call your good Dinon such names before Baby. See how he's staring at you. (*to the child*) It's all right, Zopy, my pet. It's not dad-dad she's talking about.

Praxinoa: Upon my word, the child understands.

Gorgo: Nice dad-dad.

Praxinoa: And yet that dad-dad of his the other day—the other day, now, I tell 'Daddy, get mother some soap and rouge from the shop,' and, would you believe it? back he came with a packet of salt, the great six feet of folly!

Gorgo: Mine's just the same. Diocleidas is a perfect spendthrift. Yesterday he gave seven shillings apiece for mere bits of dog's hair, mere pluckings of old handbags, five of them, all filth, all work to be done over again. But come, my dear, get your cloak and gown. I want you to come with me (*grandly*) to call on our high and mighty Prince Ptolemy to see the Adonis. I hear the Queen's getting up something quite splendid this year.

Praxinoa (hesitating): Fine folk, fine ways.

Gorgo: Yes; but sightseers make good gossips, you know, if you've been and other people haven't. It's time we were on the move.

Praxinoa (still hesitating): It's always holidays with people who've nothing to do. (*suddenly making up her mind*) Here, Eunoa, you scratch-face, take up the spinning and put it away with the rest. Cats always *will* lie soft. Come, bestir yourself. Quick, some water! (*to Gorgo*) Water's wanted first, and she brings the soap. (*to Eunoa*) Never mind; give it me. (*E. pours out the powdered soap*) Not all that, you wicked waste! Pour out the water. (*E. washes her mistress's hands and face*) Oh, you wretch! What do you mean by wetting my bodice like that? That's enough. (*to Gorgo*) I've got myself washed somehow, thank goodness. (*to Eunoa*) Now where's the key of the big cupboard? Bring it here. (*Takes out a Dorian pinner—a gown fastened with pins or brooches to the shoulders and reaching to the ground, with an overfold coming to the waist—and puts it on with Eunoa's aid over the inner garment with short sleeves which she wears indoors)*

Gorgo (referring to the style of the overfold): Praxinoa, that full gathering suits you really well. Do tell me what you gave for the material.

Praxinoa: Don't speak of it, Gorgo; it was more than eight golden sovereigns, and I can tell you I put my very soul into making it up.

Gorgo: Well, all I can say is, it's *most* successful.

Praxinoa: It's very good of you to say so. *(to Eunoa)* Come, put on my cloak and hat for me, and mind you do it properly. *(Eunoa puts her cloak about her head and shoulders and pins the straw sun-hat to it).* *(taking up the child)* No; I'm not going to take *you,* Baby. Horsebogey bites little boys. *(the child cries)* You may cry as much as you like; I'm not going to have you lamed for life. *(to Gorgo, giving the child to the nurse)* Come along. Take Baby and amuse him, Phrygia, and call the dog indoors and lock the front-door.

(in the street) Heavens, what a crowd! How we're to get through this awful crush and how long it's going to take us, I can't imagine. Talk of an antheap! *(apostrophising)* I *must* say, you've done us many a good turn, my good Ptolemy, since your father went to heaven. We have no villains sneaking up to murder us in the streets nowadays in the good old Egyptian style. They don't play those awful games now—the thorough-paced rogues, every one of them the same, all queer!

Gorgo dearest! what *shall* we do? The Royal Horse! Don't run me down, my good man. That bay's rearing. Look, what temper! Stand back, Eunoa, you reckless girl! He'll be the death of that man. Thank goodness I left Baby at home!

Gorgo: It's all right, Praxinoa. We've got well behind them, you see. They're all where they ought to be, now.

Praxinoa (recovering): And fortunately I can say the same of my poor wits. Ever since I was a girl, two things have frightened me more than anything else, a horrid slimy snake and a horse. Let's go on. Here's ever such a crowd pouring after us.

Gorgo (to an old woman): Have you come from the palace, mother?

Old Woman: Yes, my dears.

Gorgo: Then we can get there all right, can we?

Old Woman: Trying took Troy, my pretty; don't they say where there's a will there's a way?

Gorgo: That old lady gave us some oracles, didn't she?

Praxinoa (mock-sententiously): My dear, women know everything. They know all about Zeus marrying Hera.

Gorgo: Do look, Praxinoa; what a crowd there is at the door!

Praxinoa: Marvellous. Give me your arm, Gorgo; and you take hold of Eutychis' arm, Eunoa; and you hold on tight, Eutychis, or you'll be separated. We'll all go in together. Mind you keep hold of me, Eunoa. Oh dear, oh dear, Gorgo! my summer cloak's torn right in two. (*to a stranger*) For Heaven's sake, as you wish to be saved, mind my cloak, sir.

First Stranger: I really can't help what happens; but I'll do my best.

Praxinoa: The crowd's simply enormous; they're pushing like a drove of pigs.

First Stranger: Don't be alarmed, madam; we're all right.

Praxinoa: You deserve to be all right to the end of your days, my dear sir, for the care you've been taking of us. (*to Gorgo*) What a kind considerate man! Poor Eunoa's getting squeezed. (*to Eunoa*) Push, you coward, can't you? (*they pass in*)
That's all right. All inside, as the bridegroom said when he shut the door.

Gorgo (*referring, as they move forward towards the dais, to the draperies which hang between the pillars*): Praxinoa, do come here. Before you do anything else I insist upon your looking at the embroideries. How delicate they are! and in such good taste! They're really hardly human, are they?

Praxinoa: Huswife Athena! the weavers that made that material and the embroiderers who did that close detailed work are simply marvels. How realistically the things all stand and move about in it! they're living! It *is* wonderful what people can do. And then the Holy Boy; how perfectly beautiful he looks lying on his silver couch, with the down of manhood just showing on his cheeks,—(*religioso*) the thrice-beloved Adonis, beloved even down below!

Second Stranger: Oh dear, oh dear, ladies! do stop that eternal cooing. (*to the bystanders*) They'll weary me to death with their ah-ah-ah-ing.

Praxinoa: My word! where *does* that person come from? What business is it of yours if we do coo? Buy your slaves before you order them about, pray. You're giving your orders to Syracusans. If you *must* know, we're Corinthians by extraction, like Bellerophon himself. What we talk's Peloponnesian. I suppose Dorians may speak Doric, mayn't they? Persephone! let's have no more masters than the one we've got. I shall do just as I like. Pray don't waste your breath.

Gorgo: Be quiet, Praxinoa. She's just going to begin the song, that Argive person's daughter, you know, the "accomplished vocalist" that was chosen to sing the dirge *last* year. You may be sure *she'll* give us something good. Look, she's making her bow.

(THE DIRGE)

Lover of Golgi and Idaly and Eryx' steepy hold,
O Lady Aphrodite with the face that beams like gold,
Twelve months are sped and soft-footed Heav'n's pretty laggards, see,
Bring o'er the never-tarrying stream Adonis back to thee.
The Seasons, the Seasons, full slow they go and come,
But some sweet thing for all they bring, and so they are welcome home.
O Cypris, Dion's daughter, of thee anealed, 'tis said,
Our Queen that was born of woman is e'en immortal made;
And now, sweet Lady of many names, of many shrines Ladye,
Thy guerdon's giv'n; for the Queen's daughter, as Helen fair to see,
Thy lad doth dight with all delight upon this holyday;
For there's not a fruit the orchard bears but is here for his hand to take,
And cresses trim all kept for him in many a silver tray,
And Syrian balm in vials of gold; and O, there's every cake
That ever woman kneaded of bolted meal so fair
With blossoms blent of every scent or oil or honey rare—
Here's all outlaid in semblance made of every bird and beast.
   Two testers green they have plight ye, with dainty dill well dressed,
Whereon, like puny nightingales that flit from bough to bough
Trying their waxing wings to spread, the Love-babes hovering go.
How fair the ebony and the gold, the ivory white how fair,
And eagles twain to Zeus on high bringing his cup-bearer!
Aye, and the coverlets spread for ye are softer spread than sleep—
Forsooth Miletus town may say, or the master of Samian sheep,
"The bridal bed for Adonis spread of my own making is;
Cypris hath this for her wrapping, Adonis that for his."
   Of eighteen years or nineteen is turned the rose-limbed groom;
His pretty lip is smooth to sip, for it bears but flaxen bloom.
And now she's in her husband's arms, and so we'll say good-night;
But to-morrow we'll come wi' the dew, the dew, and take hands and bear
      him away
Where plashing wave the shore doth lave, and there with locks undight
And bosoms bare all shining fair will raise this shrilling lay:—
"O sweet Adonis, none but thee of the children of Gods and men
'Twixt overworld and underworld doth pass and pass agen;
That cannot Agamemnon, nor the Lord o' the Woeful Spleen,
Nor the first of the twice-ten children that came of the Troyan queen,
Nor Patroclus brave, nor Pyrrhus bold that home from the war did win,
Nor none o' the kith o' the old Lapith nor of them of Deucalion's kin—
E'en Pelops line lacks fate so fine, and Pelasgian Argos' pride.

      Adonis sweet, Adonis dear,
      Be gracious for another year;
      Thou'rt welcome to thine own alway,
      And welcome we'll both cry to-day
         And next Adonis-tide."

Gorgo: O Praxinoa! what clever things we women are! I do envy her knowing all that, and still more having such a lovely voice. But I must be getting back. It's Diocleidas' dinner-time, and that man's all pepper; I wouldn't advise anyone to come near him even, when he's kept waiting for his food. Goodbye, Adonis darling; and I only trust you may find us all thriving when you come next year.

PASTORAL LOVE[1]

From As You Like It[2]

William Shakespeare

Enter SILVIUS *and* PHEBE

Sil. Sweet Phebe, do not scorn me; do not, Phebe:
Say that you love me not, but say not so
In bitterness. The common executioner,
Whose heart the accustom'd sight of death makes hard,
Falls not the axe upon the humbled neck
But first begs pardon: will you sterner be
Than he that dies and lives by bloody drops?

Enter ROSALIND, CELIA, *and* CORIN, *behind.*

Phe. I would not be thy executioner:
I fly thee, for I would not injure thee.
Thou tell'st me there is murder in mine eye:
'Tis pretty, sure, and very probable,
That eyes that are the frail'st and softest things,
Who shut their coward gates on atomies,
Should be call'd tyrants, butchers, murderers!
Now I do frown on thee with all my heart;
And, if mine eyes can wound, now let them kill thee;
Now counterfeit to swound; why now fall down;
Or, if thou canst not, O! for shame, for shame,
Lie not, to say mine eyes are murderers.
Now show the wound mine eye hath made in thee:
Scratch thee but with a pin, and there remains
Some scar of it: lean but upon a rush,
The cicatrice and capable impressure
Thy palm some moment keeps; and now mine eyes,
Which I have darted at thee, hurt thee not.
Nor, I am sure, there is no force in eyes
That can do hurt.
  Sil.   O dear Phebe,

---

[1] Before you attempt to read these scenes from Shakespeare be sure that you have made yourself thoroughly familiar with the plays from which they are taken.
[2] Act III, Scene 5.

If ever,—as that ever may be near,—
You meet in some fresh cheek the power of fancy,
Then shall you know the wounds invisible
That love's keen arrows make.
  Phe.   But, till that time
Come not thou near me; and, when that time comes,
Afflict me with thy mocks, pity me not;
As, till that time I shall not pity thee.
  Ros. (*Advancing.*) And why, I pray you?
Who might be your mother,
That you insult, exult, and all at once,
Over the wretched? What though you have no beauty,—
As by my faith, I see no more in you
Than without candle may go dark to bed,—
Must you be therefore proud and pitiless?
Why, what means this? Why do you look on me?
I see no more in you than in the ordinary
Of nature's sale-work. Od's my little life!
I think she means to tangle my eyes too.
No, faith, proud mistress, hope not after it:
'Tis not your inky brows, your black silk hair,
Your bugle eyeballs, nor your cheek of cream,
That can entame my spirits to your worship.
You foolish shepherd, wherefore do you follow her,
Like foggy south puffing with wind and rain?
You are a thousand times a properer man
Then she a woman: 'tis such fools as you
That make the world full of ill-favour'd children:
'Tis not her glass, but you, that flatters her;
And out of you she sees herself more proper
Than any of her lineaments can show her.
But, mistress, know yourself: down on your knees,
And thank heaven, fasting, for a good man's love:
For I must tell you friendly in your ear,
Sell when you can; you are not for all markets.
Cry the man mercy; love him, take his offer:
Foul is most foul, being foul to be a scoffer.
So take her to thee, shepherd. Fare you well.
  Phe. Sweet youth, I pray you, chide a year together:
I had rather hear you chide than this man woo.
  Ros. He's fallen in love with her foulness, and she'll fall in love with
my anger. If it be so, as fast as she answers thee with frowning looks,
I'll sauce her with bitter words. Why look you so upon me?
  Phe. For no ill will I bear you.
  Ros. I pray you, do not fall in love with me,
For I am falser than vows made in wine:
Besides, I like you not. If you will know my house,

'Tis at the tuft of olives here hard by.
Will you go, sister? Shepherd, ply her hard.
Come, sister. Shepherdess, look on him better,
And be not proud: though all the world could see,
None could be so abus'd in sight as he.
Come, to our flock.

(*Exeunt* ROSALIND, CELIA, *and* CORIN)

Phe. Dead shepherd, now I find thy saw of might:
'Who ever lov'd that lov'd not at first sight?'
Sil. Sweet Phebe,—
Phe.   Ha! what sayest thou, Silvius?
Sil. Sweet Phebe, pity me.
Phe. Why, I am sorry for thee, gentle Silvius.
Sil. Wherever sorrow is, relief would be:
If you do sorrow at my grief in love,
By giving love your sorrow and my grief
Were both extermin'd.
Phe. Thou hast my love: is not that neighbourly?
Sil. I would have you.
Phe.   Why, that were covetousness.
Silvius, the time was that I hated thee;
And yet it is not that I bear thee love;
But since that thou canst talk of love so well,
Thy company, which erst was irksome to me,
I will endure, and I'll employ thee too;
But do not look for further recompense
Than thine own gladness that thou art employ'd.
Sil. So holy and so perfect is my love,
And I in such a poverty of grace,
That I shall think it a most plenteous crop
To glean the broken ears after the man
That the main harvest reaps: loose now and then
A scatter'd smile, and that I'll live upon.
Phe. Know'st thou the youth that spoke to me erewhile?
Sil. Not very well, but I have met him oft;
And he hath bought the cottage and the bounds
That the old carlot once was master of.
Phe. Think not I love him, though I ask for him.
'Tis but a peevish boy; yet he talks well;
But what care I for words? yet words do well,
When he that speaks them pleases those that hear.
It is a pretty youth: not very pretty:
But, sure, he's proud; and yet his pride becomes him:
He'll make a proper man: the best thing in him
Is his complexion; and faster than his tongue
Did make offence his eye did heal it up.

He is not very tall; yet for his years he's tall:
His leg is but so so; and yet 'tis well:
There was a pretty redness in his lip,
A little riper and more lusty red
Than that mix'd in his cheek; 'twas just the difference
Betwixt the constant red and mingled damask.
There be some women, Silvius, had they mark'd him
In parcels as I did, would have gone near
To fall in love with him; but, for my part,
I love him not nor hate him not; and yet
I have more cause to hate him than to love him:
For what had he to do to chide at me?
He said mine eyes were black and my hair black;
And, now I am remember'd, scorn'd at me.
I marvel why I answer'd not again:
But that's all one; omittance is no quittance.
I'll write to him a very taunting letter,
And thou shalt bear it: wilt thou, Silvius?
　　Sil.　Phebe, with all my heart.
　　Phe.　　　　　　　　　　I'll write it straight;
The matter's in my head and in my heart:
I will be bitter with him and passing short.
Go with me, Silvius.

ROMEO AND JULIET

From ROMEO AND JULIET[3]
William Shakespeare

　　Romeo.　He jests at scars, but never felt a wound.
But, soft! what light through yonder window breaks?
It is the east, and Juliet is the sun!
Arise, fair sun and kill the envious moon,
Who is already sick and pale with grief,
That thou her maid art far more fair than she:
Be not her maid, since she is envious;
Her vestal livery is but sick and green,
And none but fools do wear it; cast it off.
It is my lady; O! it is my love:
O! that she knew she were.
She speaks, yet she says nothing: what of that?
Her eye discourses; I will answer it.
I am too bold, 'tis not to me she speaks:
Two of the fairest stars in all the heaven,
Having some business, do entreat her eyes

---

[3] Act II, Scene 2.

To twinkle in their spheres till they return.
What if her eyes were there, they in her head?
The brightness of her cheek would shame those stars
As daylight doth a lamp; her eyes in heaven
Would through the airy region stream so bright
That birds would sing and think it were not night.
See! how she leans her cheek upon her hand:
O! that I were a glove upon that hand:
That I might touch that cheek.
    Juliet.   Ay me!
    Romeo. She speaks.
O! speak again, bright angel; for thou art
As glorious to this night, being o'er my head,
As is a winged messenger of heaven
Unto the white-upturned wond'ring eyes
Of mortals, that fall back to gaze on him
When he bestrides the lazy-pacing clouds,
And sails upon the bosom of the air.
    Juliet. O Romeo, Romeo! Wherefore art thou Romeo?
Deny thy father, and refuse thy name;
Or, if thou wilt not, be but sworn my love,
And I'll no longer be a Capulet.
    Romeo. Shall I hear more, or shall I speak at this?
    Juliet. 'Tis but they name that is my enemy;
Thou art thyself though, not a Montague.
What's Montague? it is nor hand, nor foot,
Nor arm, nor face, nor any other part
Belonging to a man. O! be some other name:
What's in a name? that which we call a rose
By any other name would smell as sweet;
So Romeo would, were he not Romeo call'd,
Retain that dear perfection which he owes
Without that title. Romeo, doff thy name;
And for that name, which is no part of thee,
Take all myself.
    Romeo. I take thee at thy word.
Call me but love, and I'll be new baptiz'd;
Henceforth I never will be Romeo.
    Juliet. What man art thou, that, thus bescreen'd in night,
So stumblest on my counsel?
    Romeo.   By a name
I know not how to tell thee who I am:
My name, dear saint, is hateful to myself,
Because it is an enemy to thee:
Had I it written, I would tear the word.
    Juliet. My ears have not yet drunk a hundred words
Of that tongue's uttering, yet I know the sound:

Art thou not Romeo, and a Montague?

    Romeo. Neither, fair maid, if either thee dislike.

    Juliet. How cam'st thou hither, tell me, and wherefore?
The orchard walls are high and hard to climb,
And the place death, considering who thou art,
If any of my kinsmen find thee here.

    Romeo. With love's light wings did I o'erperch these walls;
For stony limits cannot hold love out,
And what love can do that dares love attempt;
Therefore thy kinsmen are no stop to me.

    Juliet. If they do see thee they will murder thee.

    Romeo. Alack! there lies more peril in thine eye
Than twenty of their swords: look thou but sweet,
And I am proof against their enmity.

    Juliet. I would not for the world they saw thee here.

    Romeo. I have night's cloak to hide me from their eyes;
And but thou love me, let them find me here;
My life were better ended by their hate,
Than death prorogued, wanting of thy love.

    Juliet. By whose direction found'st thou out this place?

    Romeo. By Love, that first did prompt me to inquire;
He lent me counsel, and I lent him eyes.
I am no pilot; yet, wert thou as far
As that vast shore wash'd with the furthest sea,
I would adventure for such merchandise.

    Juliet. Thou know'st the mask of night is on my face,
Else would a maiden blush bepaint my cheek
For that which thou hast heard me speak tonight.
Fain would I dwell on form, fain, fain deny
What I have spoke: but farewell compliment!
Dost thou love me? I know thou wilt say 'Ay';
And I will take thy word; yet, if thou swear'st,
Thou mayst prove false; at lovers' perjuries,
They say, Jove laughs. O gentle Romeo!
If thou dost love, pronounce it faithfully:
Or if thou think'st I am too quickly won,
I'll frown and be perverse and say thee nay,
So thou wilt woo; but else, not for the world.
In truth, fair Montague, I am too fond,
And therefore thou mayst think my 'haviour light:
But trust me, gentleman, I'll prove more true
Than those that have more cunning to be strange.
I should have been more strange, I must confess,
But that thou over-heard'st, ere I was 'ware,
My true love's passion: therefore pardon me,
And not impute this yielding to light love,
Which the dark night hath so discovered.

Romeo. Lady, by yonder blessed moon I swear
That tips with silver all these fruit-tree tops,—
    Juliet. O! swear not by the moon, the inconstant moon,
That monthly changes in her circled orb,
Lest that thy love prove likewise variable.
    Romeo. What shall I swear by?
    Juliet.   Do not swear at all;
Or, if thou wilt, swear by thy gracious self,
Which is the god of my idolatry,
And I'll believe thee.
    Romeo.   If my heart's dear love—
    Juliet. Well, do not swear. Although I joy in thee,
I have no joy of this contract to-night:
It is too rash, too unadvis'd, too sudden;
Too like the lightning, which doth cease to be
Ere one can say it lightens. Sweet, good-night!
This bud of love, by summer's ripening breath,
May prove a beauteous flower when next we meet.
Good-night, good-night! as sweet repose and rest
Come to thy heart as that within my breast!
    Romeo. O! wilt thou leave me so unsatisfied?
    Juliet. What satisfaction canst thou have to-night?
    Romeo. The exchange of thy love's faithful vow for mine.
    Juliet. I gave thee mine before thou didst request it;
And yet I would it were to give again.
    Romeo. Wouldst thou withdraw it? for what purpose, love?
    Juliet. But to be frank, and give it thee again.
And yet I wish but for the thing I have:
My bounty is as boundless as the sea,
My love as deep; the more I give to thee,
The more I have, for both are infinite.
I hear some noise within; dear love, adieu!
Anon, good nurse! Sweet Montague, be true.

HOTSPUR'S REVOLT

From KING HENRY IV, PART I[4]

William Shakespeare

Northumberland. Yea, my good lord.
Those prisoners in your highness' name demanded,
Which Harry Percy here at Holmedon took,
Were, as he says, not with such strength denied
As is deliver'd to your majesty:
Either envy, therefore, or misprision

---

[4] Act I, Scene 3.

Is guilty of this fault and not my son.

 Hotspur. My liege, I did deny no prisoners:
But I remember, when the fight was done,
When I was dry with rage and extreme toil,
Breathless and faint, leaning upon my sword,
Came there a certain lord, neat, and trimly dress'd,
Fresh as a bridegroom; and his chin, new reap'd,
Show'd like a stubble-land at harvest-home:
He was perfumed like a milliner,
And 'twixt his finger and his thumb he held
A pouncet-box, which ever and anon
He gave his nose and took't away again;
Who therewith angry, when it next came there,
Took it in snuff: and still he smil'd and talk'd;
And as the soldiers bore dead bodies by,
He call'd them untaught knaves, unmannerly,
To bring a slovenly unhandsome corpse
Betwixt the wind and his nobility.
With many holiday and lady terms
He question'd me; among the rest, demanded
My prisoners in your majesty's behalf.
I then all smarting with my wounds being cold,
To be so pester'd with a popinjay,
Out of my grief and my impatience
Answer'd neglectingly, I know not what,
He should, or he should not; for't made me mad
To see him shine so brisk and smell so sweet
And talk so like a waiting-gentlewoman
Of guns, and drums, and wounds,—God save the mark!—
And telling me the sovereign'st thing on earth
Was parmaceti for an inward bruise;
And that it was great pity, so it was,
This villainous saltpetre should be digg'd
Out of the bowels of the harmless earth,
Which many a good tall fellow had destroy'd
So cowardly; and but for these vile guns,
He would himself have been a soldier.
This bald unjointed chat of his, my lord,
I answer'd indirectly, as I said;
And I beseech you, let not his report
Come current for an accusation
Betwixt my love and your high majesty.

 Sir Walter Blunt. The circumstance consider'd, good my lord,
Whatever Harry Percy then had said
To such a person and in such a place,
At such a time, with all the rest re-told,
May reasonably die and never rise

To do him wrong, or any way impeach
What then he said, so he unsay it now.
    King Henry. Why, yet he doth deny his prisoners,
But with proviso and exception,
That we at our own charge shall ransom straight
His brother-in-law, the foolish Mortimer;
Who, on my soul, hath wilfully betray'd
The lives of those that he did lead to fight
Against the great magician, damn'd Glendower,
Whose daughter, as we hear, the Earl of March
Hath lately married. Shall our coffers then
Be emptied to redeem a traitor home?
Shall we buy treason, and indent with fears,
When they have lost and forfeited themselves?
No, on the barren mountains let him starve;
For I shall never hold that man my friend
Whose tongue shall ask me for one penny cost
To ransom home revolted Mortimer.
    Hotspur.   Revolted Mortimer!
He never did fall off, my sovereign liege,
But by the chance of war: to prove that true
Needs no more but one tongue for all those wounds,
Those mouthed wounds, which valiantly he took,
When on the gentle Severn's sedgy bank,
In single opposition, hand to hand,
He did confound the best part of an hour
In changing hardiment with great Glendower.
Three times they breath'd and three times did they drink,
Upon agreement, of swift Severn's flood,
Who then, affrighted with their bloody looks,
Ran fearfully among the trembling reeds
And hid his crisp head in the hollow bank
Blood-stained with these valiant combatants.
Never did base and rotten policy
Colour her working with such deadly wounds;
Nor never could the noble Mortimer
Receive so many, and all willingly:
Then let him not be slander'd with revolt.
    King Henry. Thou dost belie him, Percy, thou dost belie him:
He never did encounter with Glendower:
I tell thee,
He durst as well have met the devil alone
As Owen Glendower for an enemy.
Art thou not asham'd? But, sirrah, henceforth
Let me not hear you speak of Mortimer:
Send me your prisoners with the speediest means,
Or you shall hear in such a kind from me

As will displease you. My Lord Northumberland,
We license your departure with your son.
Send us your prisoners, or you'll hear of it.

Exeunt KING HENRY, BLUNT, *and train.*

Hotspur. And if the devil come and roar for them,
I will not send them: I will after straight
And tell him so; for I will ease my heart,
Albeit I make a hazard of my head.

Northumberland. What! drunk with choler? stay, and pause awhile:
Here comes your uncle.

Re-enter WORCESTER.

Hotspur.   Speak of Mortimer!
'Zounds! I will speak of him; and let my soul
Want mercy if I do not join with him:
In his behalf I'll empty all these veins,
And shed my dear blood drop by drop i' the dust,
But I will lift the down-trod Mortimer
As high i' the air as this unthankful king,
As this ingrate and canker'd Bolingbroke.

Northumberland. Brother, the king hath made your nephew mad.

Worcester. Who struck this heat up after I was gone?

Hotspur. He will, forsooth, have all my prisoners;
And when I urg'd the ransome once again
Of my wife's brother, then his cheek look'd pale,
And on my face he turn'd an eye of death,
Trembling even at the name of Mortimer.

Worcester. I cannot blame him: was he not proclaim'd
By Richard that is dead the next of blood?

Northumberland. He was; I heard the proclamation:
And then it was when the unhappy king,—
Whose wrongs in us God pardon!—did set forth
Upon his Irish expedition;
From whence he, intercepted, did return
To be depos'd, and shortly murdered.

Worcester. And for whose death we in the world's wide mouth
Live scandaliz'd and foully spoken of.

Hotspur. But, soft! I pray you, did King Richard then
Proclaim my brother Edmund Mortimer
Heir to the crown?

Northumberland. He did; myself did hear it.

Hotspur. Nay, then I cannot blame his cousin king,
That wish'd him on the barren mountains starve.
But shall it be that you, that set the crown
Upon the head of this forgetful man,
And for his sake wear the detested blot

Of murd'rous subornation, shall it be,
That you a world of curses undergo,
Being the agents, or base second means,
The cords, the ladder, or the hangman rather?
O! Pardon me that I descend so low,
To show the line and the predicament
Wherein you range under this subtle king.
Shall it for shame be spoken in these days,
Or fill up chronicles in time to come,
That men of your nobility and power,
Did gage them both in an unjust behalf,
As both of you—God pardon it!—have done,
To put down Richard, that sweet lovely rose,
And plant this thorn, this canker, Bolingbroke?
And shall it in more shame be further spoken,
That you are fool'd, discarded, and shook off
By him for whom these shames ye underwent?
No; yet time serves wherein you may redeem
Your banish'd honours, and restore yourselves
Into the good thoughts of the world again;
Revenge the jeering and disdain'd contempt
Of this proud king, who studies day and night
To answer all the debt he owes to you,
Therefore, I say,—

   Worcester. Peace, cousin! say no more:
And now I will unclasp a secret book,
And to your quick-conceiving discontents
I'll read you matter deep and dangerous,
As full of peril and adventurous spirit
As to o'er-walk a current roaring loud,
On the unsteadfast footing of a spear.

   Hotspur. If we fall in, good night! or sink or swim:
Send danger from the east unto the west,
So honour cross it from the north to south,
And let them grapple: O! the blood more stirs
To rouse a lion than to start a hare.

   Northumberland. Imagination of some great exploit
Drives him beyond the bounds of patience.

   Hotspur. By heaven methinks it were an easy leap
To pluck bright honour from the pale-fac'd moon,
Or dive into the bottom of the deep,
Where fathom-line could never touch the ground,
And pluck up drowned honour by the locks;
So he that doth redeem her thence might wear
Without corrival all her dignities:
But out upon this half-fac'd fellowship!

   Worcester. He apprehends a world of figures here,

But not the form of what he should attend.
Good cousin, give me audience for a while.
    Hotspur. I cry you mercy.
    Worcester.   Those same noble Scots
That are your prisoners,—
    Hotspur.   I'll keep them all;
By God, he shall not have a Scot of them:
No, if a Scot would save his soul, he shall not:
I'll keep them, by this hand.
    Worcester.   You start away,
And lend no ear unto my purposes.
Those prisoners you shall keep.
    Hotspur. Nay, I will; that's flat:
He said he would not ransom Mortimer;
Forbade my tongue to speak of Mortimer;
But I will find him when he lies asleep,
And in his ear I'll holla 'Mortimer!'
Nay,
I'll have a starling shall be taught to speak
Nothing but 'Mortimer,' and give it him,
To keep his anger still in motion.
    Worcester. Hear you, cousin; a word.
    Hotspur. All studies here I solemnly defy,
Save how to gall and pinch this Bolingbroke:
And that same sword-and-buckler Prince of Wales,
But that I think his father loves him not,
And would be glad he met with some mischance,
I'd have him poison'd with a pot of ale.
    Worcester. Farewell, kinsman: I will talk to you
When you are better temper'd to attend.
    Northumberland. Why, what a wasp-stung and impatient fool
Art thou to break into this woman's mood,
Tying thine ear to no tongue but thine own!
    Hotspur. Why, look you, I am whipp'd and scourg'd with rods,
Nettled and stung with pismires, when I hear
Of this vile politician, Bolingbroke.
In Richard's time,—what do you call the place?—
A plague upon't—it is in Gloucestershire;—
'Twas where the madcap duke his uncle kept,
His uncle York; where I first bow'd my knee
Unto this king of smiles, this Bolingbroke,
'Sblood!
When you and he came back from Ravenspurgh.
    Northumberland. At Berkeley Castle.
    Hotspur. You say true.
Why, what a candy deal of courtesy
This fawning greyhound then did proffer me!

Look, 'when his infant fortune came to age,'
And 'gentle Harry Percy,' and 'kind cousin.'
O! the devil take such cozeners. God forgive me!
Good uncle, tell your tale, for I have done.
   Worcester. Nay, if you have not, to't again;
We'll stay your leisure.
   Hotspur. I have done, i' faith.

CARDINAL WOLSEY'S FALL

From KING HENRY VIII[5]

William Shakespeare

   Wolsey. Farewell! a long farewell, to all my greatness!
This is the state of man: to-day he puts forth
The tender leaves of hopes; to-morrow blossoms,
And bears his blushing honours thick upon him;
The third day comes a frost, a killing frost;
And, when he thinks, good easy man, full surely
His greatness is a-ripening, nips his root,
And then he falls, as I do. I have ventur'd,
Like little wanton boys that swim on bladders,
This many summers in a sea of glory,
But far beyond my depth: my high-blown pride
At length broke under me, and now has left me,
Weary and old with service, to the mercy
Of a rude stream, that must for ever hide me.
Vain pomp and glory of this world, I hate ye:
I feel my heart new open'd. O! how wretched
Is that poor man that hangs on princes' favours!
There is, betwixt that smile we would aspire to,
That sweet aspect of princes, and their ruin,
More pangs and fears than wars or women have;
And when he falls, he falls like Lucifer,
Never to hope again.

Enter CROMWELL, *amazedly.*

Why, how now, Cromwell!
   Cromwell. I have no power to speak, sir.
   Wolsey.   What! amaz'd
At my misfortunes? can thy spirit wonder
A great man should decline? Nay, an you weep,
I am fall'n indeed.
   Cromwell. How does your Grace?
   Wolsey.   Why, well;

[5] Act III, Scene 2.

Never so truly happy, my good Cromwell.
I know myself now; and I feel within me
A peace above all earthly dignities,
A still and quiet conscience. The king has cur'd me,
I humbly thank his Grace; and from these shoulders
These ruin'd pillars, out of pity taken
A load would sink a navy, too much honour
O! 'tis a burden, Cromwell, 'tis a burden
Too heavy for a man that hopes for heaven.
  Cromwell. I am glad your Grace has made that right use of it.
  Wolsey. I hope I have: I am able now, methinks,—
Out of a fortitude of soul I feel,—
To endure more miseries and greater far
Than my weak-hearted enemies dare offer.

    . . . . .

Go, get thee from me, Cromwell;
I am a poor fall'n man, unworthy now
To be thy lord and master: seek the king;—
That sun, I pray, may never set!—I have told him
What, and how true thou art: he will advance thee;
Some little memory of me will stir him—
I know his noble nature—not to let
Thy hopeful service perish too. Good Cromwell,
Neglect him not; make use now, and provide
For thine own future safety.
  Cromwell.   O my lord!
Must I then leave you? must I needs forego
So good, so noble, and so true a master?
Bear witness all that have not hearts of iron,
With what a sorrow Cromwell leaves his lord.
The king shall have my service; but my prayers
For ever and for ever, shall be yours.
  Wolsey. Cromwell, I did not think to shed a tear
In all my miseries; but thou hast forc'd me,
Out of thy honest truth, to play the woman.
Let's dry our eyes: and thus far hear me, Cromwell;
And, when I am forgotten, as I shall be,
And sleep in dull cold marble, where no mention
Of me more must be heard of, say, I taught thee,
Say, Wolsey, that once trod the ways of glory,
And sounded all the depths and shoals of honour,
Found thee a way, out of his wrack, to rise in;
A sure and safe one, though thy master miss'd it.
Mark but my fall, and that that ruin'd me.
Cromwell, I charge thee, fling away ambition:
By that sin fell the angels; how can man then,

The image of his Maker, hope to win by't?
Love thyself last: cherish those hearts that hate thee;
Corruption wins not more than honesty.
Still in thy right hand carry gentle peace,
To silence envious tongues: be just, and fear not.
Let all the ends thou aim'st at be thy country's,
Thy God's, and truth's; then if thou fall'st, O Cromwell!
Thou fall'st a blessed martyr. Serve the king;
And,—prithee, lead me in:
There take an inventory of all I have,
To the last penny; 'tis the king's: my robe,
And my integrity to heaven is all
I dare now call mine own. O Cromwell, Cromwell!
Had I but serv'd my God with half the zeal
I served my king, he would not in mine age
Have left me naked to mine enemies.
    Cromwell. Good sir, have patience.
    Wolsey. So I have. Farewell
The hopes of court! my hopes in heaven do dwell.

A CEMETERY AT HOGA POINT[6]

James A. Michener

I was flown down to Konora to recruit aviation replacements for LARU-8, which had been destroyed at Kuralei. As always, there were ten volunteers for each job up front. The skipper said, "Isn't LARU-8 the unit that waited almost a year for something to do?"

"Yes," I said. "Then it hurried to Kuralei just in time to catch a bomb in the belly."

"You're stealing my best men, but go ahead."

We flew the key men north. The rest of us waited for a transport. Tired and sweating, I leaned forward on the table. "Was Kuralei that tough?" the skipper asked.

"Not for me," I said. "Some of the fellows on the beaches, yes. But I did see a lot. You ever know Tony Fry?"

"Sure! He had that beer-bottle TBF didn't he? Used to see him in Guadal. He get it?"

"Yes," I said. I looked away. My right eye was twitching. I couldn't make it stop.

"Commander," the skipper said. "You're getting a case of nerves. What you need is a fishing party. I got some old togs. We'll go out and soak up some sun."

Konora was peaceful. As I gazed at it from the ammunition scow on

which we fished, the island seemed asleep. Its low hills were beautiful
against the deep sky. In the bend of the island there was a white slash
across the green hill. "That's where Pearlstein ripped away the coral," I
recalled. A gaunt steam shovel worked by the bay, lifting live coral for
patching the airstrip. From time to time silvery bombers, white against
the dark sky, settled down on the strip or rose from it in graceful circles.

Far out at sea slim birds of passage dived breathlessly at schools of
fish. At the edge of the reef breakers shot silvery spume into the air.
Along the horizon the ultramarine sky joined the gray-blue sea. I closed
my eyes from this enchanting beauty. It was so remote from the torn
coconut trees of Kuralei.

"It's not bad from out here," the skipper said.

It was difficult to believe that on Konora nine hundred and seventeen
Japs were buried in graves patiently dug by Marines and SeaBees. Nor
did it seem possible that two hundred and eighty-one Americans lay on
that island in timeless sleep. Only a few weeks before this peaceful land
had been torn and twisted like Kuralei.

Our ammunition barge now lay opposite Hoga Point. I said to the
skipper, "Would you think me crazy if I asked you to put me ashore here?
I can't seem to get things under control. I'd like to walk back to camp
through the trees."

"You're the visitor," he said indulgently. He had the coxswain row me
ashore. In a few minutes I was standing at the head of a small promon-
tory which climbed slightly from the sea until it reached a height of sixty
or seventy feet above the waves. At that level it formed a plateau which
overlooked the vast Pacific on one side and the soft lagoon on the other.
Here, on the ruins of their enemy, the Americans had built their cemetery.

A white picket fence surrounded the burial ground. From one corner
rose a slim steel flagpole. From it fluttered an American flag. Because
the air was so clean, the white stripes and the stars shone more beautifully
than any I had ever seen before.

Before me lay the dead, the heroic dead who took the island. Upon
a strange plateau, on a strange island, in a strange sea, far from their farms
and villages, they slept forever beside the lagoon which bore them to their
day of battle. Over them the sea birds dipped in endless homage. Above
them the deep sky erected a cathedral. I cannot put into words the emotions that captured me as I looked upon the graves of my friends. Never
once during the five weeks I helped to plan the operations that engulfed
Konora, not once at Kuralei, did I believe that I would die. No more did
any man who now lay still in death. The Marine in the prow of the ship,
he might die. The SeaBee who made noises when he ate, he might topple
from the crane. But not I!

Yet there before me lay almost three hundred Americans who thought
as I had thought. They could not die. But there were the white crosses.
I was appalled by the relentless manner in which one dead plus one dead
plus one dead add up to three white crosses. If you sit at home and read
that two hundred and eighty-one men die in taking an island, the number

is only a symbol for the mind to classify. But when you stand at the white crosses, the two hundred and eighty-one dead become men: the sons, the husbands, and the lovers.

Lonely and bitter, I leaned against the picket fence. It was then that I noticed a tall, very thin Negro ambling toward me. He walked like one of the mechanical ducks which dull-eyed men sell on the street corners of New York, a waddle-walk obtained by never lifting either foot completely from the ground. But the Negro gave the shuffle a certain dignity. He looked as if he owned Hoga Point, as if he had lived there all his life.

"Aftanoon, suh," he drawled. He was dragging a rake which he pushed against the picket fence. Holding it with both hands before his chest, he leaned forward. "Yo'-all lookin' fo' sumbuddy, suh? Or you jes' lookin'?"

"I'm just looking," I replied. "May I come in?"

"You certainly kin, suh!" the tall Negro replied. He pointed to the gate in the white pickets. "Won't you please come in, suh? It's a real pleasure to have officers visit the cemetery. Me 'n' Denis, we doan' see much people up dis yere way. Please to come in!"

I followed him to the gate, he on the inside of the pickets, I on the outside. Graciously he opened the gate and then carefully closed it. "I finds sittin' under dem trees mos' beneficial," he said, indicating several tall trees whose shadows fell within the fence. He slowly showed me to a rude hassock, probably the stump of an old tree overgrown with moss. He was correct. The seat in the shadows was beneficial.

"Me 'n' Denis, we sits here right often when de sun get too hot. Sun in dese yere latitudes is pow'ful strong sometimes." He spoke with a calm drawl which matched his gait. Gripping the rake handle firmly, he let himself down upon the earth beside me.

"Who is Denis?" I inquired.

"Me 'n' Denis, we runs dis yere place," the Negro replied.

"What do you mean?" I asked.

"Well, me 'n' Denis we is de only people dat works yere," he drawled. "Seem lak nobody else want to work in a place lak dis yere." With a languid sweep of his hand he indicated the white crosses.

"Is Denis a colored man, too?" I asked.

"Yes," he answered. "Me 'n' Denis, we is bof' cullud. He f'um Geo'gia. I f'um Mississippi."

"Isn't it strange," I asked, "for colored men to like work in a cemetery?"

My guide laughed, gently and easily. "Yes! Yes! I knows jes' what yo'-all means," he said. "All dem jokes about ghos's and cullud men. But what yo'-all doan' see," he added quietly, "is dat dey ain' no ghos's up here!"

He waved his hand once more across the graves. I waited for him to speak again.

"Up here," he continued, "dey is only heroes. Me 'n' Denis has often remarked dat never again will we be surrounded only by heroes. I 'spect we likes our work better'n any other men on dis yere rock. Would you like to walk among de graves, suh?" he inquired. "We got some mighty in'erestin' graves in here." Slowly, by means of the rake handle, he pulled himself to his feet. He led me to a small corner of the cemetery.

"Dese yere is de men dat took de las' Jap charge," he said softly, like the verger of the cathedral at Antwerp. "Wiped out. Ever'one of dem." He dropped his voice still lower. "Some of dem we couldn't even find. Dat is, not all of dem. We jes' had to bury arms and legs and call 'em bodies." He raised his voice. "But here dey all lie. Sleepin'. It doan' make no difference to 'em now. Bodies or no bodies. Dey all heroes!"

"Over here," he said proudly, "we got de bes' man of 'em all. Dat grave wid de flowers. Me 'n' Denis, we planted dem flowers." I looked at the garlanded grave. The plots around it were vacant, and the flowers grew in rich profusion, right up to the austere white cross: "Commander Hoag."

"As you kin see," the caretaker said solemnly, "dis here de commander. Commander Hoag hisse'f. Finer man never lived this side o' heaven. Ever'body says that. You know de commander?"

I replied that I had. The Negro droned on. "He about de bes' man I met in all de Navy. He kind to ever'body. Always greet you wid a smile. Wasn't afraid of bawlin' you out, neither. I remembers 'specially one time he give me 'n' Denis a bad time. Mighty bad time he give us. Had to do wid de officers' mess. We was mighty mad, at de time. But we got over it. 'N' here he lies. Daid lak de res'. Tell me, suh? What we gonna do if men lak de commander is killed all de time? Where we gonna git good men lak him? You 'spect there's men lak him ready to take his job?"

I slipped into Sunday school maxims. "Isn't it pretty true," I asked, "that good men always show up when they're needed? You don't think the SeaBees will fall apart just because Commander Hoag died?"

"Da's mah point!" the Negro cried. "Da's jes' mah point! Already we got a new skipper. Sure. But he ain' a good man! Not at all he ain'." The tall Negro looked about him slowly. "Lemme show you jes' what I mean." He placed his rake among the flowers on Commander Hoag's grave and leaned upon it. We talked across the grave of the fallen leader. Whenever the caretaker mentioned Hoag he would release one hand from the rake and point languidly downward.

" 'Bout two month ago we git an officer in de unit dat hated cullud folk. He give us a mighty bad time in de mess hall. One morning I tell him twice we doan' have no eggs. He git very mad. 'Won't have no —— eight ball tellin' me what to do and what not to do!' He shouted. Later in de day Commander Hoag he hear about dis yere ruckus. He call us into his office. All us cullud boys. He stand up when we come in. 'Men,' he says, 'I'm mighty sorry to hear about what happen dis mornin'. Yo'-all know we doan' act lak dat in de 144th. You men got rights jes' lak ever'one else. I ain't gonna stand by and see 'em abused.' " The Negro pointed at the grave with his thumb. "He was a good man. Where we gonna git good men lak him?"

I repeated my former argument and the Negro disagreed violently.

"No, suh!" he replied. "I cain' believe dat. Dey's only so many good men, and if you uses 'em up, where you gonna git de others? Take de 144th! When Commander Hoag died, who dey put in his place? De officer dat give us black boys all dat trouble. What he say de first day? 'Gonna be some changes here! Ain' gonna take no mo' nonsense f'um a lot of —— niggers!' Da's why me 'n' Denis works up here. Ain' nobody to push us aroun'. Ain' nobody always tellin' us what to do. We is de boss!" He surveyed his lonely acres. "Up here ever'body is easy to get along wid. Doan' make no difference is you cullud or white. When yo' daid you fo'get all dat stuff." He lifted his rake from Commander Hoag's grave and ambled down the long lines.

"Dat one ova' dere," he said, pointing with his rake to a small white cross at the end of a row. "He git drunk. Run off'n de cliff one night and kill hisse'f. All his own fault. But now he daid. Back home I guess he a big hero. I kin jes' hear his folks sayin' kinda proud and heartbreakin' at de same time, 'Our boy, he died on Konora.' Da's one reason why I likes to work here. Up here dey all heroes. Ain' a mean man in de bunch." We walked among the fresh graves. Already their brutal outlines were softened by wisps of tender grass. Along the fence yellow flowers were in bloom.

"Dis boy over here what I mean," the caretaker continued, pointing with his rake to a grave undistinguishable from the others. "He quite a man!" I followed the rake past the graves of two Marine privates and a SeaBee carpenter's mate to an officer's grave. In the cemetery at Hoga Point distinctions end. There are no officers and men. There are only men. This was the grave of First Lt. Joe Cable, USMCR.

"He got hisse'f into some kind of trouble down south," the Negro droned on, pointing at the grave with a lazy thumb. "Had a fight on de boat wid some his own men. Ever'body called him Fo' Dolla'. Made him mighty mad. Well, dey kep' de fight sort of hushed up. But two nights before we land here, I und'stand dey was another fight. Dis time de lieutenant he slug another officer. De colonel hear about dis one. He furious. Say dey ain' got no right fightin' among deyselves when de Japs so near. De colonel he want to th'ow de lieutenant in de brig right den. But instead he give de young fellow one mo' chance. Say if he pull hisse'f together on de beach, he goin' to forget all about it. What de colonel doan' know is dat de boy, he pretty heartsick. Trouble he got into down south. He pretty well fed up wid things in general." The caretaker paused and reflected upon the grave. "Seem lak sometime it's de officers doan' know how to take care of theyselves."

"Well, come de beachhead," he continued. "And dis yere Marine, he about de bes' we got on our side. He go after them Japs plenty tough. Lot of wise guys dat been plaguin' him, dey keep dey big mouf' shut. Finally, he git his. Go down all in a lump. Dey tell me de colonel see him go. Some time de colonel come up here and look around. I figger he pretty glad he let de lieutenant outen de brig. But maybe he ain' so glad either. 'Cause if he keep de young man locked up, he be alive now."

The caretaker wandered to the end of the cemetery and shuffled over to the cool mound under the trees. Easing himself down by means of his rake handle, he waited for his partner Denis to appear.

I did not join him but stayed among the graves.

Like the Negro I wondered where the men would come from to take Commander Hoag's place. Throughout the Pacific, in Russia, in Africa, and soon on fronts not yet named, good men were dying. Who would take their place? Who would marry the girls they would have married? Or build the buildings they would have built? Were there men at home ready to do Hoag's job? And Cable's? And Tony Fry's? Or did war itself help create replacements out of its bitterness?

I thought of Hoag as I knew him, a man who never buttoned his shirt properly. He was from Atlanta, but he championed the Negro. He was a rich man, but he befriended his meanest enlisted man. He was a gentile, but he placed Jews in positions of command. He was a man tired with responsibility, but he saw to it that others got rest. Yet when he died a loud-mouthed bully came along to take his place. One night he called Pearlstein a kike. Threatened to have no more trouble with a bunch of —— niggers. Called hardworking young De Vito a "grease ball, and you know how they stand up in war!" If he stayed in command much longer, all the patient work Hoag had done would be dissipated. The 144th SeaBees would be unfit to hit another beachhead. Already they were beginning to fall apart at the seams. The guiding spirit of their team was dead.

Each man who lay on Hoga Point bore with him to his grave some promise for a free America. Now they were gone. Who would take their places? Women? Old men? Or were those who lived committed to a double burden? Theirs and the dead men's?

From the picket fence I heard a cheerful voice. It was Denis lugging a bucket of cold water. He laughed when he saw me by the graves. "You comin' up to see about movin' all dese yere bodies back to the States?" he asked.

"No," I replied. "Are they going to do that?"

"Da's what dey say," Denis laughed, wiping his jet forehead. "Seem lak nonsense to me. If'n I die out here, where I goin' to sleep happier dan wid de men I fought wif'? Where I goin' to get a more peaceful dreamin' place dan dis yere spot? Look at dem birds!" I followed the flight of four dazzling birds as they dipped toward the lagoon. "I s'pose you been talkin' to de preacher?" Denis inquired.

"Who's that?" I asked, and Denis pointed to his friend under the tree.

"Da's him. Da's de preacher! In Mississippi he call hisse'f a preacher!" He laughed and took the water to his friend. The caretaker took a long drink, and what was left in the cup he swished into the flowers.

"Doan' you mind what Denis say," he whispered to me. "Denis, he quite a cutup. Sometime he run off at de mouf'."

DRAMA AT SEAL LAKES[7]

Arthur C. Twomey and *Nigel Herrick*

[This incident is from the adventures of two scientists, J. K. Doutt and Arthur C. Twomey, in their search for the mysterious fresh water seal, *kasagea*, in the unexplored wastes of central Labrador. They rode by train and plane to the eastern shore of Hudson Bay, but the last two hundred and fifty miles inland from there they had to make on foot, dragging their supplies over the snow on Indian toboggans. With them were their guide and interpreter, George Moore; four Indians, Daniel, Jacob, Luk Cashe, and Boyshish; and a little Eskimo, Ekumiak, with his dog. *Kingmee.* They established their camp at one of the Seal Lakes, and for twelve discouraging days they watched and waited in the bitter cold without seeing a sign of a seal.]

On March the twenty-first, from nine in the morning until five at night, we and the Indians and Ekumiak covered every hole that we knew of, for every minute of the time, without finding any sign of a seal. During all these hours everyone was perfectly quiet, sitting in the separate 'hides' of snow which Ekumiak had built for us.

While I sat in my own 'hide,' I heard a pair of jays fussing in a clump of trees behind me. The sun was out again but it was stinging cold. A red-poll flew over, giving his clear ringing song as he passed into the distant hills. A single Hudsonian chickadee winged above our strange community—as it must have seemed to him—stopping for a moment's rest on a large rock boulder which stuck up from the ice only a few feet from me, and was off again with an excited chirp. Two flocks of rock ptarmigan whizzed by like bullets, flying but a few scant feet above the ground. I sat almost motionless through the whole day, until the fading light and bitter evening chill drove us all at last in a common misery back to camp. George and Jacob Rupert had got in from their far searches before me and with the same old story: 'no *kasagea*.'

That night we did not hear Jacob's rich tenor voice singing 'In the Land of the Sweet By and By.' The Indians' food condition was precarious, and only our own woes and the intentness of our search for the seal had kept us from inquiring much into it. We did not dare to let them shoot within sound of the shrub-bordered lake or river for fear of alarming *kasagea*, and beyond the shrubs there were no birds. According to our calculations, there should still have been reserves of food from the toboggans, but Daniel said he had given out the last they had. We were too absorbed in our schemes to ask why. We simply split our remaining rations, giving half to the Indians, and prepared to quit. Twenty-five pounds of flour, fifteen pounds of beans, ten pounds of split peas, and a

[7] From *Needle to the North, the Story of an Expedition to Ungava and the Belcher Islands,* by Arthur C. Twomey. In collaboration with Nigel Herrick. Houghton Mifflin Co., Boston, 1942. By permission of the authors.

little bacon would keep them alive until we could all reach the cache of abandoned supplies just beyond Clearwater Lake Island. My heart was like lead that night and I could hardly look at Doutt, knowing what he must feel. The Indians had been on the point of mutiny long before this, and we knew now that they could not be kept inland any longer. Later on that day we meant to let the Indians shoot, but the wind was up and all the birds were under cover.

For the *kingmee* Ekumiak was still in tortures of fear, but he himself was no longer afraid of the Indians. At least he was no longer afraid of young Boyshish. Boyshish knew a little Husky, so that the two of them could have a glimmering of conversation together, and sometimes Ekumiak had gone so far as to sit in the Indians' tent singing hymns with them, for they knew the same tunes, though in different language. On the night of March the twenty-first, he furnished them with a drama, a pantomimed story from traditional Eskimo life.

The Indians lounged around the tent walls in various postures, looking positively gaunt. They were all muttering among themselves when I came in and they continued to mutter. George was there, having come like me in restless aimlessness. I sat down at George's invitation, and against our general policy, being too tired and careless now to take heed of dignity or of lice any longer. The red stove glowed and crackled. The row of swinging mitts, fantastically dangling from the drying-rack near the ceiling, grew enormous in my eyes, hanging there as a horrible symbol of our sufferings and our defeat. Twelve tired, wet, frozen, *empty* hands. Empty stomachs. Tired, baneful, bloodshot eyes, I thought, watching them. What could we do, except quit?

Were the Indians talking of risking it just one more day, George asked Daniel, but Daniel had already told Doutt that they wouldn't. They hadn't wanted to risk it for the last week or more. And who could blame them? As to the food stores, weird suspicions were always crossing our minds, dark and unprovable. The fact remained that there were not even rations enough to make the home-going easy, and the men were in no shape to bear much more suffering. *'Undyeskosen'* ('I am sick'), *'Kewaida!'* ('Let's go home!') they were muttering on all sides.

Their voices rose in malevolence as Daniel's rose in argument. There was a pause presently, with things apparently hopeless. All sat dejected and most of them silent. *'Sheewadan'* ('I am hungry'), added Luk Cashe simply, summing it all up in a nutshell.

But Ekumiak and Boyshish, who had been speaking together, suddenly held up their hands, motioning to the Indians to move back out of the way, and Boyshish began explaining to the group excitedly that Ekumiak was going to show them all the *pibors dowhoon*—'the winter hunt' of the Innuit.

'He will show them,' whispered George for my benefit, 'how the Eskimos used to hunt seals long ago.'

The Indians were looking up with an amazing show of interest—for *them*—as Ekumiak, holding out his hand to me, asked, *'sernuhuti?'*—for the watch out of my pocket. He put the watch on the food-box near him, first holding it up to show the dial and pointing to four o'clock. His body sagged, his eyes closed, his face dropped. He stretched himself on the floor and slept.

'*Tabiscow*' ('darkness'), murmured Boyshish in hushed tones as the actor indicated that it was night.

Ekumiak's pantomime was very realistic. He sat up, yawned, shivered. He stood up, turned to the stove to warm his hands a moment. . . . He pulled on a pair of pants, and then pulled on another, holding up two fingers so that we understood.

'Two pairs,' whispered George to me helpfully as Boyshish explained again to the Indians. Then Ekumiak donned a parka and repeated the operation also. Two parkas! He put on several pairs of socks and pulled on high boots (tightening the drawstring high at the top so that we understood he meant the Eskimo *Komik*). He put on two pairs of mitts. He pulled up one parka hood. Then he pulled up the other. Again he went to the stove. Again he shivered. Then he gave a great sigh of resignation. After that he acted swiftly, gathering up objects, first a *long* one as he measured it for us by his arms. ('The harpoon,' whispered George, entranced.) Then he hastily revolved one hand about the other in cylindrical fashion, as though winding the long harpoon line about his arm. Down on his hands and knees, he moved forward in a determined crawl, out through the long low tunneled entrance of the imaginary igloo. Turning to us with a smile, which served very well for the first act curtain, he rose and showed us the watch again, pointing to only a little past four.

There was nothing startling in what Ekumiak did at any time, but somehow we felt that there was. The little Innuit had that subtle inborn quality of being able to command attention. Like many fine actors he was not much when he was himself, but given license to be somebody else, his strength was tremendous. Once he had decided to entertain us, he threw his whole soul into it, and was rewarded with a complete success. No Broadway prize play was ever more hung upon by a gaping audience than was Ekumiak's little drama in that drab tent in the Ungava wilderness.

For almost half an hour in reality (and for many hours as revealed upon the watch), we sat in spirit beside an Eskimo's seal hole, with tension in the tent rising to an ever higher pitch. Even the Indians lost themselves in Ekumiak's acted story. Shifting his feet with incredible care among the spruce boughs on the tent floor, the Eskimo would indicate strained muscles—so tired that they must be moved, but moved without the slightest sound. Intermittently, he would show us the watch dial, solemnly and painfully moving his finger completely around the face of it, indicating that the seal hunter in the drama had waited one hour, then that he had waited two, then three, four, five, six, seven and eight.

At the end of ten imaginary hours, Ekumiak picked up the fingers of one hand and let the hand fall limply, as though it were frozen. Then the little Innuit scooped up some snow, very cautiously, very silently, as always, and began rubbing the limp hand back and forth, slowly, over and over. A gasp went up from the watching Indians at the look of suffering on the fat Eskimo face of Ekumiak, as he sat clasping the supposedly frozen fingers tightly between his legs.

Five more hours went by, as he made plain on the clock. Ekumiak's body was drawn into a knot of misery. His eyes stared, yet he seemed to see nothing. It was his *right* hand now that he clasped between his legs. He even wrinkled his face up once, and felt of it tenderly to show that it too was freezing. When the whole drama had become so painful that I thought I couldn't stand any more of it, Ekumiak suddenly straightened. With a theatrical pause, wherein he riveted our attention, his hand began to move. Almost imperceptibly, he was lifting up his clenched right fist. But he did not strike. He kept us waiting there with him, while the empathy which I myself felt in my muscles strained my back so much that I felt sore afterward. And then, suddenly, he struck. The suspense in the audience had been terrible. A great sigh went up from the Indians, as the hunter at last began to pull and pull and pull the imaginary body of the seal out of the water.

'Kosigwan' ('heavy'), growled out a deep Indian voice in tones of the most intense satisfaction.

It was accomplished. It was done. Then simply, in a pathetic gesture, Ekumiak knelt beside the seal for a moment and bowed his head and clasped his hands together. To my amazement, a tear was running down the cheek of one of the Indians. He had been *so* hungry! And now he was *so* thankful.

Rising, flushed with success, Ekumiak murmured something to Boyshish, still in fanciful and hysterical spirit.

'Now the seal is in his stomach!' cried Boyshish wildly, almost beside himself with pleasure, and all the other Indians loudly laughed. They really *laughed*. I could hardly believe it.

I took note of myself and of the whole scene. For twenty-three hours, Ekumiak had told us, an Eskimo used to sit waiting for his seal. Twenty-three hours by the seal hole, without once leaving it! And we were going home tomorrow, from our warm tents—with nothing.

I went back to my tent and to sleep, somehow purged of those dreadful emotions that had beset all of us for the last few days. The situation had not changed, but I had. And so apparently had the Indians. The next morning Daniel brought us their decision; they would stay another twenty-four hours. We would all risk it for one more day.

MR. SHAW'S CHRISTMAS[8]

George Bernard Shaw

The only music I have heard this week is Waits. To sit up working until two or three in the morning, and then, just as I am losing myself in my first sleep, to hear *Venite adoremus*, more generally known as Ow, cam

[8] From Hesketh Pearson, *G. B. S. A Full Length Portrait.* Reprinted by permission of Hesketh Pearson.

let Haz adore Im, welling forth from a cornet (English pitch), a saxhorn (Society of Arts pitch, or thereabouts), and a trombone (French pitch), is the sort of thing that breaks my peace and destroys my good will toward men. Coming on top of a very arduous month, it reduced me last Saturday to a condition of such complete addledness, that it became evident that my overwrought brain would work itself soft in another fortnight unless an interval of complete mental vacuity could be induced.

Obviously the thing to do was to escape from the magnetic atmosphere of London, and slow down in some empty-headed place where I should be thoroughly bored. Somebody suggested Broadstairs. I had always supposed Broadstairs to be a show place at Wapping; but I found that it was half-way between Margate and Ramsgate, in neither of which famous watering-places had I ever set foot.

So to Broadstairs I went. Let no man henceforth ever trifle with Fate so far as actually to seek boredom. Before I was ten minutes here I was bored beyond description. The air of the place is infernal. In it I hurry about like a mouse suffocating in oxygen. The people here call it "ozone" and consider it splendid; but there is a visible crust over them, a sort of dull terra-cotta surface which they pretend to regard as a sign of robust health. As I consume in the ozone, this terrible limekiln crust is forming on me too; and they congratulate me already on "looking quite different." As a matter of fact I can do nothing but eat: my brain refuses its accustomed work. The place smells as if someone had spilt a bottle of iodine over it. The sea is absolutely dirtier than the Thames under Blackfriars Bridge; and the cold is hideous. I have not come across a graveyard yet; and I have no doubt that sepulture is unnecessary, as the houses are perfect refrigerating chambers, capable of preserving a corpse to the remotest posterity.

I am staying in Nuckell's Place; and they tell me that Miss Nuckell was the original of Betsy Trotwood in *David Copperfield*, and that the strip of green outside is that from which she used to chase the donkeys. A house down to the left is called Bleak House; and I can only say that if it is any bleaker than my bedroom, it must be a nonpareil freezer. But all this Dickensmania is only hallucination induced by the ozone. This morning a resident said to me, "Do you see that weatherbeaten old salt coming along?" "Yes," I replied; "and if you will excuse my anticipating your reply, I may say that I have no doubt that he is the original of Captain Cuttle. But, my dear madam, I myself am Corno di Bassetto; and in future Broadstairs anecdotage will begin to revolve round Me." Then, impelled to restless activity by the abominable ozone, I rushed off to the left; sped along the cliffs; passed a lighthouse, which looked as if it had been turned into a pillar of salt by the sea air; fell presently among stony ground; and finally reached Margate, a most dismal hole, where the iodine and ozone were flavored with lodgings.

I made at once for the railway station, and demanded the next train. "Where to?" said the official. "Anywhere," I replied, "provided it be far inland." "Train to Ramsgit at two-fifteen," he said: "nothing else till six."

I could not conceive Ramsgit as being so depressing, even on Christmas day, as Margit; so I got into that train; and lo, the second station we came to was Broadstairs. This was the finger of fate; for the ozone had made me so ragingly hungry that I burst from the train and ran all the way to Nuckell's Place, where, to my unspeakable horror and loathing, they triumphantly brought me up a turkey with sausages. "Surely, sir," they said, as if remonstrating with me for some exhibition of depravity, "*surely* you eat meat on *Christmas* day." "I tell you," I screamed, "that I never eat meat." "Not even a little gravy, sir? I think it would do you good." I put a fearful constraint on myself, and politely refused. Yet they came up again, as fresh as paint, with a discolored mess of suet scorched in flaming brandy; and when I conveyed to them, as considerately as I could, that I thought the distinction between suet and meat, burnt brandy and spirits, too fine to be worth insisting on, they evidently regarded me as hardly reasonable. There can be no doubt that the people here are mentally enfeebled. The keen air causes such rapid waste of tissue that they dare not add to it by thinking. They are always recuperating—that is to say eating—mostly cows.

Nevertheless it was with some emotion that I trod sea sand for the first time for many years. When I was a boy I learnt to appreciate the sight and sound of the sea in a beautiful bay on the Irish coast. But they have no confounded ozone in Ireland, only ordinary wholesome sea air. You never see an Irishman swaggering and sniffing about with his chest expanded, mad with excessive ozone, and assuring everybody that he feels —poor devil—like a new man.

By the way, I did not escape the Waits by coming down here. I had not walked fifty yards from the railway station when I found them in full cry in a front garden. However, I am bound to confess that the seaside vocal Wait is enormously superior to the metropolitan instrumental one. They sang very well: were quite Waits off my mind, in fact. (This is my first pun: let who can beat it.)

JOHN ADAMS, COLLEGE SENIOR[9]

Catherine Drinker Bowen

In Braintree, Mr. Josiah Quincy was deeply concerned [over the French invasion of the Ohio Valley]. He had spent many years in Europe, knew the North American situation from a broad angle. He was a friend and correspondent of Dr. Franklin, who a year ago had devised a plan of strong colonial union for better protection against the growing French menace. . . . Had John Adams heard of this plan, Mr. Quincy demanded one day in his living room at the old parsonage? He flung out the ques-

[9] From *John Adams and the American Revolution.* Copyright, 1949, 1950, by Catherine Drinker Bowen. Reprinted by permission of Little, Brown & Co. and the Atlantic Monthly Press.

tion as if he were addressing not a Harvard Senior, but town meeting and town meeting were hostile.

It was a November afternoon of 1753. John had walked down to tea on invitation of Hannah [Quincy]. She was in the room, presiding over the tea table, very distracting in a dress of yellow wool, cut tight to her figure, with a wide, flowing skirt. Sam and Ned were there. Young Josiah [aged ten] lay sprawled on the floor before the fire, roasting chestnuts in a long-handled skillet. Outside, a northeast wind was blowing; the day had threatened snow. Crimson damask curtains were drawn against the dusk; the candles were lighted. Mr. Quincy turned in his highbacked chair. John's father, he remarked, was a man who knew matters of practical government. What did Mr. Adams think of this plan of union, proposed last June at Albany . . . ? Had John seen Dr. Franklin's motto for the colonies: JOIN OR DIE?

Yes, John replied. The Boston *Gazette* had printed the motto with the accompanying drawing, reproduced from a Philadelphia paper. A clever device of a snake, broken into parts. Each part bore the initials of a colony or section: New England, New York, Pennsylvania, North Carolina, South Carolina. Underneath was written in bold letters: JOIN OR DIE.

"The colonies," Mr. Quincy retorted bitterly, "seem to prefer the latter contingency."

It was true. When the Albany Plan had been put to vote in the various provincial Assemblies, one by one they had turned it down. Most of them protested that it gave too much power to the home government in England. Connecticut objected violently to the veto privilege of a President appointed by the crown. Benjamin Franklin, pondering these contrary opinions, declared them proof positive of how necessary some plan of union had become. When local sovereignties grew fixed and angry, it was imperative to find some kind of balance between them. England, moreover, had not so much as hinted at a declaration of war against the French. Suppose she left us to fend for ourselves, could we act at all unless we learned to act together?

Mr. Josiah Quincy, addressing his living room of young people, seized the tongs and poked angrily at the fire, looking over his nose. "How near must the French come," he demanded, "before the colonies forget their eternal boundary squabbles? And which is more important—a slice of the Green Mountains for Hampshire, or King Lewis's grenadiers walking down into Ticonderoga?"

"God in his heaven!" shouted Mr. Quincy suddenly, staring straight at John—or what he thought was straight. [Mr. Quincy was cross-eyed.] John cleared his throat and looked away. "God in heaven! Here are three university men—Ned—Sam—John Adams. What does our precious Harvard College have to say about Franklin's plan of union and the French on the Ohio? Or does the Discussion Club"—Mr. Quincy's lip curled—"prefer to debate the governments of Greece and Rome, as it did in my time, keeping life on a high classical plane altogether?"

John smiled, but he was much struck by what Mr. Quincy had said. Walking home that night, guarding his lantern under his greatcoat—it had begun to snow in brief, gusty flurries—he went over the conversation in his mind. It was true, about Harvard's remoteness from the present scene. John was due back at college tomorrow. He had come to love the university, felt more at home there, sometimes, than in the farmhouse on the Coast Road.

As for the Harvard Discussion Club, John enjoyed it more than anything he had ever taken part in, or so he told himself now, climbing the hill toward home, his head lowered against the wind. He had not always enjoyed the club. As a Junior last year, he had been surprised to be invited to join. He was among the first four scholars in his class, but he knew himself as an awkward speaker, and the members were chosen for their skill in elocution and declamation. President Holyoke encouraged the use of rhetoric and graceful phrase, embellished with quotations from the classics. The boys read aloud the latest books and plays, which last they were careful to refer to as "dramatic compositions"—Massachusetts having just passed a new law forbidding stage plays.

When John's turn came to declaim for the first time, he had been terrified. His part was assigned to him: Oedipus's first speech from Pope's translation of the *Thebais*. John practiced for hours in his room, striding up and down, hurling out the words, now loud, now suddenly *pianissimo*. One gesture in particular he favored. Raising his right hand high, the index finger extended, he brought his arm down slowly until thumb and forefinger pointed directly at the middle man in an imaginary front row. This telling gesture John synchronized exactly with the climax of his hero's speech: "*Go, and a parent's heavy curses bear!*"

The club met in the library, with an audience of perhaps fifty. Several graduate students had been invited, as well as old Tutor Flynt, who after sixty years' service had resigned as a teacher but lived nearby and liked to be included in these celebrations. John had practiced so hard and so long that he had forgotten his original terror—until his name was called and he rose. As he walked to the rostrum, his stomach turned over agonizingly. Panic gripped him from head to foot. He faced the audience, cleared his throat, opened his mouth. No sound emerged. He cleared his throat again, loudly. His eyes, fixed upward in a glassy stare, saw nothing, his arms stuck rigid to his sides. In a voice wholly unrecognizable, he began to speak, stumbled on toward the climax. As he approached it he gasped, inhaled noisily as if he were choking, then lifted his arm automatically above his head, brought it down slowly and pointed. . . .

There was a shout. "Don't shoot, Adams! . . . For God's sake spare a mother's son!"

Laughter broke like a hurricane in the room. Boys howled, wept, fell on each other's shoulder, leaned helpless over their knees, hugging their stomachs with expressions of agony. Even Tutor Flynt was in a state of collapse and made no effort at rescue. John, his notes crumpled in his hands, fled the rostrum in utter, completest defeat.

It had taken him months to forget it. Perhaps he would never, he thought, forget it. He knew his turn to speak would soon come round again. He practiced doggedly in his room with the door barricaded. This time he would speak his piece if the room burst into flames and the ceiling fell in. He would not be driven from that rostrum by the jeers of one man or fifty. He chose, from Shakespeare's *Coriolanus,* words of the hero's that breathed defiance in every line. The more John practiced, the more he felt at one with this soldier who refused to beg favors from the politicians.

The evening arrived. John rose and made his way to the rostrum. Even before he took his place, the titter started. John's palms were wet. The book, when he raised it, shook miserably in his hands. He began to read Coriolanus's speech to the tribune. The old soldier, scarred with battle, is a candidate for the consulship:

> What must I say?
> "I pray, sir"—Plague upon't. I cannot bring
> My tongue to such a pace . . .

The titter increased. Sudden anger gripped John. He threw the book on the table and walked round to the front. Standing with his legs apart, hands gripped behind him, head flung back, he began Coriolanus's speech from memory:

> Look, sir, my wounds!
> I got them in my country's service, when
> Some certain of your brethren roar'd and ran
> From the noise of our own drums.

Utterly careless as to effect, John spat each word as if every man who heard it were his own personal, desperate antagonist:

> You common cry of curs! whose breath I hate
> As reek o' the rotten fens . . .
>   Despising,
> For you, the city, thus I turn my back:
> *There is a world elsewhere.*

John finished and stood a moment in angry defiance, his round face scarlet, his blue eyes flashing. With a reckless gesture he shook the hair back from his brow, then swung round abruptly and marched to his seat, to the sound of—what was this roaring, overwhelming noise? The audience was clapping, pounding its feet on the floor! Friends rushed up, whacked John on the back. . . . "Adams!" they cried. "You'll make the best speaker of us all, someday." . . . "Coriolanus angry," Sam Locke told the room, "is surely better than Oedipus scared."

John all but wept with surprise and pleasure. His collar was wilted, his fine brown hair awry. The black ribbon at his neck had slipped off altogether. John stuffed it in his pocket. He walked home across the court, arm in arm with Locke and Sewall, singing a song convivial and forbidden. Tutor Mayhew, hearing it from his study, smiled, and did not move from his chair.

From ROUGHING IT WITH GRAMP[10]

Stephen Longstreet

That year 1919 when Gramp and Mama and myself were crossing America the hard way, via a Model T, was a year of sun and dust in the Middle West. Mama's spine was a little unstrung from riding in the back, and Gramp almost lost half of his mustache trying to crank life into Emma (as we called the car) on a back road when his mustache was caught in the crank. Gramp shot up a full series of purple curses, danced, and held his face. Mama stuffed her fingers in my ears. After that, we were all hungry, tired, and dusty.

Mama said, "We should stop for the night."

"Not 'til we get to Ohio. No decent food 'til we hit the river."

"My spine aches."

"Only a few miles more."

We got real lost just before dark, and Gramp got out under an apple tree and looked around him. "Well, you'd think the natives would put up signs for strangers."

"Can't they read themselves?" I asked.

Gramp looked at me and motioned me into the car, and we went on and came to an old white bridge and crossed. It was warm and dusty in the hot night on the other side. But Gramp put his cap on and said, "It's certainly cooler in Ohio."

Mama, who was getting that hard look around her little mouth, said, "It must be even cooler in hell."

Gramp winked at me as if to say "women!" and drove on. The road got worse, and the moon failed us, and far off a dog howled at something until someone kicked him. We could hear the kick and then the talky dog stopped his monologue. It was pretty bad in those days—the bad roads, the bad maps, the worse food, the far places, and the closeness to death— but the worst was the nighttime far from a town. It's an America that is gone now and I don't have too much nostalgia for it; only people who grew up in big cities and never saw the rural old days collect wagon wheels and cobblers' benches and say "those were the days."

After a while, of course, Emma ran out of gas and water, and one tire ran out of air. "They built great cars in those days," I always hear. We stood on foot, Mama gathering her clothes around her, and Gramp, his last match gone, chewed into the neck of a cold cigar.

Far ahead a light gleamed and we started toward it over a field laid

[10] By permission of Stephen Longstreet and *Gourmet Magazine*.

out in young peach trees. We came to a barbed-wire fence and went through it; I lost the seat of my pants. Then we waded across a shallow creek, Gramp carrying Mama and I carrying Gramp's gold watch—for some reason I now forget.

We were on a wide, wild-grown lawn, and beyond was a huge white house, looking bone-white in the night. A pack of hund dogs ran towards us, scenting meat, I suppose, and Gramp swung his cane, shouting at the top of his lungs.

"Get back, you hounds of hell, get back! Hello there . . . damn it . . . hello!"

Mama, who was very brave when her young were in danger, had placed me behind her and was whacking hound dogs over the head with a small shoe she had removed, hopping gracefully on the other foot.

Some big doors were flung open in the white house and a voice said, "What you doin' out there?"

"Call off your dogs!" Gramp shouted, banging his cane down on a liver-colored hound's head.

"Git off, Nero, git off, Ruffas, git off, Nellie, Cleo. Damn it, Pompey!" We saw a tall thin man with a gun under his arm drop-kick one of the dogs at least ten feet. The rest got back and sat down with their tongues out, waiting. Mama had fainted and the tall man picked her up, gun and all, and carried her towards the house.

"Really sorry," the man said to Gramp, "but this isn't the kind of road many people use these days."

"What road?" asked Gramp.

Inside the house the tall man set Mama down on a sofa and rubbed her hand. He was a handsome young man, and there were more dogs in the house, watching us with big dark eyes. Mama opened her eyes and saw the dogs and said, "Oh, I wasn't dreaming. Dogs!"

"Gaylord is the name," said the young man. "This is Gaylord House."

"I get the connection," said Gramp, growling. "We're lost, and its no way to treat strangers."

"I agree," said the young man. "Will you join me at dinner?"

"Yes, damn it," said Gramp. "We forgive you the dogs. How about you, Sari?"

Mama sat up and smiled. "I am hungry. Stevie, comb the hair out of your face."

The dining room was huge, the service fine, and the food—after all these years, I still remember it. I can't tell you who was President then or who won the World Series or the name of the famous murderer of that year, but I remember that meal.

River oysters Rockefeller, made with minced bacon, spinach, parsley, green onion, lemon, cayenne, bread crumbs, and a little real absinthe. Gramp told me later they don't have absinthe any more, but the Gaylords did. Gramp's journal of our trip says the wine was Clos de Vougeot, 1919. The main course was *tournedos* of beef à la Gaylord, an old family way of cooking it, the young man told us. His name was Dennis. Small filets were cut from the heart of a good section of beef, sautéed in butter, placed on thin croutons of toast fried in a little garlic butter, and served with hearts of artichoke, stuffed mushrooms, and grilled tomatoes from which the skin had been peeled.

Mama and I were very hungry and Gramp was always a good man with a plate of food. Dennis smiled at us.

"I'm sorry about the dogs, but we raise them, you know. The Gaylord is a famous breed. Has been for hundreds of years in this state."

Gramp nodded. "The Ohio Gaylord, a fine hound," he said, kicking at a dog under his feet.

Dennis said, "Ohio? This is Kentucky, suh . . ." I noticed a slight Southern tone suddenly in his voice and I looked up at the dueling pistols nailed to the wall.

"Kentucky?" said Gramp. "Damn, I was drifting south more than I thought. Must get that steering wheel fixed."

Mama looked at Gramp as if she hadn't come with him and went on eating. When it came time to serve coffee, a tall, very pretty girl came in (with two dogs, naturally), and she was wearing jodhpurs, those imported Indian riding pants. It was the first time I had ever seen any, and I found them amazing, but in this case form-fitting.

"My sister Dora," said Dennis, making the introductions. "She's been at a dog show. How did we do?"

"Lost," said Dora, throwing her dog whip into the corner. "They're importing their own judges, Dennis. We haven't a chance any more."

Dennis nodded. "It's hard to find honest men among dogs."

Gramp agreed. "Show me a man who loves a dog too much and I'll show you a person who lacks respect for the human race. Present company, of course, left out."

"I'm hungry," said Dora.

I don't remember much more that night. I slept in a big bed all alone, and I heard the dogs in the hall all night sporting a mouse hunt. In the morning we sent out for help to get Emma, our car, in order, but something had snapped someplace and it would be some days before the local wagonsmith could fix it. The Gaylords invited us to stay on and we did. They were fine people. Much too proud a sister and brother to marry with the decaying stock around them, they raised hounds, kept up the big white family house, and expected to be the last of their line. It was all rather run-down and a little foolish, but to a kid raised on mid-Victorian novels it seemed very romantic and exciting; today we would call the Gaylords snobs, Dennis a secret drinker, and Dora frigid. But this was before Freud and Marx had flavored our lives too much, and we saw the Gaylords as wonderful people upholding the family motto, *Disce pati,* "Learn to Endure."

I was in the garden the next day helping the colored man water the plants, and Gramp was smoking his morning cigar when Dennis came out and spoke to Gramp.

"You know the points of a good dog, don't you, Captain?"

Gramp who had not been expecting to be hailed by his military title (even if he had spoken of his war efforts at dinner), nodded. "But certainly. They all have four legs, a tail more or less, and enough ears to hear with."

Dennis said, "Frankly, we're short of judges. And I'm on the committee, and I haven't been able to find a really good judge. Would you, sir, like to judge in the hound class this afternoon at the Club?"

"You flatter me," said Gramp, looking at his cigar as if it were a prize dog. "I know a good dog but not a dog's good parts according to the texts."

Dennis rubbed a hound's ears. "You yourself saw the points of these dogs. You remarked at breakfast that you'd never seen such hounds."

Gramp had said "hounds of hell," but Dennis hadn't heard it all. Gramp was a sport. He threw up his hand and nodded. "I'll judge. You can say I will judge and judge . . ."

They shook hands and went inside to try some prime bourbon and branch water. By the time lunch came around they were fairly glowing, and Gramp was explaining the kind of dogs Caesar had in Gaul and the breeding of lap dogs in London according to the shape of their noses.

No matter how the Gaylord hounds did, the food never went to the dogs. Gramp's journal lists baked ham with *sauce bigarade* and chicken wings *fricassée à l'ancienne*. The apple pie was a delight and the men had more bourbon, but Mama and Dora had some *Spritzer,* which was a Rhine wine with seltzer.

Mama and Dora went upstairs after lunch to wave each other's hair, and Gramp and Dennis and I went to the front lawn to pick up the winning team of three hounds Dennis was entering in the show. Dudley, Montez, and Mac were their names, I remember, and they looked just like any other set of three hounds. But Gramp and Dennis were very pleased with them. The bourbon had mellowed them neatly. We put Dudley and Mac in the back of a blue Jordan roadster with me and Montez in the front between Gramp and Dennis. Mama and Dora would follow later in another car.

We drove off in a clash of gears, the blue Jordan being a very fine car. For the young folk I might explain the Jordan was a real fancy car of the period. This one had a low slung blue body, red wire wheels, and on the hood Dennis had welded in silver a running hound with flapping ears. The horn had been tuned to sound like a braying dog in sight of prey, and the dusty roads saw us pass in gray clouds of glory. Montez in the front seat sat on her round little bottom and howled politely, and Mac and Dudley in the back seat licked my face from time to time and flogged me with their tails.

It was a very nice trip, the car rolling along and the dogs yipping. The towns we passed got out of our way, and it was no time at all before we were at the Club.

It had once been a fox hunting club, but someone had quoted Oscar Wilde about fox hunting being "the unspeakable in full pursuit of the uneatable," and anyway the few remaining foxes got too wise for the dogs. So, Dennis told us, it became a dog and horse club. All the members raised dogs or horses or knew people who did.

Gramp was taken over to a lot of fine gentlemen who shook his hand and pinned a blue ribbon on him almost as large as the ribbons they awarded the dogs. He wasn't a winner, however, I saw—just a "Judge," as the ribbon read.

Gramp and Dennis left me in charge of the dogs, who got on my lap, and I sat holding the dogs while they went inside. They were big dogs, and I only had room for one at a time, so the cutest one won, and she kissed me on the nose, but I was too shy to kiss her back. I just wished I had her in the city and could walk her in the flower gardens. Mama and Dora got to the show at last and they took the hounds and entered them in their groups. At least Mama, who disliked all animal life except raccoon coats from Harvard, went along.

It was a gay time, and they served a few things to charm all dog lovers. A big table had been set up on the front lawn of the club, and while it was just then against the law to drink certain forms of stuff men swallow, they did have a nice odor of bourbon and rye whiskey all over the place, and *plats du jour* of smoked ox tongue in almond and raisin sauce, *mignonnettes* of lamb with chicken livers, and what Mama called *mollusque hors-d'oeuvre*. Also fried chicken and the expected ham.

Gramp and Dennis did their duty here, and then Gramp went off with some red-faced characters with notebooks to judge some dogs. All the dogs and all the people loved each other, and when they saw anyone they knew they either barked or said, "Hi, Roger," "good doggie, Eddie," or "down, Mike."

Gramp was in great form; at least he was doing a fine job of acting as if he knew dog life and its fine points. A large hound was standing in a dazed way in the sun, and Gramp went up to him and grabbed his tail and some skin under his neck and pulled; then he felt along the chest lines. Then he got down for an eye level view (the eye level of a worm) and scouted the hound dog's angle shots. Then he rolled over almost like a garage mechanic rolling under an ailing car and studied the dog.

Every one seemed very impressed. "There never was any judging like *this* before!" The dog seemed bored, then he looked at Gramp as if he were wondering if Gramp were another dog. Gramp got that look and I think for a moment felt a little foolish because he got up, dusted his knees, and said, "*This* is a dog."

People clapped their hands and some of the other judges came over and talked with Gramp and they agreed on something—that it *was* a dog most likely. Mama and Dora lowered their eyes when two Gaylord dogs got ribbons, but the Best of Show, and the Best in Class went to a big red dog with red eyes and a sensual leer.

On the way home Gramp said, "They outvoted me, Dennis. But your dogs should have won first. Frankly, the other judges were carpetbaggers, not real judges of dog flesh." . . .

We left right after dinner, of which I can't remember a thing any more. I guess the day had worn me down to a mental nub.

We promised to come back real soon, but of course we never did go back. That's the sad part about traveling: You make fast friends so quickly and then it's all over. Dora kissed Mama and kissed me, and Gramp handed out a cigar and shook hands with Dennis, who looked very handsome in white, his nose just a little red.

Emma, our car, was fixed and we piled in and drove off. Mama held a gift ham, the bottles of gift bourbon were at her feet, and Dudley and Mac, the good hound dogs, sat in the road as we pulled away.

"Sorry I couldn't win first for them," said Gramp.

"It was only dogs," said Mama, reverting to type.

"The best dogs in Kentucky," I said.

"Don't be too sure, Stevie," said Mama. "It might be Ohio after all."

Gramp scowled. "I suppose I'll never hear the end of how I mistook Kentucky for Ohio."

"No," said Mama cheerfully.

A WRITER'S CHILDHOOD[11]

Jean-Paul Sartre

There is no good father, that's the rule. Don't lay the blame on men but on the bond of paternity, which is rotten. To beget children, nothing better; to *have* them, what iniquity! Had my father lived, he would have lain on me at full length and would have crushed me. As luck had it, he died young. Amidst Aeneas and his fellows who carry their Anchises on their backs, I move from shore to shore, alone and hating those invisible begetters who bestraddle their sons all their life long. I left behind me a young man who did not have time to be my father and who could now be my son. Was it a good thing or a bad? I don't know. But I readily subscribe to the verdict of an eminent psychoanalyst: I have no Superego. Never in my life have I given an order without laughing, without making others laugh. It is because I am not consumed by the canker of power; I was not taught obedience.

Whom would I obey? I am shown a young giantress, I am told she's my mother. I myself would take her rather for an elder sister. That virgin who is under surveillance, who is obedient to everyone, I can see very well that she's there to serve me. I love her, but how can I respect her if no one else does? There are three bedrooms in our home: my grandfather's, my grandmother's, and the "children's." The "children" are we: both alike are minors and both alike are supported.

There remained the patriarch. When my grandfather's beard had been black, he had been Jehovah. But I appeared at the end of his long life; his beard had turned white, tobacco had yellowed it. He was the

---

[11] George Braziller, Inc.—from *The Words* by Jean-Paul Sartre reprinted with permission of the publisher. © 1964 by George Braziller, Inc.

God of Love with the beard of the Father and the Sacred Heart of the Son. There was a laying on of hands, and I could feel the warmth of his palm on my skull. He would call me his "tiny little one" in a voice quavering with tenderness. His cold eyes would dim with tears. Everybody would exclaim, "That scamp has driven him crazy!" He worshiped me, that was manifest. Did he love me? In so public a passion it's hard for me to distinguish sincerity from artifice. I don't think he displayed much affection for his other grandchildren. It's true that he hardly ever saw them and that they had no need of him, whereas I depended on him for everything—what he worshiped in me was his generosity.

I am adored, I thought, hence I am adorable. What can be more simple, since the world is well made? I am told that I am good-looking, I believe it. For some time my right eye has had a white speck that will make me half-blind and walleyed, but this is not yet apparent. Dozens of photos are taken of me, and my mother retouches them with colored pencils. In one of them which has survived, I am pink and blond, with curls; I am round-cheeked, and my expression displays a kindly deference toward the established order; my mouth is puffed with hypocritical arrogance—I know my worth. . . .

My truth, my character, and my name were in the hands of adults. I had learned to see myself through their eyes. I was a child, that monster which they fabricate with their regrets. I reflected back to them the unity of the family and its ancient conflicts; they were using my divine childhood to become what they were. I lived in a state of uneasiness: at the very moment when their ceremonies convinced me that nothing exists without a reason and that everyone, from the highest to the lowest, has his place marked out for him in the universe, my own reason for being slipped away; I would suddenly discover that I did not really count, and I felt ashamed of my unwonted presence in that well-ordered world.

My begetter, had he lived, would have determined my future. But if Jean-Baptiste Sartre had ever known my destination, he had taken the secret with him. My mother remembered only his saying, "My son won't go into the Navy." For want of more precise information, nobody, beginning with me, knew why the hell I had been born. Had he left me property, my childhood would have been changed. I would not be writing now, since I would be someone else. House and field reflect back to the young heir a stable image of himself. He touches himself on *his* gravel, on the diamond-shaped panes of *his* veranda, and makes of their inertia the deathless substance of his soul. Once, in a restaurant, I heard the owner's son, a little seven-year-old, cry out to the cashier, "When my father's not here, *I'm* the boss!" There's a man for you! At his age, I was nobody's master and nothing belonged to me. In my rare moments of lavishness, my mother would whisper to me, "Be careful! We're not in our own home!" We were never in our own home, neither on the Rue Le Goff nor later, when my mother remarried. This caused me no suffering since everything was loaned to me, but I remained abstract. Worldly possessions reflect to their owner what he is; they taught me what I was not. *I was not* substantial or permanent, *I was not* the future continuer of my father's work, *I was not* necessary to the production of steel. In short, I had no soul. . . .

All my grandfather's colleagues held up the sky. Those Atlases included grammarians, philologists, and linguists, M. Lyon-Caen, and the editor of the *Pedagogic Review*. He spoke of them sententiously so that we would realize their full importance, "Lyon-Caen knows his business. His place is at the Institute," or, "Shurer is getting old. Let's hope they won't be so foolish as to pension him off. The Faculty doesn't realize what it would be losing." Surrounded by irreplaceable old men whose approaching demise was going to plunge Europe into mourning and perhaps the world into barbarism, what would I not have given to hear a fabulous voice proclaim solemnly in my heart, "That little Sartre knows his business. France doesn't realize what she'd be losing if he passes away." I wanted to be an Atlas right away, forever, and since the beginning of time. It did not even occur to me that one could work to become one.

Good friends said to my mother that I was sad, that they had seen me dreaming. My mother hugged me to her, with a laugh. "You who are so gay, always singing! What could you possibly complain about? You have everything you want." She was right. A spoiled child isn't sad; he's bored, like a king. Like a dog. . . .

Everything took place in my head. Imaginary child that I was, I began defending myself with my imagination. When I examined my life from the age of six to nine, I am struck by the continuity of my spiritual exercises. Their content often changed, but the program remained unvaried. I had made a false entrance; I withdrew behind a screen and began my birth over again at the right moment, the very minute that the universe silently called for me.

I became a hero. I cast off my charms. I abandoned my family. Sated with gestures and attitudes, I performed real acts in my reveries. Instead of work and need, about which I knew nothing, I introduced danger. Never was I further from challenging the established order. Assured of living in the best of worlds, I made it my business to purge it of its monsters. As cop and lyncher, I sacrificed a gang of bandits every evening. I never engaged in a preventive war or carried out punitive measures. I killed without pleasure or anger, in order to save young ladies from death. Those frail creatures were indispensable to me; they called out for me. Obviously they could not have counted on my help since they did not know me. But I thrust them into such great perils that nobody could have rescued them unless he were I. When the janissaries brandished their curved scimitars, a moan went through the desert and the rocks said to the sand, "Someone's missing here. It's Sartre." A that very moment, I pushed aside the screen. I struck out with my saber and sent heads flying. I was being born in a river of blood. Oh, blessed steel! I was where I belonged. . . .

The bourgeois of the last century never forgot their first evening at the theatre, but I defy my contemporaries to tell me the date of the first movie they saw. Movies were an amusement for women and children. My mother and I loved them. . . . I wanted to see the films *as close up as possible.* I had learned in the equalitarian discomfort of the neighborhood houses that this new art was mine, just as it was everyone else's. We had the same mental age: I was seven and knew how to read; it was twelve and did not know how to talk. I liked the incurable muteness of my heroes. But no, they weren't mute, since they knew how to make themselves understood. We communicated by means of music; it was the sound of their inner life. Persecuted innocence did better than merely show or speak of suffering: it permeated me with its pain by means of the melody that issued from it. I would read the conversations, but I heard the hope and bitterness; I would perceive by ear the proud grief that remains silent. I was compromised; the young widow who wept on the screen *was not I,* and yet she and I had only one soul: Chopin's funeral march; no more was needed for her tears to wet my eyes.

The virgin's desperate struggle against her abductor, the hero's gallop across the plain, the interlacing of all those images, of all those speeds, and, beneath it all, the demonic movement of the "Race to the Abyss," an orchestral selection taken from *The Damnation of Faust* and adapted for the piano, all of this was one and the same: it was Destiny. What joy when the last knife stroke coincided with the last chord! I was utterly content, I had found the world in which I wanted to live, I touched the absolute.

I decided to lose the power of speech and to live in music. I had an opportunity to do this every afternoon around five o'clock. My grandfather was teaching his classes at the Modern Language Institute; my grandmother had retired to her room and was reading Gyp; my mother had given me my afternoon snack; she had got dinner under way and given final instructions to the maid; she would sit down at the piano and play Chopin's *Ballades,* a Schumann sonata, Franck's *Symphonic Variations,* sometimes, at my request, the overture to *Fingal's Cave.* I would slip into the study; it was already dark there; two candles were burning on the piano. The semidarkness served my purpose. I would seize my grandfather's ruler; it was my rapier; his paper cutter was my dagger; I became then and there the flat image of a musketeer. Sometimes I had to wait for inspiration; to gain time, I the illustrious swashbuckler would decide that an important matter obliged me to remain incognito. I had to receive blows without hitting back and to display my courage by feigning cowardice. I would walk around the room, my eyes glowering, my head bowed, shuffling my feet. I would indicate by a sudden start from time to time that I had been slapped or kicked in the behind, but I was careful not to react; I made a mental note of my insulter's name. Finally, the music, of which I had taken a huge dose, began to act. The piano forced its rhythm on me like a voodoo drum. The *Fantasia Impromptu* substituted for my soul; it inhabited me, gave me an unknown past, a blazing and mortal future. I was possessed; the demon had seized me and was shaking me like a plum tree. To horse! I was mare and rider, bestrider and bestridden. I dashed over hill and dale, from the door to the window.

As a heartsore vagabond seeking justice, I resembled, like a twin brother, the child who was at loose ends, a burden to himself, in search of a reason for living, who prowled about, to a musical accompaniment, in his grandfather's study. Without dropping the role, I took advantage of the resemblance to amalgamate our destinies; reassured as to the final victory, I would regard my tribulations as the surest way to achieve it. I would see through my abjection to the future glory that was its true cause. Schumann's sonata would finally convince me: I was both the creature who despairs and the God who has always saved him since the beginning of time.

APPENDIX

PLATO'S "ION"

(Translation by Benjamin Jowett)

Persons of the Dialogue: SOCRATES, ION.

Socrates. Welcome, Ion. Are you from your native city of Ephesus?

Ion. No, Socrates; but from Epidaurus, where I attended the festival of Asclepius.

Soc. And do the Epidaurians have contests of rhapsodes at the festival?

Ion. O, yes; and of all sorts of musical performers.

Soc. And were you one of the competitors—and did you succeed?

Ion. I obtained the first prize of all, Socrates.

Soc. Well done; and I hope that you will do the same for us at the Panathenaea.

Ion. And I will, please heaven.

Soc. I often envy the profession of a rhapsode, Ion; for you have always to wear fine clothes, and to look as beautiful as you can is a part of your art. Then, again, you are obliged to be continually in the company of many good poets; and especially of Homer, who is the best and most divine of them; and to understand him, and not merely learn his words by rote, is a thing greatly to be envied. And no man can be rhapsode who does not understand the meaning of the poet. For the rhapsode ought to interpret the mind of the poet to his hearers, but how can he interpret him well unless he knows what he means? All this is greatly to be envied.

Ion. Very true, Socrates; interpretation has certainly been the most laborious part of my art; and I believe myself able to speak about Homer better than any man; and that neither Metrodorus of Lampsacus, nor Stesimbrotus of Thasos, nor Glaucon, nor any one else who ever was, had as good ideas about Homer as I have, or as many.

Soc. I am glad to hear you say so, Ion; I see that you will not refuse to acquaint me with them.

Ion. Certainly, Socrates; and you really ought to hear how exquisitely I render Homer. I think that the Homeridae should give me a golden crown.

Soc. I shall take an opportunity of hearing your embellishments of him at some other time. But just now I should like to ask you a question: Does your art extend to Hesiod and Archilochus, or to Homer only?

Ion. To Homer only; he is in himself quite enough.

Soc. Are there any things about which Homer and Hesiod agree?

Ion. Yes; in my opinion there are a good many.

Soc. And can you interpret better what Homer says, or what Hesiod says, about these matters in which they agree?

Ion. I can interpret them equally well, Socrates, where they agree.

Soc. But what about matters in which they do not agree?—for example, about divination, of which both Homer and Hesiod have something to say,—

Ion. Very true.

Soc. Would you or a good prophet be a better interpreter of what these two poets say about divination, not only when they agree, but when they disagree?

Ion. A prophet.

Soc. And if you were a prophet, would you not be able to interpret them when they disagree as well as when they agree?

Ion. Clearly.

Soc. But how did you come to have this skill about Homer only, and not about Hesiod or the other poets? Does not Homer speak of the same themes which all other poets handle? Is not war his great argument? and does he not speak of human society and of intercourse of men, good and bad, skilled and unskilled, and of the gods conversing with one another and with mankind, and about what happens in heaven and in the world below, and the generations of gods and heroes? Are not these the themes of which Homer sings?

Ion. Very true, Socrates.

Soc. And do not the other poets sing of the same?

Ion. Yes, Socrates; but not in the same way as Homer.

Soc. What, in a worse way?

Ion. Yes, in a far worse.

Soc. And Homer in a better way?

Ion. He is incomparably better.

Soc. And yet surely, my dear friend Ion, in a discussion about arithmetic, where many people are speaking, and one speaks better than the rest, there is somebody who can judge which of them is the good speaker?

Ion. Yes.

Soc. And he who judges of the good will be the same as he who judges of the bad speakers?

Ion. The same.

Soc. And he will be the arithmetician?

Ion. Yes.

Soc. Well, and in discussions about the wholesomeness of food, when many persons are speaking, and one speaks better than the rest, will he who recognizes the better speaker be a different person from him who recognizes the worse, or the same?

Ion. Clearly the same.

Soc. And who is he, and what is his name?

Ion. The physician.

Soc. And speaking generally, in all discussions in which the subject is the same and many men are speaking, will not he who knows the good know the bad speaker also? For if he does not know the bad, neither will he know the good when the same topic is being discussed.

Ion. True.

Soc. Is not the same person skilful in both?

Ion. Yes.

Soc. And you say that Homer and the other poets, such as Hesiod and Archilochus, speak of the same things, although not in the same way; but the one speaks well and the other not so well?

Ion. Yes; and I am right in saying so.

Soc. And if you knew the good speaker, you would also know the inferior speakers to be inferior?

Ion. That is true.

Soc. Then, my dear friend, can I be mistaken in saying that Ion is equally skilled in Homer and in other poets, since he himself acknowledges that the same person will be a good judge of all those who speak of the same things; and that almost all poets do speak of the same things?

Ion. Why then, Socrates, do I lose attention and go to sleep and have absolutely no ideas of the least value, when any one speaks of any other poet; but when Homer is mentioned, I wake up at once and am all attention and have plenty to say?

Soc. The reason, my friend, is obvious. No one can fail to see that you speak of Homer without any art or knowledge. If you were able to speak of him by rules of art, you would have been able to speak of all other poets; for poetry is a whole.

Ion. Yes.

Soc. And when any one acquires any other art as a whole, the same may be said of them. Would you like me to explain my meaning, Ion?

Ion. Yes, indeed, Socrates; I very much wish that you would; for I love to hear you wise men talk.

Soc. O that we were wise, Ion, and that you could truly call us so; but you rhapsodes and actors, and the poets whose verses you sing, are wise; whereas I am a common man, who only speak the truth. For consider what a very commonplace and trivial thing is this which I have said —a thing which any man might say: that when a man has acquired a knowledge of a whole art, the enquiry into good and bad is one and the same. Let us consider this matter; is not the art of painting a whole?

Ion. Yes.

Soc. And there are and have been many painters good and bad?

Ion. Yes.

Soc. And did you ever know any one who was skilful in pointing out the excellences and defects of Polygnotus the son of Aglaophon, but incapable of criticizing other painters; and when the work of any other painter was produced, went to sleep and was at a loss, and had no ideas; but when he had to give his opinion about Polygnotus, or whoever the painter might be, and about him only, woke up and was attentive and had plenty to say?

Ion. No, indeed, I have never known such a person.

Soc. Or did you ever know of any one in sculpture, who was skilful in expounding the merits of Daedalus the son of Metion, or of Epeius the son of Panopeus, or of Theodorus the Samian, or of any individual sculptor; but when the works of sculptors in general were produced, was at a loss and went to sleep and had nothing to say?

Ion. No indeed; no more than the other.

Soc. And if I am not mistaken, you never met with any one among flute-players or harp-players or singers to the harp or rhapsodes who was able to discourse of Olympus or Thamyras or Orpheus, or Phemius the rhapsode of Ithaca, but was at a loss when he came to speak of Ion of Ephesus, and had no notion of his merits or defects?

Ion. I cannot deny what you say, Socrates. Nevertheless I am conscious in my own self, and the world agrees with me in thinking that I do speak better and have more to say about Homer than any other man. But I do not speak equally well about others—tell me the reason for this.

Soc. I perceive, Ion; and I will proceed to explain to you what I imagine to be the reason of this. The gift which you possess of speaking excellently about Homer is not an art, but, as I was just saying, an inspiration; there is a divinity moving you, like that contained in the stone which Euripides calls a magnet, but which is commonly known as the stone of Heracles. This stone not only attracts iron rings, but also imparts to them a similar power of attracting other rings; and sometimes you may see a number of pieces of iron and rings suspended from one another so as to form quite a long chain; and all of them derive their power of suspension from the original stone. In like manner the Muse first of all inspires men herself; and from these inspired persons a chain of other persons is suspended, who take the inspirations. For all good poets, epic as well as lyric, compose their beautiful poems not by art, but because they are inspired and possessed. And as the Corybantian revellers when they dance are not in their right mind, so the lyric poets are not in their right mind when they are composing their beautiful strains; but when falling under the power of music and metre they are inspired and possessed; like Bacchic maidens who draw milk and honey from the rivers when they are under the influence of Dionysus but not when they are in their right mind. And the soul of the lyric poet does the same, as they themselves say; for they tell us that they bring songs from honeyed fountains, culling them out of the gardens and dells of the Muses; they, like the bees winging their way from flower to flower. And this is true. For the poet is a light and winged and holy thing, and there is no invention in him until he has been inspired and is out of his senses, and the mind is no longer in him: when he has not attained to this state, he is powerless and is unable to utter his oracles. Many are the noble words in which poets speak concerning the actions of men; but like yourself when speaking about Homer, they do not speak of them by any rules of art: they are simply inspired to utter that to which the Muse impels them, and that only; and when inspired, one of them will make dithyrambs, another hymns of praise, another choral strains, another epic or iambic verses—and he who is good at one is not good at any other kind of verse: for not by art does the poet sing, but by power divine. Had he learned by rules of art, he would have known how to speak not of one theme only, but of all; and therefore God takes away the minds of poets, and uses them as his ministers, as he also uses diviners and holy prophets, in order that we who hear them may know them to be speaking not of themselves who utter these priceless words in a state of unconsciousness, but that God himself is the speaker, and that through them he is conversing with us. And Tynnichus the Chalcidian affords a striking instance of what I am saying: he wrote nothing that any one would care to remember but the famous paean which is in every one's mouth, one of the finest poems ever written, simply an invention of the Muses, as he himself says. For in this way the God would seem to indicate to us and not allow us to doubt that these beautiful poems are not human, or the work of man, but divine and the work of God; and that the poets are only the interpreters of the Gods by whom they are severally possessed. Was not this the lesson which the God intended to teach when by the mouth of the worst of poets he sang the best of songs? Am I not right, Ion?

Ion. Yes, indeed, Socrates, I feel that you are; for your words touch my soul, and I am persuaded that good poets by a divine inspiration interpret the things of the Gods to us.

Soc. And you rhapsodists are the interpreters of the poets?

Ion. There again you are right.

Soc. Then you are the interpreters of interpreters?

Ion. Precisely.

Soc. I wish you would frankly tell me, Ion, what I am going to ask of you: When you produce the greatest effect upon the audience in the recitation of some striking passage, such as the apparition of Odysseus leaping forth on the floor, recognized by the suitors and casting his arrows at his feet, or the description of Achilles, rushing at Hector, or the sorrows of Andromache, Hecuba, or Priam,—are you in your right mind? Are you not carried out of yourself, and does not your soul in an ecstasy seem to be among the persons or places of which you are speaking, whether they are in Ithaca or in Troy or whatever may be the scene of the poem?

Ion. That proof strikes home to me, Socrates. For I must frankly confess that at the tale of pity my eyes are filled with tears, and when I speak of horrors, my hair stands on end and my heart throbs.

Soc. Well, Ion, and what are we to say of a man who at a sacrifice or festival, when he is dressed in holiday attire, and has golden crowns upon his head, of which nobody has robbed him, appears weeping or panic-stricken in the presence of more than twenty thousand friendly faces, when there is no one despoiling or wronging him;—is he in his right mind or is he not?

Ion. No, indeed, Socrates, I must say that, strictly speaking, he is not in his right mind.

Soc. And are you aware that you produce similar effects on most of the spectators?

Ion. Only too well; for I look down upon them from the stage, and behold the various emotions of pity, wonder, sternness, stamped upon their countenances when I am speaking: and I am obliged to give my very best attention to them; for if I make them cry I myself shall laugh, and if I make them laugh I myself shall cry when the time of payment arrives.

Soc. Do you know that the spectator is the last of the rings which, as I am saying, receive the power of the original magnet from one another? The rhapsode like yourself and the actor are intermediate links, and the poet himself is the first of them. Through all these the God sways the souls of men in any direction which he pleases, and makes one man hang down from another. Thus there is a vast chain of dancers and masters and under-masters of choruses, who are suspended, as if from the stone, at the side of the rings which hang down from the Muse. And every poet has some Muse from whom he is suspended, and by whom he is said to be possessed, which is nearly the same thing; for he is taken hold of. And from these first rings, which are the poets, depend others, some deriving their inspiration from Orpheus, others from Musaeus; but the greater number are possessed and held by Homer. Of whom, Ion, you are one, and are possessed by Homer; and when any one repeats the words of another poet you go to sleep, and know not what to say; but when any one recites a strain of Homer you wake up in a moment, and your soul leaps within you, and you have plenty to say; for not by art or knowledge about Homer do you say what you say, but by divine inspiration and by possession; just as the Corybantian revellers too have a quick perception of that strain only which is appropriated to the God by whom they are possessed, and have plenty of dances and words for that, but take no heed of any other. And you, Ion, when the name of Homer is mentioned have plenty to say, and have nothing to say of others. You ask, "Why is this?" The answer is that you praise Homer not by art but by divine inspiration.

Ion. That is good, Socrates; and yet I doubt whether you will ever have eloquence enough to persuade me that I praise Homer only when I am mad and possessed; and if you could hear me speak of him I am sure you would never think this to be the case.

Soc. I should like very much to hear you, but not until you have answered a question which I have to ask.   In what part of Homer do you speak well?—not surely about every part.

Ion.   There is no part, Socrates, about which I do not speak well; of that I can assure you.

Soc.   Surely not about things in Homer of which you have no knowledge?

Ion.   And what is there in Homer of which I have no knowledge?

Soc.   Why, does not Homer speak in many passages about arts?   For example, about driving; if I can only remember the lines I will repeat them.

Ion.   I remember, and will repeat them.

Soc.   Tell me then, what Nestor says to Antilochus, his son, where he bids him be careful of the turn at the horse-race in honour of Patroclus.

Ion.   "Bend gently," he says, "in the polished chariot to the left of them, and urge the horse on the right hand with whip and voice; and slacken the rein.   And when you are at the goal, let the left horse draw near, yet so that the nave of the well-wrought wheel may not even seem to touch the extremity; and avoid catching the stone."

Soc.   Enough.   Now, Ion, will the charioteer or the physician be the better judge of the propriety of these lines?

Ion.   The charioteer, clearly.

Soc.   And will the reason be that this is his art, or will there be any other reason?

Ion.   No, that will be the reason.

Soc.   And every art is appointed by God to have knowledge of a certain work; for that which we know by the art of the pilot we do not know by the art of medicine?

Ion.   Certainly not.

Soc.   Nor do we know by the art of the carpenter that which we know by the art of medicine?

Ion.   Certainly not.

Soc.   And this is true of all the arts;—that which we know with one art we do not know with the other?   But let me ask a prior question: You admit that there are differences of arts?

Ion.   Yes.

Soc.   You would argue, as I should, that when one art is of one kind of knowledge and another of another, they are different?

Ion.   Yes.

Soc.   Yes, surely; for if the subject of knowledge were the same, there would be no meaning in saying that the arts were different,—if they both gave the same knowledge.   For example, I know that here are five fingers, and you know the same.   And if I were to ask whether I and you became acquainted with this fact by the help of the same art of arithmetic, you would acknowledge that we did?

Ion.   Yes.

Soc.   Tell me, then, what I was intending to ask you,—whether this holds universally? Must the same art have the same subject of knowledge, and different arts other subjects of knowledge?

Ion. That is my opinion, Socrates.

Soc. Then he who has no knowledge of a particular art will have no right judgment of the sayings and doings of that art?

Ion. Very true.

Soc. Then which will be a better judge of the lines which you were reciting from Homer, you or the charioteer?

Ion. The charioteer.

Soc. Why, yes, because you are a rhapsode and not a charioteer.

Ion. Yes.

Soc. And the art of the rhapsode is different from that of the charioteer?

Ion. Yes.

Soc. And if a different knowledge, then a knowledge of different matters?

Ion. True.

Soc. You know the passage in which Hecamede, the concubine of Nestor, is described as giving to the wounded Machaon a posset, as he says,

"Made with Pramnian wine; and she grated cheese of goat's milk with a grater of bronze, and at his side placed an onion which gives a relish to drink."

Now would you say that the art of the rhapsode or the art of medicine was better able to judge of the propriety of these lines?

Ion. The art of medicine.

Soc. And when Homer says,

"And she descended into the deep like a leaden plummet, which, set in the horn of ox that ranges in the fields, rushes along carrying death among the ravenous fishes,"—

will the art of the fisherman or of the rhapsode be better able to judge whether these lines are rightly expressed or not?

Ion. Clearly, Socrates, the art of the fisherman.

Soc. Come now, suppose that you were to say to me: "Since you, Socrates, are able to assign different passages in Homer to their corresponding arts, I wish that you would tell me what are the passages of which the excellence ought to be judged by the prophet and prophetic art"; and you will see how readily and truly I shall answer you. For there are many such passages, particularly in the Odyssey; as, for example, the passage in which Theoclymenus the prophet of the house of Melampus says to the suitors:—

"Wretched men! what is happening to you? Your heads and your faces and your limbs underneath are shrouded in night; and the voice of lamentation bursts forth, and your cheeks are wet with tears. And the

vestibule is full, and the court is full, of ghosts descending into the darkness of Erebus, and the sun has perished out of heaven, and an evil mist is
spread abroad."

And there are many such passages in the Iliad also; as for example
in the description of the battle near the rampart, where he says:—

"As they were eager to pass the ditch, there came to them an omen;
a soaring eagle, holding back the people on the left, bore a huge bloody
dragon in his talons, still living and panting; nor had he yet resigned the
strife, for he bent back and smote the bird which carried him on the
breast by the neck, and he in pain let him fall from him to the ground
into the midst of the multitude. And the eagle, with a cry, was borne afar
on the wings of the wind."

These are the sort of things which I should say that the prophet ought to
consider and determine.

Ion. And you are quite right, Socrates, in saying tthat.

Soc. Yes, Ion, and you are right also. And as I have selected from the
Iliad and Odyssey for you passages which describe the office of the
prophet and the physician and the fisherman, do you, who know Homer
so much better than I do, Ion, select for me passages which relate to the
rhapsode and the rhapsode's art, and which the rhapsode ought to examine and judge of better than other men.

Ion. All passages, I should say, Socrates.

Soc. Not all, Ion, surely. Have you already forgotten what you were
saying? A rhapsode ought to have a better memory.

Ion. Why, what am I forgetting?

Soc. Do you not remember that you declared the art of the rhapsode
to be different from the art of the charioteer?

Ion. Yes, I remember.

Soc. And you admitted that being different they would have different
subjects of knowledge?

Ion. Yes.

Soc. Then upon your own showing the rhapsode, and the art of the
rhapsode, will not know everything?

Ion. I should exclude certain things, Socrates.

Soc. You mean to say that you would exclude pretty much the subjects of the other arts. As he does not know all of them, which of them
will he know?

Ion. He will know what a man and what a woman ought to say, and
what a freeman and what a slave ought to say, and what a ruler and what
a subject.

Soc. Do you mean that a rhapsode will know better than the pilot
what the ruler of a sea-tossed vessel ought to say?

Ion. No; the pilot will know best.

Soc. Or will the rhapsode know better than the physician what the
ruler of a sick man ought to say?

Ion. He will not.

Soc. But he will know what a slave ought to say?

Ion. Yes.

Soc. Suppose the slave to be a cowherd; the rhapsode will know better than the cowherd what he ought to say in order to soothe the infuriated cows?

Ion. No, he will not.

Soc. But he will know what a spinning-woman ought to say about the working of wool?

Ion. No.

Soc. At any rate he will know what a general ought to say when exhorting his soldiers?

Ion. Yes, that is the sort of thing which the rhapsode will be sure to know.

Soc. Well, but is the art of the rhapsode the art of the general?

Ion. I am sure that I should know what a general ought to say.

Soc. Why, yes, Ion, because you may possibly have a knowledge of the art of the general as well as of the rhapsode; and you may also have a knowledge of horsemanship as well as of the lyre: and then you would know when horses were well or ill managed. But suppose I were to ask you: By the help of which art, Ion, do you know whether horses are well managed, by your skill as a horseman or as a performer on the lyre—what would you answer?

Ion. I should reply, by my skill as a horseman.

Soc. And if you judged of performers on the lyre, you would admit that you judged of them as a performer on the lyre, and not as a horseman?

Ion. Yes.

Soc. And in judging of the general's art, do you judge of it as a general or a rhapsode?

Ion. To me there appears to be no difference between them.

Soc. What do you mean? Do you mean to say that the art of the rhapsode and of the general is the same?

Ion. Yes, one and the same.

Soc. Then he who is a good rhapsode is also a good general?

Ion. Certainly, Socrates.

Soc. And he who is a good general is also a good rhapsode?

Ion. No; I do not say that.

Soc. But you do say that he who is a good rhapsode is also a good general.

Ion. Certainly.

Soc. And you are the best of Hellenic rhapsodes?

Ion. Far the best, Socrates.

Soc. And are you the best general, Ion?

Ion. To be sure, Socrates; and Homer was my master.

Soc. But then, Ion, what in the name of goodness can be the reason why you, who are the best of generals as well as the best of rhapsodes in all Hellas, go about as a rhapsode when you might be a general? Do you think that the Hellenes want a rhapsode with his golden crown, and do not want a general?

Ion. Why, Socrates, the reason is, that my countrymen, the Ephesians, are the servants and soldiers of Athens, and do not need a general; and you and Sparta are not likely to have me, for you think that you have enough generals of your own.

Soc. My good Ion, did you never hear of Apollodorus of Cyzicus?

Ion. Who may he be?

Soc. One who, though a foreigner, has often been chosen their general by the Athenians: and there is Phanosthenes of Andros, and Heraclides of Clazomenae, whom they have also appointed to the command of their armies and to other offices, although aliens, after they had shown their merit. And will they not choose Ion the Ephesian to be their general, and honour him, if he prove himself worthy? Were not the Ephesians originally Athenians, and Ephesus is no mean city? But, indeed, Ion, if you are correct in saying that by art and knowledge you are able to praise Homer, you do not deal fairly with me, and after all your professions of knowing many glorious things about Homer, and promises that you would exhibit them, you are only a deceiver, and so far from exhibiting the art of which you are a master, will not, even after my repeated entreaties, explain to me the nature of it. You have literally as many forms as Proteus; and now you go all manner of ways, twisting and turning, and like Proteus, become all manner of people at once, and at last slip away from me in the disguise of a general, in order that you may escape exhibiting your Homeric lore. And if you have art, then, as I was saying, in falsifying your promise that you would exhibit Homer, you are not dealing fairly with me. But if, as I believe, you have no art, but speak all these beautiful words about Homer unconsciously under his inspiring influence, then I acquit you of dishonesty, and shall only say that you are inspired. Which do you prefer to be thought, dishonest or inspired?

Ion. There is a great difference, Socrates, between the two alternatives; and inspiration is by far the nobler.

Soc. Then, Ion, I shall assume the nobler alternative; and attribute to you in your praises of Homer inspiration, and not art.

INDEX OF SELECTIONS

495

INDEX OF TOPICS AND NAMES